I0837097

PICTORIAL HISTORY AMERICAN REVOLUTION.

ROBERT SEARS, No. 128. NASSAU St.
NEW-YORK

THE

PICTORIAL HISTORY

OF THE

AMERICAN REVOLUTION;

WITH A

SKETCH OF THE EARLY HISTORY OF THE COUNTRY.

THE

CONSTITUTION OF THE UNITED STATES,

AND A CHRONOLOGICAL INDEX.

ILLUSTRATED WITH SEVERAL HUNDRED ENGRAVINGS.

THIRTY-FIRST THOUSAND.

NEW YORK:

PUBLISHED BY ROBERT SEARS, 128 NASSAU STREET.

BURGESS, STRINGER, & CO.; W. H. GRAHAM; JUDD & TAYLOR.—BOSTON: REDDING, & CO.—PHILADELPHIA: ZEIBER, & CO.; COLON & ADRIANCE.—BALTIMORE: SHURTZ & TAYLOR.—CINCINNATI: ROBINSON & JONES.—LOUISVILLE: J. H. BAGBY.—NEW ORLEANS: J. B. STEEL, & CO.—MOBILE: T. P. MILLER, & CO.—CHARLESTON, S. C.: SILAS HOWE.—PENFIELD, GA.: WM. RICHARDS.—ATHENS, GA.: J. J. RICHARDS.—AND SOLD BY BOOKSELLERS AND PERIODICAL AGENTS GENERALLY, THROUGHOUT THE UNITED STATES.

1850.

PREFACE.

No portion of the world's history can be more interesting to the present generation, than that recorded in this volume; and although of comparatively recent occurrence, it has acquired by neglect much of the freshness and fascination of novelty. The AMERICAN REVOLUTION is an event calculated to exercise a great influence on the present and future destinies of other nations.

To write an authentic "HISTORY OF THE AMERICAN REVOLUTION," is no light, irresponsible task. We have endeavored to be impartial, and to be careful that no fact should be distorted, or receive a false coloring. Where, as is frequently the case, a considerable difference exists between various authorities, we have endeavored to exercise an unbiased judgment, and to adopt that statement which appeared on the whole, most consistent with TRUTH. The great principles of civil and religious freedom, the contest for which, in America, aroused the slumbering nations of Europe, can not fail engaging our ardent admiration; and every Friend of Human Rights, at the present day, can have no hesitation in adopting the words of the immortal CHATHAM, "*I rejoice that they have resisted.*" At this moment, the whole English nation, which then, with a few honorable exceptions, was willing to aid her rulers in trampling on the necks of her transatlantic sons, is now sealing her approval of the principles which actuated American Patriots, by her own efforts to establish the truth, that "TAXATION, WITHOUT REPRESENTATION, IS TYRANNY."

In the preparation of a volume like the present, however, it is impossible to give universal satisfaction. Is it not enough that our fathers suffered, without the strife being bequeathed, as an heirloom, to their children? Wisdom suffers antipathies to die with the generation which has fostered them; and we believe that, were it not for the noxious influence of a portion of the periodical press, both in America and England, the only rivalry between the two greatest countries on the face of the globe would be, in the knowledge and practice of those principles of moral and political science, which are adapted to promote the happiness and welfare of mankind at large. HISTORY requires a distant eminence, from which to take an impartial view of the character and transactions of the recording pen: but little more than half a century has now elapsed since the Colonists first asserted their independence; and the generation, whose arduous struggles achieved so important a result, has passed away to the silent tomb. To give a just and impartial view of the rise, progress, and establishment of the American Republic, has been the design of the work The editor has aimed to do justice without asperity; to applaud patriotism, but not to justify its excesses; to condemn tyranny, but not to overlook the virtues of many of its instruments; and to exhibit the kindly prospect of the FUTURE, more strongly than the irritating aspect of the PAST.

The study of HISTORY can not be appreciated too highly; it tells to the YOUTH of our country a story full of wisdom, and replete with many a moral—it shows the influence and success of honor and virtue—that vice and dishonor go hand in hand together; and it excites them to noble deeds of patriotism, and calls upon them to do all, and suffer all, for their country.

To the YOUTH OF AMERICA, especially, the present Narrative is invaluable. It tells the price at which all their present rights were purchased—it teaches them their incomparable value; and thus renders those in whose hands the destinies of America are hereafter to be intrusted, alive to every encroachment upon them. It relates to a country of greater extent, resources, and beauty, than is possessed by any other single nation under heaven; and to a people, of recent origin indeed, but developing immense powers, and making gigantic progress; to a people above all others interesting to the nations of Europe—presenting a refuge for their distressed children—exhibiting a noble example for their imitation; and as exercising no feeble influence on their destiny.

It is not, however, for YOUTH, alone, that this volume has been prepared. It has been written for ALL—for every age. To mankind at large the subject can not fail to be interesting; and if the preparation of these pages has been executed with a competent measure of industry, candor, and carefulness, they can scarcely fail of being valuable. These the editor has endeavored to exercise, and he hopes not altogether without success. R. S

New York, May 1, 1845.

CHRONOLOGICAL INDEX.

INTRODUCTION.

EARLY HISTORY OF THE AMERICAN COLONIES.

HISTORY OF THE REVOLUTION.

CHAPTER I.

CHAPTER II.

CHAPTER III.

CHAPTER IV.

CHAPTER V.

CHAPTER VI.

CHAPTER VII.

CHAPTER VIII.

CHAPTER IX.

CHAPTER X.

CHAPTER XI.

CHAPTER XII.

CHAPTER XIII.

CHAPTER XIV.

LIST OF ILLUSTRATIONS.

INTRODUCTORY CHAPTER.

HISTORY OF THE REVOLUTION.

THE

PICTORIAL HISTORY

OF THE

AMERICAN REVOLUTION.

INTRODUCTION.

We propose to give a brief history of the war of the American Revolution, a contest waged by the American colonies, then in their infancy, but relying on the justice of their cause, against the fleets and armies of a mighty kingdom, unequalled for its giant strength and resources. That important event has brought a powerful nation into active life; it laid the foundation of the American republic, the pattern model of a democratic form of government, which proves to every candid inquirer that man is capable of governing himself, and which shines brightly, as the beacon-fire of liberty, to the whole world. Before proceeding directly to the war, it will be useful to glance at the earlier history and discoverers of America.

I. Eric the Red, with his household, emigrated from Iceland to Greenland, where they formed a settlement. Among those who accompanied him was Heriulf Bardson, whose son Biarne happened at this time to be on a trading voyage to Norway. Eric established himself at Brattalid in Ericsfiod, and Heriulf Bardson settled at Heriulfsnes.

When Biarne returned to Eyrar in Iceland, and found that his father had departed, he determined upon spending the following winter with him, as he had done the preceding ones, although he and all his people were entirely ignorant of the navigation of the Greenland sea. To this determination the original discovery of America appears to be owing.

They commenced their voyage; fogs and northerly winds arose, and for many days they were driven they knew not whither. At length they descried a land without mountains, overgrown with wood, and presenting many gentle elevations; but as it did not correspond with the descriptions which they had received of Greenland, they left it to the larboard, and pursued their course for two days, when they came to another land, which was flat and overgrown with wood. They again stood out to sea, and, after three days' sailing with a southwest wind, perceived a third land, which Biarne discovered to be an island; but as it did not present an inviting aspect, being mountainous and covered with glaciers, he did not go on shore, but bore away with the same wind, and, after four days' sailing, arrived at Heriulfsnes in Greenland. This was in the summer of 986.

About eight years after this Biarne went on a visit to Eric, Earl of Norway, and related to him his voyage, with an account of the strange lands he had discovered. Biarne's description of the coasts was very accurate, but he was much blamed for not having made himself better acquainted with the country.

In Greenland his voyage had excited much interest, and, on his return, a voyage of discovery was projected.

Among those whose curiosity had been excited by the discovery of the un known lands, was Leif, one of the sons of Eric the Red. This enterprising navigator purchased Biarne's ship, and, having manned it with a crew of thirty-five men, set sail in quest of strange lands, in the year 1000. The first land they made was that which Biarne had seen last. Here they went on shore; not a blade of grass was to be seen, but everywhere mountains of ice, and between these and the shore one barren plain of slate (hella). This country not appearing to possess any good qualities, they called it Helluland, and put to sea again. This was the land which Biarne had discovered to be an island, and was doubtless Newfoundland, which in modern descriptions is said partly to consist of naked rocky flats where not even a shrub can grow, and therefore called Barrens; thus corresponding to the island of Helluland first discovered by Biarne. The next land they came to, and where they went on shore, was level, covered with woods, and characterized by cliffs of white sand and a low coast; they called it Markland (Woodland). This country, southwest of Helluland, and distant from it about three days' sail, is Nova Scotia, of which the descriptions given by later writers answers completely to that given by the ancient Northmen of Markland. Leif left this country, and, after two days' sailing with a northeast wind, came to an island eastward of the mainland. They sailed westward, and went on shore at a place where a river issued from a lake and flowed into the sea. Here they first raised some log-huts, but when they had determined upon passing the winter there, they built commodious houses, which were afterward called Leifsbudir (Leif's booths). Leif then divided his people into two companies, which were alternately to be employed in guarding the houses and in making short excursions. He gave them special instructions not to go farther than would admit of their return on the same evening. It happened one day that one of his followers, a German named Tyrker, was missing. Leif, with a small party, went out to seek him, but they soon met him returning. He informed them that he had not been far, but had discovered vines and grapes, with which he was well acquainted, having been born in a country where vines grew. They had now two employments—hewing of timber for loading the ship, and collecting grapes, with which they filled the long boat. Leif named the country Vinland (Vineland), and in the spring departed thence for Greenland.

The country thus named Vineland, and which is proved to be identical with Massachusetts and Rhode Island, naturally became the theme of much conversation in Greenland; and Leif's brother, Thorwald, thinking it had not been sufficiently explored, was desirous of making a voyage thither, with a view to more extensive researches. In pursuance of this object he borrowed Leif's ship, and having received his instructions and advice, set sail in the year 1002. They reached Vineland at Leifsbooths, and spent the winter there. In the spring of 1003 Thorwald equipped the ship's long-boat with a party of his followers for the purpose of making a voyage of discovery southward. They found the country extremely beautiful, but without any appearance of men having been there before them, except on an island to the westward, where they discovered a wooden shed. They did not return to their companions at Leifsbooths until autumn.

In the summer of 1004 Thorwald left a party at Leifsbooths, and steering his course first eastward and then northward, passed a remarkable headland enclosing a bay. They called it Kialarnes (Keelcape), from its resemblance to the keel of their ship. This promontory, which modern geographers have sometimes likened to a horn and sometimes to a sickle, is Cape Cod. They sailed along the eastern coast into one of the nearest firths, until they arrived at a promontory entirely overgrown with wood, where they all landed. Thorwald was so much pleased with this spot, that he exclaimed to his companions, "Here it is beau tiful, and here I should like well to fix my dwelling." He little thought that, instead of being his dwelling, it was so soon to be his burial-place. As they were preparing to go on board, they descried on the sandy beach three hillocks, which, on a near approach, were found to be three canoes, and under each three Skrellings (Esquimaux). A fight ensued: eight of the Skrellings were killed; the ninth escaped with his canoe. Afterward a numerous party rushed upon them from the interior of the bay, and discharged arrows at them. Thorwald and his party endeavored to shield themselves by raising little screens on the ship's side, and the Skrellings at length retired, but not till Thorwald had received a wound under the arm from an arrow. Finding the wound to be mortal, he said to his followers, "I now advise you to prepare for your departure as soon as possible, but me ye shall bring to the promontory where I thought it good to dwell; it may be that it was a prophetic word which fell from my mouth about my abiding there for a season; there shall ye bury me, and plant a cross at my head and also at my feet, and call the place Krossanes (Crossness) in all time coming." He died, and they buried him as he had directed. (Krossanes is, in all probability, Gurnet Point.) After this they rejoined their companions at Leifsbooths, where they spent the winter; but in the spring of 1005 set sail for Greenland to communicate to Leif the fate of his brother.

When the circumstance of the death and burial of Thorwald was made known in Greenland, Thorstein, Eric's third son, determined on making a voyage to Vineland to fetch his brother's body. He equipped the same ship, and was accompanied by his wife Gudrida: but his design was frustrated; for, after having been tossed about and driven they knew not whither during the whole summer, they landed in the western settlements of Greenland, where Thorstein shortly after died. In the spring Gudrida returned to Ericsford.

This unsuccessful expedition was soon after followed by another, on a larger scale than any of the preceding ones; for it happened that, in the summer of 1006, two ships arrived from Iceland, the one commanded by Thorfinn Karlsefne, a wealthy and powerful man, of illustrious birth; the other by Biarne Grimolfson. Thorfinn was accompanied by Snorre Thorbradson, and Biarne by Thorhall Gamlason. At this time a festival was held at Brattalid, on which occasion the Vineland voyage was the leading topic of conversation, and Thorfinn, being captivated by Gudrida, asked and obtained the consent of her brother-in-law, Leif, to their union, which took place in the course of the winter. On the celebration of these nuptials the Vineland voyage was again the subject of discussion, and Karlsefne was prevailed on, by his wife Gudrida and others, to prosecute a voyage thither and plant a colony. Accordingly three ships were fitted out, and all kinds of live stock taken on board. The first ship was commanded by Thorfinn Karlsefne and Snorre Thorbradson, the second by Biarne Grimolfson and Thorhall Gamlason, and the third by Thorward, who had married Freydisa, the natural daughter of Eric the Red. They mustered one hundred and sixty men, and, being furnished with what was necessary for the occasion, departed in the spring of 1007. After touching at Helluland and Markland, they came to Kialarnes (the Nauset of the Indians), where the trackless deserts, long beaches, and sands, so much excited their wonder, that they called them Furdustrandir (Wonder strands). They passed these, and came to a firth which ran far into the country, and which they called Straumfiördr (Stream firth). On the shore of this firth they landed: the country was beautiful, and they made preparations for a winter residence; but Thorhall wished to go in quest of Vineland in a north direction. Karlsefne, however, decided on going to the southwest. Thorhall, therefore, with eight men, quitted them, and was driven by westerly gales to the coast of Ireland, where, according to some accounts, they were taken and made slaves. Karlsefne and those that remained with him, in all one hundred and fifty-one men, sailed in a southerly direction till they entered a river which fell into the sea from a lake. They steered into this lake, and called the place Hóp, which, in Icelandic, signifies a bay, or the land bordering on such a bay Here they landed, and found wheat growing wild on the low grounds, and on the rising lands grape-vines. To this place Mount Hope's bay corresponds; and it was at this Hóp that Leifsbooths were situated. Above this, and most probably on the beautifully-situated elevation afterward called by the Indians Mont Haup, Karlsefne and his companions erected their dwellings and passed the winter. They had no snow, and the cattle fed in the open fields. One morning, in the beginning of 1008, they perceived a number of canoes coming from the southwest past the cape. Karlsefne exhibited friendly signals by holding up a white shield, and the natives, a sallow-colored and ill-looking race, drew nigh, and commenced bartering furs and squirrel-skins for pieces of red cloth, and afterward for milk-soup.

While this traffic was proceeding, a bull, which Thorfinn had brought with him, came out of the wood and bellowed loudly. This terrified the Skrellings; they rushed to their canoes, and rowed away. About this time Gudrida gave birth to a son, who received the name of Snorre. At the commencement of the following winter the Skrellings appeared again in much greater numbers, and menaced hostility by loud yellings. They advanced—a battle took place; the Skrellings had war-slings, and a galling discharge of missiles fell upon the land; one, enormously large, fell with a crash that filled the Northmen with dismay, and they fled into the woods. Freydisa, the wife of Thorward, a bold and artful woman, upon perceiving the retreat of her countrymen, called to them, and reproached them with their cowardice, saying, if she had a weapon she would defend herself better than any of them. She followed them into the wood, where she saw the dead body of Snorre Thorbradson; a flat stone was sticking in his head, and his drawn sword was lying by his side. This she seized, and by her frantic gestures so terrified the Skrellings, that they in turn fled to their canoes and rowed away. Thorfinn and his people now rallied; they came up to her and praised her courage; but they became convinced that they could not continue in the country without being in constant alarm from the powerful hostility of the natives, and therefore determined upon returning to their own country. They freighted their ships, sailed eastward, and came to Straumfiord, where they passed the third winter; Karlsefne's son Snorre being then three years old.

At Markland they met with five Skrellings, two of which (boys) th caught and carried away with them. These children, after they had been taught the Norse language, informed them that the Skrellings were ruled by chieftains (kings), that there were no houses in the country, but that the people dwelled in holes and caves. Karlsefne, after having gone in quest of Thorhall, pursued his voyage to Greenland, and arrived at Ericsfiord in 1011.

The next voyage was undertaken at the instigation of Freydisa, who prevailed on two brothers, commanders of a ship from Iceland, to make a voyage to Vineland, and share equally with her in all the profits. To this the brothers, Helge and Finnboge, assented, and a mutual agreement was entered into that each party should have thirty-five able-bodied men on board their ship; but Freydisa concealed five additional men, whom she took with her. They reached Leifsbooths in 1012, where they remained during the winter. But the deceitful conduct of Freydisa caused an estrangement between the parties, and she at length succeeded, by subtlety and artifice, in persuading her husband to effect the murder of the two brothers and their followers. After this atrocious act they returned to Greenland in the spring of 1013.

At this time Thorfinn Karlsefne was waiting for a fair wind to sail for Norway. His ship was laden with a more valuable cargo than was ever before known to leave Greenland. When the wind was favorable, he sailed to Norway, and sold his goods. The next year he proceeded to Iceland, and in the year following, 1015, purchased the Glaumboe estate, where he resided during the remainder of his life. Snorre, his American-born son, also dwelled and ended his days there.

Among the numerous and illustrious descendants of Karlsefne was the learned bishop Thorlak Runolfson, born in 1085, of Snorre's daughter Halfrida, who was probably the original compiler of the account of the foregoing voyages. After these, many voyages were undertaken, and the last piece of information preserved in the ancient MSS. relates to a voyage, in the year 1347, from Greenland to Markland, undertaken for the purpose of bringing home timber and other supplies. On her voyage homeward the ship was driven out of her course, and arrived, with loss of anchors, at Straumfiord, in the west of Iceland. From the accounts of this voyage, written by a contemporary nine years after the event, it appears that the intercourse between Greenland and America Proper had been maintained to so late a date as 1347; for it is expressly stated that the ship went to Markland, which must have been thus mentioned as a country still known and visited in those days.

Thus it appears that, during the tenth and eleventh centuries, the ancient Northmen discovered a great extent of the eastern coasts of North America, and made frequent visits to Massachusetts and Rhode Island; and that, during the centuries immediately following, the intercourse was never entirely broken off. As confirmatory of these statements, Dr. J. V. C. Smith, of Boston, has written an account of a remarkable rough stone cemetery, discovered about fifty years ago in Rainsford island, in the bay of Boston, which contained a skeleton and a sword-hilt of iron. Dr. Smith argues that, as the body could not have been that of a native Indian nor of a settler posterior to the re-discovery, it was most probably that of one of the early Scandinavians. Dr. Webb, of Providence, has also furnished an account of a skeleton found at Fall river Massachusetts, on or near which were a bronze breast-plate, bronze tubes belonging to a belt, &c., none of which appear to be of Indian or of a comparatively modern European manufacture.

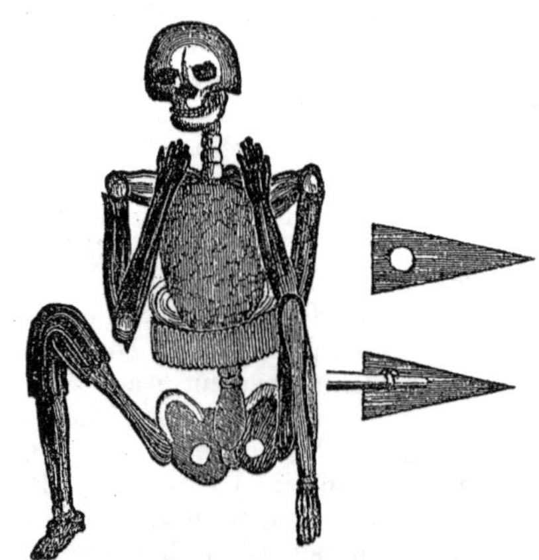

Fig. 3.—Skeleton and Arrow-heads found at Fall River

A Runic inscription is also still to be seen on Dighton rock, on the east side of Taunton river, which is exposed and covered at every ebb and flow of the tide.

At Newport, Rhode Island, there is a stone tower built of rough pieces of

Fig. 4.—Runic Inscription on Dighton Rock.

Fig. 5.—Old Stone Tower, at Newport, R. I.

greywacke stone, laid in courses, strongly cemented by a mortar of sand and gravel of excellent quality, which nearly equals the stone itself in hardness. It appears to have been at some former period covered with a stucco of similar character to the cement with which the stone is held together. It is nearly twenty-five feet in height; its diameter outside is twenty-three feet, and inside eighteen feet nine inches. It is circular, and is supported upon eight arches resting on thick columns about ten feet high; the height of the centres of the arches from the ground is twelve feet six inches. The foundation extends to the depth of four or five feet.

The columns are peculiar, having only half capitals, which seem to have been simply rounded slabs of stone, of which the part projecting on the inside had been cut away. According to Professor Râfn, the architecture of this building is in the ante-Gothic style, which was common in the north and west of Europe from the eighth to the twelfth centuries. The circular form, the low columns, their thickness in proportion to their distance from each other, and the entire want of ornament, all point out this epoch. He imagines it was used for a baptistery, and accounts for the absence of buildings of a similar character by the abundance of wood in America.

II. From the time of the Northmen nothing seems to have been known of the western continent till the birth of Christopher Columbus.

Fig. 6.—Christopher Columbus.

The territory of Genoa had the honor of giving birth to him, and the traveller in Italy is still gratified by beholding at the little village of Cocoletto, the humble mansion, where, in a narrow room in the rear, looking out upon the deep blue Mediterranean, and over which the troubled sea often throws its spray, Christopher Columbus, called by the Spaniards Colon, first saw the light. He appears to have had an early attachment to sea affairs; he studied navigation with the utmost industry, and supported himself by making charts for the sea-service He had the universal character of a sober, temperate, and devout man; he was a good mathematician, and had, in other respects, a tolerable share of learning.

The fame of the Portuguese in naval affairs having drawn him to Lisbon, he there settled, carried on a trade to the coast of Guinea, and at length married a woman of considerable fortune.

The reasons which, probably, determined Columbus to attempt the discovery of America, were the following: he had observed, when at the Cape de Verd slands, that at a particular season, the wind always blew from the west, which he thought was occasioned by a large tract of land lying that way; and he thought that the spherical figure of the earth demanded, that the land on the one side should be balanced by an equal quantity on the other.

He flattered himself that by sailing west, he should find a nearer passage to the Indies, than that which the Portuguese hoped to discover, by sailing round the coast of Africa, of a great part of which they had already made themselves masters. When he was fully convinced of the possibility of carrying his scheme into execution, he proposed it to the state of Genoa as early as the year 1484; but they having rejected it, he applied in the year 1485 to John the Second king of Portugal, in whose dominions he had now resided some years, and commissioners were appointed to treat with him; who, having artfully drawn his secret from him, advised the king to fit out a ship to try the practicability of the plan, and to rob Columbus of the honor and advantage of it; but the design failed; and when the king would have treated with Columbus a second time, his indignation at the treatment he had received, determined him to apply elsewhere; and that very year he sent his brother Bartholomew with proposals to Henry VII., king of England, while he himself proceeded to Spain, to offer his services to Ferdinand and Isabella.

Bartholomew had the misfortune to fall into the hands of pirates, who, stripping him of all he had, he arrived in England in a very miserable condition where he was taken ill of a fever, and reduced to great distress. On his recovery, he applied himself with great industry to the making and selling of maps and charts, by which he at length, in the year 1488, put himself into a proper equipage to appear before the king (Henry VII.), with whom he entered into an agreement, in the name and on the behalf of his brother.

When Christopher Columbus arrived in Spain, he communicated his plan to Martin Alonzo Pinzon, a celebrated pilot, who saw the force of his arguments, and readily agreed to go with him, if his application at court should be successful; but so much difficulty attended the prosecution of his suit, and he met with so many delays and insults, that he was actually on the point of leaving Spain for England, to see what success his brother had met with, and in case his applications had been equally fruitless, to offer his proposals to the court of France

At this interval Queen Isabella was prevailed upon to encourage his plan; and articles of agreement were signed at Santa Fe, in the kingdom of Grenada, on the seventeenth of April, 1492.

By this agreement, Columbus was to be admiral of the seas, and viceroy of all the countries he should discover: he was to have a tenth part of the profits redounding to their majesties from his labors; and an eighth of what he should bring home in his ships; himself furnishing one eighth of the expense of the equipment.

When this agreement was concluded, he was allowed three vessels; the Galega, which he named the Santa Maria, a carrac, or ship with a deck, commanded by himself; the Pinta, of which Martin Alonzo Pinzon was captain; and the Nina, under the command of Vincent Yanez Pinzon, brother to Martin Alonzo, who furnished half of Columbus's share of the expense. These two vessels were called caravels, that is, ships without decks; and the whole fleet, which carried but one hundred and twenty men, put to sea from Palos. on Friday the third day of August, 1492.

On the next morning the rudder of the Pinta breaking loose, they made it fast in the best manner they were able with cords, till they had an opportunity effectually to repair it. Several of the seamen began to consider this as an ill omen; but the admiral told them that "no omen could be evil to those whose designs were good."

They arrived at the Canaries on the eleventh of August, where they remained, refreshing themselves, till the sixth of September; when they weighed anchor, and proceeded on their voyage, for fear of the Portuguese, who had fitted out three caravels to attack them.

On the seventh they lost sight of land, and with it all their courage, bitterly bemoaning their fate, as that of wretches destined to certain destruction. Columbus comforted these cowards in the best manner he was able; setting before them the certain prospect of wealth and happiness, as the reward of their labors; and that they might not think themselves so far from home, as they really were, he resolved, during the whole voyage, to deceive them in the reckoning; and having this day sailed eighteen leagues, he pretended they had made no more than fifteen.

On the fourteenth of September, they took notice of the variation of the compass, and the people on board the Nina saw a heron, and some tropic birds, and the next day the sea was covered with yellow and green weeds, among which they saw a live lobster; and as they advanced they found the sea-water less salt, from which circumstances they imagined they were near land.

Alonzo Pinzon, who had been ahead, lay by for the captain on the eighteenth, acquainting him that he had seen a large number of birds flying westward, and imagined he saw land fifteen leagues to the north; but Columbus, having no doubt but he was mistaken, would not alter his course, though most earnestly solicited so to do by the sailors.

On the nineteenth, the sight of a great number of sea-gulls, which it was imagined could not fly far, began to give the admiral himself some hopes of seeing land speedily; but on sounding with a line of two hundred fathoms, no bottom could be found. They now saw abundance of weeds, and three days afterward took a bird like a heron, web-footed, of a dark color, with a white tuft on the head; and in the evening, saw three small singing-birds, which flew away at break of day.

They now encountered such a quantity of weeds, that they were apprehensive the ships would not long be able to make their way. Till this time the wind had been always right astern; but now shifting to the southwest, gave the admiral an opportunity of exposing the groundless fears of the sailors, who had imagined they should never have a fair wind to carry them back; but notwithstanding all he could say to them, they loudly complained of the danger they were in of perishing at sea, and a mutiny would, in all probability, have been the consequence of their clamors, but for a strong gale, which sprung up at west-northwest, and convinced them that there was no danger of their having no opportunity to return.

Several flights of small birds, which they observed coming from the west, and a pigeon, which flew over the ship, gave them fresh hopes of making land; but when they found themselves disappointed, their mortification was the greater, and their complaints increased.

They censured the admiral as a person, who, from an idle ambition of aggrandizing himself, and his own family, had led them into dangers and difficulties, in search of a country which nowhere existed; they said they had given suffi-

FIG. 7.—Mutiny on board the Santa Maria.

cient proofs of their courage, by venturing so far from home, and began to entertain serious thoughts of compelling Columbus to return. In a word, so great were their fears, that some of them were for throwing the admiral overboard, and asserting, on their return to Spain, that he fell into the sea, as he was gazing at the stars.

Columbus was not insensible of the spirit of mutiny, by which they were actuated, and exerted himself, partly by representing their duty to the king, partly by threats of punishment in case of disobedience, and partly by promises of the reward of their perseverance; so that the enterprise received no detriment from their ill-grounded fears and apprehensions.

The men were, however, extremely anxious and disconsolate, till on the twenty-fifth of September, about sunsetting, while Columbus was talking to Vincent Yanez Pinzon, he cried, "Land! Land! Let me not lose the reward for this good news!" and immediately pointed toward the southwest, where there was something which looked like an island, at the distance of twenty-five leagues.

This, which was afterward looked on as a contrivance between Columbus and Pinzon, so animated the men, that they returned thanks to God with the utmost fervency, and the admiral, at the earnest entreaty of the crew, steered toward the supposed island most part of the night; but in the morning no island was to be seen, and the men were as loud in their complaints as ever.

Columbus continued on his course with the utmost resolution; and on the twenty-ninth they saw many flying fishes, some of which fell into the ship. They also saw a gull, several wagtails, and other birds, and were encompassed with so great a quantity of weeds, that the men thought they were near land, and in danger of running aground.

On the thirtieth they also saw many wagtails, and observed that the weeds lay in a line from west-northwest, to east-southeast.

At break of day, on the first of October, a wagtail came on board the admiral, and that day the pilot told the admiral, that they were five handred and seventy-eight leagues west of the island of Ferro; but by Columbus's account they were seven hundred and seven; but he took no notice of the error, because he would not discourage the sailors.

On the second they killed a tunny fish, and some birds; but seeing no birds on the third day, they feared they had missed some islands, and the men begged the admiral to steer either to the right or left; but regardless of their entreaties, he resolved to keep right on his course, that the credit of his undertaking might not suffer by an idle compliance with their demands.

Hereupon the men began to mutiny, and would probably have taken some desperate measures, had not the flight of upward of forty sparrows, and other birds, from the west, again given them hopes that they were near land. Some signs of land appeared to the westward on the seventh of October, but the weather being hazy, no one would venture to cry land.

An annuity of ten thousand marvadies, or thirty crowns, for life, had been offered by their catholic majesties to the person who should first discover land; but if any one cried out land, and it did not prove to be so, he was to be excluded from the reward, even though he should afterward discover it. But the people of the Nina, which was generally ahead, fired a gun, and hoisted colors, concluding it was certainly land; but as they sailed farther they were soon undeceived.

Next day they saw many birds, both large and small, among which were some land-fowl, flying from the west to the southwest, and Columbus, thinking they could not fly far, imitated the Portuguese, who, by following such flights of birds, had discovered several islands; he therefore changed his course, and stood for the west; and having already sailed seven hundred and twenty leagues to the westward of the Canaries, imagined he should soon find land; and he had often told the sailors to expect it at that distance.

They saw twelve singing-birds, and many ducks, gulls, and jays, on the eighth of October; and on the eleventh, when all the admiral's skill and address would have been insufficient to withstand much longer the mutinous disposition of the crew, he was comforted with indubitable proofs of their being near land; for on this day they saw a green rush, and a large rock-fish swim near the admiral's ship; and those on board the Pinta took up a staff most curiously wrought, and saw a cane floating, and a number of weeds fresh torn from the shore.

On the evening of this day the admiral represented to his men, how merciful God had been to them, in conducting them safe so long a voyage; and said, that since the tokens he now saw were proofs they were near land, he would have them watch all night, and they would most likely discover it before the morning; and he promised to give a velvet doublet, as an addition to their majesties' reward, to the person who should make the discovery.

Two hours before midnight, Columbus standing on the poop, saw a light on shore, and called Guitierres, groom of the privy chamber to the king, who also saw it. It appeared like a candle, or other light carried in a person's hand from one house to another.

About two o'clock in the morning land was discovered, at the distance of two leagues, by Roderic de Trians, on board the Pinta, which was considerably ahead; but the reward was afterward paid to Columbus, by order of their catholic majesties, for having first discovered the light.

The ships now lay too, and the people waited with the utmost anxiety for a sight of that land of which they had been so long in search; and at the break

Fig. 8.—Lisbon.

of day they had the pleasure to behold an island about fifteen leagues in length; of a flat surface, well covered with wood and watered, with a large lake in the middle of it. It appeared to be full of inhabitants, who waited on the shore, astonished at the sight of the ships, which they took for prodigious sea monsters

The sailors were extremely eager to be on shore; and as soon as the vessels were brought to an anchor, the admiral went on shore, with the royal colors flying, as did the captains, carrying the colors of their enterprise, being a green cross with crowns, and the names of their catholic majesties.

They were no sooner on shore, than they fell on their knees, and kissing the ground, with tears of joy, gave thanks to God for his goodness, when the admiral stood up, and gave the island the name of St. Salvador, which the natives called Guanihani; but it is now known by the name of Cat-island.

Columbus having taken possession of the island, for the king and queen of Spain, the sailors acknowledged his authority, begged pardon for their former behavior, and promised the utmost obedience for the future.

On his return, when near the coast of Portugal, a terrible storm arose, and he found it expedient to anchor off Lisbon, where he was warmly solicited by the king of Portugal to re-enter his service, but this was declined. Columbus again made sail, and in a few days came to anchor in the port of Palos.

Columbus gave their majesties an account of his voyages and discoveries, showed the Indians as they appeared in their own country, and exhibited all the curiosities he had brought. When he had concluded his account, their majesties knelt down, and with tears in their eyes, returned thanks to God, and immediately the choristers of the chapel sung Te Deum.

The articles heretofore concluded with the admiral were only in form of a contract; but as he had performed what he engaged to do, their majesties now passed grants, making good what they had before promised him.

When his majesty rode through Barcelona, he would make the admiral ride by his side, an honor, till then, peculiar to the princes of the blood. The importance of his discoveries induced their majesties to despatch an ambassador to Pope Alexander VI., requesting his authority for an exclusive title to the countries which had been, or might be discovered; this the pope readily complied with, drawing a line from pole to pole, one hundred leagues westward from the Cape de Verd islands, granting to their majesties all the dominions beyond that part of the globe.

The son of the poor wool-comber of Genoa was laden with every honor that power could bestow. His patroness, Isabella, received him with open arms, the very courts that had denied him aid now solicited his presence, and at the tables of the noblest he became an honored guest.

Among many others of the grandees of Spain, Pedro Gonzales de Mendoza, the grand cardinal of Spain, invited Columbus to a banquet. He gave him the most honorable place at table, and, notwithstanding etiquette to its fullest extent was at that time punctiliously observed, he served him with ceremonies which were observed toward sovereigns. It was at that banquet that the anecdote of the egg is said to have occurred, which scene is graphically delineated in our engraving. A courtier who was present, possessing more impudence than wit, and jealous of Columbus because he was a foreigner, and so highly honored by his master, abruptly asked him whether he thought that in case he had not discovered the Indies, there were not other men who would have been capable of the enterprise? Columbus, looking with proper contempt upon the fellow, deigned no reply, but taking an egg, invited the company to make it stand upon one end. All attempted it, but in vain, whereupon he struck it upon the table so as to break the end, and left it standing upon the broken part. This, in the most simple manner, illustrated the fact, that when he had once shown the way

Fig. 9.—Columbus Breaking the Egg

to the new world, it was a very easy thing to follow. The rebuke was felt, and the courtier held his peace. "This anecdote," says Irving, "rests on the authority of the Italian historian Benzoni. It has been condemned as trivial, but the simplicity of the reproof constituted its severity, and was characteristic of the practical sagacity of Columbus. The universal popularity of the anecdote is a proof of its merit."

On the twenty-fifth of September, 1493, Columbus sailed on his second voyage, in which he discovered more of the West India islands.

On the thirteenth of May, 1498, Columbus commenced his third voyage, from the bay of St. Lucas, and after seeing some new islands, on the first of August he discovered the continent, but imagining it to be an island, he termed it Isla Santa. From this cruise Columbus was brought back in chains to Cadiz in consequence of false charges made against him by interested individuals; but he was soon restored to the favor of his king and master.

A new voyage was now projected, which was commenced on the fourth of May, 1502. In this he was very successful as a discoverer, but on his return home his health failed, and he died May 15, 1506. His body was taken to the Carthusian convent, and thence to St. Domingo. His bones, however, were afterward removed to Cuba, and are still preserved in the cathedral at Havana.

In the cathedral of Seville, fig. 8, there is a flat stone with an inscription, which, when translated, states,

To Castile and Leon
Columbus gave a new world.

Such was the end of this great man, to whom the Spaniards are indebted for all their American possessions, and who, from the boldness of his undertakings, and the greatness of his achievements, may, in a great degree, be considered as the Father of Navigation.

Columbus was in stature tall, his face long, his aspect majestic, his nose aquiline, his eyes gray, his complexion ruddy and clear; his beard and hair were fair in his youth, but the many hardships he suffered soon turned them gray. He was a man of wit and pleasantry, yet modestly grave, and eloquent in discourse. He was affable to strangers, and kind to his own family. He had an air of authority and grandeur that commanded respect; he was temperate in eating and drinking, and modest in his dress. He was strict in religion, according to the mode of his country, and obliged those under him to pay, at least, a decent regard to it. He much desired the conversion of the Indians, and did what he could to allure them, by obliging the Spaniards to lead a life, in some measure agreeable to the faith they professed. He was a man of undaunted courage, and fond of great enterprises; he remained unmoved amidst the many troubles and adversities that attended him, ever relying on the Divine Providence.

This is the account given of the famous Columbus, by a Spanish writer of knowledge and fidelity, who adds, that

"His name will be renowned as long as the world endures."

III. Sebastian Cabot, who claims with Columbus to have been the first discoverer of the continent of America, was the son of John Cabot, a Venetian. He was born at Bristol in 1477; and was taught by his father arithmetic, geometry, and cosmography. Before he was twenty years of age he made several voyages. The first of any consequence seems to have been made with his father, who had a commission from Henry VII. for the discovery of a northwest passage to India. They sailed in the spring of 1497; and proceeding to the northwest, they discovered land, which for that reason they called Primavista, or Newfoundland. Another smaller island they called St. John, from its being discovered on the feast of St. John Baptist; after which, they sailed along the

FIG. 10.—Tomb of Columbus.—Seville Cathedral.

FIG. 11.—Portrait of Sebastian Cabot.

coast of America as far as Cape Florida, and then returned to England with a good cargo, and three Indians aboard. Stowe and Speed ascribe these discoveries wholly to Sebastian, without mentioning his father. It is probable that Sebastian, after his father's death, made several voyages to these parts, as a map of his discoveries, drawn by himself, was hung up in the privy garden at Whitehall. However, history gives but little account of his life for near twenty years, when he went to Spain, where he was made pilot-major, and intrusted with reviewing all projects for discoveries, which were then very numerous. His great capacity and approved integrity induced many eminent merchants to treat with him about a voyage by the new-found straits of Magellan to the Moluccas. He therefore sailed in 1525, first to the Canaries, then to the Cape Verd islands, thence to St. Augustine and the island of Patos; when some of his people beginning to be mutinous, and refusing to pass through the straits, he laid aside the design of sailing to the Moluccas, left some of the principal mutineers upon a desert island, and, sailing up the rivers of Plate and Paraguay, discovered and built forts in a large tract of fine country, that produced gold, silver, and other rich commodities. He thence despatched messengers to Spain for a supply of provisions, ammunition, goods for trade, and a recruit of men; but his request not being readily complied with, after staying five years in America, he returned home, where he met with a cold reception, the merchants being displeased at his not having pursued his voyage to the Moluccas, while his treatment of the mutineers had given umbrage at court. Hence he returned to England; and being introduced to the Duke of Somerset, then lord protector, a new office was erected for him; he was made governor of the mystery and company of the merchant adventurers for the discovery of regions, dominions, islands, and places unknown; a pension was granted him, by letters patent, of £166 13*s*. 4*d*. per annum; and he was consulted in all affairs relative to trade. In 1522, by his interest, the court fitted out some ships for the discovery of the northern parts of the world. This produced the first voyage the English made to Russia, and the beginning of that commerce which has ever since been carried on between the two nations. The Russia company was now founded by a charter granted by Philip and Mary; and of this company Sebastian was appointed governor for life. He is said to be the first who took notice of the variation of the needle, and who published a map of the world. The exact time of his death is not known, but he lived to be above seventy years of age.

FIG. 12.—Portrait of Americus Vespucius.

IV. Although America was discovered by the Northmen, Columbus, and the Cabots, yet it was reserved for Amerigo Vespucci to give a name to the soil; that name AMERICA, which is already synonymous with liberty and independence throughout the whole world; where the genius of freedom finds her dearest place of abiding while living, and which, if she be ever conquered by the strong

Fig. 13.—Pizarro

arm of imperial tyranny and royal despotism, will be for her a magnificent sepulchre.

Americus Vespucius, or more properly Amerigo Vespucci, a Florentine gentleman, was born March 9, 1451, of an ancient family. His father, who was an Italian merchant, brought him up in this business, and his profession led him to visit Spain and other countries. Being eminently skilled in all the sciences subservient to navigation, and possessing an enterprising spirit, he became desirous of seeing the new world, which Columbus had discovered in 1492. He accordingly entered as a merchant on board the small fleet of four ships, equipped by the merchants of Seville, and set out under the command of Ojeda. The enterprise was sanctioned by a royal license.

He sailed May 20, 1499, under the command of Ojeda, and proceeded to the Antilles islands, and thence to the coast of Guiana and Venezuela, and returned to Cadiz in November, 1500. After his return, Emanuel, king of Portugal, who was jealous of the success and glory of Spain, invited him to his kingdom, and gave him the command of three ships to make a third voyage of discovery. He sailed from Lisbon, May 10, 1501, and ran down the coasts of Africa as far as Sierra Leone and the coast of Angola, and then passed over to Brazil in South America, and continued his discoveries to the south as far as Patagonia. He then returned to Sierra Leone and the coast of Guinea, and entered again the port of Lisbon, September 7, 1502.

King Emanuel, highly gratified by his success, equipped for him six ships, with which he sailed on his fourth and last voyage, May 10, 1503. It was his object to discover a western passage to the Molucca islands. He passed the coasts of Africa, and entered the bay of All Saints in Brazil. Having provision for only twenty months, and being detained on the coast of Brazil by bad weather and contrary winds five months, he formed the resolution of returning to Portugal, where he arrived June 14, 1504. As he carried home with him considerable quantities of the Brazil wood, and other articles of value, he was received with joy. It was soon after this period, that he wrote an account of his four voyages. The work was dedicated to Rene II., duke of Lorraine, who took the title of the king of Sicily, and who died December 10, 1508. It was probably published about the year 1507, for in that year he went from Lisbon to Seville, and King Ferdinand appointed him to draw sea-charts with the title of chief pilot. He died at the island of Terceira in 1514, aged about sixty-three years, or agreeably to another account, at Seville, in 1512, having published the first book and chart describing the new world.

V. The Mississippi, that broad and majestic river, as it rushes onward with resistless current to the sea, contains within its deep bosom the abode of no more daring or gallant spirit than that which animated the proud Hernando de Soto.

He was born at Barcarota in 1501; his family was respectable, but poor, and De Soto was obliged to depend upon his bravery for his subsistence. With this view he accompanied Davila to America, and distinguished himself so much that he had command given him of a troop of horse, with which he followed Pizarro (fig. 13) to Peru, and in that severe battle which took place between Pizarro and Almagro, (fig. 14), he displayed great prowess, and distinguish himself for his valor and prudence.

On his return to Spain, he appeared at the court of the emperor Charles V. in magnificent style, and was attended by a knot of brave cavaliers, many of whom had been with him in Peru; he was in the prime of manhood, about thirty-six years old, commanding in figure, and of a dark, animated, and expressive countenance. With such advantages of person and reputation he soon succeeded in gaining the affections and hand of a lady of distinguished rank and merit, Isabella de Bobadilla, which marriage strengthened his influence at court. About this

Fig. 14.—Battle between Pizarro and Almagro.

FIG. 15.—Portrait of Hernando de Soto.

time tne fate of Pamphilo de Narvaez and his followers, who had gone on an expedition to Florida, reached Spain. The imagination of De Soto became excited by the narrative of this expedition; his ambition was roused by the desire of rivalling the fame of Cortez and Pizarro, and his reputation, wealth, past services, and marriage connexions, all gave him the means of attaining his wishes. He therefore asked permission of the emperor to undertake the conquest of Florida at his own expense and risk. His prayer was granted; numerous privileges were conferred upon him, and he was created captain-general for life, of Florida as well as of Cuba; the control of the latter island being important to him in fitting out his armament for the conquest of Florida. The news of this expedition was soon promulgated throughout Spain, and in a little more than a year from the time that this enterprise was first proclaimed, nine hundred and fifty Spaniards of all degrees had assembled in the port of San Lucar de Barrameda, to embark in the expedition. Never had a more gallant and brilliant body of men offered themselves for conquest in the new world. All were young and vigorous, and fitted for the toils, hardships, and dangers, of so adventurous an undertaking. De Soto was magnificent in his offers of pecuniary assistance, to aid the cavaliers in fitting themselves out according to their rank and station. Many were compelled, through necessity, to accept of these offers ; others, who had means, generously declined them, deeming it more proper that they should assist than accept aid from him. Many came splendidly equipped with rich armor, costly dresses, and a train of domestics. Indeed, some young men of quality had spent a great part of their property in this manner. This brilliant armament embarked at San Lucar de Barrameda, on the sixth of April, 1538, in seven large and three small vessels. The governor, his wife, together with all his family and retinue, embarked in the largest vessel, called the San Christoval, of eight hundred tons burden. They quitted the Spanish shore in company with a fleet of twenty-six sail bound to Mexico, amid the braying of trumpets and the thunder of artillery. The armament of De Soto was so bountifully supplied with naval stores, that each man was allowed double rations. This led to useless waste, but the governor was of a munificent spirit, and so elated at finding in his train such noble and gallant spirits, that he thought he could not do enough to honor and gratify them.

The armament arrived at Cuba about the last of May. Here the fleet remained for a long period; during which De Soto despatched a vessel to St. Augustine to select a safe harbor. This having been accomplished, he sailed from Havana on the twelfth of May, 1539, and on the twenty-fifth of the same month arrived at Espiritu Santo, and took formal possession of the country in the name of Charles V

The troops disembarked, and not a single Indian was to be seen ; the soldiers, remained all night on shore in careless security, when in the morning they were suddenly attacked by a large body of Indians ; several of the Spaniards were wounded by arrows, but reinforcements arriving from the ships, the savages were repulsed and the army took up their residence in the deserted village, the houses of which were large, built of wood, and thatched with palm-leaves Leaving a garrison in this village of Herrihigua, De Soto proceeded for several leagues into the interior, although constantly harassed by the Indians.

The fertile province in which the army was now encamped lay twenty leagues to the north of that governed by Urribarracaxi, and was governed by a cacique named Acuera, who, on the approach of the Spaniards, had fled with his people to the woods. Hernando de Soto sent Indian interpreters to this chief, representing the power of the Spaniards to do injury in war, and confer benefits in peace ; declaring his disposition to befriend the natives ; his only object being, by amicable means to bring the people of this great country into obedience to his sovereign, the powerful emperor and king of Castile. He invited the cacique, therefore, to a friendly interview, in order to arrange a peaceful intercourse. The cacique returned a haughty reply : " Others of your accursed race," said he, " have, in years past, disturbed our peaceful shores. They have taught me what you are. What is your employment ? To wander about like vagabonds from land to land ; to rob the poor ; to betray the confiding ; to murder the defenceless in cold blood. No ! with such a people I want neither peace nor friendship. War—never-ending, exterminating war—is all I ask. You boast yourselves to be valiant—and so you may be ; but my faithful warriors are not less brave ; and of this you shall one day have proof, for I have sworn to maintain an unsparing conflict while one white man remains in my borders ; not openly in the battle-field, though even thus we fear not to meet you, but by stratagem, ambush, and midnight surprisal." In reply to the demand that he should yield obedience to the emperor, the chief replied : " I am king in my own land, and will never become the vassal of a mortal like myself. Vile and pusillanimous is he who submits to the yoke of another when he may be free !"

As for me and my people, we prefer death to the loss of liberty, and the subjugation of our country!" The governor, filled with admiration at the spirit of this savage chieftain, was more pressing than ever to gain his friendship; but to all his overtures the cacique's answer was, that he had already made the only reply he had to offer. The army remained in this province twenty days, recruiting from the fatigues and privations of their past journey. During this time, the governor sent persons in every direction to explore the country; and they returned with favorable reports. During this time the Indians were not idle. To justify the bravadoes of their cacique, they lurked in ambush about the camp, so that a Spaniard could not stray a hundred steps from it without being shot and instantly beheaded; if his companions hastened to his rescue, they found nothing but a headless trunk. The Christians buried the bodies of their unfortunate comrades wherever they found them; but the savages invariably returned the following night, disinterred them, cut them up, and hanged them upon trees. The heads they carried as trophies to their cacique, according to his orders. Thus fourteen Spaniards perished, and a great number were wounded. In these skirmishes the Indians ran comparatively little risk, as the Spanish encampment was skirted by a thicket, whither, after making an assault, the assailants could easily escape. In this manner the Spaniards saw effectually verified the threats of their ferocious foes, who had hung upon their rear during the march. "Keep on, robbers and traitors!" they cried, "in Aucera and Apalachee we will treat you as you deserve. We will quarter and hang up every captive on the highest trees along the road." Notwithstanding their great vigilance, the Spaniards did not kill more than fifty Indians, for the latter were extremely wary in their ambuscades.

The foregoing will enable our readers to judge of the difficulties encountered by De Soto. He however continued his route through the province of Osachile, and the army passed the winter of 1539 in the province of Apalachee. In the spring of 1540, De Soto continued his route; and in the province of Cosachriqui, which is thought to be near the seacoast of Georgia and South Carolina, he obtained, it is said, fourteen bushels of pearls. At length he came to the dominions of the cacique Tuscaloosa, which must have comprised a great part of Alabama and Mississippi. Here a disastrous battle ensued on the site as it is thought of Mobile; a battle in which forty-two Spaniards were killed, and many thousand Indians perished. After this battle the situation of the Spaniards was most deplorable. The army had been much reduced by the march into the interior; most of the soldiers were severely wounded, all were exhausted by fatigue and hunger. The village around them was reduced to ashes, and all the baggage with the supplies of food and medicine had been consumed in the house. At this time, too, the spirit and ardor of De Soto were damped by the dissatisfaction among his troops: on the sixteenth of November, he therefore broke up his encampment and turned his face to the northward; after a march of five days he entered the province of Chicazo, where he remained through the winter. Early in 1541, the army of De Soto was attacked in the encampment, and although the Indians were driven off and defeated, yet it was with the loss of forty Spaniards with their horses. Three days after this battle the army moved to a more advantageous position, about a league distant, called Chicacilla; here they spent the rest of the winter, in great suffering from the cold, having lost all their clothing in the late battle. They now erected a forge, and busied themselves in newly tempering their swords, and in making saddles, shields, and lances, to replace those which they had lost. On the first of April, the army again moved forward till they came in sight of the Mississippi, which they crossed (probably at the lowest Chickasaw bluff), and came to the village called Casquin or Casqui, (Kaskaskias), situated in the province of the same name. The same fortune still awaited the Spaniards: the Indians were constantly attacking them; and although always subdued and cut off in great numbers, yet their enmity against the conquerors remained firm and implacable. De Soto, however, continued his march through the province of Palisema, passed through a village called Tanied (Tunicas), and came among the tribe of Tula Indians, and wintered in the village of Uttanque. Here their interpreter died, and his death was a severe loss to the service, as throughout the expedition he had served as the main organ of communication between the Spaniards and the natives. In the spring of 1542, the views of De Soto were changed; his hopes of finding gold regions were disappointed; he had lost nearly half his troops by fighting and hardships of various kinds; the greater part of his horses too had perished, and all had been without shoes for more than a year for the want of iron. He now resolved to return to the Mississippi; select a suitable village on its banks for a fortified post, establish himself there and build two vessels, in which some of his most confidential followers might descend the river, carry tidings of his safety to his wife and friends in Cuba, procure reinforcements of men and horses, together with flocks, herds, seeds, and everything else necessary to colonize and secure the possession of the vast and fertile country he had overrun. As soon as the spring was sufficiently advanced, therefore, De Soto broke up his winter cantonment and set out in the direction of the Mississippi; after a time he came to the village of Guachoya, which contained three hundred houses, and was situated about a bowshot from the Mississippi in two contiguous hills with a small intervening plain that served as a public square, the whole way fortified with palissades. The inhabitants had fled across the river in their canoes, but abundance of provisions was found in the adjacent country. Here the melancholy which had long preyed upon the spirits of De Soto, the incessant anxiety of mind and fatigue of body, added perhaps to the influence of climate, brought on a slow fever, which continued until the seventh day, when he felt convinced that his last hour was at hand. He now made his will, and appointed his successor. When this was done, the dying chief called to him by two and two, and three and three, the most noble of his army, and after them he ordered that the soldiery should enter, twenty and twenty, thirty and thirty, and of all of them he took his last farewell. He charged them to convert the natives to the Catholic faith, and to augment the power of the crown of Spain. He thanked them for their affection and fidelity to him, and regretted that he could not show his gratitude by rewards such as they merited. He begged forgiveness of all whom he had offended, and finally entreated them, in the most affectionate manner, to be peaceful and loving to one another. Having confessed his sins with much humility, he died like a catholic Christian, imploring mercy of the most Holy Trinity. His body was placed in the trunk of an evergreen oak and sunk in the Mississippi.

VI. Francis I., a powerful monarch, ambitious of every kind of glory, was animated also with eager rivalry of Charles V., who derived much lustre from his possessions in the new world. He therefore ardently desired to follow successfully in the same career; and with this view he supplied to Giovanni Verazzano, a noble Florentine, four vessels destined to America. This chief, after being driven back by a storm, was refitted, and engaged in some successful naval operations on the Spanish coast; and it was then determined, that in the Dolphin, with fifty men, provisioned for eight months, he should prosecute his original design of discovery. After a severe tempest, he came, in the middle of March, upon a coast which, with great probability, is supposed to be that of North Carolina; and having sailed fifty leagues southward in search of a port without success, he turned again toward the north with the same object. He was once more disappointed as to a harbor; but seeing a fine populous country, he landed

Fig. 16.—View on the Mississippi.—Maiden's Rock.

FIG. 17.—Portrait of Verazzano.

in boats, and held some friendly intercourse with the natives. He next proceeded in an eastern direction along a low coast, where even a boat could not touch; but a sailor swam ashore, and though alarmed by some strange gestures, found the natives kind. A change of course to the northward marks the rounding of Cape Hatteras; and a run of fifty leagues brought him to a fertile region, covered with rich verdure and luxuriant forests. This was Virginia, near the mouth of the Chesapeake, though no mention is made of that great inlet. A sail of one hundred leagues in the same direction led to a spacious bay receiving a noble river, evidently the Hudson. They ascended it a short way in boats, and were delighted with its banks. The coast then tended eastward; and after following it fifty leagues, they reached an island of pleasing aspect, which, being of a triangular form, and about the size of Rhodes, clearly appears to be that named Martha's Vineyard. The weather prevented his landing; and, fifteen leagues farther, he found a very convenient port, where he had again much satisfaction in communicating with the people. Though the latitude of forty-one degrees forty minutes be about half a degree too low, it seems impossible not to recognise Boston. He then made a course of 150 leagues along a country of similar character, but somewhat more elevated, without landing at any point. Another stretch of fifty leagues, first west and then north, brought him to a bolder territory (Nova Scotia), covered with dense forests of fir, pine, and other trees of a northern climate. The inhabitants were fiercer, and carried on trade only under jealous precautions. In a subsequent run of the same extent, he discovered thirty small islands, with narrow channels running between them, being such as are known to stud the northern coast of that country and the adjacent one of Cape Breton. Lastly, by sailing 150 leagues farther, he reached in fifty degrees the land discovered by the Britons (Newfoundland or Labrador). His stock of victuals being spent, he here took in water, and returned to France.

Verazzano, on the eighth of July, 1584, wrote to the king from Dieppe a narrative of this voyage. Ramusio heard from different quarters that he had submitted to that monarch the plan of a colony; and the general belief is, that he was again employed by him. Mr. Biddle, indeed, urges the improbability that, amid the disasters caused by the battle of Pavia in February, 1525, Francis could engage in any such undertaking. Down, however, to that fatal day, his career was triumphant; and there was ample time to have authorized another expedition, though there is a total absence of any positive notice on the subject Ramusio, without mentioning either place or date, states that in his last voyage, having landed with some companions, he was killed by the savages in presence of his crew still on shipboard. In a modern narrative, which, from its full genealogical details, appears to have been furnished by his relatives, Coronelli, an eminent Venetian hydrographer, is quoted, expressing his belief that the catastrophe took place off Cape Breton, in 1525. In the portrait from which our sketch is taken, the inscription positively bears "Dead in 1525." It was engraved in 1767 after a picture by Zocchi, in the possession of the family, whose opinion is thus decidedly expressed. Yet Tiraboschi has drawn attention to a letter of Annibal Caro, apparently directed to him when living at Florence in 1537. There seems a mystery round his fate, which can not be unravelled.

Claims so extensive and so feebly supported as those of Spain to North America, were not likely to remain long undisputed. Other European nations were then rapidly advancing in maritime skill and enterprise, among whom for some time France took the lead. The defeat and captivity of the king, followed by an humiliating peace, naturally diverted his mind from distant enterprises, especially such as would have been considered hostile by his rival, Charles. The troubles which agitated the country after his death were also unfavorable to such undertakings; nevertheless, the spirit of adventure was cherished among the people, especially the Huguenots, an industrious class, who almost alone raised her commerce and manufactures to a flourishing condition. Admiral Coligni, one of the leaders in that eventful time, formed the scheme of a transatlantic settlement, which might at once extend the resources of his country, and afford an asylum to his Protestant brethren. While the civil war was yet only impending, he enjoyed intervals of favor at court, which enabled him to obtain permission, first to establish one in Brazil; and when that proved unfortunate, to plant another in Florida. He fitted out two vessels in 1562, and placed them under John Ribault of Dieppe, a seaman of experience. The object was to reach the mouth of the river called by Ayllon the Jordan, now Combahee, in South Carolina; but, steering in too low a latitude, the discoverers reached the St. John, near St. Augustine. On reaching Port Royal, they were so pleased with its noble harbor, the magnificent trees, and beautiful shrubs, that they determined to choose it for the site of their colony. Having seen a fort erected, and the settlement in a promising state, Ribault left twenty-six men, and returned to France for reinforcements and supplies. This seems an imprudent step. The establishment, in its unsettled state, stood in peculiar need of being well governed; whereas it fell into the hands of Albert, a rash and tyrannical officer, who, finding it difficult to maintain authority, where all thought themselves nearly equal, enforced it in the most violent manner. He addressed them in opprobrious language; hanged one of them with his own hands, and threatened others with the same fate. At length they rose in mutiny, put him to death, and appointed a new commander, Nicholas Barre, who restored tranquillity.

Ribault, meantime, in consequence of the breaking out of the great civil war, was unable to make good his expectations and promises. After long waiting for him, the colonists were seized with an extreme desire to return to their native country; and, having no ship, they resolved to build one, and constructed a brigantine fit for the passage; but they laid in a slender stock of provisions, which, during the delay of a tedious calm, was entirely consumed. The last extremities of famine were suffered; and one had been actually sacrificed to preserve the rest, when an English vessel appeared, and received them on board.

This project was still cherished by Coligni; and in 1564, he fitted out three vessels, abundantly supplied, and gave the command to René Laudonniere an able officer who had accompanied Ribault. Taking a circuitous course by the Canaries and the West Indies, he made for Florida, which he chose to term New France; and at Ribault's first station on the river St. John (named May from the month of its discovery), the party resolved to stop and settle. The fort of La Carolina was erected, and expeditions sent up the river, where small quantities of gold and silver were seen; reports being also received as to the mountainous country in the interior, where these metals abounded. The hopes thus kindled were quite illusory, and diverted attention from the solid labors of agriculture. Alarming symptoms of insubordination appeared; many of the party, notwithstanding their religious profession, were of a reckless character, and had gone out with the most chimerical hopes of suddenly realizing a large fortune. Seeing no such prospect, they formed the criminal resolution of seeking it by piracy. They confined their commander, and extorted from him, by threats of immediate death, a commission to follow this unlawful vocation; while, by rifling his stores, they obtained materials for its prosecution. After various fortune, they were successful in capturing a vessel, richly laden, and having the governor of Jamaica on board. Hoping for a large ransom, they sailed to the island, and unguardedly allowed him to send messengers to his wife; through whom he conveyed a secret intimation, in consequence of which an armed force surrounded the pirates, captured the larger of their vessels, while the other escaped by cutting her cables. Those on board the latter being reduced to extremity from want of food, were obliged to return to the settlement, where Laudonniere condemned four of the ringleaders to be executed.

That chief meantime continued to make incursions to the interior, and entered into various transactions with the natives in the vain hope of arriving at some region rich in gold and silver. Neglecting to establish themselves on the solid basis of agriculture, the settlers depended for food on the Indians, whose own stock was scanty. They were therefore obliged to undertake long journeys, without obtaining a full supply; and the natives, seeing them thus straitened, raised the price, disdainfully telling them to eat their goods, if they did not choose to give them for grain and fish. Amid these sufferings, and no prospect of realizing their fond dreams of wealth, they were seized, as was usual, with the ardent desire of returning home, and shrunk not from the laborious task of constructing vessels for that purpose. Amid their painful labor, they were cheered by a visit from Sir John Hawkins, who gave them a liberal supply of provisions. They did not, however, intermit their task, and on the twenty-eighth of August, 1565, were on the point of sailing, when several ships were descried approaching; which proved to be a new expedition, under Ribault, sent to supersede Laudonniere, of whose severity complaints had been made. He brought a reinforcement, with ample supplies, which induced the colonists to remain.

VII. The name of Sir Walter Raleigh is dear to Americans, for to him is due the honor of projecting and of keeping up, by his persevering efforts and expensive expeditions, the idea of permanent British settlements in America. His name is thus associated with the origin of the independent states of North America, and must be reverenced by all who, from liberal curiosity or pious affection, study the early history of their country.

Walter Raleigh was born at Hayes, on the coast of Devonshire: when young, he was sent to Oriel college, Oxford, where he exhibited a restless ambition, which prompted him to seek distinction rather in the stirring scenes of the world, than the cloistered solitude of a college; and this natural inclination to adventure was fostered by the study of books relating to the conquests of the Spaniards in the new world, a species of reading which was the delight of his early years, and undoubtedly gave a color to the whole tenor of his life.

Fig. 18.—Birthplace of Sir Walter Raleigh.

FIG. 19.—Portrait of Sir Walter Raleigh.

His stay at Oxford, therefore, was short; and in 1559 he seized the opportu uity of the civil wars in France, between the Huguenots and Catholics, to visit that kingdom and commence his military education; but although engaged in war, he found leisure to study the histories of the discoveries of Columbus, the conquests of Cortes, and the sanguinary triumphs of Pizarro, which books were his especial favorites. By the study of the Spanish voyages, and his conversations with some skilful mariners of that nation, whom he met in Holland and Flanders, he had learned that the Spanish ships always went into the gulf of Mexico by St. Domingo and Hispaniola, and directed their homeward course by the Havana and the gulf of Florida, where they found a continued coast on the west side, tending away north, which, however, they soon lost sight of by standing to the east, to make the coast of Spain. Upon these grounds, and for reasons deduced from analogy and a knowledge of the sphere, he concluded there must be a vast extent of land north of the gulf of Florida, of which he resolved to attempt the discovery.

Probably, also, during his residence in France he might have become acquainted with the particulars of the voyage of Verazzano, or have seen the charts constructed by that navigator, who had explored the same coast nearly as far south as the latitude of Virginia. Having fully weighed this project, he laid a memoir before the queen and council, who approved of the undertaking; and in the beginning of 1584 her majesty granted, by letters patent, all such countries as he should discover in property to himself and his heirs, reserving to the crown the fifth part of the gold or silver ore which might be found. The patent contained ample authority for the defence of the new countries, the transport of settlers, and the exportation of provisions and commodities for their use.

Sir Walter selected for the command of his projected voyage two experienced officers—Captain Philip Amadas and Arthur Barlow—to whom he gave minute written instructions, and who sailed with two ships, well manned and provisioned, on the twenty-seventh of April, 1584. On the tenth of May they arrived at the Canaries; after which, keeping a southwesterly course, they made the West Indies; and, departing thence on the tenth of July, found themselves in shoal-water, discerning their approach to the lands by the delicious fragrance with which the air was loaded—"as if," to use the words of their letter to Raleigh, "we had been in the midst of some delicate garden, abounding with all kinds of odoriferous flowers."

Arrived upon the coast, and sailing along upward of one hundred and twenty miles, they at length found a haven, and disembarked. Their first step was to take possession of the country in the name of the queen; after which they ascended a neighboring eminence, and discovered to their surprise that they had not landed on the continent, but on the island of Okakoke, which they found running parallel to nearly the whole coast of North Carolina. The valleys were finely wooded with cedars, around whose trunks wild vines hung in rich festoons; and the grape seemed so native to the soil, that the clusters covered the ground, and dipped into the sea. For two days no inhabitants were seen; but on the third a canoe with three men approached. One of them was easily prevailed on to come aboard, when the present of a shirt and some trinkets gained his confidence. On returning to his boat he began to fish, and having loaded it heavily, paddled back to the English, and, dividing his cargo into two parts, intimated that one was for the ship, and the other for the pinnace.

Next day they received a visit from some canoes, in which were forty or fifty men, among whom was Granganimeo, the king's brother. Having first rowed within a short distance, they landed on the beach; and the chief, attended by his suite, who were handsome and athletic persons, fearlessly approached opposite the ship. A long mat was spread for him, on which he sat down; and four men of his followers, apparently men of rank, squatted themselves on the corner. Signs were made for the English to come forward; and on doing so, Granganimeo desired them to sit down beside him, showing every token of joy and welcome, first striking his own head and breast, and afterward those of the strangers, as if to express that they were all brethren. Presents were exchanged; and such was the reverence with which these people treated their prince, that while he made a long harangue, they remained perfectly still, standing at a distance; even the four chiefs only venturing to communicate their feelings to each other in a low whisper. The gifts were received with delight; but on some trinkets being offered to the chiefs, Granganimeo quietly rose up, and, taking them away, put them into his own basket, intimating by signs that everything ought to be given to him, these men being no more than his servants—a proceeding to which they submitted without a murmur. A trade was soon opened, in which the strangers made good profit, by exchanging beads and other trifles for rich furs and skins. On exhibiting their wares, Granganimeo's eye fixed with delight upon a pewter dish, for which he conceived the strongest desire. It became his at the price of twenty skins; and, having pierced a hole in the rim, he hung it round his neck, making signs that it would serve as a breastplate to protect him against the arrows of his enemies.

It was now found that these people were engaged in hostilities with a neighboring nation, and that the absence of the king was occasioned by severe wounds lately received in battle, of which he lay sick at the chief town, six miles off. His brother, after a few days, again visited the English, attended by his wife and

Fig. 20.—Landing of the English at Roanoke.

children, coming aboard and partaking of a collation, which they seemed to enjoy. Their manners were remarkable for ease and civility. The lady was a handsome little woman, extremely bashful. She wore a leathern mantle, with the fur next her skin, and her hair, which was long and black, was confined in a band of white coral; strings of pearls, as large as peas, hung from her ears, reaching to her middle. Her children had ear-rings of the same precious material, while those of her attendants were of copper. Granganimeo was dressed much in the same fashion as his wife. On his head he wore a broad plate of metal; but, not being permitted to examine it, they were uncertain whether it was copper or gold.

A brisk trade now began with the natives; but no one was allowed to engage in it when the king's brother was present, except such chiefs as were distinguished by having plates of copper upon their heads. When this prince intended to visit the ship, he invariably intimated the number of boats which were to accompany him, by lighting on the shore an equal number of beacons. The navigators learned that about twenty years before their arrival, a vessel belonging to a Christian country had been wrecked on the coast, all hands on board perishing; out of the planks cast ashore, the people had drawn the nails and bolts, with which they had formed some edgetools, not having possessed any previous to this accident; but these were very rude, and their common instruments consisted of shells and sharp flints. Considering such imperfect means, their canoes were admirably made, and large enough to hold twenty men. When they wished to construct one, they either burned down a large tree, or selected such as had been blown down by the wind, and laying a coat of gum and resin on one side, set fire to it, by which it was hollowed out; after which they scraped and polished it with their shells; and if found too shallow, laid on more resin, and burnt it down to the required depth.

The soil of the country was rich, the air mild and salubrious, and they counted fourteen kinds of sweet-smelling trees, besides an underwood of laurel and box, with oaks whose girth was greater than those of England. The fruits were melons, walnuts, cucumbers, gourds, and esculent roots; and the woods were plentifully stocked with bucks, rabbits, and hares. After a short while, the adventurers, by invitation of the natives, explored the river, on whose banks was their principal town; but the distance to be travelled being twenty miles, they did not see the city. They reached, however, an island called Aonoak, where they found a village of nine houses, built of cedar, the residence of their friend Granganimeo, who was then absent. His wife, with whom they were already acquainted, received them with distinguished hospitality, running out to meet them, giving directions to her servants to pull their boats on shore, and to carry the white strangers on their backs to her own house, where she feasted them with fish and venison, and afterward set before them a desert of various kinds. These people were gentle and faithful, void of all deceit, and seemed to live after the manner of the golden age.

As the surf beat high on the landing they got wet, notwithstanding their mode of transport; but this inconvenience was soon remedied; a great fire being kindled, and their clothes washed and dried by the princess' women, while their feet were bathed in warm water. The natives expressed astonishment at the whiteness of their skins, and kindly patted them as they looked wonderingly at each other. During the feast, two men, armed with bows and arrows, suddenly entered the gate, when the visiters, in some alarm, took hold of their swords, which lay beside them, to the great annoyance of their hostess, who at once detected their mistrust. She despatched some of her attendants to drive the poor fellows out of the gate, and who, seizing their bows and arrows, broke them in an instant. These arrows were made of small canes, pointed with shell or the sharp tooth of a fish. The swords, breastplates, and war-clubs, used by the natives, were formed of hardened wood; to the end of this last weapon, they fastened the horns of a stag or some other beast, and their wars were carried on with much cruelty and loss of life.

The name of the country where the English landed was called Wingandaeoa, and of the sovereign Wingina; but his kingdom was of moderate extent, and surrounded by states under independent princes, some of them in alliance and and others at war with him. Having examined as much of the interior as their time would permit, they sailed homeward, accompanied by two of the natives, named Wanchese and Manteo, and arrived in England in the middle of September.

Raleigh was highly delighted with this new discovery, establishing, in so satisfactory a manner, the results of his previous reasoning, and undertaken at his sole suggestion and expense. His royal mistress, too, was scarcely less gratified; she gave her countenance and support to the schemes for colonization, which he begun to urge at court, and issued her command, that the new country, so full of amenity and beauty, should, in allusion to her state of life, be called Virginia.

Not long after this, Raleigh received the honor of knighthood, a dignity bestowed by Elizabeth with singular frugality and discrimination, and, about the same period, the grant of a patent to license the vending of wines throughout the kingdom; a monopoly extremely lucrative in its returns, and which was probably bestowed by Elizabeth to enable him to carry on his great schemes for the improvement of navigation, and the settlement of a colony in Virginia.

Sir Walter now fitted out a new fleet for America, the command of which he gave to Sir Richard Grenville; the fleet consisted of seven vessels; part of these were fitted out at Sir Walter's expense, the remainder by his companions in the adventure; one of whom was Thomas Candish or Cavendish, afterward so eminent as a navigator, who now served under Grenville.

On the nineteenth of April the mariners reached the Canaries, from which they steered to Dominica in the West Indies, and landed at Puerto Rico, where they constructed a temporary fort. On the twenty-sixth of June, after some delays at Hispaniola and Florida, they proceeded to Wohoken in Virginia; and having sent notice of their arrival by Manteo, one of the two natives who had visited England, they were soon welcomed by their old friend Granganimeo, who displayed much satisfaction at their return. Mr. Ralph Lane, who had been invested with the dignity of chief-governor, now disembarked with one hundred and eight men, having as his deputy Philip Amadas, one of the original discoverers. Grenville does not appear to have been sufficiently impressed with the difficulties attending an infant colony in a new country; and, accordingly, after a short stay, during which was collected a valuable cargo of skins, furs, and pearls, he returned to England, carrying into Plymouth a Spanish prize, which he had captured on the homeward voyage, of three hundred tons burden, and richly laden.

The first survey of their new country delighted the English; and the governor, in a letter to Hakluyt, who appears to have been his intimate friend, informs him that "they had discovered the mainland to be the goodliest soil under the cope of heaven; abounding with sweet trees, that bring sundry rich and pleasant gums; * * and, moreover, of huge and unknown greatness: well peopled and towned, though savagely, and the climate so wholesome, that they had not one person sick since their arrival."

Lane fixed his abode on the island of Roanoke, and thence extended his researches eighty miles southward to the city of Secotan. He also pushed one hundred and thirty miles north, to the country of the Chesepians, a temperate and fertile region; and northwest to Chawanook, a large province, under a monarch named Menatonon. These proceedings, however, were soon interrupted by the threatening aspect of affairs at headquarters. Even before the departure of Grenville for England, an accident occurred, in which the conduct of the settlers appeared rash and impolitic. A silver cup had been stolen, and a boat was despatched to Aquascogok to reclaim it. Alarmed at this visit, the savages fled into the woods, and the enraged crew demolished the city and destroyed the cornfields. A revenge so deep for so slight an injury incensed the natives; and although they artfully concealed their resentment, from that moment all cordiality between them and the strangers was at an end.

Not long after, Menatonon and his son Skyco were seized and put in irons; but the monarch was soon liberated, while the youth was retained as a hostage for his fidelity. To all appearance, this precaution had the desired effect. But the king, although an untaught savage, proved himself an adept in dissimulation. Working upon the avarice and credulity of the English, he enticed them into the interior of the country by a flattering report of its extraordinary richness and amenity. He asserted that they would arrive at a region where the robes of the sovereign and his courtiers were embroidered with pearl, and the beds and houses studded with the same precious material. Menatonon described also a remarkably rich mine, called by the natives chaumis temoatan, which was situated in the country of the Mangaoaks, and produced a mineral similar to copper, although softer and paler.

By these artful representations, Lane was persuaded to undertake an expedition by water, with two wherries and forty men. Instead, however, of the promised relays of provisions, they found the towns deserted, and the whole country laid waste. Their boats glided along silent and solitary banks; and after three days, during which they had not seen a human being, their last morsel of food was exhausted, and the governor, now aware of the treachery of Menatonon, proposed to return. His men, however, entreated him to proceed, still haunted by dreams of the inexhaustible riches of the Mangaoaks' country, and declaring they could not starve as long as they had two mastiffs, which they might kill, and make into soup. Overcome by such arguments, Lane continued the voyage; but for two days longer no living thing appeared. At night, indeed, lights were seen moving on the banks, demonstrating that their progress was not unknown, though the observers were invisible. At last, on the third day, a loud voice from the woods suddenly called out the name of Manteo, who was now with the expedition. As the voice was followed by a song, Lane imagined it a pacific salutation; but the Indian seized his gun, and had scarcely time to warn them that they were about to be attacked, when a volley of arrows was discharged into the boats. The travellers now landed and assaulted the savages, who fell back into the depths of the wood, and escaped with little injury; upon which it was resolved to return to the settlement. On their homeward bound voyage, which, owing to their descending with the current was performed with great rapidity, they had recourse to the mastiff broth, or, as the governor terms it, "dog's porridge," and arrived at Roanoke in time to defeat a formidable conspiracy.

The author of the plot was Wingina, who, since the death of his brother Granganimeo, had taken the name of Pemisapan. His associates were Skyco and Menatonon; and these two chiefs, pretending friendship, but concealing under its mask the most deadly enmity, had organized the plan of a general massacre of the colony. The design, however, was betrayed to Lane by Skyco, who had become attached to the English; and, aware of the necessity of taking immediate measures before Pemisapan could muster his forces, the governor gave instructions to seize any canoes which might offer to depart from the island.

In executing this order, two natives were slain, and their enraged countrymen rose in a body, and attempted to overpower the colonists, but were instantly dispersed. Not aware, however, that his secret was discovered, and affecting to consider it as an accident, Pemisapan admitted Lane and his officers to an interview, which proved fatal to him. The Virginian monarch was seated in state, surrounded by seven or eight of his principal weroanees, or high chiefs; and after a brief debate, upon a signal given, the Europeans attacked the royal circle, and put them all to death.

This alarming conspiracy had scarcely been put down, when the natives made a second attempt to get rid of the strangers, by neglecting to sow the adjacent lands, hoping, in this manner, to compel them to leave the country. At this decisive moment, a fleet of twenty-three vessels came in sight, which turned out to be the squadron of Sir Francis Drake, who had fortunately determined to visit the colony of his friend Sir Walter, and carry home news of their condition, on his return from an expedition against the settlements in the Spanish Main. It was now long past the time when supplies had been expected from England, and Drake generously offered every sort of provisions. Lane, however, only requested a vessel and some smaller craft to carry them home, which was immediately granted; but before they could get on board, a dreadful tempest, which continued for four days, dashed the barks intended for the colonists to pieces, and might have driven on shore the whole fleet, unless, to use the language of the old despatch, " the Lord had held his holy hand over them." Deprived in this way of all other prospect of return, they embarked in Sir Francis's fleet, and arrived in England on the 27th of July, 1586.

Scarcely, however, had they sailed, when the folly of their precipitate conclusion, that Raleigh had forgotten or neglected them, was manifested by the arrival, at Roanoke, of a vessel of one hundred tons, amply stored with every supply. Deeply disappointed at finding no appearance of the colony, they sailed along the coast, and explored the interior. But all their search was in vain, and they were compelled to take their departure for Europe. This, however, was not all. Within a fortnight after they weighed anchor, Sir Richard Grenville, with three well-appointed vessels, fitted out principally by Raleigh, appeared off Virginia, where, on landing, he found, to his astonishment, everything deserted and in ruins. Having made an unsuccessful effort to procure intelligence of his countrymen, it became necessary to return home. But, unwilling to abandon so promising a discovery, he left behind him fifteen men, with provisions for two years, and, after some exploits against the Spaniards and the Azores, arrived in England.

It is asserted by Camden, that tobacco was now, for the first time, brought into England by these settlers, and there can be little doubt that Lane had been directed to import it by his master, who must have seen it used in France, during his residence there. There is a well-known tradition, that Sir Walter first began to smoke privately in his study, and the servant coming in with his tankard of ale and nutmeg, as he was intent upon his book, seeing the smoke issuing from his mouth, threw all the liquor in his face by way of extinguishing the fire, and running down stairs, alarmed the family with piercing cries, that his master, before they could get up, would be burnt to ashes. " And this," continued Oldys, " has nothing in it more surprising than the mistake of those Virginians them, selves, who, the first time they seized upon a quantity of gunpowder, which belonged to the English colony, sowed it for grain, or the seed of some strange vegetable in the earth, with full expectation of reaping a plentiful crop of combustion by the next harvest, to scatter their enemies."

On another occasion, it is said that Raleigh, conversing with his royal mistress upon the singular properties of this new and extraordinary herb, assured her that he had so well experienced the nature of it that he could tell her the exact weight of the smoke in any quantity proposed to be consumed. Her majesty immediately fixed her thoughts upon the most impracticable part of the experiment, that of bounding the smoke in a balance; suspecting that he was playing the traveller with her, and laying a wager that he could not solve the doubt. Upon this Raleigh selected the quantity agreed on, and having thoroughly smoked it, set himself to weighing—but it was of the ashes; and in conclusion, demonstrating to the queen the difference between this and the weight of the tobacco, her majesty could not deny that this must be the weight of what was evaporated in smoke. Upon this, Elizabeth, paying down the money, remarked, that she had heard of many laborers in the fire who had turned their gold into smoke, but that Raleigh was certainly the first who had turned his smoke into gold.

Raleigh, however, was by no means discouraged by the unfortunate results of these expeditions; but again turned his attention to his Virginian colony, the failure of which was rather owing to the precipitate desertion of Lane, than to any fault in the original plan; and he determined to make a new attempt for the settlement of a country which held out so many encouragements from its salubrious climate and fertile soil. Hariot, who accompanied Lane, had by this time published his "True Report of the New-found Land of Virginia," which created much speculation; so that he experienced little difficulty in procuring one hundred and fifty settlers. He appointed as governor, Mr. John White, with twelve assistants, to whom he gave a charter, incorporating them by the name of the "Governor and Assistants of the City of Raleigh in Virginia." These, in three vessels, furnished principally at his own expense, sailed from Portsmouth on the twenty-sixth of April, 1587, and on the twenty-second of July anchored in Hatorask harbor. White, with forty men, proceeded in the pinnace to Roanoke to confer with the fifteen colonists, left by Sir Richard Grenville; but to his dismay found the place deserted, and human bones scattered on the beech; the remains, as was afterward discovered, of their countrymen, all of whom the savages had slain. A party then hastened to the fort on the north side of the island. But here the prospect was equally discouraging No trace of a human being was to be seen; the building was razed to the ground, and the wild deer were couching in the ruined houses, and feeding on the herbage and melons which had overgrown the floor and crept up the walls.

Although the governor held Raleigh's written orders to make the settlement on the bay of Chesapeake, he was obliged to abandon that plan, and commenced repairing the buildings at Roanoke. But disaster attended all their proceedings. Dissensions broke out among them; and White, either from want of firmness, or not being intrusted with sufficient authority, found it impossible to carry on his operations with success. The natives of Croatoan were friendly; those of Secota and Aquascogok, who had murdered the former colonists, completely hostile; but all were clothed alike; and before going to war, the Crotoans anxiously begged for some badge by which they might be recognised. In the confusion, this was neglected, and it led to unhappy consequences. Howe, an English sailor, while engaged in fishing, was slain by the savages, being pierced with sixteen arrows; and White, having in vain attempted to open a pacific communication with the weroansees, or chief men of Secota, and Pomeiock, determined not to delay his revenge. Guided, therefore, by Manteo, he set out at midnight, with Captain Stafford and twenty-four men, and stealing in the dark upon the natives as they sat round a fire, shot some of them dead upon the spot, while others fled shrieking into a thicket, and one savage, who knew Stafford, rushed up, calling out his name and embracing his knees. To the grief and horror of the governor, it was then discovered that they had attacked a party of friends instead of enemies.

Soon after, Manteo, in obedience to Raleigh's directions was christened, and created Lord of Roanoke and Dasamonwepuk; while Mrs. Eleanor Dare, the wife of one of the assistants, having given birth to a daughter, the infant was named Virginia, being the first Christian born in that country.

White was now anxious to fulfil Sir Walter's instructions; but disputes arose with renewed bitterness among the settlers. Though they were not in want of stores, many demanded permission to go home; others violently opposed this; and at last, after stating a variety of projects, all joined in requesting the governor to sail for England, and return with a supply of everything requisite for the establishment of the colony. To this he reluctantly consented; and departing from Roanoke on the twenty-seventh of August, 1587, where he left eight-nine men, seventeen women, and eleven children, he arrived in England on the fifth of November.

Our limits do not allow us to follow Sir Walter in his discovery of Guiana, and voyage up the Oronoko, and in his brave exploits against the fleets of Philip of Spain, nor in the vicissitudes which he experienced at the court of Elizabeth; at one time we find him enjoying her utmost confidence, exerting his influence in the cause of benevolence; and it is reported, that Elizabeth, somewhat irritated by his applications for the unfortunate, on his telling her one day he had a favor to ask, impatiently exclaimed: "When, Sir Walter, will you cease to be a beggar?" To which he made the noted answer, "When your gracious majesty ceases to be a benefactor."

Soon after, he was committed to the tower for presuming to marry without the queen's consent; he, however, was again restored to favor, and continued to aid the state by his services and counsel, till the death of Elizabeth, in 1602.

On the accession of James to the throne, Sir Walter was not only treated with coolness and neglect, but became the victim of a conspiracy; was tried for treason against the crown, found guilty, and condemned to death. Having been warned to prepare for execution, he sent a manly and affecting letter to his wife, from which the following is an extract:—

"When I am gone, no doubt you shall be sought to by many, for the world thinks I was very rich. But take heed of the pretences of men, and their affections; for they last not but in honest and worthy men, and no greater misery can befall you in this life than to become a prey, and afterward to be despised. I speak not this, God knows, to dissuade you from marriage; for it will be best for you, both in respect of the world and of God. As for me, I am no more yours, nor you mine. Death has cut us asunder, and God hath divided me from the world, and you from me. Remember your poor child for his father's sake, who chose you and loved you in his happiest time. Get those letters, if it be possible, which I writ to the lords, wherein I sued for my life. God is my witness it was for you and yours that I desired life. But it is true that I disdain myself for begging it; for know it, dear wife, that your son is the son of a true man, and one who, in his own respect, despiseth death in all his misshapen and ugly forms. I can not write much. God he knoweth how hardly I steal this ime while others sleep; and it is also high time that I should separate my thoughts from the world. Beg my dead body, which, living, was denied thee, and either leave it at Sherborne, if the land continue, or in Exeter church, by my father and mother. I can say no more, time and death call me away.

"The everlasting, powerful, infinite, and omnipotent God, who is goodness itself, the true life and true light, keep thee and thine, have mercy on me, and teach me to forgive my persecutors and accusers, and send us to meet in his glorious kingdom. My dear wife, farewell! Bless my poor boy; pray for me, and let my good God hold you both in his arms! Written with the dying hand of some time thy husband, but now, alas! overthrown. Yours that was, but now not my own,

"RALEIGH."

Fig. 21—Sir Walter Raleigh taking leave of his Family.

Sir Walter, however, was reprieved at this time, but was confined in the tower for many years after, during which his History of the World was composed. On regaining his liberty, in 1615, a new expedition to Guiana was projected, of which Raleigh took command, but it was unsuccessful; and on his return to England, he was again arrested, imprisoned, and executed. His conduct, while on the scaffold, was extremely firm. The morning being sharp, the sheriff offered to bring him down off the scaffold to warm himself by the fire before he should say his prayers; "No, good Mr. Sheriff," said he, "let us despatch, for within this quarter of an hour my ague will come upon me, and if I be not dead before that, mine enemies will say I quake for fear." He then, to use the words of a contemporary and eyewitness, made a most divine and admirable prayer; after which, rising up, and clasping his hands together, he exclaimed, "Now I am going to God!" The scaffold was soon cleared; and having thrown off his gown and doublet, he bid the executioner show him the axe, which not being done immediately, he was urgent in his request. "I prithee," said he, "let me see it. Dost thou think I am afraid of it?" Taking it in his hand, he kissed the blade, and passing his finger slightly along the edge, observed to the sheriff, "'Tis a sharp medicine, but a sound cure for all diseases." He then walked to the corner of the scaffold, and kneeling down, requested the people to pray for him, and for a considerable time remained on his knees engaged in silent devotion; after which he rose, and carefully examined the block, laying himself down to fit it to his neck, and to choose the easiest and most decent attitude. In all this he would receive no assistance; and having satisfied himself, he rose and declared he was ready. The executioner now came forward, and kneeling, asked his forgiveness, upon which Raleigh laid his hand smilingly on his shoulder, and bade him be satisfied, for he most cheerfully forgave him, only entreating him not to strike till he himself gave the signal, and then to fear nothing, and strike home. Saying this, he lay down on the block, and on being directed to place himself so that his face should look to the east, he answered, "It mattered little how the head lay, provided the heart was right." After a little while, during which it was observed, by the motion of his lips and hands, that he was occupied in prayer, he gave the signal; but whether from awkwardness or agitation, the executioner delayed; upon which, after waiting for a short time, he partially raised his head, and said aloud, "What dost thou fear? strike, man!" The axe then descended, and at two strokes the head was severed from the body, which never shrunk or altered its position, while the extraordinary effusion of blood evinced an unusual strength and vigor of constitution, though when he suffered, Sir Walter was in his sixty-sixth year. The head, after being, as usual, held up to the view of the people on either side of the scaffold, was put into a red bag, over which his velvet night-gown was thrown, and the whole immediately carried to a mourning-coach which was waiting, and conveyed to Lady Raleigh. This faithful and affectionate woman, who never married again, though she survived him twenty-nine years, had it embalmed and preserved in a case, which she kept with pious solicitude till her death.

The body was buried privately near the high altar of St. Margaret's church in Westminster, but no stone marks the spot.

VIII. The series of voyages to which allusion has been made, conveyed to England a much higher idea than had yet been entertained of her transatlantic dominion. It was found to include a range of territory stretching over eleven degrees of latitude, all in the temperate climates, diversified with noble rivers and harbors, and, wherever visited, displaying a luxuriant fertility. This prospect rekindled all the enthusiasm of enterprise and hopes of wealth. An association was formed by Sir Thomas Gates, Sir George Summers, Wingfield, Popham, with other men of rank, and eminent merchants, for the purpose of colonizing this vast region. James I., who was fond of such undertakings, and had employed them successfully for the improvement of some ruder parts of Scotland and Ireland, was ready to give every encouragement. The adventurers were divided into two companies; the one from London for the southern, the other from Bristol and the west for the northern parts of Virginia. The former were allowed to choose any spot between the thirty-fourth and forty-first degrees of latitude; the latter between the thirty-eighth and forty-fifth. Three degrees were thus common between both; but collision was prevented by enacting that wherever one had fixed its seat, the others should choose theirs at least 100 miles distant. From that first station each company was to possess fifty miles of coast on each side; their territory was thence to stretch the same distance inland, and the same out to sea, including all islands within the range. The coast was not divided between the companies, nor had either an exclusive right to their own portions beyond the space of 100 miles square, which they were allowed to choose. This may serve to acquit successive princes of the repeated infractions of the charter with which they have been charged. Within this range the associations obtained full property in all the lands, natural resources, and objects of every kind, with only the usual exception of a fifth of the gold and a fifteenth of the copper. The revenue produced by fines and light import-duties was to be enjoyed by them for twenty-one years, after which it was to be paid into the royal treasury. They were not, however, invested with those kingly attributes which had been lavished on Raleigh. James lodged the government in two councils, one resident in England, the other in the colony, and claimed the right of appointing both; but, having exercised it in regard to the first, he allowed them to nominate the Virginian members. He busied himself moreover in preparing a code of "orders and instructions," a proceeding, as Mr. Chalmers observes, decidedly unconstitutional, but controverted by no one. The colonists and their posterity were declared English subjects, yet were invested with no political rights, not even trial by jury, unless in capital charges; minor offences were punished arbitrarily by the council. The English church was exclusively established. Strict and laudable injunctions were given for the mild and equitable treatment of the natives.

The year 1606 was spent in collecting funds and adventurers, which last amounted then to one hundred and five, including persons of distinction, particularly George Percy, brother to the Earl of Northumberland. There were also Gosnold and Mr. Hunt a clergyman, while Captain Newport, an officer of skill and experience, undertook the naval command. But the individual destined to exercise the happiest influence on the new colony was Captain John Smith, who already, in the Turkish war, had displayed a firmness and intrepidity peculiarly fitting him for this arduous appointment. The fleet of three vessels, none exceeding one hundred tons, sailed from London on the nineteenth of December, taking again the circuitous route of the West Indies, rendered necessary perhaps through the lateness of the season. The arrangements, however, had been injudicious. James, by a ridiculous caprice, had caused the names and instructions of the council to be enclosed in a box, not to be opened till after the arrival in Virginia; and thus the crew, in going out, knew not whom to obey. The energy of Smith, with his frank and manly bearing, soon led them to recognise him as their leader. This was envied by others higher in rank, who charged him with a design to set aside the council, to usurp the government, and to become king. On these unsupported charges he was arrested, and confined during the voyage, and for some time longer; so that his services, when most wanted, were lost to the colony.

The expedition did not reach the coast of America till April, 1607, and in making for Roanoke, a violent tempest drove them quite out of their reckoning.

Fig. 22.—Portrait of Capt. John Smith.

Being tossed about several days without sight of land, they became despondent, and some even urged to return to England. Suddenly they came in view of an unknown promontory, which marked the entrance into a spacious gulf. This was the magnificent opening of the Chesapeake, the opposite capes of which were named after the young princes, Henry and Charles. The view of this coast at once dispelled their gloom, and made them rejoice in their enforced change of direction. "They were almost ravished with the sight thereof. It seemed to them to claim the prerogative over the most pleasant places in the world. Heaven and earth seem never to have agreed better to frame a place for man's commodious and delightful habitation." They soon reached a noble river, which they named James, and after ascending and examining its shores during seventeen days, they chose for their colony a spot fifty miles up, and called it Jamestown. The difficulties of treating with the natives soon began. The very first night "came the savages creeping upon all-fours from the hills, like bears, with their bows in their mouths." These they discharged against the strangers and wounded two; but as soon as "they had felt the sharpness of our shot" they retreated with loud cries into the woods. Afterward five, who were met near Cape Henry, though showing some signs of fear, were reassured by seeing "the captain lay his hand on his heart," and invite them across the river to the town. Their welcome was signally expressed "by a doleful noise, laying their faces to the ground, and scratching the earth with their nails." Mats were then spread on the ground, and covered with maize-bread, while tobacco was presented, with long ornamented pipes. They then danced for the amusement of their guests, shouting, howling, and stamping, "with many antic tricks and faces, making noise like so many wolves or devils." The English received a pressing invitation from a great Indian chief, the weroanee of Rappahana, whom they found rich in rude ornament, his person painted red and blue, with various embellishments, seemingly of pearl and silver, and a metal which was either copper or gold. "He entertained us in so modest a proud fashion, as though he had been a prince of civil government." His palace, on a hill watered by fine springs, was surrounded by as rich corn-fields as they had ever seen.

As soon as the party had landed, the box of instructions was opened, and the names of the council were found, including Smith; who, though he was kept out by the jealousy of his rivals, nevertheless accompanied Newport up the river, as high as the great falls, where they visited Powhatan, a sort of petty emperor over all the surrounding tribes. Smith reckons them at 7,000, of whom nearly 2,000 were warriors; but he never saw more than 700 together. Powhatan received them well; and when some of his people murmured at the land being thus occupied by a party of strangers, he replied, it was only waste ground, and, so long as they injured no one, they were welcome.

On their return to Jamestown affairs were found in evil plight. The colonists, not we fear without blame, had incurred the hostility of the savages, while they neglected to fortify their position. A general attack, which was made, was repulsed with great difficulty, seventeen being wounded, and one boy killed. By great exertion, about the middle of June, a palisaded fort was erected, secure against those rude assailants, who, however, continued to hover round, cutting off stragglers, and obliging the settlers to keep constant watch. The charges against Smith were still pressed, and a party wished to send him to England; but he, loudly demanding a trial on the spot, was supported by a majority of the colonists. He was triumphantly acquitted, and Wingfield, his accuser, condemned to pay him a fine of £200, which he generously threw into the common stock. Mr. Hunt, the clergyman, succeeded in producing at least an appearance of harmony, cemented by partaking together the Christian communion.

On the 15th June, Newport with the vessels sailed for England, leaving the settlers in the midst of that vast wilderness which they had undertaken to cultivate. In this situation the brilliant hopes which had lured them thither quickly vanished. The fruitfulness of the soil indeed fully equalled expectation; but all the machinery by which it could be made capable of producing individual wealth was still to be created. The land required not only a laborious culture, for which they were little prepared; but a still harder task remained, that of hewing down the forest which covered the whole of it. By an unhappy arrangement, all the produce for the first five years was to be in common, and distributed by the council according to their respective wants. But, as Chalmers shrewdly observes, "when men are not to profit, they will labor little; and when all are fed from a common granary, few will concern themselves how it is filled." Raising scarcely any crop the first year, they were dependant on the supplies from home, which had been much diminished during the long voyage, and are alleged to have been originally of inferior quality. A slender allowance of this unwholesome food, bad river-water, and exposure to a new climate, soon spread disease so widely, that there were often not ten men fit for service. "There were never," says Percy, "Englishmen left in a foreign country in such misery as we were." Before autumn, fifty died, nearly half their number, among whom was Gosnold, the projector of the settlement. Discontent naturally arose; Wingfield, the president, was accused of living in plenty while others were perishing, and even of meditating a departure. On these charges he was deposed, and his place supplied by Ratcliffe, who, being of an easy temper, left the whole management to Smith, which was what the colonists desired.

This gentleman justly considered sustenance the most important object, in search of which he proceeded with a party down the river. The natives treated them with derision, "as famished men, and holding out morsels of bread, asked

Fig. 23.—Indian Warrior.

for them swords, muskets, and other valuables." Unable to succeed by fair means, he discharged a volley, which caused them immediately to seek the shelter of the woods. Landing at a village, he found food in abundance; but forbade his people to encumber themselves with it, foreseeing the immediate return of the Indians. Accordingly there soon issued forth, amid hideous noises, sixty or seventy painted savages, bearing in front their *okee*, an image of skins stuffed with moss, and hung with copper chains. They advanced upon the English, but met so *kindly* a reception, that " down fell their god," divers of his worshippers lay sprawling, and the rest disappeared. Their spirit being now humbled, they sent presently a venerable character, a *quiyoughcasuck*, to treat for peace, and for the restoration of their idol. Smith answered, that if they would load his boat, they should be welcome not only to their okee, but to a stock of beads, hatchets, and other valuables. They cheerfully assented, and amidst singing and dancing brought not only the stipulated grain, but presents of turkey, venison, and wild fowl.

Smith returned just in time to prevent Wingfield and another from seizing a vessel and sailing to England. His supplies, with the flocks of water-fowl which came at the approach of winter, relieved their wants ; and having in his rambles discovered the great river Chickahominy, he determined to explore it to its source, not, it is said, without a hope of thereby reaching the South sea, viewed then as the grand source of wealth. He was impelled, it was imagined, by the taunts of some of his enemies in the colony, but we rather think only by his own adventurous spirit. He ascended first in his barge, then in a canoe, and twenty miles on foot attended only by his Indian guides. But three hundred natives, who had traced his steps, surprised and dispersed his party, and then came suddenly upon himself. He made astonishing efforts for safety, and fastening with his garters a native ally to his person, presented him to the enemy as a buckler ; then he ran to the canoe, which he would have reached, had he not suddenly sunk in a deep morass, where he was overtaken, and, to escape from perishing with cold, obliged to surrender.

He had now reason to consider his last hour approaching, and a circle had in fact been formed to shoot him. With characteristic presence of mind he asked for the chief, showed his compass-dial, pointed out its singular movements, and endeavored to explain the corresponding phenomena of the earth and sky. Whether they understood these indications or not, they were awed with astonishment as if admitted to contemplate a supernatural object. On a signal from their leader, they laid down their bows and arrows, and led him under strict guard to their capital. He was there exhibited to the women and children ; and a wild war-dance was performed round him, in fantastic measures, and with frightful yells and contortions. He was then shut up in a long house, and supplied at every meal with as much bread and venison as would have dined twenty men ; but, receiving no other sign of kindness, he began to dread that they were fattening in order to eat him. Even without such a precise purpose, this festive entertainment is known among savages to be no uncommon prelude to torture and death. They asked his aid in reducing Jamestown, while he sought an opportunity of making his way thither. In the course of this manœuvring, a message sent to that place gave him an opportunity to display the powers of writing, which was considered by them as a species of magical spell. At length, after being paraded and exhibited in various villages, he was led to Pamunkey, the residence of Powhatan. It was here his doom was sealed. The chief received him in pomp, wrapt in a spacious robe of rackoon skins, with all the tails hanging down. Behind appeared two long lines of men and women, with faces painted red, heads decked with white down, and necks quite encircled by chains of beads. A lady of rank presented water to wash his hands, another a bunch of feathers to dry them. A long deliberation was then held, and the result proved fatal. Two large stones were placed before Powhatan, and by the united efforts of the attendants Smith was dragged to the spot, his head laid on one of

Fig. 24.—Frontlet of the Queen of Pamunkey.

FIG. 25.—Portrait of Pochahontas.

them, and the mighty club was raised, a few blows of which were to terminate his life. In this last extremity, when every hope seemed past, a very unexpected interposition took place. Pocahontas, the youthful and favorite daughter of this savage chief, was seized with those tender emotions which form the ornament of her sex. Advancing to her father, she in the most earnest terms supplicated mercy for the stranger: and though all her entreaties were lost on that savage heart, her zeal only redoubled. She ran to Smith, took his head in her arms, laid her own upon it, and declared that the first death-blow must fall upon her. The barbarian's breast was at length softened, and the life of the Englishman was spared.

Our adventurer, being naturally expected to render some services in return for so great a boon, employed himself in making hatchets, beads, and other ornaments for the father and daughter. At the end of two days he was conducted into a large house, where, amid hideous and doleful noises, Powhatan rushed in, with two hundred attendants, strangely disguised and their faces blackened.

Fig. 26.—Pocahontas saving the Life of Smith.

Smith again thought his last hour had come, but the chief announced these as signs of peace and friendship; and he was forthwith sent to Jamestown on the sole condition of transmitting thence two culverins and a millstone, a promise faithfully fulfilled.

He again arrived at a critical moment. A majority of the colonists, impatient of continued hardship and privation, had determined to prepare a pinnace, and set sail for their native country. He took the most energetic steps to arrest this course, having, with the aid of some faithful adherents, pointed a gun at the vessel, and declared she must either stop or sink. A conspiracy was then formed against him; but by his vigilance he detected it, and sent the ringleaders to England. The fair Pocahontas continued her generous kindness, and came every four or five days with provisions, which relieved their wants and revived their spirits. They were soon still farther cheered by the arrival of Captain Newport, with one hundred and twenty emigrants and liberal supplies. The company, however, now impatiently endured their heavy expenses, and the absence of all prospect of marketable returns. Gold was still viewed as the main source of wealth, and many of the new-comers had been selected on account of their supposed skill in its discovery. Naturally desiring to satisfy their employers, they thought they perceived in a certain yellow glittering earth this precious ore. Thenceforth all sober industry was thrown aside: "Dig gold, wash gold, refine gold," was the universal cry. Smith lamented to see the whole attention of the settlers attracted by this "gilded dirt," but could not prevent them from putting a large portion on board, and some time elapsed before they were apprized that a skilful examination had proved it utterly worthless. Fortunately perhaps, no rumor seems ever to have reached them of the real gold in the mountainous country, whence they were indeed more distant than the first colonists.

Newport, on learning the friendly intercourse with Powhatan, sent liberal presents, and was invited to visit that savage potentate. He found the monarch surrounded by twenty-two fair ladies, lavishly painted and decked with beads. A courteous traffic was opened, in which Smith considered the captain as overreached, particularly in afterward acceding to a request for twenty swords, dangerous weapons to put into such hands. The latter, after remaining fourteen weeks, departed without being able to collect any other cargo besides cedarwood, and the yellow earth of which such illusory hopes were entertained.

Smith now undertook the important task of exploring the Chesapeake to its head, not only with the view of tracing the limits of the colony, but still more from the hope of an inlet opening into the South sea, and affording a passage to India. In a small barge of only two tons, he steered across to Cape Charles, and began to survey the eastern shore. Here, and at other places, he had sharp conflicts with the natives; and, we suspect, did not altogether follow that conciliatory course ascribed to him by his panegyrists. On meeting any new tribe, his first step is stated to have been to demand their arms and one of their children; and, on refusal, they were treated as enemies. It can not surely appear surprising that there should have been some hesitation in complying with such requisitions. In general the people received the English with much surprise, asking "what they were, and what they would." Finding the eastern coast obstructed by rocks and other difficulties, he crossed to the western and proceeded upward. The men, however, tired with twelve days' rowing, and finding their bread wet and spoiled, became extremely discontented. He endeavored to rouse them to an emulation of Lane's crew and their canine diet, but was soon obliged to yield and return. Proceeding along an unexplored part of the western coast, they came unexpectedly upon the magnificent estuary of the Potomac, seven miles broad; and this grand object reviving their spirits and energies, they cheerfully undertook to explore it. They ascended as high as the barge could carry them, and then made a journey by land. Mr. Bancroft has traced them beyond the future site of Washington to the falls above Georgetown. They were led to a mine of a substance like antimony, which, though black, glittered like silver, and was believed by some to contain a large portion of that metal; but, on being examined, it proved of no value whatever. After escaping several ambuscades laid by the natives, they made a short survey of the Rappahannock, and then returned to Jamestown.

Smith, having been prevented from reaching the head of this great inlet, set out afresh in a few days for that destination. He accordingly made his way thither, and ascended the Susquehanna, till stopped by the cataracts. Having learned that two days' journey higher there was a powerful people named the Sasquesahanocks, he sent a message requesting a visit. After an interval of nearly a week there appeared sixty, a giant-like race, with presents of arms, venison, and tobacco-pipes nearly three feet long; and their deportment was quite peaceable and courteous. He then returned to Jamestown, examining in his way the river Patuxent. This voyage of about three thousand miles, performed by twelve men in a small open barge, " with such watery diet, in those great waters and barbarous countries," was extremely creditable to the parties. Although unproductive as to the South sea or to gold, it made an important addition to the knowledge of this part of America.

On his arrival, Smith was installed as president, and began, with characteristic activity, to improve the buildings, strengthen the forts, and train the men to military exercises; but he was interrupted by the arrival of Newport with a fresh colony of about seventy, including two females. The company having spent at least £2,000 in the equipment, expressed an earnest desire and expectation of being somewhat reimbursed. They pointed out particularly, as objects to be attained, a lump of gold, the discovery of the South sea, or a member of Raleigh's lost company. The second being seemingly the main object, a bark was sent in frame to ascend one of the great rivers, to be thence carried over the mountains, and launched on a stream flowing into the Pacific. In estimating the want of geographical knowledge which this scheme displayed, we must allow for their imperfect resources. The discoveries of Drake and Cavendish could not yet be connected with the eastern side of America. The impression probably was, that the moderate breadth of the continent in Mexico would be prolonged northward; while in point of fact the idea of wealth attached to the South sea was founded on vague and illusory associations. Its shores in Mexico and Peru were indeed rich in the precious metals; but this afforded no presumption as to what might be the productions of a more northern latitude. As, in furtherance of this object, Powhatan's favor was to be courted, there had been sent handsome presents, with materials to crown him with splendor in the European style. Smith viewed the Pacific and the coronation of Powhatan as alike absurd; but was obliged to yield to Newport, who came with instructions direct from the company. With only four companions he courageously repaired to the residence of the monarch, inviting him to come and be crowned at Jamestown. The party were extremely well received, though once they heard in the adjoining wood outcries so hideous as made them flee to their arms; but Pocahontas assured them they had nothing to fear. Accordingly, there issued thence thirty damsels of such strange aspect that he uncourteously terms them fiends. They were covered only with green leaves bedaubed with shining colors, the leader wearing on her forehead a pair of stag's horns. For an hour they danced round the fire, with wild shouts and strange contortions. They then retired; and the table was spread with an abundance of savage dainties, when the ladies with whom he hoped to have done, rushed in, and, crowding round him, lavished

FIG. 27.—Ruins of Jamestown.

compliments with which he would have gladly dispensed, each calling out, "Love you not me?" When, however, the unsophisticated monarch received the invitation, he proudly replied, "If your king has sent me presents, I also am a king, and this is my land—your father is to come up to me, not I to him."

Newport was not discouraged; but, taking with him Smith and fifty men, repaired to this sylvan court. The coronation took place; but Powhatan appears to have been more surprised than delighted. He made a difficulty even in putting on the scarlet dress from a fear of some magical effect. He strenuously objected to kneeling; on which they long absurdly insisted, but were obliged to be contented with his merely bending the shoulders. A volley fired at the close made him start up in alarm, but he soon recovered his composure.

The king assured them that all their ideas of a salt water beyond the mountains were erroneous, and refused guides for so wild a search. Newport, how ever, goaded probably by his employers, set out, leaving Smith at Jamestown. The party ascended to the falls, and even forty miles farther by land. Finding, however, provisions scanty, and their toils always increasing, they commenced a retreat before they had reached the Allegany. They returned to the town, oppressed "with toil, famine, and discontent;" and the chimera of the South sea was finally relinquished.

Meantime all hands were employed in preparing some kind of cargo that might not wholly disappoint the company; but this was very difficult. Persons had been sent over to teach the art of making pitch, tar, glass, and ashes, objects unfit for so distant a market; however some specimens were prepared. The larger number applied themselves to the cutting of timber for boards and wainscot; and even the gentlemen endeavored to make an amusement of this hard task. Thus a cargo was at length made up, though its value little accorded with expectation.

Smith, having despatched the vessel, applied himself to the procuring of food. In this search he employed an unjustifiable violence toward the Indians, and formed a plot for seizing the person of Powhatan, with whom the colonists had long been in amity. As a preparation he sent six men, four of them Germans, to build for him a sylvan palace. These persons, however, being extremely well treated, became attached to their host, and betrayed to him the meditated conspiracy. Powhatan, though highly incensed, was unwilling to encounter the English in open war, but dissembling, endeavored to catch the president in his own toils. When the latter, therefore, approached with a large party, he declined, on plausible pretences, to receive them armed. Smith replied in a similar tone; and there began between the two a game of courtesy and treachery, in which, however, the savage proved the better performer. Not only was the Englishman foiled, but was himself repeatedly in danger, and once only saved by a second interposition of Pocahontas, who, at the risk of her father's displeasure, ran through the woods in a dark night to give him warning. At another time he was surrounded by a large body under Powhatan's brother, but extricated himself by energy and address. In this way, however, he had placed his countrymen in a position of rooted enmity with the natives, which continued to produce distressing consequences.

Meantime events occurred at home deeply affecting the interests of the colony. Although the company had been disappointed of their expected returns, the accounts of the extent, beauty, and fertility of the regions just discovered, kindled in that enterprising age an extraordinary enthusiasm. Pamphlets were published, apparently on high authority, painting it as completely an earthly paradise. On a larger scale, and under more enlightened views, it was hoped that the errors which had cramped its progress would be avoided. Many distinguished individuals were ready to embark their fortunes in this enterprise; and, with the consent of the old members, the company was remodelled on a larger scale, and under a new charter. Their territory was augmented from the former one hundred miles of coast to four hundred; being two hundred on each side of Cape Comfort; and it was extended in breadth to the South sea. James, yielding to some influence which does not distinctly appear, was induced to waive those high claims of sovereignty before so strictly reserved. He allowed the council in England to be chosen by the proprietors, with power to nominate a governor. The Episcopal church was exclusively established, and all emigrants required to take the oath of supremacy. There appears a peculiar anxiety to exclude Roman Catholics, respecting whom it is observed, in a pamphlet addressed to Sir Thomas Smith, the treasurer, "I would have none seasoned with the least taint of that leaven to be settled on this plantation, or any part of that country; but if once perceived, such a one, weed him out; for they will ever be plotting and conspiring to root you out if they can. If you will live and prosper, harbor not this viperous brood in your bosom."

The exertions of the patentees, and the general enthusiasm kindled throughout the nation, enabled the company to equip an expedition of nine vessels and five hundred emigrants. Lord Delaware, distinguished by his talents and virtues, was named governor for life; and as he could not depart immediately, Sir Thomas Gates and Sir George Summers were to rule in the meantime. The vessels set sail on the 15th May, 1609, and seven arrived on the 11th August at Jamestown; but unfortunately they had encountered a violent storm, in which two, having on board Gates and Summers, were separated and thrown upon the Bermudas. In their absence, Smith justly claimed the rule; but many of the new-comers, being bankrupts, spendthrifts, or others sent for doing no good at home, were indisposed to obey him. For some time total anarchy reigned; but its evils at length became so great, that he was entreated to resume the government. He exerted himself to locate advantageously the emigrants, of whom two parties, one hundred and twenty each, were settled at Nansemond, and at the Falls of James river. Both, however, mismanaged their affairs, quarrelled with the Indians, and lost a number of their men; while they rejected all his efforts to remedy these disorders. In returning from the latter place, a bag of gunpowder burst and severely mangled his person, so that he reached home in extreme torture. Here he was told that plots were forming against his life. Unable in his debilitated state to struggle against so many difficulties, he returned to England, quitting for ever the colony which had been so much indebted to him. He received at home neither honors nor rewards. The company, prepossessed by his numerous enemies, complained that he had brought no wealth into their coffers, and had acted severely toward the Indians. Posterity has done him justice, perhaps somewhat beyond his merits. His bold and active spirit, with sound practical judgment, eminently qualified him for the station; though, being somewhat hot and uncompromising in his temper, he excited bitter enmities. A conciliatory disposition and persuasive powers were, in such a situation, almost indispensable to render his exertions effective. His conduct toward the Indians was in general culpable, and by the hostility which it created, neutralized in a great measure his eminent services.

His eulogium, however, was found in the state of the colony after his departure. Only about thirty or forty acres were cultivated; the ships had brought grain in limited quantity, and much spoiled during the unfortunate voyage. The Indians, no longer overawed by the late president, not only refused victuals, but killed many settlers. Thus there ensued a dreadful famine, long fearfully remembered under the name of the "Starving Time." Many were impelled to the horrid resource of devouring the bodies of the dead; nay there are dark imputations of murder committed under this fearful impulse. Vessels sent along the rivers were either sunk, or the crews beaten by the savages. Virginia seemed a devoted soil. Of the flourishing colony of five hundred persons, there remained only sixty "most miserable and poor creatures." After a large expenditure, and successive arrivals of emigrants, it had returned almost into its original insignificance.

IX. The Virginian company, by their second charter, had assigned to them a region of vast extent, including, doubtless, the heads of the great bays of Delaware and Chesapeake. This grant, we have seen, was forfeited; yet the colonists continued anxiously to claim and consider the whole as Virginia, though their title could not stand against the regal power influenced by the solicitations of a favorite. Sir George Calvert had been secretary of state under James I., but having become a convert to the Romish religion, he was excluded from the direction of the government. He now turned his attention to America, and obtained from the king a large grant of land, which was termed Maryland, in honor of the queen Henrietta Maria, who had warmly seconded his views.

The influence and favor enjoyed by Calvert, now created Lord Baltimore, are strikingly proved by the terms of the grant. Charles, notwithstanding his despotic feelings, reserved neither the right of taxation nor of giving laws; these were to be exercised by the proprietor, with the assent of the freemen or their deputies, whose assembly was to be made "in such sort and form as to him should seem best." Moreover, in emergencies, when there was not time to call them together, he might of himself make "fit and wholesome ordinances," not stated as temporary, but "to be inviolably observed." By a very singular clause, meant, it should seem, to blind the public at home, he was empowered to found churches and chapels, "according to the ecclesiastical law of England." He might also train, muster, and call out troops, exercise all the functions of captain-general, and, in case of rebellion or sedition, proclaim martial law. He had likewise the nomination of the judges and all other officers. Nothing being left to the crown but the usual empty claim of the royal mines, Maryland became, what indeed the proprietor terms it, a separate monarchy.

FIG. 28.—Portrait of Cecil Calvert, Lord Baltimore.

George, the first Lord Baltimore, died before the completion of the charter, which was therefore granted to his son Cecil, on whom devolved the establishment of the colony. He appears to have applied himself to the task with activity and judgment; and states that he spent upon it above £20,000 from his own funds, and an equal sum raised among his friends. Warned by Virginian disasters, he avoided from the first all chimerical projects, and placed his establishment entirely on an agricultural basis. Every one who carried out five persons, male or female, paying their expenses, estimated at £20 each, was to receive 1,000 acres. Those defraying their own charges got 100 for themselves, and the same for each adult member of their family; for children under six years, 50 acres. The rent was two shillings for each 100 acres. Lord Baltimore did not rule in person, nor, so far as we can trace, even visit the colony, at least till after the restoration. Two of his brothers, however, acted successively as governors, and died there.

In November, 1633, Leonard Calvert set sail with the first emigrants, consisting of about two hundred persons, including a son of Sir Thomas Gerard, one of Sir Thomas Wiseman, and two of Lady Wintour. In February he touched at Point Comfort in Virginia, where his arrival was by no means acceptable; nevertheless, Sir John Harvey, in obedience to the express orders of Charles, gave him a courteous reception. Early in March he entered the Potomac, to the people on the shores of which the sight of so large a vessel was quite new, and caused the utmost astonishment. The report was, that a canoe was approaching as big as an island, with men standing in it as thick as trees in a forest; and they thought with amazement how enormous must have been the trunk out of which it had been hollowed. A piece of ordnance, resounding for the first time on the shores of this mighty river, caused the whole country to tremble. The intercourse, however, appears to have been judiciously conducted, and was, on the whole, very amicable. Calvert sailed up to Piscataqua, an Indian settlement nearly opposite the present site of Mount Vernon, where the chief received him with kindness, saying, "he would not bid him go, neither would he bid him stay; he might use his own discretion." On reflection, he considered the place too far up the river, and therefore the vessel was moved down to a tributary named then St. George's, and now St. Mary's. Ascending it four leagues, he came to a considerable Indian town, named Yoacomoco; and being hospitably received, as well as pleased with the situation, he determined to fix his colony there. The weroanee accepted an invitation on board, and Sir John Harvey having just arrived from Virginia, the chief was led down to the cabin, and seated at dinner between the two governors. An alarm having spread among the people on shore that he was detained as a prisoner, they made the banks echo with shouts of alarm; the Indian attendants durst not go to them, but when he himself appeared on deck, they were satisfied. He became so much attached to the English as to declare, that if they should kill him he would not wish his death avenged, being sure that he must have deserved his fate. Amid these dispositions, it was not difficult to negotiate the formation of a settlement. For hatchets, hoes, knives, cloth, and other articles of probably very small original cost, the strangers not only obtained a large tract of land, but were allowed by the inhabitants to occupy immediately half of their village, with the corn growing adjacent to it, and, at the end of harvest, were to receive the whole. Thus the English were at once comfortably established, without those severe hardships which usually attend an infant settlement.

This good understanding was prolonged for a number of years; but at length, in 1642, the emigrants had the usual misfortune of being involved in a war with the natives. For two years they suffered all its distressing and harassing accompaniments, which, in 1664, were happily terminated by a treaty, the conditions of which, and some acts of assembly immediately following, seem to prove that the evil had arisen entirely from the interested proceedings of individuals

The prohibition of kidnapping the Indians, and of selling arms to them, show the existence of these culpable practices. This peace was of long duration, and the Maryland government seem, on the whole, to have acted more laudably toward this race than any other, that of Penn excepted.

X. All the efforts both of government and of powerful companies to people the district of New England had proved nearly abortive, when, from an unexpected quarter, a tide of population poured into it, which rendered it the most prosperous of all the colonies on the American continent.

The Reformation, though it doubtless involved an extensive exercise of private judgment, was not accompanied by any express recognition of that right, or of any general principle of toleration. These, which, as Mr. Bancroft observes, were its tardy fruits, were long wanting in England, where the change was introduced, not by the people, though conformable to their wishes, but by the most arbitrary of their monarchs, consulting chiefly his own passion and caprice. Substituting himself for the head of the Catholic church, Henry VIII. exacted the same implicit submission. Elizabeth trode in his steps, equally despotic, and attached, if not to popery, as has sometimes been suspected, at least to a pompous ritual and powerful hierarchy. But the nation in general, considering the Romish religion as contrary to Scripture, and shocked by the bloody persecutions of Mary, and other sovereigns on the continent, were disposed to go into the opposite extreme. From Geneva they imbibed the Calvinistic doctrine and discipline, with the strict manners usually imbibed with them. The queen, whose views were irreconcilably opposed to these innovations, claimed the right of putting them down by main force. The most severe laws were enacted under the sanction of Whitgift, Archbishop of Canterbury, a prelate sincerely but bigotedly attached to the English church. The wisdom of Cecil viewed with much dissatisfaction the discontents thus engendered, and, on reading twenty-four queries drawn up by the primate, told him, "he thought the Inquisition of Spain used not so many questions to comprehend and to trap their preys." He was seconded by the lords of the council, and the queen was not insensible to his remonstrances; but whenever she showed a disposition to relent, Whitgift threw himself on his knees, and prevailed upon her not to sacrifice her own power and the unity of the church. The high court of commission was established; several nonconformists were fined or imprisoned, and a few suffered death.

But under all these persecutions, the party continually increased, and even assumed a bolder character. The Puritans, while they sought to reform the church, had no wish to withdraw from her bosom; but there sprang up a new sect named Brownists, who, denying the authority of her doctrine and discipline, sought for the first time to found an independent communion. Upon them all the vials of persecution were poured forth. Brown himself could boast that he had been shut up in thirty-two prisons, and several of his followers were put to death; but his own firmness at length failed, and he accepted a living in that church which he had so strenuously opposed. Although much condemned by his more zealous adherents, his desertion broke for some time the union of the party. Toward the end of Elizabeth's reign, however, there was formed in a northern county a congregation of separatists, under two respectable clergymen, Robinson and Brewster. During a certain interval they escaped notice; but James, who soon began to follow his predecessor's steps, took such measures as convinced them that it would be vain to attempt the exercise of their profession at home. In looking for an asylum, they fixed upon Holland, the first country where toleration was publicly sanctioned by law; and thither they made their escape amid much difficulty and hardship, their families being for some time detained behind them. Having reached that foreign land, they found the protection denied at home, and remained eleven years unmolested, and even respected. But they never became fully naturalized; their original occupation of agriculture was more congenial to their taste than the mechanical arts, by which alone they could earn a subsistence among the Dutch. They turned their eyes, therefore, to a transatlantic region, where they would not merely enjoy toleration, but might form a society founded on their favorite plan of church-government.

Animated by these views, the exiles applied to the Virginian company, then under the management of Sandys, Southampton, and other liberal members, who zealously espousing their cause, obtained, though not without difficulty, from King James a promise to wink at their heresy, provided they remained otherwise tranquil. Smith, deeply interested in this transaction, tendered and even pressed his services; which would doubtless have been extremely valuable. His religious views, however, were materially different, and instead of the subordination which he required, he found in them a rooted determination "to be lords and kings of themselves." It was necessary, therefore, that they should "make trial of their own follies;" for which, he mentions with a mixture of regret and triumph, that "they paid soundly, and were beaten with their own rod." They also wanted capital adequate to the founding of a plantation. Several London merchants agreed to advance the necessary sums, to be repaid out of the proceeds of their industry; but the terms were very high, and till the liquidation of the debt the produce of their labor was to be thrown into a common stock for the benefit of the creditors; hence their exertions were not stimulated by the salutary impulse of personal interest.

With the means thus procured, the emigrants purchased one vessel of sixty, and hired another of 180 tons; the former of which sailed to Delfthaven to take on board the brethren. The two joined at Southampton, and thence proceeded on their western voyage; but before they reached the Land's End, the master of the smaller one, declaring her to be too leaky to cross the Atlantic, put back to Dartmouth for repairs. After another trial, the captain again pronounced her unfit for the voyage, and made sail for Plymouth. These disasters and alarms, though involving the loss of much precious time, "winnowed their number of the cowardly and the lukewarm;" and they finally set sail in one vessel on the 6th September, 1620, being in all one hundred and two persons, with the firm determination of braving every hardship. They had a tempestuous voyage, and though their destination was the mouth of the Hudson, they arrived on the 9th November in view of a great promontory, which proved to be Cape Cod. The captain, it has been alleged, had received a bribe from the Dutch to avoid a place where they had projected a settlement. Of this, however, the adventurers being ignorant, were comforted by the view of a goodly land wooded to the water's edge. Whales so abounded, that had the crew possessed means and instruments, which, to their great regret, were wanting, they might have procured £4,000 worth of oil. They sailed on toward their destination, but being driven back by contrary winds, determined to go ashore. Previously, however, they sought to obviate the danger of discord by a mutual agreement, in the name of God, to combine into a body politic; framing and duly observing laws for the general good.

They landed on the 11th, but being informed that more commodious spots might be found to the northwest, in the interior of the great bay of Massachusetts, they determined that a select party should proceed in the shallop in search of them. The boat, however, was in such disrepair that it could not sail till the end of two or three weeks: sixteen of them, therefore, resolved to make an excursion into the interior. They met no natives, but found on a hill, half buried in the ground, several baskets filled with ears of corn, part of which they carried away, meaning to satisfy the owners on the first opportunity, which unluckily never occurred. They saw many geese and ducks, but were unable to reach them; and being exposed to severe cold, hastily returned. Soon after they started for the same spot, named Cornhill, in the neighborhood of which they collected ten bushels of grain, esteemed a providential supply. They lighted upon a village without inhabitants; but the houses were neatly constructed of young saplings bent at top, as in an arbor, and covered without and within with fine mats. Eagles' claws, deers' feet, and harts' horns, were stuck into them as charms and ornaments. They then regained their boat and sailed round to the ship. Some of their number urged that they should remain at least during the winter in this creek, where corn and fish could be procured, while many were disabled by sickness for further removal. The majority, however, observed that water was scarce, and the anchorage for ships too distant; that they had every chance of finding a better situation, and to fix here and then remove would be doubling their labor. On the 6th December, therefore, the shallop being at length ready, a chosen party set sail. After proceeding six or seven leagues, they reached a bay forming a good harbor, but without a stream falling into it. Seeing some Indian wigwams, they followed, but could not reach the people, and found only a large burial-place. They returned to sleep at the landing-place, but at midnight were wakened by "a great and hideous cry," which they flattered themselves proceeded only from wolves or foxes. Next morning, just after prayers, the sound was heard with redoubled violence, and was most dreadful. A straggler rushed in, crying, "They are men—Indians." Though the party ran to their arms, before they could be mustered the arrows were flying thick among them. A brisk fire checked the assailants; but the chief, shooting from a tree, stood three discharges, till at the fourth he screamed out and ran, followed by his men. They were reckoned at thirty or forty, and numerous arrows were picked up; but providentially not one Englishman was hurt.

They sailed fifteen leagues farther, and on the 9th reached a harbor that had been strongly recommended. The weather was dark and stormy, and the entrance encumbered with rocks; yet they fortunately run in on a fine sandy beach. This being Saturday, they did not land till Monday the 11th, when they were highly pleased, finding a commodious harbor, a land well wooded, vines, cherries, and berries, lately planted, and a hill cleared for corn. There was no navigable stream, but several brooks of fresh water fell into the sea. They advanced seven or eight miles into the country without seeing any Indians.

They now finally fixed upon this spot, to which, on the 19th, the vessel was brought round; and they named it New Plymouth, to commemorate hospitalities received at home. The erection of houses, however, was a hard task, amid severe weather, short days, and very frequent storms. By distributing the unmarried among the several families, they reduced the buildings wanted to nineteen, and by the 10th January had completed one, twenty feet square, for public meetings. The exposure, however, and wading through the water in such inclement weather, brought on severe illnesses, to which Carver, a governor highly esteemed, and many others, fell victims. But on the 3d March a south wind sprung up; the weather became mild; the birds sung in the woods most pleasantly; the invalids quickly recovered; and many of them lived to a good old age.

In the autumn of 1621, the merchants sent out another vessel with thirty-five settlers; but misled by "prodigal reports of plenty" sent home by certain colonists, they supplied no provisions; nay, the crew required to be provided with a portion for their return voyage. The consequence was, that in the course of the winter the colonists were reduced to a half allowance of corn daily, then to five kernels a-piece; lastly, to entire want. Equally destitute of live stock, they depended wholly on wild animals. Till May, 1622, fowls abounded; but there remained then merely fish, which they had not nets to catch; and it was only by feeding on the shell species, collected among the rocks, that they were preserved from absolute starvation.

The emigrants had seen the natives only in the short hostile encounter, but afterward learned that a severe pestilence had thinned their numbers. The crime of Hunt also had filled the country with horror and dread of the strangers. To their surprise, on the 16th March, 1621, a savage almost naked, in the most confident manner, walked through the village, and addressed those he met in broken English. They crowded round him, and on their eager inquiry, learned that his name was Samoset; that he belonged to the Wampanoags, a somewhat distant tribe; and that their immediate neighbors were the people of Massassoit and the Nausites, the latter of whom had been the assailants in the late conflict. They treated him liberally with strong waters and food, presented him with a great-coat, knife, and ornaments, and begged him to return with some of his countrymen. After a brief absence, he appeared with "five proper men," pre

Fig. 29.—Tattooed Indian.

senting the usual grotesque attire and ferocious aspect. They all heartily danced and sung. A few days later he brought Squanto, whose restoration to his native country had rendered him extremely friendly to the English. Being ready to act as interpreter and mediator, he opened a communication with Massassoit; and on the 22d March, that great sagamore, with Quadequina his brother, and sixty men, was announced as in the vicinity. Difficulties were felt as to the meeting from want of mutual confidence; however, Squanto having brought an invitation to parley, Edward Winslow went with presents, and was kindly received. The governor, then, after obtaining some Indians as hostages, marched out at the head of six musketeers, kissed hands with the great chief, and presented a bottle of strong waters, of which he drank somewhat too copiously. A treaty was concluded, both of abstinence from mutual injury, and protection against others; and it was long faithfully observed.

Two of the settlers now accepted an invitation to visit his residence. After a laborious journey of fifteen miles through trackless woods, they were received with great courtesy, but found a total deficiency of victuals, of which it seems the king's absence had prevented any supply. At night they were honored by sharing the royal couch, which consisted of a large board, covered with a thin mat. At the other end lay his majesty and the queen; and they had soon the additional company of two chiefs, who, with a large colony of fleas and other insects, and the uncouth songs with which their bedfellows lulled themselves to rest, rendered their slumbers very brief. Next day, two large bream were spread on the table; but "forty expected a share." Though strongly urged, they declined to partake any longer of these hospitalities.

It was discovered, however, that Squanto was completely abusing their confidence; telling his countrymen that but for him the English would kill the Indians; and that they kept the plague locked up in their store-house, which only his intercession prevented from being let loose. On this being known, the utmost pains were taken, and successfully, to undeceive the people. In February, 1622, the settlers had completely enclosed their town, forming four bulwarks and three gates. They were some time after alarmed by hearing that Massassoit, now at the point of death, was likely to be succeeded by his son Coubatant, whose disposition was far from friendly. Edward Winslow hastened to the spot, and found the magicians busy at their incantations, and six or eight woman chafing him amidst hideous yells. The chief, already blind, cried out: "Oh, Winslow, I shall never see thee again!" That gentleman, however, by suitable medicines, gave present relief, and in a few days effected a cure. Even the heir-apparent being promised similar aid in case of need, became greatly reconciled to them.

Meantime, Weston, one of the London adventurers, had sent out a settlement consisting of sixty individuals to a place which they named Weymouth; but they behaved so ill to the Indians, that the latter entered into a general confederacy to cut off all the English. This was revealed by Massassoit to his friends at Plymouth, who succeeded in saving both themselves and their rivals, though the latter were obliged to relinquish their establishment, some returning home, and others joining the first colony.

This last made such progress that, though reduced in the spring of 1621 to fifty or sixty persons, in 1624 it amounted to a hundred and eighty. They were, as Winslow observes, "by God's providence safely seated, housed, and fortified." They had escaped those tyrannical governors, and "bestial yea diabolical" settlers, who had ruined so many colonies, though he admits that it was vain as yet to hope for profit. The merchants, however, complained most loudly, that they had laid out a large capital without receiving or having any prospect of the slightest return. After much discussion, it was determined that the colonists should now supply themselves with everything, and for past services should, during nine years, pay £200 annually. Eight adventurers, on receiving a monopoly of the trade for six years, undertook to meet this engagement; so that the settlers were now established in the full property of their lands. In six years more their number had risen to three hundred.

The Plymouth company meantime continued their abortive efforts to derive some benefit from their vast domains; being particularly solicitous to stop the active trade and fishery carried on in defiance of them. Francis West was appointed admiral, and Robert Gorges lieutenant-general of New England, with strict injunctions to restrain interlopers; but in an ocean and continent almost equally wide and waste, they could effect little. The most important grant was to Robert, son of Sir Ferdinand Gorges, who, obtaining a large portion of what is now called New Hampshire, employed Captain Mason, a person of great activity, to colonize it; and hence were built Dover and Portsmouth on the Piscataqua. These, however, made only a slow progress; nor was it till the death of their founders, that, being left nearly to themselves, they drew gradual accessions both from home and the adjoining colony. The crews also, who sought timber and fish on the coast of Maine, began to form fixed stations on the Penobscot and Kennebec. Levett, who visited America in 1623, strongly recommends this course, asserting that a settlement on shore might take twice the quantity of fish that a ship can do at sea, and have still seven months for other employment. He gives a warning, at that time too much neglected, that they must carry out eighteen months' provisions, and work hard for a fresh supply.

The emigration, however, which was to render New England a flourishing colony, was again derived from the suspicion and dread which always attend religious persecution. It seems to have abated toward the end of James's reign, Abbot, the primate, being a man of mild temper, and averse to violent measures. In 1625, Charles I. succeeded, a young prince of virtuous dispositions, but of obstinate and despotic temper, attached with a conscientious but blind zeal to the English church, and probably imbibing from his queen Henrietta some favor for popish ceremonies. He threw himself into the arms of Laud, bishop of London, a zealot in the same cause, and they entered together on a career oppressive to the nation, and ultimately fatal to themselves. The body of the people and clergy having become more and more Calvinistic, that creed had obtained among both a great majority. It was accompanied with a strictness, and even preciseness as to morals and conduct, which procured them the name of Puritans; also with a peculiar aversion to everything which had the least aspect of popery. Laud proceeded with the utmost severity not only against the new doctrine, but against any particular display of it, such as preaching on week-days, enforcing a rigid observance of the sabbath, rebuking for drunkenness, or other open sin. These steps were sufficient, according to circumstances, to produce censure, suspension, and deprivation. Nor was he content with the church as he had found it, but introduced new ceremonies and vestments, closely approximating to the Romish standard. These mandates, though the most odious, were also the most strongly urged, and their omission the most rigidly punished. All the popular ministers in the kingdom were thus either silenced or under immediate peril of this sentence; and hence a great part of the nation was deprived of any ministration which they considered profitable or edifying. Yet loyalty was still powerful, and they were not ripe for that terrible resistance, to which they were afterward impelled. Their only refuge seemed to be in some distant region, whither the power of Laud could not reach, and where they might enjoy a form of worship which they esteemed pure and scriptural.

In 1625, Roger Conant, with some mercantile aid, but chiefly inspired by religious zeal, had established a body of settlers near Cape Anne; their sufferings, however, were so severe, that they determined to return to England. White, however, an eminent minister of Dorchester, entreated him to remain, promising that he should receive a patent, friends, goods, provisions, and everything he could desire. This zealous clergyman held communication with many persons in his own neighborhood, in London, and other quarters, particularly Lincolnshire; who, with zeal for religious purity, united energy of character, and in many cases considerable property. They found no difficulty in purchasing from the Plymouth company an extensive tract, including all the coast between the rivers Charles and Merrimac, and across to the Pacific ocean. They even obtained, though not without cost and trouble, a charter from Charles, under the title of "The Company of the Massachusetts Bay." On the delicate topic of religion, the governor was empowered, but not required, to administer the oath of supremacy; and there was no other mention of the subject. Some eminent historians have therefore thought that the colonists went out without any secu-

Fig. 30.—Portrait of Charles I.

rity whatever on a matter deemed by them so supremely important. To us it appears evident that, under all the circumstances, this silence implied a full assurance of their not being disturbed. In fact, they took with them a silenced minister, and on their arrival immediately began to exercise uncontrolled liberty, without drawing upon themselves any penal proceedings. We have seen, on every occasion, the vast sacrifices which princes were willing to make, in order to people their distant possessions; and the backwardness hitherto visible as to New England rendered the necessity of encouragement more urgent. It was probably also imagined, that a few of the most discontented spirits being thus removed, the nation in general might become more peaceable.

On the 1st May, 1629, six vessels, having on board about two hundred passengers, including four clergymen, sailed from the Isle of Wight. Smith would evidently have been glad to co-operate; but difference of religious views seems again to have prevented negotiation. He describes them "an absolute crew, only of the elect, holding all but such as themselves as reprobate;" and before sailing, all those persons were dismissed whose character was thought to make them unsuitable companions. The seamen were surprised and edified by the new scene which their ships presented—prayer and exposition of the Word two or three times a day; the sabbath entirely spent in preaching and catechising; repeated and solemn fasts for the success of the voyage. They arrived on the 24th June, and found only eight or ten hovels, which, with others scattered along the coast, contained about one hundred settlers. A site, already marked out, had its name changed from Nahumkeik to Salem; while a large party removed to Mishaum, which they called Charlestown.

The colonists suffered severely during the winter under the usual evils of a new settlement, especially in so rigorous a climate. No fewer than eighty died; yet the spirits of the rest continued unbroken, and they transmitted by no means unfavorable reports to England. Mr. Higgeson, the principal clergyman, was one of the victims; yet he had previously prepared a narrative, which painted the country under the most flattering colors, as "a wonderment, outstripping the increase of Egypt—yielding from thirty to sixty fold; the ears of corn nowhere so great and plentiful." He adds, "Shall such a man as I lie? It becometh not a preacher of the truth to be a writer of falsehood in any degree." Yet the picture was much too highly colored, though we hope not intentionally. At home it was extensively read, and produced a strong impression. An extraordinary movement had in fact taken place among those to whom their religious welfare was an object of paramount interest; and their promptitude to remove was greatly increased by an arrangement, according to which the meetings of the company might be held in New England. The colonists thus carried the charter along with them, and were entirely released from all dependance upon Great Britain. A body of emigrants was formed, much superior to their predecessors in numbers, wealth, education, and intelligence. The principal lay members were Winthrop, Dudley, and Johnston; the two first of whom were successively governors, while the other was accompanied by his wife, Lady Arabella, a daughter of the house of Lincoln.

The party thus assembled from various quarters was ready to sail early in the spring of 1630. The expedition consisted of seventeen vessels, and nearly fifteen hundred settlers, who were respectable as well for their intelligence as for their rank in society. They published an account of their motives for removal, taking an affectionate leave of their friends in England, in which they said, "Our eyes shall be fountains of tears for your everlasting welfare, while we are in our poor cottages in the wilderness." They went, however, with little experience in the mysteries of settlement, and without any suspicion of their own ignorance. Smith intimates that he saw clearly the errors which they were

FIG. 31.—Portrait of Governor Winthrop.

committing, but no regard was paid to his warning voice. They had received a false impression, for which Mr. Higgeson must be partly blamed, that they were going to a land already in the enjoyment of plenty; whereas the existing settlers were looking anxiously to them for supplies. Want of food and shelter, and a change in the habits of life, which with many of them had been those of ease and comfort, produced the usual distressing consequences; and in the first month from eighty to one hundred died, among whom Lady Arabella and her husband were particularly lamented. The hopes of religion, the firmness of the leaders, and the high motives by which they were inspired, carried them through this period of heavy trial. They spread themselves over the coast—a large proportion going to Charleston. Part of these were attracted by a situation at the very head of the bay, named by the Indians Shawmut, where they founded a town called first Trimountain, and afterward Boston, under which name it has become a populous and flourishing city.

The relations of the colonists with the Indian tribes were not so satisfactory as the character of the settlers might have led us to hope. Almost from the first establishment of Connecticut, mutual wrongs had created an animosity between the settlers and the Pequods, the most powerful of all the tribes, who sought, by an alliance with their enemies, the Narragansets, to form a general league against them. This scheme had nearly succeeded, when it was frustrated by the generous exertions of Williams. The English at first were taken by surprise, had several small detachments cut off, and were so closely hemmed in, that they could not go to their work or even to church without a strong escort. Captains Mason and Underhill, however, having come up with seventy men, determined to attack their main fort, surrounded by a palisade of strong trees, but so loosely put together that musketry could penetrate it. The assailants having forced an entrance, set fire to the camp, which was soon reduced to ashes, and above three hundred Indians, men, women, and children, perished in the ruins. The English, whose loss was trifling, pursued the remnant of the tribe from place to place, till the whole were either killed or taken prisoners. Forty who had sought refuge among the Mohawks, were given up by these savages, and the few others who remained alive surrendered in despair.

After the terror inspired by this dreadful overthrow, tranquillity continued nearly forty years. The Massachusetts government maintained friendly relations with the Indians, allowing them even when unconverted to settle within its jurisdiction. The conditions required, as stated by Winthrop, with their answers, are somewhat curious :—They were not to blaspheme, but to revere the true God.—Ans. They would always desire to speak reverentially of the Englishmen's God, who did so much better for them than other gods did for their worshippers. They should not work on the sabbath.—Ans. They worked so little any day, that they need not object to this article. They should not swear falsely.—Ans. They never swore at all. They should not permit murder, lying, or other crimes.—Ans. All these they condemned already. A number of them, as will be afterward observed, were even converted to Christianity. A disposition arose to imitate the English, and even to assume their names ; those of King Philip, Stonewall John, and Sagamore Sam, were borne by powerful chiefs.

As the colonists multiplied, and the circle of settlement extended, the natives could not but feel for how paltry a price they had sold their once spacious birthright. The enlarged frontier afforded new occasions of dispute ; and the Indians, when wronged, instead of appealing to the general court, took vengeance with their own hands. When charged with offences, they were tried according to the rigor of English law—a treatment altogether foreign to their ideas. There was no general confederacy, nor even any deliberate purpose of commencing hostilities. A member of one of the tribes, having given information against certain of his countrymen, fell a victim to their resentment ; but the murderers were condemned to death by a jury, of whom half were Indians. In revenge, a small party of English were surprised and slain ; and immediately war broke out along the whole border.

The Indians were now much more formidable than in the first contest. During the long interval they had eagerly sought to procure the superior arms wielded by Europeans ; and commercial avidity had supplied them. They had attained no discipline, and could not contend in the open field ; but the English soon learned to dread an enemy whose habitations, says Mather, " were the dark places of the earth ;" who, at moments the most unexpected, rushing from the depth of forests, surrounded and overwhelmed them. The war began with the burning of frontier villages, and the slaughter of detached parties. Beers, one of the bravest captains, was surprised and killed with twenty of his followers. Then came a more " black and fatal day." Lothrop commanded with reputation a body of fine young men, the flower of the county of Essex, who, having piled their arms on wagons, were securely reposing and plucking grapes when the alarm was given. After a desperate resistance they were cut off, only a mere handful escaping. This was followed by the " Springfield misery." That village, the most important on the boundary, was broken into, and every building reduced to ashes, except a large one, which, being slightly fortified supplied a refuge to the inhabitants. Others soon shared the same fate, in circumstances still more tragical. A boast was at first made that no place with a church had been sacked, but this was soon belied ; and the Indians, according to ideas prevalent among savages, considered themselves at war at once with the English and with their gods. In a captured village, their first step was to reduce the meeting-house to ashes ; and in torturing their captives, they derided the objects of their worship, for the want of power to save them. After killing the men, they carried away the women and children ; and, though the honor of the former was not threatened, they were treated with dreadful cruelty. For example they were compelled to follow rapid marches, which at this time were frequent, and when found unequal to the effort, were killed at once by blows on the head.

The colonists were doubly perplexed and dismayed by these disasters. Imbued with a belief, beyond what the usual course of Providence justifies, that every calamity was a judgment for some great iniquity, they anxiously sought why "the Lord no longer went forth with their armies." Mather quotes a letter from a leading man in the camp, imputing it to the luxury which wealth had produced among the citizens of Boston—"their intolerable pride in clothes and hair," and the multiplication of taverns. The neglect of religion and of its ministers was of course blamed; unfortunately, too, the increase of schism and even the slender toleration which had begun to be granted. Days of fasting were appointed; but they were astounded when one of the most solemn was followed by the catastrophe of Lothrop, from which they drew the salutary inference that "praying without reforming would not do." These views did not prevent them from using regular means of warfare, of which the attack of the fortified villages was found the most effective. In the midst of winter, one thousand men marched against the mainhold of the Narragansets. They rushed to the onset; and after a dreadful conflict it was carried, and reduced to ashes—the Indians perishing in vast numbers. But the colonists, appalled by their own loss of three hundred killed and wounded, including their six bravest leaders, retreated in great confusion: the enemy, however, were overwhelmed by their disaster, which they never fully recovered. In spring, indeed, they resumed their wonted warfare, but with diminished means and spirit; and in May, another of their principal settlements was destroyed. Driven from their cultivated spots, and finding shelter only in woods and marshes, they suffered increasing hardships and privations. Discontent and disunion were the consequence; several of the tribes began to make their submission, when pardon was granted. Two hundred laid down their arms at Plymouth; and Sagamore John came in with one hundred and eighty, bringing also Matoonas, accused as the author of this dreadful war. In the course of it had been formed skilful officers, particularly Captain Church, who displayed singular talents in this desultory contest. In August he came up with Philip himself, who was completely routed, and fled almost alone. Hunted from place to place, he was traced to the centre of a morass, where he was betrayed and shot by one of his own people. The spirit of the Indians then entirely sunk; and all who survived either emigrated to a distance, or submitted without reserve to the English power.

XI. Notwithstanding the paramount importance to which New York has attained, its early settlement was not accompanied by such striking circumstances as marked those of some other colonies.

About the year 1600, the attention of the English and Dutch had been directed to the discovery of a northern passage to India, which they hoped might at once be shorter, and enable them to escape the still formidable hostility of Spain. After this object had been vainly pursued by Frobisher, Davis, Barentz, and other navigators, it was resumed by Henry Hudson. Though a native of Holland, he was first employed by a company of English merchants, when he made the daring effort to cross the pole itself, and penetrated farther in that direction than any of his predecessors; but the icy barriers compelled him to return. He next attempted an eastern passage, between Nova Zembla and Spitzbergen, but again failed. His patrons in London then lost courage; but he, animated by the same ardor, solicited and obtained from the Dutch East India Company a small vessel named the Crescent, to renew his researches. After another abortive endeavor at an eastern passage, he appears to have finally renounced that object; and steering toward the west, began to explore the American coast, from Newfoundland southward. It had, indeed, been to a great extent both discovered

FIG. 32.—Portrait of King Philip, the last of the Wampanoags.

and settled, yet not in such continuity as to preclude the hope of finding a deep bay leading to the Pacific, and through it to the East Indies. In the beginning of July, he reached the Great bank, and continued his course cautiously along the shores of Acadia. In forty-four degrees he touched at the mouth of a spacious river, which appears to have been the Penobscot, where the French were found carrying on a very active trade. In passing Cape Cod, his people landed at several points, and held intercourse with the natives. They then pursued their course through the open sea, till, on the 17th of August, they came in sight of a low land, and soon afterward found themselves off the bar of James river, where they understood that the English had formed a settlement. No opening having yet occurred, it seemed expedient to return northward, keeping closer to the coast. They found it running northwest, and entered a great bay with rivers evidently that of Delaware. The water was so shoally, however, as to prevent its exploration, unless in pinnaces drawing only four or five feet. They proceeded therefore to the coast now called New Jersey, and were involved in the range of islands running parallel to it. The navigation was very difficult on account of storms and frequent shallows. At length Hudson came to a continuous land, good and pleasant, rising boldly from the sea, and bounded by high hills. He appeared to discover the mouths of three great rivers, which, however, could only be different channels, separated by islands, of the great stream now bearing his name. Boats were sent to sound the most northern of them, which was found to afford a good depth of water. They entered it, and were soon visited by large parties of natives in canoes, when a friendly exchange took place, of tobacco and maize for knives and beads. Unfortunately, a boat being sent to examine one of the other channels, was assailed by twenty of the savages in two skiffs, one of the seamen killed, and two wounded. This unhappy event poisoned the future intercourse with the Indians, whose friendly professions were henceforth considered as made only with a view to betray them. At one place, twenty-eight canoes, full of men, women, and children, approached and made overtures for trade; but their intentions being considered evil, they were not allowed to come on board. In ascending, the Hudson was found to be a noble stream, a mile broad, and bordered by lofty mountains. Seventeen days after entering it, the vessel, being embarrassed by shoals, stopped at a point where a small city has since been built, bearing the name of the discoverer. A boat sailed eight or nine leagues higher, somewhat above the site of Albany, where it was clear that the ship could not proceed farther. In this upper tract, the intercourse with the natives was very friendly, and even the suspicions of the crew were lulled. One party came on board, who, being freely treated with wine and aquavitæ, became all merry, and one completely tipsy, the effects of which caused to his companions the greatest surprise. On the way down, they were repeatedly attacked by the large body which in ascending had excited their jealousy. On each occasion, a discharge of musketry, killing two or three, caused all the rest to take flight. On leaving the river, Hudson made directly for Europe, and arrived at Dartmouth on the 7th November, 1609.

He transmitted to the Dutch company a flattering report of the country which he had discovered, strongly recommending a settlement. It has even been said, that he sold his rights to them, which seems quite erroneous, as in fact he could not be said to possess any. He was not even allowed to follow up this important discovery, but was obliged again to seek employment from the English merchants. By them, in 1610, he was sent out on that remarkable voyage, during which he explored the great bay to which his name is attached, but unhappily fell a sacrifice to the mutiny of a turbulent crew.

The Dutch, however, in virtue of this discovery, claimed the country, and in 1610, a few individuals fitted out a vessel for traffic. Several stations were

Fig. 33.—The Palisades on the Hudson River.

formed on the island of Manhattan (the name then given to New York), but no attempt was made to colonize. In 1613, they were visited by Argall, the adventurous English captain, who compelled them to own the dominion of his country; but as no steps were taken to follow up this advantage, they continued as before to trade with the natives, and consider the land their own. In 1614, a grant of exclusive commerce was made to a company of merchants, who thereupon erected a rude fort, and pushed their operations as high as Albany. They appear at the same time to have formed a station at the mouth of the Connecticut.

In 1620, an American settlement was attempted on a grander scale, by the formation of the Dutch West India Company, incorporated for twenty-four years. Their privileges included the whole western coast of Africa, as far as the Cape, with all the eastern shores of America, from Newfoundland to the Straits of Magellan. Over this vast extent they had the exclusive right to conclude treaties, carry on war, and exercise all the functions of government. No notice was taken in the grant, that the whole of this territory was claimed, and many parts occupied, by other European nations; nor did the government, in making this vast donation of what was not their own, promise the means of placing it in the company's hands. Their possessions, accordingly, were fiercely disputed, and most precariously held. The weakness of the Portuguese crown enabled them to grasp large portions of its territory in Brazil and on the African coast. In North America, they did not venture to measure their strength with the English but were content silently to enlarge their stations on the Hudson, which the latter showed no disposition to occupy. The country was called New Netherlands; and an increasing cluster of cottages, where New York now stands, was named New Amsterdam.

As yet there was nothing that could be denominated a colony; but in 1629, government interposed to establish one on a considerable scale. It was planned on quite an aristocratic basis; for though lands were granted to detached settlers, the chief dependance was on opulent individuals, who were expected to carry out bodies of tenants at their own expense; and those who should transport fifty became lords of manors, holding the absolute property of the lands thus colonized. They might even possess tracts sixteen miles long, and be furnished with negroes, if they could profitably do so. Several of them began to found these manors; two, Godyn and De Vries, led out thirty settlers to the head of the Delaware, laying the first foundation of that state; but the latter having visited home, found on his return that it had been attacked by the Indians, and totally destroyed. The whole colony was unprosperous, and very hard pressed on different sides. The New England settlement in Connecticut soon surrounded their little station, obliged them to give way, and even to abandon part of Long Island. At the same time, the Swedes, then in the height of their power, under Gustavus Adolphus, planned a settlement, which was zealously supported by that great monarch, who subscribed 400,000 dollars in its favor. They fixed on the bay of Delaware; and though Kieft, the governor sent from Holland, entered a protest, he did not venture to employ force against the conqueror of Lutzen. Moreover, Lord Baltimore, having just obtained his patent extending northward to the latitude of forty degrees, intimated his claim to nearly the whole of the Dutch territory. All these annoyances, however, were small compared to the Indian war, in which the atrocious violence of Kieft involved the colony. Attacking by surprise a party who had shown some hostile dispositions, he commenced a general massacre, in which nearly a hundred perished. Hence raged during two years a contest, accompanied by the usual horrors and calamities, and which effectually checked the progress of New Netherlands. At length a treaty was negotiated, in which the five nations were included.

A few years after, in 1646, the governor was recalled, to the great satisfaction of the people, and was succeeded by Stuyvesant, a military officer of distinction, brave, honest, and with some tincture of letters. Adopting a wise and humane policy toward the Indians, he succeeded in obviating any disturbance from that quarter. By negotiation with the company, he obtained a release from those trammels by which commerce had hitherto been fettered, substituting moderate duties on exports and imports. He suffered, however, much trouble from the English, who were continually extending their frontier on and beyond the Connecticut, and set scarcely any limit to their claims. The settlers discouraged greatly any idea of going to war with so powerful a neighbor, and exhorted him to gain the best terms he could by treaty. By large concessions he obtained a provisional compact, which was never indeed ratified in England, yet obtained for his people some security. Stuyvesant then turned his eyes on the other side to the Swedish colony, which had prospered and become a commercial rival. It was much inferior, however, to New Netherlands, while the death of Gustavus and of his great ministers and generals, succeeded by the fantastic sway of Christina, rendered her country no longer formidable. He, therefore, with the sanction of his employers, determined to reannex it, for which some violent proceedings on the part of Rising, the governor, afforded a fair pretext. Having assembled a force of 600 men, he marched into New Sweden, as it was termed, which, after a short resistance, renounced that name, and became incorporated with the Dutch dependency. A few of the settlers returned to their native country; the rest yielded to the mild sway of the conqueror. Stuyvesant was next annoyed by Lord Baltimore, who could boast that his charter entitled him to extend his borders to New England, leaving no room whatever for New Netherlands; but as his pretensions were not supported by any adequate force, they were easily evaded.

The company, though they did not grant any political franchises to the colonists, took great care to have them well governed, and to check those despotic practices in which Stuyvesant, from his military habits, was prone to indulge. They prohibited likewise all persecution, and studied to make the country a refuge for professors of every creed. From France, the Low Countries, the Rhine, Northern Germany, Bohemia, the mountains of Piedmont, the suffering protestants flocked to this transatlantic asylum. Even the New Englanders, allured by the fine climate and fertile soil, arrived in great numbers, and formed entire villages. It therefore became expedient to have a secretary of their nation, and to issue proclamations in French and English, as well as Dutch. To augment the variety, the company introduced as many negro slaves as they conveniently could. New York became, as Mr. Bancroft terms it, a city of the world; its inhabitants termed themselves a blended community of various lineage. Unluckily for the Dutch, the protestants of that age carried generally with them an ardent attachment to civil liberty, which was pushed to its utmost height by those of New England. Their views soon found favor in the eyes even of the Hollanders; for, though some of the more opulent were adverse to any very broad popular institutions, they could not forbear joining in the objection to be taxed without their own consent. Innovations of this nature, it appeared, were agreeable neither to the company nor the governor. The colonists, having sent over a deputation to the former, obtained a few municipal privileges, but none of the rights of a representative government. Such was their perseverance, however, that they erected one for themselves, by calling two deputies from each village; and the body thus assembled presented a remonstrance to Stuyvesant, claiming that their consent should be necessary to the enactment of new laws, and even to the appointment of officers. He received this address extremely ill, and bitterly reproached them with yielding to the visionary notions of the

Fig. 34.—Portrait of Peter Stuyvesant.

New Englanders ; stating that the laws were good, and would continue to be well executed, but could not be allowed to emanate from the wavering multitude He derived his authority only from God and the West India Company, who would never become responsible to their own subjects. The remonstrants were therefore commanded, under a severe penalty, immediately to disperse. In this the company firmly supported their governor, directing that the people should no longer indulge the visionary dream that taxes could be imposed only with their own consent. They, however, cherished a deep dissatisfaction, which, though it did not break out into open violence, indisposed them to make any exertions in support of a government under which they enjoyed no rights. This became of a serious consequence in the crisis that was now approaching.

Considering the long and embittered hostility of England against the Dutch, it may appear wonderful that she did not sooner attempt the conquest of a valuable possession, to which she had so plausible a title. Cromwell, in fact, had projected

Fig. 35.—Portrait of Oliver Cromwell.

it, but was diverted by other objects. Charles II., always prejudiced against that people, soon adopted the same resolution ; and even before any measure was taken for conquering the country, he included it in a grant made to his brother James, of the territory from the Kennebec to the St. Croix, and from the Connecticut to the Delaware. To make good this donation, Sir Robert Nichols was sent out with an expedition, to be reinforced by a detachment from another colony. The Dutch had for some time foreseen the crisis ; but unwilling to ex pend their funds in sending troops, they urged the governor to seek means of defence within his own dominions. This, from circumstances already stated, was exceedingly difficult ; and though Stuyvesant, in this emergency, granted their demand for a representative assembly, it was too late to inspire confidence. and the people declined making any sacrifices to repel a power from whom they hoped more liberal treatment. In August, 1664, Nichols cast anchor in face of New Amsterdam, having landed part of his troops on Long Island. He immediately summoned the city to surrender, guarantying to the people their property, the rights of citizens, their ancient laws and usages. The governor attempted by delay and negotiation to parry the blow; but the other declined all discussion, and the principal inhabitants, headed by Winthrop from Connecticut, assembling in the town-hall, determined against offering any resistance. They drew up articles of surrender conformable to the demand of the English officer, which, however, Stuyvesant refused to sign till the place was actually in the enemy's hands.

XII. The history of New England exhibits the extravagance indulged in by the quakers. Carrying to an undue length that religious movement which produced the Reformation, they relinquished a proper regard not only to forms and ordinances, but to reason, and, in some degree, to scripture, yielding themselves in a great measure to the guidance of visions and inward illuminations. They constituted at this period, as already observed, the extreme of the ultra-protestant section, which thenceforth began to recede from its too forward position. Not only did no similar sects spring up, but they themselves gradually pruned away the exaggerated features of their system. They assumed even a remarkably sedate character, and retaining still their deep devotional feeling, with only a few outward peculiarities, distinguished themselves in the walks of life by practical philanthropy. In this chastened and reformed quakerism, the lead was taken by William Penn, one of the most illustrious characters of modern

Fig. 36.—Portrait of William Penn.

times. Born to rank and distinction, son of an admiral who had attained celebrity under Cromwell by the conquest of Jamaica, he embraced at college his persecuted cause, and devoted himself to it throughout his whole life. Refusing to retract or compromise his views, he was expelled from his father's house, becoming amenable to all the rigors then enforced against eccentric modes of religious worship and teaching. He indulged at first in certain extravagances; but [illegible]ening years, combined with extensive study, and travel over a great part [illegible] Europe, enlarged his mind, and while retaining the same devoted attachment to what was valuable in his system, he purified it from its principal errors. His steady course of christian kindness gained for him the general esteem of the public, and ultimately led to a reconciliation with his parent, who bequeathed to him the whole of his property.

Among the tenets of this school, which Penn at all times advocated with the utmost zeal, was that of complete liberty in religious opinion and worship. It became, indeed, a leading object of his life to render himself a shield not only to his own people but to all who on this ground were exposed to suffering and persecution. Unable as yet fully to accomplish his end in the old world, he conceived the plan of providing for them, in the new continent, an asylum similar to that of their pilgrim ancestors. By founding there a state open to the votaries of every faith, he might, he hoped, fulfil his benevolent purpose, and at the same time secure for himself a degree of importance and wealth. He possessed, in virtue of his father's services, a claim on government, estimated at £16,000; but after a long delay, amid the exigencies of the court, he could not without difficulty have rendered it effective in any shape, except for one favorable circumstance. He enjoyed the favor both of Charles II. and James II., and was always a welcome guest at Whitehall. This intercourse with princes whose character was so unlike his own, excited in that age a feeling of surprise which we can scarcely avoid sharing. The most injurious surmises arose—he was represented as a papist, and even a jesuit. He seems, however, to have clearly proved, that he never concurred in any of the illegal measures of those rulers, but employed his influence almost solely with the view of obtaining protection for those numerous sufferers in whom he took so deep an interest. Had his object been money, he must have encountered many obstacles in obtaining it from the dilapidated treasury of Charles. It was much easier to get the royal assent respecting a desert region beyond the Atlantic, whence no immediate benefit was to be derived. His petition, being presented in June, 1680, was referred to the agents of the Duke of York and Lord Baltimore, who declared it to be unobjectionable, provided the rights of these individuals were preserved inviolate. Penn, therefore, submitted the draft of a charter, which, after being revised by Chief Justice North and the Bishop of London, was passed under the seal-royal. It granted to him the tract in America extending northward from the 40th to the 43d degree of latitude, and five degrees of longitude westward, from a boundary line drawn twelve miles from Newcastle on the Delaware. Nearly the same privileges were conceded as were formerly granted to Lord Baltimore. The proprietor was empowered to dispose of the lands in fee-simple, to levy taxes with consent of the freemen or their delegates, to erect courts of justice, and (what one might scarcely have expected) to raise forces for the defence of the province by sea and land. There was reserved, however, the sovereignty of the crown, and its claim to allegiance, also an appeal from the courts to the king in council, and the right of parliament to levy custom-duties. The acts passed by the assembly and the owner were to be transmitted within five years to his majesty, and if considered unconstitutional, might be disallowed. The Bishop of London stipulated for the reception of a preacher, as soon as one should be requested by twenty of the settlers.

Invested with these ample powers, Penn proceeded to give to the colony a constitution, on a very liberal footing. A council of seventy-two, elected by the body of the people, and having a third of their number renewed every year, carried on the executive government, in conjunction with the proprietor, who was allowed three votes. This body was divided into four committees, of plantation, trade, justice, and education. They prepared the bills and propositions which were submitted to the general assembly, also elected by the people. They were to sit nine days only, during eight of which they were to consider the proposals made by the council, and on the ninth to pronounce their decision. This system, said to have been copied chiefly from the Oceana of Harrington, was not very well fitted for practical purposes, and had not a long duration.

Penn now circulated widely his proposals through Britain, France, and Germany; the oppressed and impoverished of every class being invited to this land of promise He recommended it not only to those who suffered under religious persecution, but "to industrious laborers and handicraftsmen—ingenious spirits low in the world—younger brothers of small inheritances, instead of haging on as retainers on their elder brothers' table and charity—lastly, to men of an universal spirit, who have an eye to the good of posterity." The necessary expense of conveyance was stated to be—for an adult £5, a child under twelve £2, 10*s*., goods £2 per ton. Those who could not afford even this moderate amount, were informed that, on engaging with emigrants of property for a service of four years, not only would their passage be defrayed, but at the end of the term they would receive 50 acres, at 2*s*. quitrent. An extent of 5,000 acres was sold for £100, with 50*s*. quitrent, commencing only in 1684. Those who preferred might pay merely a quitrent of 1*d*. an acre, or £20, 16*s*. 8*d*. Smaller tracts were disposed of at corresponding prices. Poor men were allowed 50 acres at ½*d*. per acre.

These advantageous terms, the troubled state of Europe, and the high character of the proprietor, caused his proposals to be received with general favor. An influx into America took place, such as had never been equalled since the days of the first settlers. Between 1682 and 1685, there arrived ninety sail, conveying an average of eighty passengers, in all 7,200, beside 1,000 who had landed in 1681. They had been sent under his kinsman Markham, to take possession of the country, and prepare the way for the larger colony. He found no difficulty in completing the purchase of an extensive tract of land from the Indians on terms satisfactory to them, yet moderate for the buyer.

In October, 1682, Penn arrived with a body of 2,000 emigrants. After some time spent in surveying his new possessions, he, in the beginning of 1683, arranged a meeting with the native chiefs, under the canopy of a spacious elm tree, near the present site of Philadelphia. They appeared on the day appointed, in their rude attire, and with brandished weapons, beneath the shadow of those dense woods which covered what is now a fine and cultivated plain. On learning that the English approached, they deposited their arms and sat down in groups, each tribe behind its own chieftain. Penn then stepping forward in his usual plain dress and unarmed, held forth in his hand the parchment on which the treaty was engrossed. In a simple speech, he announced to them those principles of equity and amity upon which he desired that all their future intercourse should be conducted. He besought them to keep this parchment during three generations. The Indians replied, in their usual solemn and figurative language, that they would live in peace with him and with his children while the sun and moon should endure. A friendly display like this is by no means unusual in the first opening of intercourse between civilized and savage nations; but seldom indeed does it long continue unbroken, or fail even of being succeeded by an embittered enmity. Pennsylvania afforded at least one happy exception. Her founder continued with this savage people on terms not only of peace, but of intimate union; he visited them in their villages, he slept in their wigwams; they welcomed him almost as a brother. Forty years afterward they said to the governor, Sir William Keith, as the highest possible compliment: "We esteem and love you as if you were William Penn himself." What was still more wonderful, the colonists, though they had to struggle with many uncongenial spirits in their own body, succeeded in maintaining good terms with the natives; and for nearly a century, the Indian tomahawk was never lifted against a people who would have considered it unlawful to return the blow.

His next object was to found a capital for his new settlement. He chose a site upon a neck of land between the Schuylkill and Delaware, in a situation which appeared at once agreeable and healthy, abounding in water, and with

FIG. 37.—Treaty of William Penn with the Indians.

convenient river communications. He gave to it the name of Philadelphia (brotherly love), under which it has become one of the most flourishing cities in the new world. Combining the taste for neatness and regularity characteristic of his people, with a love of rural nature, he planned a town composed of parallel streets, each a hundred feet broad, crossed by others also spacious, and some indicating by their very names, Vine, Mulberry, Chestnut, that the verdure of the country was still to enliven them. The purchasers of 5,000 acres were to have a house in one of the two principal streets, with a garden and orchard ; those of 1,000 in the three next ; such as were under 1,000 acres in the cross streets. In 1684, fifty villages, arranged in regular squares, had sprung up, on a similar plan, though on a smaller scale.

In December, 1682, Penn proceeded to Maryland, to adjust with Lord Baltimore the boundaries of their respective provinces. His lordship received him, as he had before received his agent Markham, with the utmost politeness ; yet the arrangement was found very difficult and vexatious. The specified limit of the 40th degree had, in the maps of that age, been made to run across the Bay of Chesapeake, about the latitude of Pool's Island. Thus the head of that great inlet was left within the bounds assigned to Pennsylvania, and afforded an advantageous outlet for her commerce. Lord Baltimore, however, caused a new and more scientific survey to be made, showing that this limit really lay considerably to the north of any part of the bay, from which the new province was thus wholly excluded. This circumstance bore heavily upon the philanthropist, whose colony was thus deprived of all direct maritime trade. He earnestly urged, that the space in question was a hundred times more valuable to him than to the other party, of whose territory this was only an outer tract, scarcely at all known or settled ; that the proprietor of Maryland must probably have gained by the error in settling his own boundaries with Virginia ; and that the understanding upon which the grant had been made ought to be taken into consideration. Their interests came into collision on another point. Penn had obtained a grant from the Duke of York of the whole coast of the river and bay of Delaware southward from Newcastle to Cape Henlopen, which would in some degree have supplied his want of a seacoast. But the other party claimed all the shores of this bay also, as included within the 40th degree. Both parties, during their personal intercourse, maintained their claims with extreme pertinacity, yet with politeness ; but the correspondence which afterward ensued is tinctured with considerable bitterness, each accusing the other of forwarding his views in an unfair manner. Historians are even still much divided. Mr. Chalmers derides the claim of Penn, whom, in truth, he always mentions in the most depreciating terms ; indeed, to have been engaged in any dispute with a Baltimore, was enough in his eyes to efface the brightest qualities that could adorn a human being. Mr. Bancroft, on the contrary, has in this particular forsaken his first love, and admits nothing to interfere with the absolute perfection of the Pennsylvania legislator. It became necessary to refer the question to the committee of plantation, who, in November, 1685, came to the decision that the 40th degree in its real direction, must be the boundary, thus excluding the quaker from the Chesapeake. But while they allowed that the Maryland patent had extended indeed to the Delaware, they considered that it had been granted only in respect to such countries as were not occupied by any Christian people, while that region had been already colonized in considerable numbers by the Dutch and Swedes. Hence it was determined that the eastern part belonged of right to the crown, including Penn's domain, which was thereby rendered valid, and gave him the command of that fine estuary, thus in a great measure compensating his loss on another side.

In 1684, Penn was induced by this and other affairs to return to England leaving the administration in the hands of commissioners; a body who did no' by any means work harmoniously. Moore, a leading proprietary officer, was accused by the assembly of corruption and other high misdemeanors; which charge being strenuously resisted by the executive, a violent collision ensued. The proprietor, while he felt disposed to grant a liberal government to his settlers, was probably little prepared to make over to them the whole political power, which yet they seem to have been determined to grasp. In 1686, he sent instructions to his officers to dissolve the constitution, which he had so studiously constructed. The assembly, however, foreseeing that the change was proposed with a view to the abridgment of their privileges, resolutely opposed his views. He then determined to supersede the commission, and appoint a deputy governor, as more likely to support his authority.

The person selected was Blackwell, who is admitted to have been no quaker, and indeed to have had nothing akin to the character. The apology made seems singular, namely, that no one of that profession could be found fit for the office, and willing to undertake it. We may rather suspect that, being a dexterous politician and high advocate for power, he was expected to beat down the democratic opposition. His efforts for this purpose were carried to an extreme. White, who, as former speaker, had been active in the persecution of Moore, having been re-elected as delegate, was thrown into prison, and his claim under the habeas corpus act evaded. The most embittered messages passed between the governor and assembly. He contrived, however, to gain over a part of the members, and thus to carry on the government.

On these proceedings being represented to him, Penn was not disposed to support them; and he now threw almost everything into the hands of the council, on whom he conferred the power of choosing the executive officers and deputy governor: they elected Thomas Lloyd, a quaker preacher of great merit. But neither did this arrangement work well. Schisms arose among the too numerous body; and violent protests were made. The chief conflicts, which were between the old territory of Pennsylvania and the new counties on the Delaware, rose to such a height, that the proprietor was obliged reluctantly to separate the two territories; appointing Markham governor of the latter, which ultimately formed a small state, bearing the name of that great bay. Peace did not reign among the quakers themselves. George Keith, one of the most eminent among them as a preacher and writer, disappointed perhaps at not himself obtaining a lead in the government, proclaimed that no one of his sect could lawfully act as an executive officer or magistrate, and if he did, had no claim to any obedience. These doctrines, enforced not in the mildest terms, brought him under the cognizance of the authorities. His adherents allege that their proceedings were violent and irregular; that without hearing or inquiry he was proclaimed in the market-place a seditious person, and an enemy to the king and queen; and that the ministers, with as little ceremony, denounced him as not having the fear of God before his eyes. The actual penalty was only a moderate fine, and not even enforced; but the finding himself proscribed among his brethren, both in the colony and at home, seems to have exasperated him; he became an enemy to the quakers, abandoned their communion, and finally accepted an episcopal benefice. He was lamented by them as a mighty man fallen from the high places of Israel; and the noise made by these feuds seriously injured the colony in the crisis which now arose.

The Pennsylvanians, who had owed everything to James II., did not share the general joy at his abdication in 1688. The news was unwillingly believed; and the government, till September, 1789, was still administered in his name. This was carefully reported in New York; while in England, charges were

Fig. 38.—Monument of the great Treaty of Penn, at Shackamaxon.

brought against the proprietor as adhering to popery, or at least strongly attached to the exiled house. William, after some hesitation, deprived him of his patent; and in April, 1693, Benjamin Fletcher, governor of New York, assumed authority also over Pennsylvania. The assembly professed their willingness to obey, provided they were used in the usual manner, and by laws founded on letters-patent. But he intimated that they were much mistaken; that the change had been made on account of neglects and miscarriages; and that his majesty's mode of governing would be in direct opposition to that of Mr. Penn. It was even maintained that all the former laws had been abrogated, though a willingness was expressed to re-enact the greater number.

Penn, however, on reaching England, was gratified to find that the trials he encountered had not deprived him of all his friends. He acquired considerable favor with Queen Anne; but circumstances prevented his return. Hamilton, appointed his deputy, was still troubled by internal dissensions. These were not abated by the nomination, in 1703, of Evans, in whom we see a character the most opposite to that of the proprietor himself. This officer, young, lively, fond of frolic and revelry, and inflamed with military ardor, was utterly opposed to the quaker assembly, and treated with derision their pacific dispositions. He began to erect forts without their permission, and endeavored, but in vain, to rouse them by a false alarm of a French invasion. On having three of their bills presented to him, he told them, "they were very great absurdities." They sent home loud remonstrances, complaining also that under the new frame their liberties were greatly abridged. Penn listened unwillingly, and it was not till 1709 that this unsuitable ruler was removed. He was succeeded by Gookin, an Irish gentleman, of good age and mild manners; yet the discontents still continued. The war with Canada having broken out, he had the ungracious task of demanding a supply of £4,000 and 150 men. It was privately intimated that the money would suffice; but the assembly declared that they could not in conscience either fight or hire others to do so; however, they offered the queen a present of £500. The chief objection made was to the amount; but on this point, pleading poverty, they stood firm. An equal sum was afterward, in a similar manner, extracted from them.

In 1710, Penn, having reached the age of sixty-six, sent out a solemn remonstrance on the feuds and discontent in which the settlers had so long indulged Amid the satisfaction of seeing the colony free and flourishing, their disputes had been to him a source of grief, trouble, and poverty. Recapitulating the whole train of his proceedings, he appealed to them whether he had given any real cause for this conduct; he lamented the unhappiness they were bringing on themselves, as well as the scandal they were causing in the eyes of Europe, by such incessant contention. This appeal was not unsuccessful; and in the next year an assembly much more friendly to him was elected. It is doubtful, however, if this news ever reached him. Oppressed with embarrassments and losses incurred seemingly without blame, he had entered into a treaty with government for transferring his territorial rights, and had agreed to accept for them £12,000. A series of apoplectic shocks, however, entirely deprived him of his faculties, and disabled him from completing the bargain, so that the property remained in his family.

The favor restored to Penn was not extended to Gookin, whom the assembly accused of arbitrary measures, and of favoring the non-quaker part of the population. In 1716, he was succeeded by Sir William Keith, who, during the illness of the founder, was named by the king. This governor enjoyed a much greater degree of favor than any of his predecessors, though he is accused of purchasing it by too entire an acquiescence in the demands of the assembly, and allowing almost the whole power to pass into their hands. Such, at least, was the opinion of the proprietaries, who considered him also as neglecting their interest, and at the end of nine years removed him. He then attempted to raise a factious opposition, but was obliged to leave the colony. After a peaceable administration of several years by Major Gordon, Thomas, and afterward John Penn, sons of the late owner, went out in 1732 and 1734. They were received with the most cordial welcome, though the former did not altogether preserve his popularity.

XIII. While emigration proceeded so actively in various parts of North America, the regions south of Virginia, though of vast extent, and presenting many natural advantages, had attracted little attention. The Spaniards, as long as they could, jealously guarded this coast; and the bloody catastrophe of the first French settlement was long remembered with terror. Raleigh's original establishment had been formed within this range; and its tragical results, though not connected with the situation, threw a gloom over all the recollections associated with it. Yet flattering rumors were still spread; and as the older settlements became crowded, detachments began to overflow into this unoccupied tract. The river Nansemond, on the immediate border of Virginia, had been very early settled; and colonists thence found their way to the banks of the Chowan and the shores of Albemarle Sound. Much farther to the south, a body of enterprising New Englanders had purchased from the Indians a district around Cape Fear. Sir Robert Heath, in 1630, obtained a patent; but having been unable to fulfil the conditions, it was declared forfeited.

The reign of Charles II. was a period of large grants; for, having many claims upon him while he had little to give, he was ready to bestow colonial rights. On the 24th March, 1663, the whole coast, from the 36th degree of latitude to the river San Matheo, was granted under the name of Carolina to a body of highly distinguished personages, among whom were Monk, duke of Albemarle, Lord Clarendon, Lord Ashley Cooper afterward Earl of Shaftesbury, Lord Berkeley, and his brother Sir William, governor of Virginia. Their privileges were as usual extensive, and seem to have been in a great measure copied from those granted in the case of Maryland. The present occupants could only be considered as squatters; yet as men were much wanted, the utmost encouragement was given to them to remain, while others were invited. Political and personal immunities, more ample than were possessed by the neighboring colonies, or were satisfactory to the views of some of the proprietors, were not withheld. Berkeley, who brought additional emigrants from Virginia to Albe-

FIG. 39.—Squatters.

marle Sound, placed them under Drummond, a prudent and popular governor A party of planters from Barbadoes, induced to remove to this congenial climate were settled on Cape Fear river, near the New Englanders, and ruled by Sir John Yeamans, one of their own number. A few shipbuilders were also obtained from the Bermudas.

In 1665, the proprietors, still in high favor with Charles, obtained a new patent with much larger privileges. Their territory was now, without regard to Spanish claims, extended to the Pacific, while they were empowered to create titles and orders of nobility. This appears to have been preparatory to the formation of what was intended to be a monument of human wisdom—a constitution for the new colony. It was undertaken by Shaftesbury, the ablest statesman of the age, who employed upon it Locke, the illustrious philosopher; and its object was to transport into the New World the varied ranks and aristocratic establishments of Europe. Two orders of nobility were to be instituted, the higher of landgraves or earls, the lower of caciques or barons. The territory was to be divided into counties, each containing 480,000 acres, with one landgrave and two caciques, a number never to be increased nor diminished. There was also to be lords of manors, entitled, like the nobles, to hold courts, and exercise judicial functions. Those possessing 50 acres were to be freeholders; but the tenants held no political franchise, and could never attain any higher rank. All the estates were to sit in one chamber. The proprietary were always to continue eight in number, to possess the whole judicial power, and have the supreme direction of all the tribunals. One was to take cognizance of ceremonies and pedigrees, of fashions and sports. But it is needless to enter into further details of a constitution which never did nor could have any practical existence. It must remain a striking proof how unfit the ablest men are to legislate for a society with whose condition and circumstances they are not intimately acquainted.

Nothing could exceed the surprise of the colonists when this elaborate system was transmitted to them, with an urgent call for its immediate adoption. Albemarle, the chief settlement, could scarcely number 1,400 *working hands;* how then was it to furnish its landgraves, its caciques, its barons? The proprietors, on a representation of this state of affairs, were obliged to own that their magnificent system could not yet be carried into full execution; but they required its introduction so far as circumstances allowed, and its completion to be kept constantly in view. Meanwhile, a series of temporary laws were established, until the inhabitants should be ripe for the fundamental constitutions. They had formed, however, a simple code adapted to their circumstances, which they preferred to one by which the popular privileges were materially abridged; and its abrogation for a merely provisional system would have taken away everything stable and permanent in their political position. As Miller, who acted as administrator and collector of the revenue, had not given them satisfaction, they rose in a body, imprisoned him and most of the council, seized the public funds, appointed magistrates and judges, called a parliament, and in short took into their hands all the functions of government. Culpepper, the ringleader, came to England to plead their cause, a step which certainly does not seem to indicate consciousness of guilt; but he was arrested and brought to trial for high treason. Shaftesbury, by his eloquence and popular influence, procured his acquittal, pleading that there had been no regular government in Albemarle, so that these disorders could only be considered as feuds among the several planters.

The proprietors found themselves in an embarrassing situation, unwilling to yield to the colonists and renounce their darling constitutions, yet neither desirous nor very able to reduce them by force. They resolved, therefore, to send out as governor Seth Sothel, one of their own body, who had previously purchased Lord Clarendon's share, and whose territorial rights would, they hoped, command respect. According to Chalmers, the annals of delegated authority include no name so infamous as that of this new administrator; a remark which is probably too strong, for he had to deal with persons not easily pleased. It would appear, however, that his sole object was to advance his fortune, at the expense both of the colonists and of his fellow-proprietors. The former soon practised the lesson which they had already learned. They deposed him, seized his person, and were about to send him to England to answer to the owners for the charges brought against him. Sothel preferred to abide the judgment of the assembly themselves; a circumstance which, joined to the sentence, seems to indicate that his conduct was not extremely atrocious. After finding all the accusations proven, they merely banished him from the colony for a single year, and declared him incapable of ever again holding the office of governor. The proprietors, though troubled at these stretches of power, yet owning the complaints to be just, and having been themselves wronged, sanctioned the proceedings, and nominated Philip Ludwell as their representative.

Meantime they were bestowing a more special attention to the southern colony. In 1670, they sent out a considerable number of settlers under William Sayle, who was named governor. He died soon after, and his place was supplied by Sir John Yeamans, once a Barbadoes planter, who had acquired a good reputation in his command at Cape Fear. He was speedily accused, however, of sordid proceedings, in carrying on all the little trade of the colony for his own advantage. Affairs were in many respects unsatisfactory. The proprietors, like other similar bodies, already discovered that the colony, instead of a mine of wealth, was a constant drain; they had expended upon it upward of £18,000, without any return, but, on the contrary, had to encounter new demands. They were therefore not unwilling to remove Yeamans in order to make room for West, a favorite of the settlers. During his residence of eight years, he enjoyed a popularity rare among transatlantic rulers. The colony flourished; for beside emigrants sent over by the proprietors, a considerable tide flowed in from various quarters. The poor cavaliers, considering it to have been founded upon their own principles, sought it as a place where they might retrieve their fortunes. A number of Dutch in New York, dissatisfied with their transference to British rule, thought, it scarcely appears for what reason, that they would be more at ease in this new settlement; and some of their countrymen from Europe were induced to follow. The revocation of the edict of Nantz, and the persecution of the protestants by Louis XIV. during his bigoted dotage, drove out a large body of most respectable emigrants. A small party proceeded from Ireland, and another from Scotland under Lord Cardross; but the latter was unfortunate, being nearly all destroyed by the Indians. This influx was considered to afford an inducement for the erection of a city. One was early founded on a high ground, above Ashley River, named Charleston; but afterward another spot, called Oyster Point, at the junction of that stream with the Cooper, was considered so much more eligible, that the site was changed. The choice was happy; and it has since become the chief emporium of the southern states.

West was succeeded, in 1682, by Moreton, and the latter, in 1686, by Colleton, a brother of one of the proprietors, and endowed with the rank of landgrave. Under these governors, the spirit of faction, which had in some degree slumbered, broke forth with extreme violence. An obstinate dispute was waged between the three counties of Berkeley, Craven, and Colleton, respecting the number of members that should be sent from each to the assembly: that body also proposed two acts which can not be applauded, with a view to relieve the scarcity of money. It was the purpose of the one to raise the value of the coin, and of the other to suspend the payment of foreign debts. The first was carried, whence arose the depreciation of the Carolina currency, which afterward became extreme. The other was rejected by the proprietors with reprobation. This was not well brooked by the assembly, who began to contest the legality of the fundamental constitutions, and to demand their original charter. Discontents ran so high, that the people, in 1687, elected an assembly, expressly to resist whatever the governor should propose; and, in 1690, they passed an act banishing him from the province. Amid this ferment, appeared Seth Sothel, the rejected of North Carolina; and such was the influence of party, that he found no difficulty in occupying the place of his unpopular predecessor, and in calling a parliament, which sanctioned all his proceedings. The proprietors were beyond measure astonished to hear of such a person setting up against them as a leader supported by the people. They sent out the strictest orders for his immediate recall, appointing in his place Philip Ludwell, with instructions, however, to examine and report as to any real grievances. The chief complaint was found to be against "the fundamental constitutions;" and as there appeared no serious prospect of carrying into execution that famous code, it was, in 1693, finally abrogated. Caciques, landgraves, and barons were swept away, and the labors of Shaftesbury and Locke were given to the winds. It may be observed that James II., on his usual despotic principle, had prepared a *quo warranto* against the charter; but the proprietors, opening a treaty for its surrender, on condition of replacing the funds expended on it, spun out the affair till that monarch became no longer an object of dread.

These arrangements did not fully secure tranquillity; and a new source of dissension was afforded by the numerous body of French protestant refugees. Most of the original settlers, zealously attached to the church of England, viewed with aversion both their religious and national peculiarities, and refused to admit them to the rights of citizenship. At this treatment they were justly indignant; and disputes rose so high, that the proprietors sent out one of their own body, John Archdale, a quaker, with full power to investigate and redress grievances. He conducted himself with great prudence, and, though he could not procure for the new comers all the desired privileges, succeeded in greatly allaying their discontent. After remaining a year, he left as his successor Joseph Blake, who steadily pursued the same system, by which, in a few years, the parties were reconciled, and the French admitted to all the rights of citizens.

Blake died in 1700, and was succeeded by Moore, who, two years after, sought to distinguish himself by the capture of the French capital of St. Augustine. He himself, with the main force, proceeded by sea, while Colonel Daniel, with a party of militia and Indians, marched by land. The latter arrived first, and took possession of the town, obliging the enemy to retreat into the castle; but the governor considered that post so strong, as to render it necessary to send to Jamaica for more artillery. On the appearance, however, of two Spanish ships, he was seized with a panic alleged to be groundless, and precipitately raising the siege, returned by land to Carolina. This repulse was not only very mortifying, but entailed on the colony a heavy debt, which it could ill bear.

In 1706, the Spaniards endeavored to retaliate, and, aided by their French allies, equipped a considerable armament. Their admiral, Le Feboure, with five ships-of-war, forthwith summoned the capital; but the governor, Sir Nathaniel Johnson, who had, with great spirit, though inadequate means, prepared for defence, sent an indignant defiance. The invader, whose main land force had not yet arrived, imprudently sent on shore a small detachment, which was immediately attacked and cut off. This success inspired such courage, that Captain Rhett, with six small vessels, sailed against the enemy, who struck with

F.s.—40.—View of the Public Square in St. Augustine, Florida.

alarm, immediately retired. Soon after, an additional armament appeared, and a body of troops were landed; but the English, flushed with victory, attacked them with such resolution, that both they and their ships were captured.

After some years of repose, the colony was involved in all the horrors of Indian war; the origin of which is difficult to trace, though the settlers throw the whole blame upon the natives. It is manifest that they waged it with deep treachery and ferocity, and yet there seems room to suspect that they had heavy wrongs to avenge. The first burst was from the Tuscaroras, on the frontier of North Carolina, whose attack against the settlements on the Roanoke was made with the usual secrecy and rapidity, and above a hundred perished before measures of defence could be adopted. This was all that could be done till aid was procured from South Carolina, whence Captain Barnwell, with 600 militia and 360 Indians, penetrated the intervening wilderness, defeated the enemy, and pursuing them to their main fortress, obliged them to surrender. They soon after migrated northward, and formed a union with the Five Nations.

A more formidable struggle awaited South Carolina. The Indians on its

Fig. 41.—Male and Female Indian.

border had long been united with the colonists in alliance and common hostility to the Spaniards. When the treaty of Utrecht had terminated the European war with the latter people, the natives soon announced that they had dined with the governor of Florida, and washed his face—a sure pledge of alliance The colonists, who did not suspect that the enmity was to be transferred to them, allege that it was fomented by their old enemies; but the charge seems scarcely supported by any overt act. Certain it is, that the Yemassees, Creeks, Cherokees, and all the tribes from Cape Fear to the shores of the gulf, amounting to 6,000 men, became united in one grand confederacy to exterminate the English name. Their preparations were enveloped as usual in profound secrecy; and, even on the previous evening, when some suspicious circumstances were noticed, they gave the most friendly explanation. In the morning the work of blood commenced in the vicinity of Port Royal, where about ninety of the planters perished; but the people of the place, happily finding a vessel in the harbor crowded on board, and were conveyed to Charleston. The Indians collected from all sides, and advanced upon that capital; two detachments, which attempted to stop their progress, were surprised or ensnared, and suffered severely. Craven, the governor, however, having mustered 1,200 men fit to bear arms, succeeded in stopping their progress; upon which, having collected all his strength, and receiving a reinforcement from North Carolina, he marched to the attack of their grand camp. The struggle was long and fierce—the Indians having stationed themselves in a broken and entangled spot, fitted for their wild manœuvres. At length they were completely defeated, and soon after driven beyond the limits of the colony.

The termination of this contest was immediately followed by violent internal disturbances. The settlers had many grounds of complaint against the proprietors, who had not afforded any pecuniary aid during the late sanguinary contest. At its close the assembly passed acts bestowing the lands whence the Indians had been expelled upon such persons as might choose to occupy them; on the faith of which a party of 500 emigrated from Ireland. But the proprietary annulling this grant, caused them to be ejected, and the tract divided into baronies for their own benefit. They disallowed other laws, which the colonists were extremely desirous to obtain, and sent orders to the governor to sanction none which had not been previously submitted to themselves. They reposed their entire confidence in Trott, the chief-justice, who was even accused of malversation in his office; but the complaints against him from the people, and even the governor, were disdainfully rejected. This discontent, long fomenting, broke out openly on a report of invasion from the Havana. In this emergency the assembly refused to vote any supplies; a bond of union was drawn up, and signed by almost all the inhabitants. They transmitted a proposal to Johnson that he should contiue to hold his office in the name of the king; but as he declined the offer, Colonel Moore was elected. The other made some attempts to compel submission, but found his force inadequate. The issue of the whole transaction, however, depended on the view which might be taken by the crown, always disposed to favor any arrangement that might extend its prerogative. The king, being absent in Hanover, had left the government in the hands of a regency, who, on examining the case, decided that the proprietors had forfeited their charter, and ordered proceedings to be instituted for its dissolution. Acting certainly with great promptitude, as if this were already effected, they named Sir Francis Nicholson governor, under a commission from his majesty. That person, distinguished in other stations for his active talents, had been accused of arbitrary maxims; but in Carolina he seems to have laid these aside, and rendered himself extremely acceptable. He made great exertions to provide for religious instruction, and the diffusion of education. Through an alliance with the Creeks and Cherokees, he secured the frontier, which had been considerably harassed by Indian incursions.

We may here pause to mention, that at the end of the seventeenth and the beginning of the eighteenth century, the American coast, and particularly Carolina, was dreadfully infested by piracy. The long war between France and Spain, aided by the vicinity of the West Indies, afforded large scope for privateers. After the peace, they were unwilling to relinquish so lucrative an occupation; and, exercising it equally on friends and foes, spread desolation over all those shores. The governors, it is said, instead of striving to suppress the disorder, often secretly favored it, and shared in the profits. James II., in 1687, equipped a small fleet under Sir Robert Holmes, who considerably checked the evil; but it again broke out with augmented violence, especially after the treaty of Utrecht. John Theach, called Blackbeard, equally frightful in his aspect and character, became a sort of pirate-king—the idol of his followers, and the terror of all peaceable merchants. In 1718, George I. despatched a squadron under Woodes Rogers, who took the island of New Providence in the Bahamas, long a kind of outlawed capital. The pirates attempted to form another stronghold at the mouth of Cape Fear river, but were driven from it by the governor of Carolina. Rogers was empowered, in case of submission, to offer pardon to those who should surrender, of which most availed themselves; though some afterward resumed their vocation, and among them Theach himself, who was soon, however, defeated and killed. In the course of the five subsequent years, twenty-six suffered death for this offence.

In 1729, the transactions of the proprietors were finally closed by a deed surrendering all their rights into the hands of the crown. They received in return £17,500, with £5,000 for arrears of rent amounting to £9,000; but Lord Carteret, while resigning all political power, preferred to retain his claim to property in the soil, of which an ample portion was assigned to him. The colonists were gratified by the entire remission of their quit-rents. In 1694, the captain of a vessel from Madagascar, having touched at Carolina, had presented the governor with a bag of rice, which, being distributed among several farmers, throve so remarkably, that it had already become a staple of the settlement; and the privilege was now granted of exporting this article direct to any part of Europe southward of Cape Finisterre. North and South Carolina, too, which in point of fact had always been distinct, and their occupied parts even distant from each other, were now finally declared to be two colonies, each to have its separate governor.

From this era their affairs held a pretty uniform course, diversified only as the character of the successive governors was popular or otherwise. They continued to draw numerous bodies of emigrants; and their career, both of agriculture and commerce, was extremely prosperous. This, it is painful to add, was in a great measure effected by large importations of negro slaves, which enabled the wealthy to cultivate plantations on an extensive scale, and without personal labor. It appears also that reproach was incurred by the harshness with which these captives were treated; and serious alarms of insurrection were entertained. To guard against this danger, they petitioned, in 1742, to be allowed to raise and maintain three independent companies; a boon which, though refused at first, was finally granted. These colonies derived a considerable accession from the rebellion of 1745, at the close of which many adherents of the vanquished cause were allowed to seek shelter in the western plantations, and induced by various circumstances to prefer the Carolinas. The discovery of indigo, as a native production, afforded, in addition to rice, another article for which a sure demand would be found in Europe. About the middle of the eighteenth century, too, when the other colonies began to have at least their best lands appropriated, this, which was still comparatively unoccupied, drew settlers from them, especially from Pennsylvania. Although estates along the coast were become scarce, valuable tracts remained in the interior, to which these American emigrants were pleased to resort.

After all that had been done before 1732 for the peopling of Carolina, there remained a large district between the Savannah and the Alatamaha, claimed by Britain, yet completely uninhabited. This disadvantage was more felt from its being bordered, not only by powerful Indian tribes, but by the Spaniards in Florida and the French in Louisiana; both having claims which, if circumstances favored, they could plausibly advance. The planters were particularly anxious to have a settlement formed, that might stand like a wall between them and these troublesome neighbors, but were much at a loss for persons who would voluntarily station themselves in a situation so unpleasant. Circumstances arose in England which afforded a prospect of supplying this want. A body of dis tinguished individuals, under the impulse of humanity,

> " Redressive searched
> Into the horrors of the gloomy jail."

General Oglethorpe, a soldier, brave, honorable, and humane, moved an inquiry, in 1728, into the treatment and condition of persons confined in the pris-

Fig. 42.—Portrait of General Oglethorpe.

ons of England, and in the following year presented a report upon this subject. It was found that, under the extremely bad management then prevalent, many persons imprisoned for debt or minor offences were treated most tyrannically, deprived of common comforts, and their morals farther injured by the associates with whom they were compelled to mingle. Many of them, even if liberated, could not have returned to the world with any prospect of comfort or advantage; and hence it occurred that to them a residence in the new continent might form an extremely desirable change. They could not be fastidious as to the situation, and might there be formed into military colonies, as a barrier to the other states. The conversion and improvement of the Indians entered into this generous plan. It was entrusted to a body of eminent persons, who undertook to act as trustees, not entering, like former associations, into a mercantile speculation for profit, but from philanthropic motives devoting their time and contributions to the object. They were to administer the colony during twenty-one years, after which it was to revert to the crown. It was named Georgia, from the reigning monarch; and Oglethorpe, with whom the whole scheme had originated, undertook to act gratuitously as governor. A general enthusiasm prevailed throughout the nation; large sums were subscribed by benevolent individuals; and parliament, in the course of two years, voted £36,000 for the purpose.

In the end of 1732, Oglethorpe, with a party of a hundred and sixteen, sailed for the new settlement. Having touched on their way at South Carolina, his followers were most hospitably received; and on their arrival, he made it his first object to conciliate the neighboring Indians, belonging to the powerful race of the Creeks. His efforts, guided by sincerity and discretion, were crowned with success. He prevailed upon Tomochichi, the head of this savage confed eracy, to meet him at Savannah, accompanied by fifty other petty chiefs, called kings. This aged person, expressing his ideas as usual by outward symbols, presented to the governor the skin of a buffalo, on the inside of which the head and feathers of an eagle were painted. This indicated the swiftness and power of the English, and also, by its softness and warmth, the love and protection which the Indians expected from them. This chief was even induced to visit Britain, where he met with many attentions, and had an audience of George II., whom he presented with a bunch of eagles' feathers, saying, "These are a sign of peace in our land, and have been carried from town to town there. We have brought them over to leave them with you, O great king, as a token of everlasting peace. O great king, whatever words you shall say unto me, I will faithfully tell them to all the kings of the Creek nations." In 1734, the town of Augusta was founded on the Upper Savannah, with a view to local trade. During the same year, two successive parties went out, amounting to 500 or 600, of whom 100 defrayed their own expenses. About 150 Highlanders were induced to join the colony, being well fitted for its military objects. A party of Moravians also arrived, whose industrious habits were likely to be of great advantage; and by a report of the trustees in 1740, it appeared that 2,500 emigrants had been sent out, at an expense of £80,000. John and Charles Wesley, then only known as zealous clergymen, were prevailed upon to accept livings in the colony.

Notwithstanding these promising appearances, and this most zealous support, Georgia did not prosper. The proprietors began with a series of regulations, well meant indeed, but carried to an extreme, and with little attention to existing circumstances. A complete prohibition was imposed on the introduction of rum, and even on all commercial intercourse with the West Indies. The importation of negroes was forbidden; a laudable measure, but indignantly endured by the colonists, who saw much wealth accruing to Carolina from their employment. The lands were most injudiciously granted in small lots of twenty-five acres, on condition of military service, and with that view descending only to heirs male. The settlers soon began to display those faults which, from their previous condition, might have been anticipated. Complaints were made against the Wesleys for their extreme rigidness, their peculiar forms of worship, and for giving their confidence to unworthy persons, who made false pretences of piety. Feuds rose so high that both left the colony. Whitefield, founder of the rival sect of Methodists, went out in 1740, with a particular view to establish an orphan asylum, which did not succeed; but his zealous and eloquent, though somewhat rude address, produced a strong impression, and were supposed to effect considerable good.

Affairs were rendered still further critical by the Spanish war, which, after long irritation and petty aggression, broke out in 1738. Oglethorpe determined to attack St. Augustine, the capital of Florida. Great preparations were made for this enterprise; Virginia and the Carolinas furnished a regiment, as well as £120,000 currency; and an Indian force undertook to assist. The governor, who was thus enabled to make an invasion with 2,000 men, reduced two successive forts; but the castle of St. Augustine itself was found too strongly fortified to allow a reasonable hope of reducing it unless by blockade. This he expected to accomplish by the aid of a strong flotilla, which came to co-operate with him. It proved, however, a very discouraging service for his undisciplined warriors; and the Indians, disgusted by an expression which escaped him, of horror at their cruelty, went off. The Highlanders, his best troops, were surprised, and a number cut to pieces; while the militia lost courage, broke the restraints of discipline, and deserted in great numbers. It proved impossible to prevent the enemy from procuring a reinforcement and large supply of provisions. In short matters were so adverse a state, that he had no alternative but to raise the siege, and return with his armament seriously shattered, and his reputation impaired.

The Spaniards, in two years after, in 1742, attempted to retaliate, and Monteano, governor of St. Augustine, with thirty-two vessels and 3,000 men, advanced to attack Frederica. Oglethorpe's force was very inadequate, and the aid from the north both scanty and very slow in arriving; yet he acted so as completely to redeem his military character. By skilfully using all the advantages of his situation, he kept the enemy at bay; then by various stratagems conveyed such an exaggerated idea both of his actual force and expected reinforcements, that they ultimately abandoned the enterprise, without having made one serious attack.

Georgia was thus delivered from foreign dangers; but she continued to suffer under her internal evils. The colonists complained that absurd regulations debarred them from rendering their productions available, and kept them in poverty. Numbers removed to South Carolina, where they were free from restraint; and the Moravians, being called upon to take up arms contrary to their principles, departed for Pennsylvania. Great efforts were made, as formerly, in Virginia, to produce silk, but for the same reasons without any success. In 1752, the twenty-one years had expired; and the trustees finding that their well-meant endeavors had produced only misery and discontent, relinquished the charge. Georgia became a royal colony, and the people were left at full liberty to use all the means, good and bad, of advancing themselves; lands were held on any tenure that best pleased them; and a free intercourse was opened with the West Indies. Thenceforth it was on a footing with South Carolina, and advanced with equally rapid steps.

XIV. The colonies, of which we have thus delineated the origin and progress, down to the close of the war in 1763 were altogether unconnected. Each had been founded on a separate basis, by distinct and even hostile classes. Between neighboring communities, where no sentiment of unity reigns, jealousies almost inevitably arise; and these were aggravated by boundary disputes and other contending claims. Some governors, particularly Nicholson, recommended the union of several of them under one head; but these were men of arbitrary temper, who urged this measure on the home administration as a mode of extending the power of the crown, and keeping down the increasing spirit of independence. Such communications, when they transpired, heightened not a little the antipathy already felt to the proposed measure.

There was, however, one object by which all the colonies were roused to a most zealous co-operation. It might have seemed a hardship that the successive wars between Britain and France should be transferred to their rising settlements beyond the Atlantic; but the inhabitants by no means felt it as such, and required only permission, in order to rush with fury against each other. The old national antipathy was remarkably strong in this ruder society; the difference of creed made the contests be viewed somewhat as religious wars; and the contrast between an absolute and a free government appeared peculiarly striking on the English side, where maxims almost republican prevailed. At first the colonies followed in the footsteps of the mother country; but as their magnitude and importance increased, the flame arose among themselves, and was thence communicated to Europe.

Even so early as 1629, Sir David Kirk, having equipped a fleet, surprised and took Quebec; but that infant settlement, to which little value was then attached, was restored at the peace of 1632. A severe collision, however, arose in consequence of the support afforded by the English from New York to the Five Nations, in the long and terrible war waged by them against the French in Canada. It was mostly carried on by skirmishes, in a covert manner, and without regular sanction from either power. But after the revolution of 1688, open hostilities ensued between the two nations, and Britain again determined to strike a blow against the enemy's power beyond the Atlantic. Acadia was subdued with little resistance, and Sir William Phipps, with thirty-four vessels and a large body of troops, reached Quebec. He did not, however, display the requisite promptitude; and through the able defence made by Count Frontenac, was obliged to re-embark without effecting his object. An attempt against Montreal was also defeated by the ability of Des Callierès. The contest was suspended by the peace of 1697, when, to the great discontent of the inhabitants, Acadia was restored to France. During the war of the Spanish succession, two expeditions, the one in 1704, and the other in 1707, failed in achieving the conquest of that province; but General Nicholson, in September, 1710, finally annexed it, under the title of Nova Scotia, to the British crown. He proceeded afterward to make a grand effort against the Canadian capital, which was frustrated by the shipwreck of his squadron near the Seven Islands. Still the force of England was considered so superior, that she must ultimately have triumphed, had not the contest been terminated in 1713 by the peace of Utrecht. France retained Canada, but was obliged to cede Acadia and Newfoundland; also to make over to Britain her claims to the sovereignty of the Five Nations.

A long peace now followed, and though jealousies continued, no open hostilities ensued till 1744, when the war which Britain had for several years waged with Spain was extended to France. The latter power, though deprived of Nova Scotia by the treaty of Utrecht, had retained Cape Breton, and erected upon it Louisburg, which, by an expenditure of £1,200,000, was supposed to have been rendered one of the strongest of modern fortresses. The New England colonies, however, having, with characteristic ardor, determined to attack it, raised 4,000 men, and placed them under the command of Colonel Pepperel, who, on the 30th April, 1745, took the enemy somewhat by surprise. Being seconded by the fleet under Admiral Warren, he in seven weeks reduced this grand bulwark of their power in America; and though they made several vigorous efforts, they did not succeed in retrieving this disaster. Nevertheless, at the treaty of Aix-la-Chapelle in 1748, the colonists had the mortification to see the fruits of their valor snatched from them, Cape Breton being restored in exchange for some continental advantages, which were more highly prized by the British king and ministry. They expressed the deepest discontent, and hesitated not even to charge the government at home with a desire to maintain the power of Louis, in order to check the spirit of internal independence.

The French, meantime, had become inspired with an eager desire to extend their North American possessions. Having at various points been brought into contact with the back settlements of their rival, they had been generally successful in gaining the alliance of the Indians, from whose warlike character important aid was expected. They made the most active movements in New Brunswick, hoping thence to penetrate into Nova Scotia, where they would find a population originally French, and still strongly attached to the country of their fathers. But the enterprises which caused the greatest inquietude took place along the Ohio and the Mississippi. The colonists had already, at different points, penetrated the barrier of the Alleghany, and began to discover the value of the country extending to those mighty streams. The enemy, on the other hand, in virtue of certain voyages made in the preceding century by Marquette and La Salle, claimed the whole range of the Mississippi, by attaining which, their settlements in Canada and New Orleans would be formed into one continuous territory. This pretension, if referred to that peculiar law according to which Europeans have divided America among themselves, seems not wholly unfounded. They had added, however, a more exorbitant claim of all the streams falling into the great river, which would have carried them to the very summit of the Alleghany, and have hemmed in the British colonists in a manner to which they were by no means disposed to submit. The banks of the Ohio became the debateable ground on which this collision mainly took place.

The British were so confident in their right, that in 1749, an association was formed of merchants in London, combined with Virginian planters, called the Ohio Company, who received from the crown a grant of 600,000 acres on that river. Similar donations were made to other parties, who could not with any degree of safety turn them to account, in the face of such pretensions as the French advanced and showed a determination to support. These assumed so menacing a character, that Mr. Dinwiddie, governor of Virginia, under instructions from home, judged it necessary to send a commissioner to examine the state of affairs on that frontier, to confer with the French commander and urge him to desist from farther encroachment. This little expedition is memorable from the command being intrusted to Major George Washington.

Fig. 43.—Washington. From an early Print by Trumbull.

George Washington, whose name will descend to the latest posterity as the Father of his Country, as first in war, first in peace, and first in the hearts of his countrymen, was born near the banks of the Potomac, in Westmoreland county, in Virginia, on the 22d of February, 1732. He was great-grandson to John Washington, a gentleman of a respectable family, who had emigrated from the north of England about the middle of the preceding century, and had settled on the place where George Washington was born. George was the third son of his father, Augustine Washington, who died when he was very young. After receiving a very plain education, he learned something of the business of land surveying, and was in his eighteenth year appointed surveyor of the western part of the territory called the Northern Neck of Virginia, by Lord Fairfax, the proprietor of that country, whose niece had been married to George Washington's eldest brother. Two years later, and through the same influence, when the provincial militia was to be trained for actual service, he was appointed one of the adjutant generals of the Virginia militia, with the rank of major. Two years after this, in 1753, when the designs of the French in Canada began to create alarm in all our colonies, he was despatched on a half diplomatic mission to the French commandant on the Ohio, and acquitted himself with great judgment and ability, failing, indeed, in his remonstrances with M. Le Gardeur de St. Pierre, but informing himself fully of the condition of the French force, surveying with a careful eye the vast tract of country—then almost an unexplored wilderness—he had to pass through, and winning over the wild Indian tribes to the interests of the colonies. On his return to Virginia Washington became, in a small and very modest way, an author; for he published the journal of his very interesting expedition. In the course of 1754, when it was determined to dislodge the French, without declaration of war by England, from some forts they were building on the Ohio and at the confluence of the Monongahela and Alleghany rivers, he was appointed lieutenant colonel of a provincial regiment, and sent with Colonel Fry toward the scene of action, which he had carefully examined on his former journey. Fry died in the wilds, and then Washington took the sole command. He was joined by some of the Indian tribes, whose friendship he had captivated, and was further reinforced by two independent companies of regulars; but, instead of taking the French and their forts by surprise, he was taken by surprise himself, and was compelled to retreat to a stockade or fort at the Great Meadows, now termed Fort Necessity, where he was soon surrounded by the French, and, after a gallant resistance, compelled to capitulate. It is quite clear that he had been rash and over-hazardous—an inherent defect in his military conduct which he was quick in correcting. Being allowed the honors of war, and suffered to march without molestation into the inhabited parts of Virginia, he returned home with his little detachment considerably reduced. The legislature of Virginia, in admiration of the courage displayed, passed a vote of thanks to him and the officers under his command.

By this time the colonists began seriously to feel the absence of some general co-operation against this formidable enemy. Those who stood most immediately exposed to attack, complained that upon them alone was thrown the whole burden of repelling it; and the government at home were at length induced to recommend a convention of delegates being held at Albany, to concert with each other, and with the chiefs of the Six Nations, a plan of united defence. The New England states, Pennsylvania, Maryland, and New York, complied with the advice, and appointed deputies, who assembled in June, 1754; when the lead was taken by Benjamin Franklin, who ranked already as one of the most intelligent and distinguished citizens of America. Rising from a humble station, he had acquired a paramount influence in his own state of Pennsylvania, and been appointed postmaster general for the colonies. He soon submitted to his colleagues a very bold and important project. A general government, consisting of a president appointed by the crown, and of a council of representatives from the respective colonies, were to be invested with the general direction of war, peace, treaties, and transactions with the Indians. They were to have the power of imposing such taxes as might be deemed necessary for these purposes; and their acts, if not disallowed by the king within three years, were to acquire the force of law. They might also levy troops, the commanding officers being appointed by the president, subject to the approbation of the council. For this scheme Franklin gained the approbation of all the delegates, except those from Connecticut; but when submitted to the respective governments, it met a very different fate. They all considered these powers, especially that of taxation, as far too great to be placed in the hands of a body over whom each had so little control. Its reception was equally unfavorable in the British cabinet, who viewed it, not without reason, as an arrangement rendering America almost en-

tirely independent. Thus the plan, recommended as it was by such high authority, proved wholly abortive ; though perhaps it had some small influence in paving the way for a similar union, which future emergencies induced the colonies to form.

The British ministry were, however, determined to support their cause with the utmost vigor. Warm remonstrances were made to the court of France, which lavished in return pacific professions and even promises ; but they were directly contradicted by actions, which left no doubt of a firm determination to maintain her lofty pretensions. It was resolved, therefore, to employ force in driving the French from their present advanced position ; and in the beginning of 1755, General Braddock, with two regiments, was despatched from Ireland to co-operate with the Virginia forces in obtaining the command of the Ohio. His arrival excited enthusiastic hopes, and at Alexandria he met the governors of five colonies, assembled to concert the general plan of a campaign. Washington had quitted the army on account of a regulation by which the colonial officers were made to rank under those of the regular army ; but, at the solicitation of Braddock, he consented to act as his aid-de-camp, in the character of a

FIG. 45.—Defeat of General Braddock—9th, July 1755.

volunteer. Yet their movements were almost arrested by the failure of the Virginian contractors to furnish the wagons necessary for transporting the baggage and artillery. In this emergency, Franklin, by great exertions, and by influence with the farmers of Pennsylvania, succeeded in procuring these supplies ; but before they could be transported across the rugged Allegany, a long time would necessarily elapse, during which the enemy might strengthen Duquesne and reinforce the garrison. At the earnest entreaty of Washington, it was therefore determined to press forward with 1,200 well-appointed men, and that Colonel Dunbar, with the heavy artillery and baggage, should remain behind. Washington, however, was dismayed to find that Braddock, though a brave and experienced officer, was wedded to the forms of regular European warfare. Instead of causing his troops to push briskly across the intervening obstacles, he employed them in levelling every hillock, and throwing bridges over every brook. Again, though advised to accept the offered aid of some Indians, at least for scouring the woods and guarding against surprise, he despised such auxiliaries, and treated them so coldly that they quickly dropped off. Washington being unfortunately seized with a violent illness, was unable by his utmost efforts to keep up with the army, but rejoined it on the evening of the 8th July, within fifteen miles of Fort Duquesne, against which this laborious movement was directed. The garrison was understood to be small, and quite inadequate to resist the great force now brought to bear upon it ; exulting hope filled every heart ; and no one doubted to see the British flag waving next day over the battlements, and the enemy rooted out from all Western America. The march next morning is described as a splendid spectacle ; being made in full military array, with a majestic river on one hand, and deep woods on the other. Not an enemy appeared, and the most profound silence reigned over this wild territory. They proceeded, forded the stream, and were passing a rough tract covered with wood, which led direct to the fort, when suddenly a destructive fire was poured in upon the front, while another rapidly followed on the right flank. The assault was continued by an enemy who remained invisible, closely hidden behind trees and ravines. The vanguard fell back in a confusion which soon became general. Their only hope would now have been to quit their ranks, rush behind the bushes, and fight man to man with their assailants ; but Braddock insisted on forming them into platoons and columns, in order to make regular discharges, which struck only the trees. After some time spent in these fruitless efforts, with the hidden fire still unabated, a general flight ensued, that of the regulars being the most precipitate and shameful, while the only stand was made by the Virginian hunters. The officers in general remained on the field while there seemed any hope of rallying their troops, and, consequently, out of eighty-six engaged, sixty-three were killed or wounded ; the commander himself mortally. Of the privates, 714 fell ; the rout was complete, and the more disgraceful, in that it was before an inferior enemy, whose number did not exceed 850, of whom only 250 were Europeans. During this disastrous day, Washington displayed an admirable courage and coolness. After the fall of so many officers, he alone remained to convey orders, and was seen galloping in every direction across the field, amid the thickest fire ; yet, by a dispensation which seemed providential, though four balls passed through his clothes, and two horses were killed under him, he escaped unhurt ; and very contrary to his wish, this melancholy disaster greatly elevated his reputation. The remnant of the army retreated precipitately into the low country, whither the French considered themselves too weak to pursue them.

Meantime, a militia force of about 5,000 men was assembled at Albany, for an expedition against the important fortress of Crown Point, on the borders of Canada. The commander was William Johnson, an Irishman, who had risen

FIG. 46.—A Western Hunter in proper Costume.

from the ranks, and whose uncommon bodily strength, with a rude energy of character, had enabled him to acquire a greater influence over the Indian tribes than any other British officer. Having reached the southern extremity of Lake George, and learned that the enemy were erecting an additional fort at Ticonderoga, he resolved to push forward, hoping to reduce it before the works were completed. Intelligence, however, was soon received, which required him to stand on the defensive. Baron Dieskau, an able commander, had carried out from France a large reinforcement, and having added to them a considerable body of Indians, was advancing to attack the British settlements. He at first proceeded toward Oswego, but on learning the advance of Johnson, hastened to direct his operations against him. The latter had fortified his camp, but through defective information, sent forward an advanced party of 1,000 men, who at a distance of about three miles unexpectedly met the enemy, and were driven back with great loss. Dieskau then marched forward to assault the main camp, which he seemed to have a fair prospect of carrying; but Johnson received him with the utmost firmness, and opening a brisk fire, caused the Indians and militia to fall back. The French regulars maintained the contest for several hours with great vigor, and the British general was even obliged by a severe wound to leave the command to Lyman, his second. The final result however was, that the assailants were completely repulsed, with the loss of nearly 1,000 men. Dieskau himself was mortally wounded and made prisoner; and his retreating forces, being suddenly assailed by a small detachment from New York, abandoned their baggage and took to flight. It was thought by many, that if Johnson had followed up his victory by an attack on Crown Point, or at least on Ticonderoga, he would have succeeded; but he did not choose to hazard the laurels already gained.

It may be mentioned also that in this busy campaign, Shirley, the governor of Massachusetts, led an expedition against Niagara; but the difficulties of the march, and the discouragement spread by the tidings of Braddock's defeat, prevented his engaging in any undertaking. It would seem, indeed, that the British forces were scattered in too many quarters, instead of concentrating themselves in one united effort against some important position or commanding stronghold.

The war which had thus for some time been covertly waged between the two nations, was, in 1756, openly declared; and increased exertions were made on both sides. In a council of governors held at New York, three expeditions were planned, in which 21,000 men were to be employed. Abercromby and Lord Loudon, however, who successively went out as commander-in-chief, did not possess the requisite energy; and discontents arose among the provincial officers, from being compelled to take rank under the regulars. The French force, meantime, was united under Montcalm, an officer of high spirit; and while the British were deliberating, he hastened against the two forts at Oswego, which, as they protected Lake Ontario, formed their principal bulwark in that quarter. On the 10th of August he began the siege of the first, which was soon evacuated by its defenders, owing to the failure of their ammunition, and he then assailed the other with such vigor, that it surrendered on the 14th, Colonel Mercer, the commander, having been killed in the attack. The garrison, amounting to 1,400, became prisoners of war, while 121 pieces of cannon, with a quantity of stores, sloops, and boats, fell into his hands. In the following year, he marched against Fort William Henry, on Lake George, commenced the siege in the beginning of August, and compelled it, in six days, to surrender. The defenders stipulated to march out with the honors of war, and rejoin their countrymen; but these terms were completely violated by the Indians, who barbarously massacred a great number of them. Montcalm's friends have studiously defended him against any charge, even of neglect, on this dreadful occasion, but blame was attached, at the time, both to him and his officers, and there was accordingly kindled throughout the colonies a deep thirst for vengeance.

Hitherto this war had been an almost continued series of disaster and disgrace; and in Europe similar results were seen to follow the feeble measures of the cabinet. But the spirit of the nation, being now aroused, forced into power William Pitt, perhaps the most energetic war minister who has ever swayed the British councils. Adverse to military operations in Germany, he turned his main attention to the North American colonies, and by vigorously announcing his resolution, drew forth from themselves strenuous exertions. Lord Loudon was superseded by Amherst, a more able commander; while the most active part was assigned to Wolfe, a young officer, in whom the discerning eye of Pitt discovered a rising military genius. It being determined to strike the first blow against Louisburg, considered the centre of French power in that quarter, an expedition sailed against it in May, 1757, and by the end of July, chiefly through his exertions, it was compelled to surrender. This success was followed up next year by a more formidable attempt, under the same commander, against Quebec, capital of New France. On the 13th September, 1759, a splendid victory, dearly purchased indeed by the death of that gallant officer, placed the city in the undisputed possession of Britain.

After this triumph, France could with difficulty maintain her posts in the interior. In 1758, General Abercromby, with 16,000 regulars and provincials, marched against Crown Point and Ticonderoga. The first skirmish was marked by the fall of Lord Howe, a young officer of high promise, and much beloved in America. The commander, having soon after made a premature assault on the last-mentioned fort, was repulsed with considerable loss, when he raised the siege and precipitately retreated. Colonel Bradstreet, however, at the head of a detachment, captured Fort Frontignac, a post of some consequence on Lake Ontario.

Meantime the Virginians, notwithstanding their most earnest wishes, had in vain attempted to renew the expedition against Fort Duquesne; having placed under the command of Washington a force barely sufficient to check the incursions of the French and Indians. In 1758, however, under the auspices of Pitt, General Forbes arrived with a body of troops, which the provincials soon raised to 6,000; but, contrary to the urgent advice of the American, instead of pushing on by a track already formed, he undertook to cut a new one through forests almost impracticable. He accordingly failed to reach the scene of action till November, when the season was too late for active operations, and the provisions were nearly exhausted. A party under Major Grant, having rashly advanced, were defeated with great loss. The situation of the army appeared very serious, when news arrived that the garrison, reduced to 500, and discouraged probably by the fall of Louisburg and the dangers menacing Canada, had set fire to the fort, and retreated in boats down the river. The Indians, who had already abandoned their cause, readily entered into terms with the British, and tranquillity was established along the whole line of the back settlements. By the peace of Paris, France ceded it and all the adjacent countries. Spain was also obliged to yield Florida; and Britain acquired a vast, compact, and flourishing empire, reaching from the arctic zone to the Gulf of Mexico.

It would have been satisfactory could we have added a particular view of the progress made during this period by the colonies, in population, industry, and wealth. Their advance was certainly most rapid; yet the details are scanty and in many cases doubtful. They were favored by a combination of circumstances almost unprecedented. An industrious race, skilled in agriculture, were transported to a country where land to any extent could be easily obtained.

The abundance of the necessaries of life thus produced, removed all check to marriage and the rearing of children; while the same circumstances invited a continual iuflux of emigrants from Europe. Hence arose a rapid increase of population, of which the modern world at least had never seen any example; doubling, it was supposed, in twenty-five or even twenty years.

The commercial progress of the colonies was equally rapid, and excited a still greater interest. Their exports consisted almost exclusively of the rude productions of land; a circumstance most grateful to the English people, since it naturally led to the desire to take their commodities in exchange. Their progress in agriculture, by absorbing at once their capital and their labor, prevented them from making any attempt to manufacture goods for themselves; while, by increasing their wealth, it induced them to prefer the fabrics of Britain to the rude home-made stuffs with which they had been at first contented. There was, however, a difficulty in finding articles, such as the rich products of the West Indies, which would obtain a place in the market of Europe. Silk and wine, the early objects of hope and pride, never succeeded; and though, in 1731, there were exported from Virginia three hundred weight of the former, their expectations from this source proved ultimately fallacious. What they vainly sought, however, came upon them from unexpected quarters; and we have seen how tobacco forced itself into the place of a leading export. During the present period, Virginia and Maryland became the chief sources whence all Europe was supplied. In 1744 and the two succeeding years, Britain imported 40,000,000 pounds, whereof 30,000 were re-exported. Rice also was accidentally introduced in the manner already mentioned; and so congenial was the swampy soil of Carolina to its culture, that nearly the whole quantity consumed in Europe was raised in that plantation. The productions of the northern colonies being nearly the same with those of Britain, met with no demand from our merchants; but the surplus of grain found a market in Spain and Portugal; provisions and timber were sent to the West Indies; and thence they obtained the means to pay for foreign manufactures. To New England again, the fisheries and shipbuilding were a continual source of ever-increasing wealth. The following exhibits a view of the progressive increase of imports and exports from 1700 to 1763:—

	1701		1730		1750		1763	
	British Imports.	Exports.	Imports.	Exports.	Imports.	Exports.	Imports.	Exports.
	£	£	£	£	£	£	£	£
New England...	32,656	86,322	54,701	208,196	48,455	343,659	74,815	258,854
New York......	18,547	31,910	8,740	64,356	35,634	267,130	53,988	238,560
Pennsylvania....	5,220	12,003	10,582	48,592	28,191	217,713	38,228	284,152
Virginia, and Maryland....	235,738	199,683	346,823	150,931	508,939	349,419	642,294	555,391
Carolina.......	16,973	13,908	151,739	64,785	191,607	133,037	282,366	250,132
Georgia.........	–	–	–	–	1,942	2,125	14,469	44,908
	309,134	343,826	572,585	536,860	814,768	1,313,083	1,106,160	1,631,997

In 1769, a merchant, under the title of The American Traveller (4to, London, 1769), published a very detailed statement of the commerce of the colonies, on an average of the preceding three years; and as this does not seem to be generally known, we here present a summary, which may interest some classes of readers:—

	Massa-chusetts	Rest of N. E.	New York.	Pennsyl-vania.	Virg'a & Maryl'd.	North Carolina	South Carolina	Georgia.	Total.
	£	£	£	£	£	£	£	£	£
Dry Cod . . .	100,000	—	—	—	—	—	—	—	100,000
Pickled Fish . .	8,000	7,000	—	—	—	—	—	—	15,000
Timber	45,000	30,000	25,000	35,000	55,000	15,000	20,000	11,000	236,000
Ships	49,000	—	14,000	17,500	30,000	—	6,000	—	116,500
Whale and Cod Oil, &c. . . .	114,000	22,500	—	—	—	—	—	—	136,500
Live Stock . .	12,000	25,000	17,000	20,000	—	—	15,000	—	89,000
Salted Beef and Pork	13,500	15,000	26,000	55,000	15,000	—	25,000	—	149,500
Potash	20,000	15,000	14,000	—	—	—	—	—	49,000
Beeswax, &c. .	9,000	—	1,500	1,000	—	—	—	—	11,500
Flour and biscuit	—	—	250,000	350,000	—	—	—	—	600,000
Grain	—	—	110,000	112,000	70,000	—	12,000	—	304,000
Skins	—	—	35,000	50,000	25,000	—	45,000	17,000	172,000
Copper and Iron	—	—	20,000	35,000	35,000	—	—	—	90,000
Tobacco . . .	—	—	—	—	768,000	14,000	—	—	782,000
Rice	—	—	—	—	—	—	220,000	36,000	256,000
Indigo	—	—	—	—	—	—	50,000	1,700	51,700
Tar	—	—	—	—	—	17,800	2,600	—	20,400
Hemp	—	—	—	—	21,000	—	—	—	21,000
Flaxseed . . .	—	—	14,000	30,000	14,000	—	—	—	58,000
Sassafras . . .	—	—	—	—	7,000	—	—	—	7,000
Silk	—	—	—	—	—	—	—	2,500	2,500
Sundries . . .	—	—	—	—	—	21,500	—	6,000	27,500
Exports . . .	370,500	114,500	526,500	705,500	1,040,000	68,300	395,600	74,200	3,295,100
Imports . . .	395,000	12,000	531,000	611,000	865,000	18,000	365,000	49,000	2,846,000

THE

AMERICAN REVOLUTION

CHAPTER I.

The triumphant issue of the contest with France seemed to have placed the British empire in America on a foundation at once solid and permanent. The possession of the whole eastern coast, from the Gulf of Mexico to the Arctic ocean, secured it almost completely against any other European power, without whose support the natives could make only a very feeble and desultory resistance. The population, the wealth, and advancing commerce of these colonies, inspired sanguine and indeed chimerical hopes of future advantage. They had co-operated most cordially, by strenuous efforts and great sacrifices, in the arduous contest waged on their soil by Britain and her powerful rival; and the exultation of common success cemented still more closely the mutual ties. The most friendly feelings appeared to be mutually cherished; and nothing indicated the approach of that fatal crisis which was to rend the empire asunder, and to begin the separation between the Old and the New Worlds.

There were not wanting, indeed, circumstances secretly tending toward this result. The colonies had always professed a firm and zealous allegiance to the king; and even Mr. Marshall admits, that to the very latest period they did not generally dispute the supreme legislative power of parliament: yet they had at the same time shown an extreme anxiety to manage their affairs in their own way; and during their silent growth, when communication was tedious and unfrequent, they generally attained this object. Occasionally the monarchs were seized with jealous feelings, and sent out strict and imperious mandates; but the planters, by delay, coupled with firm and respectful remonstrance, usually contrived to evade their execution. The discouragement to their manufactures, though unfair, was of little consequence, when such branches of industry would at all events have been premature. The monopoly of their commerce, though a more serious evil, was so accordant with the contracted views of the age, that they never thought of disputing the right, or expecting it not to be enforced. It was, besides, executed with so much laxness, that the most lucrative dealings were carried on clandestinely with very little interruption. On this point British jealousy was at length roused; customhouses were erected, and cruisers stationed along the coast.

In Great Britain, meanwhile, the light under which the colonies were viewed underwent a material alteration. Free nations, it has been often observed, are peculiarly apt to domineer over subject states. The people regarded with the highest complacency their sway over a vast transatlantic empire: according to Lord Chatham, even the chimney-sweepers on the streets talked boastingly of their subjects in America. The entire subservience of the settlers, the power of parliament to impose upon them both laws and taxes, had always at home been held undisputed. In their infant state, however, when struggling with poverty and danger, there had been neither motive nor disposition to enforce these claims; and the occasional attempts to subvert their privileges, having been made in a violent manner by arbitrary and unpopular monarchs, had excited sympathy among the great body of the nation. The case was altered, when they had attained a degree of prosperity which enabled them undoubtedly to make a certain contribution toward the general interests of the empire; and some benefit might reasonably be expected from the vast exertions made in order to promote their security. The effect of these, indeed appeared in a serious derangement of the national finances. The budget of 1764 exhibited an expenditure hitherto unprecedented, leaving a deficiency of about three millions, which was with difficulty supplied by temporary resources and by encroachment on the sinking fund. Successive changes in the ministry had raised to its head George Grenville, an honest statesman, of great political knowledge and indefatigable application; but his mind, according to the able view of his character drawn by Burke, could not extend beyond the circle of official routine, and was unable to estimate the result of untried measures. He saw only the emptiness of the British exchequer, the capability of the Americans to pay a certain revenue, and the supposed unquestionable right to levy it.

Under these views, the minister, on the 10th March, 1764, introduced a series of resolutions, asserting the right and expediency of requiring America to contribute to the general exigencies of the empire, and specifying a stamp-duty as an eligible mode. These formidable propositions, which were to shake Europe and America to their foundations, were passed by parliament in the most thoughtless and careless manner. There is no record of speech or vote against them in either house. Mr. Grenville proceeded, on the 5th May, with as little opposition as before, to bring in an act imposing the intended duty. He showed considerable indulgence toward the colonies, having, on the first moving of the resolutions, sent for their agents, and stated his intention not to push the measure through that session, but to give them an opportunity of passing it themselves, or of raising in any other manner the required sum of £100,000.

These resolutions, being transmitted to America, excited the strongest and most hostile feeling; and the colonial assemblies almost unanimously advanced the claim of having the sole right of imposing taxes on their fellow-citizens. They maintained that recent duties on imported goods had materially encroached on this right, which the proposed act would entirely extinguish, and thus reduce them completely to the condition of slaves. The assembly of Massachusetts, however, after passing resolutions to the full extent of this principle, were induced by Mr. Hutchinson so to modify them as to rest their opposition solely on the ground of expediency. The other states, particularly Virginia and New York, took also a decided part, and petitions of the same tenor were forwarded from many of them to Great Britian. Dr. Franklin, already a highly distinguished person, appeared in London as agent for Pennsylvania. He and the others endeavored to impress strongly upon the minister the hopelessness of the Americans ever submitting to this arbitrary mode of taxation.

Mr. Grenville, early in February, 1765, brought his Stamp Act again before parliament. Voices, few indeed, but loud, were now raised against it. General Conway and Alderman Beckford denied the right of taxing America: Colonel Barré, with others, condemned it only as highly inexpedient, and even unjust, while the monopoly of her trade was retained. The latter gentleman began a course of most energetic and persevering opposition to the measure. He repelled the alleged obligations of the colonies to the mother country, describing

Fig. 47.—Portrait of Colonel Barré.

them as driven from her bosom by persecution, and raised up by their own energies amid many oppressions; as a people at once noble and truly loyal, but jealous of their liberties, which they were determined to vindicate. The act, however, passed in the Commons by a majority of 250 to 50, and in the Lords with scarcely any opposition. The petitions had been generally rejected, on account of their denying the parliamentary right of taxation; that of New York was so intemperate, that no one dared to present it. The act received the royal assent on the 22d March, though it was not to take effect till November following.

Virginia had always been an aristocratic colony, and hitherto considered peculiarly loyal; but her opulent planters now appeared animated by a most daring spirit of independence. The assembly being then in session, Patrick Henry, at that time one of the most eloquent men in America, brought forward a series of resolutions against the proposed measure, supported by a speech, in which he said, "Cæsar had his Brutus, Charles I. his Cromwell, and George III.—" being interrupted by loud cries of treason, he added, "may profit by their example." The resolutions were modified, and different versions are given of those finally adopted; but they certainly denied, in the most unqualified terms, the right of taxation claimed. Similar sentiments flew like lightning through the other states, which had at first displayed some degree of apathy. The most momentous step was taken by the assembly of Massachusetts, which, on the 6th June, 1766, circulated among the others the proposition for a general congress, to meet at New York, and arrange in concert the means of averting the threatened evil. Nine colonies responded to this call, the others being prevented chiefly by the difficulty of convoking their assemblies. The deputies from Boston, on their arrival, waited upon the governor, and, representing their meeting as regular, informed him of its object and nature. He warned them against it as quite unconstitutional, and which could in no shape be sanctioned; yet without attempting to obstruct the proceedings. In a series of fourteen resolutions they denounced the injustice and ruinous consequences of their being taxed without being represented; a privilege which, from their distance, they declared

FIG. 48.—Portrait of Patrick Henry.

it impossible for them to enjoy. They did not intimate any willingness to raise a revenue themselves, but maintained that the great advantages derived by Britain from the monopoly of American commerce formed an ample contribution. In an address to the throne, and petitions to both houses of parliament, these sentiments were forcibly expressed; yet they declared that their connexion with the empire formed their greatest happiness and security, and that its harmonious maintenance was the object of their most ardent desire. These documents were signed by only six commissioners; while others had authority only to report to their state assemblies. All those bodies, however, ultimately approved the proceedings; and this first united act of the colonies against the mother country bore certainly a most portentous aspect.

But the dreaded crisis arose when the first cargo of stamped paper was landed upon the American shores. Boston was the centre of tumult. On the 15th of August, the multitude hung on a tree the effigy of Mr. Oliver, the stamp-master; and the sheriff, when ordered to take it down, declared it was impossible, without hazarding the lives of those employed. At dusk, the people carried the figure to the town-house, where the council were assembled, and raised three loud huzzas in token of defiance. They then took it to the front of his house, where they cut off the head, after which, notwithstanding the defence made by his friends, they burst open the door, proclaiming their intention to seize him; but he had escaped. The council, having sent orders to a colonel of militia to beat an alarm, was told that it would signify nothing, for the drummer would be knocked down, and that probably every one belonging to the regiment was among the mob. Next morning, Mr. Oliver, to save his life, resigned his office, and whenever any one was heard of who defended or was likely to succeed him, a day was fixed for mobbing his house; a measure which was preceded by a bonfire in front of the dwelling, and cries of "liberty and property." The mob, meeting no resistance, proceeded to still greater extremities. On the 26th they demolished the residences of the registrar-deputy and comptroller of the customs; after which they hastened to that of the governor, who not having the slightest apprehension, was with difficulty persuaded by his family to quit it. The people rushed in, and immediately began its total destruction, involving that of a fine library, together with important manuscripts illustrative of the history of the state from its earliest settlement. Next morning, the street was found strewed with plate, rings, money, and other valuable articles. Boston being now threatened with entire destruction, the principal inhabitants repaired to the governor, and offered to restore the dominion of law, on condition that no penal proceedings should be held on account of the first commotion, directed solely against the stamps; and it was only by this compact that order was restored. In New York the people advanced in arms to attack the fort in which the obnoxious article had been lodged, and this post not being deemed tenable, the commander thought it necessary to deposite the object of their resentment in the hands of the magistrates. Movements somewhat similar were organized at every place of landing; at the same time, combinations were proposed for discontinuing the use of all British manufactures.

In England, meanwhile, affairs took a favorable turn for the colonists, through circumstances wholly independent of the merits of the question. From certain causes, an account of which falls not within our range of inquiry, ministerial affairs were in a very unsettled state. A turn of the political wheel brought into power the Marquis of Rockingham, a nobleman professing principles decidedly liberal. The colonial department was entrusted to General Conway, who had

Fig. 49.—Portrait of General Conway.

stood forward as the zealous advocate of the Americans. His views were seconded by petitions from London, Liverpool, Manchester, Birmingham, Newcastle, Glasgow, and other great commercial towns, deprecating the loss of their lucrative commerce. Yet ministers were beset with considerable difficulties, having to maintain the honor of the British government, which would be seriously compromised and its authority weakened, by yielding to a resistance thus violently urged. In the debate on the address, Mr. Grenville maintained that if Great Britain yielded, America was lost; what was now almost rebellion would become revolution. "The seditious spirit in the colonies owed its birth, he said, to factions in the house. We were bid to expect disobedience; what was this but telling the Americans to resist—to encourage their obstinacy with the expectation of support?" This argument, however, seems untenable, when we consider the apathy shown in parliament till the disturbances had actually arisen. Mr. Nugent, afterward Lord Clare, insisted that the colonies should at least be obliged to own the right of taxation, and to solicit the repeal of the late act as a favor. The opposite cause was most strenuously advocated by Mr. Pitt, who, after a long illness, reappeared on the scene. On the proposal to tax America, so great he said had been his agitation for the consequences, that if he could have been carried in his bed, and placed on the floor of the house, he would come to bear testimony against it. He maintained the supremacy of Great Britain in all matters of government and legislation; the greater must rule the less; but taxes were a gift or grant from the people; and how could any assembly give or grant what was not their own. "I rejoice," said he, "that America has resisted. Three millions of people, so dead to all the feelings of liberty as voluntarily to submit to be slaves, would have been fit instruments to make slaves of the rest."—"In a good cause, on a sound bottom, the force of this country can crush America to atoms. But on this ground your success would be hazardous. America, if she fell, would fall like the strong man; she would embrace the pillars of the state, and pull down the constitution along with her."

The ministers, after a good deal of consideration, determined to bring in a bill for the repeal of the Stamp Act, combined with a declaration of the power of Britain to bind the colonies *in all cases whatsoever.* This pointed expression, meant to soothe the opposite party, appeared to imply the power of taxation, and was indeed so explained by Conway, though as one only to be exercised in extreme cases. Yet very great difficulty was found in carrying it through the houses. In the Commons the minority was 167 to 275; in the Lords, 71 to 105. Thirty-three of the latter joined in a protest, stating, that after the declaration already made, "such a submission of King, Lords, and Commons, in so strange and unheard-of a contest," would amount to an entire surrender of British supremacy.

The news of this repeal was received in the colonies with gratitude and satisfaction; and they passed over the declaratory portion of the act, as merely intended to save the honor of the British legislature. The assembly of Massachusetts passed a vote of thanks to the king, to whom the house of burgesses in Virginia voted the erection of a statue. The greatest difficulty respected compensation to the sufferers by the disturbances, which was demanded in mild but urgent terms by General Conway. Though not absolutely repelled, great backwardness was shown in fulfilling it, especially in Massachusetts, where complaints were made that Governor Bernard made the requisition in a more peremptory manner than his dispatches had authorized. After long delay the measure was agreed to, but combined with a general pardon to all concerned in the riots, a proceeding considered by the government as wholly irrelevant and beyond their jurisdiction. Notwithstanding these obstacles, the compensation was at length everywhere adjusted. A new clause in the Mutiny Act, however, by which it was required that the troops sent out should be furnished not only with quarters but with beer, salt, and vinegar, was represented as only a disguised form of taxation. In New York, where it came first into operation, the assembly refused to issue orders for its enforcement.

The colonies had thus shown a disposition to remain attached on certain terms to the mother country, yet combined with an extreme and determined jealousy of any encroachment. In such circumstances, prudence evidently enjoined the strictest caution and a study to maintain things as they were, rather than attempt novel and doubtful measures. Unhappily, though there was no want of talent among the statesmen of the day, ministerial arrangements continued very fluctuating and unsettled. An entirely new cabinet came into power, at the head of which indeed was nominally Mr. Pitt, the friend of America; but his health was so broken, that he took no share whatever in public measures, and not being expected to recover, had lost his wonted influence. The lead was taken by Charles Townshend, a man of the most brilliant wit and eloquence, and whose power over the House of Commons was almost unbounded; yet destitute of solid and statesman-like views, and, according to Burke, impelled by an inordinate vanity to the hopeless attempt of pleasing the most opposite parties. He soon found that concession to America was in bad odor among the majority of the house, and was stung, it is said, by taunts from his old colleague, Mr. Grenville, who reproached him with cowardice in not daring to act on his own principles. Under these impulses, he determined to undertake this perilous measure in a different shape, which might, it was hoped, be less offensive and more efficacious.

In May, 1767, he introduced a bill imposing a duty on tea, glass, paper, and painters' colors, exported from England to America. As the colonists could receive these articles only from Britain, a tax was thus inevitably entailed, to which, after what had passed, their submission could never be expected. Yet we have again to wonder at the supine apathy of parliament, and particularly of those members who afterward impugned the measure with the greatest vehemence. The bill passed rapidly through both houses, and on the 29th June received the royal assent. By another act, resident commissioners of customs were established in the colonies, and other regulations made for the more strict collection of the revenue. The principle of these arrangements could not be objected to; yet, as in fact a very extensive contraband trade had long entered into the traffic of the Americans, they pressed upon them with a new severity, which they could scarcely brook.

On intelligence of these acts being received among them, all the elements of opposition were again in movement. A number of publications, particularly Mr. Dickinson's "Letters of a Pennsylvania Farmer," taught the people to regard them as a decided attack on their liberties. The general assembly of Massachusetts, having met in January, 1768, drew up a petition to the king, asserting in decided though not violent terms the right of not being taxed without their own consent. They took the more obnoxious measure of sending a circular, embodying the same sentiments, to the assemblies of the other colonies, inviting their co-operation. This last step excited the utmost jealousy in the British ministers, who instructed Governor Bernard to call upon them to rescind their resolution, and, in case of non-compliance, to dissolve them. The house, however, in June, 1768, by a vote of 92 to 17, adhered in the most positive manner to these proceedings; when their immediate dissolution followed. The government sent a counter circular to the other assemblies, warning them to beware of the dangerous and factious conduct of Massachusetts. It failed, however, to prevent a cordial concurrence of all the leading bodies, several of whom repelled with vehemence the attempt to dictate to them, or to control their proceedings.

At Boston, meantime, fresh grounds of irritation continually arose. The commissioners of customs arrived, and one of their officers was placed on board the sloop LIBERTY, belonging to John Hancock, a zealous patriot, laden with wines from Madeira. The functionary, on attempting to exercise his duties, was confined in the cabin, and the whole cargo was landed during the night. The vessel was in consequence condemned and seized; upon which the people rose in tumult, burned a customhouse boat, and compelled the commissioners to flee for safety on board the Romney ship of war. The assemblies strongly condemned these proceedings, inviting even the government to prosecute; but there appeared

Fig. 50.—Portrait of John Hancock.

so little prospect of obtaining either witnesses or juries who would convict, that no such attempt was made.

The agitation excited by this event was heightened by another, which was in a great degree its consequence. Two regiments were ordered from New York to be quartered at Boston. The first rumor of this measure raised an extraordinary ferment; a town meeting was held, and a committee appointed, who waited on the governor to ascertain the truth of the report, and solicit him to convene the assembly. He did not deny the fact, but declared that he was unable to comply with the request without instructions from home. The people then proceeded to the very serious measure of finding a substitute for the assembly, by inviting the other towns to nominate deputies, and thus form a convention. Pretending, too, the dread of a war with France, they issued orders that every inhabitant, according to an alleged law of the state, should provide himself with a musket and the requisite ammunition. All the towns except one sent deputies, who assembled in the beginning of September. They immediately despatched three members to the governor, with a petition, disclaiming any idea of assuming an authoritative character, but professing merely to have met "in this dark and distressing time to consult and advise as to the best means of preserving peace and good order;" and concluded with a request to call the assembly. He refused to receive the message, or in any shape recognize the meeting, and next day wrote a letter, admonishing them to separate without delay. They did not immediately comply; yet not being actuated by the violent temper which prevailed among the citizens, they merely prepared a petition to the king, expounding their grievances, but professing the most decided loyalty, and a desire to cultivate harmony with Great Britain. In a report addressed to the people, while setting forth the alarming state of the country, they earnestly inculcated submission to legal authority, and abstinence from all acts of violence and tumult. They then separated after a session of five days. The troops now arrived, and as the council and inhabitants refused to take any steps for their accommodation, the governor was obliged to encamp part on the common, and assign to some quarters in the market-hall and state-house; positions that greatly aggravated the odium with which they were regarded.

Another important step to which the Americans were now impelled was an agreement for the non-importation of British goods. This, however, was accomplished with great difficulty, the people being thereby deprived of nearly all the conveniences and luxuries of life; while the merchants, the most active opponents of the mother country, were threatened with ruin. The proposition, after being suggested, lay some time dormant, nor, till August, 1768, was it fully determined upon, even in Massachusetts. Virginia next followed the example which Lord Bottetourt, the governor, vainly endeavored to prevent by dissolving the assembly. In this measure Washington took an active part, and his confidential letters intimate that he already contemplated a resort to arms as inevitable. Other colonies were induced to join.

In the beginning of 1769, these proceedings being brought under the view of the British parliament, excited in a great majority the most decided reprobation Both houses passed a series of resolutions declaring the pretension of not being bound by the acts of the legislature "illegal, unconstitutional, and derogatory of the rights of the crown and parliament of Great Britain." The circular letter of the Massachusetts assembly, the assemblage and proceedings of the Boston convention, were characterized as daring insults on his majesty's authority, and audacious usurpations of the powers of government. In an address to the king, the lords assured him of support in maintaining the laws in Massachusetts Bay, and prayed information respecting all persons accused of treason in the said colony, that they might be dealt with according to the act 35 Henry VIII., which directs such to be brought to England, and tried under a special commission. The resolution and address, when brought down to the Commons, encountered a warm opposition. Governor Pownall, intimately acquainted with the colonies, and actuated seemingly by patriotic motives, strongly advised ministers to pause, and do nothing to inflame the Americans, whom he described as sincerely attached to the mother country, yet jealous in the extreme of those liberties for which their ancestors had made such sacrifices. Yet the resolution was passed by 161 to 65.

At this time, however, another entire change took place in official arrangements, when Lord North began his long and eventful career. He possessed extensive and varied knowledge, considerable eloquence, with peculiar skill in debate, and address in managing the house. Yet he wanted the decisive character of mind which would have fitted him for that formidable crisis he could not avoid. He was incapable of originating or of acting upon any comprehensive plan, while, on the other hand, he was easily hurried into hasty and inconsiderate measures, from the effects of which he had not skill to extricate himself.

Almost every new minister had opened his career by concession to the provincials; and one of Lord North's temper was not likely to form an exception. The merchants, too, who were beginning to suffer severely by the non-importation proceedings, petitioned earnestly in favor of the colonies. The exports, which in 1768 had amounted to £2,378,000, of which £132,000 was in tea, had fallen in 1769 to £1,634,000, the tea being only £44,000. On the 5th March, 1770, his lordship proposed to withdraw the duties recently imposed, as contrary to sound commercial principles, and tending to discourage their own manufactures. He retained only that on tea as an assertion of the British right of taxation. Even George Grenville condemned this plan as inconsistent and imperfect, urging that one system or other ought to be thoroughly adopted; while several members reprobated all concession, and insisted that the acts should be enforced with the united powers of the nation. An amendment by Governor Pownall, that the tea duty also should be repealed, was negatived by 204 to 142, and the original motion carried.

This measure in a great degree tranquilized America; though considerable materials of irritation were left. The more zealous patriots contended, that as their objection had been to the principle, not the amount of the taxes, the retention of any one was equivalent to a continuance of the whole. The resolution, also, respecting the conveyance of offenders to England for trial, though never in fact intended to be acted upon, excited rumors and alarms. The Massachusetts assembly advanced new and bolder claims, altogether denying the power of parliament even to legislate; they complained also of the laws restraining their manufactures, which were doubtless impolitic, but had hitherto been quietly submitted to, and in their actual state were of very small practical injury. A new arrangement, making the salaries of the governor and judges independent of the assembly, gave rise to strong remonstrances. They declared that no arrangement would satisfy them except the restoration of everything to the same footing as at the close of the late war. The removal of their body to Cambridge, and its long prorogations, heightened the discontent; while the presence of the military was a continued source of complaint and irritation.

During these parliamentary transactions, an occurrence happened in Boston, the source and centre of opposition to British authority, which greatly exasperated the Americans and removed the hopes of reconciliation to a greater distance than ever. Frequent quarrels had arisen between the inhabitants and the soldiers, who had been stationed there in the autumn of 1768; but the public peace was preserved till the evening of the 5th of March, 1770, when a scuffle ensued, near the barracks, between a few soldiers and some young men of the town: the soldiers pursued the young men through the streets; the townsmen took the alarm; the bells of the churches were rung; the multitude assembled at the customhouse, and insulted and threatened the sentinel stationed there. Captain Preston, the officer on duty at the time, hastened with a party to support the sentinel: he endeavored to persuade the people to disperse; but his efforts were unavailing. The mob became more riotous than before, throwing stones and other missiles at the military. At length a soldier who had been struck fired on the multitude; some of his comrades soon followed his example: four persons were killed, and several wounded. The crowd fled, but soon collected in another street. The drums beat to arms; the troops were drawn out; and the utmost agitation and confusion prevailed in the town.

A meeting of the inhabitants was held, and a deputation sent to the governor, requesting him to remove the troops. He assembled the council, who were of opinion that the removal of the troops would be for the good of his majesty's service. The troops were accordingly removed to Castle William. Captain Preston surrendered himself for trial; and the soldiers who had been under his command at the customhouse were taken into custody.

Some days afterward, the bodies of those who had been killed in the riot, accompanied by a great concourse of people, displaying emblematical devices calculated to inflame the popular mind, were carried in funeral procession through the town to the place of sepulture. The colonial newspapers gave an inflammatory account of the transaction, representing it as an atrocious massacre of the peaceable inhabitants. The trial of Captain Preston and his party was delayed till the month of October, and Samuel Adams was assigned to him by the court as his defender. Before that time the irritation of the public mind had somewhat abated; and Captain Preston and six of his men, were acquitted by a Boston jury. Two of the party were found guilty of manslaughter.

The news of the discontinuance of the American duties reached Boston while the minds of the people were much irritated by the death of their townsmen; but in the inflamed state of the public mind the intelligence had little effect in soothing their angry passions, or cherishing a spirit of conciliation. The ex-

Fig. 51.—Boston Massacre.

Fig. 52.—Portrait of Samuel Adams.

asperation and firm resolution to resist all parliamentary taxation, which prevailed in Massachusetts, did not exist, in the same degree, in the other colonies; and, therefore, in them the repeal of the duties had considerable influence on the public mind. In all the provinces much inconvenience had been felt in consequence of the non-importation associations, and many of the people were glad to be released from them. Accordingly, they now held those associations no longer binding, except in regard to tea: some, indeed, wished to interpret them more rigorously, and to consider them obligatory till the tax on every article was abrogated. But the general sense of the colonists was that they ceased in regard to every article from which the tax was removed, and that now they operated against tea only. Hence, during the remainder of this year and the whole of the next, the commerce of Britain with America was in a flourishing condition.

In the southern and middle colonies, although the people were not entirely satisfied with parliament, yet, for the sake of peace, they were generally inclined to acquiesce in what it had done. The same spirit did not prevail in the

FIG. 53.—Residence of the Adams' Family, Quincy, Mass.

north; for there the colonists were indignant at the restrictions laid on their commerce by the establishment of an American board of admiralty, and the powers granted to the officers of the navy, in order to enforce the revenue laws. The zeal of these petty officers was often much greater than their prudence; and they highly provoked the people by the vexatious activity and insolence with which they executed their commission.

Lieutenant Dudington, commander of the armed vessel Gasper, stationed off Rhode Island, was remarkably active in searching for contraband goods. By this conduct, and by compelling the packets to lower their colors in passing him, he had become the object of much ill will. On the evening of the 9th of June, 1772, the Providence packet, with passengers on board, came up with colors flying, and refusing to lower them, the lieutenant fired a shot at her; which being disregarded, he gave chase. It was near full tide, and the packet stood closely in to the land, for the purpose of drawing the Gasper into shallow water: the design succeeded, and the schooner got fast aground about seven miles below Providence. The packet proceeded to the town, where the resolution was soon formed of attacking and destroying the Gasper. Accordingly, about two in the morning, a body of armed men, in several whale-boats, boarded the Gasper, which was still aground, forced the lieutenant, who was wounded in the scuffle, with his crew, ashore, and burned the schooner and her stores.

The British ministry were incapable of deriving wisdom from experience; for, after all the mischief which had resulted from their American acts, they still indulged the passion for colonial legislation. Hitherto the assembly of Massachusetts Bay had voted a scanty allowance to the judges and to law officers of the crown; but about the beginning of 1772, in order to render the judges more independent, the crown granted them liberal salaries out of the American revenue. The measure was unseasonable; for every act of government was looked on with distrust and jealousy by the colonists; and in the irritable state of the public mind at that time, the grant of salaries to the judges, being viewed as the wages of subserviency, created much alarm and agitation.

The inhabitants of Boston met on the 25th of October. Mr. Hutchinson was then governor, having succeeded Sir Francis Bernard in 1770: to him they presented a petition, setting forth the evil tendency of the new regulation respecting the judges, and the alarm which it had occasioned, and praying him to call an assembly. He refused: the people, therefore, appointed a committee to consider what was to be done in that season of danger, and to report to a subsequent meeting. The committee prepared a report more extensive than any that had hitherto been framed, comprehending the rights of the colonists as men, as citizens, and as Christians

The inhabitants of Boston met to receive the report, which was read and agreed to. It was ordered to be printed and circulated in the province, accompanied by an exhortation to the people no longer to doze or sit in supine indifference, while the hand of oppression was tearing the choicest fruits from the tree of liberty.

When the assembly met in January, 1773, the governor imprudently expatiated on the supreme legislative authority of the king and parliament. This fanned the dying embers; and the assembly, instead of qualifying the claims contained in the resolutions of the people of Boston, avowed them in all their extent. In their address they openly denied the right of parliament to tax or to legislate for them in any respect whatsoever; and added that, if in any late instances there had been a submission to acts of parliament, it had arisen rather from want of consideration, and a reluctance to contend with the parent state, than from a conviction of the supreme legislative authority of parliament.

CHAPTER II.

The independent spirit which had so often manifested itself in the assembly and colony of Massachusetts Bay, had been gradually working its way into the other provinces. Since the time of the first congress, a mutual correspondence had been maintained between the leading men of the several colonies. The measures of the British ministry had tended to promote among them an approximation of political sentiment, and to make them feel the importance of union and co-operation in giving consistency and vigor to their measures. But although the colonies were determined to resist taxation by a British parliament, yet there was not at this time among the great body of the people, nor even among their leaders, unless with perhaps a very few exceptions, the remotest intention of a separation from Great Britain. But an act of parliament was passed this session, which brought matters to a crisis, and severed the American colonies for ever from the British empire.

The East India Company enjoyed a monopoly, and, having allowed their affairs to fall into disorder, they applied to parliament for relief, complaining that their embarrassments were partly owing to the American disturbances, which had lessened the demand for their tea, and left nearly 17,000,000 lbs. lying in their warehouses for want of a market; but unhappily the ministry resolved to relieve them. For this purpose parliament empowered the company to export their tea to the colonies free from all duties payable in Britain. The ministry seem to have imagined that the company, by exporting the tea to America in their own ships, would be enabled to relieve their overstocked warehouses; that the colonial non-importation associations would be rendered ineffectual; and that the tax of three pence on the pound would necessarily be paid in America. But the quarrel had already proceeded too far to admit of the success of such a scheme. The Americans easily foresaw, that if the tea were landed in the provinces it would be impossible to check the sale and consumption of it; they, therefore took measures to prevent the discharging of their cargoes.

In November news reached Boston that three ships, loaded with tea, on account of the East India Company, were on their way to that port. The information threw the people into great commotion; the consignees were threatened, and fled for safety to Castle William. On the arrival of the tea, a meeting of the inhabitants of Boston and of the neighboring towns was held, at which it was resolved to send back the ships without permitting them to discharge their cargoes. Notice of this resolution was given to the consignees and others interested in the ships; and the meeting adjourned to afford them time to return their answer. The captains wished to put to sea, without running the risk of losing their cargoes. But the governor, who had always recommended coercive measures, found it easy to throw difficulties in the way of an amicable arrangement. The clearance from the customhouse, which was necessary to authorize the sailing of the ships, could not be obtained; besides, the vessels could not be allowed to pass Castle William without the governor's permission, which he refused to grant. The people, however, were too resolutely bent on their purpose to be diverted from it by such management. On the 16th of December the adjourned town meeting, after having heard an account of al the proceedings in the affair, dissolved itself amid cries of "A mob, a mob!" and in the evening a number of armed men, disguised like Mohawk Indians, boarded the three tea ships, and in about the space of two hours, broke open 342 chests of tea, valued at 18,000*l.* sterling, and discharged the contents into the sea. The work was deliberately performed, and no property but the tea injured.

The determined spirit of resistance to the introduction of this article was not confined to Boston, but manifested itself in other places also, although it was not attended with similar violence. In most instances the ships were obliged to return without having discharged their cargoes. In Charlestown, after much opposition, the tea was permitted to be landed, but was immediately lodged in damp cellars, where it long remained, and was finally spoiled.

Information of the destructive proceedings at Boston reached Britain while parliament was sitting, and was communicated to both houses by messages from the crown. The people of that town had on so many occasions shown an independent spirit, and had resisted oppression so often, that it was determined to make them feel the weight of parliamentary vengeance. For that purpose a bill was introduced on the 14th of March, 1774, and received the royal assent on the 31st of the same month, prohibiting the lading or unlading of any goods or merchandise, excepting stores for his majesty's service, and provisions and fuel for the use of the inhabitants, at any place within the port of Boston, after the 1st day of June, until the king was satisfied that good order and obedience to the laws were restored, and until the East India Company and others should be indemnified for the loss they had sustained. Then, and not till then, might the king by proclamation open the harbor of Boston. In order to enforce obedience to the enactments of this bill, four ships-of-war were ordered to sail for the proscribed town. General Gage, commander-in-chief in America, was appointed governor of Massachusetts Bay, in the room of Mr. Hutchinson; and he was authorized to grant pardons for treasons and all other crimes, and to remit forfeitures to all such offenders as he should think fit objects of royal clemency.

But the British ministry were not satisfied with shutting up the harbor of Boston; they resolved not only to punish the people for past offences, but also to prevent future misconduct. For these purposes, they determined to annul the charter of the colony, and give it a new constitution. They accordingly procured an act of parliament which deprived the lower house of assembly in Massachusetts Bay of the power of electing the council, and vested that privilege in the crown, authorizing the king, or the governor acting in his name, to appoint judges, magistrates, and sheriffs. The act also empowered the sheriff to summon and return juries, and prohibited town meetings, unless with the consent of the governor. The charter was considered by the colonists as the compact between them and the king, and as the only bond of union between them. They admitted that if they had violated the charter they were justly liable to punishment; but thought neither king nor parliament had any right to annul the charter. The attempt to do so, in their opinion, broke the bond of union, and set the people free from their allegiance. From that moment the parties became independent of each other, and the king could reign over the colony only as a conquered province, reduced to unconditional submission.

But with these two acts the ministry were not satisfied. For the consummation of their plan, they added a third, empowering the governor, with the advice of the council, when any person in the discharge of his duty as an officer of revenue, or as a magistrate in the suppression of riots, or in the support of the laws of revenue, or when any person acting under the authority of a magistrate for any of those purposes, should be charged with the crime of murder, or with any other capital offence while so acting, to send the person so charged to any

FIG. 54. Destruction of Tea in Boston Harbor.

other colony, or to Britain, to be tried, if it should appear to the governor and his council that an impartial trial could not be had in the province. Those acts did not pass without opposition. There were persons in parliament who had discernment enough to perceive the pernicious tendency of such measures ; but the plan of the ministry was supported by docile majorities in both houses.

On the 10th of May intelligence of the port bill reached the town. Such a rigorous measure was wholly unexpected, and excited the liveliest indignation against its authors. The act was immediately printed on paper with a black border, and hawked about the streets as a bloody, cruel, and inhuman murder.

The inhabitants of Boston were not long left in uncertainty and suspense with respect to the sentiments and conduct of the other provinces concerning the port bill. The rest of the colonies had opposed the introduction of the tea as firmly as they, although, from peculiar circumstances, the proceedings had not been equally vigorous at any other port. They were considered as suffering in the common cause ; and the other colonies gave them prompt assurances of co-operation and support. The people of the other sea-port towns of Massachusetts Bay, instead of taking advantage of the calamity of their neighbors in Boston to increase their own commerce, generously offered them the use of their wharves and warehouses for carrying on their trade.

Before the 7th of June the people of Boston had received assurances of the lively sympathy of the other colonies, and of their active co-operation in the cause of American freedom. Emboldened by such support, they determined to act with unabated vigor. The assembly met at Salem on the 7th of June ; resolved on a general congress, to meet at Philadelphia on the 1st of September ; nominated five of their members to attend it ; voted the sum of 500*l.* for defraying their expenses ; and recommended to the several towns and districts of the province to raise this sum, according to their proportion of the last provincial tax, which was readily complied with. On being informed of these proceedings the governor dissolved the assembly.

An active correspondence was now carried on between the leading men of the several provinces ; and corresponding committees were everywhere established. The cause of the inhabitants of Boston daily became more popular ; and the sentiments of the people of New England rapidly gained ground throughout the continent. There were a few persons not unfriendly to the claims of the British government ; but at town meetings their efforts were vain, as they were opposed by overwhelming majorities.

Throughout the country the press was chiefly in the hands of persons friendly to the people ; and that powerful engine was actively employed in supporting the cause of the colonies, and contributed not a little to fan the growing flame. The sufferings occasioned by the port bill, in Boston and its vicinity, exasperated the people without either intimidating or subduing them ; they saw that it was intended either to terrify or compel them to unconditional submission ; and they determined to repel force by force. They seized every opportunity of providing themselves with muskets, and other military accoutrements. Many of them, indeed, in conformity to the militia laws, were already in possession of firearms, and all were desirous of improving themselves in the use of them. With the musket they were familiarly acquainted from their earliest years ; and having been much exercised in hunting, were dexterous marksmen. Many imagined that this, combined with patriotic ardor, would supply the defects of military discipline and want of military habits. A warlike spirit pervaded the provinces, and the note of preparation for battle was everywhere heard. The parties had ill calculated each other's strength ; the colonists had but a very imperfect knowledge of the formidable power of Britain, and the British government had formed no just estimate of the unanimity and vigor of the colonists; else both parties would have been much more cautious.

While the people were so active in their preparations, General Gage was not an inattentive or idle spectator of their proceedings. Apprehensive of resistance to his authority, he had soon after entering on his government ordered two regiments of infantry and a detachment of artillery to Boston. This body of troops was gradually increased by reinforcements from Ireland, New York, Halifax, and Quebec, and was encamped on the common and narrow neck which connected Boston with the main land. The presence of these troops alarmed the townsmen, and greatly increased the jealousy of the country people. The Boston committee did everything in their power to render the situation of the military disagreeable; and privately counteracted every measure tending to promote their comfort. They dissuaded the farmers and others from selling them straw, timber, boards, and every other article, except the provisions necessary for their subsistence. If purchases were made by the agents of government, care was taken that the articles did not reach the camp in safety: the straw was burned; vessels with bricks were sunk; carts with wood were overturned; and, in one way or other, purchases were either prevented, or the commodities destroyed before they reached the camp.

A guard was stationed on Boston Neck, ostensibly with a view to prevent the desertion of the soldiers; but it was considered by the Americans as intended to cut off the communication between the town and country, and to compel the inhabitants of Boston to submit unconditionally to the acts of the British parliament. Inflamed by rumors of this kind, the inhabitants of Worcester county assembled, and despatched messengers to Boston, to ascertain what degree of credit was due to these reports. Those messengers assured the people of the town that, if any attempt should be made to compel them to surrender their rights, several thousands of armed men were ready to march to their assistance; and that if they should yield up their liberties, the people in the country would not consider themselves parties in their submission, nor bound by their deed.

The events of almost every day tended not only to keep alive but to increase the mutual irritation. The inhabitants of Salem were invited by a hand-bill to meet on the 25th of August, in order to concert measures for opposing the late acts of parliament. On the 24th, the governor issued a proclamation prohibiting the meeting. But the proclamation was disregarded: the people assembled Troops were sent to disperse them; but before the arrival of the troops the business was finished, and the assembly dissolved.

Everything wore a portentous aspect. The people were highly exasperated; the governor was irritated and alarmed. Perhaps no human prudence could have long delayed hostilities without abandoning the British claims; but the conduct of the governor hastened matters to a crisis. He fortified Boston Neck; and before daybreak, on the 1st of September, sent a party of soldiers across the river Charles, and removed a quantity of provincial powder which had been lodged in the arsenal at Charlestown, a small town opposite Boston. The news of this transaction spread rapidly through the country; and several thousands of the inhabitants of the neighboring towns, mostly armed, soon assembled at Cambridge. They proceeded to the houses of several gentlemen who had been named counsellors under the late act; and those gentlemen found it expedient to resign their appointments, and to declare that they would not fill any office under the obnoxious bills. It was with difficulty that this multitude was dissuaded from marching to Boston, to demand the restoration of the powder, and to attack the troops in case of refusal.

This tumultuary meeting gave rise to a rumor, which circulated throughout New England with amazing rapidity, that the troops were firing on the town of

Boston; and in less than twenty-four hours, between thirty and forty thousand men were in arms, some of whom marched upward of twenty miles on their way toward Boston before they were satisfied that the rumor was false. This circumstance greatly encouraged the most daring of the popular leaders, who resolved to keep up and cherish the public agitation by holding an assembly of delegates from the several towns and districts of the county of Suffolk, of which Boston is the capital, to consider what course was to be pursued in the present posture of affairs. This assembly met on the 9th of September; and after a spirited preamble, daringly resolved, "That no obedience is due from this province to the late acts, but that they be rejected as the attempts of a wicked administration to enslave America: that so long as the justices are appointed or hold their places by any other tenure than that which the charter and the laws of the province direct, they must be considered as unconstitutional officers; and, as such, no regard ought to be paid to them by the people of this country; that it be recommended to the collectors of taxes, and all other officers who have public money in their hands, to retain the same, and not to make any payment thereof to the provincial county treasurer, until the civil government of the province be placed upon a constitutional foundation, or it shall be otherwise ordered by the proposed provincial congress: that the persons who have accepted seats at the council-board, by virtue of a *mandamus* from the king, have acted in direct violation of the duty they owe to their country: that this county do recommend it to all who have so highly offended, and have not already resigned, to make public resignation on or before the 20th day of this month of September: that all refusing so to do shall, after said day, be considered as obstinate and incorrigible enemies to this country: that the fortifications begun and carrying on at Boston Neck give reason to apprehend some hostile intentions against that town: that the late act establishing the Roman catholic religion in Quebec is dangerous in an extreme degree to the protestant religion, and to the civil rights and liberties of America: that whereas our enemies have flattered themselves that they shall make an easy prey of this numerous and brave people, from an apprehension that they are unacquainted with military discipline; we therefore, for the honor and security of this county and province, advise that such persons be elected n each town, as officers in the militia, as shall be judged of sufficient capacity, and who have evinced themselves the inflexible friends of the rights of the people; and that the inhabitants do use their utmost endeavors to acquaint themselves with the art of war, and do, for that purpose, appear under arms at least once every week."

After passing these decisive resolutions, the meeting despatched copies of them to the general congress, which had met at Philadelphia on the 5th of the month, for their opinion and advice on the subject. The congress approved of the Suffolk resolutions, and resolved unanimously, "That this assembly deeply feels the sufferings of their countrymen in the Massachusetts Bay, under the operation of the late unjust, cruel, and oppressive acts of the British parliament, that they most thoroughly approve the wisdom and fortitude with which opposition to these wicked ministerial measures has hitherto been conducted; and they earnestly recommend to their brethren a perseverance in the same firm and temperate conduct as expressed in their resolutions; trusting that the united efforts of North America in their behalf will carry such conviction to the British nation of the unwise, unjust, and ruinous policy of the present administration, as quickly to introduce better men and wiser measures."

The Suffolk resolutions openly set government at defiance; and congress, by approving their resolutions, virtually raised the standard of rebellion, and set the colonies in hostile array against the parent state. Thus, step by step, the provinces were brought into a condition which a short time before they would have contemplated with regret. Many of the colonists, however, still fondly cherished the hope that the quarrel would be settled without an appeal to arms.

Between the unwary and obstinate policy of his superiors, and the determined opposition of the subjects of his government, General Gage was placed in unpleasant and difficult circumstances; but to the committee from the county of Suffolk, which waited upon him, his language was firm and temperate.

The people of New England, who had impatiently waited for the opinion of congress on the Suffolk resolutions, were much elated with the approbation of that body; and, considering its resolutions as a pledge of support from the other colonies, they proceeded with increased courage in the bold career on which they had entered.

Georgia had not yet joined the confederation; but twelve colonies had sent delegates to the general congress, which consisted of fifty-two members, beside the president. All these delegates had received instructions from their respective constituents; and some of the instructions were more moderate than others: but all of them authorized the delegates to concur in any measures which the majority thought it expedient to adopt. In the congress each colony had only one vote, although it had several delegates present.

The congress chose Peyton Randolph as their president, and Charles Thomson secretary. The resolution in approbation of the Suffolk meeting was the first business in which they engaged. In a subsequent resolution, passed on the 8th of October, they declared, "That if the late acts of parliament shall be attempted to be carried into execution by force, in such case all America ought to support the inhabitants of Massachusetts Bay in their opposition: that if it be found absolutely necessary to remove the people of Boston into the country, all America ought to contribute toward recompensing them for the injury they may thereby sustain; and that every person who shall accept, or act under any commission or authority derived from the act of parliament, changing the form of government and violating the charter, ought to be held in detestation."

The congress deliberated with shut doors, and consequently none of its proceedings were known, except such as it thought proper to publish; but the papers which it communicated to the world were important, and had a powerful influence on subsequent events. They published a declaration of rights to which the colonists of North America were entitled by the immutable laws of nature, the principles of the British constitution, and their several charters or compacts. As the first of these rights, they mentioned life, liberty, and property; the power to dispose of any of which, without their consent, they had never ceded to any sovereign power whatever. Their ancestors, they said, at the time of their emigration, were entitled to all the rights, liberties, and immunities of free and natural-born subjects of the realm of England: that by their emigration they had not forfeited, surrendered, or lost any of those rights; but that they and their descendants were entitled to all of them which their circumstances enabled them to exercise. They stated, that the foundation of English liberty, and of all free government, is a right in the people to participate in their legislative council; that as the colonists are not, and from various causes can not be represented in the British parliament, they are entitled to a free and exclusive power of legislation in their several provincial legislatures, where only their right of representation can be preserved, in all cases of taxation and internal policy, subject only to the negative of their sovereign, in such manner as had heretofore been used.

They asserted their right to trial by their peers of the vicinage; pronounced a standing army, kept up in time of peace in any colony, without the consent of the legislature of that colony, illegal; and maintained that a legislative council, appointed during pleasure by the crown, was unconstitutional: they also entered into a non-importation agreement.

At the same time they prepared an address to the people of Britain, in which they warned them that, if they supported ministers in attempting to subdue and enslave the American colonies, they would forge chains for themselves. "Take care," said they, "that you do not fall into the pit preparing for us." . . . "But if you," they afterward add, "are determined that your ministers shall wantonly sport with the rights of mankind; if neither the voice of justice, the dictates of the law, the principles of the constitution, nor the suggestions of humanity, can restrain your hands from shedding human blood in such an impious cause, we must then tell you that we will never submit to be hewers of wood and drawers of water for any ministry or nation in the world. Place us in the same situation that we were in at the close of the last war, and our former harmony will be restored."

Congress addressed a memorial to their constituents, replete with serious and temperate argument. In this paper, they detailed the causes which had led to the unhappy differences, and labored to convince the colonists that their liberty would be destroyed, and the security of their persons and property annihilated, by submission to the claims of Great Britain. They addressed a letter to the inhabitants of Canada also, and endeavored to interest them in their cause.

That they might in no respect be wanting to themselves, congress prepared a petition to the king, in which they gave a succinct statement of their grievances, implored his clemency for protection against them, and imputed all their distresses, dangers, and fears, to the destructive system of colonial administration which had been adopted since the conclusion of the last war. They expressed their belief that, as his majesty enjoyed the singular distinction of reigning over freemen, the language of freemen could not be displeasing to him "Your royal indignation," say they, "we hope will rather fall on those designing and dangerous men who daringly interpose themselves between your royal person and your faithful subjects, and, by abusing your majesty's authority, misrepresenting your American subjects, and prosecuting the most desperate and irritating projects of oppression, have at length compelled us, by the force of accumulated injuries, too severe to be any longer tolerated, to disturb your majesty's repose by our complaints."

The addresses of congress were written with much ability, and its recommendations were revered and obeyed as sacred laws throughout the colonies.

The congress having finished their labors, and recommended the appointment of a similar assembly, to meet on the 10th of May next, unless a redress of grievances had before that time been obtained, dissolved themselves on the 26th day of October.

Originally formed of heterogeneous materials, differing in manners, religious sentiments, and civil constitutions, the colonies, for a long time, had no common feelings and interests. They had even been alienated from each other by local prejudices and provincial jealousies; but the dread of a common danger had gradually overcome all those principles of repulsion, and united the twelve provinces, from New Hampshire to South Carolina, in one compact body. They were embarked in a common cause, and relied on each other for mutual support. By meeting in congress, the leading men in the several provinces had become personally acquainted; and their sentiments of reciprocal respect and friendship strengthened the bonds of political union. It was not, therefore, to be expected that they would recede from their claims without a violent struggle.

The province of Massachusetts Bay was the more immediate seat of the quarrel; and the popular leaders in that colony, assured of the co-operation and support of the other provinces, were not intimidated by the menacing attitude of the governor, but persevered steadily in the execution of their purposes.

The violence of the people against all whom they considered unfriendly to American freedom was so great, that the commissioners of the customs, and all the officers of government, deemed it expedient to quit Salem, and to repair to Boston for safety; so that all the apparatus of a customhouse was transferred to a port which an act of parliament had pronounced it unlawful for any vessel to enter.

Having formed a council under the new act for the government of Massachusetts Bay, General Gage, by its advice, issued writs for holding an assembly in Salem, on the 5th of October; but was induced by subsequent events to countermand the elections by a second preclamation, and to suspend the meeting of the members already returned. The colonists, considering the second proclamation illegal, utterly disregarded it, and chose their representatives in obedience to the first.

The assembly, to the number of ninety, met at the time and place appointed They waited a day for the governor to open the session; but finding he did not appear, they, on the third day, resolved themselves into a provincial congress, and adjourned to Concord, a town about twenty miles distant from Boston. They chose John Hancock president; and appointed a committee to wait on the governor with a remonstrance, in which they apologized for their meeting by representing the distressed state of the colony; mentioned the grievous apprehensions of the people; asserted that the rigor of the Boston port bill was increased by the manner of its execution; complained of the late laws, and of the hostile preparations on Boston Neck; and adjured him to desist immediately from the construction of a fortress there.

The governor was at a loss how to act. He could not recognise the meeting at Concord as a legal assembly, and was sensible of the imprudence of increasing the public irritation by declining to take notice of their remonstrance. He was constrained by the pressure of circumstances to return an answer: and, in that answer he expressed his indignation at the suspicion that the lives, liberty, or property of any but avowed enemies, were in danger from English troops; and observed, that notwithstanding the hostile dispositions manifested toward them, by withholding almost every necessary accommodation, they had not discovered that resentment which such unfriendly conduct was calculated to provoke. He told them that, while they complained of alterations in their charter by act of parliament, they were themselves, by their present assembling, subverting that charter, and acting in direct violation of their own constitution: he therefore warned them of their danger, and called on them to desist from such unconstitutional proceedings.

But the warnings f the governor made no impression on the provincial congress. On the 17th of October, that assembly adjourned to Cambridge, a town about four miles from Boston. They resolved to purchase military stores; and to enlist a number of *minute* men, so named from their engaging to take the field in arms on a minute's warning. But the greater part of the members, although sufficiently zealous in the cause, had no conception of the expense attending such proceedings; and were alarmed at the mention of the most trivial sums. They were in easy circumstances, but had little money; living on the produce of their farms, their expenditure was trifling, and they were utter strangers to large accounts. They were prevailed on, however, at first to vote £750 sterling, and afterward to add £1,500 more, for purchasing warlike stores. By cautious management, their leaders ultimately induced them to grant £16,000 sterling for the purpose of maintaining their liberties. Such was the sum with which they were to resist the power of the British empire!

They appointed a *committee of safety*, with authority to call out the militia when thought necessary for the defence of the inhabitants of the province; and a committee of *supplies*, to purchase ammunition, ordnance, and other military stores. They elected Jedidiah Pribble, Artemas Ward, and Colonel Pomeroy, who had seen some service in the late war, general officers, and appointed them to the chief command of the minute-men and militia, if they should be called into actual service. On the 27th of October, the congress adjourned to the 23d of November.

On the approach of winter, the governor ordered temporary barracks for the troops to be erected: but he found much difficulty in the execution of his pur pose; as, through the influence of the select-men and committees, the mechanics were unwilling or afraid to engage in the work, and the merchants declined to execute his orders.

The mutual suspicions of the governor and people of Massachusetts Bay were now so strong that every petty incident increased the irritation. Each party made loud professions of the best intentions; and each watched the other with a jealous eye. In a proclamation, the governor forbade the people to pay any regard to the requisitions, directions, or resolutions of the provincial congress, and denounced that body as an illegal assembly; but the proclamation was disregarded, and the recommendations of congress were revered and promptly obeyed.

Instead of being intimidated by the governor's proclamation, the provincial congress of Massachusetts Bay, on reassembling after their adjournment, pro ceeded with greater boldness than ever, and gave decisive evidence of their de termination to carry matters to extremities, rather than submit to the late acts of parliament. They resolved to have 12,000 men in readiness to act on any emergency, and ordered a fourth of the militia to be enlisted as minute-men, and empowered them to choose their own officers. They despatched agents to New Hampshire, Rhode Island, and Connecticut, to concert measures with the leading men in those provinces, and to engage them to provide their contingents for an army of 20,000 men. They resolved to bring their force into action, and to oppose General Gage whenever he should march his troops out of Boston, with their baggage, ammunition, and artillery; and they applied to the ministers of religion, throughout the province, desiring their countenance and co-operation. They also added Colonels Thomas and Heath to the number of generals whom they had formerly nominated. Toward the end of November the congress dissolved itself, having appointed another to be held in the month of February.

Alarmed by the proceedings in the several provinces, the ministry had issued a proclamation prohibiting the exportation of military stores from Britain. On hearing of this proclamation, the inhabitants of Rhode Island removed above forty pieces of cannon from the batteries about the harbor for the avowed purpose of preventing them from falling into the hands of the king's troops, and of employing them against such persons as might attempt to infringe their liberties. About the same time, the assembly of the province passed resolutions for purchasing arms and military stores at the public expense, and for carefully training the militia in military exercises.

The people of New Hampshire, who had hitherto been moderate, surprised a small fort at Portsmouth, and carried off the military stores which it contained.

The beginning of the year 1775 presented a gloomy prospect to England: all the provincial assemblies, except that of New York, approved of the resolutions of the general congress; and even the assembly of New York joined in the complaints of the other provinces, although it was less resolute in its opposition to the obnoxious laws. The passions of the people were everywhere roused, and great agitation prevailed. The inhabitants were all in motion; forming county meetings; entering into associations; recommending measures for carrying into execution the resolutions of the general congress, and choosing committees of inspection and observation, to take care that the public resolutions should be universally attended to, and to guard against the practices of those selfish individuals who, for interested purposes, might wish to elude them. In the midst of all this bustle, the militia were everywhere carefully trained.

Meanwhile, the privations and sufferings of the inhabitants of Boston were grievous, and their passions were highly excited; but their resentful spirit was kept in check by the presence of the troops. Supplies of provisions were sent them from the other colonies: these, however, formed but a partial and precarious resource; but the people were encouraged by the sympathy of their brethren, and by the thought that they were considered martyrs in the common cause.

Notwithstanding the portentous aspect of affairs, many of the colonists still believed that there would be no appeal to arms. Formerly their non-importation associations had produced the desired effect; and they flattered themselves that similar measures would again be followed with similar results; that the British ministry would never come to an open rupture with the best customers of their merchants and manufacturers, but would recede from their pretensions when convinced of the determined opposition of the Americans. On the other hand, the British ministry expected the colonists would yield; and thus both parties persisted in their claims till neither could easily give way; and in the debates on American affairs, in parliament, the partisans of the ministry spake of the colonists in the most contemptuous manner; affirmed that they were undisciplined, and incapable of discipline, and that their numbers would only increase their confusion and facilitate their defeat.

Meanwhile the colonists were not idle. On the 1st of February, the provincial congress of Massachusetts Bay met at Cambridge, and, apprehensive of being too much within the reach of General Gage, toward the middle of the month they again adjourned to Concord. They thus took decisive measures for resisting the obnoxious acts of parliament. They earnestly exhorted the militia in general, and the minute-men in particular, to be indefatigable in improving themselves in military discipline; they recommended the making of firearms and bayonets; and they dissuaded the people from supplying the troops in Boston with anything necessary for military service. The committee of safety resolved to purchase powder, artillery, provisions, and other military stores, and to deposite them partly at Worcester and partly at Concord.

In this agitated posture of public affairs, General Gage conceived it to be his duty to seize the warlike stores of the colonists wherever he could find them. With this view he ordered a small detachment, under the command of Lieutenant Colonel Leslie, on Sunday the 26th of February, to bring off some field-pieces which he understood the provincial congress had at Salem. The party landed at Marblehead, and marched to Salem, but found no cannon there. Believing they had been removed only a short time before, the commanding officer determined on pursuit. He reached a small river, on the way to Danvers, over which was a draw-bridge; but, on his approach, some people on the other side drew it up, and alleged that, as both the bridge and road were private property, the soldiers had no right to pass that way. The party were about to use some boats, but the owners instantly scuttled them. The bridge was at length let down; but the day was so far spent, that Colonel Leslie, deeming it inexpedient to proceed much farther, returned to Boston. This ineffectual attempt showed the designs of the governor, and gave fresh activity to the vigilance of the people.

The colonies were now all in commotion; and preparations were everywhere making for the general congress, which was to assemble in the month of May. New York was the only place which discovered much backwardness in the matter; and perhaps the timid and selfish policy of that province contributed no less to the war, than the audacious turbulence of the people of Massachusetts Bay; for the British ministry were encouraged by the irresolution of the people of New York to persist in their plan of coercion, from which they had been almost deterred by he firm attitude and united counsels of the other colonies But hoping, by the compliance of New York with their designs, to separate the middle and southern from the northern provinces, and so easily subjugate them all, they determined to persevere in strong measures. The active exertions, however, of the adherents of the British ministry were defeated, even in New York, by the resolute conduct of their opponents ; and that province sent deputies to the general congress.

Although some of the persons most obnoxious to the British government had withdrawn from Boston, yet many zealous Americans still remained in the town, observed every motion of General Gage with a vigilant eye, and transmitted to their friends in the country notices of his proceedings and probable intentions. The American stores at Concord had attracted the general's attention, and he determined to seize them. But, although he had been careful to conceal his intention, yet some intimations of it reached the ears of the colonists, who took their measures accordingly.

At eleven o'clock at night, on the 18th of April, General Gage embarked 800 grenadiers and light infantry, the flower of his army, under the command of Lieutenant Colonel Smith and Major Pitcairn, on Charles river, at Boston Neck.

They sailed up the river, landed at Phipp's farm, and advanced toward Concord. Of this movement some of the friends of the American cause got notice, just before the embarcation of the troops ; and they instantly despatched messengers by different routes, with the information The troops soon perceived, by the ringing of bells and firing of musketry, that notwithstanding the secrecy with which they had quitted Boston, they had been discovered, and that the alarm was fast spreading throughout the country. Between four and five o'clock, on the morning of the 19th of April, the detachment reached Lexington, thirteen miles from Boston. Here about seventy of the militia were assembled, and were standing near the road ; but their number being so small they had no intention of making any resistance to the military. Major Pitcairn, who had been sent forward with the light infantry, rode toward them, calling out, "Disperse, you rebels ! throw down your arms and disperse !" The order was not instantly obeyed : Major Pitcairn advanced a little farther, fired his pistol, and flourished his sword, while his men began to fire, with a shout. Several Americans fell ; the rest dispersed, but the firing on them was continued ; and, on observing this, some of the retreating colonists returned the fire. Eight Americans remained dead on the field.

At the close of this rencounter, the rest of the British detachment, under Lieutenant Colonel Smith, came up ; and the party, without further violence, proceeded to Concord. On arriving at that place, they found a body of militia drawn up, who retreated across the bridge before the British light infantry. The main body of the royal troops entered the town, destroyed two pieces of cannon with their carriages, and a number of carriage-wheels ; threw 500 pounds of balls into the river and wells and broke in pieces about sixty flour-barrels. These were all the stores they found.

While the main body of the troops was engaged in these operations, the light infantry kept possession of the bridge, the Americans having retired to wait for reinforcements. Reinforcements arrived ; and Mr. John Butterworth, of Concord, who commanded the Americans, ordered his men to advance ; but ignorant of what had happened at Lexington, enjoined them not to fire, unless the troops fired first. The matter did not long remain in suspense. The Americans advanced ; the troops fired on them ; the Americans returned the fire ; a smart skirmish ensued, and a number of men fell on each side.

The troops, having accomplished the object of their expedition, began to retreat. But blood had been shed, and the aggressors were not to be allowed to

Fig. 55.—American Militia and Minute Men at Lexington.

escape with impunity. The country was alarmed; armed men crowded in from every quarter; and the retreating troops were assailed with an unceasing but irregular discharge of musketry.

General Gage had early information that the country was rising in arms; and, about eight in the morning, he despatched 900 men, under the command of Earl Percy, to support his first party. According to Gordon, this detachment left Boston with their music playing *Yankee Doodle*, a tune composed in derision of the inhabitants of the northern provinces; an act which had no tendency to subdue, but which was well calculated to irritate the colonists.

Earl Percy met Colonel Smith's retreating party at Lexington much exhausted; and being provided with two pieces of artillery, he was able to keep the Americans in check. The whole party rested on their arms till they took some refreshment, of which they stood much in need. But there was no time for delay, as the militia and minute-men were hastening in from all quarters to the scene of action. When the troops resumed their march, the attack was renewed; and Earl Percy continued the retreat under an incessant and galling fire of small arms. By means of his field-pieces and musketry, however, he was able to keep the assailants at a respectful distance. The colonists were under no authority; but ran across the fields from one place to another, taking their station at the points from which they could fire on the troops with most safety and effect. Numbers of them, becoming weary of the pursuit, retired from the contest; but their places were supplied by new comers, so that, although not more than 400 or 500 of the provincials were actually engaged at any one time, yet the conflict was continued without intermission, till the troops, in a state of great exhaustion, reached Charlestown Neck, with only two or three rounds of cartridges each, although they had thirty-six in the morning.

On this memorable day, the British had 65 men killed, 180 wounded, and 28 taken prisoners. The provincials had 50 men killed, 34 wounded, and 4 missing.

The appeal to arms was now made; and the struggle about to ensue was one of the most momentous recorded in the annals of the human race; not on account of the number of combatants engaged, for neither party had at any one time above thirty or forty thousand men in the field, and often not the half of those numbers; but because of the principles involved in it, and the consequences which it has produced.

At the opening of this interesting contest, the parties seemed very unequally matched. Great Britain was the most formidable state in the world. In the preceding war she had humbled the pride of the Bourbons, and triumphed over every enemy; her fleets commanded the ocean, and victory hovered over her standards. She carried on a lucrative commerce in every quarter of the globe; her flag waved in the ports of every nation; and her merchants occupied the most distinguished place in the great mart of the world. Her resources seemed inexhaustible, and her fame encircled the earth. On the other hand, the Americans were an infant people, only between two and three millions in number; they were thinly scattered over a vast extent of country, from the borders of Florida on the south to the Bay of Fundy on the north, and from the Atlantic on the east to the Alleganies on the west. Till lately, the intercourse between the provinces had been slender, and respect for the parent state was their only common feeling, and the only bond of union among them. Their pursuits, manners, and sentiments were different. They were without armies; they had a militia very partially acquainted with manual exercise. Having been much employed in hunting, many of them were expert marksmen; but to military tactics, to the subordination, prompt obedience, and patient endurance of soldiers, they were entire strangers. They had no ships but those which were employed in the peaceful pursuits of commerce. They had no exchequer, and but little money; and that little, having been gained by persevering industry and frugal habits, they were loth to expend. Their savings were chiefly laid out in the improvement of their farms.

But, unpromising as their prospects were, the Americans determined not to be wanting to themselves, and took their measures with promptitude and vigor. Intelligence of the events of the 19th of April spread rapidly over the country; and the militia, from every quarter, hastened toward Boston. On the 20th, the provincial congress chose General Ward commander in chief of the forces in Massachusetts Bay, and soon afterward named John Thomas lieutenant general Both of those officers had seen some service during the preceding war.

The provincial congress, having adjourned from Concord to Watertown, resolved that an army of 30,000 men be immediately raised, and wrote to the colonies of New Hampshire, Rhode Island, and Connecticut, informing them of the events of the 19th, and earnestly requesting them to send forward as many troops as they could spare, with provisions, arms, and military stores. The Connecticut militia marched to join their countrymen in arms, under the command of Benedict Arnold and Israel Putnam—as brave a man as ever walked the earth, and who was known to his countrymen by many deeds of daring, two of which we shall here mention.

Putnam's neighbors had long been annoyed by a ferocious wolf, and in one night Putnam lost seventy fine sheep and goats, and many lambs and kids were wounded.

This wolf at length became such an intolerable nuisance, that Mr. Putnam entered into a combination with five of his neighbors to hunt alternately until they could destroy her. Two, by rotation, were to be constantly in pursuit. It was known, that, having lost the toes from one foot by a steel trap, she made one track shorter than the other. By this vestige, the pursuers recognised, in a light snow, the route of this pernicious animal. Having followed her to Connecticut river, and found she had turned back in a direct course toward Pomfret, they immediately returned, and by ten o'clock the next morning the bloodhounds had driven her into a den, about three miles distant from the house of Mr. Putnam. The people soon collected with dogs, guns, straw, fire, and sulphur, to attack the common enemy. With this apparatus, several unsuccessful efforts were made to force her from the den. The hounds came back badly wounded and refused to return. The smoke of blazing straw had no effect. Nor did the fumes of burnt brimstone, with which the cavern was filled, compel her to quit the retirement. Wearied with such fruitless attempts (which had brought the time to ten o'clock at night), Mr. Putnam tried once more to make his dog enter, but in vain. He proposed to his negro man to go down into the cavern and shoot the wolf; the negro declined the hazardous service. Then it was, that their master, angry at the disappointment, and declaring that he was ashamed to have a coward in his family, resolved himself to destroy the ferocious beast, lest she should escape through some unknown fissure of the rock. His neighbors strongly remonstrated against the perilous enerprise: but he knowing that wild animals were intimidated by fire, and having provided several strips of birch bark, the only combustible material which he could obtain, that would afford light in this deep and darksome cave, prepared for his descent. Having, accordingly, divested himself of his coat and waistcoat, and having a long rope fastened round his legs, by which he might be pulled back, at a concerted signal, he entered head foremost, with the blazing torch in his hand.

The aperture of the den, on the east side of a very high ledge of rocks, is about two feet square; thence it descends obliquely fifteen feet, then running horizontally about ten more, it ascends gradually sixteen feet toward its termination. The sides of this subterraneous cavity are composed of smooth and solid

›6.—Putnam killing the Wolf.

rocks, which seem to have been divided from each other by some former earthquake. The top and bottom are also of stone, and the entrance, in winter, being covered with ice, is exceedingly slippery. It is in no place high enough for a man to raise himself upright; nor in any part more than three feet in width.

Having groped his passage to the horizontal part of the den, the most terrifying darkness appeared in front of the dim circle of light afforded by his torch It was silent as the house of death. None but monsters of the desert had ever before explored this solitary mansion of horror. He, cautiously proceeding onward, came to the ascent, which he slowly mounted on his hands and knees, until he discovered the glaring eyeballs of the wolf, who was sitting at the extremity of the cavern. Startled at the sight of fire, she gnashed her teeth and gave a sullen growl. As soon as he had made the necessary discovery, he kicked the rope as a signal for drawing him out. The people at the mouth of the den, who had listened with painful anxiety, hearing the growling of the wolf, and supposing their friend to be in the most imminent danger, drew him forth with such celerity, that his shirt was stripped over his head and his skin severely lacerated. After he had adjusted his clothes and loaded his gun with nine buckshot, holding a torch in one hand and the musket in the other, he descended the second time. When he drew nearer than before, the wolf, assuming a still more fierce and terrible appearance, howling, rolling her eyes, snapping her teeth, and dropping her head between her legs, was evidently in the attitude and on the point of springing at him. At this critical instant, he levelled and fired at her head. Stunned with the shock, and suffocated with the smoke, he immediately found himself drawn out of the cave. But having refreshed himself, and permitted the smoke to dissipate, he went down the third time Once more he came within sight of the wolf, who appearing very passive, he applied the torch to her nose; and perceiving her dead, he took hold of her ears, and then kicking the rope (still tied round his legs), the people above, with no small exultation, dragged them both out together.

In the winter of 1757, when Col. Haviland was commandant of Fort Edward, the barracks adjoining to the northwest bastion took fire. They extended within twelve feet of the magazine, which contained three hundred barrels of powder. On its first discovery, the fire raged with great violence. The commandant endeavored, in vain, by discharging some pieces of heavy artillery against the supporters of this flight of barracks, to level them with the ground. Putnam arrived from the island where he was stationed, at the moment when the blaze approached that end which was contiguous to the magazine. Instantly, a vigorous attempt was made to extinguish the conflagration. A way was opened by a postern gate to the river, and the soldiers were employed in bringing water; which he, having mounted on a ladder to the eaves of the building, received and threw upon the flame. It continued, notwithstanding their utmost efforts, to gain upon them. He stood, enveloped in smoke, so near the sheet of fire, that a pair of thick blanket-mittens were burnt entirely off his hands—he was supplied with another pair dipped in water. Col. Haviland, fearing that he would perish in the flames, called to him to come down. But he entreated that he might be suffered to remain, since destruction must inevitably ensue if their exertions should be remitted. The gallant commandant, not less astonished than charmed at the boldness of his conduct, forbade any more effects to be carried out of the fort, animated the men to redoubled diligence, and exclaimed, "If we must be blown up, we will all go together." At last, when the barracks were seen to be trembling, Putnam descended, placed himself at the interval, and continued from an incessant rotation of replenished buckets to pour water upon the magazine. The outside planks were already consumed by the proximity of the fire, and as only one thickness of timber intervened, trepidation now became general and extreme Putnam, still undaunted, covered with a cloud of cinders, and scorched with the intensity of the heat, maintained his position until the fire subsided, and the danger was wholly over. He had contended for one hour and a half with that terrible element. His legs, his thighs, his arms, and his face were blistered; and when he pulled off his second pair of mittens, the skin from his hands and fingers followed them. It was a month before he recovered. The commandant, to whom his merits had before endeared him, could not stifle the emotions of gratitude due to the man who had been so instrumental in preserving the magazine, the fort, and the garrison.

A large body of men was soon collected before Boston; but they were in great want of everything necessary for the equipment of an army. They had muskets, many of them old and rusty; but were ill provided with bayonets. They had a few pieces of artillery and a few mortars, with some balls and shells; but had only forty-one barrels of gunpowder in the public store.

The battle of Lexington operated like an electrical shock throughout the provinces. On hearing of that event, even in New York, where the friends of the ministry were more numerous than in any other place, the people espoused the cause of their countrymen. They shut up the customhouse, and stopped all vessels preparing to sail to Quebec, Newfoundland, Georgia, or Boston.

The colonists of New Jersey took possession of the treasury of the province, containing about £20,000, to employ it in their own defence. The inhabitants of Philadelphia followed the example of New York, and prevented the sailing of vessels to any port on the continent that acknowledged the authority or was subject to the power of Britain.

In six days intelligence of the action of the 19th of April reached Baltimore, in Maryland. The people instantly seized the provincial magazine, containing about 1,500 stand of arms, and stopped all exports to the fishing islands, to such of the colonies as had declined to join the confederacy, and to the British army and navy at Boston.

In Virginia a provincial congress had met in the month of March, which took measures for training the militia, and recommended to each county to raise a volunteer company for the better defence of the country. At Williamsburgh, the capital of the colony, there was a small provincial magazine, containing upward of 1,000 pounds of gunpowder. On the night of the 20th of April, Lord Dunmore, the governor, employed the captain of an armed vessel to convey the greater part of that powder on board his ship. Having got notice of the transaction, the citizens took the alarm, and the mayor and corporation addressed his lordship on the subject. He answered that he had removed the powder to a place of security; and assured them that if it should be needed in order to suppress an insurrection, he would restore it in half an hour.

When news of this affair reached Hanover county, captain Patrick Henry, at the head of more than 150 volunteers, marched toward Williamsburgh, to demand restitution of the powder, and to protect the public treasury against a similar depredation. When within about fifteen miles of the capital, he was assured that the receiver-general would pay for the powder, and that the citizens would guard the public treasury and magazine. The party then dispersed.

Lord Dunmore, greatly alarmed by Henry's march, converted his palace into a garrison, and issued a proclamation charging the people with the design of altering the established constitution. This was a new cause of exasperation; and the people, in their county meetings, not only approved of Mr. Henry's proceedings, but retorted upon the governor, attributing all the disturbances to his misconduct, and declaring that they only vindicated their rights, and opposed innovation. While the public mind was in this feverish state, intelligence of the battle of Lexington arrived in Virginia. It greatly increased the apprehensions and irritation of the people, and made them far more active in arming and training the militia and volunteer companies than they had formerly been. In Virginia, as well as in the other colonies, many were much alarmed; but the apprehensions of impending danger were overpowered by feelings of indignation.

In this critical posture of affairs, Lord Dunmore convened the house of burgesses. His intention was to procure their approbation of Lord North's conciliatory plan; and in his speech at the opening of the session, he employed all his address to gain his end. But, instead of complying with his recommendations, the house immediately appointed a committee to inquire into the causes of the late disturbances, and to examine the state of the public magazine. For the defence of the magazine Lord Dunmore had ordered spring guns to be placed in it, without giving any public warning of the measure. Some inconsiderate young men, unapprized of their danger, attempted to furnish themselves with arms out of it; and one of them was wounded. This circumstance occasioned a violent ferment. A multitude of people assembled, broke into the magazine, and took out many of the arms; but some members of the house of burgesses, having repaired to the spot, by their remonstrances prevailed on the people to restore them.

On the 7th of June, a report was spread about Williamsburgh, that Captain Collins, of the British vessel Magdalen, was coming up the river, with about 100 men in several boats, to take possession of the town. A number of armed persons instantly assembled to defend the place and its inhabitants; but on learning that there was no occasion for their services, they quietly dispersed. The

Fig. 57.—View of Yorktown.

circumstance, however, made such an impression on the governor's mind, that, with his lady and family, he quitted Williamsburgh, proceeded to Yorktown, and went on board the Fowey man of war.

A correspondence now took place between his lordship and the council and burgesses. He accused: they recriminated. They rejected Lord North's conciliatory plan; but passed the necessary bills, and entreated the governor's attendance to give his assent to them, and to close the session. His lordship declined meeting them in the capital, and they did not choose to wait upon him on board a man of war. The correspondence terminated about the middle of July, when the burgesses were obliged to separate, in order to attend to their private affairs; but they appointed a convention of delegates to meet and supply their place. In August this convention met, and showed itself animated by the common spirit of the country; and before dissolving issued a declaration, setting forth the reasons of its meeting, and showing the necessity of immediately putting the country in a posture of defence.

Having been joined by a number of loyal colonists and fugitive slaves, Lord Dunmore very imprudently began a system of predatory warfare. By mutual insults and injuries, the minds of both parties became much exasperated. At length the governor attempted to burn the town of Hampton; but on the morning of the 27th of October, just as he began a furious cannonade upon it, a body of riflemen from Williamsburgh, who had marched all night, entered the place, and being joined by some of their countrymen, took such an advantageous position, that, with their small arms, they compelled his lordship to retreat, with the loss of some of his men and one of his vessels.

Lord Dunmore now issued a proclamation declaring the province under martial law; requiring all persons capable of bearing arms to repair to the royal standard, under the penalty of being considered traitors if they disobeyed, and promising freedom to all indented servants, negroes, and others belonging to rebels, on their joining his majesty's troops.

In consequence of this proclamation, his lordship soon found himself at the head of some hundreds of fugitive negroes and others at Norfolk; but the proclamation highly incensed the great body of the Virginians, and alienated the minds of many who had hitherto been friendly to the British claims. Being informed that a number of armed colonists were rapidly advancing against him, Lord Dunmore took possession of the great bridge near Norfolk; a post of much importance for protecting his friends, and frustrating the designs of his enemies. On arriving near the bridge, the Virginians, commanded by Colonel Woodford, instead of attempting to force a passage, fortified themselves at a short distance on the other side of Elizabeth river; and in this position the two parties faced each other for several days.

The impatient impetuosity of Lord Dunmore's temper could ill brook to be thus braved by the colonists, and he determined to dislodge them. Accordingly, early in the morning of the 8th of December, Captain Fordyce of the 14th regiment, at the head of a royalist detachment, left Norfolk, and reached the bridge before daybreak. He silently replaced the planks of the bridge which had been removed. The road between the bridge and the American breastwork, which was on the south of the river, was a narrow causeway, through swampy ground; and on the right, within musket-shot of the causeway, was a thicket, where the Americans had posted a small party. At daybreak, Captain Fordyce, at the head of his detachment, with fixed bayonets, passed the bridge, and proceeded rapidly toward the enemy. But the Americans were not unprepared: they however allowed the troops to advance a good way without molestation; and when near the works poured upon them a destructive discharge of musketry, both from the entrenchment and thicket at the same time. Undismayed by this warm reception, Captain Fordyce steadily advanced: but on the second fire, he fell dead within a few yards of the American works. His party instantly retreated, sixty-two of their party being either killed or wounded, while the Americans had only one man slightly hurt.

Next night Lord Dunmore quitted his post, and with his adherents sought refuge on board the shipping in the river. The Americans took possession of the town, and refused to supply the ships with provisions ; therefore, early in the morning of the 1st of January, 1776, Lord Dunmore began a furious cannonade on the town, and sent parties of sailors and marines ashore, who set fire to the houses nearest the water. The flames spread rapidly among the wooden buildings ; a great part of the town was consumed ; and the Americans themselves afterward destroyed the rest of it, that it might afford no shelter to the royal troops. Thus perished Norfolk, the most flourishing commercial town in Virginia.

While these operations were going on, Lord Dunmore entertained hopes of subduing the colony by the agency of an adventurer named John Connelly, a native of Pennsylvania. This man, having concerted measures with his lordship, and having received encouragement from General Gage also, communicated with such militia officers as he thought most likely to enter into his views, promising them, in the name of his lordship, ample rewards. He engaged the Indians on the Ohio to act in concert with him ; and he was to be assisted by the garrisons of Fort Detroit and Fort Gage on the Illinois. Having collected a force on the western frontier, he was to penetrate through Virginia, and meet his lordship at Alexandria, on the Potomac, in April. But about ten days after taking leave of Lord Dunmore, Connelly was apprehended; his papers were seized; the plot was fully discovered, and entirely frustrated. Lord Dunmore finding all his efforts ineffectual, and being unable to remain any longer on the coast, sailed with the force under his command to join General Howe.

We shall now glance at the occurrences in the southern provinces during 1775.

From the beginning of the troubles, the people of South Carolina had flattered themselves that their non-importation and non-exportation agreements would induce the mother country to recede from her high pretensions; but the arrival at Charleston of a packet from London, on the 19th of April, dissipated the illusion, and gave them a glimpse of the real difficulties of their situation. In the midst of the gloomy forebodings which depressed their minds, information of the skirmish at Lexington arrived, and filled them with grief and indignation. They felt their circumstances embarrassing and perilous. Their means were feeble, and their enemies powerful; but they determined not to abandon themselves to despair. Next night they seized twelve hundred stand of arms, with the accoutrements, which were in the magazine; and afterward distributed them among the men enlisted for the public service.

The provincial congress resolved that " in their distressed circumstances they would be justified before God and man in resisting force by force." They solemnly engaged to defend their injured country against every foe ; and to support, with their lives and fortunes, every measure which the provincial or continental councils should recommend. They resolved to raise two regiments of infantry and a regiment of rangers, and to put Charleston in a respectable state of defence. Money was wanting ; but bills of credit were issued, which, by a consent produced by the enthusiasm of the people, served the immediate purpose.

But notwithstanding the military enthusiasm of the South Carolinians, they were ill provided with ammunition ; for never having contemplated the possibility of actual war, they had made no provision for such a contingency. They now determined, however, by the promptitude and vigor of their measures, to compensate their past inactivity. There were not above 3,000 pounds of gunpowder in the colony, and no supply could be obtained directly from Britain.

But the inhabitants of East Florida had never joined in the opposition to British policy, and therefore that province still enjoyed an unfettered commerce with the mother country.

The committee of safety at Charleston, which had been appointed by the provincial congress, authorized twelve persons to sail to the coast of Florida, where they surprised a ship with twelve British soldiers on board; took out 15,000 pounds of gunpowder, for which they gave the captain a bill of exchange; and although pursued, escaped safely to Charleston with their prize. In that agitated state of the public mind, and while the provincial congress was sitting, Lord William Campbell, governor of the province, arrived, and was received with the usual demonstrations of joy. The congress waited upon him with an address, in which they represented the cause of their proceedings; declared that love of innovation had no influence on their councils; that they had been forced to associate and take up arms, with no other view than that of defending their lives, liberties, and properties; and they entreated his excellency to assure his majesty of their loyal attachment. His lordship returned a prudent and conciliatory answer.

The people of Georgia, who had hitherto declined a participation in the colonial policy, about this time abandoned their cautious neutrality; espoused the cause of their countrymen; and appointed delegates to attend the continental congress. Thus the whole of the thirteen provinces were arrayed in opposition to Britain.

CHAPTER III.

The British house of commons had been dissolved in September, 1774; and a new parliament met on the 30th of November following. On opening the session, the king's speech related chiefly to the insubordination in the province of Massachusetts Bay, and the refractory spirit manifested in the other colonies; and it concluded by expressing his majesty's determination to maintain the authority of the legislature over every part of the British empire.

On the 1st of February, the Earl of Chatham made another attempt toward reconciliation; and brought in the outlines of "a provisional act for settling the troubles in America; and for asserting the supreme legislative authority and superintending power of Great Britain over the colonies." But, after a keen discussion, the bill was rejected, without being allowed to lie upon the table. The house of commons refused to receive any petition from congress; and the ministry, encouraged chiefly, it has been said, by the representations of Mr. Hutchinson, late governor of Massachusetts Bay, resolved to enforce obedience to the obnoxious acts.

The plans of the cabinet, being now fully formed, soon developed themselves. Lord North, who had the management of the house of commons, moved an address to the king, and a conference with the lords upon it, in order that it might be the joint address of both houses. The address thanked the king for the communication of the American papers; declared that, from those papers, parliament found that a rebellion actually existed within the province of Massachusetts Bay; that the parties concerned in it had been countenanced and encouraged by unlawful combinations and engagements entered into in several of the other colonies; that parliament could never relinquish any part of the sovereign authority over all the dominions by law vested in his majesty and the two houses

Fig. 58.— Statue of the Earl of Chatham.

of parliament; that they ever have been and always will be ready to pay attention and regard to any real grievances of his majesty's subjects, which shall in a dutiful and constitutional manner be laid before them; but at the same time they beseech his majesty to take the most effectual measures to enforce due obedience to the authority of the supreme legislature; and in the most solemn manner they assured him that, at the hazard of their lives and fortunes, they would stand by him against all rebellious attempts, in the maintenance of the just rights of his majesty and of the two houses of parliament.

The address wore such a portentous aspect, that it roused all the energies of the members in opposition, and appalled some even of the staunch adherents of the ministry; but it was carried by large majorities, and, on being presented, met with a gracious reception.

Every motion in parliament tending toward conciliation was rejected; and every petition against the coercive acts was disregarded. To one from the city of London, presented to the king on the 10th of April, his majesty replied, "It is with the utmost astonishment that I find any of my subjects capable of encouraging the rebellious disposition which unhappily exists in my colonies in North America. Having entire confidence in the wisdom of my parliament, the great council of the nation, I will steadily pursue the measures which they have recommended for the support of the constitutional rights of Great Britain, and the protection of the commercial rights of my kingdom." A few petitions in favor of the ministerial policy were presented; but as it was easy to procure them from dependants and expectants, at any time, and in any cause, they made no impression on the public mind, and afforded but a feeble support to the measures of the cabinet.

The administration having exhausted their legislative sagacity on America, began without delay to display their military talents against the colonists. Toward the end of April, they despatched Generals Howe, Clinton, and Burgoyne to that country, and soon afterward ordered a number of transports to sail from Cork with reinforcements to General Gage.

Near the end of May the session of parliament was closed; and on the evening of the 28th of that month, Captain Derby, who had been despatched by the colony of Massachusetts Bay with an account of the events of the 19th of April, to their agent in London, reached that city. Rumors of the tidings which he brought soon circulated; but it was not till the 9th of June, when Captain Brown of the Silkey, who had sailed four days before Captain Derby, with despatches from General Gage to government, arrived in London, that the public was fully apprized of the transactions in the vicinity of Boston. For those events the public mind was in some measure prepared by what had before happened; and consequently, although the news was unpleasant, yet they excited no great surprise. The ministry prepared for active operations, and ordered six regiments of infantry to hold themselves in readiness to embark for America.

The blood shed at Lexington loosened the social bond in America, and almost dissolved the fabric of society. The great mass of the people was held together by their common apprehensions and common indignation; but in the provinces of New England, the people, for a short time, acknowledged no supreme authority to direct their operations. Every man considered himself his own master, and at liberty to pursue such measures as he deemed most expedient for the common welfare. Accordingly, a gentleman of the name of Ethan Allen, a militia colonel, in conjunction with some others, planned an expedition against Ticonderoga.

The importance of securing the communication between Quebec and the refractory colonies, by the Lakes Champlain and George, had been early perceived by the Americans; and Colonel Allen, without waiting for instructions from any constituted authority, successfully executed the project. At the head of a body of armed men he hastened toward Ticonderoga, and on his march was joined by Arnold, already raised to the rank of colonel. The commandant of Ticonderoga, without the least suspicion of his post being in danger, was somewhat remiss in the discipline of his small garrison; and, early on the morning of the 10th of May, he was surprised in bed by Allen, Arnold, and a few of their followers, who had entered the fort, and made themselves masters of it without any loss. On being ordered to surrender, he asked by what authority he was required to do so. Allen replied, "I demand it in the name of the great Jehovah, and of the continental congress." The congress, however, knew nothing of the matter; nor was its first meeting held till some hours after the transaction. The same party made themselves masters of Crown Point, situated near the southern extremity of Lake Champlain, as Ticonderoga is at the north end of Lake George. They also surprised Skenesborough, and a sloop of war, the only vessel belonging to the royal navy on those lakes. In this way, Allen and Arnold took upward of 100 pieces of cannon, and some ammunition and stores; and gained possession of Lake Champlain.

On the 10th of May the general congress met, when deputies from twelve colonies appeared. Georgia had not yet joined the confederacy. The congress chose Peyton Randolph president; but that gentleman being obliged to return home on the 24th of the month, they placed John Hancock in the chair. On receiving information of the enterprise and success of Allen and Arnold, the congress earnestly recommended it to the people of New York and Albany to remove the cannon and stores of Crown Point and Ticonderoga to the south of Lake George; and to take an exact inventory of them, that they might be returned on the restoration of the former harmony between Britain and the colonies.

They agreed to present a second petition to the king, similar to that of the preceding year; but, at the same time, resolved that the colonies be put in a pos ture of defence. They recommended to the colonists to collect saltpetre and sulphur, and to manufacture gunpowder for the use of the united provinces They resolved to raise troops, and made every preparation for maintaining their privileges by force, if humble representations and petitions should prove unsuccessful.

But, amid all these warlike preparations, the greater number of the deputies had no intention of separating from Britain, or of aspiring to independence. They were resolutely determined to defend their privileges, but aimed at nothing more ; although, even at this early period, a few were fully convinced that the contest must terminate either in absolute submission or complete independence. The congress addressed a letter to *the oppressed* inhabitants of Canada, styling themselves their *friends* and *countrymen.* Its obvious design was to inspire the Canadians with jealousy or hatred of the British government, and to gain their good will and co-operation in the measures which they were then pursuing.

On the 15th of June congress proceeded to choose, by ballot, a commander-in-chief of the provincial or continental forces, and unanimously elected George Washington to that arduous office. We have already alluded briefly to his early history, and to his early military services. These had established his character as a sagacious warrior, a man of sound understanding, undaunted courage, and inflexible integrity. In addition, he enjoyed, in a high degree, the confidence of his countrymen, and had been chosen one of the deputies to congress for his native province of Virginia. He had used neither solicitation nor influence of any kind to procure the appointment ; and when the president informed him of his election, and of the request of congress that he would accept the office, he stood up in his place, and addressed the president in the following terms : " Though I am truly sensible of the high honor done me by this appointment, yet I feel great distress from a consciousness that my abilities and military experience are not equal to the arduous trust. But, as the congress desire it, I will enter on the momentous duty, and exert every power I possess in their service, and for the support of the glorious cause. I beg they will accept my cordial thanks for this high testimony of their approbation." He besought congress to remember that he thought himself unequal to the command with which they had honored him ; that he expected no emolument from it, but that he would keep an exact account of his expenses, and hoped they would reimburse him.

The congress afterward chose Artemas Ward, Charles Lee, Philip Schuyler, and Israel Putnam, major-generals, and Horatio Gates adjutant-general. On the 22d of June they appointed Seth Pomeroy, Richard Montgomery, David Wooster, William Heath, Joseph Spencer, John Thomas, John Sullivan, and Nathaniel Greene, brigadier-generals.

While the continental congress was busily employed in taking such measures as they deemed best for the general safety, the provincial congress of Massachusetts Bay, and the colonial troops encamped before Boston, were not without their cares and toils The American army being entirely unaccustomed to military subordination, many of the militia came to camp, stayed a few days, and then returned home. The army, which at first amounted to 20,000 men, dwindled down to less than a third of that number, and gave no flattering prospect of success in a protracted contest with regular troops. But some skirmishes happened, on occasion of bringing off cattle from the islands in the vicinity of Boston, in which the Americans were successful; and this encouraged them.

In the end of May and beginning of June, Generals Howe, Burgoyne, and Clinton, with reinforcements from Britain, arrived at Boston. The British general, in common with his troops, indignant at being cooped up by a force which all despised, resolved on active operations ; but every movement which they made was watched with an attentive eye by zealous Americans in Boston, who found means to penetrate into every design before it was carried into execution, and to transmit secret intelligence to the American headquarters. About the middle of June, it was suspected that General Gage intended to cross the river Charles, on the north side of Boston, and take possession of Breed's or Bunker's Hill, in the peninsula of Charlestown. That peninsula has the river Mystic, or Medford, on the north, and the river Charles on the south, separating it from the peninsula of Boston. It is level toward the sea ; but, nearly opposite Boston, a considerable eminence runs across the peninsula, between the rivers Medford and Charles, at the bottom of which, on the banks of the last-named river, stood Charlestown, opposite Boston.

On the night of the 16th of June, upward of 1,000 Americans, under Colonel William Prescott, were ordered to proceed to this eminence, and entrench themselves upon it. The movement was not without difficulty and danger; for British vessels of war were lying both in the Medford and Charles, on each side of the narrow peninsula. But the provincials marched to the place in profound silence; and about midnight began their operations. They labored with such assiduity, that before the dawn of day they had thrown up a breastwork nearly across the peninsula, and constructed a small redoubt on their right.

FIG. 59.—Throwing up Entrenchments on Bunker's Hill.

About four in the morning of the 17th of June, the American works were observed by the captain of the Lively sloop of war, lying in the river Charles, who instantly began a heavy fire upon them, and was soon joined by the other ships, and by the battery on Copp's Hill at Boston. The Americans steadily continued their labors under a furious cannonade and an incessant shower of balls and bombs; but so harmless was this fearful noise that they lost only one man in the course of the morning. As in this post the Americans overlooked Boston, it was thought necessary to dislodge them; and for this purpose, soon after midday a detachment of British troops, under the command of Generals Howe and Pigot, crossed the river in boats, and landed near the point of the peninsula; but on observing the formidable position of the Americans, they waited for a reinforcement, which soon arived. Meanwhile the steeples and the roofs of the houses in Boston, the eminences in the adjacent country, and the ships in the rivers were crowded with anxious spectators, agitated by different hopes and fears, according to their different attachments and interests. The main body of the American army encamped beyond Charlestown Neck, were looking on; and Generals Clinton and Burgoyne, and other British officers of high rank, took their station in the battery on Copp's Hill to view the approaching conflict.

Fig. 60.—Encampment on Breed's Hill.

While General Howe waited for his reinforcement, the Americans received an accession of strength, under Generals Warren and Pomeroy, who crossed Charlestown Neck under a brisk cannonade from the shipping in the rivers, to join their countrymen and take part in the battle. By their arrival the provincial force was increased to 1,500 at least. The Americans also took advantage of General Howe's halt to strengthen part of their position, by pulling down some rail-fences, forming the stakes into two parallel lines at a small distance from each other, and filling the interval with hay.

The British detachment, consisting of upward of 2,000 men, advanced toward the American line. The light infantry commanded by General Howe, was on the right; the grenadiers, under General Pigot, on the left. They began the attack by a brisk cannonade from some field-pieces and howitzers, the troops proceeding slowly, and sometimes halting, to give time to the artillery to produce some effect. On advancing, the left set fire to Charlestown, a thriving town, containing about 300 wooden houses, besides other buildings, and entirely consumed it. The rising flames added not a little to the grandeur and solemnity of the scene.

Secure behind their entrenchments, the Americans reserved their fire, and silently waited the approach of the British, till the whites of their eyes could be discerned, when they poured upon them an incessant and well-directed discharge of musketry. The British returned the fire for some time, without attempting to advance: but the discharge from the American line was so close and so destructive, that the troops at length gave way, and fell back toward the landing-place. By the vigorous exertions of their officers, however, they were again brought to the charge: and the Americans, again reserving their fire till the troops were very near, directed it against them with the same deadly aim as before. Many fell: at one time General Howe for a few seconds was left

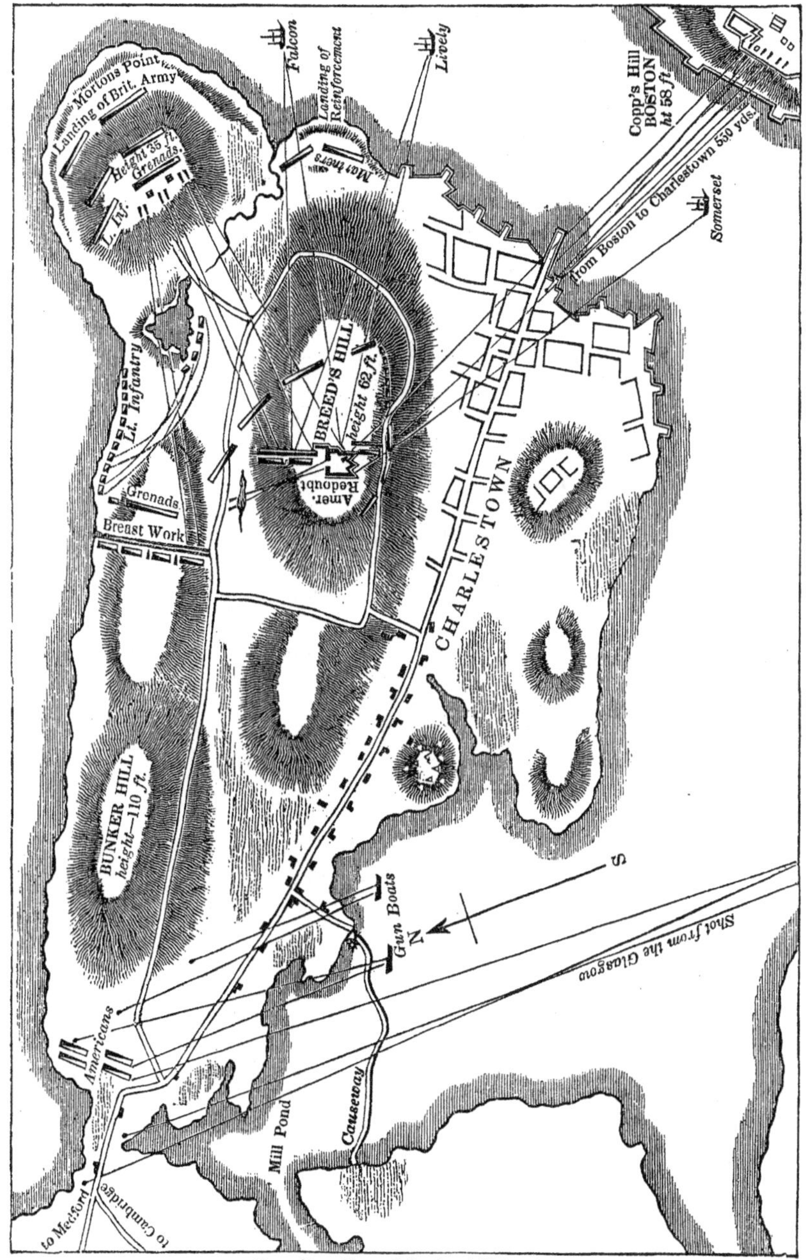

Fig. 61.—Plan of Bunker hill battle.

alone, every officer and soldier near him having been killed or wounded. The troops gave wav a second time; but at that critical moment Sir Henry Clin n

FIG. 62.—Portrait of General Clinton, from a picture by J. Smart.

arrived from Boston, and was very active in leading them back to a third and more successful attack, in which they entered the American lines with fixed bayonets. The colonists had nearly exhausted their powder, and hence their fire had slackened. Being mostly armed with old rusty muskets, and ill-provided with bayonets, they were unprepared for a close encounter, but they met the British with clubbed muskets, until overcome by numbers and destitute of ammunition, they were compelled to retreat. In passing Charlestown Neck, they were exposed to the fire of the Glasgow sloop of war, and two floating batteries, from which they sustained their greatest loss.

The British troops had suffered so severely in the engagement, that no pursuit was ordered; and indeed a pursuit could have served no good purpose, as the main body of the American army was at a small distance beyond the Neck, and the royal troops were in no condition to encounter it. They were protected merely by the ships of war and floating batteries in the rivers Charles and Medford. The battle lasted about an hour, during the greater part of which time there was an incessant blaze of musketry from the American line.

This was a severe battle; and considering the numbers engaged, extremely destructive to the British; for nearly one half of the detachment fell. According to the return made by General Gage, they lost 1,054 men; 226 of whom were slain on the field, and 828 wounded. Nineteen commissioned officers were killed, and seventy wounded; among the former was Major Pitcairn, whose inconsiderate conduct at Lexington had occasioned the first shedding of blood.

The Americans had 139 killed, 278 wounded, and thirty-six missing; in all 453. Among the killed were several provincial officers; but the death of General Warren was particularly regretted by his countrymen. He was seen by a British officer, a personal acquaintance, to rally the Americans in their retreat: the officer borrowed a musket, took deliberate aim, and Warren fell. In this engagement the Americans discovered far more courage and steadiness than could

Fig. 63.—Monument on Bunker's Hill.

have been expected from an ill-disciplined militia, few of whom had before seen the face of an enemy; but their hearts were nerved by the consciousness of being in the right, and their arms were strengthened by the desire of obtaining liberty and independence.

After the engagement the British entrenched themselves on Bunker's Hill, the scene of action; and the Americans on Prospect Hill, at a small distance in front of them. The colonists had been driven from their entrenchments; the royal troops had suffered severely in the battle, and neither party was forward to renew the conflict. Each fortified his post, and stood on the defensive.

On the 2d of July, General Washington, accompanied by General Lee and several other officers of rank, arrived at Cambridge, the headquarters of the provincial army. On his journey he had everywhere been received with much respect, and escorted by companies of gentlemen, who volunteered their services on the occasion.

General Washington found between fourteen and fifteen thousand men encamped before Boston; and he and the other generals exerted themselves in establishing more exact discipline than had been observed before. Under their care the colonists in arms soon acquired somewhat of the mechanism and movements, as well as the name of an army; but still they were ill-disciplined, and ill-armed.

The Americans, who had been made prisoners at Bunker's Hill, were indiscriminately thrown into jail at Boston, and treated with little humanity. On the 11th of August, General Washington addressed a letter to General Gage on the subject, and informed him that his treatment of British prisoners should be regulated by that which the Americans experienced. General Gage replied that the prisoners had been treated with care and kindness, but indiscriminately, because he acknowledged no rank that was not derived from the king; and at the same time retorted on the Americans the charge of cruelty. General Washington replied: "I have taken time, sir, to make a strict inquiry, and find the intelligence you have received has not the least foundation in truth. Not only your officers and soldiers have been treated with the tenderness due to fellow-citizens and brethren; but even those execrable parricides, whose council and aid have deluged this country with blood, have been protected from the fury of a justly enraged people. You affect, sir, to despise all rank not derived from the same source with your own; I can not conceive one more honorable than that which flows from the uncorrupted choice of a brave and free people, the purest source and original fountain of all power."

This epistolary correspondence did not suspend military operations: some skirmishing took place between the advanced parties of the two armies; and the Americans fortified themselves on an eminence within half a mile of the British post on Bunker's Hill. There was a good deal of firing on the occasion, without much loss to either side; but it in some measure accustomed the colonists to the use of arms, the noise of artillery, and the operations of war.

The American army was extremely deficient in gunpowder; but in the beginning of September it received a supply of 7,000 pounds from Rhode Island, procured, it is said, from the British forts on the coast of Africa. Saltpetre was collected in all the colonies; powder-mills were erected at Philadelphia and New York; and upward of 100 barrels of powder were obtained by American agents from the magazine at Bermuda.

General Washington soon began to feel the difficulties of his situation. He perceived that the expense of maintaining the army far exceeded any estimate of congress, and was very uneasy on the subject. The time for which the continental soldiers were engaged to serve was drawing to a close, and the danger of very short enlistments was felt. A council of war, therefore, unanimously

Fig. 64.—Washington's Headquarters at Cambridge.

agreed that the men about to be levied should be engaged till the 1st of December, 1776. This was a very inadequate remedy for the evil, which was severely felt in the course of the war; but some hopes of a reconciliation between Britain and the colonies were still entertained.

On the 10th of October, General Gage sailed for Britain, and the command of the British army devolved on General (afterward viscount) Howe, who issued a proclamation condemning to military execution such of the inhabitants of Boston as should be caught attempting to leave the town without a written permission. About that time the royal cruisers on the coasts of New England began a system of piratical and predatory warfare against the inhabitants, which considerably injured, but neither intimidated nor subdued them. Captain Wallace, of the Rose man of war, with two tenders, pursued a vessel which took refuge in the port of Stonington, in Connecticut; and on the morning of the 1st of September, he began to fire on the town, and continued his hostilities, with little intermission, throughout the day. He killed two men, damaged the houses, and carried off some vessels. At Rhode Island some firing took place between the minute-men and the ships, on occasion of carrying off some cattle. Captain Wallace afterward sailed to Bristol, and demanded 300 sheep, which not being complied with, he began a heavy cannonade on this unprotected place, and continued it till some persons went on board and purchased the peace of the town with forty sheep.

On the 18th of October Captain Mowat, with a few armed vessels, in a cowardly manner, burnt the town of Falmouth, in the northern part of Massachusetts Bay, and declared that his orders were to set on fire all the seaport towns between Boston and Halifax. The destruction of unprotected towns alarmed and exasperated, but did not intimidate the colonists.

Meanwhile the troops in Boston were reduced to a very uncomfortable condition: they could not procure provisions and other necessaries from the country, and their maritime supplies were much interrupted; for, on the 9th of October, the assembly of Massachusetts Bay resolved to fit out armed vessels for the defence of the American coast; and afterward appointed courts of admiralty, to condemn such captured vessels as should be proved to belong to persons hostile to the united American colonies. Privateers were soon at sea, and in a few days took an ordnance ship from Woolwich, and several store-ships, with valuable cargoes, which afforded a seasonable supply to the American camp, while the loss was severely felt by the British army in Boston. A military transport, having been becalmed off Cohassett, was gallantly captured by Isaiah Doane, at the head of twenty men; who boarded her at night, attacking in two whale boats with muffled oars. She was carried into Cohassett and her stores were found to be very useful to the American army. Congress also soon resolved to fit out and commission ships of war.

But although the British army in Boston was in very disagreeable circumstances, and success attended the naval operations of the Americans, yet the affairs of the provinces wore no flattering aspect. The term for which many of the men had enlisted was about to expire. Irritation of spirit had made them fly to arms; and, in the fervor of their zeal, they would at first have readily engaged to serve during the war: but the opportunity was lost, and congress severely felt the error in the course of the struggle. At the same time the colonial treasury was but ill-replenished, and the provincial paper-money soon became depreciated. In these circumstances congress, wishing by a bold movement to put an end to the war, or at least by the splendor of a successful operation to reanimate the zeal of the people, was desirous that an attack should be made on Boston; but a council of war deemed the measure inexpedient.

FIG. 65.—Yankee Privateersman

Congress early turned its attention toward Canada, and endeavored to gain the co-operation, or at least to secure the neutrality of the inhabitants, in its dispute with Britain. The congress of the preceding year, although professing allegiance to the British crown, had circulated an address to the Canadians, evidently intended to render them disaffected to the British administration, and to make them enter into the sentiments and measures of the other provinces. Although that address did not make on the minds of the Canadians all that impression which was intended and desired, yet it was not altogether without effect; for the great body of the people wished to remain neutral in the contest.

Congress mistook the reluctance of the Canadians to engage in active operations against them for a decided partiality to their cause, and resolved to anticipate the British, by striking a decisive blow in that quarter In this purpose they were encouraged by the easy success of the enterprise against the forts on the lakes, and by the small number of troops then in Canada. They appointed General Schuyler commander of the expedition, with General Montgomery under him. Early in September, those officers, with about 1,000 men, made a feeble attempt on Fort St. John, situated on the river Sorel, which flows from Lake Champlain and joins the St. Lawrence, but found it expedient to retire to Isle aux Noix, at the entrance of the lake, about twelve miles above the fort, and wait for reinforcements.

Fig. 66.—St. John, on the Sorel.

Meanwhile General Schuyler was taken ill, and returned to Albany, leaving the command in the hands of General Montgomery, with instructions to prosecute the enterprise, on receiving the expected reinforcements. The reinforcements arrived: the attack on Fort St. John was renewed; and after a vigorous defence, it surrendered about the middle of November. In it the Americans found a considerable number of brass and iron cannon, howitzers, and mortars a quantity of shot and small shells, about 800 stand of small-arms, and some naval stores; but the powder and provisions were nearly exhausted.

During the siege of Fort St. John, Fort Chamblée had been taken, which furnished General Montgomery with a plentiful supply of provisions, of which he stood greatly in need. General Carleton, who was on his way from Montreal to relieve the garrison, had been defeated; and Colonel Allen, who had made an attack on Montreal, was overcome and taken prisoner.

On the fall of Fort St. John, General Montgomery advanced against Montreal, which was in no condition to resist him. Governor Carleton, sensible of his inability to defend the town, quitted it, and next day General Montgomery entered the place. A body of provincials, under Colonel Eaton, took post at the mouth of the Sorel, and by means of an armed vessel and floating batteries, commanded the navigation of the St. Lawrence. The British force, which had retreated down the river from Montreal, consisting only of about 120 soldiers, with several officers, under General Prescott, and accompanied by Governor Carleton, in eleven vessels, seeing it impracticable to force the passage, surrendered by capitulation. The vessels contained a considerable quantity of provisions, arms, and ammunition, which furnished a seasonable supply to the Americans. About midnight of the day before the capitulation, Governor Carleton escaped down the river in a boat with muffled oars, and safely reached Quebec.

It was now the 19th of November, and the severe weather which had set in was very unfavorable to military operations. General Montgomery, a young man of superior talents and high spirit, found himself in extremely unpleasant circumstances. He was at the head of a body of armed men, many of whom were not deficient in personal courage, but all of them were strangers to military subordination. The term of service for which numbers of them were engaged was near an end; and already weary of the hardships of war, they clamorously demanded a discharge. Nothing but devotion to his country could have made him continue in the irksome command. Hitherto his career had been successful, and he was ambitious of closing the campaign by some brilliant achievement which might at once elevate the spirits of the Americans and humble the pride of the British ministry. With these views, even at that rigorous season of the year, he hastened toward Quebec, although he found it necessary to weaken his little army, which had never exceeded 2,000 men, by discharging such of his followers as had become weary of the service.

About the middle of September a detachment of 1,100 men, under Colonel Arnold, was sent from the camp in the vicinity of Boston, with orders to proceed across the country against Quebec, by a route which had not been explored, and was little known. The party embarked at Newbury, steered for the Kennebec, and ascended that river. But their progress was impeded by rapids, by an almost impassable wilderness, by bad weather, and by want of provisions. They separated into several divisions. After encountering many difficulties, the last division, under Colonel Enos, was unable to proceed, and returned to the camp in the vicinity of Boston. But the other divisions, under Arnold, pressed forward amid incredible hardships and privations, and triumphed over obstacles nearly insuperable. For a month they toiled through a rough, barren, and uninhabited wilderness, without seeing a human habitation, or the face of an individual, except those of their own party, and with very scanty provisions. At length, on the 9th of November, Arnold, with his force much diminished, arrived at Point Levi opposite Quebec.

His appearance was not unexpected; for the lieutenant governor had been for some time apprized of his march. In the early part of his progress, Arnold had met an Indian, to whom, although a stranger, he had imprudently entrusted a letter to General Schuyler, under cover to a friend in Quebec. The Indian, instead of faithfully delivering the letter according to the directions which he had received, carried it to the lieutenant governor, who, in order to prevent the Americans from passing the river, immediately removed all the canoes from Point Levi, and began to put the city in a posture of defence, which before might easily have been surprised. On discovering the arrival of Arnold at Point Levi, the British commander stationed two vessels of war in the river to guard the passage; and, at that interesting crisis, Colonel M'Lean, who had retreated before Montgomery, arrived from the Sorel, with about 170 newly-raised troops, to assist in the defence of the place.

Fig. 67.—Arnold crossing the River.

Notwithstanding all the vigilance of the British, on the night of the 14th of November Arnold crossed the river with 500 men, in thirty-five canoes, and landed unperceived near the place where the brave and enterprising Wolfe had landed about sixteen years before, thence named Wolfe's Cove. He had provided scaling ladders, but was unable to carry them over the river with his troops, and consequently was not in a condition to make an immediate attempt on the town. Instead, however, of concealing himself till he could bring forward his scaling ladders, and then make a sudden and unexpected attack by night, he marched part of his troops in military parade in sight of the garrison, and so put the British fully on their guard. He wished to summon them to surrender, but they fired on his flag of truce, and refused to hold any intercourse with him. He, therefore, on the 19th of the month, turned his back on Quebec, and marched to Point aux Trembles, about twenty miles above the city, where General Montgomery, with the force under his command, joined him on the first of December.

Soon after Arnold's retreat, Governor Carleton arrived in Quebec, and made every exertion to put the place in a state of defence. Having brought the scaling ladders across the river, General Montgomery, with the whole of the Amer-

Fig. 68.—Quebec.

ican force, appeared before Quebec on the 5th of December. The garrison was then more numerous than the army which came to take the place. So greatly was the American force reduced, that it scarcely amounted to 1,000 men; while General Carleton had about 1,500 soldiers, militia, seamen, and volunteers, under his command.

General Montgomery sent a flag of truce to summon the garrison to surrender; but, contrary to usage among civilized nations, it was fired upon, as that of Arnold had been. He therefore, in the depth of a Canadian winter, and in the most intense cold, erected batteries; but his artillery was too light to make any impression on the fortifications. He therefore determined to storm the town; and the assault was made on the morning of the 31st of December.

Fig. 69.—British Soldiers firing at the Flag of Truce.

About four o'clock in the morning, in the midst of a violent storm of snow, two feints and two real attacks were simultaneously made. The real attacks were conducted by Montgomery and Arnold. Montgomery, advancing at the head of about 200 men, fell by the first discharge of grape-shot from the works. Several of his best officers being killed, his division retreated. Arnold, at the head of about 300 men, in a different quarter, maintained a fierce and obstinate conflict for some time; but was at last wounded and repulsed. The death of Montgomery was the subject of much regret, as he had been universally loved and esteemed. On assembling after the assault, the provincials could not muster many more than 400 effective men, who chose Arnold their commander; and, in the hope of receiving reinforcements, resolved to remain in the vicinity of Quebec.

Thus perished this gallant Irishman, a martyr to his love for liberty, fighting bravely in defence of his adopted country.

In front of the church of St. Paul's, in Broadway, at the corner of Fulton street, New York, may be seen a very plain monument with the following inscription:—

"This monument is erected by order of congress, 25th January, 1776, to transmit to posterity a grateful remembrance of the *patriotism, conduct, enterprise,* and *perseverance* of Major-General Richard Montgomery, who, after a series of successes, amid the most discouraging difficulties, fell in the attack on Quebec, 31st December, 1775, aged 37 years.

"The State of New York caused the remains of Major-General Richard Montgomery to be conveyed from Quebec and deposited beneath this monument, the 8th day of July, 1818."

Sir Guy Carleton acquired much honor by the humanity with which he treat

FIG.—70. View of St. Paul's Church, New York, and the Tomb of Montgomery.

Fig. 71.—Montgomery Leading on his Men.

ed all his prisoners. He fought as a soldier, and felt as a man. The Americans were not ignorant of their own great inferiority in point of numbers to the garrison, and were not without apprehensions of being attacked; but, although the garrison was three times more numerous than the blockading army, yet it was of such a mixed and precarious nature, that Sir Guy Carleton did not deem it prudent to march out against the enemy.

A small reinforcement from Massachusetts reached the American camp, and all the troops that could be spared from Montreal marched to join their countrymen before Quebec; but the month of February was far advanced before the army amounted to 960 men. Arnold, however, resumed the siege; but his artillery was inadequate to the undertaking, and made no impression on the works. Although unsuccessful against the town, he defeated a body of Canadians who advanced to relieve it.

While the American army lay before Quebec, the troops caught the small-pox from a woman who had been a nurse in an hospital of the city; and the loathsome disease spread rapidly among them. In order to mitigate the ravages of this destructive malady, many of the men inoculated themselves, regardless of orders to the contrary. The reinforcements, which were daily arriving, had recourse to the same practice; and so general was the infection, that, on the first of May, although the army amounted to 2,000 men, yet not more than 900 were fit for duty. In this diseased state of the troops, medicines and everything necessary for the sick were wanting. The men were also scattered for want of barracks. Major-General Thomas, who had been appointed to the command of the American army in Canada, arrived in camp on the 1st of May. He found the troops enfeebled by disease, ill-supplied with provisions, and with only a small quantity of ammunition. The river was opening below; and he was well aware that as soon as ships could force their way through the ice, the garrison would be reinforced. On the 5th of May, therefore, he resolved to retreat toward Montreal; and on the evening of the same day, he received certain information that a British fleet was in the river. Next morning some of the ships, by great exertion and with much danger, pressed through the ice into the harbor, and landed some troops.

The Americans were preparing to retire: General Carleton marched out to

Fig. 72.—Portrait of General Carleton.

attack them; and as there was no hope of successfully resisting a force so mucn superior, they made a precipitate retreat, leaving behind them their sick, baggage, artillery, and military stores. Many of those who were ill of the small-pox escaped from the hospitals and concealed themselves in the country, where they were kindly entertained by the Canadians till they recovered, and were able to follow their countrymen. General Carleton could not overtake the American army; but he took about 100 sick prisoners.

The Americans retreated about forty-five miles, and then halted a few days; but afterward proceeded to Sorel, in a deplorable condition, and encamped there. In this interval some reinforcements arrived; but General Thomas was seized with the small-pox, and died. He was succeeded in command by General Sullivan.

The British had several military posts in Upper Canada; and the Americans established one at the Cedars, a point of land which projects into the St. Lawrence, about forty miles above Montreal. Captain Forster, who had marched from Oswyatchie, appeared before this post with a company of regulars and a considerable number of Indians; and the American commanding officer surrendered the place after a short resistance. An American party of about 100 men, under Major Sherburne, left Montreal to assist their countrymen at the Cedars; but as they approached that place, on the day after the surrender, and ignorant of that event, they were suddenly and unexpectedly attacked by a body of Indians and Canadians. After defending themselves for some time, the Americans were overpowered, and many of them fell under the tomahawks of the Indians The rest were made prisoners.

Arnold, who in the month of January had been raised to the rank of brigadier-general, and who then commanded at Montreal, was desirous of recovering the

..., and of relieving the prisoners there; and for these purposes marched toward that place, at the head of about 800 men. But on his approach Captain Forster gave him notice, that unless he agreed to a cartel, which had already been signed by Major Sherburne and some other officers, the Indians would put all the prisoners to death. In these circumstances, Arnold reluctantly signed the cartel, and retired.

Before the end of May, the British force in Canada was greatly increased; and, including the German mercenaries, was estimated at 13,000 men. That force was widely dispersed; but Three Rivers, about ninety miles above Quebec and as much below Montreal, was the general point of rendezvous. A considerable detachment, under General Frazer, had already arrived there. That detachment General Sullivan wished to surprise; and appointed General Thompson to command the troops in the expedition sent out for that purpose. The enterprise failed; Thompson was made prisoner, and his detachment dispersed, but without any great loss.

The royal military and naval forces having been collected at Three Rivers, a long village so named from its contiguity to a river which empties itself into the St. Lawrence by three mouths, advanced by land and water toward the Sorel. General Sullivan had retreated up that river; and General Burgoyne was ordered cautiously to pursue him. On the 15th of June, General Arnold quitted Montreal, crossed the river at Longueille, marched on Chamblée, and conducted the army to Crown Point, with little loss in the retreat. Thus terminated the invasion of Canada, in which the American army endured great hardships, and sustained considerable loss, without any advantage to the cause in which it was engaged.

Historical annals rarely furnish so striking and interesting occurrences as might be recorded, were the detail fully given of the memorable march of the Americans in order to penetrate Quebec. Honorably as it has been commemorated, its difficulties, dangers, and privations, can never be sufficiently appreciated. We read of the passage of the Alps with a just sentiment of admiration; yet it is not certain but that the privations and difficulties of those enterprises were surpassed in the expedition of Arnold. Their batteaux had to be dragged by the soldiers over water-falls, portages, and rapid streams, and such parts of the march as was not made by rivers, was performed for a distance of three hundred miles through thick woods, over lofty mountains, and deep morasses. A part of the detachment actually abandoned the undertaking and returned to Cambridge to avoid starvation. Those who persevered were actually compelled, in order to appease the torments of hunger, to devour dogs, reptiles, and their very cartridge-boxes. Among the patriots of this tried corps of invincibles were the late Col. Burr and Col. Samuel Ward, recently deceased in the city of New York.

Although the Americans had failed in their attempt on Canada, they still occupied Crown Point and Ticonderoga. General Carleton resolved to drive them from those posts; but that was an arduous task, for the British had not a ship on Lake Champlain to oppose the American navy; and it was deemed unadvisable to advance, without first gaining the command of the lakes. The great aim was to obtain possession of the upper parts of the Hudson, to march to Albany, make themselves masters of the country in General Washington's rear, and open a communication between the British army in Canada and that at New York. The task was arduous; and General Carleton labored with unwearied assiduity in providing the means of gaining a superiority on the lakes. In about three months, his efforts were crowned with success. Early in October, he had a formidable fleet, which rose, as if by magic, upon Lake Champlain. It consisted of the Inflexible, carrying eighteen 12-pounders, one schooner, mounting fourteen 12-pounders, and another having twelve 12-pounders ; a flat-bottomed vessel, carrying six 24 and six 12-pounders, besides howitzers ; a vessel having seven 9-pounders ; twenty gun-boats, each mounting a brass cannon, from 9 to 24-pounders ; with other armed vessels, and a great number of transports and tenders. This fleet had been constructed with immense labor, part of the materials having been brought from a distance, and many of the boats dragged up the rapids of the Sorel. The fleet was manned with 700 choice seamen, and under the command of Captain Pringle.

The Americans were sensible of the importance of maintaining a superiority on the lakes, and had made every effort in their power for that purpose ; but, from want of money, materials, and artificers, their exertions had not been successful. Their fleet amounted only to fifteen vessels, consisting of two schooners, one sloop, one cutter, three galleys, and eight gondolas. The largest schooner mounted only 12, 6, and 4-pounders. Arnold, as a man of desperate courage, was appointed to command this little fleet, which was, in every respect, greatly inferior to that of the British.

About the middle of October, the royal fleet, commanded by Captain Pringle, and having General Carleton on board, proceeded up Lake Champlain in quest of the Americans. The armed vessels were in front ; the army, in many transports, brought up the rear. The whole had a gay and magnificent appearance. They found Arnold in an advantageous position, forming a line to defend the passage between the island of Valicour and the western bank. A warm engagement ensued ; and the Inflexible and some other large British ships being

FIG. 73.—Engagement on Lake Champlain.

hindered by an unfavorable wind from coming so near as to take an efficient part in the battle, Arnold was able, notwithstanding the great inferiority of his force, to maintain the conflict for some hours ; when, night approaching, Captain Pringle withdrew his ships from the action, but stationed them at a little distance only, with a view to prevent the escape of the Americans. In this engagement Arnold's largest schooner was burnt, and a gondola sunk.

Arnold, feeling his inability to renew the conflict next day, made his escape during the night, in the hope of reaching Ticonderoga, and finding shelter under the guns of the fort. The wind was favorable, and next morning he was out of sight of the British fleet. Captain Pringle ordered an immediate pursuit, overtook the Americans, and brought them to action before they reached Crown Point. Arnold fought with his usual resolution for about two hours; during which time, such of his fleet as were most ahead fled under a press of sail, and escaped to Ticonderoga. Two galleys and five gondolas, which remained with him, made a desperate defence. At length one of them was compelled to strike her colors. Arnold was unable any longer to maintain the unequal conflict but, disdaining to surrender, he ran his ships ashore, landed his men, and set his vessels on fire and blew them up. In the face of the most active and vigorous opposition, he preserved his crews, and prevented his ships from falling into the hands of the British.

General Carleton advanced with the fleet, and appeared off Crown Point on the 15th of October. On his approach, a small American detachment, stationed there as an advanced post, set fire to the houses, and retired to Ticonderoga, which Generals Schuyler and Gates had determined to defend to the last extremity. General Carleton took possession of Crown Point, sent forward part of his fleet in sight of Ticonderoga, and advanced with his army toward that place; but after viewing the works, and considering that winter was setting in, and the difficulty of bringing provisions from Canada to supply his army during that inclement season, he prudently resolved to retire; and put his army into winter quarters on the Sorel and its vicinity. Isle aux Noix was his advanced post.

While their armies were blockading Boston and fighting in Canada, congress were actively employed in devising and adopting such measures as they thought most conducive to the general welfare. On the 6th of July, 1775, they published a declaration, setting forth the causes and necessity of their having taken up arms, and alleged that they were reduced to the painful alternative of unconditional submission to the tyranny of an irritated ministry, or of resistance by force. "The latter," said they, "is our choice: we have counted the cost of the contest, and find nothing so dreadful as voluntary slavery."

On the 8th of July, the members signed their famous second petition to the king. It was expressed in respectful language, well written, and declared their sentiments in a firm but dutiful manner. On the same day, they agreed to an address to the inhabitants of Great Britain, in which they said: "We have again presented an humble and dutiful petition to our sovereign; and, to remove every imputation of obstinacy, have requested his majesty to direct some mode by which the united supplications of his faithful colonists may be improved into a happy and permanent reconciliation. We are willing to treat on such terms as can alone render an accommodation lasting; and we flatter ourselves that our pacific endeavors will be attended with a removal of ministerial troops, and the repeal of those laws of the operation of which we complain, on the one part; and the disbanding of our army and a dissolution of our commercial associations on the other." At the same time, they hinted at the danger to which British freedom would be exposed, if the spirit of liberty were crushed in America.

They also wrote a letter of thanks to the lord mayor, aldermen, and livery of the city of London, for their virtuous and spirited opposition to the oppressive and ruinous system of colonial administration adopted by the British cabinet. These several papers were transmitted to Richard Penn, whom congress requested to present their petition to the king. Mr. Penn sailed for England without delay.

Congress appointed commissioners to superintend Indian affairs, to prepare proper *talks* for the tribes, and to watch over the interests of the colonies in relation to them. While congress was attentive to guard against Indian hostility, and to gain Indian friendship, they exerted themselves to put the provinces in a posture of defence, and recommended to all able-bodied men in the colonies, between sixteen and fifty years of age, immediately to form themselves into regular companies of militia, to acquire a knowledge of military exercise, and to select a fourth part of the militia in every colony as minute-men, ready to march, on a minute's notice, wherever their assistance might be required. They also recommended to each colony to appoint a committee of safety to watch over the public welfare, during the recess of their respective assemblies and conventions, and to make all the provision in their power for the protection of their harbors and coasts.

Amid the noise of arms and the contrivances of policy, the ceremonials of religion were not forgotten. The 20th of July was appointed as a general fast; and, on that day, the members of congress, in a body, attended public worship, both forenoon and afternoon. The day was observed in Philadelphia as the most solemn fast that had ever been held in that city; and it was punctually kept throughout the united colonies.

The congress appointed the establishment of a post-office, to extend from Falmouth in New England to Savannah in Georgia, and elected Benjamin Franklin postmaster-general. They also resolved to form an hospital for an army of 20 000 men, and nominated Dr. Church director and physician of it.

CHAPTER IV.

On the 1st of August, congress adjourned to the 5th of September; and the adjournment not only gave the members an opportunity of attending to their private affairs, but also of consulting their constituents; and it enabled those who secretly looked forward to independence to disseminate their opinions more freely by personal intercourse than they durst attempt by written correspondence.

The congress re-assembled at the appointed time, and resumed their labors. Their situation was difficult; and they were distracted and alarmed by many cares, apprehensions, and dangers. The great body of the people was on their side; but they were not ignorant of the fickleness of the multitude, or of their irresolution and instability in the course of a severe and protracted struggle. Many of the colonists were not unfriendly to the claims of Britain, or so lukewarm in the cause of the provinces as to be unwilling to hazard much in its support. The supporters of royal authority made hostile movements in several of the colonies; but they were crushed by the superior power of their opponents.

In New York, the British interest was stronger than in any of the other provinces; and the intrigues of Mr. Tryon, governor of that colony, gave congress considerable uneasiness; so that, with a view to his apprehension, they recommended to the several provincial assemblies, or committees of public safety, to arrest every person within their respective jurisdictions, whose being at large might endanger the safety of the colony, or the liberties of America. Of this recommendation Mr. Tryon seems to have been early apprized by Mr. Duane, one of the New York delegates, who was far from giving a cordial assent to the

FIG. 75.—View on the Hudson.

measures of congress; and the governor sought security on board the Halifax packet, then lying in the river.

In the month of August, the New York convention resolved to remove the cannon from the battery in the city, and appointed Captain Sears to execute the measure. Captain Vandeput, of the Asia man-of-war, was privately informed of the intention; and, about midnight, when Captain Sears entered on his work, Captain Vandeput opened a heavy fire upon the place; but the Americans accomplished their purpose, without losing a man. The firing, during the silence of the night, greatly alarmed the inhabitants of the adjacent towns.

The congress was fully aware of the importance of preserving the command of the Hudson, or North River; and, for that purpose, gave directions to erect batteries and place garrisons in the highlands; and they used all the means in their power to keep the royal party in New York in check, by stationing troops, on whom they could depend, in the vicinity of that city.

The convention of New Hampshire applied to congress for directions how to carry on the administration of the colony, in the circumstances in which they were placed. Congress recommended to them to call a full and free representation of the people, to establish such a form of government as they deemed most conducive to the good order, peace, and happiness of the province; thus setting an example of popular and independent government for the imitation of the colonies.

Congress recommended that Charleston, in South Carolina, be defended against all the enemies of America; that the army before Boston consist of 20,000 men; and that particular colonies raise battalions at the expense of the continent; that four armed vessels be fitted out for the purpose of intercepting transports laden with warlike stores and other supplies to the enemy, and for the protection and defence of the united colonies. Congress deliberated with shut doors, and agreed, "That every member consider himself under the ties of virtue, honor, and love of his country, not to divulge, directly or indirectly, any matter or thing agitated or debated in congress before the same shall have been determined, without the leave of congress; or any matter or thing determined in congress, which the majority of congress shall order to be kept secret; and that, if any member shall violate this agreement, he shall be expelled this congress, and be deemed an enemy to the liberties of America, and liable to be treated as such; and that every member signify his assent to this agreement by signing the same." In this way, the proceedings of congress remained entirely unknown, except in so far as that body chose to publish them.

Congress appointed a committee to correspond with their friends in Britain and Ireland; and recommended that no colony should separately petition the king: they resolved to secure and bring away a quantity of powder in the island of Providence; to retaliate, on such British soldiers as fell into their hands, any sufferings that might be inflicted on American prisoners; and to provide thirteen armed ships, carrying from thirty-two to twenty-four guns each, of which Ezekiel Hopkins was appointed commander. Thus, before the end of the year 1775, although congress still made professions of loyalty to the king, yet everything throughout the colonies was in a state of the most active preparation for war.

At Boston the hostile armies remained quiet during the severity of winter; but early in the morning of the 14th of February, 1776, General Howe sent a detachment over the ice to Dorchester Neck, and burnt a few houses. This expedition merely served to make the Americans more sensible of the importance of establishing themselves on Dorchester heights. General Washington was inclined to make an attack on Boston: to that, however, a council of war did not agree, but proposed to take possession of Dorchester heights, which are on the south of Boston, as Bunker's Hill is on the north, and so render the Brit-

Fig. 75.—Ruins of the Fort on Dorchester Heights

ish post in Boston untenable. The measure was resolved on, and preparations made for carrying it into execution. Accordingly, on the evening of the 4th of March, a strong detachment silently crossed Dorchester Neck, arrived at their places of destination, and labored incessantly in raising fortifications. In order to conceal this movement, the Americans had, for some days before, kept up a heavy fire on Boston, with little effect; and it had been as ineffectually returned by the British.

The noise of artillery prevented the pick-axes and other implements of the Americans from being heard, although the ground was hard frozen, and could not easily be penetrated. So incessantly did they labor, that during the night they raised two forts, with other defences, which in the morning presented to the British a very formidable appearance. On viewing these works, General Howe remarked, that the Americans had done more in one night than his whole army would have done in a month. He determined to dislodge them, and made the necessary preparations for attacking them next day. But in the night a violent storm arose, which drove some of his vessels ashore on Governor's Island; and in the morning it rained so heavily that the attack could not be made.

General Howe called a council of war, which was of opinion that the town of Boston ought to be evacuated as soon as possible, since the Americans had got time to strengthen their works, so as to render an attack on them very hazardous. For their own defence, the provincials had provided a number of barrels filled with stones and sand, ready to be rolled down on the assailants as they ascended the hill; a device which would have broken the line of the most steady and intrepid troops, and thrown them into confusion. That the heights of Dorchester had been so long neglected may appear surprising; but during winter the American army was both weak and ill provided, and General Howe had no troops to spare.

In Boston all was bustle and confusion; the troops and the friends of the British government preparing to quit the town. General Howe was desirous of removing all his stores of every kind; and his adherents wished to carry off all their effects. In the view of abandoning the town, the soldiery were guilty of the most shameful excesses, plundering the shops and houses, and destroying what they could not take away. About four o'clock in the morning of Sunday the 17th of March, the troops, about 7,000 in number, and some hundreds of loyal inhabitants, began to embark; and they were all on board and under sail before ten. The evacuation of the place was so sudden that an adequate number of transports had not been prepared, and much confusion and inconvenience were experienced on board. The fleet, however, remained several days in Nantucket roads, and burnt the block-house on Castle Island, and demolished the fortifications. A considerable quantity of stores was left behind in Boston.

As the last of the British party were marching out of Boston, General Washington entered it, amid the triumphant gratulations of the citizens, whose joy on their deliverance from the degrading oppression of a British army was enthusiastic. At first it was not known to what quarter General Howe would direct his course; but, apprehensive of an immediate attack on New York, General Washington, on the day after the evacuation, despatched five regiments, under General Heath, toward that city, and soon followed with the main body of his army.

In a few days it was ascertained that General Howe, instead of sailing to the southward, had steered to Halifax. But he left some cruisers to watch the entrance into Boston, and to give notice of the evacuation to such British vessels as were destined for that port. Notwithstanding that precaution, however, several ships and transports, ignorant of what had happened, sailed into the harbor, and became prizes to the Americans, who, by their naval captures, procured a

FIG. 76.—A view of Boston taken on the road to Dorchester. From a print published in London, May, 1776.

most seasonable supply of arms and ammunition. In this way Lieutenant Colonel Campbell, with nearly 300 Highlanders, after a brave resistance, was taken by some American privateers.

General Howe remained a considerable time at Halifax, to refresh his troops, exhausted by the fatigues and privations of the blockade; and General Washington marched to New York.

A considerable time elapsed before the armies under General Howe and Washington again confronted each other; but while there was a pause in military operations in the north, events of importance happened in the south. In South Carolina the friends of congress were decidedly most numerous; but the adherents of the British ministry were neither few nor inactive. The supporters of colonial measures, however, had their system far better organized, their communications more regular, their union more complete, and their zeal was more enthusiastic.

The zealous provincialists, wished to force all to join the non-importation associations, and afterward to enrol in the militia. Many refused, and quarrels arose. Camp was pitched against camp; but, after some negotiation, a treaty was entered into by the parties, in which it was agreed that the royalists should remain in a state of neutrality. A temporary calm ensued: but Mr. Robert Cunningham, who had been a principal leader among the royalists, persisted in encouraging opposition to popular measures, and declared that he did not consider himself bound by the treaty which had been entered into. The popular leaders, instead of giving him time to carry his hostile purposes into execution, apprehended and imprisoned him. His brother, Patrick Cunningham, armed his friends in order to release him. In that design they did not succeed; but they seized 1,000 pounds of gunpowder, which was public property, and which was passing through their settlements as a present to the Cherokees; and propagated the most calumnious reports against the provincial leaders, for sending powder to the Indians at a time when the colonists could not procure that important article for their own defence.

Major Williamson marched against Cunningham and his party, but was obliged to retreat before their superior force, and at last found it necessary to take refuge in a stockade fort, where Cunningham besieged him. But after a few days a sort of truce was entered into, and both parties dispersed. At that time internal divisions in the province were extremely dangerous, for a formidable invasion from Britain was daily expected; and a British force in front, with disaffected colonists and unfriendly Indians in the rear, threatened the adherents of congress with ruin.

Lord William Campbell, governor of the province, had uniformly recommended to the royalists to remain quiet till the arrival of a British force. His advice was not followed; and the friends of congress were eager to crush all internal opposition before the arrival of foreign troops. They, therefore, despatched a considerable army into the settlements of the royalists; some of whom fled beyond the mountains or into Florida, and they who remained were completely overawed.

Meanwhile the province formed for itself a temporary constitution of government, established boards and courts for conducting public business, and provided as well as it could against the impending storm from Britain.

Charleston, the capital of South Carolina, stands on a point of land which lies between the rivers Cooper and Ashley, which fall into a bay of the Atlantic; and in the bay there are several islands. The people resolved to fortify the capital of the province; and for that purpose erected a fort on Sullivan's Island, which lies in the bay, about six miles below the town, and near the channel leading to it. The fort was constructed with the wood of the palmetto; a

Fig. 77.—Made to commemorate the evacuation of Boston by the British.

tree peculiar to the southern states, which grows from twenty to forty feet high, without branches, and terminates in a top resembling the head of a cabbage The wood of the tree is remarkably spongy; and a ball entering it makes nc extended fracture, but buries itself in the wood, without injuring the adjacent parts. The fort was mounted with about thirty cannon; 32, 18, and 9 pounders.

In the latter part of 1775 and beginning of 1776, great exertions had been made in Britain to send an overwhelming force into America; and on the 2d of June the alarm guns were fired in the vicinity of Charleston, and expresses sent to the militia officers to hasten to the defence of the capital with the forces under their command. The order was promptly obeyed; and some continental regiments from the neighboring states also arrived. The whole was under the direction of General Lee, who had been appointed commander of all the forces in the southern states, and had under him the continental generals, Armstrong and Howe.

The utmost activity prevailed in Charleston. The citizens, abandoning their usual avocations, employed themselves entirely in putting the town in a respectable state of defence. They pulled down the valuable storehouses on the wharfs, barricaded the streets, and constructed lines of defence along the shore. Relinquishing the pursuits of peaceful industry and commercial gain, they engaged in incessant labor, and prepared for bloody conflicts. The troops, amounting to between five and six thousand men, were stationed in the most advantageous positions. The second and third regular regiments of South Carolina, under Colonels Moultrie and Thomson, were posted on Sullivan's Island

Fig. 78.—William Moultrie, Major General U. S. A.

A regiment commanded by Colonel Gadsden was stationed at Fort Johnson, about three miles below Charleston, on the most northerly point of James's Island, and within point blank shot of the channel. The rest of the troops were posted at Haddrel's Point, along the bay near the town, and at such other places as were thought most proper. Amid all this bustle and preparation, lead for bullets, was extremely scarce, and the windows of Charleston were stripped of their weights, in order to procure a small supply of that necessary article.

While the Americans were thus busily employed, the British exerted themselves with activity. About the middle of February, an armament sailed from he Cove of Cork, under the command of Sir Peter Parker and Earl Cornwalis, to encourage and support the loyalists in the southern provinces.

After a tedious voyage, the greater part of the fleet reached Cape Fear, in North Carolina, on the 3d of May. General Clinton, who had left Boston in December, took the command of the land forces, and issued a proclamation promising pardon to all the inhabitants who laid down their arms; but that proclamation produced no effect. Early in June, the armament, consisting of between forty and fifty vessels, appeared off Charleston bay, and thirty-six of the transports passed the bar, and anchored about three miles from Sullivan's Island. Some hundreds of the troops landed on Long Island, which lies on the west of Sullivan's Island, and which is separated from it by a narrow channel, often fordable. On the 10th of the month the Bristol, a fifty-gun ship, having taken out her guns, got safely over the bar; and on the 25th, the Experiment, a ship of equal force, arrived, and next day passed in the same way. On the part of the British everything was now ready for action. Sir Henry Clinton had nearly 3,000 men under his command. The naval force, under Sir Peter Parker, consisted of the Bristol and Experiment, of fifty guns each; the Active, Acteon, Solebay, and Syren frigates, of twenty-eight guns each; the Friendship, of twenty-two, and the Sphinx, of twenty guns; the Ranger sloop, and Thunder-bomb, of eight guns each.

On the forenoon of the 28th of June, this fleet advanced against the fort on Sullivan's Island, which was defended by Colonel Moultrie, with 344 regular troops, and some militia who volunteered their services on the occasion. The Thunder-bomb began the battle. The Active, Bristol, Experiment, and Solebay, followed boldly to the attack, and a terrible cannonade ensued. The fort returned the fire of the ships slowly, but with deliberate and deadly aim. The contest was carried on during the whole day with unabating fury. All the forces collected at Charleston stood prepared for battle; and both the troops and the numerous spectators beheld the conflict with alternations of hope and fear, which appeared in their countenances and gestures. They knew not how soon the fort might be silenced or passed by, and the attack immediately made upon themselves; but they were resolved to meet the invaders at the water's edge, to dispute every inch of ground, and to prefer death to what they considered to be slavery.

The Sphinx, Acteon, and Syren, were ordered to attack the western extremity of the fort, which was in a very unfinished state; but as they proceeded for that purpose, they got entangled with a shoal, called the Middle Ground. Two of them ran foul of each other: the Acteon stuck fast; the Sphinx and Syren got off, the former with the loss of her bowsprit, the latter with little injury; but that part of the attack completely failed.

It had been concerted, that during the attack by the ships, Sir Henry Clinton, with the troops, should pass the narrow channel which separates Long Island from Sullivan's Island, and assail the fort by land: but this the general found impracticable, for the channel, though commonly fordable, was at that time, by a long prevalence of easterly winds, deeper than usual. The seamen, who found themselves engaged in such a severe conflict, often cast a wistful look toward Long Island, in the hope of seeing Sir Henry Clinton and the troops advancing against the fort; but their hope was disappointed, and the ships and the fort were left to themselves to decide the combat. Although the channel had been fordable, the British troops would have found the passage an arduous enterprise; for Colonel Thomson, with a strong detachment of riflemen, regulars, and militia, was posted on the east end of Sullivan's Island to oppose any attack made in that quarter.

In the course of the day the fire of the fort ceased for a short time, and the British flattered themselves that the guns were abandoned; but the pause was occasioned solely by the want of powder, and when a supply was obtained tho cannonade recommenced as steadily as before. The engagement, which began about eleven o'clock in the forenoon, continued with unabated fury till seven in the evening, when the fire slackened, and about nine entirely ceased on both sides. During the night all the ships, except the Acteon, which was aground, removed about two miles from the island. Next morning the fort fired a few shots at the Acteon, and she at first returned them; but in a short time her crew set her on fire and abandoned her. A party of Americans boarded the burning vessel, seized her colors, fired some of her guns at Commodore Parker, filled three boats with her sails and stores, and then quitted her. She blew up shortly afterward.

FIG. 79.—Sir Peter Parker.

In this obstinate engagement the Americans fought with great gallantry. The loss of the British was 64 killed and 161 wounded. The garrison lost ten men killed and twenty-two wounded. Although the Americans were raw troops, yet they behaved with the steady intrepidity of veterans. In the course of the engagement the flag-staff of the fort was shot away; but the brave Serjeant Jasper leaped down upon the beach, snatched up the flag, fastened it to a sponge staff, and, while the ships were incessantly directing their broadsides upon the fort, he mounted the merlon and deliberately replaced the flag. Next day President Rutledge presented him with a sword, as a testimony of respect for his distinguished valor. Colonel Moultrie, and the officers and troops on Sullivan's island, received the thanks of their country for their bravery; and in honor of the gallant commander, the fort was named Fort Moultrie.

The failure of the attack on Charleston was of great importance to the American cause, and contributed much to the establishment of the popular government. The friends of congress triumphed; and numbers of them fondly imagined that their freedom was achieved. The diffident became bold: the advocates of the irresistibility of British fleets and armies were mortified and silenced; and they. who from interested motives had hitherto been loud in their professions of loy-

FIG. 80.—Capture of the Acteon.

alty, began to alter their tone. The brave defence of Fort Moultrie saved the southern states from the horrors of war for several years.

The government of South Carolina wisely took advantage of the moment of success to conciliate the good-will of their opponents in the province. Cunningham and other adherents of royal power, who for a considerable time had been closely imprisoned, on promising fidelity to their country, were set at freedom and restored to all the privileges of citizens. The repulse of the British fleet at Fort Moultrie left the Americans at liberty to turn their undivided force against the Indians, who had attacked the western frontier of the southern states with all the fury and carnage of savage warfare.

In 1775, when the breach between Great Britain and her colonies was daily becoming wider, one, Stuart, the agent employed in conducting the intercourse between the British authorities and the Cherokees and Creeks, used all his influence to attach the savages to the royal cause, and to inspire them with jealousy and hatred of the Americans. He found little difficulty in persuading them that the Americans, without provocation, had taken up arms against Britain, and were the means of preventing them from receiving their yearly supplies of arms, ammunition, and clothing from the British government.

Moses Kirkland, an inhabitant of South Carolina, whose vanity and ambition had not been sufficiently gratified by his countrymen, was employed by Stuart and other royalists to concert measures with General Gage for a joint attack, by sea and land, on the southern states, while the savages should fall upon their rear. Kirkland was taken on his voyage to Boston, his papers were seized, and the plot was fully discovered. The Americans endeavored to conciliate the good-will of the Indians, but their scanty presents were unsatisfactory, and the savages resolved to take up the hatchet. Accordingly, when the British fleet under Sir Peter Parker appeared in Charleston Bay, the Cherokees invaded the western frontier of the province, marking their course, as usual, with murder and devastation. The speedy retreat of the British fleet left the savages exposed to the vengeance of the Americans, who, in separate divisions, entered their country at different points, from Virginia and Georgia, defeated their warriors, burned their villages, laid waste their corn-fields, and rendered the Cherokees incapable, for the meantime, of giving the settlers further annoyance. Thus, in the south, the Americans at this time triumphed over the arms both of the British and of the Indians.

Intelligence of the rejection of their second petition, and of the cold indifference observed toward Mr. Penn by the British government, reached congress in November, and awakened a strong sensation throughout the provinces. It convinced the colonists in what light their conduct was viewed by the British cabinet, and what they had to expect from the parent state. It appeared obvious that there was no medium between unconditional submission and absolute independence. The colonists saw that they must either abandon everything for which they had hitherto been contending, or assert their freedom by force of arms; and many of them were struck with the incongruity of professing allegiance to a power which their marshalled battalions were opposing with all their might.

That men who had been accustomed to no rigorous subordination, and to few restraints, and many of whom entertained enlarged notions of the extent of their rights and privileges, should, without a struggle, submit to descend from the proud rank of freemen to what they considered the degradation of slavery—that they should abandon everything which they held dear, and become the crouching subjects of a suspected, despised, and oppressed dependancy of the British empire—was scarcely to be expected. The colonists spurned the thought of such degradation. Entirely emancipated from the antiquated notions of prerog

FIG. 81.—Carpenter's Hall, Philadelphia.

ative which guided the councils of the British cabinet, the provincial leaders took the most prompt and efficacious measures in order to give a new bias to the public mind, and to prepare the people for a new state of things. Independence, which, in the earlier stages of the quarrel had only been casually and obliquely hinted, was now made a topic of public discussion. At first it alarmed timid and moderate men, who had a glimpse of the calamitous scenes which such a course would open before them. But the partisans of independence were bold and indefatigable; they labored incessantly in rendering the subject more familiar to the popular ear and mind; the number of their adherents daily increased; and such was the posture of affairs, that many who had hitherto been hostile to a separation from Britain, became friendly to that measure, or ceased to oppose it. They thought circumstances so desperate that matters could not be rendered worse by the attempt, and success might be beneficial.

At that time Thomas Paine, who had shortly before arrived in America from England, published a pamphlet under the title of Common Sense, which had a prodigious influence in promoting the cause of independence; it was widely circulated and eagerly read. To his confident and popular manner of writing, the extraordinary effect of this pamphlet on the public mind may be traced.

The subject was discussed in a variety of ways in the different provinces; in several of them it met with more or less opposition, and the members of congress having received instructions on the point from their respective constituents, it was solemnly taken under consideration on the 4th of July, 1776; and a declaration of independence was unanimously passed at Carpenter's Hall, Philadelphia.

Of the far-famed committee appointed by congress to draft this celebrated instrument, John Adams, Thomas Jefferson, and Robert R. Livingston, were

FIG. 82.—John Adams. From an Anonymous American Portrait

members. So early as the 6th of May preceding, Mr. Adams offered a preliminary resolution to the declaration of independence, which was a recommendation to all colonies to form state governments of their own, based on the happiness and safety of the people. This was soon followed by the resolution of Mr. Lee, of Virginia, declaring that the colonies ought to be free and independent. After full discussion on the 8th and 10th of June, the further consideration was postponed until the 1st of July, and on that day it passed, and a committee was cho-

Fig. 83. Monticello.—Residence of Thomas Jefferson.

sen to prepare the declaration. It was the good fortune of Mr. Jefferson to have been the author of the draught. Jefferson always gave Adams credit of being the ablest advocate of the measure, and Mr. Adams, it is known, was a member of every important committee while he remained in congress. "Mr. Livingston," says his biographer, Dr. Francis, "represented with earnestness the feelings and interest of the people of New York; with Roger Sherman, Benjamin Franklin John Adams, and Thomas Jefferson, his patriotism in that consecrated assembly was universally acknowledged."

This declaration was signed by each of the members of congress, and by it the thirteen United States of North America separated themselves for ever from the crown of Great Britain, and declared themselves an independent people.

This measure entirely altered the aspect of the contest, and gave a clear and definite view of the point at issue between the contending parties. We no longer see colonists complaining and petitioning with arms in their hands, and vigorously resisting an authority which they did not disavow; but a people asserting their independence, and repelling the aggressions of an invading foe

---

CHAPTER V.

We formerly left General Howe at Halifax, and General Washington on his way to New York, where he soon arrived with his army. In that city the struggle between the friends of British domination and of American freedom had been more doubtful than in any other quarter. But by superior numbers and more daring activity, the Americans had gained the ascendency. On his arrival in the city, General Washington endeavored to put it into a posture of defence; and as the British, by means of their fleet, had the command of the waters, he attempted to obstruct the navigation of the East and North rivers, by sinking vessels in the channels. He also raised fortifications at New York and on Long Island, and made every preparation in his power for giving the British army a vigorous reception.

General Howe remained some time at Halifax; but after the recovery of his troops from the fatigue and sickness occasioned by the blockade of Boston, he embarked, sailed to the southward, and on the 2d of July landed, without opposition, on Staten Island, which lies on the coast of New Jersey, and is separated from Long Island by a channel called the *Narrows*. His army amounted to 9,000 men; and his brother, Lord Howe, commander of the British fleet, who had touched at Halifax expecting to find him there, arrived soon afterward, with a reinforcement of about 20,000 men from Britain. Thus General Howe had the command of nearly 30,000 troops, for the purpose of subjugating the American colonies; a more formidable force than had ever before visited those shores. General Washington was ill prepared to meet such a powerful army. His force consisted of about 9,000 men, many of whom were ill-armed, and about 2,000 more without any arms at all; but new levies were daily coming in.

On his arrival, Lord Howe, by a flag, sent ashore to Amboy a circular letter to several of the late royal governors, and a declaration mentioning the powers with which he and his brother the general were invested, and desiring their publication. These papers General Washington transmitted to congress, who ordered them to be published in the newspapers, that the people as they alleged, might be apprized of the nature and extent of the powers of these commission-

Fig. 84.—Liberty and Independence.

ers, with the expectation of whom it had been attempted to amuse and disarm them. General Howe wished to open a correspondence with General Washington, but without acknowledging his official character as commander-in-chief of the American armies; and for this purpose he sent a letter to New York, addressed "George Washington, Esquire." That letter the general refused to receive, because it was not addressed to him in his official character. A second letter was sent, addressed to "George Washington, &c., &c., &c." That also the general declined to receive, but acted in the most polite manner toward Adjutant-General Paterson, the officer who bore it. Congress approved of the conduct of General Washington on the occasion; and ordered that none of their officers should receive letters or messages from the British army unless addressed to them according to their respective ranks. But this dispute about a point of form was soon succeeded by the din of arms and the horrors of active warfare. The American army was not very formidable. In the month of July, indeed, it amounted to about 17,000 men, but a much greater number had been expected; of 15,000 new levies that had been ordered, only 5,000 had arrived in camp. But the quality and equipment of the troops were more discouraging than their numbers: they were ill-disciplined, ill-armed, and little accustomed to that subordination and prompt obedience, which are essential to the efficiency of an army. They were as deficient in ammunition as in armor; and were distracted by jealousies, prejudices, and animosities.

This raw and ill-armed multitude was opposed to 30,000 troops, many of them veterans, all of them excellently equipped, and provided with a fine train of artillery. The Americans soon found that all their endeavors to obstruct the navigation of the rivers were ineffectual; for several British ships of war passed up the North river, without receiving any considerable damage from a heavy cannonade directed against them from the shore.

The American army was posted partly at New York, and partly on Long Island. General Greene commanded in the latter place; but that officer being taken ill, General Sullivan was appointed in his room. General Howe, having collected his troops on Staten Island, and finding himself sufficiently strong to commence active operations, on the 22d of August crossed the Narrows without opposition, and landed on Long Island, between two small towns, Utrecht and Gravesend.

The American division on the island, about 11,000 strong, occupied a fortified camp at Brooklyn, on a peninsula, opposite New York. Their right flank was covered by a marsh, which extended to the East river near Mill Creek; their left, by an elbow of the river named Wallabout Bay. Across the peninsula, from Mill creek to Wallabout Bay, the Americans had thrown up entrenchments, secured by abattis, or felled trees with their tops turned outward, and flanked by strong redoubts. In their rear was the East river, about 1,300 yards wide, separating them from New York. In front of the fortified camp, and at some distance from it, a woody ridge obliquely intersected the island; and through that ridge there are passages by three different defiles: one at the southern extremity near the Narrows; another about the middle, on the Flatbush road; and a third near the northeast extremity of the hills on the Bedford road. Those defiles General Greene had carefully examined; and as it was evident that the British army must debark on the farther side of the ridge, he resolved to dispute the passage of the defiles. General Sullivan, who succeeded to the command on the illness of General Greene, was not equally sensible of the importance of those passes. On the landing of the British, however, he sent strong detachments to guard the passes near the Narrows, and on the Flatbush road; but the more distant pass he did not duly attend to, merely sending an officer with a party to observe it, and give notice if the enemy should appear

Fig. 85.—New York from Long Island.

there. That was no adequate precaution for the security of the pass; and the officer appointed to watch it discharged his duty in the most slovenly manner.

General Howe soon learned that there would be little difficulty in marching by the most distant defile, and turning the left of the Americans.

At half past two o'clock, passing clouds obscured the harvest-moon; the night waxed gloomy, and the air chill. Suddenly, a sharp report of musketry, in the direction of Yellow Hook, alarmed the American camp. It was a startling sound, in the stillness of the morning, and the troops sprang to their arms, as the *reveillé* summoned each man to his duty. Many a brave lad awoke from dreams of peaceful home, of the father-house, and its loved inmates, where, in presence of the glad crops, the warlike sounds that lulled him to sleep seemed but as dream-notes, and the danger he anticipated one that was passed. He had obeyed the watchward of liberty, which called him to the hardships of war; but his heart told him life was sweet, and his cottage home a paradise. The drum rattled in his ear, and aroused him to the stern reality he feared not, courted not.

Ere the alarm ceased beating, the men had seized their muskets. Word had been passed from the remote pickets on the coast, that the enemy were approaching. Lord Stirling was instantly directed by General Putnam to march with the two nearest regiments to their rencounter. These proved to be the Pennsylvania and Maryland troops, under Colonels Haslet and Smallwood; with whom, proceeding over the uneven ground in the direction of the attack, he found himself on the road to the Narrows, toward daybreak, and soon met Colonel Altee with his Delaware regiment, retiring before the British, with the pickets to whose aid they had advanced. Stationing this officer on the left of the road by which the enemy were approaching, Lord Stirling formed his two regiments along an advantageous ridge, ascending from the road to a piece of wood on the top of a hill. The British were received with two or three warm rounds by the Delawares, who, as their ground became untenable, withdrew to a wood on Lord Stirling's left, where they formed.

The assailants, now in sight, proved to be two brigades, of four regiments each, under the command of General Grant. They proceeded to occupy the elevation opposite Lord Stirling, at a distance of three hundred yards. Their light troops came one hundred and fifty yards nearer, with a view to gain possession of a superior eminence on his left. As they marched up this hill, they were met by the deadly fire of Kichline's rifle corps, who had just reached the ground in time to protect this important point, and who mowed them down as fast as they appeared. The Americans brought up two field-pieces to oppose the *ten* of their opponents. A sharp cannonade ensued and was vigorously sustained on both sides, to a late hour; until when let us shift the scene.

While the Americans were occupied, as we have seen, on the previous evening, there was, about dusk, an unusual stir among the troops in the British right wing. The regiments already at Flatlands, under Earl Percy, were joined at nightfall by those under Lord Cornwallis and General Clinton, who left the Hessians masters at Flatbush. The dark forms of the tall soldiery, the play of their muskets in the moonlight, the whispered order and firm tread of discipline, all announced some sudden or adventurous movement. One by one the companies filed off in the direction of New Lots, and before night was far advanced, Flatlands was deserted. As they moved farther and farther away from the American lines, the furrows became relaxed on the brows of the British commanders, and toward daybreak, half a triumph already gleamed in the eye of Clinton, who led the van.

Shortly after daylight, the Hessians at Flatbush opened a moderate cannonade upon General Sullivan, who, with a strong detachment, had advanced on the

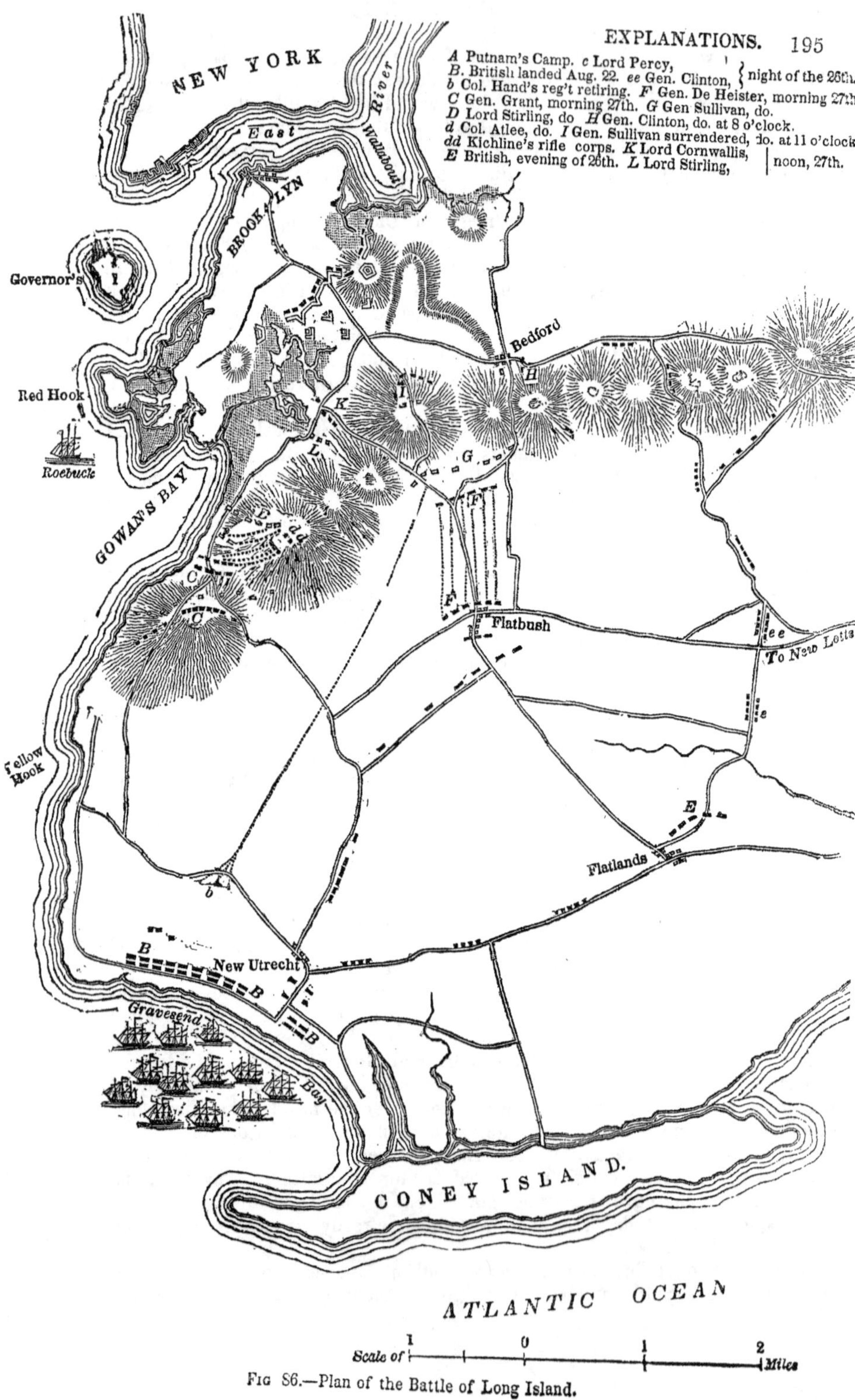

FIG. 86.—Plan of the Battle of Long Island.

direct road from Brooklyn thither, and now occupied the breastworks thrown up by General Greene, for the defence of this important pass. Colonels Miles and Williams were strongly posted on the Bedford road. At half past eight, Count Donop was detached to attack the hill, by General De Heister, who soon followed with the centre of the army.

With levelled pieces and eyes fixed on the enemy, the Americans stood firm on their vantage ground, nerved for the assault, and prepared to enact a second drama of Bunker's Hill. From behind breastwork and tree, soldier and rifleman looked down upon the ascending foe with a feeling of conscious security, when lo ! a report of artillery, in the rear of their left, flew with its own velocity along the line. A second volley revealed to them, with fearful truth, that the enemy had turned their left flank, and placed them between two fires. Horror, dismay, confusion, ensued ! The advancing Hessians were no longer faced by the whole band stationed to oppose them; and vain the efforts of General Sullivan to rally the dispersing continentals, who hastened to regain the camp, while there yet was time. It was, alas, too late ! As regiment after regiment emerged from the wood, they encountered the bayonets of the British, and all retreat was cut off. Driven back into the forest, after desperate efforts to cleave their way through the close ranks of the enemy, they were met by the Hessians, a part of whom were at the same time detached toward Bedford, in which quarter the cannon of Clinton announced that he also was attacking the American rear. The British pushed their line beyond the Flatbush road, and when our brave troops found their only outlet was through the enemy, skirmish after skirmish ensued in which they displayed signal bravery. Many forced their way through the camp, some escaped into the woods, and many were slain. Colonel Parry was shot through the head while encouraging his men.

Can the reader imagine the disastrous consequences of this surprise to the Americans, when, hemmed in by the surpassing numbers and co-operating wings of the British, they saw inevitable death or capture on every side ! Here, striking again through the wood, and lured by an enticing path, which promised safety, they rushed from its shelter upon the drawn sabres of the enemy ; there, retiring to its recesses before a superior force, they fell upon the levelled muskets of the Hessians ; bullets and balls sought victims in every direction ; and many a brave soldier sank to die beneath the tall forest tree, offering up with his parting breath, a prayer for his country, consecrated by his life-blood.

Against the hottest of the enemy's fire, General Sullivan, on the heights above Flatbush, made a brave resistance for three hours. Here the slaughter was thickest on the side of the assailants. Fairly covered by the imperfect entrenchment, the Americans poured many a deadly volley upon the approaching foe.

Leaving Generals Clinton and Percy to intercept the Americans in this quarter, Lord Cornwallis proceeded toward the scene of General Grant's engagement with Lord Stirling. We left this gallant officer bravely opposing a superior force. He continued the resistance until eleven o'clock, when, hearing a sharp firing in the direction of Brooklyn, it flashed upon him that the British were getting between him and the American lines. Discovering the position of Lord Cornwallis, he instantly saw that unless they forded the creek near the Yellow Mills, the troops under him must all become prisoners. The reader will see that he had some distance to gain before this could be effected. Hastening back, he found the enemy much stronger than he anticipated ; and, that his main body might escape, he determined in person to attack Lord Cornwallis, who was posted at a house near the upper mill. This movement he performed with the utmost gallantry, leading half of Smallwood's regiment five or six several times to the charge, and nearly dislodging the British commander, who, but for the arrival of large reinforcements, would have been driven from his station. This band of four hundred, composed, say the British accounts, of youths, the flower of the best families in Maryland, sustained severe loss. But the object was attained, and the regiments, whose retreat it was designed to favor, effected their escape over marsh and creek, with the loss of a single man drowned. In his official report, Lord Howe speaks of numbers who perished in crossing the inlet. But this is incorrect. The self-devoted heroes of this exploit were surrounded, and made prisoners of war.

We may readily conceive with what feelings their brethren in the camp beheld the undeserved ill fortune of the troops engaged in the action. General Putnam, a warrior of the true stamp, constrained to remain within the fortifications, and so little prepared for the events of the day, as to be only able, where the enemy appeared, to detach troops to meet them, saw with dismay the manœuvre which made them masters of the field. His efforts had all along been directed to General Grant's motions. For the defence in front, he relied on General Sullivan to provide, and great was his surprise, on seeing the enemy turn that officer's flank. As the engagement between Lord Stirling and General Grant grew warmer, his attention was attracted by the broadside which the British frigate Roebuck opened upon the Redhook battery in his rear. Too late aware of his mistake, he was compelled to await the issue.

At this juncture, General Washington reached the lines, and beheld, with infinite grief, the discomfiture of his beloved troops. Wringing his hands, he is said, when he saw no aid could reach them, to have given vent to the keenest anguish. From the height he stood upon, the movements of both parties were revealed to him. Here, was seen Lord Stirling, gallantly attacking Cornwallis; there, a troop of Americans, escaping with thinned numbers through the British ranks, were pursued to the very entrenchments. By the creek, soldiers plunging into the unknown depths of its waters, or struggling through the miry bog, were fired upon by the foe; toward Flatbush, the Hessians and British were combining to enfold, in a still narrower circle, the few and undaunted continentals.

Lest the foregoing imperfect description should have left obscure some of the details of this affair, let us briefly recapitulate its successive disasters. We have supposed the reader to be, where all would have chosen to stand on that occasion, on the American side. A glance at the motions of the British, will show how admirably their manœuvres were planned and executed. The success of the concerted movement was insured by the unforeseen malady of General Greene. All the passes to Brooklyn were defended, save one; and it was by this that the troops, which decided the fortunes of the day, and were the same we left filing off from Flatland to New-Lots, on the previous night, turned the American flank. The road from Jamaica to Bedford was left unprotected; the enemy early ascertained this fact; and, to enable them to profit by our neglect, General Grant's advance, which was a diversion, had been devised. The fleet and General de Heister co-operated with him in this manœuvre. General Putnam, taking this feint for a *bonafide* attack, was deceived; and the Americans were entrapped by forces superior in discipline, in tactics, in numbers, in good fortune, but not in courage; for though eleven hundred were either killed or taken, near four thousand fought their way back to the camp.

To the absence of General Greene, who had studied, and would doubtless have guarded, all the approaches to the camp, and to the want of a general commanding officer throughout the day, may this disaster be attributed. General Putnam could not leave his lines, and the double care of New York and Long Island devolved upon the commander-in-chief. General Woodhull, who had been ordered to guard the road from Bedford to Jamaica, with the Long Island militia, remained at Jamaica. The neglect which lost us the day, cost him his life. Riding home, after disbanding the volunteers under his command, he was captured by the British, and imediately cut to pieces, on his refusing to say "God save the king."

Impartiality must award high praise, on this occasion, to the bravery of the enemy's troops, who followed so hotly in pursuit, that they were with difficulty withheld from attacking the American trenches. At night, the patriots within them told their missing brethren; and when their loss became known, and uncertainty veiled the fate of the absent ones, gloom and despondency pervaded the camp. The victorious British, on the contrary, hastened to secure the ground they had gained, and flushed with victory, passed the night in exultation.

On the twenty-eighth, a violent rain kept the two armies in their respective encampments. That night the enemy broke ground within about six hundred yards of Fort Greene, and on the following day were busily engaged in throwing up entrenchments. Their main force was advancing, by slow but sure approaches, to besiege the American fortifications, and their superior artillery would doubtless soon silence our batteries. The advanced sentinel of the British army was surprised, on the morning of the thirtieth, by the unwonted stillness within the American lines. Calling a comrade or two around him, they proceeded to reconnoitre. Emboldened by the silence, they crept near the embankment, and cautiously peeping into our camp, perceived not a vestige of the army to whose challenges they had listened the night before. The alarm was given, and the party who first rushed in, to take possession of the works, saw in the midstream, out of gun-shot, and filled with well-pleased Americans, the last of the barges which had borne their comrades across the waters that night. Beyond it, in a small boat, there sat an American officer, of calm and dignified mien. On his pale countenance the anxious muscles were relaxing into a heavenly smile. This bark bore Cesar and his fortunes; and a prayer seemed to escape the lips of Washington, as a glance at the distant shore told him the American army was beyond the reach of danger.

Nine thousand men with all their stores and ammunitions, crossed the East river during the night, unperceived by the enemy. For four-and-twenty hours previous, the commander-in-chief had not left the saddle. The immediate embarcation of the troops was under the direction of General McDougall, to whose vigilant activity high praise is due.

The raw troops of the Americans were easily affected by a check; and their spirits were much depressed by the defeat on Long Island; which disappointed their hopes, and sunk them almost into a state of despondency. Indeed, at that time, the army was in an alarming condition. In its zeal for liberty, the assembly of Massachusetts Bay had granted the soldiers the choice of their own officers; and the consequence was, that those troops were disorderly. The militia had no conception of military subordination, were often very inefficient in the field, and frequently withdrew from the service at a most critical moment. Besides, the army was agitated by provincial jealousies and quarrels. The errors in the constitution of the American military force were now evident to every man of observation; but it was more easy to perceive than to rectify them.

After the battle of Brooklyn, General Sullivan was despatched, at his own request, to Philadelphia, with a verbal communication from Lord Howe to congress, expressing a wish to hold a conference with some of the members, as private gentlemen of influence in the country. General Sullivan was instructed to inform Lord Howe that congress, being the representatives of the free and independent states of America, could not, with propriety, send any of their members to confer with him in their private characters; but that, ever desirous of establishing peace upon reasonable terms, they would send a committee of their body to learn the authority with which he was invested, to hear what propositions he had to make, and to report. On the 6th of September, they chose, as their committee, Benjamin Franklin, John Adams, and Edward Rutledge. This committee met Lord Howe on Staten Island, opposite Amboy, on the 14th of the same month. He received them politely, but the conference proved fruitless; for the committee explicitly informed his lordship, that neither they, nor the congress which sent them, had authority to treat in any other capacity than as *independent states.* On that subject Lord Howe had no instructions: the conference, of course, soon came to an end; and the committee reported to congress, that, in their opinion, Lord Howe's commission contained no other powers than granting pardon, and receiving the colonies under the protection of the British government, on their submission.

When the hope of an amicable accommodation vanished, General Howe, who had already taken possession of the islands lying in the sound between New York, Long Island, and the shore of Connecticut, resumed his military operations. The British army was on Long Island, and the Americans about New York separated from each other by the East river. The city of New York stands on the southeast end of an island, anciently named Manhattan, but now called by the name of the city. The Hudson, or North river, bounds it on the southwest. It is about fifteen miles long, and only two broad. After a brisk cannonade between the British batteries on Long Island and those of the Americans about New York, General Howe resolved to transport his army into the island of New York; and accordingly, on the 15th of September, General Sir Henry Clinton, with 4,000 men, crossed the East river in flat-bottomed boats, landed at Kipp's bay, under cover of the fire of some ships-of-war, and, without opposition, took post on some high ground, now called Bloomingdale, about five miles above New York. The American detachment appointed to defend the place, terrified by the cannonade of the ships, fled on the approach of the enemy, without firing a shot. General Washington met the fugitives on the road, drew his sword, threatened, and endeavored to rally them: but his efforts were ineffectual; and his attendants seized the reins of his horse, and turned him away from the enemy. The rest of the British army soon followed General Clinton's detachment, and, after some slight skirmishing, took possession of New York, the American parties retreating to their main body posted at Harlem, about nine miles distant.

Some miles in front of New York, the British army formed a camp quite across the island, having its flanks covered by ships-of-war, which the Americans attempted, in vain, to destroy by fire-ships. The American army, amounting to about 23,000 men, ill-provided, however, and ill-disciplined, was posted on advantageous ground, opposite to it, but at some distance. On the morning of the 16th of September, General Washington sent a detachment into a wood, in front of the left of the British line. General Howe despatched three companies of light infantry to dislodge them. A sharp conflict ensued; each party was reinforced; a severe firing was for some time kept up; and a number of men fell on each side. The Americans maintained their ground; and this trifling circumstance greatly raised their depressed spirits. This encounter demonstrated the value of brave and steady officers; for on the preceding day, at the landing of the British, the officers had been the first who ran; but, on the present occasion, the officers did their duty, and the troops steadily maintained their post.

On the 21st of September, a destructive fire broke out in New York, and reduced almost a fourth part of the city to ashes. It began in a dram shop, near the river, about one o'clock in the morning; and, as everything was dry, and the houses covered with shingles instead of tiles or slates, the flames spread rapidly, and raged with great fury. Many of the citizens had removed from the

FIG. 87.—East River, from New York in 1834

town before the entrance of the British, the pumps and fire-engines were in bad order, and a brisk south wind fanned the flame. Two regiments of soldiers and many men from the fleet were employed to arrest the progress of the devouring element, and at length succeeded in extinguishing the fire, but not till it had consumed about 1,000 houses.

Probably the fire was occasioned by the inconsiderate revelry of the British sailors, who had been permitted to regale themselves on shore

The Americans were strongly posted toward the northern extremity of the island of New York. To attack them in front was unadvisable, but General Howe resolved to make an attempt on their rear, or to hem them in on the island without the possibility of escape. For this purpose, leaving three brigades of British and one of Hessian troops to guard New York, early in the morning of the 12th of October he embarked the rest of the army in flat-bottomed boats, and, in the course of the same morning, landed at Thog's Neck, in the county of West Chester. But finding that place unsuitable to his purpose, he again embarked, proceeded to the mouth of Hutchinson's river, and landed there ; when the troops had a skirmish with an American party, and succeeded in dislodging them from a narrow pass of which they had taken possession.

On the 21st of October, the main body of the British army marched to New Rochelle, lying on the sound which separates Long Island from Connecticut There the second division of foreign troops, consisting of upward of 5,000 Hessians and Waldeckers, under General Knyphausen, with about 2,000 baggage-horses, which had arrived in a fleet of seventy-two sail, joined General Howe.

General Washington's first intention was to maintain his position on the island of New York ; but General Lee, in whose military talents and experience the army had great confidence, on joining the army after the successful defence of Charleston, strongly remonstrated against that resolution, asserting that the British, by a chain of works, would completely hem in the Americans, and compel them to surrender, even without a battle. His representations induced General Washington, with the consent of a council of war, to alter his plan, and move his army from Kingsbridge to White Plains, on the left of his present position, maintaining a line parallel to that in which the British army was marching, and separated from it by the river Bronx. On the 26th of October, the main body of the American army, consisting of about 17,000 ill-disciplined men, took possession of a slightly fortified camp on the east side of the Bronx, which an advanced detachment had been employed in preparing. A bend in the river covered their right flank, and General Washington posted a body of about 1,600 men, under General McDougall, on a hill in a line with his right wing, but separated from it by the Bronx.

The British general having collected his troops, brought forward his artillery with considerable difficulty ; and having got everything ready for active operations, advanced in two columns toward the American camp. He accompanied the left column in person ; General Clinton led the right. A distant cannonade began, with little effect on either side. The detachment on the hill, under Mc Dougall, attracted the notice of General Howe, and he resolved to dislodge it. He ordered General Leslie, with the second brigade of British troops, and Colonel Donop, with the Hessian grenadiers, on that service. On their advance, the American militia fled with precipitation ; but about 600 regulars, who were under McDougall, vigorously defended themselves for some time. They were compelled, however, to retreat, and the British took possession of the hill ; but they were at too great a distance to be able to annoy any part of the American line.

Three days afterward, General Howe, having received reinforcements from New York and other quarters, resolved to attack the American camp. But a heavy rain during the whole night rendered the ground so slippery, that in the morning it would have been very difficult to ascend the acclivity of the hills on which the Americans were posted; and therefore it was deemed unadvisable to make the attempt.

General Washington, apprehensive of an attack, and doubtful of the issue on the ground which he then occupied, early in the morning of the 1st of November left his camp, retired toward North Castle, and took a strong position behind the river Croton. General Howe, perceiving that it was the purpose of his adversary to avoid a general engagement, and finding it out of his power to force a battle, in such a country, unless in very disadvantageous circumstances, ceased to pursue the American army. He well knew that soon it would be almost dissolved, on the expiration of the term for which many of the men had engaged to serve; and therefore he turned his attention to the reduction of Forts Washington and Lee; the first on the island of New York, not far from Kingsbridge and the other on the Jersey side of the North river, nearly opposite the former. The Americans had flattered themselves, that by means of these two forts they would be able to command the navigation of the North river; but that had proved an illusion, as several British vessels had passed the forts without sustaining any injury from their fire. It had been debated in an American council of war, whether, in the present posture of their affairs, those two places ought to be retained. General Lee was decidedly of opinion that they ought to be abandoned; but General Greene urged the propriety of defending them, and his opinion prevailed.

Fig. 88.—Fort Washington.

Fort Washington was garrisoned by about 3,000 men, under the command of Colonel Magaw, who thought he could defend the place till about the end of December. On the 15th of November, General Sir William Howe summoned the garrison to surrender, on pain of being put to the sword; but received for answer, that they would defend themselves to the last extremity. Early next morning, a vigorous attack was begun by the British and Hessian troops, in four divisions; and, after a severe engagement, in which the assailants lost about 1,000 men in killed and wounded, Colonel Magaw was compelled to surrender as prisoners-of-war, himself and his garrison, amounting to two thousand six hundred men, inclusive of the country militia. The fall of Fort Washington was a heavy blow to the infant republic, and greatly discouraged its raw and disorderly army.

Fort Lee, on the Jersey side of the river, nearly opposite to Fort Washington, next engaged the attention of the British general. That fort stood on a slip of land, about ten miles long, lying between the Hudson and the Hackensack, and English Neighborhood. Early on the morning of the 18th of November, Earl Cornwallis, with a strong detachment, in flat-bottomed boats, passed through the communication between the East and North rivers, by Kingsbridge, with the intention of cutting off the retreat of the troops in Fort Lee. General Greene, however, who commanded in those parts, being apprized of his movement, by a rapid march escaped with the main body of the garrison, but left behind some stragglers, and also his heavy artillery and baggage, which fell into the hands of the British. Thus the Americans were driven, with considerable loss, from the island of New York, and from the Jersey bank of the North river.

On the 12th of November, General Washington had crossed the North river with part of his army, and taken a position not far from Fort Lee, having left upward of 7,000 men at North Castle, under the command of General Lee. At that time, the American army was in a critical and alarming state. It was composed chiefly of militia and of men engaged for a short time only. The term of service of many of them was about to expire; and the republican military force was on the point of dissolution, in the presence of a well-disciplined, well-appointed, and victorious enemy.

In that threatening posture of public affairs, General Washington applied to the state of Massachusetts for 4,000 new militia; and General Lee besought the militia under his command to remain for a few days after their term of service was expired. But the application of the commander-in-chief was not promptly answered; and the earnest entreaties of General Lee were almost utterly disregarded.

On the fall of Forts Washington and Lee, General Washington, with his little army, of about 3,000 effective men, ill-armed, worse clad, and almost without tents, blankets, or utensils for cooking their provisions, took a position behind the Hackensack. His army consisted chiefly of the garrison of Fort Lee, which had been obliged to evacuate that place with so much precipitation as to leave behind them the tents and most of the articles of comfort and accommodation in their possession. But although General Washington made a show of resistance by occupying the line of the Hackensack, yet he was sensible of his inability to dispute the passage of that river; he therefore retreated to Newark. There he remained some days, making the most earnest applications in every quarter for reinforcements, and pressing General Lee to hasten his march to the southward and join him.

On the advance of Earl Cornwallis, General Washington abandoned Newark, and retreated to New Brunswick, a small village on the Raritan. While there, the term of service of a number of his troops expired, and he had the mortification to see them abandon him. From New Brunswick the Americans retreated to Trenton. There General Washington received a reinforcement of about 2,000 men from Pennsylvania. He had taken the precaution of collecting and guarding all the boats on the Delaware from Philadelphia for seventy miles higher up the river. He sent his sick to Philadelphia, and his heavy artillery and baggage across the Delaware. Having taken these precautionary measures, and being somewhat encouraged by the reinforcements which he had received, he halted some time at Trenton, and even began to advance toward Princeton; but being informed that Earl Cornwallis, strongly reinforced, was marching against him, he was obliged to seek refuge behind the great river Delaware. On the 8th of December he accomplished the passage at Trenton Ferry, the van of the British army making its appearance just as his rear-guard had crossed.

General Washington was careful to secure all the boats on the south side of the river, and to guard all those places where it was probable that the British army might attempt to pass; so that his feeble army was secured from the danger of an immediate attack. The British troops made demonstrations of an intention to cross the river, and detachments were stationed to oppose them; but the attempt was not seriously made. In this situation the American commander anxiously waited for reinforcements, and sent some parties over the river to observe and annoy the enemy.

While General Washington was retreating through the Jerseys, he earnestly desired General Lee, who had been left in command of the division of the army at North Castle, to hasten his march to the Delaware and join the main army. But that officer, notwithstanding the critical nature of the case, and the pressing orders of his commander, was in no haste to obey. He marched slowly to the southward, at the head of about 3,000 men; and his sluggish movements and unwary conduct proved fatal to his own personal liberty, and excited a lively sensation throughout America. He lay carelessly without a guard, and at some distance from his troops, at Baskenridge, in Morris county, where, on the 13th of December, Colonel Harcourt, who, with a small detachment of light horse, had been sent to observe the movements of that division of the American army, by a gallant act of partisan warfare, made him prisoner, and conveyed him rapidly to New York. For some time he was closely confined, and considered not as a prisoner-of-war, but as a deserter from the British army. The capture of General Lee was regarded as a great misfortune by the Americans; for at that time he enjoyed, in a high degree, the esteem and confidence of the friends of congress; on the other hand, the British exulted in his captivity, as equal to a signal victory, declaring that "they had taken the American palladium."

General Sullivan, who on the 4th of September had been exchanged for General Prescott, when Lord Stirling also had been exchanged for General McDonald, succeeded to the command of Lee's division, and soon conducted it across the Delaware to General Washington's army. At the same time General Gates, with part of the army of Canada, arrived in camp. But even after the junction of those troops, and a number of militia of Pennsylvania, General Washington's force did not exceed 5,000 men; for though many had joined the army, yet not a few were daily leaving it; and of those who remained, the greater part were raw troops, ill-provided, and all of them dispirited by defeat.

General Howe, with an army of 27,000 men, completely armed and disciplined, well-provided, and flushed with success, lay on the opposite side of the Delaware; stretching from New Brunswick to the vicinity of Philadelphia, and ready, it was believed, to pass over as soon as the severity of the winter was set in, and the river completely frozen. To the Americans this was the most gloomy period of the contest; and their affairs appeared in a very hopeless condition. To deepen the gloom of this period, so alarming to the Americans, and to confirm the confidence of the British army, General Clinton, with two brigades of British and two of Hessian troops, escorted by a squadron of men-of-war under Sir Peter Parker, was sent against Rhode Island. The American force, incapable of making any effectual resistance, abandoned the island on General Clinton's approach; and on the day that General Washington crossed the Delaware, he took possession of it without opposition or loss. At the same time the British fleet blocked up Commodore Hopkins' squadron, and a number of privateers at Providence.

When the American army retreated through the Jerseys, dejection took possession of the public mind. General Washington called on the militia of that state to take the field; but his call was not obeyed. Fear triumphed over patriotism; and every one was more anxious to provide for his personal safety than to support the national cause.

On the 30th of November, when the sun of American independence seemed fast setting, Lord Howe and the general issued a proclamation, promising pardon to those who should return to their allegiance, and subscribe a suitable obligation. Many took advantage of the proclamation, and submitted to the British government; and among these were all the richer inhabitants of the province, with a few exceptions. It was the middle class chiefly that remained steadfast in the day of trial and adversity. The consequence of this apathy, fear, and defection, was the retreat of General Washington across the Delaware, at the head of only 2,000 men; and in a day or two afterward even that small number was considerably diminished.

On the 12th of December, congress quitted Philadelphia and retired to Baltimore, in Maryland. But under all the reverses which their cause had suffered, and in the most unpromising state of their affairs, they manifested an unshaken firmness. Their energy did not forsake them; there was no humiliation in their attitude, no despondency in their language, and no inactivity in their operations. Their fortitude was well supported by their brave, sagacious, and persevering commander-in-chief.

At first, the Americans fondly hoped that the war would not be of long duration; and, influenced partly by that deceitful expectation, and more perhaps by a wish not to discourage their adherents, congress had enlisted their soldiers for a year only. That error in their military system, which gave them much uneasiness, and exposed them to no small danger in the course of the war, now began to be severely felt, by the almost total dissolution of their army, in the presence of a victorious enemy. In order to remedy that defect in future, congress resolved that their soldiers should be bound to serve for three years, or during the continuance of the war; and, on this principle, they ordered a new army of eighty-eight battalions to be raised, each state furnishing its due proportion. Virginia and Massachusetts were each to raise fifteen battalions; Pennsylvania, twelve; North Carolina, nine; South Carolina, six; Connecticut and Maryland, eight each; Rhode Island, two; Delaware and Georgia, one each; New Hampshire, three; New York and the Jerseys, being partly in possession of the enemy, were rated at only four battalions each. The appointment of officers in the battalions, and the filling up of vacancies, except in the case of general officers, was left to the several provincial governments.

But the first ebullition of popular patriotism had evaporated; and, while all clamored about freedom, each wished to make as few sacrifices as possible in order to obtain it. Of this state of things congress were fully sensible, and therefore endeavored to overcome the general reluctance to the service, by present bounties and the prospect of future rewards. To induce men to enlist and fill up the battalions that had been ordered, congress promised a bounty of twenty dollars to each soldier, and an allotment of land, at the end of the war, to all who survived, and to the families of such as had fallen in the service. The allotments were proportioned to the rank of the individuals: a common soldier was to have 100 acres; an ensign, 150; a lieutenant, 200; a major, 400; a lieutenant-colonel, 450; and a colonel, 500. They who enlisted for three years only were not entitled to an allotment. No person was permitted to purchase another's allotment, which was to remain secure to him as a means of decent subsistence, when the public should no longer need his professional services.

Congress also offered a bounty to such foreign troops in British pay as should desert, and enlist under the republican banners: to a colonel, 1000 acres of land; to a lieutenant-colonel, 800; to a major, 600; to a captain, 400; to a lieutenant, 300; to an ensign, 200; and to every non-commissioned soldier, 100. This measure was intended as a counterpoise to the promise of large grants of vacant land, at the close of the troubles, made by the British government to the highland emigrants, and other new troops raised in America, as a reward for their loyalty and zeal in the reduction of the country. In order to provide for the maintenance of their army, congress resolved to borrow five millons of dollars, and pledged the faith of the United States for the payment of principal and interest.

Although the continental governments of Europe felt no good-will toward the progress of liberty, and took no interest in the happiness of mankind; yet, from jealousy of the power and glory of Britain, they looked on the cause of the Americans with no unfavorable eye. Some indirect communications appear to have taken place between the cabinet of Versailles and congress; and, toward the end of September, congress elected Benjamin Franklin, Silas Deane, and Arthur Lee, their commissioners to the court of France, with powers to enter into a treaty with the French king: they sailed for France soon afterward. At this time also commissioners were sent to Canada to induce the inhabitants of that province to join the Americans, and Charles Carroll went as one of them but returned without success.

FIG. 89.—Charles Carroll, of Carrollton.

In the course of the campaign, General Washington had severely felt the want of cavalry, and of artillerymen and engineers. Therefore congress having assembled according to adjournment, at Baltimore on the 20th of December, resolved that General Washington shall be, and hereby is, vested with full, ample, and complete powers to raise and collect together, in the most speedy and effectual manner, from any or all of these United States, sixteen battalions of infantry, in addition to those already voted; and to appoint officers for the said battalions of infantry; to raise, officer, and equip 3,000 light horse, three regiments of artillery, and a corps of engineers, and to establish their pay; to apply to any of the states for such aid of the militia as he shall judge necessary; to form such magazines of provisions, and in such places as he shall think proper, to displace and appoint all officers under the rank of brigadier-general, and to fill up all vacancies in every other department in the American army; to take, wherever he may be, whatever he may want for the use of the army, if the inhabitants will not sell it, allowing a reasonable price for the same; to arrest and confine persons who refuse to take the continental currency; and that these powers be vested in General Washington for the period of six months, unless sooner determined by congress. At the same time, congress turned its attention toward the Canadian frontier, and ordered works to be constructed for the security of the lakes George and Champlain.

While active in using all means for internal security and defence, congress were not careless of foreign relations. They resolved, without delay, to send commissioners to the courts of Vienna, Spain, Prussia, and the grand duke of Tuscany, to assure those powers that the United States were determined to maintain their independence; to solicit the friendly aid of those courts, or their good offices in preventing any more foreigners in the pay of Great Britain from being sent against the states, and in procuring the recall of those that had been already sent.

Richard Stockton, a member of congress, had been made prisoner by the British, and thrown into a common jail. Congress was indignant at the treatment he received, and ordered General Washington to open a correspondence on the subject with General Howe, that it might be ascertained in what manner prisoners were to be treated, as the Americans were determined to retaliate on British prisoners any ill-usage which their adherents who fell into the hands of the British might meet with.

Congress also made a solemn and animated appeal to all the provinces of the union. They reminded the people of their grounds of complaint against the British government, and of the treatment which they had received from it. They assured them that nothing less than absolute submission would satisfy their enemies; and emphatically asked them whether they chose resistance or slavery. The appeal produced the desired effect, and the people prepared to continue the struggle with renewed vigor.

The British parliament met on the 26th of October, 1775, and was opened by a speech from the throne, in which the king set forth that he had it in contemplation to engage some foreign troops which had been offered him to serve in America; that it was necessary to compel the colonists to submission, but that he would be ready to receive them with tenderness and mercy, on their becoming sensible of their error. Ministry moved an address in full accordance with the speech, which was strenuously resisted by the opponents of the administration in both houses of parliament, and keen debates ensued; but ministry carried their point by large majorities, and the far greater number of the people fully concurred in the war.

The employment of foreign mercenaries against the colonists was strongly opposed in parliament; but the measure was adopted, which awakened a lively sensation in the provinces, where it was considered as an avowal that the mother country had entirely shaken off the remembrance of their propinquity, and indulged a spirit of rancorous hostility against them. Hence, numbers who had hitherto been moderate in their political sentiments, became steady adherents of the republican cause; while they who had formerly been refractory, became more determined in their opposition to the measures of the British government.

The second petition of congress, to which no answer had been returned, was brought under the notice of parliament, and Mr. Penn, formerly governor of Pennsylvania, was examined at the bar of the house of lords; but his examination was followed by no conciliatory results. About that time Mr. Edmund Burke, an eloquent member of parliament under the banners of the opposition, introduced into the house of commons his conciliatory bill, which proposed to renounce the exercise of taxation in the colonies, without entering on the consideration of the question of right; reserving, however, to Great Britain, the power of levying commercial duties, to be applied to those purposes which the general assembly of each province should judge most salutary and beneficial. The bill also proposed the repeal of all the laws complained of by the colonists and the passing an immediate act of amnesty. But this, like every other con ciliatory proposition, was unsuccessful.

Fig. 90.—Edmund Burke.

The rejection of Mr. Burke's bill was followed by the introduction of one by ministry, prohibiting all intercourse with the colonies, which, after a keen opposition, passed both houses of parliament, and received the royal sanction.

CHAPTER VI.

When General Washington crossed the Delaware, winter was fast setting in, and it was no part of General Howe's plan to carry on military operations during that inclement season of the year. Fearless of a feeble enemy, whom he had easily driven before him, and whom he confidently expected soon to annihilate, he cantoned his troops rather with a view to the convenient resumption of their march, than with any regard to security against a fugitive foe. As he entertained not the slightest apprehension of an attack, he paid little attention to the arrangement of his several posts for the purpose of mutual support. He stationed a detachment of about 1,500 Hessians at Trenton, under Colonel Rhalle, and about 2,000 at Bordentown, farther down the river, under Count Donop; the rest of his army was quartered over the country, between the Hackensack and the Delaware.

General Howe certainly had little apparent cause of apprehension; Washing ton had retreated beyond the Delaware at the head of only about 2,000 men, while he had an army of nearly 30,000 fine troops under his command. The congress had withdrawn from Philadelphia; and, by their retreat, had thrown that city into much confusion. Their presence had overawed the disaffected, and maintained the tranquillity of the place; but, on their removal, the friends of the British claims, to whom belonged the great body of the quakers, a timid sect, began to bestir themselves; and General Putnam, who commanded there, needed

FIG. 91.—Portrait of General Putnam.

a considerable force to preserve the peace of the city. The country was dejected; the friends of congress were filled with the most gloomy apprehensions; and many of the inhabitants repaired to the British posts, expressed their allegiance to the British crown, and claimed protection; so that in those circumstances General Howe seemed perfectly secure.

But in that alarming state of affairs the American leaders still maintained an erect posture, and their brave and persevering commander-in-chief did not despair. Congress actively employed all the means in their power for supporting their independence, and General Washington applied in every quarter for reinforcements. He perceived the security of the British commander-in-chief, and the advantages which the scattered cantonment of his troops presented to the American arms. "Now," exclaimed he, on being informed of the widely dispersed state of the British troops, "is the time to clip their wings, when they are so spread;" and, accordingly, resolved to make a bold effort to check the progress of the enemy. For that purpose he planned an attack on the Hessians at Trenton. General Putnam, who was stationed in Philadelphia, might have been useful in creating a diversion on that side; but in that city the friends of Britain were so strong, that it was deemed inexpedient to withdraw, even for a hort time, the troops posted there. But a small party of militia, under Colonel Griffin, passed the Delaware near Philadelphia, and advanced to Mount Holly. Count Donop marched against them, but, on their retreat, he returned to Bordentown.

General Washington formed his troops into three divisions, which were almost simultaneously to pass the Delaware, at three different places, on the evening of the 25th of December, hoping to surprise the enemy after the festivities of Christmas. One division, under General Cadwallader, was to pass the river

FIG. 92.—Washington approaching the Delaware.

in the vicinity of Bristol, but failed through inattention to the state of the tide and of the river, as they could not land on account of the heaps of ice accumulated on the Jersey bank. The second division, under General Irving, was to pass at Trenton Ferry, but was unable to make its way through the ice. The third and main division, under the command of General Washington in person, assisted by Generals Sullivan and Greene, and Colonel Knox of the artillery,

FIG. 93.—Portrait of Colonel Knox.

accomplished the passage, with great difficulty, at McKenzie's Ferry, about nine miles above Trenton. The general had expected to have his troops on the Jersey side about midnight, and to reach Trenton about five in the morning. But the difficulties arising from the accumulation of ice in the river, were so great, that it was three o'clock in the morning before the troops got across, and nearly four before they began to move forward. They were formed into two divisions, one of which proceeded toward Trenton by the lower or river road and the other by the upper or Pennington road

Colonel Rhalle had received some intimation that an attack on his post was meditated, and probably would be made on the evening of the twenty-fifth. Captain Washington, afterward much distinguished as an officer of cavalry, had for some days been on a scouting party in the Jerseys with about fifty foot soldiers; and, ignorant of the meditated attack on the evening of the twenty-fifth, had approached Trenton, exchanged a few shots with the advanced sentinels, and then retreated. The Hessians concluded that this was the threatened attack, and became quite secure. Captain Washington, in his retreat, met the general advancing against Trenton by the upper road, and joined him. Although some apprehensions were entertained that the alarm excited by Captain Washington's appearance might have put the Hessians on their guard, yet, as there was now no room either for hesitation or delay, the Americans steadily continued their march. The night was severe: it sleeted, snowed, and was intensely cold, and the road slippery. But General Washington advanced firmly, and at eight o'clock in the morning reached the Hessian advanced posts, which he instantly drove in; and, so equal had been the progress of the columns, that in three minutes afterward the firing on the river road announced the arrival of the other division.

Colonel Rhalle, who was a courageous officer, soon had his men under arms, and prepared for a brave defence; but, early in the engagement, he received a mortal wound, and his men, being severely galled by the American artillery, about 1,000 of them threw down their arms and surrendered themselves prisoners of war; but a considerable body of them, chiefly light horse, retreated toward Bordentown and made their escape.

In this attack not many Hessians were killed, and the Americans lost only four or five men, some of whom were frozen to death by the intense cold of the night. Some of General Washington's officers wished him to follow up his success, and he was inclined to pursue that course; but a council of war was averse to this measure, and he did not think it advisable to act contrary to the prevailing opinion. On the evening of the twenty-sixth he repassed the Delaware, carrying his prisoners along with him, and their arms, colors, and artillery.

This enterprise was completely successful in so far as it was under the immediate direction of the commander-in-chief, and it had a happy effect on the affairs of America. It was the first wave of the returning tide. It filled the British with astonishment; and the Hessians, whose name had before inspired the people with fear, ceased to be terrible. The prisoners were paraded through the streets of Philadelphia to prove the reality of the victory, which the friends of the British government had denied. The hopes of the Americans were revived, and their spirits elevated: they had a clear proof that their enemies were not invincible; and that union, courage, and perseverance, would ensure success.

The British troops in the Jerseys behaved toward the inhabitants with all the insolence of victory, and plundered them with indiscriminate and unmerciful rapacity. Filled with indignation at such insults, injustice, and oppression, the people were everywhere ready to flee to arms; and the success of their countrymen at Trenton encouraged their resentment and patriotic feelings.

Although General Cadwallader had not been able to pass the Delaware at the appointed time, yet, believing that General Washington was still on the Jersey side, on the twenty-seventh he crossed the river with 1,500 men, about two miles above Bristol; and even after he was informed that General Washington had again passed into Pennsylvania, he proceeded to Burlington, and next day marched on Bordentown, the enemy hastily retiring as he advanced.

The spirit of resistance was again fully awakened in Pennsylvania, and considerable numbers of the militia repaired to the standard of the commander-in chief, who again crossed the Delaware and marched to Trenton, where, at the beginning of January, he found himself at the head of 5,000 men.

The alarm was now spread throughout the British army. A strong detachment under General Grant marched to Princeton; and Earl Cornwallis, who was on the point of sailing for England, was ordered to leave New York, and resume his command in the Jerseys.

FIG. 94.—Portrait of Lord Cornwallis.

On joining General Grant, Lord Cornwallis immediately marched against Trenton. On his approach, General Washington crossed a rivulet named the Assumpink, and took post on some high ground, with the rivulet in his front. On the advance of the British army on the afternoon of the 2d of January, 1777, a smart cannonade ensued, and continued till night, Lord Cornwallis intending to renew the attack next morning; but soon after midnight General Washington silently decamped, leaving his fires burning, his sentinels advanced, and small parties to guard the fords of the rivulet, and, by a circuitous route through Allen town, proceeded toward Princeton.

It was the most inclement season of the year, but the weather favored his movement. For two days before it had been warm, soft, and foggy, and great apprehensions were entertained lest, by the depth of the roads, it should be found impossible to transport the baggage and artillery with the requisite celerity; but about the time the troops began to move, one of those sudden changes of weather which are not unfrequent in America happened. The wind shifted to the northwest, while the council of war which was to decide on their ulterior operations was sitting. An intense frost set in; and instead of being obliged to struggle through a miry road, the army marched as on solid pavement. The American soldiers considered the change of weather as an interposition of Heaven in their behalf, and proceeded on their way with alacrity.

Earl Cornwallis, in his rapid march toward Trenton, had left three regiments, under Lieutenant-Colonel Mawhood, at Princeton, with orders to advance on the third of the month to Maidenhead, a village about half way between Princeton and Trenton. General Washington approached Princeton toward daybreak and shortly before that time Colonel Mawhood's detachment had began to advance toward Maidenhead, by a road at a little distance from that on which the Americans were marching. The two armies unexpectedly met, and a smart engagement instantly ensued. At first the Americans were thrown into some confusion; but General Washington, by great personal exertions, restored order, and renewed the battle. Colonel Mawhood, with a part of his force, broke through the American army, and continued his route to Maidenhead; the remainder of his detachment, being unable to advance, retreated by different roads to New Brunswick.

In this rencounter a considerable number of men fell on each side. The Americans lost General Mercer, whose death was much lamented by his countrymen. Captain Leslie, son of the Earl of Leven, was among the slain on the side of the British; and he was buried with military honors by the Americans, in testimony of respect not to himself merely, but to his family also. In this battle Colonel Monroe, who was afterward elected president of the United States, took an active part.

It was immediately after the sharp conflict at the fence, between the advance guard of the American army, led by General Mercer, and the British seventeenth regiment, and the retreat of the Americans through the orchard near to Clark's house and barn, that General Mercer, while exerting himself to rally his broken troops, was brought to the ground by a blow from the butt of a musket. He was on foot at this time—the gray horse he rode at the beginning of the action having been disabled by a ball in the fore leg. The British soldiers were not at first aware of the general's rank, for the morning being cold, he wore a surtout over his uniform. So soon as they discovered that he was a general officer, they shouted that they had got the rebel general, and cried, "Call for quarters, you d—d rebel!" Mercer to the most undaunted courage united a quick and ardent temperament; he replied with indignation to his enemies, while their bayonets were at his bosom, that he deserved not the name of rebel; and determining to die as he had lived, a true and honored soldier of liberty, lounged with his sword at the nearest man. They then bayoneted him, and left him for dead.

Upon the retreat of the enemy, the wounded general was conveyed to Clark's house, immediately adjoining the field of battle. The information that the commander-in-chief first received of the fall of his old companion in arms of the war of 1775, and beloved officer, was that he had expired under his numerous wounds; and it was not until the American army was in full march for Morristown that the chief was undeceived, and learned, to his great gratification, that Mercer, though fearfully wounded, was yet alive. Upon the first halt, at Somerset courthouse, Washington despatched the late Major George Lewis, his nephew, and captain of the Horse Guards, with a flag and a letter to Lord Cornwallis, requesting that every possible attention might be shown to the wounded general, and permission that young Lewis should remain with him to minister to his wants. To both requests his lordship yielded a willing assent, and ordered his staff-surgeon to attend upon General Mercer. Upon an examination of the wounds, the British surgeon remarked that, although they were many and severe, he was disposed to believe that they would not prove dangerous. Mercer, bred to the profession of an army surgeon in Europe, said to young Lewis, "Raise my right arm, George, and this gentleman will there discover the smallest of my wounds, but which will prove the most fatal. Yes, sir, that is a fellow that will very soon do my business." He languished till the twelfth, and expired in the arms of Lewis, admired and lamented by the whole army. During the period that he languished on the couch of suffering, he exonerated his enemies from the foul accusation which they bore not only in 1777, but for half a century

FIG. 95.—Birthplace of Ex-President Munroe.

since, viz: of their having bayoneted a general officer after he had surrendered his sword, and become a prisoner of war—declaring that he only relinquished his sword when his arm had become powerless to wield it. He paid the homage of his whole heart to the person and character of the commander-in-chief, rejoiced with true soldierly pride in the triumphs of Trenton and Princeton, in both of which he had borne a conspicuous part, and offered up his fervent prayers for the final success of the cause of American independence.

Thus lived and died Hugh Mercer, a name that will for ever be associated with momentous events in the history of the War of the Revolution. When a grateful posterity shall bid the trophied memorial rise to the martyrs who sealed with their blood the charter of an empire's liberties, there will not be wanting a monument to him whom Washington mourned as the worthy and brave General Mercer.

We shall give a single anecdote of the subject of the foregoing memoir, to show the pure and high minded principles that actuated the patriots and soldiers of the days of our country's first trial.

Virginia at first organized two regiments for the common cause. When it was determined to raise a third, there were numerous applications for commissions; and, these being mostly from men of fortune and family interest, there was scarcely an application for a rank less than a field officer. During the sitting of the house of burgesses upon the important motion, a plain but soldierly-looking individual handed up to the speaker's chair a scrap of paper, on which was written, "Hugh Mercer will serve his adopted country and the cause of liberty in any rank or station to which he may be appointed." This, from a veteran soldier, bred in European camps, the associate of Washington in the war of 1755, and known to stand high in his confidence and esteem, was all-sufficient for a body of patriots and statesmen, such as composed the Virginia house of burgesses in the days of the revolution. The appointment of Mercer to the command of the third Virginia regiment was carried instanter.

It was was while the commander-in-chief reined up his horse, upon approaching the spot in a ploughed field where lay the gallant Colonel Haslett mortally wounded, that he perceived some British soldiers supporting an officer, and upon inquiring his name and rank, was answered, Captain Leslie. Doctor Benjamin Rush, who formed a part of the general's suite, earnestly asked, "A son of the earl of Leven?" to which the soldiers replied in the affirmative. The doctor then addressed the general-in-chief: "I beg your excellency to permit this wounded officer to be placed under my care, that I may return, in however small a degree, a part of the obligations I owe to his worthy father for the many kindnesses received at his hands while I was a student in Edinburgh." The request was immediately granted; but, alas! poor Leslie was soon "past all surgery." He died the same evening, after receiving every possible kindness and attention, and was buried the next day at Pluckemin, with the honors of war; his soldiers, as they lowered his remains to the soldier's last rest, shedding tears over the grave of a much loved commander.

The battle of Princeton, for the time it lasted and the numbers engaged, was the most fatal to our officers of any action during the whole of our revolutionary war; the Americans losing one general, two colonels, one major, and three captains, killed—while the martial prowess of our enemy shone not with more brilliant lustre in any one of their combats during their long career of arms than did the courage and discipline of the seventeenth British regiment on the third of January, 1777. Indeed, Washington himself, during the height of the conflict, pointed out this gallant corps to his officers, exclaiming, "See how those noble fellows fight! Ah! gentlemen, when shall we be able to keep an army long enough together to display a discipline equal to our enemies?"

The regular troops that constituted the grand army at the close of the campaign of '76, were the fragments of many regiments, worn down by constant and toilsome marches, and suffering of every sort, in the depth of winter. The fine regiment of Smallwood, composed of the flower of the Maryland youth, and which, in the June preceding, marched into Philadelphia eleven hundred strong, was, on the third of January, reduced to scarcely sixty men, and commanded by a captain. In fact, the bulk of what was then called the grand army, consisted of the Pennsylvania militia and volunteers, citizen soldiers who had left their comfortable homes at the call of their country, and were enduring the rigors of a winter campaign. On the morning of the battle of Princeton, they had been eighteen hours under arms, and harassed by a long night's march. Was it then to be wondered at that they should have given way before the veteran bayonets of their fresh and well-appointed foe ?

The heroic devotion of Washington was not wanting in the exigencies of this memorable day. He was aware that his hour was come to redeem the pledge he had laid on the altar of his country when first he took up arms in her cause : to win her liberties or perish in the attempt. Defeat at Princeton would have amounted to the annihilation of America's last hope ; for, independent of the enemy's forces in front, Cornwallis, with the flower of the British army eight thousand strong, was already panting close on the rear. It was, indeed, the very crisis of the struggle. In the hurried and imposing events of little more than one short week, liberty endured her greatest agony. What, then, is due to the fame and memories of that sacred band, who, with the master of liberty at their head, breasted the storm at this fearful crisis of their country's destiny ?

The heroic devotion of Washington on the field of Princeton is matter of history. We have often enjoyed a touching reminiscence of that ever-memorable event from the late Colonel Fitzgerald, who was aid to the chief, and who never related the story of his general's danger and almost miraculous preservation, without adding to his tale the homage of a tear.

The aid-de-camp had been ordered to bring up the troops from the rear of the column, when the band under General Mercer became engaged. Upon returning to the spot where he had left the commander-in-chief, he was no longer there, and, upon looking around, the aid discovered him endeavoring to rally the line which had been thrown into disorder by a rapid onset of the foe. Washington, after several ineffectual efforts to restore the fortunes of the fight, is seen to rein up his horse, with his head to the enemy, and, in that position to become immoveable. It was a last appeal to his soldiers, and seemed to say, " Will you give up your general to the foe ?" Such an appeal was not made in vain. The discomfited Americans rally on the instant, and form into line ; the enemy halt, and dress their line ; the American chief is between the adverse posts, as though he had been placed there, a target for both. The arms of both lines are levelled. Can escape from death be possible ? Fitzgerald, horror-struck at the danger of his beloved commander, dropped the reins upon his horse's neck, and drew his hat over his face, that he might not see him die. A roar of musketry succeeds, and then a shout. It was the shout of victory. The aid-de-camp ventures to raise his eyes, and oh, glorious sight, the enemy are broken and flying, while dimly amid the glimpses of the smoke is seen the chief, " alive, unharmed, and without a wound," waving his hat, and cheering his comrades to the pursuit.

Colonel Fitzgerald, celebrated as one of the finest horsemen in the American army, now dashed his rowels in his charger's flank, and, heedless of the dead and dying in his way, flew to the side of his chief, exclaiming, " Thank God ! your excellency is safe," while the favorite aid, a gallant and warm-hearted son of Erin, a man of thews and sinews, and " albeit unused to the melting mood," gave loose to his feelings, and wept like a child for joy.

Washington, ever calm amid scenes of the greatest excitement, affectionately grasped the hand of his aid and friend, and then ordered, "Away, my dear Colonel, and bring up the troops; the day is our own!"

Early in the morning Earl Cornwallis discovered that General Washington had decamped, and soon afterward the report of the artillery in the engagement with Colonel Mawhood near Princeton, convinced him of the direction which the American army had taken. Alarmed for the safety of the British stores at New Brunswick, he advanced rapidly toward Princeton. In the American army it had indeed been proposed to make a forced march to New Brunswick, where all the baggage of the British army was deposited; but the complete exhaustion of the men, who had been without rest, and almost without food for two days and nights, prevented the adoption of the measure. General Washington proceeded toward Morristown, and Lord Cornwallis pressed on his rear; but the Americans, on crossing Millstone river, broke down the bridge at Kingston, to impede the progress of their enemies; and there the pursuit ended. Both armies were completely worn out, the one being as unable to pursue as the other was to retreat. General Washington took a position at Morristown, and Lord Cornwallis reached New-Brunswick, where no small alarm had been excited by the advance of the Americans, and where every exertion had been made for the removal of the baggage, and for defending the place.

General Washington fixed his headquarters at Morristown, situated among hills of difficult access, where he had a fine country in his rear, from which he could easily draw supplies, and was able to retreat across the Delaware, if needful. Giving his troops little repose, he overran both East and West Jersey, spread his army over the Raritan, and penetrated into the county of Essex, where he made himself master of the coast opposite Staten Island. With a greatly inferior army, by judicious movements, he wrested from the British almost all their conquests in the Jerseys. New Brunswick and Amboy were the only posts which remained in their hands, and even in these they were not a little harassed and straitened. The American detachments were in a state of unwearied activity, frequently surprising and cutting off the British advanced guards, keeping them in perpetual alarm, and melting down their numbers by a desultory and indecisive warfare.

General Howe had issued a proclamation, calling on the colonists to support his majesty's government, and promising them protection both in their persons and property. General Washington accompanied his successful operations with a counter-proclamation, absolving the inhabitants from their engagements to Britain, and promising them protection on their submission to congress. This was a seasonable proclamation, and produced much effect. Intimidated by the desperate aspect of American affairs when General Washington retreated into Pennsylvania, many of the inhabitants of the Jerseys had taken advantage of General Howe's proclamation, and submitted to the British authority; but with respect to the promised protection, they had been entirely disappointed. Instead of protection and conciliation, they had been insulted by the rude insolence of a licentious soldiery, and plundered with indiscriminate and unsparing rapacity. Their passions were exasperated; they thirsted for vengeance, and were prepared for the most vindictive hostility against the British troops. Hence the soldiers could not venture out to forage, except in large parties; and they seldom returned without loss.

Their licentious insolence and merciless rapacity lost more than their bravery gained, and inspired the people with a deadly enmity against the British government.

In ancient warfare the vanquished who were unable to make their escape were not unfrequently put to death on the field of battle; at times their lives

Fig. 96.—Washington's headquarters, Morristown, N. J.

were spared, when they were sold as slaves, or otherwise treated with indignity and cruelty; but the mild genius of Christianity has communicated its gentle and benevolent spirit to all the relations of life, has softened even the horrid features of war, and infused sentiments and feelings of kindness amid the din of arms. Among the civilized nations of modern Europe, prisoners-of-war are commonly treated with humanity, and principles are established on which they are exchanged. The British officers, however, considered the Americans as rebels deserving condign punishment, and not entitled to the sympathetic treatment commonly shown to the captive soldiers of independent nations. They seem to have thought that the Americans would never be able, or would never dare to retaliate. Hence, at first, their prisoners were, in some instances, harshly treated. To this the Americans could not submit, but remonstrated; and, on finding their remonstrances disregarded, they adopted a system of retaliation, which occasioned much unmerited suffering to individuals, and reflected no honor on any of the contending parties. Colonel Ethan Allen, who had been defeated and made prisoner in a bold attempt against Montreal, was put in irons, and sent to England as a traitor. In retaliation, General Prescott, who had been taken at the mouth of the Sorel, was put in close confinement, for the avowed purpose of subjecting him to the same fate which Colonel Allen should suffer. Both officers and privates, prisoners to the Americans, were more rigorously confined than they would otherwise have been; and, that they might not impute this to wanton harshness and cruelty, they were distinctly told that their own superiors only were to blame for any severe treatment they might experience.

The capture of General Lee became the occasion of embittering the complaints on this subject, and of aggravating the sufferings of the prisoners-of-war. Before that event, something like a cartel for the exchange of prisoners had been established between Generals Howe and Washington; but the captivity of General Lee interrupted that arrangement. The general had been an officer in the British army; but, having been disgusted, had resigned his commission, and, at the beginning of the troubles, had offered his services to congress, which were readily accepted. General Howe affected to consider him as a deserter, and ordered him into close confinement.

General Washington had no prisoner of equal rank, but offered six Hessian field-officers in exchange for him; and required that, if that offer should not be accepted, General Lee should be treated according to his rank in the American army. General Howe replied that General Lee was a deserter from his majesty's service, and could not be considered as a prisoner-of-war, nor come within the conditions of the cartel. A fruitless discussion ensued between the commanders-in-chief. Congress took up the matter; and resolved that General Washington be directed to inform General Howe, that should the proffered exchange of six Hessian field-officers for General Lee not be accepted, and his former treatment continued, the principle of retaliation shall occasion five of the Hessian field-officers, together with Lieutenant-Colonel Archibald Campbell, or any other officers that are or shall be in possession of the Americans, equivalent in number or quality, to be detained, in order that the treatment which General Lee shall receive may be exactly inflicted upon their persons. Congress also ordered a copy of their resolution to be transmitted to the council of Massachusetts Bay, and that they be desired to detain Lieutenant-Colonel Campbell, and keep him in close custody till the further orders of congress; and that a copy be also sent to the committee of congress in Philadelphia, and that they be desired to have the prisoners, officers and privates, lately taken, properly secured in some safe place.

The honorable Lieutenant-Colonel Campbell, of the 71st regiment, with about 270 of his men, after a brave and obstinate defence, had been made prisoners in the bay of Boston, while sailing for the harbor, ignorant of the evacuation of the town by the British. Hitherto the colonel had been civilly treated ; but, on receiving the order of congress respecting him, the council of Massachusetts Bay, instead of simply keeping him *in safe custody*, according to order, with a retaliating zeal, sent him to Concord jail, and lodged him in a dungeon, about twelve or thirteen feet square. He was locked in by double bolts, and expressly prohibited from entering the prison-yard on any consideration whatever.

That officer naturally complained to the commander-in-chief of such treatment ; and General Howe addressed General Washington on the subject. The latter immediately wrote to the council of Massachusetts Bay, and said : "You will observe that exactly the same treatment is to be shown to Colonel Campbell and the Hessian officers, that General Howe shows to General Lee ; and as he is only confined to a commodious house, with genteel accommodation, we have no right or reason to be more severe to Colonel Campbell, whom I wish to be immediately removed from his present situation, and put into a house where he may live comfortably."

General Lee was kept in confinement, till the capture of General Prescott put an officer of equal rank into the hands of the Americans, when an exchange was effected. At that time the British had nearly 300 American officers prisoners ; while the Americans had not more than 50 officers belonging to the British service. In the month of January, almost all those American officers were sent to Long Island on parole, and billeted on the inhabitants at two dollars a week ; but the privates were ill-lodged and ill-fed. Many were confined in the New York jail, where they were starved to death by the keeper, Captain Cunningham,

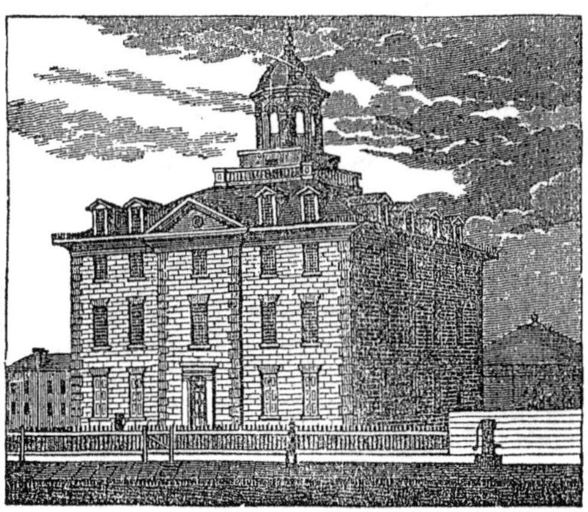

FIG. 97.—The old Jail in New York.

who was afterward hung in England for perjury, and who on the gibbet confessed the death of between two and three thousand American prisoners by starvation, in order that he might sell their rations. The provisions which they received were deficient in quantity, and of the worst quality. Many of the men died of cold and hunger. Under that ungenerous treatment, they were importuned to enlist in the British service, but generally remained faithful to their engagements, under all their privations and sufferings. Avarice and an ignorant and cruel policy seem to have operated with joint influence in the treatment of the American prisoners. The contractors, indeed, filled their pockets by their nefarious practices toward the unhappy men in their power ; but they who expected, by such measures, to increase the strength of the British army, or to deter the colonists from joining the standards of their country, were utterly disappointed. Kind treatment might have gained good will; but the harsh and unfeeling usage which many of them experienced only exasperated the passions of the Americans, and contributed to the recruiting of General Washington's army.

While General Washington was actively employed in the Jerseys in asserting the independence of America, congress could not afford him much assistance; but that body was active in promoting the same cause, by its enactments and recommendations. Hitherto the colonies had been united by no bond but that of their common danger and common love of liberty. Congress resolved to render the terms of their union more definite, to ascertain the rights and duties of the several colonies, and their mutual obligations toward each other. A committee was appointed to sketch the principles of the union or confederation.

This committee presented a report in thirteen *Articles of Confederation and perpetual Union* between the states, and proposed, that, instead of calling themselves the UNITED COLONIES, as they had hitherto done, they should assume the name of the UNITED STATES OF AMERICA; that each state should retain its sovereignty, freedom, and independence, and every power, jurisdiction, and right, which is not by the confederation expressly delegated to the United States in congress assembled; that they enter into a firm league for mutual defence; that the free inhabitants of any of the states shall be entitled to the privileges and immunities of free citizens in any other state; that any traitor or great delinquent fleeing from one state and found in another, shall be delivered up to the state having jurisdiction of his offence; that full faith and credit shall be given in each of the states to the records, acts, and judicial proceedings of every other state; that delegates shall be annually chosen, in such manner as the legislature of each state shall direct, to meet in congress on the first Monday in November, with power to each state to recall its delegates, or any of them, at any time within the year, and to send others in their stead; that no state shall be represented in congress by less than two or more than seven members, and no person shall be a delegate for more than three out of six years, nor shall any delegate hold a place of emolument under the United States; that each state shall maintain its own delegates; that in congress each state shall have only one vote; that freedom of speech shall be enjoyed by the members; and that they shall be free from arrest, except for treason, felony, or breach of the peace; that no state, without the consent of congress, shall receive any ambassador, or enter into any treaty with any foreign power; that no person holding any office in any of the United States shall receive any present, office, or title, from any foreign state; and that neither congress nor any of the states shall grant any titles of nobility; that no two or more of the states shall enter into any confederation whatever without the consent of congress; that no state shall impose any duties which may interfere with treaties made by congress; that in time of peace no vessels of war or military force shall be kept up in any of the states but by the authority of congress, but every state shall have a well-regulated and disciplined militia; that no state, unless invaded, shall engage in war without the consent of congress, nor shall they grant letters of marque or reprisal till after a declaration of war by congress; that colonels and inferior officers shall be appointed by the legislature of each state for its own troops; that the expenses of war shall be defrayed out of a common treasury, supplied by the several states according to the value of the land in each; that taxes shall be imposed and levied by authority and direction of the several states within the time prescribed by congress; that congress has the sole and exclusive right of deciding on peace and war, of sending and receiving ambassadors, and entering into treaties; that congress shall be the last resort on appeal in all disputes and differences between two or more of the states; that congress have the sole and exclusive right and power of regulating the alloy and value of coin struck by their own authority, or by that of the respective states, fixing the standard of weights and measures, regulating the trade, establishing postoffices, appointing all officers of the land forces in the service of the United States, except regimental officers, appointing all the officers of the naval forces, and commissioning all officers whatever in the service of the United States, making rules for the government and regulation of the said land and naval forces, and directing their operations ; that congress have authority to appoint a committee to sit during their recess, to be denominated a *Committee of the States*, and to consist of one delegate from each state ; that congress shall have power to ascertain the necessary sums of money to be raised for the service of the United States, and to appropriate and apply the same, to borrow money or emit bills on the credit of the United States, to build and equip a navy, to fix the number of land forces, and to make requisitions from each state for its quota, in proportion to the number of white inhabitants in such state ; that the consent of nine states shall be requisite to any great public measure of common interest ; that congress shall have power to adjourn to any time within the year, and to any place within the United States, but the adjournment not to exceed six months ; and that they shall publish their proceedings monthly, excepting such parts relating to treaties, alliances, or military operations, as in their judgment require secrecy ; that the *yeas* and *nays* of the delegates of each state shall, if required, be entered on the journal, and extracts granted ; that the *Committee of the States*, or any nine of them, shall, during the recess of congress, exercise such powers as congress shall vest them with ; that Canada, if willing, shall be admitted to all the advantages of the union ; but no other colony shall be admitted, unless such admission shall be agreed to by nine states ; that all bills of credit emitted, moneys borrowed, or debts contracted by congress before this confederation, shall be charges on the United States ; that every state shall abide by the determinations of congress on all questions submitted to them by this confederation ; that the articles of it shall be inviolably observed by every state ; and that no alteration in any of the articles shall be made, unless agreed to by congress, and afterward confirmed by the legislature of every state.

FIG. 98.—Great Seal of the United States.

Such was the substance of this confederation or union. After much discussion, at thirty-nine sittings, the articles were approved by congress, transmitted to the several state legislatures, and, meeting with their approbation, were ratified by all the delegates on the 15th of November, 1777. Congress maintained an erect posture, although its affairs then wore the most gloomy aspect. It was under the provisions of this confederation that the war was afterward carried on ;

and, considered as a first essay of legislative wisdom, it discovers a good understanding, and an extensive knowledge of the structure of society. Had peace been concluded before the settlement of this confederation, the states would probably have broken down into so many independent governments, and the strength of the union been lost in a number of petty sovereignties.

CHAPTER VII.

Let us now attend to the proceedings of congress. The colonies had been drawn into the war by a train of unforeseen events, and had made no preparation for a great and protracted struggle. Their finances soon failed; and they severely felt the want of arms and military stores. About the middle of January, congress entered on the consideration of the state of the treasury, and resolved to provide funds for maintaining the war, by issuing bills, under their authority, which were to pass current, at their nominal value, in all payments and dealings throughout the states. In the difficult and embarrassing circumstances in which they were placed, it perhaps would not have been easy to have devised any better scheme for supporting the cause of the Union; but a compulsory paper currency was certainly a pernicious expedient, destined to prove most ruinous to those who had most confidence in it, and who were most devoted to the support of their country. The paper-currency of congress soon became depreciated

Fig. 99.—Continental Money.

This led from one mistake into another, and induced them to attempt to fix the prices of commodities; a measure which must always prove abortive, and which introduced incalculable confusion and misery into America, involving many families in ruin.

Congress decreed a monument to the memory of General Warren, who fell at Bunker's Hill; and one to the memory of General Mercer, who was mortally wounded in the rencounter with Colonel Mawhood near Princeton. They were much alarmed by the langour and supineness which everywhere prevailed

During those convulsions in the colonies, the people of Great Britain, long accustomed to colonial complaints and quarrels, and attentive merely to their own immediate interests, paid no due regard to the progress of the contest, or to the importance of the principles in which it originated. Large majorities in both houses of parliament supported the ministry in all their violent proceedings; and although a small minority, including several men of distinguished talents, who trembled for the fate of British liberty if the court should succeed in establishing its claims against the colonists, vigorously opposed the measures of administration, yet the great body of the people manifested a loyal zeal in favor of the war; and the ill success of the colonists, in the campaign of 1776, gave that zeal additional energy.

But, amid all the popularity of their warlike operations, the difficulties of the ministry soon began to multiply. In consequence of hostilities with the American provinces, the British West India islands experienced a scarcity of the necessaries of life. About the time when the West Indian fleet was about to set sail, under convoy, on its homeward voyage, it was discovered that the negroes of Jamaica meditated an insurrection. By means of the draughts to complete the army in America, the military force in that island had been weakened; and the ships-of-war were detained to assist in suppressing the negroes. By this delay, the Americans gained time for equipping their privateers. After the fleet sailed, it was dispersed by stormy weather; and many of the ships, richly laden, fell into the hands of the American cruisers, who were permitted to sell their prizes in the ports of France, both in Europe and in the West Indies.

This unfriendly conduct of France was so openly manifested, that it could no longer be winked at, and it drew forth a remonstrance from the British cabinet. The remonstrance was civilly answered, and the traffic in British prizes was carried on somewhat more covertly in the French ports in Europe; but it was evident that both France and Spain were in a state of active preparation for war. The British ministry could no longer shut their eyes against the gathering storm, and began to prepare for it. About the middle of October, 1776, they put sixteen additional ships into commission, and made every exertion to man them.

On the 31st of October the parliament met, and during its session some other attempts were made for adopting conciliatory measures, but the influence of the ministry was so powerful that they were all completely defeated, and the plans of administration received the approbation and support of parliament.

During the winter, which was very severe, the British troops at New Brunswick and Amboy were kept on constant duty, and suffered considerable privations. The Americans were vigilant and active, and the British army could seldom procure provisions or forage without fighting. But although in the course of the winter the affairs of the United States had begun to wear a more promising aspect, yet there was still many friends of royalty in the provinces. By their open attachment to the British interest, numbers had already exposed themselves to the vengeance of the republicans; and others, from affection to Britain or distrust of the American cause, gave their countenance and aid to Sir William Howe. Early in the season a considerable number of these men joined the royal army, and were embodied under the direction of the commander-in-chief, with the same pay as the regular troops, besides the promise of an allotment of land at the close of the disturbances. Governor Tryon, who had been extremely active in engaging and disciplining them, was promoted to the rank of major-general of the loyal provincialists.

The campaign opened on both sides by rapid predatory incursions and bold desultory attacks. At Peekskill, on the North river, about fifty miles above New York, the Americans had formed a post, at which, during the winter, they had collected a considerable quantity of provisions and camp equipage, to supply the stations in the vicinity as occasion might require. General Washington's position was naturally strong, and during the winter he added many artificial fortifications. The most mountainous part of the district, named the Manor of Cortland, was formed into a kind of citadel, replenished with stores, and Peekskill served as a port to it. On the 23d of March, as soon as the river was clear of ice, General Howe, who thought Peekskill of more importance than it really was, detached Colonel Bird, with about 500 men, under convoy of a frigate and some armed vessels, against that post. General McDougall, who commanded there, had then only about 250 men in the place. He had timely notice of Colonel Bird's approach; and, sensible that his post was untenable, he exerted himself to remove the stores to the strong grounds about two miles and a half in his rear; but before he had made much progress in the work the British appeared, when he set fire to the stores and buildings, and retreated. Colonel Bird landed, and completed the destruction of the stores which he was unable to remove. On the same day he reimbarked, and returned to New York.

On the 13th of April, Lord Cornwallis and General Grant, with about 2,000 men, attempted to surprise and cut off General Lincoln, who, with 500 men,

Fig. 100.—Portrait of General Lincoln.

was posted at Bound Brook, seven miles from New Brunswick, and nearly succeeded in their enterprise. But, by a bold and rapid movement, Lincoln, when almost surrounded, forced his way between the British columns and escaped, with the loss of sixty men, his papers, three field-pieces, and some baggage.

At that early period of the campaign, Sir William Howe attempted no grand movement against the American commander-in-chief; but he made several efforts to interrupt his communications, destroy his stores, and impede his operations He had received information that the Americans had collected a large quantity of stores in the town of Danbury, and in other places on the borders of Connecticut. These he resolved to destroy; and appointed Major-General Tryon of the provincials, who panted for glory in his newly-acquired character, to command an expedition for that purpose; but prudently directed Generals Agnew and Sir William Erskine to accompany him.

On the 25th of April, the detachment, consisting of 2,000 men, under a proper naval escort, left New York, passed the sound, landed between Fairfield and Norwalk, and, early next afternoon reached Danbury, about twenty-three miles distant. The small American force stationed there, being unable to make any effectual resistance, carried off part of the stores, and retreated from the town. General Tryon destroyed 1,800 barrels of pork and beef; 700 barrels of flour; 200 barrels of wheat, rye, and maize; clothing for a regiment; and 1,700 tents, which, on account of their scarcity, were very valuable to the Americans. At Danbury, the troops committed some atrocities; and at other places destroyed 100 barrels of flour, and 100 hogsheads of rum.

Having achieved these feats, on the morning of the 27th General Tryon began to retire. His visit had been unexpected, and hitherto he had met with no resistance; but the alarm was now spread, and the Generals Sullivan, Wooster, and Arnold, were active in assembling the militia. General Wooster, with a small party, pursued the retreating enemy, and attacked their rear; but this brave veteran received a mortal wound, and died, much regretted, in the seventieth year of his age. Arnold rapidly crossed the country, and posted himself at Ridgefield, with 500 men, in front of the British detachment. A smart engagement ensued; the Americans were compelled to retreat; and the British troops, quite exhausted, spent the night on their arms at Ridgefield.

FIG. 101.—Retreat of General Tryon.

On the morning of the 28th they resumed their march; but were assailed by an irregular and destructive fire of musketry from houses and from behind stone fences. Arnold took possession of a bridge over the Sagatuck, by which it was expected the British would be obliged to pass the river; but their guide led them to a ford three miles above the bridge, which the Americans, deeming impassable, had left unguarded. There they crossed without opposition; but occasional skirmishing and cannonading took place till the British regained their ships.

The injury done to the Americans was considerable, but it did not compensate the loss which the British sustained in the expedition; for nearly 400 of their number were killed, wounded, or taken prisoners. The loss of the Americans amounted only to about a third of that of the British. Many of the Connecticut militia took the field on this occasion; but only 600 or 700 subjected themselves to military authority. Those who engaged actively in the contest discovered much spirit. The people of New England, by their general courage and energy in repelling such incursions, gave no encouragement to the frequent repetition of those hostile visits. The death of General Wooster was much lamented, and congress decreed a monument to his memory. General Arnold's activity and courage met with the approbation of his superiors.

The British troops were not permitted to carry on their sudden incursions and predatory attacks without retaliation. On the 8th of May, General Stevens, with a considerable force, attacked the British post at Piscataway, where the 42d regiment was stationed; but, after a furious engagement, he was repulsed. A considerable quantity of grain, forage, and other necessaries, for the use of the royal army, was collected at Sag Harbor in Long Island; where they were but slightly guarded, as the number of British cruisers in the sound seemed to secure them from all danger. Of these circumstances the American General Parsons gained information; and, on the 23d of May, he detached Colonel Meigs, with a party of 170 men, who left Guildford in Connecticut, at one o'clock in the afternoon, crossed the sound in thirteen whale-boats, attended by three sloops: landed on the north part of the island near Southhold, at six o'clock in the evening; carried his boats over a neck of land; reimbarked, and crossed the bay between the north and south parts of the island, and, at twelve o'clock at night, landed within four miles of Sag Harbor. Leaving his boats under the protection of a slender guard, he advanced silently toward the place of destination, and, about two o'clock in the morning, began the attack with fixed bayonets. The alarm soon became general, and a discharge of musketry on both sides ensued; but the Americans succeeded in burning the stores and twelve vessels. They also killed six men, took ninety prisoners, and only six of the party who guarded the place escaped. Colonel Meigs, without having a man either killed or wounded, returned with his prisoners to Guildford, where he arrived at two o'clock on the 24th; having, in the space of twenty-five hours, traversed by sea and land no less than ninety miles.

When mentioning these achievements of desultory warfare, we may here relate another enterprise of the same kind, although it did not happen till the 10th of July—the capture of General Prescott. That officer was commander of Rhode Island, and had his headquarters on the west side of the island, near Narraganset bay, about a quarter of a mile from the shore, and at some distance from any body of troops. He was but slightly guarded, trusting chiefly for security to the numerous cruisers, and to a guard-ship, which lay in the bay opposite to his quarters.

Colonel Barton, at the head of forty men, officers and volunteers, passed by night from Warwick Neck to Rhode Island; and although they had a passage of ten miles by water, yet, by keeping near the land, they eluded the vigilance of the British ships-of-war and guard-boats which surrounded the island. They conducted their enterprise with such silence and address, that, about midnight, they reached the general's quarters undiscovered, secured the sentinel, surprised the general in bed, and, without giving him time to put on his clothes, hurried him on board, with one of his aides-de-camp, and conveyed him safely to Providence. This event was very mortifying to General Prescott, and to the royal army; but occasioned much exultation among the Americans. Hitherto General Howe had absolutely refused to release General Lee, but he soon agreed to exchange him for General Prescott; and General Lee again joined the American army.

Having taken notice of these desultory enterprises, we shall now turn to the two main armies, under their respective commanders-in-chief.

In the beginning of June, General Sir William Howe, having received from England his expected reinforcements and camp equipage, left New York and passed into the Jerseys, with the intention of immediately opening the campaign. He had under his command 30,000 men, well equipped and provided; and, to resist this formidable army, General Washington, on the 9th of June could muster no more than 7,271 men fit for duty. During the winter his army had been extremely weak; but, in May, congress had been able to send him some recruits. After receiving this feeble reinforcement, toward the end of the month he left his strong camp at Morristown, and, advancing toward New Brunswick, took a good position at Middlebrook, on the north side of the Raritan, about nine miles from that place. At New Brunswick General Howe assembled his army on the 12th of June; but, judging it unadvisable to attack his adversary in the post which he had chosen, he employed every artifice to draw him into less advantageous ground. For this purpose he marched from New Brunswick, in two columns, to Middlebush and Hillsborough, on the south of the Raritan, as if he meant to advance to the Delaware. Not deceived by this feint, General Washington remained in his camp, and satisfied himself with harassing the British army by skirmishing parties.

Perceiving that this movement did not draw General Washington from his camp, General Howe returned to New Brunswick, committing terrible devastations in his march. On the 22d of June, he retreated to Amboy; an American detachment, under General Greene, hanging upon his rear, and frequently attacking it. General Washington moved his army to Quibbletown, that he might still be near the British army.

General Howe sent his heavy baggage and all the encumbrances of his army from Amboy to Staten Island, and ordered part of the troops to follow; but, being informed that General Washington had left his strong ground, and was advancing in pursuit of him, on the evening of the 25th he recalled his troops from Staten Island; and, on the morning of the 26th, suddenly and unexpectedly advanced from Amboy with his whole army, in two columns, against the Americans, with the design of cutting off their advanced detachments, bringing General Washington to an engagement on open ground, or of gaining possession of the passes in the highlands on his left, and so compelling him to abandon the advantageous position which he had hitherto occupied. For the attainment of the object last mentioned, Earl Cornwallis, with a strong detachment, set out early on the 25th of June, and, about seven o'clock in the morning, fell in with a numerous body of the enemy, under Lord Stirling and General Maxwell. After a smart engagement, the Americans retreated with some loss; and General Washington, apprized of the unexpected movement of the British army, hastily returned toward the mountains, and regained possession of these passes which it was the intention of Earl Cornwallis to seize.

Finding all his endeavors to bring the Americans to a general engagement ineffectual, on the 30th of June Sir William Howe crossed to Staten Island, and, on the 5th of July, embarked his army, consisting of about 16,000 men, on board of transports, in order to sail to the southward. To gain possession of Philadelphia was his great aim; and, instead of attempting this by marching through the Jerseys and passing the Delaware, with an unbroken though greatly inferior army in his rear, he chose to carry his army toward the place of destination by sea, leaving General Sir Henry Clinton with a respectable force to defend New York. But although the army embarked on the 5th of July, it was the 23d of the month before the fleet, consisting of 267 sail, left Sandy Hook.

The movements of General Howe greatly perplexed the American commander-in-chief, who dreaded a junction of the forces under Generals Howe and Burgoyne; and who could scarcely believe that the former would sail to the southward and abandon the latter, who was advancing from Quebec, by way of the Lakes Champlain and George, toward Albany. He also received contradictory accounts of the course which General Howe had steered; sometimes it was said that he was returning to the North river, and sometimes that the Delaware was the place of his destination, which last was the true account. But at

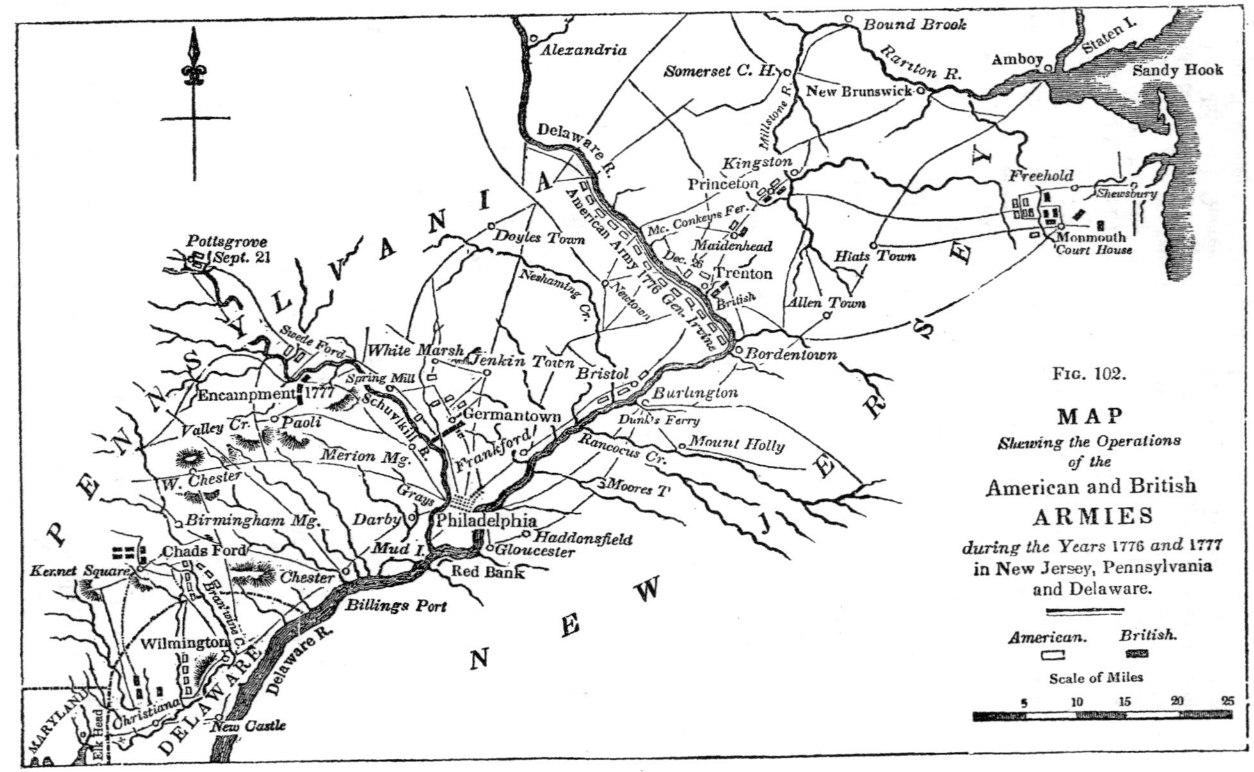

Fig. 102.

MAP
Showing the Operations
of the
American and British
ARMIES
during the Years 1776 and 1777
in New Jersey, Pennsylvania
and Delaware.

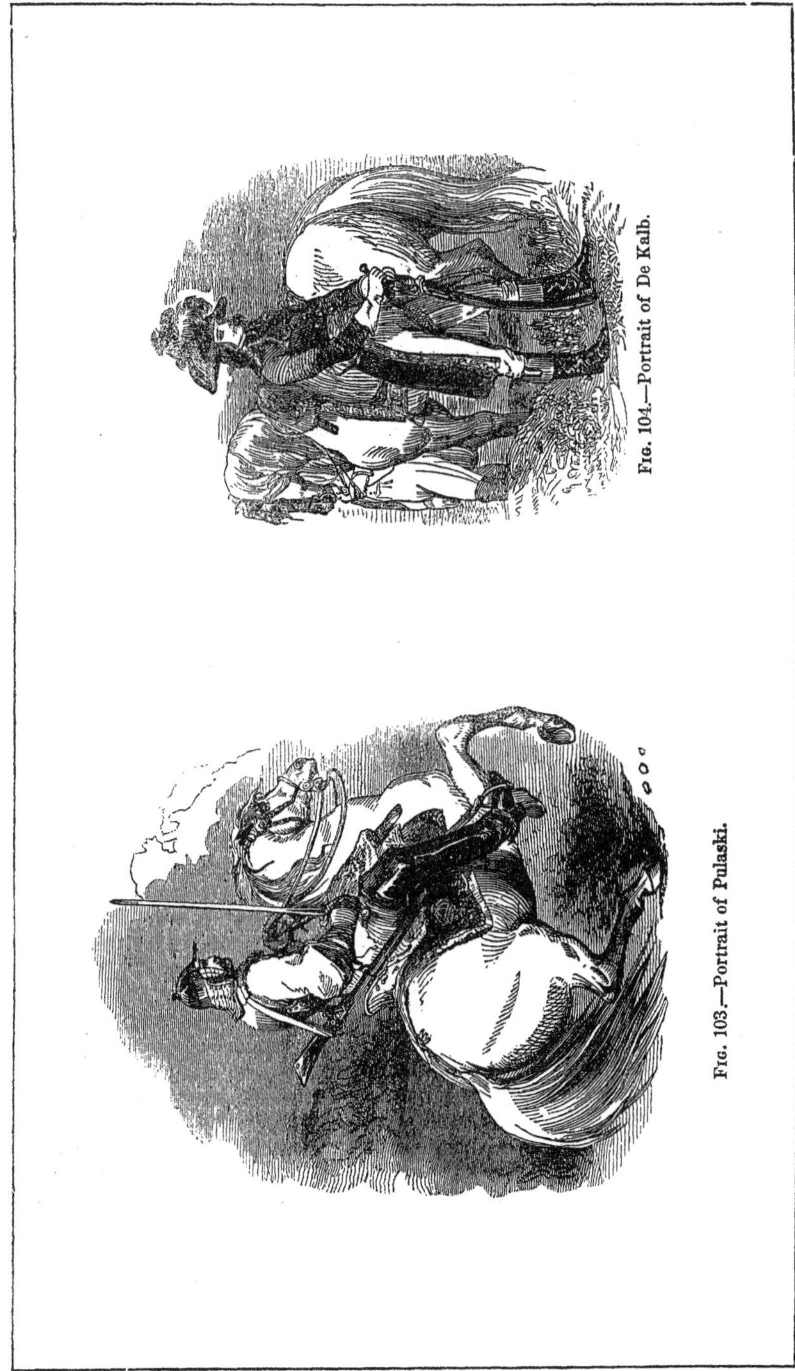

Fig. 103.—Portrait of Pulaski.

Fig. 104.—Portrait of De Kalb.

that season of the year southerly winds prevail on the coast; and it was the 30th of July before the British commander reached the capes of the Delaware.

His original intention was to sail up the river to Philadelphia; but, being informed that the Americans had obstructed the navigation, he altered his plan, and, still steering southward, entered Chesapeake bay. On the appearance of the British armament off the Delaware, General Washington moved toward Philadelphia; but, being told that the fleet had again put to sea, his perplexity returned, and he held himself in readiness to march with the the utmost rapidity toward the North river, if needful. But, on the 24th of August, he was relieved from his painful suspense by certain information that the British fleet had sailed up the Chesapeake bay, and that the army was landing at the head of the Elk river.

At the place of debarkation, the British army was within a few days' march of Philadelphia; no great rivers were in its way; and there was no very strong position of which the enemy could take possession. On landing, General Howe issued a proclamation, promising pardon and protection to all who should submit to him; but, as the American army was at hand, the proclamation produced little effect.

General Washington distinctly understood the nature of the contest in which he was engaged; and, sensible of the inferiority of his raw and disorderly army to the veteran troops under Sir William Howe, he wished to avoid a general engagement; but, aware of the effect which the fall of Philadelphia would produce on the minds of the multitude, who have no fixed principle or steady purpose, he determined to make every effort in order to retard the progress and defeat the aim of the royal army. Accordingly, he marched to meet General Howe, who, from want of horses, many of which had perished in the voyage, and from other causes, was unable to proceed from the head of the Elk before the 3d of September. On the advance of the royal army, General Washington retreated across the Brandywine, a creek which falls into the Delaware at Wilmington. He took post, with his main body, opposite Chad's Ford, where it was expected the British would attempt the passage; and ordered General Sullivan, with a detachment, to watch the fords above. He sent General Maxwell, with about 1,000 light troops, to occupy the high ground on the other side of the Brandywine, to skirmish with the British, and retard them in their progress.

On the morning of the 11th of September, the British army advanced in two columns; the right, under General Knyphausen, marched straight to Chad's Ford; the left, under Lord Cornwallis, accompanied by the commander-in-chief and Generals Grey, Grant, and Agnew, proceeded, by a circuitous route, toward a point named the Forks, where the two branches of the Brandywine unite, with a view to turn the right of the Americans and gain their rear. General Knyphausen's van soon found itself opposed to the light troops under General Maxwell. A smart conflict ensued. General Knyphausen reinforced his advanced guard, and drove the Americans across the rivulet, to shelter themselves under their batteries on the north bank. General Knyphausen ordered some artillery to be placed on the most advantageous points, and a cannonade was carried on with the American batteries on the heights beyond the ford.

Meanwhile the left wing of the British crossed the fords above the Forks. Of this movement General Washington had early notice; but the information which he received from different quarters, through his scouts, was confused and contradictory, and consequently his operations were embarrassed. After passing the fords, Lord Cornwallis took the road to Dilworth, which led him on the American right. General Sullivan, who had been appointed to guard that quarter, occupied the heights above Birmingham church, his left extending to the Brandywine, his artillery judiciously placed, and his right flank covered by woods. About four in the afternoon, Lord Cornwallis formed the line of battle and began the attack; for some time the Americans sustained it with intrepidity, but at length gave way. When General Washington heard the firing in that direction, he ordered General Greene with a brigade to support General Sullivan. General Greene marched four miles in forty-two minutes, but, on reaching the scene of action, he found General Sullivan's division defeated and fleeing in confusion. He covered the retreat; and, after some time, finding an advantageous position, he renewed the battle, and arrested the progress of the pursuing enemy.

General Knyphausen, as soon as he heard the firing of Lord Cornwallis's division, forced the passage of Chad's Ford, attacked the troops opposed to him, and compelled them to make a precipitate and disorderly retreat. General Washington, with the part of his army which he was able to keep together, retired, with his artillery and baggage, to Chester, where he halted, within eight miles of the British army, till next morning, when he retreated to Philadelphia. Night, and the exhaustion of the British troops, saved the Americans from pursuit.

In Philadelphia the American commander-in-chief remained two days, collecting his scattered troops, replacing the stores lost in the battle, and making arrangements for his future movements. On the third day after the engagement he marched up the north side of the Schuylkill, crossed it at Sweet's Ford, and proceeded toward Lancaster.

In the battle at the Brandywine the Americans suffered considerable loss having about 300 men killed, 600 wounded, and 400 taken prisoners. They also lost ten small field-pieces and a howitzer. The loss of the British was much less, not exceeding five or six hundred killed and wounded. In the battle several foreign officers of distinction served in the American army: among these was the celebrated Marquis de la Fayette; he was only about twenty years of age, and, animated by a youthful and enthusiastic love of liberty, had quitted his country, a plentiful fortune, and all the endearments of polished society, to fight under the banners of the infant republic at the most gloomy period of the contest. At his own expense he purchased and fitted out a vessel to convey him to the American continent, and sailed, notwithstanding a prohibition of the French government, which did not then deem it expedient to throw off the mask. This battle was his first military service in the American cause, and in it he received a wound in the leg, but did not leave the field. Some other French officers were in the battle on the same side, and also Count Pulaski, a Polish nobleman.

On the 16th of the month Monsieur du Coudray, with some other French gentlemen, set out to join the army. Monsieur du Coudray was mounted on a spirited young mare, on which he rode into the flat-boat used for ferrying across the Schuylkill, and being unable to stop her, she went over the boat into the river with her rider on her back. Monsieur du Coudray disengaged himself from the saddle, but was drowned, notwithstanding every effort being made to save him.

On the evening after the battle General Howe sent a party to Wilmington, who seized in bed Mr. McKinlay, governor of the state of Delaware, and took a shallop lying in the rivulet loaded with the rich effects of some of the inhabitants, together with the public records of the county, and other valuable and important property.

General Wayne, with a detachment of 1,500 men, had taken post in the woods on the left of the British army, with the intention of harassing it on its march. On the evening of the 20th of September, General Grey was despatched to surprise him, and successfully executed the enterprise; killing or wounding, chiefly

FIG. 105.—Departure of La Fayette.

Fig. 106.—Portrait of General Wayne.

with the bayonet, about 300 men, taking nearly 100 prisoners, and making him self master of all their baggage. General Grey had only one captain and three privates killed, and four wounded.

On the evening of the 18th, congress left Philadelphia for the second time, and proceeded first to Lancaster, and afterward to Yorktown. On the afternoon of the 22d, and early on the 23d of September, Sir William Howe, contrary to the expectation of the American commander-in-chief, crossed the Schuylkill at Flatland and Gordon's Ford. The main body of his army encamped at Germantown, a long village, seven miles from Philadelphia; and, on the 26th, with a detachment of his troops he took peaceable possession of the city, where he was cordially received by the quakers and other royalists. During these movements, both armies were much incommoded by cold and heavy rains.

On receiving information of the success of the royal army under his brother at Brandywine, Admiral Lord Howe left the Chesapeake and steered for the Delaware, where he arrived on the 8th of October. As soon as General Howe had gained possession of Philadelphia, he began to clear the course of the river, in order to open a free communication with the fleet.

The Americans had labored assiduously to obstruct the navigation of the Delaware; and, for that purpose, had sunk three rows of chevaux-de-frise, formed of large beams of timber bolted together, with strong projecting iron pikes, across the channel, a little below the place where the Schuylkill falls into the Delaware. The upper and lower rows were commanded by fortifications on the banks and islands of the river, and by floating batteries.

While the detachment employed in assisting to clear the course of the river weakened the royal army at Germantown, General Washington, who lay encamped at Skippach Creek on the north side of the Schuylkill, about seventeen miles from Germantown, meditated an attack upon it. Germantown consisted of one street about two miles long; the line of the British encampment bisected the village almost at right angles, and had its left covered by the Schuylkill. General Washington, having been reinforced by 1,500 troops from Peekskill, and 1,000 Virginian militia, marched from Skippach Creek on the evening of the 3d of October, and at dawn of day next morning attacked the royal army. After a smart conflict he drove in the advanced guard, which was stationed at the head of the village, and, with his army divided into five columns, prosecuted the attack; but Lieutenant-Colonel Musgrave of the 40th regiment, which had been driven in, and who had been able to keep five companies of the regiment together, threw himself into a large stone house in the village, which stood in front of the main column of the Americans, and there almost a half of General Washington's army was detained for a considerable time. Instead of masking the house with a sufficient force, and advancing rapidly with their main body, the Americans attacked the house, which was obstinately defended. This saved the British army; for the critical moment was lost in fruitless attempts on the house; the royal troops had time to get under arms, and be in readiness to resist or attack as circumstances required. General Grey came to the assistance of Colonel Musgrave; the engagement for some time was general and warm; at length the Americans began to give way, and effected a retreat with all their artillery. The morning was very foggy, a circumstance which had prevented the Americans from combining and conducting their operations as they otherwise might have done, but which now favored their retreat by concealing their movements.

In this engagement the British had 600 men killed or wounded; among the slain were Brigadier-General Agnew and Colonel Bird, officers of distinguished reputation. The Americans lost an equal number in killed and wounded, besides 400 who were taken prisoners. General Nash, of North Carolina, was among those who were killed. After the battle General Washington returned to his encampment at Skippach Creek.

But although the British army had been successful in repulsing the Americans, yet their situation was not comfortable; nor could they easily maintain themselves in Pennsylvania unless the navigation of the Delaware were opened, and a free communication established between the fleet and army. The upper line of chevaux-de-frise was protected by a work named Fort Mifflin, erected on a marshy island in the Delaware called Mud Island, formed by an accumulation of sand and vegetable mould near the Pennsylvania bank of the river, and by a redoubt, called Redbank, on the Jersey side. At a small distance below Mud Island, and nearly in a line with it, are two others, named Province and Hog's islands; between these and the Pennsylvanian bank of the river was a narrow channel, of sufficient depth to admit ships of moderate draught of water. The reduction of Forts Mifflin and Redbank, and the opening of the Delaware, were of essential importance to the British army in the occupation of Philadelphia. In order, therefore, that he might be able more conveniently to assist in those operations, General Howe, on the 19th of October, withdrew his army from Germantown, and encamped in the vicinity of Philadelphia.

He despatched Colonel Count Donop, a German officer, with three battalions of Hessian grenadiers, the regiment of Mirbach, and some light infantry, to reduce Redbank. This detachment crossed the Delaware at Philadelphia on the evening of the 21st of October, and next afternoon reached the place of its destination. Count Donop summoned the fort to surrender; but Colonel Christopher Greene, of Rhode Island, who commanded in the redoubt, answered that he would defend his post to the last extremity. Count Donop immediately led his troops to the assault, advancing under a close fire from the fort, and from the American vessels-of-war and floating-batteries on the river; he forced an extensive and unfinished outwork, but could make no impression on the redoubt. The count was mortally wounded; the second in command also was disabled; and, after a desperate conflict and severe loss, the assailants were compelled to retreat under a fire similar to that which had met them in their advance. Colonel Donop was made prisoner, and soon died of his wounds.

The disaster did not terminate here. That part of the fleet which co-operated in the attack was equally unfortunate. The Augusta, Roebuck, Liverpool, Pearl, and Merlin, vessels-of-war, had passed through an opening in the lower line of chevaux-de-frise; and, on the commencement of Count Donop's attack, moved up the river with the flowing tide. But the artificial obstructions had altered the course of the channel, and raised sand-banks where none existed before. Hence the Augusta and Merlin grounded a little below the second row of chevaux-de-frise. At the return of the tide every exertion was made to get them off, but in vain. In the morning the Americans, perceiving their condition, began to fire upon them, and sent fire-ships against them. The Augusta caught fire; and, the flames spreading rapidly, it was with the utmost difficulty that the crew were got out of her. The second lieutenant, chaplain, gunner, and some seamen, perished in the flames; but the greater part of the crew was saved. The Merlin was abandoned and destroyed.

Notwithstanding these misfortunes, the operations requisite for reducing the forts on the river were carried on with great activity. Batteries were erected on the Pennsylvanian bank opposite Mud Island; but from the difficulty of constructing works on marshy ground, and of transporting heavy artillery through swamps, much time was consumed before they could be got ready to act with effect. The British also took possession of Province Island; and, although it was almost wholly overflowed, erected works upon it.

On the 15th of November, everything was ready for a grand attack on Fort Mifflin. The Vigilant armed ship and a hulk, both mounted with heavy cannon, passed up the strait between Hog and Province islands and the Pennsylvanian bank, in order to take their station opposite the weakest part of the fort. The Isis, Somerset, Roebuck, and several frigates, sailed up the main channel, as far as the second line of chevaux-de-frise would permit them, and placed themselves in front of the work.

The little garrison of Fort Mifflin, not exceeding 300 men, had greatly exerted themselves in opposing and retarding the operations of the British fleet and army against them; and in this desperate crisis their courage did not forsake them. A terrible cannonade against Fort Mifflin was begun and carried on by the British batteries and shipping; and was answered by the fort, by the American galleys and floating-batteries on the river, and by their works on the Jersey bank. In the course of the day, the fort was in a great measure demolished, and many of the guns dismounted. The garrison, finding their post no longer tenable, retired, by means of their shipping, during the night. Two days afterward, the post at Redbank was evacuated also. Lord Cornwallis marched against it; but the garrison retreated before his arrival.

The American shipping in the river, being now left unprotected, retired up the stream: part of it, by keeping close to the Jersey side, passed the batteries at Philadelphia during the night, and escaped; the rest was set on fire, and abandoned. Even the part of it, however, which escaped at this time, was afterward destroyed. Thus the navigation of the Delaware was opened, and a free communication established between the fleet and army; but the defence of the river was so obstinate, that a considerable part of the campaign was wasted in clearing it.

General Washington having received a reinforcement from the northern army, after the termination of the campaign in that quarter, left his strong camp at Skippach Creek, and, advancing nearer the British, occupied an advantageous position at White Marsh, fourteen miles from Philadelphia. He had a valley and rivulet in front, and his right was protected by an abattis, or fence of trees cut down, with their top branches pointed and turned outward.

Sir William Howe thinking that General Washington, encouraged by his reinforcements, would hazard a battle for the recovery of the capital of Pennsylvania, or that a successful attack might be made on his position, marched from Philadelphia on the evening of the 4th of December, and next morning took post on Chestnut Hill, in front of the right wing of the American army. During the two succeeding days, General Howe made several movements in front of the hostile encampment, and some skirmishing ensued. But General Washington remained within his lines; and Sir William Howe, deeming it unadvisable to attack him there, and seeing no probability of being able to provoke him to engage on more equal terms, returned with his army, on the 8th of December, to Philadelphia. At that time the two armies were nearly equal in point of numerical force, each consisting of upward of 14,000 men. Soon afterward General Washington quitted White Marsh, crossed the Schuylkill, and took post at Valley Forge, where he spent the winter, about twenty-six miles from Philadelphia.

During the active part of the campaign the British army was most numerous; and although, in the beginning of December, the numerical force of the two armies was nearly equal, yet there was a great difference in the quality and equipment of the troops. Those under Sir William Howe were veterans, accustomed to the most exact discipline and subordination, well armed, and abundantly supplied with military stores and other necessaries; but those under General Washington were for the most part raw levies, ill-disciplined, imperfectly armed, and strangers to military subordination; hence the Americans were unable to meet the royal troops on equal terms. General Washington was obliged to occupy strong positions, and to be wary in all his movements; and although Sir William Howe was successful in all his operations, yet he gained nothing by the campaign but good winter quarters in Philadelphia.

While the events now related were happening in the middle states, most important transactions were going on in the north, to which we shall now turn our attention.

We left the retreating American army, after its unsuccessful irruption into Canada, at Ticonderoga, in the month of November, 1776. That army was composed chiefly of soldiers enlisted for a short period only, and consequently it melted away during the winter, as the term of service for which the men were engaged expired.

The cantonments of the British northern army, extending from Isle aux Noix and Montreal to Quebec, were so distant from each other that they could not readily have afforded mutual support in case of an attack; but the Americans were in no condition to avail themselves of this circumstance. They could scarcely keep up even the appearance of garrisons in their forts, and were apprehensive of an attack on Ticonderoga, as soon as the ice was strong enough to afford an easy passage to troops over the lakes.

At the close of the preceding campaign General Gates had joined the army under General Washington; and the command of the army in the northern department, comprehending Albany, Ticonderoga, Fort Stanwix, and their dependencies, remained in the hands of General Schuyler. The services of that meritorious officer had not been duly valued by congress, which was slow in discerning real and unostentatious merit. Disgusted at the injustice which he had experienced, he was restrained from leaving the army merely by the deep interest which he took in the arduous struggle in which his country was engaged; but after a full investigation of his conduct during the whole of his command, congress was at length convinced of the value of his services, and requested him to continue at the head of the army of the northern department. That army he found too weak for the services which it was expected to perform, and ill supplied with arms, clothes, and provisions. He made every exertion to organize and place it on a respectable footing for the ensuing campaign; but his means were scanty, and the new levies arrived slowly. General St. Clair, who had served under Gates, commanded at Ticonderoga, and, including militia, had nearly 3,000 men under him; but the works were extensive, and would have required 10,000 men to man them fully.

The British ministry had resolved to prosecute the war vigorously on the northern frontier of the United States, and appointed General Burgoyne, who had served under General Carleton in the preceding campaign, to command the royal army in that quarter.

General Burgoyne had visited England during the winter, concerted with ministry a plan of the campaign, and given an estimate of the force necessary for its successful execution. Besides a fine train of artillery and a suitable body of artillerymen, an army, consisting of more than 7,000 veteran troops, excellently equipped, and in a high state of discipline, was put under his command Besides this regular force, he had a great number of Canadians and savages.

General Burgoyne was assisted by a number of distinguished officers, among whom were Generals Philips, Frazer, Powel, Hamilton, Reidesel, and Specht. A suitable naval armament, under the orders of Commodore Lutwych, attended the expedition.

After detaching Colonel St. Leger with a body of light troops and Indians, amounting to about 800 men, by the way of Lake Oswego and the Mohawk river, to make a diversion in that quarter, and to join him when he advanced to the Hudson, General Burgoyne left St. John's on the 16th of June, and, preceded by his naval armament, sailed up Lake Champlain, and in a few days landed and encamped at Crown Point, earlier in the season than the Americans had thought it possible for him to reach that place.

He met his Indian allies, and, in imitation of a savage partisan, gave them a war-feast, at which, with well meant but useless zeal, he made them a speech, in order to inflame their courage and repress their barbarous cruelty. He next issued a lofty proclamation, addressed to the inhabitants of the country, in which, as if certain of victory, he threatened to punish with the utmost severity those who refused to attach themselves to the royal cause. He talked of the ferocity of the Indians, and their eagerness to butcher the friends of independence, and he graciously promised protection to those who should return to their duty. The proclamation was so far from answering the general's intention that it was derided by the people as a model of pomposity.

Having made the necessary arrangements, on the 30th of June General Burgoyne advanced cautiously on both sides of the narrow channel which connects Lakes Champlain and George, the British on the west, and the German auxiliaries on the east, with the naval force in the centre, forming a communication between the two divisions of the army; and on the 1st of July his van appeared in sight of Ticonderoga.

The river Sorel issues from the north end of Lake Champlain, and throws its superfluous waters into the St. Lawrence. Lake Champlain is about eighty miles long from north to south, and about fourteen miles broad where it is widest. Crown Point stands at what may properly be considered the south end of the lake, although a narrow channel, which retains the name of the lake, proceeds southward, and forms a communication with South river and the waters of Lake George.

Ticonderoga is on the west side of the narrow channel, twelve miles south from Crown Point. It is a rocky angle of land, washed on three sides by the water, and partly covered on the fourth side by a deep morass. On the space

Fig. 107.—Ticonderoga.

on the northwest quarter, between the morass and the channel, the French had formerly constructed lines of fortification, which still remained, and those lines the Americans had strengthened by additional works.

Opposite Ticonderoga, on the east side of the channel, which is here between 300 and 400 yards wide, stands a high circular hill, called Mount Independence, which had been occupied by the Americans when they abandoned Crown Point, and carefully fortified. On the top of it, which is flat, they had erected a fort, and provided it sufficiently with artillery. Near the foot of the mountain, which extends to the water's edge, they had raised entrenchments, and mounted them with heavy guns, and had covered those lower works by a battery about half way up the hill.

With prodigious labor they had constructed a communication between those two posts, by means of a wooden bridge which was supported by twenty-two strong wooden pillars, placed at nearly equal distances from each other. The spaces between the pillars were filled up by separate floats, strongly fastened to each other and to the pillars, by chains and rivets. The bridge was twelve feet wide, and the side of it next Lake Champlain was defended by a boom formed of large pieces of timber, bolted and bound together by double iron chains an inch and a half thick. Thus an easy communication was established between Ticonderoga and Mount Independence, and the passage of vessels up the strait prevented.

Immediately after passing Ticonderoga, the channel becomes wider, and, on the southeast side, receives a large body of water from a stream, at that point called South river, but higher up, named Wood Creek. From the southwest come the waters flowing from Lake George; and in the angle formed by the confluence of those two streams rises a steep and rugged eminence called Sugar Hill, which overlooks and commands both Ticonderoga and Mount Independence. That hill had been examined by the Americans; but General St. Clair considering the force under his command insufficient to occupy the extensive works of Ticonderoga and Mount Independence, and flattering himself that the extreme difficulty of the ascent would prevent the British from availing themselves of it, neglected to take possession of Sugar Hill. It may be remarked that the north end of Lake George is between two and three miles above Ticonderoga; but the channel leading to it is interrupted by rapids and shallows, and is unfit for navigation. Lake George is narrow, but is thirty-five miles long, extending from northeast to southwest. At the head of it stood a fort of the same name, strong enough to resist an attack of Indians, but incapable of making any effectual opposition to regular troops. Nine miles beyond it was Fort Edward, on the Hudson.

On the appearance of General Burgoyne's van, General St. Clair had no accurate knowledge of the strength of the British army, having heard nothing of the reinforcement from Europe. He imagined that they would attempt to take the fort by assault, and flattered himself that he would easily be able to repulse them. But, on the second of July, the British appeared in great force on both sides of the channel, and encamped four miles from the forts; while the fleet anchored just beyond the reach of the guns. After a slight resistance, General Burgoyne took possession of Mount Hope, an important post on the south of Ticonderoga, which commanded part of the lines of that fort, as well as the channel leading to Lake George; and extended his lines so as completely to invest the fort on the west side. The German division under General Reidesel occupied the eastern bank of the channel, and sent forward a detachment to the vicinity of the rivulet which flows from Mount Independence. General Burgoyne now labored assiduously in bringing forward his artillery and completing his communications. On the 5th of the month he caused Sugar Hill to be examined; and, being informed that the ascent, though difficult, was not impracticable, he immediately resolved to take possession of it, and proceeded with such activity in raising works and mounting guns upon it, that his battery might have been opened on the garrison next day.

These operations received no check from the besieged; because, as it has been alleged, they were not in a condition to give way. General St. Clair was now nearly surrounded. Only the space between the stream which flows from Mount Independence and South river remained open; and that was to be occupied next day.

In these circumstances it was requisite for the garrison to come to a prompt and decisive resolution; either, at every hazard, to defend the place to the last extremity, or immediately to abandon it. St. Clair called a council of war, the members of which unanimously advised the immediate evacuation of the forts: and preparations were instantly made for carrying this resolution into execution. The British had the command of the communication with Lake George; and consequently the garrison could not escape in that direction. The retreat could be effected by the South river only. Accordingly the invalids, the hospital, and such stores as could be most easily removed, were put on board 200 boats, and, escorted by Colonel Long's regiment, proceeded, on the night between the 5th and 6th of July, up the South river toward Skenesborough. The garrisons of Ticonderoga and Mount Independence marched by land through Castletown, toward the same place. The troops were ordered to march out in profound silence, and particularly to set nothing on fire. But these prudent orders were disobeyed; and, before the rear-guard was in motion, the house on Mount Independence, which General Fermoy had occupied, was seen in flames. That served as a signal to the enemy, who immediately entered the works, and fired, but without effect, on the rear of the retreating army.

General Burgoyne instantly resolved on a rapid pursuit. Commodore Lutwych began to cut the boom, and break down the bridge between Ticonderoga and Mount Independence; and so great was his activity that, although the Americans had labored ten months on the work, he opened a passage for his fleet by nine in the morning.

A number of gun-boats, under Captain Carter, were detached in pursuit of that part of the American force which had retreated up South river; and they proceeded with such rapidity, that at three in the afternoon they overtook the retreating enemy, brought them to action near the falls of Skenesborough, took two of their five galleys, and compelled them to burn the other three and their boats. At Skenesborough the Americans did not long remain; for understanding that General Burgoyne, who with part of his army had sailed up the South river in boats, had landed at South bay, below Skenesborough, they set fire to the works, and, without any considerable loss of men, retreated to Fort Ann, higher up Wood creek. But they lost all their baggage, and a great quantity of provisions and military stores, which were either destroyed by themselves or taken by the British.

The operations against the main body of the garrison, which retreated by land, were not less active. General Frazer, at the head of a body of grenadiers and light infantry, pursued them; and was supported by General Reidesel. General St. Clair, convinced that his safety lay in the rapidity of his movements, marched with great diligence, and in the evening of the day on which he abandoned the forts reached Castletown, thirty miles from Ticonderoga; but his rear-guard, consisting of 1,200 men, under Colonel Warner, on account of fatigue, halted at Hubbardtown, six miles behind the rest of the army.

On the evening of the 6th of July, General Frazer arrived near Hubbardtown; and being informed that the rear of the enemy was at no great distance, he re-

Fig. 108.—Burgoyne's attack on the American Batteaux.

dered his men to lie on their arms during the night. On the morning of the 7th he renewed the pursuit, and soon overtook the American rear-guard, under Colonel Warner, who, besides his own regiment, had with him those of Colonels Francis and Hale. But Hale fled without fighting; and afterward falling in with a small party of British troops, he surrendered himself and such of his men as adhered to him prisoners. By this defection Warner could bring only about 700 men into action. Frazer began the attack about seven in the morning, and the conflict was severe and sanguinary. Colonel Francis fell, fighting bravely at the head of his regiment; but the battle was obstinately maintained till the arrival of General Reidesel with a reinforcement, when the Americans fled with precipitation.

St. Clair, who was at Castletown, six miles distant, heard the firing when it began, and ordered two regiments of militia, which were nearest the scene of action, to support Colonel Warner; but, instead of obeying the order, those regiments sought safety in flight, and left Warner to his fate. In this encounter the Americans lost 324 men in killed, wounded, and prisoners; the royal troops had 183 men killed or wounded.

While St. Clair lay at Castletown, an officer from one of the American galleys informed him that the British were hastening forward to Skenesborough, and would reach that place before him. He therefore entered the woods on his left, and pursued his way to Fort Edward, where, after a fatiguing march, in which his troops suffered much from bad weather and want of provisions, he joined General Schuyler on the 12th of July. Two days after leaving Castle-

Colonel Hill, with the 9th regiment, was ordered to pursue the American detachment under Colonel Long, which had retreated up Wood Creek from Skenesborough to Fort Ann: two other regiments were afterward directed to support him. Colonel Long attacked Colonel Hill, and a severe skirmish ensued; but, being informed of the approach of the reinforcement to Colonel Hill, the Americans set fire to the works at Fort Ann, and retreated to Fort Edward.

Thus, in the course of a few days after the commencement of active operations, General Burgoyne made himself master of Ticonderoga and Mount Independence, drove the republicans from Lakes Champlain and George, and compelled them to seek shelter behind the Hudson.

CHAPTER VIII.

The evacuation of Ticonderoga and Mount Independence was an event entirely unexpected by the Americans, and spread surprise and alarm throughout the provinces, particularly those of New England, which were exposed to the most immediate danger. St. Clair was generally blamed, but on inquiry was acquitted, although the Americans were not too indulgent to their unsuccessful officers. His garrison was much weaker than had been commonly supposed; and the circumstances of the retreat show that a considerable number of his troops were of the worst quality; but amid the agitation and alarm occasioned by the abandonment of posts on the lakes, none of the people manifested a disposition to submit to British authority.

General Schuyler was on his way to Ticonderoga; but at Stillwater he was informed of the evacuation of the fort; and at Saratoga, on the same day, he learned the total loss of the stores at Skenesborough. Amid this disastrous in-

FIG. 109.
MAP
Showing the route
of
GEN. BURGOYNE
previous
to his surrender at
SARATOGA
October 17th,
1777.
Note. The route of the army under Gen. Burgoyne is seen by the double line
LAKE CHAMPLAIN
Crown Point
Ticonderoga
Sugar Hill
Ft. Independence
Otter Creek
July 7th
Hubberton
Fort
Castleton
East Cr.
South Bay
Skenesboro
July 6th
Pultney
Lake George
Wood Cr.
July 8th
Ft. George
formerly ft. William Henry
Fort Ann
Hudson R.
Falls
Kingsbury
Fort Edward
Pawlet
Moses Kill
Rupert
Manchester
Falls
Ft. Miller
Shallows
Batten Kill
Ft. Hardy
Oct. 10
Fish Kill
Saratoga
Sunderland
Freemans farm
Sept. 19th
Arlington
Bemus Heights
Oct. 7th
Cambridge
Shaftesborough
Still water
Hoosac R
Santcoick
Aug. 16th
Anthony's Kill
Schaticoke
Bennington
Half Moon
Mohawk R.
Cohoes Falls
Lansingburgh
Pownal
Hudson R.
Massachusetts Fort
Williamston
Deerfield R.
Connecticut R.
ALBANY

FIG. 110.—View of Lake Saratoga.

telligence, he heard nothing from St. Clair, and was apprehensive of the total loss of the garrison. He fixed his headquarters at Fort Edward, on the Hudson, a ruinous fortification, fifty-seven miles above Albany, which merely served to give a name to the place. His force, even when joined by St. Clair, did not exceed 4,400 men, about half of which was militia, and the whole was ill-clothed, ill-armed, and dispirited by the recent disasters.

With that force General Schuyler could not face the British army; and to gain time was to him a matter of the utmost importance. For this purpose, he ordered detachments of his men to obstruct the navigation of Wood Creek above Fort Ann; to break down bridges; to cut trees so as to fall across the road from opposite sides, and intermingle their branches, particularly at places where the line of road could not be altered; and to throw every obstacle in the way, in order to retard General Burgoyne's progress. He ordered all the horses and cattle out of the way of the royal army; and brought off from Fort George all the ammunition and stores, of which he stood much in need.

While General Schuyler made every effort to retard the progress of his opponent, he exerted himself vigorously to strengthen his own army. He solicited reinforcements of regular troops; he called on the militia of New England to join the army; and used all his personal influence in the surrounding country to inspire the people with military ardor and patriotic enthusiasm. As the danger was alarming, his unwearied exertions were actively seconded by Washington and the civil authorities. General Lincoln, who in a high degree possessed the confidence of the militia, was appointed to raise and command them. Arnold, who had a high reputation for gallantry in the field, was directed to join the northern army; and Colonel Morgan, with his corps of riflemen, was ordered to the same quarter. Colonel Warner, with his regiment, was sent toward the left of the British army, to threaten its flank and rear, and to assist in raising the militia. Tents, artillery, ammunition, and other necessaries, were diligently provided.

While General Schuyler made every exertion to strengthen and equip his army, General Burgoyne was obliged to halt at Skenesborough, in order to give some rest to his exhausted troops; to reassemble and reorganize his army, which had been thrown into some disorder, and considerably scattered, by his rapid movements; to bring forward his artillery, baggage, and military stores; and to make all the necessary preparations for advancing toward Albany.

During his halt at Skenesborough, General Burgoyne issued a second proclamation, summoning the people of the adjacent country to send deputies to meet Colonel Skene at Castletown, in order to deliberate on the measures which might still be adopted to save from destruction those who had not yet conformed to his first proclamation. General Schuyler issued a counter-proclamation, warning the people to be on their guard against the insidious designs of the enemy, and assuring them that they would be considered traitors, and punished accordingly, if they complied with his propositions.

But this war of proclamations was soon followed by more active measures; for, after the necessary rest to his army in the vicinity of Skenesborough, General Burgoyne, much elated with his past success, and cherishing sanguine anticipations of future victory, began to advance toward the Hudson. On proceeding up Wood creek, he was obliged to remove the impediments with which General Schuyler had encumbered the channel, and afterward to restore the roads and bridges which he had destroyed. The labor was great: above forty bridges were constructed, and others repaired, one of which, entirely of log-work, was over a morass two miles wide. This prodigious labor, in a sultry season of the year, and in a close country swarming with tormenting insects, the army performed with cheerfulness and untired perseverance. At length, with

Fig. 111.—An American backwoodsman.

little opposition from the enemy, on the 30th of July it reached Fort Edward, which General Schuyler had quitted a short time before, and retreated to Saratoga. General Burgoyne might have much more easily reached Fort Edward by the way of Lake George; but he had been led up the South river in pursuit of the fleeing enemy; and he persevered in that difficult route, lest he should discourage his troops by a retrograde movement.

FIG. 112.—Lake George.

At Fort Edward, General Burgoyne again found it necessary to pause in his career; for his carriages, which in the hurry had been made of unseasoned wood, were much broken down, and needed to be repaired. From the unavoidable difficulties of the case, not more than one third of the draught horses contracted for in Canada had arrived; and General Schuyler had been careful to remove almost all the horses and draught cattle of the country out of his way. Boats for the navigation of the Hudson, provisions, stores, artillery, and other necessaries for the army, were all to be brought from Fort George; and although that place was only nine or ten miles from Fort Edward, yet such was the condition of the roads, rendered nearly impassable by the great quantity of rain that had fallen, that the labor of transporting necessaries was incredible. General Burgoyne had collected about 100 oxen; but it was often necessary to employ ten or twelve of them in transporting a single boat. With his utmost exertions he had only conveyed twelve boats into the Hudson, and provisions for the army for four days in advance, on the 15th of August.

In order to aid and facilitate the operations of St. Leger on the Mohawk, General Burgoyne wished to make a rapid movement down the Hudson: but it was not easy to procure provisions for his army. The difficulty of drawing his supplies from Lake George was every day to increase with the distance: and his left flank and rear were threatened by General Lincoln, who had been ordered by General Schuyler to join Colonel Warner, to collect the militia of New England, to endeavor to cut off the communication of the British army with Lake George, or even to make an attempt on Ticonderoga.

In these circumstances, General Burgoyne conceived the plan of procuring a supply for his army from a different quarter. It was well known that the American army received live cattle from New England, which were collected at Bennington, twenty-four miles east from the Hudson, where a large deposite of carriages, corn, flour, and other necessaries, had been made. For this purpose he moved down the east side of the Hudson, and encamped nearly opposite Saratoga, which place the American army left on the 15th of August, and retreated to the confluence of the Mohawk and Hudson rivers. He sent his van across the river by a bridge of boats; and at the same time despatched Colonel Baume, a German officer, with 500 men, partly cavalry, two pieces of artillery, and 100 Indians, to surprise Bennington.

General Stark, with the New Hampshire militia, 400 strong, happened to be in that vicinity, on his way to join General Schuyler. He heard first of the approach of the Indians, and soon afterward was informed that they were supported by a regular force. He collected his brigade, sent expresses to the neighboring militia to join him, and also to Colonel Warner's regiment at Manchester. On the morning of the 14th of August, he marched against the enemy, at the head of 700 men; and sent Colonel Gregg, with 200 men, to skirmish in their front and retard their progress. He drew up his men in order of battle: but, on coming in sight of him, Baume halted on advantageous ground; sent an express to General Burgoyne, informing him of his situation; and fortified himself as well as circumstances would permit.

Some small skirmishing parties of the Americans killed several Germans, and two Indian chiefs, without sustaining any loss; and this slight success not a little elated them. In a council of war, it was resolved to attack Baume next day; but next day it rained incessantly, and the attack could not be made, although there was some skirmishing.

On the morning of the 16th, Stark, having received some reinforcements, sent detachments by the right and left of the enemy, with orders to unite in their rear, and begin the attack in that quarter. But before they met the Indians retreated between the columns, and receiving a fire as they passed, sustained some loss. The detachments, according to orders, began the attack on the rear of the enemy, and were assisted by Stark, who instantly advanced to the charge in front. Baume made a brave defence; the battle lasted two hours, during which he was furiously assailed on every side by an incessant discharge of musketry. He was mortally wounded; his troops were overpowered; a few of them escaped into the woods and fled, pursued by the Americans; the rest were killed or taken prisoners. Thus, without artillery, with old rusty firelocks, and with scarcely a bayonet, these militia entirely defeated 500 veterans, well armed, provided with two pieces of artillery, and defended by breastworks.

After the victory, the greater part of the militia dispersed in quest of booty, and their avidity for spoil nearly proved fatal to them; for, on receiving Baume's express, General Burgoyne ordered Colonel Brehman, who had before been sent forward to Batten hill for the purpose, to march to the assistance of his countrymen with the Brunswick grenadiers, light infantry, and chasseurs, amounting to 500 men. Colonel Brehman set out at eight in the morning of the 15th; but the roads were rendered almost impassable by incessant rains; and, although he marched with the utmost diligence, yet it was four the next afternoon before he reached the vicinity of the place where his countrymen had been defeated. The first notice which he received of Baume's disaster was from the fugitives whom he met He easily repulsed the few militia who were in pursuit of them; and, from the scattered state of Stark's troops, had the prospect of being able to make himself master of the stores, which were the great object of the expedition. But at that critical moment Colonel Warner's regiment of continentals arrived, and instantly engaged Brehman. The firing reassembled the scattered militia, who joined in the battle as they came up Colonel Brehman maintained the conflict till dark; when, abandoning his artil lery and baggage, he retreated, and, escaping under cover of night, with the shattered remnant of his detachment, regained the camp.

In those engagements the Americans took four brass field-pieces, about 1,000 muskets (a most seasonable supply to the ill-armed militia), 900 swords, and four baggage-wagons. Exclusive of Canadians and other loyalists, the loss of the royal army could not be less than 700 men in killed, wounded, and prisoners, although General Burgoyne stated it at only about 400. The Americans admitted the loss of about 100 in killed and wounded.

This was the first check which General Burgoyne's army had met with, and it was a severe one, and had a fatal influence on the campaign. The loss of a few hundred men was nothing compared with the effects which it produced upon the minds of the people: it greatly elated them, and gave the militia, who had been much dispirited by the late defeats, confidence in themselves, and encouraged them to hasten to the army in great numbers, in order to consummate the work which they had begun. Before the events in the vicinity of Bennington, dejection and alarm pervaded the northern provinces; but those events dispelled the gloom, infused spirit and vigor into the militia, and gave a new aspect to affairs on the Hudson.

The failure of the attempt on Bennington had arisen from a concurrence of circumstances which could not be foreseen. The presence of Stark was purely accidental; and the seasonable arrival of Warner saved both the stores and the disorderly militia from the hands of Brehman. But the defeat at Bennington was not the only misfortune which General Burgoyne met with: before reaching Crown Point he had despatched Colonel St. Leger, as already mentioned, with a detachment of regular troops, Canadians, loyalists, and Indians, by the way of Oswego, to make a diversion on the upper part of the Mohawk river, and afterward join him on his way to Albany.

On the 2d of August, St. Leger approached Fort Stanwix or Schuyler, a log fortification, situated on rising ground near the source of the Mohawk river, and garrisoned by about 600 continentals under the command of Colonel Gansevoort. Next day he invested the place with an army of sixteen or seventeen hundred men, nearly one half of whom were Indians, and the rest British, Germans, Canadians, and loyal Americans. On being summoned to surrender, Gansevoort answered that he would defend the place to the last.

On the approach of St. Leger to Fort Schuyler, General Herkimer, who commanded the militia of Tryon county, assembled about 700 of them and marched to the assistance of the garrison. On the forenoon of the 6th of August, a messenger from Herkimer found means to enter the fort, and gave notice that he was only eight miles distant, and intended that day to force a passage into the fort and join the garrison. Gansevoort resolved to aid the attempt by a vigorous sally, and appointed Colonel Willet with upward of 200 men to that service.

St. Leger received information of the approach of Herkimer, and placed a large body of regulars and Indians in ambush on the road by which he was to advance. Herkimer fell into the snare. The first notice which he received of the presence of an enemy was from a heavy discharge of musketry on his troops, which was instantly followed by the war-whoop of the Indians, who attacked the militia with their tomahawks. Though disconcerted by the suddenness of the attack, many of the militia behaved with spirit, and a scene of unutterable confusion and carnage ensued. The royal troops and the militia became so closely crowded together that they had not room to use their firearms, but pushed and pulled each other, and, using their daggers, fell pierced by mutual wounds. Some of the militia fled at the first onset, others made their escape afterward; about 100 of them retreated to a rising ground, where they bravely defended themselves, till Sir John Johnstone, who commanded the ambuscade, found it necessary to call off his men for the defence of their own camp. In the absence of the party against Herkimer, Colonel Willet made a successful sally, killed a number of the enemy, destroyed their provisions, carried off some spoil, and returned to the fort without the loss of a man.

The loss of Herkimer's party was computed to amount to 400 men; the general himself was among the slain. Many of the most active political characters in that part of the country were killed, wounded, or made prisoners; so that St. Leger was secured from any further trouble from the militia. St. Leger again summoned the fort to surrender, but again met with a steady refusal.

General Schuyler, deeming it a matter of importance to prevent the junction of St. Leger with General Burgoyne, despatched Arnold with a considerable body of regular troops to relieve Fort Schuyler. Arnold apprehended an American of some wealth and influence, who, he believed, had been acting the part of a traitor, but promised to spare his life and fortune on condition of his going into the British camp before Fort Schuyler, and alarming the Indians and others by magnifying the force which was marching against them. This the person undertook and executed. Some Indians, who were friendly to the Americans, communicated similar information, and even spread a report of the total defeat of General Burgoyne's army, founded, probably, on the disaster of the party sent against Bennington.

Fort Schuyler was better constructed, and defended with more courage than St. Leger had expected; and his light artillery made little impression on it. His Indians, who liked better to take scalps and plunder than to besiege fortresses, became very unmanageable. The loss which they had sustained in the encounters with Herkimer and Willet deeply affected them; they had expected to be witnesses of the triumphs of the British, and to share with them the plunder. Hard service and little reward caused bitter disappointment; and when they heard that a strong detachment of continentals was marching against them, they resolved to seek safety in flight. St. Leger employed every argument and artifice to detain them, but in vain; part of them went off, and all the rest threatened to follow if the siege were persevered in. Therefore, on the 22d of August, St. Leger raised the siege, and retreated with circumstances indicating great alarm: the tents were left standing, the artillery was abandoned, and a great part of the baggage, ammunition, and provisions, fell into the hands of the garrison, a detachment from which pursued the retreating enemy. St. Leger retired to Montreal, whence he proceeded to Ticonderoga, with the intention of joining General Burgoyne.

General Arnold reached Fort Schuyler two days after the retreat of the besiegers; but, finding no occasion for his services, he soon returned to camp. The successful defence of Fort Stanwix or Schuyler powerfully co-operated with the defeat of the royal troops at Bennington in raising the spirits and invigorating the activity of the Americans. The loyalists became timid; the wavering began to doubt the success of the royal arms; and the great body of the people was convinced that nothing but steady exertion on their part was necessary, to ruin that army which a short time before had appeared irresistible.

General Schuyler, at this critical period of the campaign, when by unwearied exertion he had brought the northern army into a respectable condition, and had the fair prospect of gaining the laurels due to his industry and talents, was superseded, and General Gates appointed to the command of the army. General Schuyler keenly felt the indignity offered him, by depriving him of the command at that critical juncture; but he faithfully discharged his duty, till the arrival in camp of his successor, on the 19th of August. The late events had greatly changed the aspect of affairs; and General Gates found the army in a far more promising state than he had expected. The harvest was over; and many of the militia, who had been kept at home by it, were arriving in camp, where there was now a respectable force, much encouraged by the recent success of the American arms.

Soon after General Gates entered on the command of the northern army, an epistolary correspondence was opened between him and General Burgoyne, not of the most pleasant or courteous kind. On the 30th of August, the British general complained of the harsh treatment experienced by the loyalists who had been made prisoners at Bennington, and hinted at retaliation. On the 2d of September the American general answered his letter, and recriminated by expatiating on the horrid atrocities perpetrated by the Indians who accompanied the armies of General Burgoyne and Colonel St. Leger, and imputed them to General Burgoyne. One barbarous act committed by an Indian attached to General Burgoyne's army, although it involved only a case of individual suffering, yet made a deep impression on the public mind, and roused indignation to the highest pitch.

Mr. Jones, an officer of the British army, had gained the affections of Miss McCrea, a lovely young lady of amiable character and spotless reputation, daughter of a gentleman attached to the royal cause, residing near Fort Edward; and they had agreed to be married. In the course of service, the officer was removed to some distance from his bride; and became anxious for her safety and desirous of her company. He engaged some Indians, of two different tribes, to bring her to camp, and promised a keg of rum to the person who should deliver her safe to him. She dressed to meet her bridegroom, and accompanied her Indian conductors; but by the way, the two chiefs, each being desirous of receiving the promised reward, disputed which of them should deliver her to her lover. The dispute rose to a quarrel; and, according to their usual method of disposing of a disputed prisoner, one of them instantly cleft the head of the lady with his tomahawk. This simple story, tragical and affecting in itself, contributed in no slight degree to embitter the minds of the people against those who could degrade themselves by the aid of such allies. The impulse given to the public mind by such atrocities more than counterbalanced any advantages which the British derived from the assistance of the Indians.

In reference to this, General Gates said: "That the savages of America should, in their warfare, mangle and scalp the unhappy prisoners who fall into their hands is neither new nor extraordinary; but that the famous Lieutenant-General Burgoyne, in whom the fine gentleman is united with the soldier and scholar, should hire the savages of America to scalp Europeans and descendants of Europeans, nay more, that he should pay a price for each scalp so barbarously taken, is more than will be believed in Europe, until authenticated facts shall, in every gazette, confirm the truth of the horrid tale.

"Miss McCrea, a young lady lovely to the sight, of virtuous character and amiable disposition, engaged to an officer of your army, was, with other women and children, taken out of a house near Fort Edward, carried into the woods, and then scalped and mangled in a most shocking manner. Two parents with their six children were all treated with the same inhumanity, while quietly residing in their once happy and peaceful dwelling. The miserable fate of Miss McCrea was particularly aggravated by her being dressed to meet her promised husband; but she met her murderer employed by you. Upward of one hundred men, women, and children, have perished by the hands of the ruffians, to whom, it is asserted, you have paid the price of blood!"

Although General Burgoyne, defeated in his attempt against Bennington, and

FIG. 113.—Murder of Miss Jane M'Crea.

disappointed in the expectation of assistance from St. Leger, was left to his own resources, yet he did not abandon the arduous enterprise in which he was engaged, but still flattered himself with the hope of being able to accomplish the great object of the campaign. In order, however, to procure subsistence for his army, he was obliged to revert to the tedious and toilsome mode of bringing supplies from Fort George; and he prosecuted this work with his usual ardor and persevering industry. Having by unwearied exertions collected provisions for thirty days, and constructed a bridge of boats over the Hudson, in place of the rafts which had been carried away by a flood, he crossed the river on the 13th and 14th of September, and encamped on the heights and plains of Saratoga, twenty miles below Fort Edward and thirty-seven above Albany.

General Gates, who was now joined by all the continental troops destined for the northern department, and reinforced by considerable bodies of militia, left the strong position which Schuyler had taken at the confluence of the Mohawk with the Hudson eight miles above Albany, proceeded sixteen miles up the river toward the enemy, and formed a strong camp near Stillwater. The two armies were only about twelve miles distant from each other; but the bridges between them were broken down, the roads were bad, and the country was covered with woods; consequently the progress of the British army, encumbered by its fine train of artillery and numerous wagons, was slow, and it was attended with some skirmishing.

On the evening of the 17th, General Burgoyne encamped within four miles of the American army, and spent the next day in repairing the bridges between the two camps, which he accomplished with some loss. About mid-day, on the 19th of September, he put himself at the head of the right wing of his army, and advanced through the woods toward the left of the American camp; General Frazer and Colonel Brehman, with the grenadiers and light infantry, covered his right flank; and the Indians, loyalists, and Canadians, proceeded in front. The left wing and artillery, commanded by Generals Philips and Reidesel, proceeded along the great road near the river.

The nature of the ground prevented the contending armies from observing the movements of each other; but General Gates, whose scouts were in constant activity, was soon informed of the advance of the British army. He detached Colonel Morgan, a bold and active partisan, with his riflemen, to observe the motions and impede the progress of the enemy. Morgan soon met the advanced parties in front of the British right wing, and drove them back. General Burgoyne supported them by a strong detachment; and, after a severe conflict, Morgan, in his turn, was compelled to give way. But General Gates reinforced him, and the engagement became more general. The Americans attempted to turn the right flank of the British army, with the view of attacking it in the rear; but, being opposed by Frazer and Brehman, they made a rapid movement, and commenced a furious attack on the left of the British right wing. The combatants were reinforced; and between three and four in the afternoon, General Arnold, with nine continental regiments and Morgan's riflemen, was closely engaged with the whole right wing of the British army. Both parties fought with the most determined courage; and the battle ended only with the day. When it became dark, the Americans withdrew to their camp; and the royal troops lay all night on their arms on the field of battle. On hearing the firing at the beginning of the engagement, General Philips with some artillery forced his way through the woods, and rendered essential service.

In this battle, in which each party had nearly 3,000 men actually engaged, the British lost upward of 500 in killed and wounded, and the Americans about 400 men. Night separated the combatants; each side claimed the victory, and each believed that with a part only of its own force it had beaten the whole of the hostile army. But although neither army was defeated, it was evident who had gained the advantage ; General Burgoyne had failed in the attempt to dislodge the enemy, and his progress was arrested. His communication with the lakes was cut off, and his resources were daily failing; while the Americans had the same opportunities of gaining supplies as before, and their strength was still increasing by the arrival of fresh troops. In such circumstances, to fight without a decisive victory was to the British nearly equivalent to a defeat; and to fight without being beaten was to the Americans productive of many of the consequences of victory.

Accordingly, the news of the battle was received with joy and exultation throughout the United States, and the ruin of the invading army was confidently anticipated. The militia were encouraged to take the field, and assist in con summating the work so auspiciously begun. At that time the army under the command of General Gates did not much exceed 7,000 men ; but it was soon considerably increased.

On the day after the engagement, information was received in the American camp, which still farther raised the spirits and confirmed the confidence of the troops. General Lincoln, who had been sent to collect the militia of New England, had assembled a considerable body of them at Manchester, whence he marched to Pawlet, a small village on a rivulet of the same name, which falls into Wood creek. From that place, he detached three parties, consisting of about 500 men each ; one, under Colonel Brown, proceeded to the north end of Lake George, chiefly with the intention of relieving a number of prisoners confined there, but with orders to carry his offensive operations as far as prudence would permit ; one, under Colonel Johnson, marched against Mount Independence ; and a third, under Colonel Woodbury, was sent to Skenesborough, to cover, if needful, the retreat of the two others. With the remainder of his troops Lincoln set out to join General Gates, and reached the camp, with about 2,000 men, before the end of September. Colonel Brown proceeded with such secrecy and address, that, at dawn of day on the 18th of September, he arrived at the north end of Lake George, and completely surprised the outposts between the landing-place and Ticonderoga. Almost in an instant, and with scarcely any loss, he made himself master of Sugar Hill, or Mount Defiance, Mount Hope, an armed sloop, several gun-boats, and 200 boats which had been employed in transporting provisions for the army. He relieved 100 American prisoners, and took nearly 300 of the enemy. He made an attempt on Ticonderoga, but failed. Johnson also was unsuccessful against Mount Independence. The party afterward sailed up Lake George in the boats which they had taken, attacked Diamond Island, which General Burgoyne had fortified and made the deposite of all the stores collected at the south end of the lake, but were repulsed. They then burned the vessels which they had taken, and returned to their former station. The success of this party in the early part of their expedition was soon proclaimed throughout New England, where it was rumored that the forts were taken ; and the militia were invited to join their countrymen in arms and ensure the ruin of the invaders.

Immediately after the battle at Stillwater, General Burgoyne took a position almost within cannon-shot of the American camp, fortified his right, extended his left along the hills, and encamped two European regiments and a corps of provincials on the low ground on the bank of the river where he placed his hospital. He used every endeavor to communicate information of his situation to Generals Howe and Clinton, and requested and expected assistance from them ; but those officers had no suspicion of his danger, and were not able to afford him any effectual aid. On the 21st, he received a letter from General Clinton informing him of the meditated attack on Forts Clinton and Montgomery; but that attack, though successful, availed him nothing.

The two armies lay in front of each other, each fortifying its camp. General Burgoyne's provisions were daily diminishing; and the events of the campaign so little answered the expectation of his savage allies, that, notwithstanding every entreaty and remonstrance, they abandoned him at that critical period of the campaign.

After the battle of Stillwater, the safety of the British army lay only in retreat It was unable to advance; to fall back on the lakes and return to Canada, although difficult, was not then impossible. But every hour lessened the probability of victory, and rendered retreat more impracticable. General Burgoyne, however, could not at once dismiss all the splendid visions of conquest and glory which had so long dazzled his imagination; and he flattered himself with the hope of a powerful co-operation on the side of New York, which had not been concerted, and was not to happen. Under those delusions he lingered in his strong camp from the 20th of September till the 7th of October. During that interval, daily skirmishes happened, which accustomed the raw troops of America to the face of an enemy. General Gates, sensible that delay was in his favor, meditated no immediate attack on the hostile camp; but diligently took measures to prevent the escape of the royal army from the toils in which it was entangled.

General Burgoyne's difficulties were great and daily increasing. His army was reduced to 5,000 regular troops; his provisions were almost exhausted, and his men put on short allowance; his horses were perishing for want of forage; he was so environed by the enemy that he could procure no fresh supplies, and he had received no recent intelligence from Sir Henry Clinton. He could not long remain in the position which he then occupied, and he was not ignorant of the difficulty and danger of a retreat. In these circumstances he resolved to try the fortune of another battle; as a victory would enable him either to advance, or to retreat with safety.

Accordingly, on the 7th of October, he led out 1,500 men, well provided with artillery, and, accompanied by Generals Philips, Reidesel, and Frazer, marched against the enemy, leaving his camp on the high grounds under the care of Generals Hamilton and Specht, and the redoubts and posts adjacent to the river under General Gell. General Burgoyne's detachment had scarcely formed within about half a mile of the enemy's entrenchments, when its left, where the grenadiers were posted, was furiously assailed. The Germans, who were on the right of the grenadiers, were also soon engaged. Three regiments, under General Arnold, proceeded to attack the right of the British detachment in front, while another division endeavored to turn its flank and gain its rear. In order to frustrate this intention, General Frazer, with the light infantry and part of the 24th regiment, was ordered to cover the right; but, while he was making a movement for that purpose, the left was overpowered and gave way. To save it from destruction, Frazer hastened to its assistance; but met with an American corps of riflemen, which briskly attacked him, and he was mortally wounded in the conflict. The whole royal detachment now gave way; and, with the loss of most of its artillery, retreated to the camp. The Americans closely pursued, and, under a tremendous fire of grape-shot and musketry, fiercely assaulted the works throughout their whole extent. Arnold, who conducted the assault, urged on his men; but was ultimately repulsed by the British under the immediate orders of General Burgoyne, after having had his horse shot under him, and being wounded in the same leg which had been injured at Quebec. The left of the American detachment, under Colonel Brooks, was more successful. It turned the right of the royal encampment, stormed the works of the German re-

Fig. 114.—Burgoyne's Retreat.

serve, under Colonel Brehman, who was killed, and his troops retreated, with the loss of all their artillery and camp equipage; while Brooks maintained the ground which he had gained.

Darkness, as on the 19th of September, put an end to the bloody conflict; and the Americans lay all night on their arms, about half a mile from the lines, with the intention of renewing the assault in the morning. The advantage which they had gained was great. Without any considerable loss, they had killed many of the enemy, made upward of 200 prisoners, among whom were several officers of distinction, taken nine pieces of brass artillery, all the baggage and camp equipage of a German brigade, obtained a large supply of ammunition, of which they stood much in need, and had entered the royal lines, and gained a position which threatened their rear. About midnight, General Lincoln with his division marched from the American camp to relieve the troops who had been engaged, and to occupy the ground which they had won.

General Burgoyne's situation was now critical and distressing. Since he had come fairly into contact with the enemy, he had met with an obstinacy of resistance and a vigor of attack wholly unexpected. In the late encounters, the Americans had shown themselves a match for the best veteran troops, and capable of improving any advantage which they might obtain. Sensible, therefore, of the danger of encountering the events of next day on the ground which he then occupied, General Burgoyne resolved on a total change of position. Accordingly, in the course of the night, in a silent and orderly manner, and without any interruption from the enemy, he moved his camp to the hills, extending his right up the river. The entire change of front extricated him from the immediate danger with which he was threatened, and induced the Americans to make new dispositions.

On the 8th, General Burgoyne made some attempts to provoke General Gates to attack him in the strong position which he had taken: but those attempts were ineffectual; for General Gates, fully aware of his own advantages and of the difficulties to which his adversary was reduced, declined an immediate attack; but was active in taking every precaution to prevent the escape of the royal army. He posted 1,400 men on the heights opposite the ford of Saratoga, and sent strong detachments to guard the fords higher up the river.

The 8th of October was spent in skirmishing and cannonading. About sunset, the body of General Frazer, who had been mortally wounded on the preceding day, was, agreeably to his own desire, carried up the hill, to be interred in the great redoubt, attended only by the officers who had lived in his family. Generals Burgoyne, Philips, and Reidesel, in testimony of respect and affection for their late brave companion in arms, joined the mournful procession, which necessarily passed in view of both armies. The incessant cannonade, the steady attitude and unfaltering voice of the chaplain, and the firm demeanor of the company during the funeral service, though occasionally covered with the earth torn up by the shot from the hostile batteries ploughing the ground around them, the mute expression of feeling pictured on every countenance, and the increasing gloom of the evening, all contributed to give an affecting solemnity to the obsequies. General Gates afterward declared, that if he had been apprized of what what was going on, he would at least have silenced his batteries, and allowed the last offices of humanity to be performed without disturbance, or even have ordered minute guns to be fired in honor of the deceased general.

General Burgoyne being informed that an American column was advancing with the intention of gaining his right flank, resolved immediately to retreat to Saratoga, about ten miles up the river. He began his march about nine in the evening of the 8th, leaving behind him several boats loaded with provisions and baggage, and his hospital, containing about 300 sick and wounded men, toward

Fig. 115.—Washington's Headquarters at Newburgh.

FIG. 116.—Burgoyne's encampment on North river.

whom General Gates behaved with his usual humanity; but the roads were so bad, and the heavy rains so incessant, that it was the evening of next day before the army, much fatigued, reached Saratoga; and it was not till the forenoon of the 10th that the rear passed the fords of Fishkill creek a little farther north. On arriving at the ground which he intended to occupy, General Burgoyne found a party of the enemy already in possession of it; but on his approach they retreated, and joined their countrymen on the east of the river.

Fig. 117.—Field of Saratoga.

The rain, which continued during the whole of the 9th, and greatly retarded the march of the royal army, kept the Americans in their camp; but it had no sooner ceased, than General Gates set out in pursuit of the retreating enemy. As the roads, however, were extremely bad, and the bridges broken down by the British, it was some time before he overtook them.

From his camp above Fishkill creek, General Burgoyne sent forward a company of artificers, escorted by a regular regiment, some riflemen, and a body of provincials, to repair the roads and bridges leading to Fort Edward, to enable the army to pursue its march to that place. This party had not long left the camp, when the Americans appeared on the heights below Fishkill creek; and made dispositions as if intending to force a passage and attack the royal army. General Burgoyne, therefore, recalled the regular troops escorting the artificers; and the provincial corps, under whose protection the workmen were left, being attacked by a small party of the enemy, who had gained the front of the royal army, fled on the first fire, and consequently the artificers were obliged to return to camp, without having performed any part of the task to which they were appointed. As the roads could not be repaired, the baggage and artillery of the army could not proceed.

The Americans not only guarded the ford of Saratoga, but lined the whole eastern bank of the river. Parties of them were advanced between the British army and Fort Edward; and they had also thrown up entrenchments, provided with artillery, on the high grounds between Fort Edward and Fort George. The detachments on the eastern bank so much annoyed the British boats in the river, that General Burgoyne was obliged to land his provisions, and carry them to camp, up a steep hill, under a galling fire from the enemy.

The British general was now in a most distressing situation. He had crossed the Hudson in the confident hope of victory and triumph, and in the expectation of a powerful co-operation from the lower parts of the river, if needful. On the 21st of September, after the battle of the 19th had in some measure made him sensible of his difficulties, he received a messenger from Sir Henry Clinton, who informed him of the intended attack on Forts Clinton and Montgomery. That messenger he immediately sent back with a letter, informing Sir Henry Clinton of his ability and determination to maintain the ground which he then occupied till the 12th of October, and requesting assistance. He had sent other messengers, by different routes, with the same information, but had heard nothing further from New York.

The attack on Forts Clinton and Montgomery, which had been delayed till the arrival of reinforcements from Europe, had been successfully made. The voyage of those reinforcements was tedious; but they arrived at New York in the end of September, and Sir Henry Clinton without delay embarked 3,000 men in vessels of different descriptions, and, convoyed by some ships-of-war under Commodore Hotham, sailed up the Hudson.

Forts Clinton and Montgomery, against which the expedition was directed, were situated on high ground of difficult access, on the western bank of the river, about fifty miles above New York. They were separated by a rivulet, which, flowing from the hills, empties itself into the Hudson. Under cover of the guns, a boom was stretched across the river from bank to bank, and strengthened by an immense iron chain in front, as well as supported by chevaux-de-frise sunk behind it. Above this strong barrier, a frigate and galleys were moored, so as to be able to direct a heavy fire against any vessels that might attempt to force a passage. This seemed to present an insuperable obstacle in the way of the British shipping toward Albany. Fort Independence stood four or five miles below, on a high point of land, on the opposite side of the river. Fort Constitution was six miles above the boom, on an island near the eastern bank: Peekskill, the headquarters of the officer who commanded on the Hudson, from Kingsbridge to Albany, was just below Fort Independence, on the same side. General Putnam then held that command, and had about 2,000 men under him.

On the 5th of October, Sir Henry Clinton landed at Verplanck's Point, a little below Peekskill, on the same side of the river. General Putnam, apprehending that the enemy intended to attack Fort Independence, and to march through the highlands on the east of the river toward Albany, retired to the heights in his rear; and, entertaining no suspicion of the real point of attack, neglected to strengthen the garrisons of the forts on the western bank.

The British fleet moved higher up the river, in order to conceal what was passing at the place where the troops had landed; and, on the evening of the day on which he had arrived at Verplanck's Point, Sir Henry Clinton embarked upward of 2,000 of his men, leaving the rest to guard that post. Early next morning he landed at Stony Point, on the west side of the river, and immediately began his march over the mountains toward the forts. The roads were difficult and the enterprise perilous; for a small body of men, properly posted, might not only have arrested his progress but repulsed him with much loss. He, however, reached the vicinity of the forts before he was discovered; there he fell in with a patrole, who immediately retreated, and gave warning of the approaching danger.

Between four and five on the afternoon of the 6th of October, the British appeared before the forts, which they summoned to surrender; and, on receiving a refusal, instantly advanced under a heavy fire to the assault. Both forts, garrisoned by about 600 men, were attacked at the same time. Fort Montgomery, by Colonel Campbell at the head of 900 men; and Fort Clinton, the stronger of the two posts, by Sir Henry Clinton with 1,200. Fort Montgomery was soon taken; but Colonel Campbell fell in the attack. Most of the garrison, favored by the darkness and by their knowledge of the passes, made their escape

Fig. 118.—Attack on Fort Montgomery.

At Fort Clinton the resistance was more obstinate; but that fort also was storm ed, and a considerable number of the garrison killed or made prisoners.

General Putnam had no suspicion of the real point of attack till he heard the firing, when he despatched 500 men to the assistance of the garrisons; but the forts were taken before they arrived, and consequently they returned to camp. In storming the forts, the British had about 150 men killed or wounded. Besides Colonel Campbell, Captain Stewart, Major Sill, and Count Grabousky, a Polish nobleman who served as a volunteer in the royal army, were among the slain. The Americans lost 300 men, in killed and wounded, and prisoners.

The American vessels-of-war in the river, being unable to escape, were burned by their crews, in order to prevent them from falling into the hands of the British, who removed the boom and chain, and opened the navigation of the river. Fort Independence was evacuated; and Fort Constitution, where the navigation was obstructed by a boom and chain, was also abandoned, without any attempt to defend it. The British proceeded up the river, destroying everything in their power. They advanced to Esopus, which they laid in ashes; but proceeded no farther. In this expedition, they took or destroyed a large quantity of American stores.

General Putnam retreated up the river; informed General Gates that he was unable to arrest the progress of the enemy, and advised him to prepare for the worst. But although his rear was threatened, General Gates was eager in improving the advantages he had gained over the British army, which was now reduced to the most distressing circumstances.

General Burgoyne, having been defeated in his intention of repairing the road to Fort Edward, called a council of war, which adopted the desperate resolution of abandoning their baggage, artillery, and stores; and with their arms only, and such provisions as they could carry on their backs, marching in the night to Fort Edward, crossing the river at the ford there, or at one a little above it, and forcing their way to Fort George. The distance was only about thirty miles; but the scouts who had been sent out to examine the route, reported that the two fords were all already guarded by strong detachments provided with artillery, so that the resolution which had been taken could not be executed. In these hopeless circumstances, General Burgoyne again summoned his council of war, and, by the unanimous advice of the members, opened a correspondence with General Gates, on the 13th of October; and, on the 16th terms of capitulation were agreed on, by which it was stipulated that the troops under General Burgoyne should next day march out of their camp, with the honors of war, and the artillery of the entrenchments, and pile their arms at the verge of the river; that a free passage should be granted them to Great Britain, on condition of not serving in North America during the war, unless exchanged; and that they should embark at Boston. To these a number of articles of less importance were added, relating to the property of the officers, Canadians, and loyalists, the march of the troops through New England, and other similar points. On the 17th, the British army piled their arms agreeably to the capitulation.

When the British army left Ticonderoga it consisted of about 10,000 men, exclusive of Indians; but, by the casualties of war, and by desertion, it was reduced to about 6,000 at the time of the surrender. It contained six members of parliament. General Gates had then under his command upward of 9,000 continentals and 4,000 militia. On this occasion the Americans gained a remarkably fine train of brass artillery, amounting to forty pieces of different descriptions, and all the arms and baggage of the troops. Such was the fate of that army which had excited high expectations in Britain, and which, at first, spread alarm and dismay throughout the United States of America.

In consequence of the capitulation at Saratoga, the British were unable to retain possession of the forts on the lakes. They therefore destroyed the works of Ticonderoga and its dependancies, threw the heavy artillery into the lake, and retreated to Isle aux Noix and St. John's.

The great error of General Burgoyne arose from his too ardent desire not to disappoint public expectation, and his unwillingness to renounce the fond hope of victory, conquest, and renown. These induced him to linger on the Hudson till retreat became impracticable. The American troops who subdued him, especially the militia, were irritated by some marauding parties of the English, who pillaged so much that the general found it necessary to threaten the culprits with the utmost severity of military law.

The convention at Saratoga ought to have induced the British cabinet to abandon the contest, on the best terms that could be obtained; for there was little probability of subjugating a people who had been able to maintain such a protracted struggle, and who, in the course of the campaign, had not only given employment to a powerful army, under Generals Sir William Howe and Sir Henry Clinton, but had also compelled another army, consisting at first of 10,000 excellent troops, commanded by active and enterprising officers, to lay down their arms. This success elevated the spirits of the friends of congress, and increased their number. At first, the British government had not a few who were friendly to it from principle, and many more who did not oppose it from prudence. The measures of the British ministry and the conduct of their agents daily diminished the number of the first of these; and every success of the troops of congress encouraged some of the second to abandon their cautious policy, and espouse the cause of their countrymen.

The surrender of the army under General Burgoyne at Saratoga was an event of great importance in the history of the war, and produced momentous consequences both in America and in Europe. It elevated the spirits of the republicans, inspired them with confidence in themselves, gave a new impulse to their exertions in the cause of independence, and taught the British troops to respect an enemy whom before they had too much despised.

The consequences of this event were not less important in Europe. The ministry and people of Great Britain had entertained the most confident expectations of the complete success of the northern army; and the easy conquest of Ticonderoga, with its dependancies, confirmed all their fond anticipations. Therefore, when they heard that General Burgoyne's army was not only defeated, but compelled to lay down its arms, they were struck with astonishment and dismay.

The great powers on the continent of Europe had been attentive observers of the struggle between Great Britain and her colonies, and to those powers the Americans had early applied for assistance. But the strength of Britain was gigantic; and to provoke her vengeance by aiding her rebellious subjects was a danger not rashly to be encountered. Although the continental cabinets, especially that of Versailles, had not discouraged the applications of the Americans, yet they had not given them any open countenance or avowed aid. They had, indeed, afforded the provinces clandestine marks of good-will, but still preserved the semblance of neutrality. The obstinate struggle, however, which the Americans had maintained, and their success at Saratoga, put an end to this wary and hesitating policy. It was now evident that the resistance of the colonies was not merely an ebullition of popular fury, likely soon to subside or to be easily overcome, but that it was a steady and organized plan, conducted with respectable ability, and likely to be crowned with ultimate success. The court of France began to throw off the mask. It became less reserved in its communications with the American agents, gave them a public reception, and at length entered into a treaty of alliance with them.

The British parliament met on the 20th of November, and the usual addresses in answer to the royal speech were moved, but they were not carried without opposition. In the house of lords, the celebrated earl of Chatham, then sinking under the infirmities of age and disease, proposed an amendment, by introducing a clause recommending to his majesty an immediate cessation of hostilities, and the commencement of a treaty of conciliation, "to restore peace and liberty to America, strength and happiness to England, security and permanent prosperity to both countries." In his speech he animadverted with much severity on the employment of the savages as auxiliaries in the war, although their aid had not been disdained under his own administration. That singular and successful man gave a striking example of the limited views and short-sighted policy even of illustrious statesmen. He believed that the prosperity of Britain depended on her American colonies, and that the loss of them would be followed by her ruin. But, in reality, the separation of those colonies from the mother-country, considered simply in itself, neither tarnished her glory nor impaired her strength. The earl of Chatham's amendment, like every other proposal of concession and conciliation, was lost; and all the measures of the cabinet were carried by great majorities. But the ministry did not long, in unmixed triumph, enjoy their parliamentary victories. The news of General Burgoyne's surrender arrived, and filled them with mortification and dismay. A deep gloom overspread the country: the formidable nature of the resistance in America to ministerial measures was demonstrated; and the movements in the ports of France rendered the interference of that country no longer doubtful, although her professions were still pacific.

The war began to assume a more portentous aspect; and the British ministry, unable to execute their original purpose, lowered their tone and showed an inclination to treat with the colonies, on any terms which did not imply their entire independence and complete separation from the British empire. In order to terminate the quarrel with America before the actual commencement of hostilities with France, Lord North introduced two bills into the house of commons: the first declared that parliament would impose no tax or duty whatever, payable within any of the colonies of North America, except only such duties as it might be expedient to impose for the purposes of commerce, the net produce of which should always be paid and applied to and for the use of the colonies in which the same shall be respectively levied, in like manner as other duties collected under the authority of their respective legislatures are ordinarily paid and applied; the second authorized the appointment of commissioners by the crown, with power to treat with either the constituted authorities or with individuals in America; but that no stipulation entered into should have any effect till approved in parliament. It empowered the commissioners, however, to proclaim a cessation of hostilities in any of the colonies; to suspend the operation of the non-intercourse act; also to suspend, during the continuance of the act, so much of all or any of the acts of parliament which have passed since the 10th day of February, 1763, as relates to the colonies; to grant pardons to any number or description of persons; and to appoint a governor in any colony in which his majesty had heretofore exercised the power of making such appointment. The duration of the act was limited to the 1st day of June, 1779.

These bills passed both houses of parliament; and as, about the time of their introduction, ministry received information of the conclusion of the treaty between France and the colonies, they sent off copies of them to America, even before they had gone through the usual formalities, in order to counteract the effects which the news of the French alliance might produce. Early in March, the earl of Carlisle, George Johnstone, and William Eden, Esquires, were appointed commissioners for carrying the acts into execution; and the celebrated

Dr. Adam Ferguson, then professor of moral philosophy in the university of Edinburgh, was nominated their secretary. The commissioners sailed without delay for America. But the present measure, like every other concession in the course of this desperate contest, came too late. What was now offered would at one time have been hailed in America with acclamations of joy, and secured the grateful affection of the colonists. But circumstances were now changed. The minds of the people were completely alienated from the parent state, and their spirits exasperated by the events of the war. Independence had been declared; victory had emblazoned the standards of congress; and a treaty of alliance with France had been concluded.

On the 16th of December, the preliminaries of a treaty between France and America were agreed on; and the treaty itself was signed at Paris on the 6th of February, 1778—an event of which the British ministry got information in little more than forty-eight hours after the signatures were affixed. The principal articles of the treaty were, that if Britain, in consequence of the alliance, should commence hostilities against France, the two countries should mutually assist each other; that the independence of America should be effectually maintained; that if any part of North America, still possessing allegiance to the crown of Britain, should be reduced by the colonies, it should belong to the United States; that if France should conquer any of the British West India islands, they should be deemed its property; that the contracting parties should not lay down their arms till the independence of America was formally acknowledged; and that neither of them should conclude a peace without the consent of the other.

Lord North's conciliatory bills reached America before the news of the French treaty, and the American legislature referred the bills to a committee of their number, which, after an acute and severe examination, gave in a report well calculated to counteract the effects which it was apprehended the bills would produce on the minds of the timid and wavering. They reported as their opinion, that it was the aim of those bills to create divisions in the states; and "that they were the sequel of that insidious plan, which, from the days of the stamp act down to the present time, hath involved this country in contention and bloodshed; and that, as in other cases, so in this, although circumstances may at times force them to recede from their unjustifiable claims, there can be no doubt but they will, as heretofore, upon the first favorable occasion, again display that lust of domination which hath rent in twain the mighty empire of Britain." They further reported it as their opinion, that any men, or body of men, who should presume to make any separate or partial convention or agreement with commissioners under the crown of Great Britain, should be considered and treated as open and avowed enemies of the United States. The committee further gave it as their opinion, that the United States could not hold any conference with the British commissioners, unless Britain first withdrew her fleets and armies, or in positive and express terms acknowledged the independence of the states.

While these things were going on, Mr. Silas Deane arrived from Paris, with the important and gratifying information that treaties of alliance and commerce had been concluded between France and the United States. This intelligence diffused a lively joy throughout America; and was received by the people as the harbinger of their independence. The alliance had been long expected; and the delays thrown in the way of its accomplishment had excited many uneasy apprehensions. But these were now dissipated; and, to the fond imaginations of the people, all the prospects of the United States appeared gilded with the cheering beams of prosperity.

On the 29th day of the preceding October, John Hancock, one of the first

Fig. 119.—Portrait of Silas Deane.

agents in the revolutionary movements, after having filled the president s chair in congress for nearly two years and a half, requested leave of absence on account of ill health. He had been chosen to succeed Peyton Randolph; and had discharged the duties of president with great ability. Henry Laurens, of South Carolina, was chosen to succeed him in the chair.

The British army in Philadelphia spent the winter in gayety and revelry, in-

Fig. 120.—Philadelphia in 1778.

juring at once their own respectability and the cause which they were employed to support. They disgusted the sober inhabitants by their irregularities, and provoked them by their insolence; so that many who had hailed their arrival with cordial gratulations, felt a lively satisfaction when the hour of their departure came.

General Washington quitted White Marsh, crossed the Schuylkill at Sweed's Ford, and, on the 19th of December, took a strong position at Valley Forge, about twenty-six miles from Philadelphia. Had he retired during the winter to the shelter of a large town, he must have gone to a great distance from the British army, and left an extensive tract of country open to their foraging parties; or had he cantoned his men in the adjacent villages, his army might have been beaten in detail and gradually destroyed. But at Valley Forge he was sufficiently near Philadelphia to check the foraging parties of the enemy, and his army was so much concentrated as to secure it from any sudden and desultory attack.

At Valley Forge the American commander-in-chief lodged his army in huts formed of logs, with the interstices filled with mud, which constituted very ac-

FIG. 121.—Village of Log-Huts.

ceptable habitations to men long unaccustomed to the conveniences of life. But, though sheltered from the storm by their rude dwellings, the sufferings of the army from want of provisions and clothing were incredible. The winter was severe, and many of the men were without stockings or shoes, and almost naked. The non-importation associations rendered cloth scarce at the commencement of hostilities; the war rendered importation difficult; and the consumption exceeded the produce of the home manufacture. Hence the army was left in a destitute and deplorable condition; and the line of march, from White Marsh to Valley Forge, over rough and frozen roads, might have been traced by the blood from the bare and mangled feet of the soldiers. Under shelter of the huts their sufferings were at first considerably alleviated; but in a short time the miseries of want, amounting almost to famine, were added to those of nakedness.

Many representations on this subject had been submitted to congress, which had authorized the commander-in-chief to seize provisions for his army wherever he could find them, within seventy miles of headquarters, paying for them with money, or giving certificates for the redemption of which the faith of the United States was pledged. This odious power General Washington was extremely backward to exercise: but at Valley Forge his necessities were so pressing that he was constrained to have recourse to it; and, notwithstanding all his precautions, the manner in which his orders were executed did not always soften the rigor of this harsh measure.

The American commander-in-chief was ill provided with money, and could make his payments only in paper of very uncertain value; but the supplies carried into Philadelphia were readily paid for by the British troops in gold and silver. It was, however, no easy matter for the country people to carry provisions into Philadelphia without detection and punishment; for the American detachments and patroles, though at a respectful distance, almost encircled the city. General Armstrong, with the Pennsylvania militia, was at the old camp at White Marsh; General Smallwood was detached to Wilmington; Colonel Morgan, whose riflemen had been so active on the Hudson during the preceding campaign, guarded the western bank of the Schuylkill; Count Pulaski, a Polish nobleman in the service of the United States, who had been appointed to command the cavalry, was posted with a part of his force at Trenton; and Major Jamieson and Captain Lee were appointed to watch both sides of the Delaware.

From the position which General Washington had taken at Valley Forge, and from the activity and vigilance of his patroles, the British army in Philadelphia was straitened for forage and fresh provisions. A considerable number of the people of Pennsylvania were well affected to the British cause, and desirous of supplying the troops, while many more were willing to carry victuals to Philadelphia, where they found a ready market, and payment in gold or silver, whereas the army at Valley Forge could pay only in paper money of uncertain value. But it was not easy to reach Philadelphia, nor safe to attempt it; for the American parties often intercepted them, took the provisions without payment, and not unfrequently added corporal chastisement. The first operations on the part of the British, therefore, in the campaign of 1778, were undertaken in order to procure supplies for the army. About the middle of March, a strong detachment, under Lieutenant-Colonel Mawhood, made a foraging excursion, for six or seven days, into Jersey, surprised and defeated the American parties at Hancock's and Quinton's bridges, on Always creek, which falls into the Delaware to the south of Reedy island, killed or took fifty or sixty of the militia, and, after a successful expedition, returned to Philadelphia with little loss.

A corps of Pennsylvania militia, daily varying in number, sometimes not exceeding fifty, sometimes amounting to 600, under General Lacy, had taken post at a place called Crooked Billet, about seventeen miles from Philadelphia, on the road to New York, for the purpose of intercepting the country people who attempted to carry provisions to the British army. Early on the morning of the 4th of May, Colonel Abercrombie and Major Simcoe, with a strong detachment, attempted to surprise this party; but Lacy escaped with little loss, except his baggage, which fell into the hands of the enemy.

On the 7th of May, the British undertook an expedition against the galleys and other shipping which had escaped up the Delaware after the reduction of Mud Island, and destroyed upward of forty vessels and some stores and provisions. The undisputed superiority of the British naval force, and the consequent command of the Delaware, gave them great facilities in directing a suitable armament against any particular point; and the movements of the militia, on whom congress chiefly depended for repelling sudden predatory incursions and for guarding the roads to Philadelphia, were often tardy and inefficient. The oads were ill-guarded; and the British commonly accomplished their foraging and returned to camp before an adequate force could be assembled to oppose them.

To remedy these evils, to annoy the rear of the British troops, in case they evacuated Philadelphia, which it was now suspected they intended to do, and also to form an advanced guard of the main army, the Marquis de la Fayette, with upward of 2,000 chosen men, and six pieces of artillery, was ordered to the east of the Schuylkill, and took post on Baron Hill, seven or eight miles in front of the army at Valley Forge. Sir William Howe immediately got notice of his position, and formed a plan to surprise and cut him off. For that purpose, a detachment of 5,000 of the best troops of the British army, under General Grant, marched from Philadelphia on the night of the 20th of May, and took the road which runs along the Delaware, and consequently does not lead directly to Baron Hill. But after advancing a few miles, the detachment turned to the left, and, proceeding by White Marsh, passed at no great distance from La Fayette's left flank, and about sunrise reached a point in his rear, where two roads diverged, one leading to the camp of the marquis, the other to Matson's ford, each about a mile distant. There General Grant's detachment was first observed by the Americans; and the British perceived by the rapid movements of some hostile horsemen, that they were seen. Both La Fayette's camp and the road leading from it to Matson's ford, were concealed from the British troops by intervening woods and high grounds. General Grant spent some time in making dispositions for the intended attack. That interval was actively improved by the marquis, who, although not apprized of the full extent of his danger, acted with promptitude and decision. He marched rapidly to Matson's ford, from which he was somewhat more distant than the British detachment, and reached it while General Grant was advancing against Baron Hill, in the belief that the Marquis de la Fayette was still there. The Americans hurried through the ford, leaving their artillery behind; but, on discovering that they were not closely pursued, some of them returned and dragged the fieldpieces across the river: a small party was also sent into the woods to retard the progress of the British advanced guard, if it should approach while the artillery was in the ford.

On finding the camp at Baron Hill deserted, General Grant immediately pursued in the track of the retreating enemy, toward Matson's ford. His advanced guard overtook some of the small American party, which had been sent back to cover the passage of the artillery, before they could recross the river, and took or killed a few of them; but on reaching the ford General Grant found the marquis so advantageously posted on the rising ground on the opposite bank, and his artillery so judiciously placed, that it was deemed unadvisable to attack him. Thus the attempt against the Marquis de la Fayette failed, although the plan was well-concerted, and on the very point of success. In the British army sanguine expectations of the favorable issue of the enterprise were entertained; and in order to insure a happy result, a large detachment under General Grey, in the course of the night, took post at a ford of the Schuylkill, two or three miles in front of La Fayette's right flank, to intercept him if he should attempt to escape in that direction, while the main body of the army advanced to Chestnut Hill to support the attack; but on the failure of the enterprise the whole returned to Philadelphia.

General Grant's detachment was seen from the camp at Valley Forge about the time it was discovered by the troops at Baron Hill: alarm-guns were fired to warn the marquis of his danger; and the whole army was drawn out, to be in readiness to act as circumstances might require. The escape of the detachment was the cause of much joy and congratulation in the American, and of disappointment and chagrin in the British army.

That a strong detachment of hostile troops should pass at a small distance from La Fayette's flank, and gain his rear unobserved, would seem to argue a want of vigilance on the part of that officer; but the Pennsylvania militia had been posted at a little distance on his left, and he relied on them for watching the roads in that quarter. The militia, however, had quitted their station, without informing him of their movement; and consequently his left flank, and the roads about White Marsh, remained unguarded.

About that time, Sir William Howe resigned the command of the army. So far back as the month of October, in the preceding year, he had requested to be relieved from the painful service in which he was engaged. On the 14th of April, 1778, he received his majesty's permission to resign; but at the same time he was directed, while he continued in command, to embrace every opportunity of putting an end to the war, by a due employment of the force under his orders. In the beginning of June he sailed for England, leaving the troops under the care of Sir Henry Clinton as his successor.

About the time when Sir William Howe resigned the command of the army, the British government ordered the evacuation of Philadelphia. While the British had an undisputed naval superiority, Philadelphia was, in some respects, a good military station. But Philadelphia is 100 miles up the Delaware; and as Sir William Howe had been unable to drive General Washington from the field, he had found some difficulty in subsisting his army in that city, even when the British ships had the full command of the sea, and could force their way up the great rivers; but when the empire of the ocean was about to be disputed by the French, Philadelphia became a hazardous post, on account of the difficulty and uncertainty of procuring provisions, receiving communications, or sending aid to such places as might be attacked. It was accordingly resolved to abandon that city; and as circumstances were changed, instead of returning by sea, to march the army through the Jerseys to New York, where the communication with the ocean is more easy.

The preparations required for this movement could not be so secretly made as to escape the notice of the Americans; and to be in readiness for it, was one reason of detaching the Marquis de la Fayette to Baron Hill, where he had been exposed to so much danger. General Washington called in his detachments, and pressed the state governments to hasten the march of their new levies, in order that he might be enabled to act offensively: but the new levies arrived slowly; and in some instances the state legislatures were deliberating on the means of raising them at the time when they should have been in the field.

Although General Washington was satisfied of the intention of the British commander-in-chief to evacuate Philadelphia, yet it was uncertain in what way he would accomplish his purpose; but the opinion that he intended to march through the Jerseys to New York gained ground in the American camp; and in this persuasion General Washington detached General Maxwell with the Jersey brigade across the Delaware, to co-operate with General Dickinson, who was assembling the Jersey militia, in breaking down the bridges, felling trees across the roads, and impeding and harassing the British troops in their retreat; but with orders to be on his guard against a sudden attack.

General Washington summoned a council of war to deliberate on the measures to be pursued in that emergency. It was unanimously resolved not to molest the British army in passing the Delaware; but with respect to subsequent operations there was much difference of opinion in the council. General Lee, who had lately joined the army after his exchange, was decidedly against risking either a general or partial engagement. The British army he estimated at 10,000 men fit for duty, exclusive of officers, while the American army did not amount to 11,000; he was therefore of opinion that, with such an equality of force, it would be criminal to hazard a battle. He relied much on the imposing attitude in which their late foreign alliance placed them, and maintained that nothing but a defeat of the army could now endanger their independence. Almost all the foreign officers agreed in opinion with General Lee; and among the American generals only Wayne and Cadwallader were decidedly in favor of attacking the enemy. In these circumstances, General Washington, although strongly inclined to fight, found himself constrained to act with much circumspection.

Having made all the requisite preparations, Sir Henry Clinton, early in the morning of the 18th of June, led the British army to the confluence of the Delaware and Schuylkill, where boats and other vessels were ready to receive them; and so judicious were the arrangements made by the admiral, that all the troops, with the baggage and artillery, were carried across the Delaware, and safely landed on the Jersey side of the river before ten in the morning. Many of the loyalists of Philadelphia accompanied the army, carrying their effects along with them. The Americans entered the city before the British rear-guard had entirely left it.

There were two roads leading from Philadelphia to New York; the one running along the western bank of the Delaware to Trenton ferry, and the other along the eastern bank to the same point. The British army had wisely crossed the river at the point where it was least exposed to molestation, and entered on the last of these two roads. In marching through a difficult and hostile country, Sir Henry Clinton prudently carried along with him a considerable quantity of baggage, and a large supply of provisions; so that the progress of the army, thus heavily incumbered, was but slow. It proceeded leisurely through Huddersfield, Mount Holly, Crosswick, and reached Allentown on the 24th; having in seven days marched less than forty miles. This slow progress made the Americans believe that Sir Henry Clinton wished to be attacked. General Maxwell, who was posted at Mount Holly, retired on his approach; and neither he nor General Dickinson was able to give him much molestation.

As the march of the British army, till it passed Crosswick, was up the Delaware, and only at a small distance from that river, General Washington, who left Valley Forge on the day that Sir Henry Clinton evacuated Philadelphia, found it necessary to take a circuitous route, and pass the river higher up, at Coryell's ferry, where he crossed it on the 22d, and took post at Hopewell, on the high grounds in that vicinity, and remained during the 23d in that position.

From Allentown there were two roads to New York; one on the left passing through South Amboy to the North river, the other on the right leading to Sandy Hook. The first of these was somewhat shorter, but the river Raritan lay in the way, and it might be difficult and dangerous to pass it in presence of the enemy. Sir Henry Clinton, therefore, resolved to take the road to Sandy Hook, by which the Raritan would be altogether avoided.

Although a great majority in the American council of war were averse from fighting, yet General Washington was strongly inclined to attack the British army. He summoned the council of war a second time, and again submitted the subject to their consideration; but they adhered to their former opinion; and General Washington, still inclined to attack the enemy, determined to act, to a certain extent, on his own responsibility.

The Jersey militia and a brigade of continentals, under Generals Dickinson and Maxwell, hovered on the left flank of the British army; General Cadwallader, with a continental regiment and a few militia, was in its rear, and Colonel Morgan, with his regiment 600 strong, was on its right. These detachments were ordered to harass the enemy as much as possible.

As Sir Henry Clinton proceeded on the route toward Sandy Hook, General Washington strengthened his advanced guard till it amounted to 5,000 men. General Lee, from his rank, had a claim to the command of that force; but, at first, he declined it, and the Marquis de la Fayette was appointed to that service. But General Lee, perceiving the importance of the command, solicited the appointment which he had at first declined, and was accordingly sent forward with a reinforcement, when, from seniority, the whole of the advanced guard became subject to his orders.

On the evening of the 27th, Sir Henry Clinton took a strong position on the high grounds about Freehold courthouse, in the county of Monmouth. His right was posted in a small wood; his left was covered by a thick forest and a morass; he had a wood in front, also a marsh for a considerable space toward his left; and he was within twelve miles of the high grounds at Middletown, after reaching which no attempt could be made upon him with any prospect of success. His position was unassailable; but General Washington resolved to attack his rear in the morning, as soon as it descended from the high grounds into the plain beyond them, and gave orders accordingly to General Lee, who was at English Town, three miles in the rear of the British army, and as much in advance of the main body of the Americans.

By the strong parties on his flanks and rear, the British commander was convinced that the hostile army was at hand; and, suspecting that an attempt on his baggage was intended, on the morning of the 28th he changed his order of march, and put all the baggage under the care of General Knyphausen, who commanded the van division of his army, in order that the rear division, consisting of the flower of the troops, under Earl Cornwallis, might be unencumbered, and ready to act as circumstances might require. Sir Henry Clinton remained with the rear division.

At daybreak on the morning of the 28th of June, General Knyphausen marched with the van division, having in charge the baggage, which was so abundant as to extend in a line nearly twelve miles. The rear of the army, that it might not press too much on the van, did not leave its ground till near eight in the morning. General Lee, who on the preceding evening had received orders to attack the British rear, which orders were repeated in the morning, with an assurance that the main body of the army would advance and support him, prepared to obey his instructions. Scarcely had the British rear-guard descended from the heights of Freehold into a plain three miles long and one broad, when the American van was seen advancing and descending from the heights which the British had just left. At the same time, Sir Henry Clinton perceived strong columns on his flanks. Convinced that his baggage was aimed at, he thought the best method of securing it was to make a vigorous attack on the division in his rear, and to press it so closely as to render the recall of the columns on his flanks necessary. He accordingly made the proper dispositions for attacking the enemy; while General Lee, who believed he had to do with a rear-guard only, and from whom the movements of the British were concealed by intervening woods, advanced over some narrow passes in a morass into the plain: but, instead of a rear-guard, he saw the flower of the British army drawn up to receive him. He perceived his mistake and danger, and instantly retreated, before the British were ready to attack him; sensible that, if beaten on that ground, his retreat across the morass would be difficult or impracticable, and that he could not be easily reinforced, he resolved to regain the rising ground, that he might receive the attack of the enemy in a more favorable position. While he was making this retrograde movement, near midday, General Washington rode forward, and, ignorant of the causes and motives of the retreat, addressed General Lee in warm terms of disapprobation. The British army advanced rapidly upon them, and Washington ordered Lee to arrest their progress while he brought up the main body of the army to his assistance.

General Lee, who had reached the ground where he intended to fight, executed his orders with characteristic courage and skill. A sharp conflict ensued; the Americans were compelled to retreat, which they did in good order. The British advanced and attacked the second line of the Americans, which was strongly posted, and made a vigorous resistance. After some severe fighting, and several movements on each side, General Washington having brought forward the main body of the American army and occupied advantageous ground, Sir Henry Clinton withdrew his troops and took a good position near the place where the battle began, at which he remained till ten at night, when he resumed his march, carrying along with him his wounded, except such as could not be moved.

In this indecisive encounter, the Americans gained a victory. The event was celebrated with rejoicings throughout the United States, and congress returned thanks to General Washington and his army. But Sir Henry Clinton was afterward allowed to pursue his march without interruption. About the time of the battle some attempts were made on the baggage, but they were easily repelled, and all the American advanced parties were recalled.

In the battle of Freehold Court House, the loss of both armies was nearly equal, amounting to about 400 men on each side. The British lost Lieutenant-Colonel Monckton, who was much lamented. The American army particularly regretted the death of Lieutenant-Colonel Bonner of Pennsylvania, and of Major Dickinson of Virginia. The day was exceedingly warm; and the heat and fatigue proved fatal to several soldiers in each army, who expired without a wound.

General Lee, conceiving himself to have been insulted by General Washington on the field of battle, in the evening addressed to him a letter, expressed in no very respectful terms. He was, therefore, put under arrest, and tried by a court-martial for disobedience of orders, and disrespect to his commander-in-chief. He was found guilty, and suspended for a year.

The sentence of the court-martial against General Lee closed the military career of that singular man, who, in the early part of the war, had been of much service to the Americans. He was bred to arms, had been a lieutenant-colonel in the British service, a colonel in the Portuguese army, and an aid-de-camp to the king of Poland, with the rank of major-general. On the breaking out of the American war he had resigned his commission in the British army, and offered his services to congress, who appointed him third in command of their forces. He had studied all the most valuable treatises on the art of war, both ancient and modern; and on military subjects his judgment was commonly correct. In the presence of the enemy he was cool and intrepid; and, notwithstanding many faults and whimsical peculiarities in his character, he was beloved both by the officers and men who served under him. His understanding was vigorous, his memory retentive, and his imagination lively. He was a classical scholar, and possessed a considerable portion of general knowledge. His temper was sour and severe; he scarcely ever laughed, and seldom smiled. He was impious and rude; a vindictive enemy, but a steady friend; extremely avaricious, but an entire stranger to deceit and dissimulation. He was at times a pleasant and instructive companion, but often capricious and disagreeable.

When the American army was encamped at White Plains, General Lee lodged in a small house near which General Washington occasionally passed when observing the dispositions of the enemy: one day, accompanied by some of his officers, he called on General Lee and dined with him; but no sooner were they gone than Lee, addressing his aid-de-camp, said: "You must look me out another place; for I shall have Washington and all his puppies continually calling upon me, and they will eat me up." Next day seeing the commander-in-chief and his suit coming that way, and suspecting another visit, he ordered his servant to write on the door with chalk, "No victuals dressed here to-day." Perceiving this inscription, General Washington and his officers rode off, not a little amused at the incident, and the oddities of Lee's character. Lee had a strong attachment to dogs, and some of these animals always accompanied him. On being informed that congress had confirmed the sentence of the court-martial against him, pointing to a dog, he exclaimed, "O that I were that animal, that I might not call man my brother!" This singular person died in Philadelphia, in the beginning of October, 1782.

After the battle of Freehold Court House, the British army continued its march without interruption to Sandy Hook, where it embarked on the 5th of July, and on the same day landed at New York.

General Washington marched to the North river, and took a position near his old camp at White Plains.

On the 5th of July, the day on which the British army arrived at New York, the Count d'Estaing, with a French fleet, appeared on the coast of Virginia.

In the month of March, the French ambassador in London, by order of his government, notified to the British court the treaties entered into between France and America. In a few days afterward he quitted London, and, about the same time, the British ambassador left Paris. This was considered equivalent to a declaration of war; and although war was not actually declared, yet both parties diligently prepared for hostilities.

The French equipped at Toulon a fleet of twelve sail of the line and six frigates, and gave the command to Count d'Estaing, who, with a considerable number of troops on board, sailed on the 13th of April; but, meeting with contrary winds, he did not reach the coast of America till the 5th of July. He expected to find the British army in Philadelphia, and the fleet in the Delaware; and it has been supposed that if this expectation had been realized, the consequences to Britain must have been calamitous. But it is needless to speculate on what might have ensued in circumstances which never existed. For the British fleet and army were at Sandy Hook or New York before the French fleet arrived on the coast.

Informed of the departure of the British from Pennsylvania, Admiral d'Estaing instantly sailed to the northward, and, on the evening of the 11th of July, came to anchor off New York. Admiral Lord Howe, whose fleet amounted only to six ships of the line, four of fifty guns each, and some frigates and smaller vessels, had been informed of D'Estaing's arrival on the coast some days before he appeared in sight, and had made a judicious disposition of his force for the defence of the harbor. For some time after D'Estaing came in sight, the wind was unfavorable to an attempt on the British fleet; however, on the 22d of July it veered to the eastward, the French squadron got under way, and the British expected to be immediately attacked. But, instead of proceeding toward the harbor, D'Estaing stood out to sea, and sailed as far south as the capes of the Delaware, where he altered his course and steered directly for Rhode Island, off which he appeared on the 29th of the month. There he meditated an attack, in which General Sullivan, with a detachment from General Washington's army, and reinforcements from New England, was to co-operate.

The Americans had been preparing for some time to attempt the reduction of Rhode Island; and Sullivan had been appointed to superintend and hasten the preparations. His measures did not escape the notice of Major-General Sir Robert Pigot, commander of the island, who, in order to impede his operations, had ordered two different incursions into Providence Plantation, one conducted by Colonel Campbell, and another under Major Eyre, in which a quantity of

Fig. 122.—Newport in 1777.

military and naval stores, some galleys and armed sloops, with upward of 100 boats prepared for the expedition, were destroyed. These losses retarded the preparations of General Sullivan; and when Count d'Estaing appeared, the Americans were not ready to co-operate with him.

Rhode Island, which consists of two parts connected by an isthmus, lies off the coast of Connecticut, not far from the main land, and has several small islands near it. Newport, the chief town of the island, stands to the west of the isthmus; and the island of Connanicut lies off it, between Rhode Island and the continent. There are three entrances to the town, one by the east or Seakonet passage; another by the west of the island, between it and Connanicut, called the Main channel; and another by the west of Connanicut, called the West or Narraganset passage, and which unites with the Main channel at the east end of Connanicut.

The British garrison, under General Pigot, amounted to 6,000 men. The main body lay at Newport; three regiments were stationed on Connanicut island; the isthmus was defended by a chain of redoubts; and each of the three entrances by sea was guarded by frigates and galleys, which were destroyed on the appearance of Count d'Estaing, to prevent them from falling into his hands. D'Estaing stationed some ships-of-war both in the Seakonet and Narraganset passages, while he effectually closed the main channel, by anchoring with his fleet at its mouth; and in that situation he remained till the 8th of August. The Americans being then ready to co-operate with him, he sailed toward the harbor, receiving and returning the fire of several batteries as he passed, and anchored between Newport and Connanicut.

On the first appearance of the French fleet at Rhode Island, information of the event was sent to New York; and Lord Howe, whose squadron was then increased to eight ships-of-the-line, five of fifty guns each, two of forty, four frigates, with three fireships, two bombs, and a number of inferior vessels, after having been detained four days by contrary winds, sailed toward Rhode Island, appeared in sight of it on the morning of the 9th, and, in the evening, anchored off Point Judith, without the entrance into the main channel, toward which the wind directly blew, and prevented the French from coming out; but it shifted to northeast during the night, and, in the morning, D'Estaing sailed toward the British fleet, before a favorable breeze. Besides his superior force, he had the advantage of the weather-gage; Lord Howe, therefore, declined a battle, and stood out to sea. D'Estaing followed him; and both fleets were soon out of sight of Rhode Island.

Lord Howe and Count d'Estaing spent two days in presence of each other, exhausting all the resources of nautical science, in order to preserve or to gain the weather-gage. Toward the close of the second day, when about to come to action, the fleets were separated by a violent storm, which dispersed and considerably injured both of them. Single ships afterward fell in with each other, and spirited encounters ensued; but no important advantage was gained on either side. Lord Howe returned to New York, and D'Estaing to Newport, both in a shattered condition.

When D'Estaing followed Lord Howe from Rhode Island, Sullivan's army, amounting to 10,000 men, chiefly militia, was ready to take the field: it was proposed, however, not to commence hostilities till the return of the French, in order that they might not offend D'Estaing, who had already discovered some jealousy and irritation on points of mere form and ceremony. But, as the American army could not be long kept together, that proposal was overruled, and it was resolved immediately to begin active operations.

On finding himself seriously threatened, General Pigot withdrew his troops from Connanicut, called in his outposts, and concentrated his force in the vicin-

Fig. 123.—Rhode Island Statehouse, Newport.

ity of Newport, where he occupied an entrenched camp. The American army was transported from the continent to the northeast end of the island, took possession of a fortified post, which the British had abandoned, and marched toward Newport, to besiege the hostile camp at that place.

But, on the 12th of August, before Sullivan had begun the siege, his army was overtaken by the furious storm of wind and rain which dispersed and damaged the fleets. It blew down, and almost irreparably injured the tents, rendered the firearms unfit for immediate use, and damaged the ammunition, of which fifty rounds had just been delivered to each man. The soldiers, having no shelter, suffered severely, and some of them perished in the storm, which lasted three days; afterward the American army advanced toward the British lines, and began the siege. But the absence of the fleet rendered the situation of General Sullivan's army precarious, as the British force at Newport could easily be increased. On the evening of the 19th, D'Estaing again appeared off the island; but the joy of the Americans on that occasion was of short duration; for he immediately informed General Sullivan that, in obedience to his orders, and agreeably to the advice of all his officers, he was about to sail to the harbor of Boston. His instructions were, to enter that port, in case he should meet with any disaster, or find a superior British fleet on the coast. The shattered condition of his ships, and the arrival of Admiral Byron with reinforcements from England, constituted the very state of things contemplated in his instructions; and therefore he resolved to proceed to Boston.

To be abandoned by the fleet in such critical circumstances, and not only deprived of the brilliant success which they thought within their reach, but exposed to imminent hazard, caused much disappointment, irritation, and alarm, in the American camp. The Marquis de la Fayette and General Greene were despatched to Count d'Estaing to remonstrate with him on the subject, and to press his co-operation and assistance for two days only, in which time they flattered themselves the most brilliant success would crown their efforts. But the count was not popular in the fleet: he was a military officer as well as a naval commander, and was considered as belonging to the army rather than to the navy. The officers of the sea service looked on him with a jealous and envious eye, and were willing to thwart him as far as they were able with safety to themselves. When, on the pressing application of La Fayette and Greene, he again submitted the matter to their consideration, they took advantage of the letter of the admiral's instructions, and unanimously adhered to their former resolution.

CHAPTER IX.

The departure of the French fleet greatly discouraged the American army; and in a few days Sullivan's force was considerably diminished by desertion. On the 26th of August he therefore resolved to raise the siege, and retreat to the north end of the island; and took the necessary precautions for the successful execution of that movement.

In the night of the 28th, General Sullivan silently decamped, and retired unobserved. Early in the morning the British discovered his retreat, and instantly commenced a pursuit. They soon overtook the light troops who covered the retreat of the American army, and who continued skirmishing and retreating till they reached the north end of the island, where the army occupied a strong

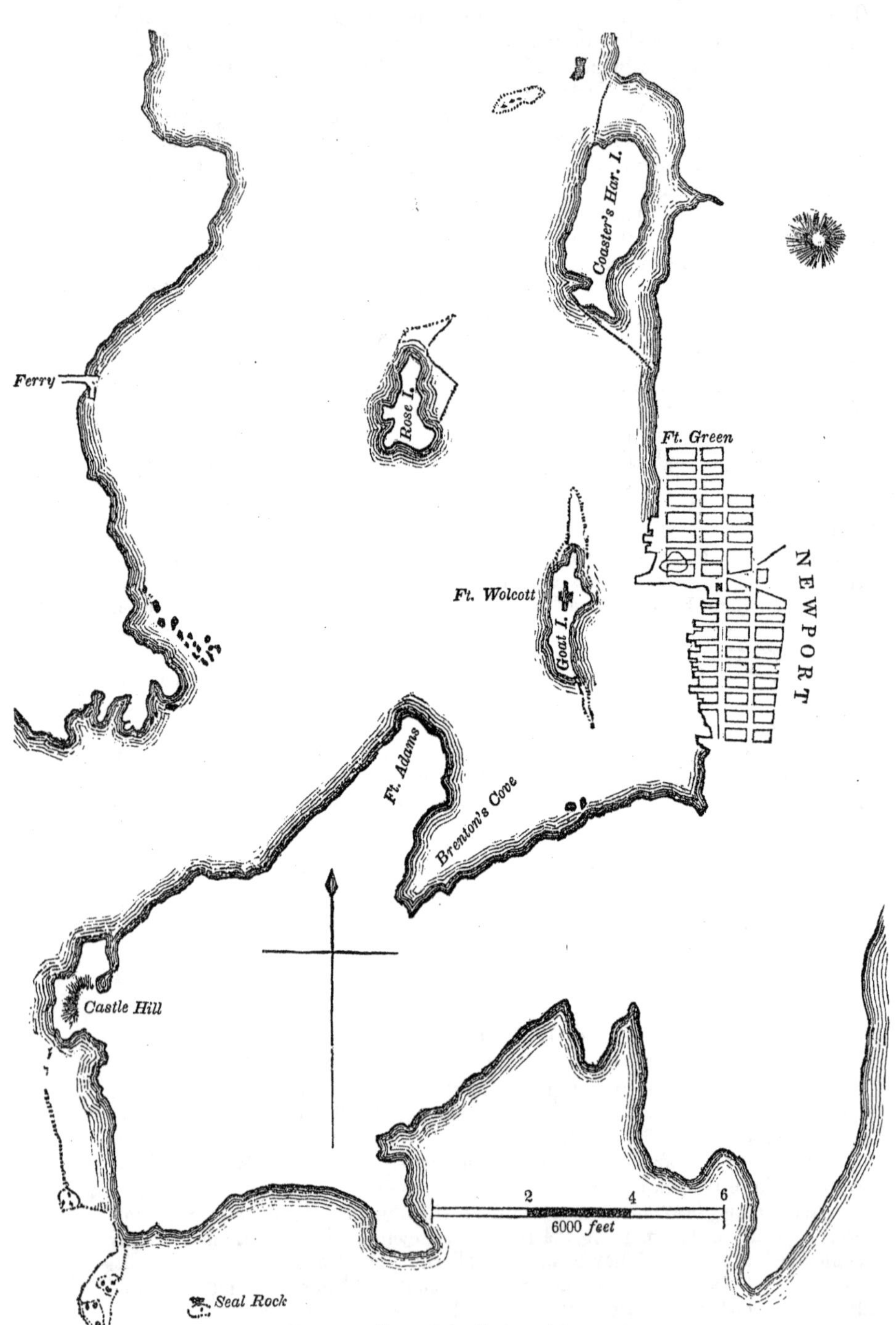

FIG. 124.—Chart of the Harbor of Newport.

position, at a place where the British formerly had a fortified post, the works of which had been strengthened during the two preceding days. There a severe conflict, for about half an hour, ensued, when the combatants mutually withdrew from the field. The loss of the armies was nearly equal, amounting to between two and three hundred killed or wounded in the course of the day.

On the 30th of August there was a good deal of cannonading, but neither party ventured to attack the other. The British were expecting reinforcements ; and Sullivan, although he made a show of resolutely maintaining his post, was busily preparing for the evacuation of the island. In the evening he silently struck his tents, embarked his army, with all the artillery, baggage, and stores, on board a great number of boats, and landed safely on the continent, before the British suspected his intention to abandon the post. General Sullivan made a timely escape ; for Sir Henry Clinton was on his way, with 4,000 men, to the assistance of General Pigot. He was detained four days in the sound by contrary winds ; but arrived on the day after the Americans left the island. A very short delay might have proved fatal to their army.

The most sanguine expectations had been entertained throughout the United States of the reduction of Rhode Island and the capture of the British force which defended it ; so that the disappointment and mortification on the failure of the enterprise were exceedingly bitter. The irritation against the French, who were considered the authors of the miscarriage, was violent. Sullivan was confident of success ; and his chagrin at the departure of the French fleet made him use some expressions, in a general order, which gave offence to D'Estaing. The American leaders felt the importance of preserving the good will of their allies. Hence Sullivan explained ; and Washington and congress employed all their influence to sooth the angry feelings of the French admiral, and to prevent that disunion and distrust which threatened to alienate the Americans and their new allies from each other. These efforts to heal the growing breach were successful ; although the ill humor of the populace manifested itself in quarrelling with the French sailors both at Boston and Charleston in South Carolina.

The British fleet had suffered considerably in the storm, but had not sustained so much damage as the French. In a short time, Lord Howe was again ready for sea ; and, having learned that D'Estaing had sailed for Boston, he left New York with the intention of reaching that place before him, or of attacking him there, if he found it could be done with advantage. But on entering the bay of Boston, he perceived the French fleet in Nantucket Roads, so judiciously stationed, and so well protected by batteries, that there was no prospect of attacking it with success. He therefore returned to New York, where, finding that, by fresh arrivals, his fleet was decidedly superior to that of the French, he availed himself of the permission which he had received some time before, and resigned the command to Admiral Gambier, who was to continue in the command till the arrival of Admiral Byron, who was daily expected from Halifax.

Sir Henry Clinton, finding that General Sullivan had effected his retreat from Rhode Island, set out on his return to New York ; but, that the expedition might not be wholly ineffectual, he meditated an attack on New London, situated on a river which falls into the sound. The wind, however, being unfavorable to the enterprise, he gave the command of the troops on board the transports to General Grey, with orders to proceed in an expedition against Buzzard's bay, and continued his voyage to New York. In obedience to the orders which he had received, General Grey sailed to Acushnet river, where he landed on the 5th of September, and destroyed all the shipping in the river, amounting to more than seventy sail. He burned a great part of the towns of Bedford and Fairhaven, the one on the west and the other on the east bank, destroying a considerable quantity of military and naval stores, provisions, and merchandise. He landed at six in the evening; and so rapid were his movements, that the work of destruction was accomplished, and the troops reimbarked before noon the next day. He then proceeded to Martha's Vineyard, where he took or burned several vessels, destroyed a salt work, compelled the inhabitants to surrender their arms, and levied from them a contribution of 1,000 sheep and 300 oxen, with which seasonable supply of provisions he returned to New York.

The return of the British fleet and of the troops under General Grey relieved the Americans from the anxious apprehensions of an attack on their allies at Boston. Under that apprehension General Washington broke up his camp at White Plains, and, proceeding northward, took a position at Fredericksburg. He detached Generals Gates and McDougall to Danbury in Connecticut, in order that they might be in readiness to move as circumstances might require; and he sent General Putnam to West Point, to watch the North river, and the important passes in the highlands. But the return of the fleet and troops to New York quieted those apprehensions.

Meanwhile the Americans perceived that an expedition was preparing at New York, the object of which they were unable to ascertain; but soon after the return of the troops under General Grey, the British army advanced in great force on both sides of the North river. The column on the west bank, consisting of 5,000 men, commanded by Lord Cornwallis, extended from the Hudson to the Hackensack. The division on the east side, consisting of about 3,000 men, under General Knyphausen, stretched from the North river to the Bronx. The communication between them was kept up by flat-bottomed boats, by means of which the two divisions could have been readily united, if the Americans had advanced against either of them. General Washington sent out several detachments to observe the movements of those columns. Colonel Baylor, who with his regiment of cavalry, consisting of upward of a hundred men, had been stationed near Paramus, crossed the Hackensack on the morning of the 27th of September, and occupied Tappon or Herringtown, a small village near New Tappon, where some militia were posted. Of these circumstances Lord Cornwallis received immediate notice, and he formed a plan to surprise and cut off both the cavalry and militia. The execution of the enterprise against Baylor was intrusted to General Grey; and Colonel Campbell, with a detachment from Knyphausen's division, was to cross the river, and attack the militia at New Tappon. Colonel Campbell's part of the plan failed, by some delay in the passage of the river; during which a deserter informed the militia of their danger, and they saved themselves by flight. But General Grey completely surprised Baylor's troops, and killed, wounded, or took the greater part of them. Colonel Baylor was wounded and made prisoner. The slaughter on that occasion, which the Americans thought unnecessarily great, excited much indignation, and was the subject of loud complaints throughout the United States.

Three days after the surprise of Baylor, the American Colonel Butler, with a detachment of infantry, assisted by Major Lee with part of his cavalry, fell in with a party of fifteen chasseurs and about 100 yagers, under Captain Donop, on whom they made such a rapid charge, that, without the loss of a man, they killed ten on the spot, and took about twenty prisoners. This advantage was very soothing to the embittered feelings of the Americans, who considered it some compensation for Baylor's loss.

The movement of the British army up the North river already mentioned, was made for the purpose of foraging, and also to cover a meditated attack on Little Egg Harbor; and having accomplished its object, it returned to New York. Little Egg Harbor, situated on the coast of Jersey, was a noted rendezvous of privateers; and being so near the entrance to New York, ships bound to that port were much exposed to their depredations. An expedition against it was therefore planned, and the conduct of the enterprise intrusted to Captain Ferguson of the seventeenth regiment, with about 300 men, assisted by Captain Collins of the navy. He sailed from New York; but, short as the passage was, he was detained several days by contrary winds, and did not arrive at the place of his destination till the evening of the 5th of October. The Americans had got notice of his design, and had sent to sea such of their privateers as were ready for sailing. They had also hauled the largest of the remaining vessels, which were chiefly prizes, twenty miles up the river to Chestnut Neck, and had carried their smaller vessels still farther into the country. Ferguson proceeded to Chestnut Neck, burned the vessels there, destroyed the storehouses and public works of every sort; and, in returning, committed some depredations on private property.

Count Pulaski, a Polish nobleman in the service of the United States, had been nominated commander of the American cavalry; but, as that appointment gave offence to the officers, he resigned his commission. Congress, however, permitted him to raise a legionary corps, consisting of three incomplete companies of infantry and three troops of cavalry, which he officered chiefly with foreigners, and commanded the whole in person. He was ordered toward Little Egg harbor, and lay, without due vigilance, eight or ten miles from the coast. One Juliet, a Frenchman, who had deserted from the British service and obtained a commission in Pulaski's corps, redeserted, joined Captain Ferguson of Little Egg harbor, after his return from Chestnut Neck, and gave him exact information of the strength and situation of Pulaski's troops. Ferguson and Collins immediately resolved to surprise the Polish nobleman; and for that purpose, on the fifteenth of October, they embarked two hundred and fifty men in boats, rowed ten miles up the river before daybreak, landed within a small distance of his infantry, left fifty men to guard their boats, and with the remainder of their force suddenly fell on the unsuspicious detachment, killed about fifty of them, among whom were the Baron de Bosc and Lieutenant de la Borderie, and retreated, with scarcely any loss, before they could be attacked by Pulaski's cavalry.

In this instance they greatly injured or ruined many individuals among the Americans; but they were useless in respect of the great object of the war—the subjugation of the country.

Admiral Byron, with a considerable number of ships, sailed from England on the ninth of June to take the command of the fleet on the American station, and to oppose Count d'Estaing in those seas: but during the summer the weather was uncommonly boisterous in the Atlantic ocean; and on the third of July he was overtaken by a storm which dispersed his fleet. Several of his ships reached New York singly; and six of them, which had kept together under Admiral Parker, arrived there on the 29th of August. Admiral Byron, in the Princess Royal, being left alone, steered for Halifax, where he anchored on the 26th of August; and in that port found the Culloden, one of his fleet. These two vessels being refitted with the utmost despatch, he sailed on the 4th of September, and arrived at New York about the middle of the month.

He made every exertion to repair his shattered squadron; but was not ready for sea till the 18th of October, when he sailed for Boston in quest of D'Estaing. His ill fortune still pursued him; for scarcely had he reached the bay of Boston, when on the 1st of November, a violent storm arose, which drove him to sea, and so disabled his ships that he was obliged to hasten to Rhode Island to refit. D'Estaing, having repaired his fleet, seized the opportunity of Admiral Byron's absence to put to sea, on the 3d of November, and steered for the West Indies. On the same day, Grant, with a detachment of six thousand men from the British army, convoyed by six sail of the line under Commodore Hotham sailed for the same quarter. Toward the end of the month a detachment of the British army under Lieutenant-Colonel Campbell, embarked with the design of invading the southern states, and was escorted by Commodore Sir Peter Parker. A sufficient force still remained at New York for its defence.

As the season for active operations in the northern and middle states was now at an end, the American army retired into winter quarters. The main body was cantoned on both sides of the North river, about West Point and Middleburgh, while light troops were posted in advance. In this situation they covered the country, and were conveniently placed for procuring subsistence. The greater part of the men were on the west side of the river, because from that quarter the supplies of bread were drawn, while the animal food was brought from the states of New England; and it was easier to drive the cattle than to transport the corn from a distance. The army was lodged in huts as in the preceding winter; but, by means of the French alliance, the men were more comfortably clothed than formerly.

During the summer of 1778 a harassing and destructive war was carried on by the Indians against the settlers on the western frontier of the United States. Congress was desirous that the numerous tribes of aboriginal inhabitants should either become their allies or remain neutral during the war. At first many of the nations seemed friendly to the United States: but congress had not the means of supplying them with those European commodities which they were in the habit of using; while the British agents in Canada liberally bestowed upon them the articles of which they stood in need, and zealously invited them to take up arms against the United States. By their presents and their councils they alienated the minds of the Indians from the Americans, and prevailed upon them to espouse the British cause; so that, from the Mohawk to the Ohio, the American frontier was threatened with the tomahawk and the scalping-knife.

Although the storm was foreseen, yet the measures of the Americans, depending on the resolutions of different states and the agency of militia, were not sufficiently prompt to prevent or anticipate the threatened aggression. The Indians, with savage fury, burst into the American territory, carrying death and desolation in their train. The happy settlement of Wyoming became, in a particular manner, the scene of carnage, misery, and ruin. That beautiful tract of country, lying on both sides of the Susquehannah, was claimed both by Connecticut and Pennsylvania; and had been settled by emigrants from the former of those states, who, it is said, purchased the land from the Indians. The settlement was in a most flourishing condition, and contained upward of 1,000 families. Unfortunately, Wyoming was not free from those political dissensions which, in a greater or less degree, agitated every province of the union, and which have such a pestilential tendency to destroy social happiness and embitter human life. A great majority of the settlers zealously espoused the cause of congress; but a few were devoted to the support of royalty. These last, considering themselves harshly treated by their political opponents, withdrew from the settlement, and sought refuge among the savages, or retired to the British posts on the frontiers of Canada. There they cherished a deadly hatred against their countrymen, and meditated sanguinary schemes of vengeance.

At the head of those refugees was Colonel John Butler, cousin of Zebulon Butler, commander of the militia of Wyoming. The hostile designs of the Indians and of the emigrants were not unknown to the settlers at Wyoming, who constructed forts, and made such other preparations for defence as they were able. But their enemies endeavored to deceive, in order more easily to destroy them. The hostile Indians sent messengers with assurances of their peaceable disposition; and, the more effectually to lull the settlers at Wyoming into a fatal security, Butler, in a numerous assembly of savages, declared that

Fig. 125.—Vale of Wyoming.

he was about to retire to Detroit, adding, agreeably to the peculiar idiom of his auditors, that "his hand was too short to do anything that year." These professions and declarations were merely intended to deceive; but the perfidious artifice was not followed with complete success. The settlers suspected the designs of their enemies, and, it is said, wrote to congress and to General Washington, representing the danger to which they were exposed; but their letters were intercepted by the royalists, or *tories*, as they were commonly called, of Pennsylvania, so that government remained ignorant of the perilous state of Wyoming. Meanwhile the settlers betook themselves to their forts for security.

On the 1st of July, a hostile force, supposed to amount to 1,500 men, composed of 300 Indians under their own chiefs, and upward of 1,000 tories painted like Indians, commanded by Colonel John Butler, burst into the settlement. They easily gained possession, by treachery, it is said, of one of the upper forts; and they took the other. The two principal forts, Kingston and Wilkesbarre, were situated near each other, but on different sides of the river. Of the first of these Colonel Zebulon Butler took possession, with the greater part of the armed force of the district; and a number of women and children took refuge in the same place. When summoned to surrender the fort, Zebulon Butler refused compliance, but proposed a parley; and a place at some distance from the fort was agreed on for a conference. At the head of 400 men, Butler left the fort and marched toward the appointed spot, but found none of the opposite party there. At a still greater distance from the fort, however, and near the foot of a mountain, he saw a flag displayed, and with imprudent confidence proceeded toward it; but, for a while, it retired as he advanced. At length he found himself almost surrounded by the enemy, who, instead of a friendly conference, commenced a furious attack upon them. In that alarming juncture the Americans displayed much firmness, and fought with such steady courage that the advantage was rather on their side, till a soldier, either through treachery or cowardice, cried out, "The colonel has ordered a retreat!" Instantly his men fell into confusion and a total rout soon ensued. The troops fled toward the river, which they endeavored to pass in order to enter Fort Wilkesbarre, The enemy pursued with savage fury, massacring without resistance all who fell in their way. So complete was their success, and so destructive their rage, that of 400 men who had marched out to the delusive parley, Zebulon Butler and about twenty others only escaped. In this transaction we are equally surprised at the unsuspecting simplicity of the one party,and the sanguinary conduct of the other.

Next day the Indians and their barbarous white allies invested Fort Kingston Colonel Dennison, on whom the command of the fort had devolved, sensible of his inability to defend the post, went out with a flag of truce to inquire what terms would be granted to the garrison on surrendering. John Butler, with savage ferocity, replied, "The hatchet." Dennison defended the fort till most of his men were either killed or wounded, when he surrendered at discretion. A few prisoners were selected; and John Butler, with his Indians and tories, to save themselves the trouble of murdering individually their vanquished enemies, with the women and children, shut them all up in the houses and barracks, set fire to the buildings, and with horrid joy saw them perish in one general conflagration.

Butler next passed over to Wilkesbarre the feeble garrison of which, trusting to the generosity of the enemy, surrendered at discretion; but they mistook the character of Butler and his associates: for the continental soldiers, amounting to about seventy, were cut in pieces; and the rest of the people in the fort, men, women, and children, were consumed in the flames, as those of

Kingston had been. All show of resistance was at an end; but the work of devastation did not cease. About 3,000 persons, without money, clothes, or provisions, precipitately abandoned their homes, and fled from the murderous tomahawk: and, in order to prevent their return, their enemies destroyed everything they had left behind. In the work of desolation and death, fire and sword were alternately employed; and the settlement, which had lately bloomed like paradise, was converted into a dreary and silent wilderness. The property of the few tories only was spared; and their thinly-scattered houses and farms smiled in the midst of surrounding ruin. Having gratified their revenge, and hearing that regular troops were advancing against them, the savage invaders retreated from the country which they had laid waste.

Congress could not spare troops to cover the whole of the western frontier, which was exposed to hostile incursions; and consequently some districts were occasionally ravaged: but the sufferings at Wyoming were so remarkable, that, on the first notice of what had happened, Colonel Hartley, with his regiment and two companies of militia, was ordered to that settlement. He marched against the Indian towns, destroyed some of them, and took a few prisoners; but soon found it expedient to retreat. He was pursued and vigorously attacked, but repulsed the assailants with loss.

The fourth Pennsylvanian regiment, with some of Morgan's riflemen, commanded by Lieutenant-Colonel William Butler, a distinguished partisan, marched for the defence of the western frontier. After a difficult and fatiguing march, in which he crossed high mountains and deep waters, he reached the Indian towns of Unundilla and Anaquaqua, near the sources of the Susquehannah, where a considerable quantity of corn was laid up for winter provisions. He destroyed both the towns and corn, drove the savages to a greater distance from the frontier, and rendered their incursions into the provinces more difficult.

On the 11th of November 500 Indians and loyalists, with a small detachment of regular troops, under the command of the notorious John Butler, made an irruption into the settlement at Cherry Valley, in the state of New York, surprised and killed Colonel Alden, commander of the American force at that place, and ten of his soldiers. They attacked a fort erected there; but were compelled to retreat. Next day they left the place, after having murdered and scalped thirty-two of the inhabitants, chiefly women and children.

During the summer, the house of Mr. John Merrill, of Nelson county, Kentucky, was attacked by the Indians, and defended with singular address and good fortune. Merrill was alarmed by the barking of a dog about midnight, and upon opening the door in order to ascertain the cause of the disturbance, he received the fire of six or seven Indians, by which his arm and thigh were both broken. He instantly sunk upon the floor, and called upon his wife to close the door. This had scarcely been done, when it was violently assailed by the tomahawks of the enemy, and a large breach soon effected. Mrs. Merrill, however, being a perfect Amazon, both in strength and courage, guarded it with an axe, and successively killed or badly wounded four of the enemy as they attempted to force their way into the cabin. The Indians then ascended the roof and attempted to enter by way of the chimney, but here, again, they were met by the same determined enemy. Mrs. Merrill seized the only feather-bed which the cabin afforded, and hastily ripping it open, poured its contents upon the fire. A furious blaze and stifling smoke instantly ascended the chimney, and quickly brought down two of the enemy, who lay for a few moments at the mercy of the lady. Seizing the axe, she quickly despatched them, and was instantly afterward summoned to the door, where the only remaining savage now appeared, endeavoring to effect an entrance while she was engaged at the chimney. He soon received a gash in the cheek, which compelled him with a loud

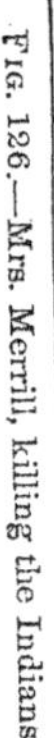

Fig. 126.—Mrs. Merrill, killing the Indians.

yell to relinquish his purpose. He returned to Chilicothe, where, from the report of a prisoner, he gave an exaggerated account of the fierceness, strength and courage of the long-knife squaw.

While the frontiers of Pennsylvania and New York were afflicted by the horrors of savage warfare, the same calamity was preparing for Virginia, but was prevented by the courage and persevering activity of Colonel George Rogers Clarke. At the head of some of the western militia of Virginia, by incredible exertions, he penetrated to the British settlements on the Mississippi, and took the town of Kaskaskias, a dependancy on Canada, which, along with that province, had been given up to the British at the peace of 1763. At Kaskaskias Clarke, with a handful of men, was far removed from all support, and surrounded by numerous fierce and hostile tribes: but his courage and talents were equal to the arduous circumstances in which he was placed; and he showed in a striking manner what difficulties a sound and enterprising mind can surmount, and what brilliant exploits it can achieve. His plans were formed with judgment, and executed with promptitude and intrepidity. At the most inclement season of the year, he suddenly attacked the Indians in their villages, turned all their military artifices against themselves, and damped the courage of their warriors.

On taking Kaskaskias, Clarke made Rocheblave, governor of the place, prisoner, and got possession of all his written instructions for the conduct of the war, from Quebec, Detroit, and Michilimackinac. From those papers he learned that Colonel Hamilton, governor of Detroit, was very active in planning and stimulating the incursions of the Indians into the United States. In the month of December Hamilton advanced to St. Vincent on the Wabash, in order to prepare an extensive expedition, not only against Clarke, but against the whole western frontier of Virginia. Clarke was in no condition to encounter the combined force of all the tribes from the lakes to the mouth of the Ohio, supported by the troops which Hamilton might be able to bring into the field; but he took the best measures in his power for maintaining his post.

Colonel Clarke soon received information that Hamilton, trusting to his distance from danger, and to the difficulty of approaching him, had sent off all his Indians to alarm and harass the frontier, and lay securely at St. Vincent with only about eighty soldiers, having three field-pieces and some swivels. Clarke, although he could muster only 130 men, determined to take advantage of Hamilton's weakness and security and to attack him, as the only means of saving himself and of disconcerting the whole of Hamilton's plan. Accordingly, about the beginning of February, 1779, he despatched a small galley which he had fitted out, mounting two four-pounders and four swivels, manned with a company of soldiers, and carrying stores for his men, with orders to force her way up the Wabash, to take her station a few miles below St. Vincent, and to allow no person to pass her. He himself marched with his little band, and spent sixteen days in traversing the country between Kaskaskias and St. Vincent, passing with incredible fatigue through woods and marshes. He was five days in crossing the drowned lands of the Wabash; and for five miles was frequently up to the breast in water. After overcoming difficulties which had been thought insurmountable, he appeared before the place, and completely surprised it. The inhabitants readily submitted, but Hamilton at first defended himself in the fort: next day, however, he surrendered himself and his garrison prisoners-of-war. By his activity in encouraging the hostilities of the Indians, and by the revolting enormities perpetrated by those savages, Hamilton had rendered himself so obnoxious, that the executive council of Virginia threw him and some of his immediate agents into prison, and put them in irons.

This enterprise of Clarke was of much advantage to congress. It disconcerted the whole of Hamilton's plan, saved the western frontier of Virginia from the extensive devastations of savage warfare which had been devised against it, cooled the ardor of many of the Indian tribes, and deterred them from engaging in their ferocious incursions into the United States.

Except the unsuccessful attack on Sullivan's island in 1776, the British force had hitherto been directed solely against the northern and middle states, the most populous and strongest parts of the Union. If the north had been subdued, the south must have yielded: but the results had not answered the expectations of the British cabinet. One army had been compelled to lay down its arms; and the army on the coast had been of little advantage to the cause. The people had indeed suffered much in the course of the contest; but their sufferings, instead of subduing their spirits, had only embittered their animosity against the mother-country.

In those circumstances, when the season for active operations in the middle and northern states terminated, the British commander-in-chief resolved to make an attempt on the southern provinces, as an experiment to ascertain the probable result of transferring the war to that quarter. If he could not subdue all the country, he might reduce a part of it to allegiance to the British crown. Success in the south might pave the way for victory in the north. The south produced the commodities most valuable in the European market; and the possession of some of the provinces would entitle the British government to better terms at a general peace. By these and similar considerations, the British commander-in-chief was induced to try the chances of war in the south. His attention was turned to that quarter by a desultory but destructive warfare which, during the preceding summer, had been carried on between Georgia and East Florida. In some degree that warfare had subsisted ever since Georgia joined the Union; but, during the preceding summer, those inroads had assumed a more serious aspect than usual: numbers of loyalists, who had fled from the Carolinas and Georgia, sought shelter in East Florida; and, animated with all the fervor of political zeal and personal revenge, they readily joined in those expeditions. One of these marauding parties advanced to Sunbury in Georgia, which they summoned to surrender; but Colonel McIntosh, commander of the fort, returned this laconic answer: "Come and take it." Understanding by this reply that they were to meet with an obstinate resistance, and being little inclined to encounter the fatigue and dangers of a siege, the party immediately retreated. Another body of those irregular warriors, by a different route, penetrated as far as the river Ogeechee, within thirty miles of Savannah. There they found Colonel Elbert, with 200 continental troops ready to dispute the passage of the river; and being informed of the retrograde movement of the other division, they also retraced their steps, marking their course by ruin and carnage.

This inroad was retaliated by an incursion into East Florida by General Robert Howe, commander of the military force of South Carolina and Georgia. But his troops were attacked by disease; and he was obliged to hasten home with considerable loss. Scarcely, however, had his army, consisting of between six and seven hundred continental soldiers and a few hundreds of militia, taken post in the vicinity of Savannah, when he had to encounter an enemy far more formidable than the irregulars of East Florida.

A plan of attack on Georgia had been concerted between Sir Henry Clinton and General Provost, who commanded in East Florida. A British detachment was to land on the banks of the Savannah, and there to be joined by the troops under General Provost, who was to command the whole. For that purpose the seventy-first regiment of foot, two battalions of Hessians, four of loyal provincials, and a party of artillery, amounting in all to about 3,500 men, under the command of Colonel Campbell, sailed from Sandy Hook on the 27th of November; and, as already mentioned, was escorted by a small squadron under Com-

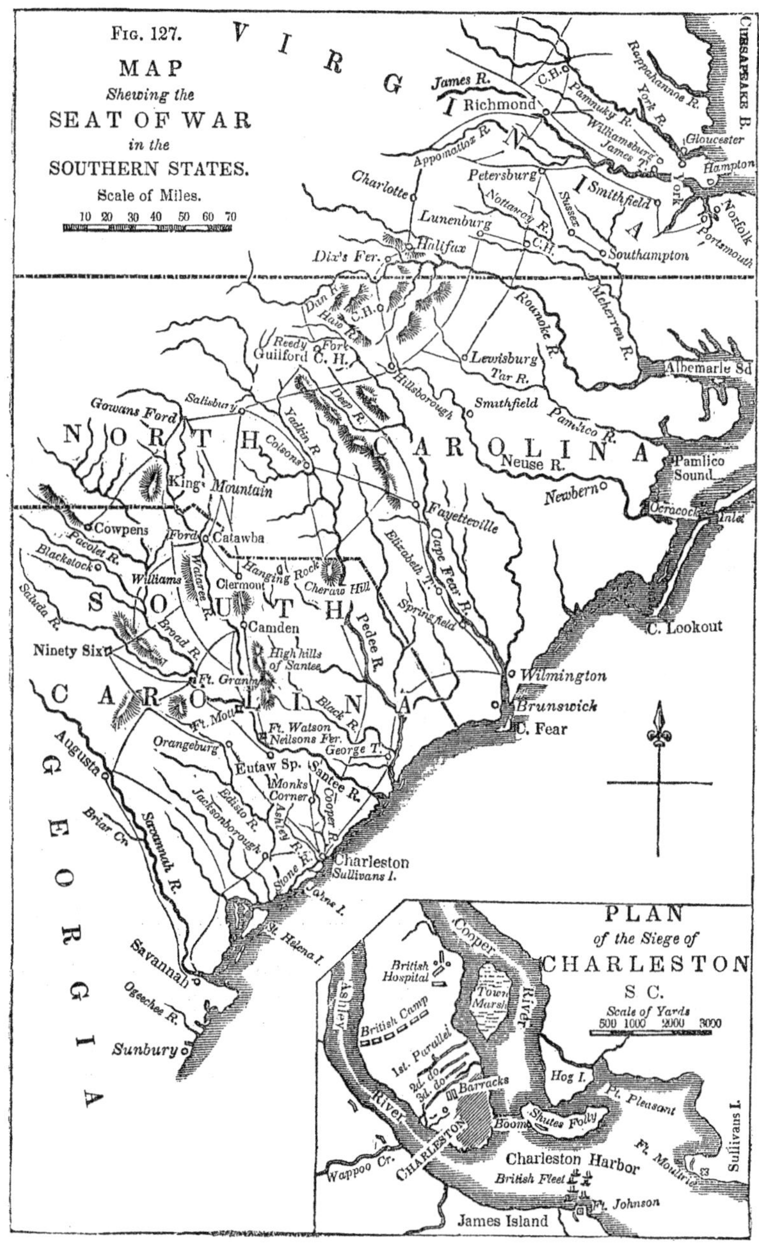
FIG. 127.
MAP
Shewing the
SEAT OF WAR
in the
SOUTHERN STATES.
Scale of Miles.
10 20 30 40 50 60 70
VIRGINIA
NORTH CAROLINA
SOUTH CAROLINA
GEORGIA
CHESAPEAKE B.
Richmond
Petersburg
Smithfield
Southampton
Norfolk
Portsmouth
Hampton
Gloucester
Halifax
Lunenburg
Charlotte
Dix's Fer.
Guilford C. H.
Reedy Fork
Hillsborough
Lewisburg
Smithfield
Salisbury
Gowans Ford
King Mountain
Cowpens
Catawba
Clermont
Hanging Rock
Cheraw Hill
Camden
Ninety Six
Ft. Granby
High hills of Santee
Ft. Motte
Ft. Watson
Neilsons Fer.
George T.
Orangeburg
Eutaw Sp.
Monks Corner
Augusta
Jacksonborough
Charleston
Sullivans I.
Savannah
Sunbury
Fayetteville
Springfield
Wilmington
Brunswick
C. Fear
C. Lookout
Newbern
Pamlico Sound
Ocracock
Inlet
Albemarle Sd
Neuse R.
Pamlico R.
Roanoke R.
Meherren R.
Tar R.
Deep R.
Yadkin R.
Pedee R.
Cape Fear R.
Broad R.
Wateree R.
Saluda R.
Santee R.
Cooper R.
Ashley R.
Edisto R.
Savannah R.
Ogeechee R.
Briar Cr.
PLAN
of the Siege of
CHARLESTON
S. C.
Scale of Yards
500 1000 2000 3000
British Hospital
British Camp
1st. Parallel
2d. do
3d. do
Barracks
Town Marsh
Hog I.
Ft. Pleasant
Shutes Folly
Boom
Charleston Harbor
British Fleet
Ft. Johnson
James Island
Ft. Moultrie
Sullivans I.
Wappoo Cr.
Ashley River
Cooper River

modore Parker. The armament appeared off the mouth of the Savannah on the 23d of December.

The river Savannah is the line of separation between the states of Georgia and South Carolina; and the country about the mouth of the river is one continued marsh, impassable by troops except over causeways extending through the swamps. Colonel Campbell had heard nothing of the movements of General Provost, who was to command the expedition; but, having received some information concerning the state of the province and its military force, he determined to commence active operations without waiting the general's arrival. He accordingly proceeded up the river to the first practicable landing-place at Gerido's plantation, about three miles below the town of Savannah, where the debarcation began early on the morning of the 29th. From the landing-place a narrow causeway, 600 yards long, with a ditch on each side of it, ran through a rice swamp to the plantation on the rising ground. Captain Cameron of the seventy-first regiment, with his light infantry, landed first, and advanced along the causeway. A small American party, stationed on the rising ground at the upper end of it, received the British detachment with a discharge of musketry, which killed Captain Cameron and two of his men, and wounded five others. The Highlanders rushed forward, and the Americans retreated, when the British landed without farther interruption.

The American General Howe, with about 900 men, had occupied a good position about half a mile below the town of Savannah, on the road leading to Gerido's plantation. The swamp and river were on his left, a morass in front extending beyond his right flank, where it was covered with wood and bushes. He had one piece of artillery on each flank, and two pointed to the road by which he expected the British troops to advance. He had broken up the road and destroyed a bridge, so that his front was well secured; and if the attack had been made in that quarter only, an obstinate conflict might have ensued. But a negro, who fell into Colonel Campbell's hands, informed him of a private path through the marsh, beyond the American right flank, and by which their rear might be gained. Colonel Campbell came in sight of the American army about three in the afternoon; and, while the inequalities of the ground partly concealed his movements, he detached Sir James Baird with the light infantry and New York volunteers to cross the morass by the private path, turn the American right, and attack their rear. Meanwhile, in order to amuse the Americans and divert their attention from the real point of attack, Colonel Campbell performed some evolutions in front; but as soon as Sir James Baird had passed the swamp by the private path, he attacked a party of Georgian militia, and the firing on that occasion informed Colonel Campbell of the success of his detachment, and gave the American general the first notice of the danger which threatened his rear. The British line was ordered to advance rapidly: the artillery, which had been concealed behind an eminence, was brought forward, and began a brisk cannonade on the Americans. Howe ordered a retreat, which was now become difficult. His men ran across a plain in front of Sir James Baird's detachment, which attacked them with great impetuosity, and did considerable execution. Such of them as escaped retreated up the Savannah, crossed the river at Zubly's ferry, and took refuge in South Carolina.

The fort, forty-eight pieces of cannon, twenty-three mortars, a quantity of military stores and provisions collected for the use of the southern army and the capital of Georgia, fell into the hands of the conquerors. The brave defence of Fort Moultrie, in 1776, had hitherto saved the southern states from the horrors of war; but the defeat of Howe at Savannah made those states the scene of fierce and desolating hostilities during the remainder of the contest.

General Prevost had been ordered to join Colonel Campbell and command the expedition; but Campbell had acted with such promptitude that the reduction of the province was almost accomplished before Prevost appeared.

Colonel Campbell, having taken the necessary measures for securing the northern frontier of Georgia, turned his attention toward the garrison of Sunbury, the retreat of which was cut off; but, when he was about to march against it, he was informed that it had surrendered to General Prevost, who advanced to Savannah, where he arrived about the middle of January, and took the command of the British force in Georgia, agreeably to the original plan of the expedition. He immediately detached Colonel Campbell, with 800 regular troops, and some provincials, against Augusta, the principal town of the interior part of the province, situated on the south bank of the Savannah, about 150 miles from the coast. Possession of it was easily acquired, and thus the reduction of Georgia was completed.

While the expedition against Georgia was preparing at New York, congress was meditating the conquest of East Florida. Having received notice from General Washington of an intended attack on the southern states, the delegates of Georgia requested that General Lincoln, who had been second in rank at Saratoga, should be appointed to the command of the southern army. Accordingly, so far back as the month of September, Howe had been ordered to repair to the headquarters of General Washington, and Lincoln was nominated commander in the south. At the same time congress passed a resolution, requesting the executive councils of Virginia and North Carolina to give all the assistance in their power to South Carolina and Georgia.

In obedience to orders, General Lincoln repaired to Charleston, the capital of South Carolina, where he found the military affairs of the country in much disorder. From inadvertency, or want of means, congress had established no continental military chest in the southern department. That defect rendered the troops dependant on the several state governments for supplies to enable the army to move on any emergency; and, in a great degree, subjected even the continental troops to the control of the civil authority in the several states. The militia, also, who had been taken into continental pay, considered themselves subject only to the military code of the province to which they belonged. Such a state of things was extremely unfavorable to the promptitude and vigor of military operations.

While General Lincoln was employed in rectifying disorders, and making preparations for the ensuing campaign, he received information of the appearance of the British armament off the coast of Georgia. So promptly had the state of North Carolina complied with the recommendation of congress to assist their southern neighbors, that 2,000 men, raised for that purpose, arrived at Charleston, under the command of Generals Ashe and Rutherford. But although the state of North Carolina had raised the men, it had not provided them with arms; and congress had no magazines in that part of the union. The troops, therefore, were dependant on South Carolina for every military equipment: but that state, though better provided than North Carolina, had no superabundance of arms; and, under the apprehension that its own territory was to be invaded, declined supplying the troops of North Carolina with arms till it was too late to save the capital of Georgia.

When it was ascertained that the British fleet had entered the Savannah, the arms were furnished, every exertion was made to put the troops of Charleston in motion, and General Lincoln at their head proceeded rapidly toward the enemy; but on his march he received information of Howe's defeat, and soon afterward met the feeble remnant of the beaten army at Perrysburg, a small town on the north bank of the Savannah, about thirty miles from the coast. At Perrysburg General Lincoln established his headquarters on the 3d of January

The force under his command amounted to between 3,000 and 4,000 men, many of them new levies and militia, who were strangers to the discipline and subordination of a camp. The army of General Prevost was somewhat more numerous, and greatly superior in the quality of the troops.

But with all his advantages it was not easy for General Prevost to advance into South Carolina; for the river Savannah flowed between the two armies. Its channel, indeed, is not wide; but for 100 miles from its mouth it flows through a marshy country, which it often inundates to the breadth of from two to four miles. At no one place is there solid ground on both sides to the brink of the river. A few narrow causeways running through the marsh are the only places where it can be passed, and on many occasions these can not be crossed by an army. This circumstance made it difficult for General Prevost to enter South Carolina, and inexpedient for General Lincoln to make any attempt on the British posts, although they extended from Savannah to Augusta.

The coast of Georgia and South Carolina is broken and irregular, abounding in islands, and intersected by arms of the sea. General Prevost detached Major Gardener, with 200 men, to take possession of the island of Port Royal; but that officer was soon attacked by General Moultrie, who compelled him to retreat with loss. Deterred by that check, General Prevost, for some time, made no farther attempts on South Carolina.

From the beginning of the war, a considerable number of the settlers on the western frontier of the three southern provinces had been well disposed toward Great Britain. They were satisfied with their condition, and wished no change. Information of the first successes of the British arms in Georgia soon reached these settlers; and emissaries were despatched to invite them to join the king's standard at Augusta, which had been erected there partly with a view to favor such movements, and to encourage the loyal settlers to co-operate with the troops in establishing the royal authority. Such of them as, on account of the notoriety of their principles and of their active hostility to independence, had been obliged to seek shelter among the Indians, were flattered with the hope of returning in triumph to the enjoyment of their possessions.

About 700 of these loyalists imbodied themselves under Colonel Boyd, and began their march from the back part of South Carolina to Augusta. Destitute of provisions, and dependant on plunder for subsistence, they resembled a disorderly banditti rather than a military force; and, by their irregularities, they armed all the peaceable inhabitants against them. The militia assembled under Colonel Pickens; pursued and attacked them near Kittle creek; and defeated them with considerable slaughter, Boyd, their leader, being among the killed. Many prisoners were taken, seventy of whom were tried and condemned as traitors, and five of the most obnoxious were executed. About 300 of them escaped, reached the British outposts, and joined the royal army. This defeat depressed the rising spirits of the loyalists, and for a while, preserved the tranquillity of the western frontier.

The British post at Augusta was too distant from the main body of the army to be easily maintained; and therefore, about the middle of February, Colonel Campbell was ordered to abandon it. By slow marches he moved down the river, till he reached Hudson's ferry, about twenty-four miles from Ebenezer, where the British headquarters were then established. There he left his detachment under the care of Lieutenant-Colonel Prevost, brother of the general, and returned to Savannah.

The American army was gradually reinforced by the arrival of militia from the Carolinas; and General Lincoln began to meditate offensive operations. He extended his posts up the river; and detached General Ashe, with 1,300 militia 100 continental soldiers, and some cavalry, to take post opposite Augusta.

His intention was to straiten the quarters of the British troops, and to cut off the communication with the Indians and the settlers on the western frontier. On arriving at his station, Ashe found Augusta already evacuated; and, agreeably to his instructions, he crossed the river, marched down the south side, and took post near the point where Brier creek falls into the Savannah, forming an acute angle with it. His position was good, and appeared secure. The Savannah with its marshes was on his left; and his front was covered by Brier creek, which is about six yards wide and unfordable at that place, as well as for several miles above it.

General Prevost resolved to dislodge the American detachment. For the purpose of amusing General Lincoln, he made a show of an intention to pass the river; and, in order to occupy the attention of Ashe, he ordered a party to appear on the opposite side of Brier creek, in his front. Meanwhile Colonel Prevost, with 900 chosen men, made an extensive circuit, passed Brier creek fifteen miles above the American station, gained their rear unperceived, and was almost in their camp before they discovered his approach. The continental troops under General Elbert, were drawn out to meet them, and began the engagement with spirit. But most of the militia threw down their arms without firing a shot, fled in confusion into the marsh, and swam across the river, in which numbers of them were drowned. General Elbert and his small band of continentals, supported by only one regiment of North Carolina militia, were not long able to maintain the unequal conflict; but being overpowered by numbers, were compelled to surrender themselves prisoner of war. The Americans lost between 300 and 400 men, who were killed or taken prisoners, with seven pieces of artillery. Among the prisoners were General Elbert and Colonel M'Intosh, officers of the continental army. The militia were dispersed; most of them who escaped returned home; and of the whole of Ashe's division not more than 450 men again joined General Lincoln.

The defeat and dispersion of Ashe's division deprived Lincoln of one fourth of his numerical force, restored to the British the entire possession of Georgia, and opened again their communications with the Indians and loyalists in the back settlements of the southern provinces. The success was complete; and General Prevost seems to have flattered himself that its effects would be permanent; for next day he issued a proclamation establishing civil government in the province, appointing executive and judicial officers for its administration, and declaring the laws, as they existed at the end of the year 1775, to be in force, and to continue till they should be altered by a legislature afterward to be assembled.

The disaster which had befallen Ashe, instead of terrifying the people of South Carolina into submission, roused them to more vigorous exertions, and to a more determined resolution to maintain their independence. They elected as their governor John Rutledge, a man of talents and influence; and delegated to him and his council powers almost dictatorial. Rutledge, who was zealous in the cause of independence, exerted much energy, and soon sent 1,000 militia to camp. Strengthened by such a large reinforcement, General Lincoln resumed his original plan of gaining possession of the upper parts of Georgia; and on the 23d of April he marched up the Savannah with the main body of his army. One design of that movement was to afford protection to the state legislature of Georgia, which was to assemble at Augusta on the 1st of May.

At that time the river was in full flood, and overflowed the marshes on its margin. The rivulets were swollen, and the swamps inundated; and therefore it was believed that a small military force would be able to defend the country against an invading enemy. Accordingly, for the protection of the lower districts, General Lincoln left only 200 continentals, under Colonel McIntosh, who

Fig. 128.—City Hall at Augusta, Georgia.

had been exchanged, and 800 militia ; the whole commanded by General Moultrie, who had distinguished himself by his brave defence of Sullivan's island in the year 1776. It was expected that if an invasion of the lower parts of South Carolina should be attempted in Lincoln's absence, the militia would promptly take the field in defence of the country.

Instead of marching up the river, and encountering General Lincoln in the interior, General Prevost considered an irruption into South Carolina the best means for recalling that officer from the enterprise in which he was engaged. Accordingly, on the 29th of April, when Lincoln was far advanced on his way to Augusta, General Prevost, with 2,500 troops and a considerable number of Indian allies, suddenly passed the river near Perrysburg. Colonel M'Intosh, who was stationed there with a small detachment, retreated to General Moultrie at Black Swamp. General Prevost advanced rapidly into the country ; and Moultrie was obliged to retire hastily before him, destroying the bridges in his rear. The militia who were in the field showed no courage, and could not be prevailed on to defend the passes with any degree of bravery. The militia of the state did not appear in arms as had been expected ; and Moultrie experienced an alarming diminution of his strength, by the desertion of many of those under his command.

Immediately after the passage of the river by the British, an express was sent to Lincoln, then nearly opposite Augusta, informing him of the event. He considered Prevost's movement as a feint to recall him from the upper parts of the river, and determined to prosecute his plan, and compel the British general to return for the defence of the capital of Georgia. Meanwhile he despatched 300 light troops, under Colonel Harris, to Moultrie's assistance ; and crossing the river at Augusta, he marched down on the south side toward the town of Savannah.

General Prevost's original plan was merely to make a temporary incursion into South Carolina, chiefly for the purpose of inducing Lincoln to retrace his steps, and return to the lower parts of the river. But meeting with a feebler resistance than he had anticipated, and encouraged by the flattering representations received from the loyalists of the good will of the people in general to the royal cause, and of the defenceless state of Charleston, his views began to enlarge, and at length he came to the resolution of making an attempt on the capital of South Carolina. He resumed his march. The plundering and devastation of his troops, and of his Indian allies, spread terror and desolation around him. Moultrie, with his handful of continentals, and his militia, retreated before the enemy, giving them little interruption, farther than breaking down the bridges on the road.

Express on express was now despatched to General Lincoln to inform him of the alarming posture of affairs in South Carolina. That officer had crossed the Savannah at Augusta, and, notwithstanding the progress of the British army, resolved to proceed down the south side of the river, because that road was almost as near to Charleston as any other, and because, by showing his army in Georgia, he hoped to rouse the courage of the intimidated inhabitants. Meanwhile all was activity and alarm in Charleston. That city, as already mentioned, is situated on a point of land between the rivers Ashley and Cooper, where they terminate in a bay of the ocean. Toward the sea the place had been fortified, and works erected on the islands in the bay to defend the entrance. An attack by land had not been anticipated; and on that side the city was entirely open. But in the present alarming crisis the inhabitants began to fortify the city on the land side, and prosecuted the work with vigor and unremitting assiduity. All hands were employed on the work ; the slave and his master labored together. Lines of defence were drawn from the Ashley to the Cooper ; artil lery was planted on them; and they were flanked by armed galleys stationed in the rivers. General Moultrie, with his feeble force, entered the town; the 300 men detached by Lincoln arrived; Governor Rutledge, who had taken post with the militia at Orangeburgh high up the north branch of the Edisto, as a central station whence he could most easily afford assistance to any place that might be threatened, hastened to the point of danger; and Pulaski's legion came in. All these troops entered the city nearly at the same time; and, together with the fortifications recently constructed, put it in a condition very different from that in which it had been only a few days before.

On the evening of the 10th of May, about the time when the several American detachments entered Charleston, General Prevost with his army arrived at Ashley ferry. Next morning he passed the river, marched down the neck between the Ashley and Cooper, and took a position just without the reach of the guns on the fortifications. The remainder of the day was spent in slight skirmishes. On the 12th General Prevost summoned the town to surrender; and Governor Rutledge, deeming it of much importance to gain time, the day was occupied in negotiation. On the part of the town a proposal was made for the neutrality of South Carolina during the war, leaving its ultimate fate to be determined by the treaty of peace; but after several messages and explanations, this proposal was entirely rejected by General Prevost, who told the garrison that, being in arms, they must surrender themselves prisoners-of-war. This closed the negotiation, and both parties seemed to prepare for an appeal to arms. But next morning the garrison was agreeably surprised to find that the British army had retreated during the night, and recrossed Ashley ferry. On surveying the American works, General Prevost perceived that, although they were unfinished, yet it was too hazardous in his circumstances to assault them; for the garrison was more numerous than his army. There was no time for delay, as he knew Lincoln was rapidly advancing against him; therefore he came to the prudent resolution of immediately retreating.

General Prevost did not return to Savannah by the direct road, as he had advanced; for in Charleston there was a numerous garrison in his rear, and Lincoln was near at hand with his army. Therefore, after passing Ashley ferry, he turned to the left and proceeded to the coast, which, abounding with islands, and being intersected by arms of the sea all the way to the mouth of the Savannah, afforded him the easiest and safest method of returning with all his baggage to Georgia. He first passed into the island of St. James, and then into that of St. John, where he took post till the arrival of a supply of provisions, which he had for some time expected from New York.

By hasty marches General Lincoln had arrived at Dorchester, not far from Charleston, before General Prevost left Ashley ferry; and when the British troops proceeded to the coast, Lincoln followed and encamped near them, both armies being about thirty miles from Charleston.

St. John's island, of which General Prevost took possession, is separated from the main land by a narrow inlet called Stone river; and the communication between the continent and the island is kept up by a ferry. On the continent, at this ferry, the British general established a post; partly for the security of the island, and partly for the protection of his foragers. For the defence of the post three redoubts were constructed, and joined together by lines of communication. For some time 1,500 men were stationed at the post under Colonel Prevost; and the communication with the island was maintained by a bridge, formed by the numerous schooners, sloops, and smaller vessels which attended the army.

So long as the whole of General Prevost's force lay on St. John's island, ready to support his detachment at Stono ferry, General Lincoln made no attempt against that post. But the British general set out on his return to Georgia transporting a large part of his troops, by means of the shipping, from island to island along the coast. Colonel Prevost, also, with part of the garrison of Stono ferry, was ordered to Savannah; and he left the remainder, amounting to about 700 men, under the command of Lieutenant-Colonel Maitland. A number of troops still remained on St. John's island, but almost all the boats were removed, and consequently the communication between the island and the main land was not nearly so open as before.

General Lincoln plainly perceived that it was the intention of the British general to evacuate that part of the country without delay; and he resolved not to allow the troops to depart unmolested. He determined to attack the post at Stono ferry; and in order to prevent it from being reinforced by the troops on the island, General Moultrie, who commanded in Charleston, was to pass over to St. James's island with a number of militia, and engage the attention of the force on St. John's island, while a real attack was made on the post at the ferry.

On the 20th of June, before seven in the morning, General Lincoln, with about 1,200 men, advanced to the attack. His right wing was composed of the militia of South and North Carolina, and his continental soldiers formed the left, to encounter the Scottish highlanders, reckoned the best troops in the British service. Colonel Maitland's advanced guards were stationed a good way in front of his works, and a smart firing between them and the Americans gave him the first warning of the approach of the enemy. He instantly put his garrison under arms, and sent out two companies of highlanders from his right, under Captain Campbell, to ascertain the force of the assailants. The highlanders had proceeded only a quarter of a mile when they met the continental troops of the American army. A fierce conflict ensued; and the highlanders persisted in the combat till all their officers were either killed or wounded. Of the two companies, eleven men only returned to the garrison. The whole American line now advanced within 300 yards of the works, and a general engagement with cannon and musketry began, and was maintained with much courage and steadiness on both sides. At length a regiment of Hessians on the British left gave way, and the Americans were on the point of entering the works; but, by a rapid movement of the remainder of the 71st regiment, their progress was checked: and as General Moultrie, from want of boats, had been unable to execute in due time his part of the enterprise, General Lincoln, apprehensive of he arrival of reinforcements to the British from the island, drew off his men, and retired in good order, carrying his wounded along with him. The battle lasted upward of an hour. The British had three officers and twenty-three privates killed, and ten officers and ninety-three privates wounded. The Americans lost five officers who died of their wounds, and thirty-five privates who were killed on the field of battle, besides nineteen officers and 120 privates wounded.

Three days after the battle the British troops evacuated the post at Stono ferry, and also the island of St. John, passing along the coast from island to island, till they reached Beaufort in the island of Port Royal, where General Prevost left a garrison under the command of Lieutenant-Colonel Maitland.

The heat, which in the southern provinces as effectually puts a stop to military operations during summer as the cold of the north in winter, was now become too intense for active service. The care of the officers, in both armies, was employed in preserving their men from the fevers of the season, and keeping them in a condition for service next campaign, which was expected to open in October. The American militia dispersed, leaving General Lincoln with about 800 men, whom he marched to Shelden, not far from Beaufort.

The alarm for the safety of the southern states was so great, that General

FIG. 129.—Hired Hessians.

Washington, weak as his army was, weakened it still farther by sending a detachment, consisting of Bland's regiment of cavalry, and the remnant of that lately under Baylor, but now commanded by Lieutenant-Colonel Washington, with some new levies, to reinforce General Lincoln.

The irruption of General Prevost into South Carolina did no credit to the British army, nor did it in any degree serve the royal cause, although it occasioned great loss to the inhabitants of the province. The British army marked its course by plunder and devastation. It spread over the country to a considerable extent: small parties entered every house; seized the plate, money, jewels, and personal ornaments of the people; and often destroyed what they could not carry away. The slaves, allured by the hope of freedom, repaired to the royal army; and, in order to ingratiate themselves with their new friends, disclosed where their masters had concealed their most valuable effects. Many of those slaves were afterward shipped off and sold in the West Indies. Some hundreds of them died of the camp fever; and numbers of them, overtaken by disease, and afraid to return to their masters, perished miserably in the woods. It has been calculated that South Carolina lost four thousand slaves. The rapine and devastation were great; and many of the inhabitants, in order to save themselves from those ravages, made professions of attachment to the royal cause; while the means which induced them to make a show of loyalty alienated all their affections from their former rulers.

While the events now related were passing in the south, several desultory operations, the object of which was devastation and plunder, rather than conquest, were projected by the British in the middle and southern states.

Admiral Gambier, who had succeeded Lord Howe in the command of the fleet on the American station, was recalled; and, in the month of April, Sir George Collier succeeded him. Between Sir George and Sir Henry Clinton, a plan was concerted for interrupting the commerce of the Chesapeake, and destroying the magazines on its shores. For those purposes, the commander-in-chief detached 1,800 men under General Matthews; and the transports in which they sailed were convoyed by the admiral himself. The fleet sailed from Sandy Hook on the 5th of May, and entered the capes of Virginia on the 8th. The lower part of Virginia is so intersected by deep creeks and rivers, as to afford those who have the command of the waters an easy passage from one place to another, and to give them a decided advantage over those who are destitute of such facil.i ies of communication.

FIG. 130.—Southern Slaves.

The fleet anchored in Hampton Road, a large basin of water formed by the confluence of the rivers James, Nansemond, and Elizabeth. On the morning of the 10th it entered Elizabeth river; and the weak American detachment in that quarter, wholly unable to resist such a formidable force, saved itself by flight. The British troops landed without opposition. General Matthews established his headquarters at Portsmouth, whence he sent small parties to Norfolk, Gosport, Kemp's landing, and Suffolk; where they took and carried off or destroyed a large quantity of naval and military stores, and a number of ships, some of them richly laden. The loss to the public and to individuals was great Having accomplished the object of the expedition, General Matthews returned to New York before the end of the month.

At the opening of the campaign of 1779, the British army at New York and Rhode Island, including the detachment under General Matthews, amounted to upward of sixteen thousand men, assisted by a powerful fleet. The complete command of the ocean and of the navigable rivers enabled the royal army to make sudden attacks on distant parts of the country, and to keep the Americans in perpetual alarm, as they knew not at what point they were to be assailed. In numerical force the northern army of congress was nearly equal to that under Sir Henry Clinton. Upward of seven thousand men were stationed at Middlebrook, under the immediate command of General Washington; the rest of the army was posted in the highlands on the Hudson, under General M'Dougall, and on the east side of the river, under General Putnam.

On the part of the Americans the plan of the campaign was necessarily defensive; for they had no probability of making any successful attack on the British army at New York or Rhode Island. That army interrupted the communication by sea, and by the lower parts of the Hudson, between the middle and northern states. To preserve that communication as far down the Hudson as possible, was a matter of much importance to the Americans; and to guard the passes of the highlands, and command the communication between New York and Albany, was always an object of anxious attention to General Washington. With a view to secure those points, the Americans began to construct fortifications on Stony point, a rocky and commanding eminence on the west bank of the river, about sixty miles above New York, and on Verplanck's point, a flat peninsula projecting a good way into the river on the opposite side. The fort at the last place, named La Fayette, was in a state of greater forwardness than the works on Stony point.

Before the return of General Matthews from his incursion into Virginia, Sir Henry Clinton had planned an attack upon those places, and the troops were embarked for that purpose. On the return of Matthews, his detachment, without being permitted to land, was joined to the expedition; and on the 30th of May the whole armament, convoyed by Sir George Collier and accompanied by the commander-in-chief, sailed up the North river. Next morning the largest division of the troops, under General Vaughan, landed on the east bank, seven miles below Fort La Fayette; the remainder, accompanied by Sir Henry Clinton, continued their course up the river, and landed on the west side, three miles below Stony point.

The position of the Americans at Stony point was strong, but the works were unfinished; and the feeble garrison, after setting fire to a blockhouse on the top of the eminence, abandoned the place. The British took possession of it in the afternoon, and, in the course of the night, with great labor, dragged some heavy cannon and mortars to the top of the hill. At five next morning a battery was ready to open on Fort La Fayette. The distance across the river was about a thousand yards; and during the day the fire from the commanding summit of Stony point, and from the armed vessels and gun-boats in the river, made a sensible impression on the works of Fort La Fayette. During the following night two galleys passed up the river, and anchored above the fort, so as to prevent the escape of the garrison by water. General Vaughan, having made a long circuit, completely invested the place by land. Therefore the garrison, unable to maintain the post against such a superior force, and finding themselves enclosed on every side, surrendered the place, and became prisoners of war. Sir Henry Clinton gave immediate directions for completing the fortifications of both posts, and putting them in a strong state of defence.

General Washington obtained early notice of preparations at New York for this expedition; and, suspecting that it was intended either against his own army at Middlebrook or the passes in the highlands, he put his troops in motion, and ordered General Putnam to be ready to make a rapid movement up the river. He strengthened the garrison of West Point, an important post on the Hudson, some miles above Verplanck's;and took a strong position, with his army, in Smith's close, so as to secure West Point on that side. But Sir Henry Clinton, perceiving that no further progress could be made up the river, and being informed that Staten Island was threatened in his absence, after garrisoning the posts which he had taken, returned with his fleet and army to New York.

The states of New England were the most populous in the Union. With them the quarrel originated; and they had given congress an active and zealous support. The activity and courage which they had displayed at the commencement of the struggle had hitherto, in a great measure, saved that part of the country from being made the theatre of war. But now Sir Henry Clinton determined to ravage the coast of Connecticut; partly with the view of drawing General Washington from his strong position in the highlands to protect the towns near the shore, and partly in order to punish the inhabitants for their active hostility to the British government. For those purposes 2,600 men, under the command of Tryon, formerly governor of the province of New York, but now a major-general in the British army, convoyed by Sir George Collier with several vessels of war, sailed from Throg's Neck in the sound, on the 4th of July, and next morning reached the vicinity of New Haven, the capital of Connecticut.

On the appearance of the armament, the militia assembled with alacrity and in considerable numbers. But the troops effected a landing several miles below the town; and, notwithstanding a continued opposition, made themselves masters of it, and took or destroyed all the artillery, ammunition, public stores, and the vessels in the harbor, but, in a great measure, spared private property.

Next day they reimbarked, and sailed along the coast to the village of Fairfield. The alarm was now widely spread; the militia assembled in greater numbers; and the opposition to the troops was more obstinate than at New Haven. But they forced their way into Fairfield; and General Tryon, determined if possible to ruin those whom he was unable to subdue, not only destroyed all the public property, but laid the flourishing village in ashes, and treated many unarmed persons with severity. Such conduct disgraced the British arms, and injured the cause which it was intended to serve. At all times war is a fearful scourge, and ought to be carried on with as much humanity as is consistent with the attainment of the main object in view. To intrust a military force to the orders of an infuriated zealot can seldom serve any good purpose.

The opposition increased as the troops advanced; and the towns of Norwalk and Greenfield, at which they successively landed, shared the same unhappy fate with Fairfield. An attack on New London, a noted place of resort for the privateers which preyed on the British trade, was the ultimate object of the expedition; but, as the resistance still increased, a formidable opposition was there anticipated, and it was therefore thought advisable to procure a reinforcement of men and a supply of provisions, before attempting that place. For this purpose the fleet returned to Huntingdon bay, in Long Island; and Sir George Collier repaired to Throg's Neck, to consult with the commander-in-chief of the army concerning their subsequent operations.

The ravages committed on the towns of the coast of Connecticut excited complaints and murmurings among the people, because they were left unprotected, and exposed to the ruthless depredations of the enemy. But General Washington's army was too feeble at once to defend the passes in the highlands and afford protection to the coast. In order, therefore, to quiet the murmuring of the people, and to withdraw the British troops from Connecticut, he was powerfully induced to undertake some enterprise on the Hudson; and the posts at King's ferry seemed the most eligible point for striking an effective blow.

General Washington procured good information concerning the state of those posts; and in person took a view of Stony point, the main object of attack. From all the information which he obtained, as well as from his own observation, he was convinced that there was little probability of success against that fort but by surprise. The attempt was hazardous; for Stony point is a commanding hill, projecting far into the Hudson, which washes three fourths of its base. The remaining fourth is in a great measure covered by a deep marsh, commencing near the river on the upper side, and continuing till it joins it below the fort. The marsh was passable only at one place; but at its junction with the river there is a sandy beach, which may be passed at ebb tide. The fort stood on the summit of the hill, and was well provided with artillery. Several breastworks and strong batteries were raised in front of the principal fortification, and there were two rows of abatis about half-way down the hill. The fort was garrisoned by about 600 men, under Lieutenant-Colonel Johnson; and several vessels of war were stationed in the river, so as to command the ground at the foot of the hill.

Fig. 131.—Washington at Stony Point.

At midday, on the 15th of July, the detachment appointed to surprise the fort marched from Sandy beach, fourteen miles distance from Stony point, under the command of General Wayne. The road was mountainous, rugged, and difficult; the heat was intense; and it was eight in the evening before the van of the party reached Spring Heels, a mile and a half from the fort. There the detachment halted and formed, while General Wayne and some of his officers proceeded to take a view of the works. At half-past eleven the party, in two columns, advanced toward the garrison. One hundred and fifty volunteers, under Colonel Fleury and Major Povey, formed the van of the right; 100 volunteers, led by Major Stewart, composed the van of the left. Both advanced with unloaded muskets and fixed bayonets, and each was preceded by a forlorn hope of twenty men, conducted by Lieutenants Gibbon and Knox, to remove the abattis and other obstructions, and to open a passage for the columns which followed close in their rear. Having taken care to secure every person on the route who could give information of their approach, the columns reached the marsh undiscovered. In crossing it, unexpected difficulties occurred; and it was twenty minutes past twelve when the attack commenced. A tremendous discharge of musketry and grapeshot immediately opened on the assailants; but both columns impetuously rushed forward with fixed bayonets, and without firing a shot soon got complete possession of the fort.

This was a brilliant exploit; and the assailants gained nobler and more permanent laurels by their humanity than their bravery; for although the place was taken by storm, and the American troops were greatly exasperated by the merciless ravages and wanton devastations committed on the coast of Connecticut yet not one individual of the garrison suffered after resistance ceased. Of the garrison twenty men were killed in the conflict, including one captain; and seventy-four wounded, among whom were six officers. The Americans had sixty-three men killed, including two officers; but their wounded did not exceed forty. Of the twenty men in Lieutenant Gibbon's forlorn hope, seventeen were either killed or wounded. The prisoners amounted to 543, and among them were one lieutenant-colonel, four captains, and twenty subaltern officers. The military stores in the fort were considerable.

An attack on Fort La Fayette also was a part of the plan; and two brigades, under General M'Dougall, were ordered to proceed toward it, and to be in readiness to attack it as soon as they should be informed of General Wayne's success against Stony point. But M'Dougall was not forward in time; and the garrison of Fort La Fayette, where Colonel Webster commanded, had time to prepare for resistance. Wayne turned the artillery of Stony point against the British ships, and compelled them to drop down the river beyond the reach of his guns. He also fired on Verplanck's point; but so great was the distance that his shot made little impression on the works. The critical moment for assaulting Fort La Fayette having been lost, the plan of operation against it was changed. M'Dougall's detachment was intrusted to General Howe, and he was provided with some battering cannon, to make a breach in the fortifications but, before he was ready to act against the place, he found it expedient to retreat.

Immediately after the conference with Sir George Collier, Sir Henry Clinton was informed of the surprise of Stony point, and of the danger of Fort La Fayette. He instantly abandoned his design against New London and the coast of Connecticut; recalled his transports and troops from the sound; moved his army to Dobb's ferry; despatched General Stirling up the river with a body of troops in transports to the assistance of Colonel Webster; and soon followed in person with a larger force, in the expectation that General Washington would be induced to leave his strong position, and hazard a battle for the possession of Stony point. But the failure of the design against Fort La Fayette rendered the possession of Stony point a matter of no great importance; because the works on Verplanck's point effectually prevented the communication by King's ferry between the states on the east and west of the Hudson; and the command of that ferry constituted the chief value of the forts on Stony point and Verplanck's Neck, as, when it was closed, the intercourse with the eastern states could be kept up only by a very circuitous route. Stony point, it was thought, could not be retained without a garrison of 1,500 men; a force General Washington could not spare from his little army, which was not more than 9,000 strong. Besides, as the British had the entire command of the river, they had fortified Stony point only on the land side; but, if the Americans had kept possession of the post, it would have been as necessary to fortify it toward the river as toward the land. Therefore General Washington deemed it expedient to evacuate the place, after having to a certain extent demolished the works.

On his arrival, Sir Henry Clinton again took possession of Stony point; ordered the fortifications to be repaired; stationed a strong garrison in the fort, under Brigadier-General Stirling; and, finding that General Washington could not be drawn from his strong position in the highlands, he again sailed down the river.

Scarcely had Sir George Collier, who had accompanied the commander-in-chief on this expedition, returned to New York, when he was informed that a fleet of armed vessels, with transports and troops, had sailed from Boston to attack a post which General M'Lean was establishing at Penobscot, in the eastern part of the province of Massachusetts Bay. He immediately got ready for sea that part of the naval force which was at New York, and on the 3d of August sailed to relieve the garrison of Penobscot.

In the month of June, General M'Lean, who commanded the royal troops in Nova Scotia, arrived in the bay of Penobscot with nearly 700 men, in order to establish a post, which might at once be a means of checking the incursions of the Americans into Nova Scotia, and of supplying the royal yards at Halifax with ship timber, which abounded in that part of the country. This establishment alarmed the government of Massachusetts Bay, which resolved to dislodge M'Lean, and, with great promptitude, equipped a fleet and raised troops for that purpose. The fleet, which consisted of fifteen vessels-of-war, carrying from thirty-two to twelve guns each, with transports, was commanded by Commodore Saltonstall; the army, amounting to between three and four thousand militia, was under the orders of General Lovell.

General M'Lean chose for his post a peninsula on the east side of Penobscot bay, which is about seven leagues wide and seventeen deep, terminating at the point where the river Penobscot flows into it. M'Lean's station was nine miles from the bottom of the bay. As that part of the country was then an unbroken forest, he cleared away the wood on the peninsula, and began to construct a fort, in which he was assisted and protected by the crews of three sloops-of-war which had escorted him thither. M'Lean heard of the expedition against him on the 21st of July, when he had made little progress in the erection of his fort. On the 25th the American fleet appeared in the bay; but, owing to the opposition of the British sloops-of-war, and to the bold and rugged nature of the shore, the troops did not effect a landing till the 28th. This interval M'Lean improved with such laborious diligence that his fortifications were in a state of considerable forwardness. Lovell erected a battery within 750 yards of the works: for nearly a fortnight a brisk cannonade was kept up, and preparations were made to assault the fort. But, on the 13th of August, Lovell was informed that Sir George Collier, with a superior naval force, had entered the bay; therefore in the night he silently embarked his troops and cannon, unperceived by the garrison, which was every moment in expectation of being assaulted.

On the approach of the British fleet, the Americans, after some show of preparation for resistance, betook themselves to flight. A general pursuit and unresisted destruction ensued. The Warren, a fine new frigate of thirty-two guns, and fourteen other vessels of inferior force, were either blown up or taken. The transports fled in confusion; and, after having landed the troops in a wild and uncultivated part of the country, were burnt. The men, destitute of provisions and other necessaries, had to explore their way for more than 100 miles through an uninhabited and pathless wilderness, and many of them perished before reaching the settled country. After this successful exploit Sir George Collier returned to New York, where he resigned the command of the fleet to Admiral Arbuthnot, who had arrived from England with some ships-of-war, and with provisions, stores, and reinforcements for the army.

On descending the river, after replacing the garrison of Stony point, Sir Henry Clinton encamped above Harlem, with his upper posts at Kingsbridge. General Washington remained in his strong position in the highlands, but frequently detached numerous parties on both sides of the river, in order to check the British foragers, and to restrain the intercourse with the loyalists. Major Lee, who commanded one of those parties, planned a bold and hazardous enterprise against the British post at Powles' Hook on the Jersey bank of the river, opposite the town of New York. That post was strongly fortified and of difficult access, and therefore the garrison thought themselves secure. But Major Lee determined to make an attempt on the place ; and chose the morning of the 20th of August for his enterprise, when part of the garrison was absent on a foraging excursion. Advancing silently at the head of 300 men, the sentinel at the gate mistook his party for that which had marched out the preceding day, and allowed them to pass unchallenged ; and, almost in an instant, they seized the block-house and two redoubts before the alarm was given. Major Sutherland, commandant of the post, with sixty Hessians, entered a redoubt, and began a brisk fire on the assailants. This gave an extensive notice of the attack ; and the firing of guns in New York, and by the shipping in the roads, proved that the alarm was widely spread. In order, therefore, not to hazard the loss of his party, Major Lee retreated, with the loss of two men killed and three wounded, carrying along with him about 150 prisoners. Notwithstanding the difficulties and dangers which he had to encounter, he effected his retreat. It was not his design to keep possession of the place ; but to carry off the garrison, reflect credit on the American arms, and encourage a spirit of enterprise in the army.

The western frontier of the United States was near the dwellings of a number of Indian tribes ; and these six nations, the Mohawks, Cayugas, Tuscaroras, Oneidas, Onondagas, and Senecas, distinguished by their confederacy, policy, and bravery, possessed the extensive and fertile country lying between the vicinity of Albany and Lake Erie. From their long intercourse with Europeans, those nations had acquired a relish for some of the comforts of civilized life, and entertained more enlarged views than most of the North American tribes of the advantages of private property. Their populous villages contained some comfortable houses, and their fertile fields and rich orchards yielded an abundant supply of maize and fruit.

To gain the friendship of these confederated nations, and of the other Indian tribes on the frontier of the United States, had, from the beginning of the war, been an object of attention both to the British government and to congress. But former habits, together with rum, presents, and promises from the agents at the British posts on the lakes, secured to the royal cause the support of the greater part of the Six Nations ; while a few, chiefly the Oneidas, espoused the interests of America.

Many of the loyalists who had been obliged to flee from the United States took refuge among the Indians, and at once increased their strength and whetted their ferocity. Even the savages were ashamed of their ruthless cruelty ; and Indian chiefs have been heard to declare that they never would permit white men to accompany them in their military expeditions, because of the horrible enormities which they perpetrated. Of the murderous cruelty of the savage whites we have a striking instance in the infamous conduct of Butler at Wyoming, during the preceding campaign. In that lamentable catastrophe the Six

Fig. 132.—A War Party of Indians.

Nations had taken an active part, and they were meditating fresh hostilities Their bloody incursions excited a strong sensation throughout the United States, and produced the resolution to lead an overwhelming force into their territory and to destroy their settlements.

The largest division of the army employed on that service assembled at Wyoming on a chief branch of the Susquehannah. Another division which had wintered on the Mohawk, marched under the orders of General Clinton, and joined the main body at the confluence of the two great sources of the Susquehannah. On the 22d of August the united force, amounting to nearly 5,000 men, under the command of General Sullivan, proceeded up the Cayuga, or western branch of the last-named river, which led directly into the Indian country. The preparations for this expedition did not escape the notice of those against whom it was directed, and the Indians seem fully to have penetrated Sullivan's plan of operation. Formidable as his force was, they determined to meet him, and try the fortune of a battle. They were about 1,000 strong, commanded by the two Butlers, Guy Johnson, M'Donald, and Brandt. They chose their ground with judgment, and fortified their camp at some distance above Chemung, and a mile in front of Newtown.

There Sullivan attacked them; and, after a short but spirited resistance, they retreated with precipitation. The Americans had thirty men killed or wounded; the Indians left only eleven dead bodies on the field; but they were so discouraged by this defeat, that they abandoned their villages and fields to the unresisted ravages of the victor, who laid waste their towns and orchards, so that they might have no inducement again to settle so near the states. The members of civilized society too faithfully imitated the savage enemy whom they assailed, in all the enormities of barbarous warfare.

This expedition gave little satisfaction to any of the parties concerned in planning or executing it, and Sullivan resigned his commission, and retired from the public service. In the course of the summer, the Indians on the southern frontier were also severely chastised; but although unable to resist the force sent against them, they made some sanguinary incursions into the provinces.

We have already seen that Admiral Count d'Estaing, after repairing his ships at Boston, sailed to the West Indies; whither he was followed by Admiral Byron with the British fleet, having on board a detachment of the army at New York, under General Grant. The French took the islands of Dominica, St. Vincent, and Grenada, and spread a general alarm throughout the West Indies. The British made themselves masters of St. Lucie; but this did not compensate for the loss of the islands already named. The season of the hurricanes approached; and D'Estaing, after an engagement with the British fleet, sailed toward the coast of North America.

Although General Prevost had been obliged to retire from Charleston, and to abandon the upper parts of Georgia; yet so long as he kept possession of the town of Savannah, and maintained a post at Beaufort, South Carolina was much exposed to hostile incursions. Therefore Governor Rutledge and General Lincoln earnestly pressed D'Estaing to repair to the Savannah, hoping by his aid to drive the British from Georgia. Plombard, the French consul at Charleston, joined in these solicitations. In compliance with their importunity, D'Estaing sailed from Cape François, in St. Domingo; and with twenty-two sail of the line, and a number of smaller vessels, having 6,000 soldiers on board, appeared off the Savannah, where he captured the Experiment, a fifty-gun ship, and some other British vessels.

General Lincoln, with about 1,000 men, marched to Zubly's ferry on the Savannah, but found more difficulty than he had anticipated in crossing the river and its marshes. On the evening of the 13th of September, however, he reach-

FIG. 133.—Portrait of Brandt.

ed the southern bank, and encamped on the heights of Ebenezer, twenty-three miles from the town of Savannah. There he was joined by Colonel M'Intosh, with his detachment, from Augusta. Pulaski's legion also arrived in camp. On the same day that Lincoln passed Zubly's ferry, D'Estaing landed 3,000 men at Beaulieu; and on the 16th of September the combined armies united their strength before the town of Savannah. That place was the headquarters of General Prevost, who commanded the British troops in the southern provinces. Apprehending no immediate danger, he had weakened his garrison by establishing some distant outposts in Georgia, and by leaving Colonel Maitland with a strong detachment at Beaufort, in the island of Port Royal in South Carolina; but on the appearance of the French fleet, he immediately called in all his outposts; and before the French landed, or the Americans crossed the river, all the British detachments in Georgia had assembled at the town of Savannah, and amounted to nearly 2,000 men.

Even before the arrival of Lincoln, D'Estaing had summoned the place to surrender. But although General Prevost had exerted himself with great activity in strengthening the defences of the place from the moment that he heard of the appearance of the French fleet on the coast, yet his works were incomplete, and he was desirous of gaining time. He requested a suspension of hostilities for twenty-four hours, which was granted him. In that critical interval, Colonel Maitland, by extraordinary efforts, arrived with the garrison of Beaufort, and entered the town. Encouraged by this accession of strength, General Prevost now informed Count d'Estaing that he was resolved to defend the place to the last extremity. The combined armies determined to besiege the town, and made the necessary preparations for that purpose. Several days were spent in bringing up heavy artillery and stores from the fleet; and on the 23d of September, the besieging army broke ground before the town. By the 1st of October, they had advanced within 300 yards of the British works. Several batteries, mounting thirty-three pieces of heavy cannon and nine mortars, had for several days played incessantly on the garrison; and a floating battery of sixteen guns had also opened upon it from the river. But this cannonade made little impression on the works.

The situation of D'Estaing became extremely unpleasant. More time had already been spent in the siege than he had allotted for the expulsion of the British troops from that province. The French West India islands were exposed to danger in his absence; the tempestuous season of the year was setting in; a superior British fleet might come against him; and his officers strongly remonstrated against remaining longer in the Savannah. By continuing their regular approaches for a few days more, the besiegers would probably have made themselves masters of the place; but these few days D'Estaing could not spare. No alternative remained but to raise the siege, or storm the place. The last of these the French commander resolved to attempt. For that purpose, on the morning of the 9th of October, a heavy cannonade and bombardment opened on the town. Three thousand French, and 1,500 Americans, led by D'Estaing and Lincoln, advanced in three columns to the assault. A well-directed and destructive fire from the batteries opened upon them; but they resolutely advanced, broke through the abatis, crossed the ditch, and mounted the parapet. The French and Americans, with emulous valor, each planted a standard on a redoubt; but fell in great numbers in endeavoring to force their way into the works. While the assailants were vigorously opposed in front, the batteries galled their flanks. Count Pulaski, at the head of 200 horsemen, galloped between the batteries toward the town, with the intention of charging the garrison in the rear; but he fell mortally wounded, and his squadron was broken. The vigor of the assailants began to abate; and, after a desperate conflict of fifty minutes, they were driven from the works, and sounded a retreat.

In this unsuccessful attack the French lost 700 men in killed and wounded, among the latter was Count d'Estaing himself; and the Americans 240. As the garrison, consisting of more than 2,000 men, fought for the most part under cover, their loss was comparatively small.

Both the French and Americans displayed much courage and steadiness in the attack; and, although unsuccessful, yet, instead of mutual accusations and reproaches, their respect for each other was increased.

After this repulse no hope of taking the town remained; and Count d'Estaing having removed his heavy artillery, both armies left their ground on the evening of the 18th of October. D'Estaing marched only two miles that evening, and remained in the same encampment next day, in order to cover General Lincoln's retreat, and secure him from a pursuit by the garrison. The Americans recrossed the Savannah at Zubly's ferry, and took a position in South Carolina. The militia returned home. The French, with all their artillery, ammunition, and baggage, embarked without delay; but scarcely were they on board when a violent storm arose, which so completely dispersed the fleet, that, of seven ships which the admiral ordered to Hampton Road in Chesapeake bay, one only was able to reach that place.

From the arrival of the French to assist in the siege of Savannah, the Americans had anticipated the most brilliant results; and the discomfiture of the combined forces at that place spread a deep gloom over the southern provinces, where the cause of independence seemed more desperate than at any former period of the war. Their paper money became more depreciated; the hopes of the loyalists revived; and many exiles returned to take possession of their estates; but they were soon obliged again to abandon their property, and to seek refuge among strangers.

On being informed by Lincoln of his circumstances, congress desired General Washington to order the North Carolina troops, and any other detachments he could spare from the northern army, to the aid of the southern provinces. At the same time they assured the inhabitants of South Carolina and Georgia of their watchful attention; and recommended to those states the filling up of their continental regiments, and a due regard to their militia while on actual service.

During the siege of Savannah, an ingenious enterprise of partisan warfare was executed by Colonel White of the Georgia line. Before the arrival of the French fleet in the Savannah, a British captain, with 111 men, had taken post near the river Ogeeche, twenty-five miles from Savannah. At the same place were five British vessels, four of which were armed, the largest with fourteen guns, the least with four; and the vessels were manned with forty sailors. Late at night, on the 30th of September, White, who had only six volunteers, including his own servant, kindled a number of fires in different places, so as to exhibit the appearance of a considerable encampment, practised several other corresponding artifices, and then summoned the captain instantly to surrender. That officer, believing that he was about to be attacked by a superior force, and that nothing but immediate submission could save him and his men from destruction, made no defence. The stratagem was carried on with so much address, that the prisoners, amounting to 141, were secured, and conducted to the American post at Sunbury, twenty-five miles distant.

The failure of the attack on Savannah, with the departure of the French fleet from the coast of America, presented a gloomy prospect, and was the forerunner of many calamities to the southern states. By their courage and vigor the northern provinces had repelled the attacks of the enemy, and discouraged future attempts against them. But, although the brave defence of Sullivan's isl-

Fig. 134.—Admiral D'Estaing.

and, in 1776, had long concealed the fact, it was now discovered that the southern colonists possessed neither the strength nor vigor of their brethren in the north. The rapid conquest of Georgia, the easy march of Prevost to the very gates of Charleston, and the timid behavior of many of the colonists, who were more inclined to save themselves by submission than to assert the independence of their country by force of arms, all pointed out the southern states as the most vulnerable part of the Union, and invited an attack in that quarter. In the north the campaigns of 1778 and 1779 had produced no important results; and, therefore, the late transactions in Georgia and South Carolina more readily drew the attention of the British commander-in-chief to those states.

Savannah, the chief town of Georgia, was in the hands of the British troops, and had been successfully defended against a combined attack of the French and Americans; and, therefore, Sir Henry Clinton resolved to gain possession of Charleston also, the capital of South Carolina, which would give him the command of all the southern parts of the Union. Having made the necessary preparations, he sailed from New York on the 26th of December, under convoy of Admiral Arbuthnot, but did not arrive at Savannah till the end of January. The voyage was tempestuous: some of the transports and victuallers were lost, others shattered, and a few taken by the American cruisers. Most of the cavalry and draught horses perished. One of the transports, which had been separated from the fleet, was brought into Charleston on the 23d of January; and the prisoners gave the first certain notice of the destination of the expedition.

As soon as it was known that an armament was fitting out at New York, many suspected that the southern states were to be assailed; and such was the unhappy posture of American affairs at that time, that no sanguine expectations of a successful resistance could be reasonably entertained. The magazines of the Union were everywhere almost empty; and congress had neither money nor credit to replenish them. The army at Morristown, under the immediate orders of General Washington, was threatened with destruction by want of provisions; and, consequently, could neither act with vigor in the north, nor send reinforcements to the south.

General Lincoln, though aware of his danger, was not in a condition to meet it. On raising the siege of Savannah, he had sent the troops of Virginia to Augusta; those of South Carolina were stationed partly at Sheldon, opposite Port Royal, between thirty and forty miles north from Savannah, and partly in Fort Moultrie, which had been allowed to fall into decay; those of North Carolina were with General Lincoln at Charleston. All those detachments formed but a feeble force, and to increase it was not easy; for the colonial paper money was in a state of great depreciation—the militia, worn out by a harassing service, were reluctant again to repair to the standards of their country. The patriotism of many of the colonists had evaporated; they contemplated nothing but the hardships and dangers of the contest, and recoiled from the protracted struggle.

In these discouraging circumstances, congress recommended it to the people of South Carolina to arm their slaves; a measure from which they were generally averse; and, although they had been willing to comply with the recommendation, arms could not have been procured. Congress ordered the continental troops of North Carolina and Virginia to march to Charleston; and four American frigates, two French ships-of-war, the one mounting twenty-six and the other eighteen guns, with the marine force of South Carolina under Commodore Whipple, were directed to co-operate in the defence of the town. No more aid could be expected; yet, even in these unpromising circumstances, a full house of assembly resolved to defend Charleston to the last extremity.

Although Sir Henry Clinton had embarked at New York on the 26th of December, 1779, yet, as his voyage had been stormy and tedious, and as some

Fig. 135.—Savannah, 1778.

time had been necessarily spent at Savannah, it was the 11th of February, 1780, before he landed on St. John's island, thirty miles south from Charleston. Had he even then marched rapidly upon the town, he would probably have entered it without much opposition; but, mindful of his repulse in 1776, his progress was marked by a wary circumspection. He proceeded by the islands of St. John and St. James, while part of his fleet advanced to blockade the harbor. He sent for a reinforcement from New York, ordered General Prevost to join him with 1,100 men from Savannah, and neglected nothing that could ensure success.

Meanwhile Governor Rutledge, with such of his council as he could conveniently consult, was invested with a dictatorial authority, and empowered to do everything necessary for the public good, except taking away the life of a citizen without legal trial. The assembly, after delegating to the governor this power till ten days after its next session, dissolved itself.

Governor Rutledge and General Lincoln were indefatigable in improving the time which the slow progress of the royal army afforded them. Six hundred slaves were employed in constructing or repairing the fortifications of the town; vigorous though not very successful measures were taken to bring the militia into the field; and all the small detachments of regular troops were assembled in the capital. The works which had been begun on Charleston Neck, when General Prevost threatened the place, were resumed. A chain of redoubts, lines, and batteries, was formed between the Cooper and Ashley. In front of each flank the works were covered by swamps extending from the rivers; these opposite swamps were connected by a canal; between the canal and the works were two strong rows of abatis, and a ditch double picketed, with deep holes at short distances, to break the columns in case of an assault. Toward the water, works were thrown up at every place where a landing was practicable. The vessels intended to defend the bar of the harbor having been found insufficient for that purpose, their guns were taken out and planted on the ramparts, and the seamen were stationed at the batteries. One of the ships, which was not dismantled, was placed in the river Cooper, to assist the batteries; and several vessels were sunk at the mouth of the channel, to prevent the entrance of the royal navy. General Lincoln hoped that, if the town could be for a while defended, such reinforcements would arrive from the north as, together with the militia of the state, would compel Sir Henry Clinton to raise the siege. As the regular troops in the town did not exceed 1,400, a council of war found that the garrison was too weak to spare detachments to obstruct the progress of the royal army. Only a small party of cavalry and some light troops were ordered to hover on its left flank and observe its motions.

While those preparations for defence were going on in Charleston, the British army was cautiously but steadily advancing toward the town. As he proceeded, Sir Henry Clinton erected forts and formed magazines at proper stations, and was careful to secure his communications with those forts and with the sea. All the horses of the British army had perished in the tedious and stormy voyage from New York to Savannah; but, on landing in South Carolina, Sir Henry Clinton procured others to mount his dragoons, whom he formed into a light corps, under the command of Lieutenant-Colonel Tarleton. That officer was extremely active in covering the left wing of the army, and in dispersing the militia. In one of his excursions he fell in with Lieutenant-Colonel Washington, who commanded the remnant of Baylor's regiment, and who beat him back with loss.

On the 20th of March the British fleet under Admiral Arbuthnot, consisting of one ship of fifty guns, two of forty-four each, four of thirty-two each, and an armed vessel, passed the bar in front of Rebellion road, and anchored in Five-Fathom hole. The American naval force, under Commodore Whipple, retreated

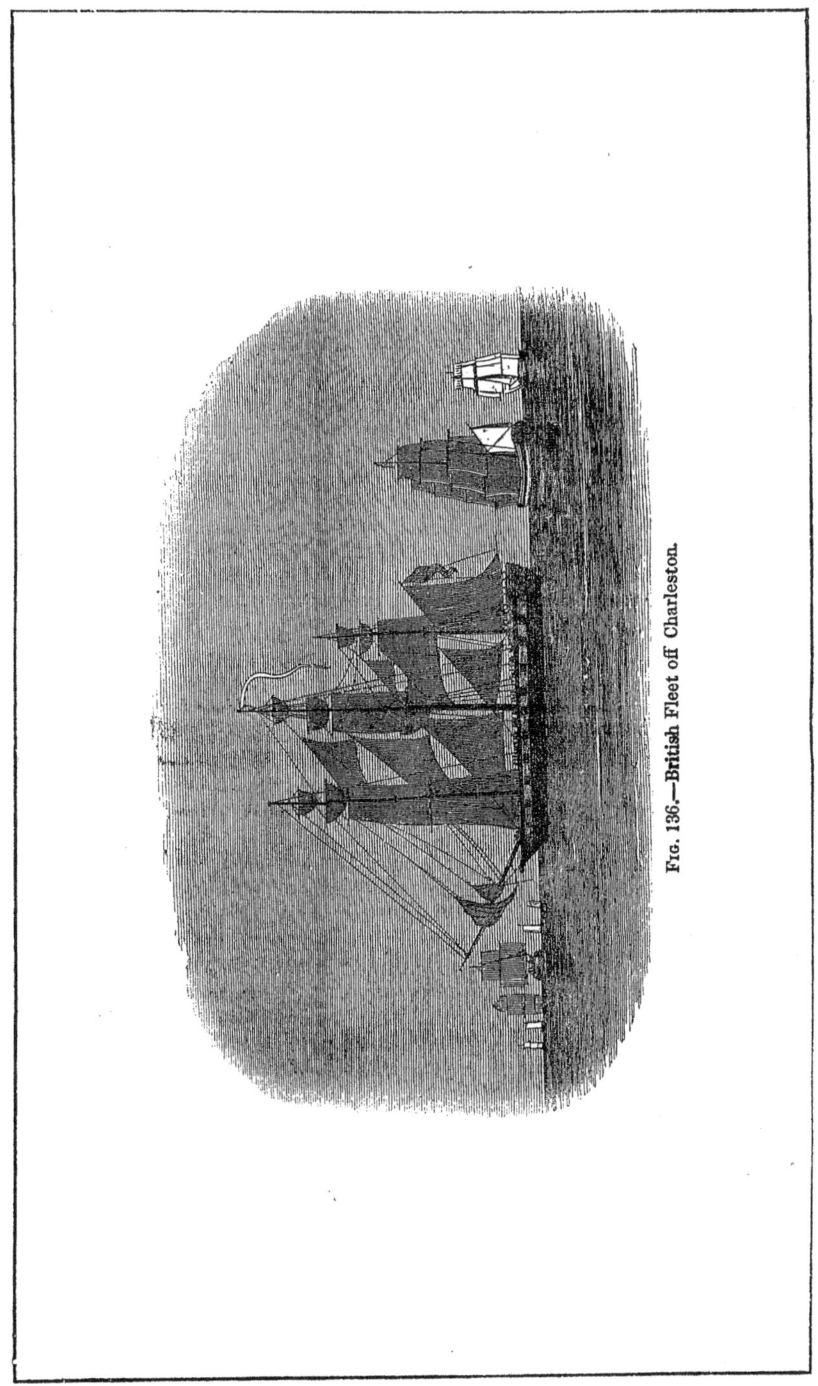

Fig. 136.—British Fleet off Charleston.

first to Sullivan's island, and afterward to Charleston, where, as already mentioned, the ships were dismantled and the crews employed on the works. On the 9th of April Admiral Arbuthnot, taking advantage of a strong southerly wind and a flowing tide, passed Fort Moultrie, and anchored just without reach of the guns of Charleston. The fort kept up a heavy fire on the fleet while passing, which did some damage to the ships, and killed or wounded twenty-seven men.

On the 29th of March, the British army reached Ashley river, and crossed it ten miles above the town without opposition; the garrison being too weak to dispute the passage. Having brought over his artillery, baggage, and stores, Sir Henry Clinton marched down Charleston Neck; and, on the night of the 1st of April, broke ground at the distance of 8,000 yards from the American works.

The fortifications of Charleston were constructed under the direction of Mr. Laumoy, a French engineer of reputation in the American service; and, although not calculated to resist regular siege, were by no means contemptible: and the British general made his approaches in due form. Meanwhile the garrison received a reinforcement of 700 continentals under General Woodford; and, after this accession of strength, amounted to somewhat more than 2,000 regular troops, besides 1,000 militia of North Carolina, and the citizens of Charleston. Governor Rutledge made every effort to raise the militia of the province, but with little success; for not more than 200 of them were in the capital.

On the 9th of April, the British commander finished his first parallel, forming an oblique line between the two rivers, from 600 to 1,100 yards from the American works, and mounted his guns in battery. He then, jointly with the admiral, summoned General Lincoln to surrender the town. Lincoln's answer was modest and firm: "Sixty days," said he, "have passed since it has been known that your intentions against this town were hostile, in which time was afforded to abandon it; but duty and inclination point to the propriety of supporting it to the last extremity."

On receiving this answer, Sir Henry Clinton immediately opened his batteries; and his fire was soon felt to be superior to that of the besieged. Hitherto the communication with the country north of the Cooper was open, and a post was established to prevent the investiture of the town on that side. After the summons, Governor Rutledge, with half of his council left the town, for the purpose of exercising the functions of the executive government in the state, and in the hope of being able to bring a large body of the militia to act on the rear or left flank of the besieging army: but the militia were as little inclined to imbody themselves as to enter the town.

For the purpose of maintaining the communication with the country north of the Cooper, of checking the British foragers, and of protecting supplies on their way to the town, the American cavalry, under General Huger, had passed the river and taken post at Monk's corner, thirty miles above Charleston. Posts of militia were established between the Cooper and Santee, and at a ferry on the last-named river, where boats were ordered to be collected in order to facilitate the passage of the garrison, if it should be necessary to evacuate the town. But the British general defeated all those precautions; for as the possession of the harbor rendered the occupation of the forts to the southward unnecessary, Sir Henry Clinton resolved to call in the troops which had been employed in that quarter, to close the communication of the garrison with the country to the northward, and to complete the investiture of the town. For those purposes, as the fleet was unable to enter the river Cooper, he deemed it necessary to dislodge the American posts, and employed Lieutenant-Colonel Tarleton to beat up the quarters of the cavalry at Monk's corner. Conducted during the night, by a negro slave, through unfrequented paths, Tarleton proceeded toward the American post; and, although the commander of the party had taken the precaution of pla-

Fig. 137.—Charleston, S. C., in 1835.

cing sentinels a mile in front of his station, and of keeping his horses saddled and bridled, yet Tarleton advanced so rapidly that, notwithstanding the alarm was given by the outposts, he began the attack before the Americans could put themselves in a posture of defence, killed or took about thirty of them, and dispersed the rest. The arrival of three thousand men from New York greatly increased the strength of the besiegers.

The second parallel was completed; and it daily became more apparent that the garrison must ultimately submit. An evacuation of the town was proposed, and General Lincoln seems to have been favorable to the measure; but the garrison could scarcely have escaped, and the principal inhabitants entreated the general not to abandon them to the fury of the enemy.

The British troops on the north of the Cooper were increased, and Cornwallis was appointed to command in that quarter. On the 20th of April, General Lincoln again called a council of war to deliberate on the measures to be adopted. The council recommended a capitulation; terms were offered, but rejected; and hostilities recommenced. After the besiegers had begun their third parallel, Colonel Henderson made a vigorous sally on their right, which was attended with some success; but, owing to the weakness of the garrison, this was the only attempt of the kind during the siege.

After the fleet passed it, Fort Moultrie became of much less importance than before, and part of the garrison was removed to Charleston. The admiral, perceiving the unfinished state of the works on the west side, prepared to storm it. On the 7th of May, everything being ready for the assault, he summoned the garrison, consisting of 200 men, who, being convinced of their inability to defend the place, surrendered themselves prisoners-of-war, without firing a gun. On the same day, the cavalry which had escaped from Monk's corner, and which had reassembled under the command of Colonel White, were again surprised and defeated by Colonel Tarleton. After Cornwallis had passed the Cooper, and made himself master of the peninsula between that river and the Santee, he occasionally sent out small foraging parties. Apprized of that circumstance, Colonel White repassed the Santee, fell in with and took one of those parties, and despatched an express to Colonel Buford, who commanded a regiment of new levies from Virginia, requesting him to cover his retreat across the Santee at Lanneau's ferry, where he had ordered some boats to be collected to carry his party over the river. Colonel White reached the ferry before Buford's arrival, and thinking himself in no immediate danger, halted to refresh his party. Cornwallis, having received notice of his incursion, despatched Tarleton in pursuit, who, overtaking him a few minutes after he had halted, instantly charged him, killed or took about thirty of the party, and dispersed the rest.

Charleston was now completely invested; all hopes of assistance had been cruelly disappointed; and the garrison and inhabitants were left to their own resources. The troops were exhausted by incessant duty, and insufficient to man the lines. Many of the guns were dismounted, the shot nearly expended, and the bread and meat almost entirely consumed. The works of the besiegers were pushed very near the defences of the town, and the issue of an assault was extremely hazardous to the garrison and inhabitants. In these critical circumstances General Lincoln summoned a council of war, which recommended a capitulation. Terms were accordingly proposed, offering to surrender the town and garrison, on condition that the militia and armed citizens should not be prisoners-of-war, but should be allowed to return home without molestation. These terms were refused; hostilities recommenced, and preparations for an assault were in progress. The citizens, who had formerly remonstrated against the departure of the garrison, now became clamorous for a surrender. In this hopeless state, General Lincoln offered to give up the place, on the terms which Sir Henry Clinton had formerly proposed. The offer was accepted; and the capitulation was signed on the 12th of May.

The town and fortifications, the shipping, artillery, and all public stores, were to be given up as they then were; the garrison, consisting of the continental troops, militia, sailors, and citizens who had borne arms during the siege, were to be prisoners-of-war; the garrison were to march out of the town, and lay down their arms in front of the works, but their drums were not to beat a British march, and their colors were not to be uncased; the continental troops and sailors were to be conducted to some place afterward to be agreed on, where they were to be well supplied with wholesome provisions till exchanged; the militia were to be allowed to go home on parole; the officers were to retain their arms, baggage, and servants, and they might sell their horses, but were not permitted to take them out of Charleston; neither the persons nor property of the militia or citizens were to be molested, so long as they kept their parole.

On these terms the garrison of Charleston marched out and laid down their arms, and General Leslie was appointed by the British commander-in-chief to take possession of the town. The siege was more obstinate than bloody. The besiegers had 76 men killed, and 189 wounded; the besieged had 92 killed, and 148 wounded; about twenty of the inhabitants were killed in their houses by random shots. The number of prisoners reported by the British commander-in-chief amounted to upward of 5,000, exclusive of sailors; but in that return all the freemen of the town capable of bearing arms, as well as the continental soldiers and militia, were included. The number of continental troops in the town amounted only to 1,777, about 500 of whom were in the hospital. The effective strength of the garrison was between 2,000 and 3,000 men. The besieging army consisted of about 9,000 of the best of the British troops.

After the British got possession of the town, the arms taken from the Americans, amounting to 5,000 stand, were lodged in a laboratory, near a large quantity of cartridges and loose powder. By some means the powder exploded and blew up the house; and the burning fragments, which were scattered in all directions, set fire to the workhouse, jail, and old barracks, and consumed them. The British guard stationed at that place, consisting of fifty men, was destroyed, and about as many other persons lost their lives on the disastrous occasion.

The fall of Charleston spread a deep gloom over the aspect of American affairs. The southern army was lost; and, although small, it could not soon be replaced. In the southern parts of the Union there had always been a considerable number of persons friendly to the claims of Britain. The success of her arms roused all their lurking partialities, encouraged the timid, drew to the British cause all those who are ever ready to take part with the strongest, and discouraged and intimidated the friends of congress.

Sir Henry Clinton was resolved to keep up and deepen the impression on the public mind, by the rapidity of his movements and the appearance of his troops in different parts of the country. For that purpose he sent a strong detachment, under Cornwallis, over the Santee, toward the frontier of North Carolina. He despatched a second, of inferior force, into the centre of the province; and sent a third up the Savannah to Augusta. These detachments were instructed to disperse any small parties that still remained in arms, and to show the people that the British troops were complete masters of South Carolina and Georgia.

Soon after passing the Santee, Cornwallis was informed that Colonel Buford was lying, with 400 men, in perfect security, near the border of North Carolina. He immediately despatched Colonel Tarleton, with his legion, to surprise that party. After performing a march of 104 miles in fifty-four hours, Tarleton, at the head of 700 men, overtook Buford on his march, at the Waxhaws, and ordered him to surrender, offering him the same terms which had been granted to the garrison of Charleston. On Buford's refusal, Tarleton instantly charged the party, who were dispirited, and unprepared for such an onset. Most of them threw down their arms, and made no resistance; but a few continued firing; and an indiscriminate slaughter ensued of those who had submitted as well as of those who resisted. Many begged for quarter, but no quarter was given. *Tarleton's quarter* became proverbial throughout the Union, and rendered some subsequent conflicts more fierce and bloody than they would otherwise have been. Buford and a few horsemen forced their way through the enemy and escaped; some of the infantry, also, who were somewhat in advance, saved themselves by flight; but the regiment was almost annihilated. Tarleton stated that 113 were killed on the spot; 150 left on parole, so badly wounded that they could not be removed; and 53 brought away as prisoners. The brutal slaughter on this occasion, and the violation of every principle of humanity and the rights of the vanquished, excited much indignation in America.

After the defeat of Buford, there were no parties in South Carolina or Georgia capable of resisting the royal detachments. The armed force of congress in those provinces seemed annihilated; and the spirit of opposition among the inhabitants was greatly subdued.

In order to secure the entire submission of that part of the country, military detachments were stationed at the most commanding points; and measures were pursued for settling the civil administration, and for consolidating the conquest of the provinces. So fully was Sir Henry Clinton convinced of the subjugation of the country, and of the sincere submission of the inhabitants, or of their inability to resist, that, on the 3d of June, he issued a proclamation, in which, after stating that all persons should take an active part in settling and securing his majesty's government, and in delivering the country from that anarchy which for some time had prevailed, he discharged from their parole the militia who were prisoners, except those only who had been taken in Charleston and Fort Moultrie, and restored them to all the rights and duties of inhabitants; he also declared that such as should neglect to return to their allegiance should be treated as enemies and rebels.

It might easily have been foreseen that the proclamation was to awaken the resentment and alienate the affections of those to whom it was addressed. Many of the colonists had submitted in the hope of being allowed, under the shelter of the British government, to attend to their own affairs in a state of peaceful tranquillity; but the proclamation dissipated this delusion, and opened their eyes to their real situation. Neutrality and peace were what they desired; but neutrality and peace were denied them. If they did not range themselves under the standards of congress, they must appear as militia in the royal service. The colonists sighed for peace; but, on finding that they must fight on one side or the other, they preferred the banners of their country, and thought they had as good a right to violate the allegiance and parole which Sir Henry Clinton had imposed on them, as he had to change their state from that of prisoners to that of British subjects without their consent. They imagined that the proclamation released them from all antecedent obligations. Not a few without any pretence of reasoning on the subject, deliberately resolved to make professions of submission and allegiance to the British government so long as they found it convenient, but with the resolution of joining the standards of their country on the first opportunity. Such duplicity is always to be reprobated; but the unsparing rapacity with which the inhabitants were plundered by the foriegn soldiery and hired Hessians made many of them imagine that no means of deception and vengeance were unjustifiable.

Hitherto the French fleets and troops had not afforded much direct assistance to the Americans, but they had impeded and embarrassed the operations of the

FIG. 138.—A French Fusileer.

British commander-in-chief. He had intended to sail against Charleston so early as the month of September, 1779; but the expected appearance of Count d'Estaing on the southern coast had detained him at New York till the latter part of December. It was his intention, after the reduction of Charleston, vigorously to employ the whole of his force in the subjugation of the adjacent provinces; but information, received about the time of the surrender of the town, that Monsieur de Ternay, with a fleet and troops from France, was expected on the American coast, deranged his plan, and induced him to return to New York with the greater part of his army; leaving Earl Cornwallis at the head of 4,000 men to prosecute the southern conquests. Sir Henry Clinton sailed from Charleston on the 5th of June.

After the reduction of Charleston, and the entire defeat of all the American detachments in those parts, an unusual calm ensued for six weeks. Zealous in the cause of his sovereign, and imagining that South Carolina and Georgia were reannexed to the British empire in sentiment as well as in appearance, Cornwallis meditated an attack on North Carolina. Impatient, however, as that active officer was of repose, he could not carry his purpose into immediate execution. The great heat, the want of magazines, and the impossibility of subsisting his army in the field before harvest, compelled him to pause. But the interval was not lost. He distributed his troops in such a manner in South Carolina and the upper parts of Georgia, as seemed most favorable to the enlistment of young men who could be prevailed on to join the royal standard; he ordered companies of royal militia to be formed; and he maintained a correspondence with such of the inhabitants of North Carolina as were friendly to the British cause. He informed them of the necessity he was under of postponing the expedition into their country, and advised them to attend to their harvest and to remain quiet till the royal army advanced to support them. Eager, however to manifest their zeal, and entertaining sanguine hopes of success, they disregarded his salutary advice, and broke out into premature insurrections, which were vigorously resisted and generally suppressed. But one party of them, amounting to 800 men under a Colonel Bryan, marched down the Yadkin to a British post at the Cheraws, and afterward reached Camden.

Having made the necessary dispositions, Cornwallis intrusted the command on the frontier to Lord Rawdon, and returned to Charleston, in order to organize the civil government of the province, and to establish such regulations as circumstances required. But that active officer showed himself more a soldier than a politician. Military government is necessarily a system of despotism and coercion, which is offensive to persons who have been accustomed to exercise their own judgment in the regulation of their conduct. Instead, however, of endeavoring to regain, by kindness and conciliation, the good will of a people whose affections were alienated from the cause in which he was engaged, Cornwallis attempted to drive them into allegiance by harshness and severity. Indeed, many of the British officers viewed the Americans merely in the light of rebels and traitors, whose lives it was indulgence to spare; treated them not only with injustice, but with insolence and insult more intolerable than injustice itself; and exercised a rigor which greatly increased the miseries, without promoting the legitimate purposes, of war.

By the capitulation of Charleston the citizens were prisoners on parole; but successive proclamations were published, each abridging the privileges of prisoners more than that which had gone before. A board of police was established for the administration of justice, and before that board British subjects were allowed to sue for debts, but prisoners were denied that privilege; they were liable to prosecution for debts, but had no security for what was owing them, except the honor of their debtors; and that, in many instances, was found a feeble guarantee. If they complained, they were threatened with close confinement: numbers were imprisoned in the town, and others consigned to dungeons at a distance from their families. In short, every method except that of kindness and conciliation, was resorted to in order to compel the people to become British subjects. A few who had always been well affected to the royal cause, cheerfully returned to their allegiance; and many followed the same course from convenience. To abandon their families and estates, and encounter all the privations of fugitives, required a degree of patriotism and fortitude which few possessed.

In that melancholy posture of American affairs, many of the ladies of Charleston displayed a remarkable degree of zeal and intrepidity in the cause of their country. They gloried in the appellation of rebel ladies, and declined invitations to public entertainments given by the British officers; but crowded to prison ships and other places of confinement to solace their suffering countrymen. While they kept back from the concerts and assemblies of the victors, they were forward in showing sympathy and kindness toward American officers wherever they met them. They exhorted their brothers, husbands, and sons, to an unshrinking endurance in behalf of their country, and cheerfully became the inmates of their prison and the companions of their exile; voluntarily renouncing affluence and ease, and encountering labor, penury, and privation.

For some time the rigorous measures of the British officers in South Carolina seemed successful; and a deathlike stillness prevailed in the province. The clangor of arms ceased, and no enemy to British authority appeared. The people of the lower part of South Carolina were generally attached to the revolution; but many of their most active leaders were prisoners. The fall of Charleston, and the subsequent events, had sunk many into despondency, and all were overawed. This gloomy stillness continued about six weeks, when the symptoms of a gathering storm began to show themselves. The oppression and insults to which the people were exposed highly exasperated them: they repented

FIG. 139.—Relieving the Prisoners.

the apathy with which they had seen the siege of Charleston carried on; and felt that the fall of their capital, instead of introducing safety and rural tranquillity, as they had fondly anticipated, was only the forerunner of insolent exactions and oppressive services. Peaceful and undisturbed neutrality was what they desired and what they had expected; but when they found themselves compelled to fight, they chose to join the provincial banners, and the most daring only waited an opportunity to show their hostility to their new masters.

Such an opportunity soon presented itself. In the end of March, General Washington despatched the troops of Maryland and Delaware, with a regiment of artillery, under the Baron de Kalb, a veteran German officer, who had early engaged in the American service, to reinforce the southern army. That detachment met with many obstructions in its progress southward. Such was the deranged state of the American finances, that it could not be put in motion when the order was given. After setting out, it marched through Jersey and Pennsylvania, embarked at the head of Elk river, was conveyed by water to Petersburgh in Virginia, and proceeded thence toward the place of its destination. But as no magazines had been provided, and as provisions could with difficulty be obtained, the march of the detachment through North Carolina was greatly retarded. Instead of advancing rapidly, the troops were obliged to spread themselves over the country in small parties, in order to collect corn and to get it ground for their daily subsistence. In this way they proceeded slowly through the upper and more fertile parts of North Carolina to Hillsborough, and were preparing to march by Cross creek to Salisbury, where they expected to be joined by the militia of North Carolina.

The approach of this detachment, together with information that great exertions were making to raise troops in Virginia, encouraged the irritation which the rigorous measures of the British officers had occasioned in South Carolina; and numbers of the inhabitants of that province, who had fled from their estates and taken refuge in North Carolina and Virginia, informed of the growing discontents in their native province, and relying on the support of regular troops, assembled on the frontier of North Carolina. About 200 of those refugees chose Colonel Sumpter, an old continental officer, as their leader. On the advance of the British into the upper parts of South Carolina, this gentleman had fled into North Carolina, but had left his family behind. Soon after his departure a British party arrived, turned his wife and family out the door, and burnt his house and everything in it. This harsh and unfeeling treatment excited his bitterest resentment, which operated with the more virulence by being concealed under the fair veil of patriotism. At the head of his little band, without money or magazines, and but ill-provided with arms and ammunition, Sumpter made an irruption into South Carolina. Iron implements of husbandry were forged by common blacksmiths into rude weapons of war; and pewter dishes, procured from private families and melted down, furnished part of their supply of balls. This little band skirmished with the royal militia, and with small parties of regular troops; sometimes successfully, and always with the active courage of men fighting for the recovery of their property. Sometimes they engaged when they had not more than three rounds of shot each; and, occasionally, some of them were obliged to keep at a distance, till, by the fall of friends or foes, they could be furnished with arms and ammunition. When successful, the field of battle supplied them with materials for the next encounter. This party soon increased to 600 men; and, encouraged by its daring exertions, a disposition manifested itself throughout South Carolina again to appeal to arms. Some companies of royal militia, imbodied under the authority of Cornwallis, deserted to Sumpter, and ranged themselves under his standards. The British commander beheld this change with surprise; he had thought the battle won, and the southern provinces completely subdued; but, to his astonishment, saw that past victories were unavailing, and that the work yet remained to be accomplished. He was obliged to call in his outposts, and to form his troops into larger bodies.

But Cornwallis was soon threatened by a more formidable enemy than Sumpter, who, though an active and audacious leader, commanded only an irregular and feeble band, and was capable of engaging only in desultory enterprises. Congress, sensible of the value and importance of the provinces which the British had overrun, made every effort to reinforce the southern army; and, fully aware of the efficacy of public opinion and of the influence of high reputation, on the 13th of June appointed General Gates to command it. He had acquired a splendid name by his triumphs over Burgoyne; and the people, whose opinions are formed by appearances, anticipated a success equally brilliant.

On receiving notice of his appointment to the command of the southern army, General Gates proceeded southward without delay, and on the 25th of July reached the camp at Buffalo ford, on Deep river, where he was received by Baron de Kalb with respect and cordiality. The army consisted of about 2,000 men; and considerable reinforcements of militia from North Carolina and Virginia were expected. In order that he might lead his troops through a more plentiful country, and for the purpose of establishing magazines and hospitals at convenient points, De Kalb had resolved to turn out of the direct road to Camden. But General Gates determined to pursue the straight route toward the British encampment, although it lay through a barren country, which afforded but a scanty subsistence to its inhabitants.

On the 27th of July he put his army in motion, and soon experienced the difficulties and privations which De Kalb had been desirous to avoid. The army was obliged to subsist chiefly on lean cattle, accidentally found in the woods; and the supply even of that mean food was very limited. Meal and corn were so scarce that the men were compelled to use unripe corn and peaches instead of bread. That insufficient diet, together with the intense heat and unhealthy climate, engendered disease, and threatened the destruction of the army. General Gates at length emerged from the inhospitable region of pine barrens, sand hills, and swamps; and, after having effected a junction with General Caswell, at the head of the militia of North Carolina, and a small body of troops under Lieutenant-Colonel Porterfield, he arrived at Clermont, or Rugely's Mills, on the 13th of August, and next day was joined by the militia of Virginia, amounting to 700 men, under General Stevens.

On the day after General Gates arrived at Rugely's Mills, he received an express from Sumpter, stating that a number of the militia of South Carolina had joined him on the west side of the Wateree, and that an escort of clothes, ammunition, and other stores, for the garrison of Camden, was on its way from Ninety-Six, and must pass the Wateree at a ford covered by a small fort, not far from Camden.

General Gates immediately detached 100 regular infantry and 300 militia of North Carolina to reinforce Sumpter, whom he ordered to reduce the fort and intercept the convoy. Meanwhile he advanced nearer Camden, with the intention of taking a position about seven miles from that place. For that purpose, he put his army in motion at ten in the evening of the 15th of August, having sent his sick, heavy baggage, and military stores not immediately wanted, under a guard to Waxhaws. On the march, Colonel Armand's legion composed the van; Porterfield's light infantry, reinforced by a company of picked men from Stevens's brigade, marching in Indian files, 200 yards from the road, covered the right flank of the legion; while Major Armstrong's light infantry of North Carolina militia, reinforced in like manner by General Caswell, in the same order, covered the left. The Maryland division, followed by the North Carolina and Virginia militia, with the artillery, composed the main body and rear guard; and the volunteer cavalry were equally distributed on the flanks of the baggage. The American army did not exceed 4,000 men, only about 900 of whom were regular troops, and 70 cavalry.

On the advance of General Gates into South Carolina, Lord Rawdon had called in his outposts, and concentrated his force at Camden. Informed of the appearance of the American army, and of the general defection of the country between the Pedee and the Black river, Cornwallis quitted Charleston and repaired to Camden, where he arrived on the same day that General Gates reached Clermont.

The British force was reduced by sickness, and Cornwallis could not assemble more than 2,000 men at Camden. That place, though advantageous in other respects, was not well adapted for resisting an attack; and as the whole country was rising against him, Lord Cornwallis felt the necessity of either retreating to Charleston, or of instantly striking a decisive blow. If he remained at Camden, his difficulties would daily increase, his communication with Charleston be endangered, and the American army acquire additional strength. A retreat to Charleston would be the signal for the whole of South Carolina and Georgia to rise in arms; his sick and magazines must be left behind; and the whole of the two provinces, except the towns of Charleston and Savannah, abandoned. The consequences of such a movement would be nearly as fatal as a defeat. Cornwallis, therefore, although he believed the American army considerably stronger than what it really was, determined to hazard a battle; and, at ten at night, on the 15th of August, the very hour when General Gates proceeded from Rugely's Mills, about thirteen miles distant, he marched toward the American camp.

About two in the morning of the 16th of August, the advanced guards of the hostile armies unexpectedly met in the woods, and the firing instantly began. Some of the cavalry of the American advanced guard being wounded by the first discharge, the party fell back in confusion, broke the Maryland regiment which was at the head of the column, and threw the whole line of the army into consternation. From that first impression, deepened by the gloom of night, the ill-disciplined militia seem not to have recovered. In the rencounter several prisoners were taken on each side; and from them the opposing generals acquired a more exact knowledge of circumstances than they formerly possessed. Several skirmishes happened during the night, which merely formed a prelude to the approaching battle, and gave the commanders some notion of the position of the hostile armies.

Cornwallis, perceiving that the Americans were on ground of no great extent, with morasses on their right and left, so that they could not avail themselves of their superior numbers to outflank his little army, impatiently awaited for the returning light, which would give every advantage to his disciplined troops. Both armies prepared for the conflict. Cornwallis formed his men in two divisions; that on the right was under the command of Lieutenant-Colonel Webster, that on the left under Lord Rawdon. In front were four field-pieces. The 71st regiment, with two cannon, formed the reserve; and the cavalry, about 300 in number, were in the rear, ready to act as circumstances might require.

In the American army, the second Maryland brigade, under General Gist, formed the right of the line; the militia of North Carolina, commanded by General Caswell, occupied the centre; and the militia of Virginia, with the light infantry and Colonel Armand's corps, composed the left; the artillery was placed between the divisions. The first Maryland brigade was stationed as a reserve 200 or 300 yards in the rear. Baron de Kalb commanded on the right; the militia generals were at the head of their respective troops ; and General Gates resolved to appear wherever his presence might be most useful.

At dawn of day Cornwallis ordered Lieutenant-Colonel Webster, with the British right wing to attack the American left. As Colonel Webster advanced, he was assailed by a desultory discharge of musketry from some volunteer militia who had advanced in front of their countrymen; but the British soldiers, rushing through that loose fire, charged the American line with a shout. The militia instantly threw down their arms and fled, many of them without even discharging their muskets; and all the efforts of the officers were unable to rally them. A great part of the centre division, composed of the militia of North Carolina, imitated the example of their comrades of Virginia: few of either division fired a shot, and still fewer carried their arms off the field. Tarleton with his legion pursued, and eagerly cut down the unresisting fugitives. Gates, with some of the militia general officers, made several attempts to rally them, but in vain. The farther they fled the more they dispersed, and Gates, in despair, hastened, with a few friends, to Charlotte, 80 miles from the field of battle.

Baron de Kalb, at the head of the continental troops, being abandoned by the militia, which had constituted the centre and left wing of the army, and being forsaken by the general also, was exposed to the attack of the whole British army. De Kalb and his troops, however, instead of imitating the example of their brethren in arms, behaved with a steady intrepidity, and defended themselves like men. Lord Rawdon attacked them about the time when Colonel Webster broke the left wing; but the charge was firmly received and steadily resisted, and the conflict was maintained for some time with equal obstinacy on both sides. The American reserve covered the left of De Kalb's division ; but its own left flank was entirely exposed by the flight of the militia; and therefore Colonel Webster, after detaching some cavalry and light troops in pursuit of the fugitive militia, with the remainder of his division attacked them at once in front and flank. A severe contest ensued. The Americans, in a great measure intermingled with the British, maintained a desperate conflict. Cornwallis brought his whole force to bear upon them; they were at length broken, and began to retreat in confusion. The brave De Kalb while making a vigorous charge at the head of a body of his men, fell pierced with eleven wounds. His aid-de-camp, Lieutenant-Colonel du Buysson, embraced the fallen general, announced his rank and nation to the surrounding enemy, and while thus generously exposing his own life to save his bleeding friend, he received several wounds, and was taken prisoner with him. De Kalb met with all possible attention and assistance from the victorious enemy, but that gallant officer expired in a few hours. Congress afterward ordered a monument to be erected to his memory.

The defeat was total. Every regiment was broken and dispersed through the woods, marshes, and brushwood. The officers lost sight of their men, and every individual endeavored to save himself in the best way he was able. General Rutherford of the North Carolina militia was made prisoner; and about 200 wagons, a great part of the baggage, military stores, small arms, and all the artillery, fell into the hands of the conquerors.

While the army under General Gates was completely defeated and dispersed, Colonel Sumpter was successful in his enterprise. On the evening in which Cornwallis marched from Camden, he reduced the redoubt on the Wateree, took the stores on their way to Camden, and made about 100 prisoners. On hearing, however, of the disastrous fate of the army under General Gates, Sumpter, fully aware of his danger, retreated hastily with his stores and prisoners up the south side of the Wateree. On the morning of the seventeenth, Cornwallis sent Tarleton, with the legion and a detachment of infantry, in pursuit of him. That officer proceeded with his usual rapidity; and, finding many of his infantry unable to keep pace with him, he advanced with about 100 cavalry and 60 of the most vigorous of the infantry; and on the 18th suddenly and unexpectedly came upon the Americans.

Sumpter, having marched with great diligence, thought himself beyond the reach of danger; and his men being exhausted by unremitting service and want of sleep, he halted near the Catawba ford, to give them some repose during the heat of the day. In order to prevent a surprise, he had placed sentinels at proper stations to give warning of approaching danger; but, overcome by fatigue, and equally regardless of duty and safety, the sentinels fell asleep at their post, and gave no alarm. Tarleton suddenly burst into the encampment of the drowsy and unsuspecting Americans; and, though some slight resistance was at first made from behind the baggage, soon gained a complete victory. The Americans fled precipitately toward the river or the woods. Many were killed or wounded. Sumpter escaped; but all his baggage fell into the hands of the enemy, while the prisoners and stores which he had taken were recovered.

By the complete defeat and dispersion of the army under General Gates and of Sumpter's corps, South Carolina and Georgia were again laid prostrate at the feet of the royal army, and the hope of maintaining their independence seemed more desperate than ever.

CHAPTER X.

THE war which was pursued with so much eagerness on land, was carried on also by sea; and there the Americans displayed that nautical skill and valor which have since enabled them to contend successfully with Great Britain upon that element where she had hitherto held undisputed supremacy, and where her victories over the Dutch, Spanish, and French, had given to her the proud title of "queen of the seas."

One of the most remarkable actions which occurred in 1779 was that of the capture of the Serapis and Countess of Scarborough by the Bon Homme Richard and Pallas, under the command of the chevalier Paul Jones.

John Paul was born at Arbigland, in Scotland, on the 6th of July, 1747, and the scenery and associations of his birthplace, and its vicinity, doubtless encouraged a restless spirit of adventure, a love of change, and an ardent enthusiasm in the objects of his pursuits, which were so strikingly manifested in his life.

His first voyage was made before he was thirteen years old; and maritime pursuits brought him to America. While here, his feelings became interested in the cause of the colonies, and fully prepared him for the active part he afterward took in their defence. In 1773, John Paul removed to Virginia, to attend to the affairs of his brother, who had died childless and intestate. He now assumed the additional surname of Jones. On the 22d of December, 1775, by a resolution of Congress, Paul Jones was appointed lieutenant in the American navy, which then consisted of the Alfred, Columbus, Andrew Doria, Sebastian Cabot, and Providence; the whole mounting 100 guns, and manned by 1,150 seamen. Jones was attached to the Alfred, and was the first to hoist the American flag, which was first displayed on board that vessel.

He was engaged in cruising among the British West India islands, where his frequent captures not only aided the cause of American independence by furnishing to the American army from the captured prizes many munitions of war

Fig. 140.—John Paul Jones

of which the states' troops were in much need, but also struck terror into the hearts of his enemies, and gained for himself the reputation of most invincible bravery and indomitable daring.

In the month of May, 1777, Congress sent him to France, where he was appointed by Franklin and his brother commissioners to the command of a French-built ship under American colors. In the course of 1778, Paul Jones sailed upon a cruise to the coast of Britain, and picked up many prizes under the very eyes of the enemy. Here his knowledge of the British coast was of much service. He made a descent at the mouth of the Dee, near to Kirkendbright; and in a visit to the house of the earl of Selkirk, retaliated for some of the many outrages committed by the British upon the defenceless shores of America; and he made another descent by night on the Cumberland coast, on the opposite side of the Frith, at the small town of Whitehaven, where he spiked the guns of the fort, and burnt one or two vessels. For some time he cruised up and down between the Solway and the Clyde, scaring the whole coast, where his name to this day is mentioned with horror; and then, returning to Brest with 200 prisoners, he boasted that with his single ship he had kept the northwestern coast of England and southern coast of Scotland in a state of alarm. In the summer of 1779, he returned to cruise along the eastern coast—no longer with a single ship, but with a squadron, manned by French and American sailors, and composed of the Bon Homme Richard of 40 guns, the Alliance of 36 guns (both American vessels), the Pallas, a French frigate of 32 guns, hired by the American Congress, and two smaller vessels. He fell in with a British merchant-fleet returning from the Baltic, convoyed by the Serapis of 44 guns, and the Countess of Scarborough of 20. Paul Jones, in his description of this contest, remarks :—

"On the 21st, we saw and chased two sail off Flamborough Head; the Pallas chased in the northeast quarter, while the Bon Homme Richard, followed by the Vengeance, chased in the southwest; the one I chased, a brigantine collier in ballast, belonging to Scarborough, was soon taken, aud sunk immediately afterward, as a fleet then appeared to the southward. This was so late in the day, that I could not come up with the fleet before night; at length, however, I got so near one of them as to force her to run ashore between Flamborough Head and the Spurn. Soon after, I took another, a brigantine from Holland, belonging to Sunderland; and at daylight next morning, seeing a fleet steering toward me from the Spurn, I imagined them to be a convoy bound from London for Leith, which had been for some time expected. One of them had a pendant hoisted, and appeared to be a ship of force. They had not, however, courage to come on, but kept back, all except the one which seemed to be armed, and that one also kept to the windward, very near the land, and on the edge of dangerous shoals, where I could not with safety approach. This induced me to make a signal for a pilot, and soon afterward two pilot-boats came off. They informed me that a ship that wore a pendant was an armed merchantman, and that a king's frigate lay there in sight, at anchor, within the Humber, waiting to take under convoy a number of merchant-ships bound to the northward. The pilots imagined the Bon Homme Richard to be an English ship-of-war, and consequently communicated to me the private signal which they had been required to make. I endeavored by this means to decoy the ships out of the port; but the wind then changing, and, with the tide, becoming unfavorable for them, the deception had not the desired effect, and they wisely put back. The entrance of the Humber is exceedingly difficult and dangerous, and as the Pallas was not in sight, I thought it imprudent to remain off the entrance—therefore steered out again to join the Pallas off Flamborough Head. In the night we saw and chased two ships until three o'clock in the morning, when, being at a very small dis-

Fig. 141.—Serapis and Bon Homme Richard.

Fig. 142.—Capture of the Countess of Scarborough.

tance from them, I made the private signal of reconnaissance, which I had given to each captain before I sailed from Groix: one half of the answer only was returned. In this position both sides lay to till daylight, when the ships proved to be the *Alliance* and the Pallas.

"On the morning of that day, the 23d, the brig from Holland not being in sight, we chased a brigantine that appeared laying to, to windward. About noon, we saw and chased a large ship that appeared coming round Flamborough Head, from the northward, and at the same time I manned and armed one of the pilot-boats to send in pursuit of the brigantine, which now appeared to be the vessel that I had forced ashore. Soon after this, a fleet of forty-one sail appeared off Flamborough Head, bearing north-northeast. This induced me to abandon the single ship, which had then anchored in Burlington bay; I also called back the pilot-boat, and hoisted a signal for a general chase. When the fleet discovered us bearing down, all the merchant-ships crowded sail toward the shore. The two ships-of-war that protected the fleet at the same time steered from the land, and made the disposition for battle. In approaching the enemy, I crowded every possible sail, and made the signal for the line of battle, to which the Alliance showed no attention. Earnest as I was for the action, I could not reach the commodore's ship until seven in the evening, being then within pistol-shot, when he hailed the Bon Homme Richard. We answered him by firing a whole broadside.

"The battle being thus begun, was continued with unremitting fury. Every method was practised on both sides to gain an advantage, and rake each other; and I must confess that the enemy's ship, being much more manageable than the Bon Homme Richard, gained thereby several times an advantageous situation, in spite of my best endeavors to prevent it. As I had to deal with an enemy of greatly superior force, I was under the necessity of closing with him, to prevent the advantage which he had over me in point of manœuvre. It was my intention to lay the Bon Homme Richard athwart the enemy's bow; but as that operation required great dexterity in the management of both sails and helm, and some of our braces being shot away, it did not exactly succeed to my wish. The enemy's bowsprit, however, came over the Bon Homme Richard's poop, by the mizzenmast, and I made both ships fast together in that situation, which by the action of the wind on the enemy's sails, forced her stern close to the Bon Homme Richard's bow, so that the ships lay square alongside of each other, the yards being all entangled, and the cannon of each ship touching the opponents. When this position took place it was eight o'clock, previous to which the Bon Homme Richard had received sundry eighteen-pound shots below the water, and leaked very much. My battery of twelve-pounders, on which I had placed my chief dependance, being commanded by Lieutenant Dale and Colonel Weibert, and manned principally with American seamen and French volunteers, was entirely silenced and abandoned. As to the six old eighteen-pounders that formed the battery of the lower gun-deck, they did no service whatever, except firing eight shots in all. Two out of three of them burst at the first fire, and killed almost all the men who were stationed to manage them. Before this time, too, Colonel de Chamillard, who commanded a party of twenty soldiers on the poop, had abandoned that station, after having lost some of his men. I had now only two pieces of cannon (nine-pounders) on the quarter-deck, that were not silenced, and not one of the heavier cannon was fired during the rest of the action. The purser, M. Mease, who commanded the guns on the quarter-deck, being dangerously wounded in the head, I was obliged to fill his place, and with great difficulty rallied a few men and shifted over one of the lee quarter-deck guns, so that we afterward played three pieces of nine-pounders upon the enemy. The tops alone seconded the fire of this little battery, and held out bravelv during the whole of the action, especially the maintop, where Lieutenant Stack commanded. I directed the fire of one of the three cannon against the mainmast, with double-headed shot, while the other two were exceedingly well served with grape and canister-shot, to silence the enemy's musketry and clear her decks, which was at last effected. The enemy were, as I have since understood, on the instant of calling for quarter, when the cowardice or treachery of three of my under-officers induced them to call to the enemy. The English commodore asked me if I demanded quarter, and I having answered him in the most determined negative, they renewed the battle with double fury. They were unable to stand the deck; but the fire of their cannon, especially the lower battery, which was entirely formed of ten-pounders, was incessant; both ships were set on fire in various places, and the scene was dreadful beyond the reach of language. To account for the timidity of my three under-officers—I mean the gunner, the carpenter, and the master-at-arms—I must observe, that the first two were slightly wounded, and, as the ship had received various shots under water, and one of the pumps being shot away, the carpenter expressed his fears that she would sink, and the other two concluded that she was sinking, which occasioned the gunner to run aft on the poop, without my knowledge, to strike the colors. Fortunately for me, a cannon-ball had done that before, by carrying away the ensign-staff; he was therefore reduced to the necessity of sinking, as he supposed, or of calling for quarter, and he preferred the latter.

"All this time the Bon Homme Richard had sustained the action alone, and the enemy, though much superior in force, would have been very glad to have got clear, as appears by their own acknowledgments, and by their having let go an anchor the instant that I laid them on board, by which means they would have escaped, had I not made them well fast to the Bon Homme Richard.

"At last, at half past nine o'clock, the Alliance appeared, and I now thought the battle at an end; but, to my utter astonishment, he discharged a broadside full into the stern of the Bon Homme Richard. We called to him for God's sake to forbear firing into the Bon Homme Richard; yet they passed along the off side of the ship, and continued firing. There was no possibility of his mistaking the enemy's ship for the Bon Homme Richard, there being the most essential difference in their appearance and construction. Besides, it was then full moonlight, and the sides of the Bon Homme Richard were all black, while the sides of the prize were all yellow. Yet, for the greater security, I showed the signal of our reconnaissance, by putting out three lanterns, one at the head, another at the stern, and the third in the middle, in a horizontal line. Every tongue cried that he was firing into the wrong ship, but nothing availed; he passed round, firing into the Bon Homme Richard's head, stern, and broadside, and by one of his volleys killed several of my best men, and mortally wounded a good officer on the forecastle. My situation was really deplorable; the Bon Homme Richard received various shots under water from the Alliance; the leak gained on the pumps, and the fire increased much on board both ships. Some officers persuaded me to strike, of whose courage and good sense I entertain a high opinion. My treacherous master-at-arms let loose all my prisoners without my knowledge, and my prospects became gloomy indeed. I would not, however, give up the point. The enemy's mainmast began to shake, their firing decreased fast, ours rather increased, and the British colors were struck at half an hour past ten o'clock.

"This prize proved to be the British ship-of-war the Serapis, a new ship of 44 guns, built on the most approved construction, with two complete batteries, one of them of eighteen-pounders, and commanded by the brave Commodore Richard Pearson. I had yet two enemies to encounter, far more formidable than the Britons: I mean fire and water. The Serapis was attacked only by

FIG 143.—Medal presented to Lafayette.

the first, but the Bon Homme Richard was assailed by both; there was five feet water in the hold, and though it was moderate from the explosion of so much gunpowder, yet the three pumps that remained could with difficulty only keep the water from gaining. The fire broke out in various parts of the ship, in spite of all the water that could be thrown in to quench it, and at length broke out as low as the powder-magazine, and within a few inches of the powder. In that dilemma, I took out the powder upon deck, ready to be thrown overboard at the last extremity, and it was ten o'clock the next day, the 24th, before the fire was entirely extinguished. With respect to the situation of the Bon Homme Richard, the rudder was cut entirely off, the stern-frame and transoms were almost entirely cut away, and the timbers by the lower-deck, especially from the mainmast toward the stern, being greatly decayed with age, were mangled beyond my power of description; and a person must have been an eyewitness to form a just idea of the tremendous scene of carnage, wreck, and ruin, which everywhere appeared. Humanity can not but recoil from the prospect of such finished horror, and lament that war should be capable of producing such fatal consequences.

"After the carpenters, as well as Captain Cottineau and other men of sense, had well examined and surveyed the ship (which was not finished before five in the evening), I found every person to be convinced that it was impossible to keep the Bon Homme Richard afloat so as to reach a port, if the wind should increase, it being then only a very moderate breeze. I had but little time to remove my wounded, which now became unavoidable, and which was effected in the course of the night and next morning. I was determined to keep the Bon Homme Richard afloat, and, if possible, to bring her into port. For that purpose, the first lieutenant of the Pallas continued on board with a party of men to attend the pumps, with boats in waiting ready to take them on board in case the water should gain on them too fast. The wind augmented in the night, and the next day, the 25th, so that it was impossible to prevent the good old ship from sinking. They did not abandon her till after nine o'clock; the water was then up to the lower deck, and a little after ten I saw, with inexpressible grief, the last glimpse of the *Bon Homme Richard.* No lives were lost with the ship, but it was impossible to save the stores of any sort whatever. I lost even the best part of my clothes, books, and papers; and several of my officers lost all their clothes and effects.

"Having thus endeavored to give a clear and simple relation of the circumstances and events that have attended the little armament under my command, I shall freely submit my conduct therein to the censure of my superiors and the impartial public. I beg leave, however, to observe, that the force put under my command was far from being well composed; and as the great majority of the actors in it have appeared bent on the pursuit of interest only, I am exceedingly sorry that they and I have been at all concerned.

"Captain Cottineau engaged the Countess of Scarborough, and took her, after an hour's action, while the Bon Homme Richard engaged the Serapis. The Countess of Scarborough is an armed ship of 20 six-pounders, and was commanded by a king's officer. In the action, the Alliance, as I am informed, fired into the Pallas and killed some men. If it should be asked why the convoy was suffered to escape, I must answer that I was myself in no condition to pursue, and that none of the rest showed any inclination; not even Mr. Ricot, who had held off at a distance to windward during the whole action, and withheld by force the pilot-boat with my lieutenant and fifteen men. The Alliance, too, was in a state to pursue the fleet, not having had a single man wounded, or a single shot fired at her from the Serapis, and only three that did execution from the Countess of Scarborough, at such a distance that one stuck in the side, and the other two just touched, and then dropped into the water. The Alliance killed one man only on board the Serapis. As Captain de Cottineau charged himself with manning and securing the prisoners of the Countess of Scarborough, I think the escape of the Baltic fleet can not so well be charged to his account.

"I should have mentioned, that the mainmast and mizzen-topmast of the Serapis fell overboard soon after the captain had come on board the Bon Homme Richard."

This brave action struck terror into the hearts of the enemies of American liberty, and contributed not a little to establish for her hardy tars a reputation for naval bravery, so well maintained afterward by a Perry, Decatur, and Hull.

CHAPTER XI.

While the transactions we have related were going on in the southern states, some interesting events happened in the more northern parts of the Union, where General Washington was beset by pressing and formidable difficulties. The finances of Congress were in a most depressed condition, and the urgent wants of the army were but ill supplied. The evils of short enlistment, though distinctly understood and strongly felt, could not be remedied; and the places of those men who were leaving the army, on the expiration of their stipulated term of service, could not easily be filled up. Besides, the troops were in danger of perishing by cold and famine. During the preceding year, General Greene and Colonel Wadsworth had been at the head of the quartermaster and commissary departments; and notwithstanding their utmost exertions, the wants of the army had been ill supplied. After being put into winter quarters, it was in great danger of being dissolved by want of provisions, or of perishing through famine. The colonial paper money was in a state of great and increasing depreciation; and in order to check the alarming evil, Congress, which, like other popular assemblies, had in it no small share of ignorance and self-sufficiency, resolved to diminish the circulation and keep up the value of their paper currency by withholding the necessary supplies from the public agents. This foolish resolution threatened the ruin of the army. Nobody was willing to make contracts with the public, and some of those entered into were not fulfilled.

Congress, jealous of the public agents, because ignorant of what was really necessary, repeatedly changed the form of its engagements with them; and at length, by its fluctuating policy, real wants, and imprudent parsimony, brought matters to such extremities, that General Washington was compelled to require the several counties of the state of New Jersey to furnish his army with certain quantities of provisions within six days, in order to prevent them from being taken by force. Although the province was much exhausted, yet the people instantly complied with the requisition, and furnished a temporary supply to the army.

Soon after Sir Henry Clinton sailed on his expedition against Charleston, toward the end of the year 1779, a frost of unexampled intensity began. The Hudson, East river, and all the waters round New York, were so completely frozen, that an army, with its artillery and wagons, might have crossed them in all directions with perfect safety. New York lost all the advantages of its insular situation, and became easily accessible on every side. This city was fortified by the British; but, on account of its insular situation, several parts, being considered of difficult access, were left undefended. By the strength of the ice, however, every point became exposed; and in that unforeseen emergency, General Knyphausen, who commanded in the city with a garrison of 10,000 men, took every prudent precaution for his own defence, and fortified every vulnerable part; but the inefficiency of the American army was his best security. General Washington easily perceived the advantages which the extraordinary frost gave him; but, from the destitute state of his army, he was unable to avail himself of them, and was obliged to see an opportunity pass away which was probably never to return. The army under his immediate command was inferior in number to the garrison of New York; it was also ill clad, scantily supplied with provisions, and in no condition to undertake offensive operations.

The British had a post on Staten Island; and, as the ice opened a free communication between the island and the Jersey coast, General Washington, notwithstanding the enfeebled condition of his army, resolved to attack the garrison, and appointed Lord Stirling to conduct the enterprise. The night of the 14th of January was chosen for the attempt; but though the Americans used every precaution, yet the officer commanding on Staten Island discovered their intention, and took effectual measures to defeat it. The attack was repulsed, but little loss was sustained on either side.

The extreme cold occasioned much suffering in New York, by want of provisions and fuel; for, as the communication by water was entirely stopped, the usual supplies were cut off. The demand for fuel in particular was so pressing that it was found expedient to break up some old transports, and to pull down some uninhabited wooden houses, for the purpose of procuring that necessary article. As the British paid in ready money for provisions or firewood carried within the lines, many of the country people, tempted by the precious metals, so rare among them, tried to supply the garrison. The endeavors of the British to encourage and protect this intercourse, and the exertions of the Americans to prevent it, brought on a sort of partisan warfare, in which the former most frequently had the advantage. In one of the most important of these rencounters, a captain and fourteen men of a Massachusetts regiment were killed on the spot, seventeen were wounded, and ninety, with Colonel Thompson, the officer who commanded the party, were made prisoners.

Congress found itself placed in very difficult circumstances. It always contained a number of men of talents, and manifested no small share of vigor and activity. Many of the members were skilful in the management of their private affairs, and, having been successful in the world, thought themselves competent to direct the most important national concerns, although unacquainted with the principles of finance, legislation, or war. In pecuniary matters they were dilatory, and never anticipated trying emergencies, or made provision for probable events, till they were overtaken by some urgent necessity. Hence they were frequently deliberating about levying troops and supplying the army when the troops ought to have been in the field, and the army fully equipped for active service. This often placed the commander-in-chief in the most trying and perilous circumstances.

Congress had solemnly resolved not to exceed $200,000,000 in continental bills of credit. In November, 1779, the whole of that sum was issued, and expended also. The demand on the states to replenish the treasury by taxes had not been fully complied with; and, even although it had been completely answered, would not have furnished a sum adequate to the expenses of government. Instead of maturely considering and digesting a plan, adhering to it, and improving it by experience, Congress often changed its measures; and, even in the midst of those distresses which had brought the army to the verge of dissolution, was busy in devising new and untried expedients for supporting it. As the treasury was empty, and money could not be raised, Congress, on the 25th of February, resolved to call on the several states for their proportion of provisions and forage for the maintenance of the army during the ensuing campaign, but specified no time within which these were to be collected, and consequently the states were in no haste in the matter. In order to encourage and facilitate compliance with this requisition, it was further resolved that any state which should have taken the necessary measures for furnishing its quota, and given notice thereof to Congress, should be authorized to prohibit any continental quartermaster or commissary from purchasing within its limits.

Every man who had a practical knowledge of the subject easily perceived the defective nature and dangerous tendency of this arrangement. It was an attempt to carry on the war rather by separate provincial efforts than by a combination of national strength; and if the army received from any state where it was acting the appointed quantity of necessaries, it had no right, though starving, to purchase what it stood in need of. Besides, the carriage of provisions from distant parts was troublesome, expensive, and sometimes impracticable.

The troops were ill clothed, their pay was in arrear, and that of the officers, owing to the great depreciation of the paper currency, was wholly unequal to their decent maintenance. These multiplied privations and sufferings soured the temper of the men; and it required all the influence of their revered commander to prevent many of the officers from resigning their commissions. The long continuance of want and hardship produced relaxation of discipline, which at length manifested itself in open mutiny. On the 25th of May, two regiments belonging to Connecticut paraded under arms, with the avowed intention of returning home, or of obtaining subsistence at the point of the bayonet. The rest of the soldiers, though they did not join in the mutiny, showed little disposition to suppress it. At length the two regiments were brought back to their duty; but much murmuring and many complaints were heard. While the army was in such want, the inhabitants of Jersey, where most of the troops were stationed, were unavoidably harassed by frequent requisitions, which excited considerable discontent.

Reports of the mutinous state of the American army, and of the dissatisfaction of the people of Jersey, probably much exaggerated, were carried to General Knyphausen, who, believing the American soldiers ready to desert their standards, and the inhabitants of Jersey willing to abandon the Union, on the 6th of June, passed from Staten Island to Elizabethtown in Jersey, with 5,000 men. That movement was intended to encourage the mutinous disposition of the American troops, and to fan the flame of discontent among the inhabitants of the province. Early next morning, he marched into the country toward Springfield by the way of Connecticut Farms, a flourishing plantation, so named because the cultivators had come from Connecticut. But even before reaching that place, which was only five or six miles from Elizabethtown, the British perceived that the reports which they had received concerning the discontent of the Americans were incorrect; for, on the first alarm, the militia assembled with great alacrity, and, aided by some small parties of regular troops, annoyed the British by an irregular but galling fire of musketry, wherever the nature of the ground presented a favorable opportunity: and although those parties were nowhere strong enough to make a stand, yet they gave plain indications of the temper and resolution which were to be encountered in advancing into the country.

At Connecticut Farms the British detachment halted. The settlers were known to be zealous in the American cause, and, therefore, with a base spirit of revenge, the British, among whom was General Tryon, laid the flourishing village, with the church and minister's house, in ashes. Here occurred one of those affecting incidents which, being somewhat out of the ordinary course of the miseries of war, make a deep impression on the public mind. Mr. Caldwell, minister of the place, had withdrawn toward Springfield, but had left his wife and family behind, believing them to be in no danger. The British advanced to the industrious and peaceful village. Mrs. Caldwell, trusting to her sex for safety, and unsuspicious of harm, was sitting in her house with her children around her, when a soldier came up, levelled his musket at the window, and shot her dead on the spot in the midst of her terrified infants. On the intercession of a friend, the dead body was permitted to be removed before the house was set on fire.

This atrocious deed excited general horror and detestation; but Tryon was present, and his conduct on other occasions was not free from acts of brutal and bloodthirsty ferocity.

After destroying the Connecticut Farms, Knyphausen advanced toward Springfield, where the Jersey brigade under General Maxwell, and a large body of militia, had taken an advantageous position, and seemed resolved to defend it. General Knyphausen, however, had met with a reception so different from what he expected, that, without making any attempt on the American post, he withdrew during the night to Elizabethtown.

On being informed of the invasion of New Jersey, General Washington put his army in motion, early on the morning of the day in which Knyphausen marched from Elizabethtown, and proceeded to the Short hills behind Springfield, while the British were in the vicinity of that place. Feeble as his army was, he made the necessary dispositions for fighting; but the unexpected retreat of Knyphausen rendered a battle unnecessary. The British were followed by an American detachment, which attacked their rear-guard next morning, but was repulsed. Instead of returning to New York, General Knyphausen lingered in the vicinity of Elizabethtown and on Staten Island; and General Washington, too weak to hazard an engagement, except on advantageous ground, remained on the hills near Springfield to watch the movements of the British army. At that time, the army under the immediate orders of General Washington did not exceed 4,000 effective men.

On the 18th of June Sir Henry Clinton returned from South Carolina, with about 4,000 men; and, after receiving this reinforcement, the British force in New York and its dependancies amounted to 12,000 effective and regular troops, most of whom could be brought into the field for any particular service; as besides them the British commander had about 4,000 militia and refugees for garrison duty. The British army was so powerful that the Americans could only follow a wary policy, occupying strong ground, presenting a bold front, and concealing their weakness as far as possible.

Sir Henry Clinton embarked troops, and awakened the fears of General Washington lest he should sail up the Hudson and attack the posts in the highlands. Those posts had always been objects of much solicitude to the American commander, and he was extremely jealous of any attack upon them. In order to be in readiness to resist any such attack, he left General Greene at Springfield, with 700 continentals, the Jersey militia, and some cavalry, and proceeded toward Pompton with the main body of the army.

Sir Henry Clinton, after having perplexed the Americans by his movements, early on the morning of the 23d of June, rapidly advanced in full force from Elizabethtown toward Springfield. General Greene hastily assembled his scattered detachments, and apprized General Washington of the march of the royal army, who instantly returned to support Greene's division. The British marched in two columns; one on the main road leading to Springfield, and the other on the Vauxhall road. General Greene scarcely had time to collect his troops at Springfield, and to make the necessary dispositions, when the royal army appeared before the town, and a cannonade immediately began. A fordable rivulet, with bridges corresponding to the different roads, runs in front of the place. Greene had stationed parties to guard the bridges, and they obstinately disputed the passage; but after a smart conflict they were overpowered, and compelled to retreat. Greene then fell back, and took post on a range of hills, where he expected to be again attacked. But the British instead of attempting to pursue their advantage, contented themselves with setting fire to the village, and laying the greater part of it in ashes. Discouraged by the obstinate resistance they had received, they immediately retreated to Elizabethtown, pursued with the utmost animosity by the militia, who were provoked at the burning of Springfield. They arrived at Elizabethtown about sunset; and, continuing their march to Elizabeth point, began at midnight to pass over to Staten Island. Before six next morning they had entirely evacuated the Jerseys, and removed the bridge of boats which communicated with Staten Island.

In the skirmish at Springfield the Americans had about twenty men killed, and sixty wounded. The British suffered a corresponding loss. Sir Henry Clinton's object in this expedition seems to have been to destroy the American magazines in that part of the country. But the obstinate resistance which he met with at Springfield deterred him from advancing into a district abounding in difficult passes, where every strong position would be vigorously defended. He seems also to have been checked by the apprehension of a fleet and army from France.

General Washington was informed of Sir Henry Clinton's march soon after the British left Elizabethtown; but though he hastily returned, the skirmish at Springfield was over before he reached the vicinity of that place.

After Sir Henry Clinton left the Jerseys, General Washington planned an enterprise against a British post at Bergen point, on the Hudson, opposite New York, garrisoned by seventy loyalists. It was intended to reduce the post, and also to carry off a number of cattle on Bergen Neck, from which the garrison of New York occasionally received supplies of fresh provisions. General Wayne was appointed to conduct the enterprise. With a respectable force he marched against the post, which consisted of a blockhouse covered by an abattis and palisade. General Wayne pointed his artillery against the blockhouse, but his field-pieces made no impression on the logs. Galled by the fire from the loop-holes, some of his men rushed impetuously through the abattis and attempted to storm the blockhouse, but they were repulsed with considerable loss. Though, however, the Americans failed in their attempt against the post, they succeeded in driving off most of the cattle.

On the commencement of hostilities in Europe, the Marquis de la Fayette, who had so early and so zealously embarked in the cause of America, returned home in order to offer his services to his king, still, however, retaining his rank in the army of congress. His ardor in behalf of the Americans remained unabated, and he exerted all his influence with the court of Versailles to gain its effectual support to the United States: his efforts were successful, and the king of France resolved vigorously to assist the Americans both by sea and land. Having gained this important point, and perceiving that there was no need for his military services in Europe, he obtained leave from his sovereign to return to America and join his former companions in arms. He landed at Boston toward the end of April; and, in his way to congress, called at the headquarters of General Washington, and informed him of the powerful succor which might soon be expected from France. He met with a most cordial reception both from congress and the commander-in-chief, on account of his high rank, tried friendship, and distinguished services.

The assistance expected from their powerful ally was very encouraging to the Americans, but called for corresponding exertions on their part. The commander-in-chief found himself in the most perplexing circumstances: his army was feeble, and he could form no plan for the campaign till he knew what forces were to be put under his orders. His troops, both officers and privates, were ill clothed, and needed to be decently apparelled before they could be led into the field to co-operate with soldiers in respectable uniforms. In order to supply these defects, and to get his army in a state of due preparation before the arrival of the European auxiliaries, General Washington made the most pressing applications to congress, and to the several state legislatures. Congress resolved and recommended; but the states were dilatory, and their tardy proceedings ill accorded with the exigencies of the case, or with the expectations of those who best understood the affairs of the Union. Even on the 4th of July, the commander-in-chief had the mortification to find that few new levies had arrived in camp, and some of the states had not even taken the trouble to inform him of the number of men they intended to furnish.

In the month of June the state of Massachusetts had resolved to send a reinforcement, but no part of it had yet arrived. About the same time a voluntary subscription was entered into in Philadelphia, for the purpose of providing bounties to recruits to fill up the Pennsylvania line; and the president or vice-president in council was empowered, if circumstances required it, to put the state under martial law. A bank also was established for the purpose of supplying the army with provisions; and a number of gentlemen engaged to support it to the amount of 189,000*l*. sterling, according to the sums affixed to their several names. The ladies of Philadelphia were ambitious of sharing the honors of patriotism with their fathers, husbands, and brothers; and a number of them visited every house in the city, in order to collect a sum of money to be presented to the army, in testimony of their esteem and approbation. The money was expended on cloth for shirts, which the ladies made.

In the midst of this bustle and preparation, the expected succors from France, consisting of a fleet of eight ships of the line, with frigates and other vessels under the Chevalier de Ternay, having about 6,000 troops on board under the Count de Rochambeau, arrived at Rhode Island on the evening of the 10th of July; and, in a few days afterward, the Marquis de la Fayette arrived at Newport from the American headquarters, to confer with his countrymen.

At the time of the arrival of the French in Rhode Island, Admiral Arbuthnot had only four sail of the line at New York; but, in a few days, Admiral Graves arrived from England with six sail of the line, which gave the British a decided superiority to the hostile squadron; and, therefore, Sir Henry Clinton without delay prepared for active operations. He embarked about 8,000 men, and sailed with the fleet to Huntington bay in Long Island, with the intention of proceeding against the French at Newport. The militia of Massachusetts and Connecticut were ordered to join their new allies in Rhode Island, and the combined army there thought itself able to give the British a good reception.

As the garrison of New York was weakened by the sailing of the armament under the British commander-in-chief, General Washington, having received considerable reinforcements, suddenly crossed the North river, and advanced toward New York; that movement brought Sir Henry Clinton back to defend the place; and, consequently, the American commander proceeded no farther in his meditated enterprise.

The want of money and of all necessaries still continued in the American camp; and the discontent of the troops gradually increased. The men, indeed, bore incredible hardships and privations with unexampled fortitude and patience; but the army was in a state of constant fluctuation; it was composed, in a great measure, of militia harassed by perpetual service, and obliged to neglect the cultivation of their farms and their private interests, in order to obey the calls of public duty, and of soldiers on short enlistments, who never acquired the military spirit and habits.

In consequence of an appointment, General Washington and suite set out to a conference with Count Rochambeau and Admiral Ternay, and, on the 21st of

FIG. 144.—Count de Rochambeau.

September, met them at Hartford in Connecticut, where they spent a few days together, and conversed about a plan for the next campaign.

The season was now far advanced: no action of importance had been achieved on the Hudson by either party, and the campaign in that quarter seemed about to close without anything remarkable, when both armies were suddenly roused, and the public mind both in Europe and America much agitated, by the execution of Major André.

In the early part of August, when General Washington meditated an attack on New York, he proposed that General Arnold should have a command in the enterprise. That Arnold declined; alleging that his lameness disqualified him for field duty. General Washington knew him to be a selfish man; but, having no suspicion of his infidelity to the American cause, for which he had professed so much zeal and made so many exertions, appointed him at his own desire, to the command of West Point and its dependancies, a most important post on the Hudson. Of the highland posts on that river General Washington was extremely jealous, and exerted himself to prevent the British from establishing a communication between Canada and New York by the lakes Champlain and George, and the river Hudson. West Point was considered a principal key of that communication; and, by the appointment to the command of it, Arnold was put into a place of high trust and confidence.

But that officer, impetuous and desperate rather than cool and intrepid, and governed more by the violence of his passions than the dictates of his understanding, had secretly determined to abandon and betray the American cause; and entered into negotiations with the British commander-in-chief for that purpose. The surrender of West Point, he was well aware, would gratify his new

FIG. 145.—West Point.

friends ; and he wished to inflict a deadly wound on his old associates, whom he hated the more because he intended to betray them. Ambitious and selfish, fond of ostentation and magnificence, his expenditure had exceeded his income ; and, in order to supply his extravagance, he had engaged in trade and privateering. His speculations proved unsuccessful ; his funds were exhausted ; and his creditors became clamorous. About the month of July, 1779, he presented heavy accounts against the public, but the commissioners rejected about one half of his demands ; he appealed to congress ; but a committee of that body reported that the commissioners had allowed him more than he had any right to demand or expect. Irritated and inflamed by this treatment, embarrassed in his circumstances, and encumbered with an expensive family, he resolved to raise a fortune on the ruins of his character, and to commit the foulest treason in order to gratify at once his ambition and revenge.

In the course of the year 1779, Major André, adjutant-general of the British

Fig. 146.—Major André.

army, a young officer of distinguished talents and acquirements, had entered into a correspondence with Mrs. Arnold, on pretence of supplying her with millinery goods ; that correspondence ripened into treason on the part of Arnold. After his nomination to the command of West Point, the Vulture sloop-of-war was stationed by Sir Henry Clinton in the North river, at such a distance from the American works as to excite no suspicion, but near enough to facilitate the correspondence which was carrying on. Before that time there had been a written correspondence, through other channels, between Arnold and André, under the assumed names of Gustavus and Anderson. In order to bring the negotiation to a speedy close, Arnold wished Sir Henry Clinton to send a confidential person to hold a conference with him ; unhappily the amiable and accomplished André was selected for the consummation of a work in which he was already too much implicated.

On the night of the 21st of September, a boat sent by Arnold carried André from the Vulture, and landed him on the bank of the river, where he met Arnold without the American posts. The day was about to dawn before the negotiation was finished ; and André was told that it was necessary he should remain concealed till next night; for that purpose he was conducted within the American lines, contrary to his previous stipulation and intention, and without his knowledge. He spent the day with Arnold. Next night the boatmen refused to carry him back to the Vulture, because she had shifted her ground in order to be beyond the reach of a cannon which had been mounted to annoy her; and he was obliged to attempt an escape by land. He now changed his uniform, which he had hitherto worn under a surtout, for a common coat; and having procured a horse, was, under the name of John Anderson, furnished with a passport by Arnold to go to the lines at White Plains, or lower if he thought proper, as he was on public business.

Thus equipped, André set out alone, and proceeded on his journey toward New York. He passed the American guards and posts on the road without suspicion; but Arnold had a scouting party, chiefly militia, scouring the country between the outposts of the two armies. As André prosecuted his journey next day, and flattered himself that all danger was past, a man suddenly sprang from a covert and seized his horse's bridle. Surprised by the unexpected onset, the major lost his presence of mind; mistaking the man for a British partisan, instead of presenting his passport, he declared himself a British officer, and asked permission to proceed: but two other militia-men coming up at the moment, the party refused to let him go, though he offered them the most tempting rewards. They conducted him to Colonel Jamieson, the officer commanding the scouting party, before whom he appeared as John Anderson; choosing rather to encounter every hazard, than, by a disclosure of his real character, to involve Arnold in jeopardy before he had warning to provide for his safety.

André had been disconcerted, and his presence of mind had forsaken him on his sudden and unexpected seizure; but, more alive to Arnold's danger than his own, he discovered his ingenuity in procuring Jamieson's permission to give that officer notice of his apprehension. Even before that time Jamieson had entertained suspicions of Arnold's fidelity; and although those suspicions must now have been strengthened or confirmed, yet he permitted a note to be sent to Arnold, giving him notice of John Anderson's detention.

Several papers were found in one of Major André's boots, all in Arnold's handwriting, which contained an exact account of the state of West Point and its dependancies, with remarks on the works, an estimate of the number of men ordinarily on duty in the place, and a copy of the state of matters which had been laid before a council of war by the American commander-in-chief on the 6th of the month. All those papers Jamieson enclosed under cover to General Washington, with a letter from the prisoner, in which he avowed himself to be Major John André, adjutant-general of the British army, related the manner of his apprehension, and endeavored to vindicate himself from the imputation of being a spy.

General Washington was then returning from his conference with the French commanders at Hartford; and Jamieson's messenger missed him by taking a different road from that in which the general was travelling. Arnold received the notice of Anderson's detention some hours before General Washington arrived at West Point, and immediately consulted his safety by hastening on board the Vulture sloop-of-war, which lay in the river some miles below Verplank's point.

On opening the packet from Jamieson at West Point, General Washington discoved Arnold's treason, and took prompt and effectual measures for the security of the post, ordering to it two brigades from the nearest division of the main army.

After allowing time for the notice of his detention to reach Arnold, Major André laid aside all disguise, and avowed who he was. His behavior was frank and ingenuous; and he seemed anxious for nothing but the vindication of his character from the imputations which the circumstances of his apprehension ap-

Fig. 147.—Benedict Arnold, the Traitor.

peared to cast upon him. General Washington appointed a board of officers, of which Greene was president, and La Fayette, Steuben, and others, were members, to inquire into the case of Major André, and to report in what character he was to be considered, and what punishment he deserved. Even during the short time that André was in the power of the Americans, and notwithstanding the unhappy circumstances in which he was placed, his behavior and talents made a highly favorable impression on their minds; and when brought before the board, the members behaved toward him with the utmost respect and delicacy, and told him not to answer any questions that might embarrass his feelings. But in that crisis of his fate, André magnanimously disregarded everything but his honor. He gave a candid recital of circumstances, concealing nothing that regarded himself; but making no disclosures to inculpate others. He acknowledged everything that was reckoned essential to his condemnation, and the board of general officers to whom his case was referred, without calling any witnesses, considered merely that he had been within their lines in disguise, and reported that in their opinion Major André was a spy, and ought to suffer death. The sentence was ordered to be carried into execution on the day after it was declared.

The apprehension of Major André excited a lively sensation in the British army, which felt a strong interest in his fate; for he was dear to all his companions in arms, and especially to the commander-in-chief, who immediately, by a flag of truce, opened a correspondence with General Washington, and urged every consideration of justice, policy, and humanity, in favor of André. Finding his letters ineffectual, he despatched General Robertson to confer with General Washington on the subject, or with any officer whom he might appoint. He was met by General Greene; but no mitigation of the doom could be procured. On the day before his execution, Major André wrote an affecting letter to General Washington, requesting to be put to death like a soldier, and not as a malefactor; but the board of general officers, to whom everything respecting him was referred, did not grant his request. The 2d of October closed the tragical scene: on that day the major was led out and hanged, supporting his high character to the last moment. He suffered amid the admiration and regrets even of the American officers; while his death was deeply lamented in the British army. He was a young man of an amiable character, engaging manners, and fine talents and acquirements. By a striking combination of circumstances, he was led to an end of which he was wholly unworthy. Sir Henry Clinton made every effort to save him, but the Americans were inexorable.

Even Arnold had the effrontery to write to General Washington on the occasion, attesting such facts as he believed favorable to André. But what reliance could be placed on the testimony of a man capable of such foul treason? He also threatened the general, and reminded him that many of the inhabitants of South Carolina had rendered themselves liable to military execution.

Arnold endeavored to vindicate his conduct by pleading hostility to the alliance with France; and he attempted to induce others to imitate his example; but no plea can justify his attempt to employ the power committed to him for the ruin of those who had trusted him; some of whom, perhaps, had been encouraged by his example and excitement to take up arms against the British authority. The name of Arnold must go down to posterity loaded with all the infamy of a traitor: and it were for the honor of human nature, and the common advantage of nations, if all governments would unite in manifesting their detestation of such villanies.

After the melancholy event now related, no military transactions of much importance were carried on in the north during the remainder of the campaign. On the 21st of November, indeed, Major Talmadge performed a brilliant exploit of desultory warfare. Being informed that the British had a large magazine of forage at Coram, on Long Island, protected by a small garrison at Fort St. George on South Haven in its vicinity, he crossed the sound where it was upward of 20 miles broad; and, with nearly 100 men, surprised the fort; made the garrison, upward of 50 in number, prisoners; burnt the magazines at Coram; and, escaping the British cruisers, recrossed the sound without losing a man. On the other hand, Major Carleton, at the head of a thousand men, Europeans, Indians, and loyalists, made a sudden irruption into the northern parts of the state of New York, took the forts Anne and George, and made the garrisons prisoners. At the same time, Sir John Johnston, at the head of a body of a similar description, appeared on the Mohawk. Several smart skirmishes were fought. But both of those parties were obliged to retire, laying waste the country through which they passed.

On the approach of winter both armies went into winter quarters. General Washington stationed the Pennsylvania line near Morristown; the Jersey line, about Pompton, on the confines of New York and New Jersey; the troops of New England, in West Point and its vicinity, on both sides of the North river; and the troops of New York remained at Albany, whither they had been sent to oppose the invasion of Carleton and Johnston.

Toward the close of the year, an agreement for an exchange of prisoners was entered into between General Philips and General Lincoln. The former had been an American prisoner since the convention of Saratoga, and the latter in the power of the British since the surrender of Charleston. Hitherto congress had shown no forwardness to enter into arrangements for a general exchange of prisoners. That body was aware of the great expense of recruiting the British army from Europe; and of the slender accession of strength which, owing to short enlistments, their own military force would derive from a release of prisoners. They considered a general exchange unfavorable to their cause; but many of their regular troops had fallen into the hands of the British, by the capitulation of Charleston, and the defeat of Gates at Camden. The complaints of the prisoners and of their friends were loud; and congress agreed to a general exchange: but the convention troops of Saratoga were detained prisoners till the end of the war.

Let us now return to the southern states. After the battle of Camden, Cornwallis was unable to follow up the victory with his usual activity. His little army was diminished by the sword and by disease. He had not brought with him from Charleston the stores necessary for an immediate pursuit of the enemy; and he did not deem it expedient to leave South Carolina till he had suppressed that spirit of resistance to his authority which had extensively manifested itself in the province. In order to consummate, as he thought, the subjugation of the state, he resorted to measures of great severity. He seemed to forget that many of the inhabitants had been received as prisoners-of-war on parole; that, without their consent, their parole had been discharged; and that, merely by a proclamation, they had been declared British subjects, instead of prisoners-of-war.

In a few days after the battle of Camden, when Cornwallis thought the country was lying prostrate at his feet, he addressed the following letter to the commandant of the British garrison at Ninety-Six: "I have given orders that all the inhabitants of this province who have subscribed, and taken part in the revolt, should be punished with the utmost rigor; and also those who will not turn out, that they may be imprisoned, and their whole property taken from them or destroyed. I have also ordered that compensation should be made out of these estates to the persons who have been injured or oppressed by them. I have ordered, in the most positive manner, that every militiaman who has borne arms with us, and afterward joined the enemy, shall be immediately hanged. I desire you will take the most vigorous measures to punish the rebels in the district you command, and that you obey, in the strictest manner, the directions I have given in this letter relative to the inhabitants of the country." Similar orders were given to the commanders of other posts.

In any circumstances, such orders given to officers, often possessing little knowledge, and as little prudence or humanity, could not fail to produce calamitous effects. In the case under consideration, where all the worst passions of the heart were irritated and inflamed, the consequences were lamentable. The orders were executed in the spirit in which they were given. Numbers of persons were put to death: many were imprisoned, and their property was destroyed or confiscated. The country was covered with blood and desolation, rancor and grief. Women and children were turned out of doors, and often slaughtered, and their houses and substance consumed.

The prisoners on parole thought they had a clear right to take arms; for from their parole they had been released by the proclamation of the 20th of June, which, indeed, called them to the duty of subjects, a condition to which they had never consented; and therefore they reckoned that they had as good a right to resume their arms as the British commander had to enjoin their allegiance. The case of those who had taken British protections, in the full persuasion that they were to be allowed to live peaceably on their estates, but who, on finding that they must fight on one side or other, had repaired to the standards of their country, was equally hard. Deception and violence were practised against both. So long as the struggle appeared doubtful, the colonists met with fair promises and kind treatment; but at the moment when resistance seemed hopeless, and obedience necessary, they were addressed in the tone of authority, heard stern commands and bloody threatenings, and received harsh usage. Hence the province, which for some time presented the stillness of peace, again put on the ruthless aspect of war.

A number of persons of much respectability remained prisoners-of-war in Charleston, since the capitulation of that town; but, after the battle of Camden, Cornwallis ordered them to be carried out of the province. Accordingly, early in the morning of the 27th of August, some of the principal citizens of Charleston were taken out of bed, put on board a guard-ship, and soon afterward transported to St. Augustine. They remonstrated with Lieutenant-Colonel Balfour, the commandant of Charleston, but experienced only the insolence of authority from that officer.

While Cornwallis endeavored, by severe measures, to break the spirits of the people, and to establish the royal authority in South Carolina, he did not lose sight of his ulterior projects. He sent emissaries into North Carolina to excite the loyalists there, and to assure them of the speedy march of the British army into that province. On the 8th of September he left Camden, and toward the end of the month arrived at Charlotte town, in North Carolina; of which place he took possession after a slight resistance from some volunteer cavalry under Colonel Davie. Though symptoms of opposition manifested themselves at Charlotte, yet he advanced toward Salisbury, and ordered his militia to cross the Yadkin. But Cornwallis was suddenly arrested in his victorious career by an unexpected disaster. He made every exertion to imbody the well-affected inhabitants of the country, and to form them into a British militia. For that purpose he employed Major Ferguson, of the 71st regiment, an officer of much merit, with a small detachment, in the district of Ninety-Six, to train the loyalists, and to attach them to his own party. From the operations of that officer he expected the most important services.

Ferguson executed his commission with activity and zeal; collected a large number of loyalists, and committed great depredations on the friends of independence in the back settlements. When about to return to the main army in triumph, he was detained by one of those incidents which occasionally occur in war, and influence the course of events and the destiny of nations. A Colonel Clarke of Georgia, who had fled from that province on its reduction by Campbell in 1779, had retired to the northward; and, having collected a number of followers in the Carolinas, he returned to his native province, at the head of about 700 men; and, while Cornwallis was marching from Camden to Charlotte town, attacked the British post at Augusta. Lieutenant-Colonel Brown, who commanded at that place with a garrison of about 150 provincials, aided by some friendly Indians, finding the town untenable, retired toward an eminence on the banks of the Savannah, named Garden Hill. But the enemy occupied it before his arrival: by bringing his artillery, however, to bear upon them, after a desperate conflict, he succeeded in dislodging them and in gaining possession of the hill, but with the loss of his cannon. There Clarke besieged him, till informed of the near approach of a British detachment from Ninety-Six, under Colonel Cruger. He then retreated, abandoning the cannon which he had taken; and, though pursued, effected his escape. Notice was instantly sent to Ferguson of Clarke's retreat, and of his route; and high hopes of intercepting him were entertained. For that purpose Ferguson remained longer in those parts, and approached nearer the mountains, than he would otherwise have done. As he had collected about 1,500 men, he had no apprehension of any force assembling in that quarter able to embarrass him.

Meanwhile the depredations committed by Ferguson exasperated many of the inhabitants of the country, some of whom, fleeing across the Allegany mountains, gave their western brethren an alarming account of the evils with which they were threatened. Those men, living in the full enjoyment of that independence for which the Atlantic states were struggling, resolved to keep the war at a distance from their settlements. The hardy mountaineers of the western parts of Virginia and North Carolina assembled under Colonels Campbell, Shelby, Cleveland, and Sevier. Other parties, under their several leaders, hastened to join them. They were all mounted, and unencumbered with baggage. Each man had his blanket, knapsack, and rifle; and set out in quest of Ferguson, equipped in the same manner as when they hunted the wild beasts of the forest. At night the earth afforded them a bed, and the heavens a covering; the flowing

Fig. 148.—Flying from Persecution.

stream quenched their thirst; their guns, their knapsacks, or a few cattle driven in their rear, supplied them with food. Their numbers made them formidable, and the rapidity of their movements rendered it difficult to escape them. They amounted to nearly 3,000 men.

On hearing of their approach, Ferguson began to retreat toward Charlotte, and sent messengers to Cornwallis to apprize him of his danger. But the messengers were intercepted; and the earl remained ignorant of the perilous situation of his detachment. In the vicinity of Gilbert town, the Americans, apprehensive of Ferguson's escape, selected 1,000 of their best riflemen, mounted them on their fleetest horses, and sent them in pursuit. Their rapid movements rendered his retreat impracticable; and Ferguson, sensible that he would inevitably be overtaken, chose his ground on King's mountain, on the confines of North and South Carolina, and waited the attack.

On the 7th of October the Americans came up with him. Campbell had the command; but his authority was merely nominal, for there was little military order or subordination in the attack. They agreed to divide their forces, in order to assail Ferguson from different quarters; and the divisions were led on by Colonels Cleveland, Shelby, Sevier, and Williams. Cleveland, who conducted the party which began the attack, addressed his men as follows:—

"My brave fellows! we have beaten the tories, and we can beat them. When engaged, you are not to wait for the word of command from me. I will show you by my example how to fight; I can undertake no more. Every man must consider himself an officer, and act on his own judgment. Though repulsed, do not run off; return, and renew the combat. If any of you are afraid, you have not only leave to withdraw, but are requested to do so."

Cleveland instantly began the attack; but was soon compelled to retire before the bayonet. But Ferguson had no time to continue the pursuit: for Shelby came forward from an unexpected quarter, and poured in a destructive fire. Ferguson again resorted to the bayonet, and was again successful. But at that moment, Campbell's division advanced on another side, and a new battle began. Campbell, like his comrades, was obliged to retreat. But Cleveland had now rallied his division, and advanced anew to the combat. The royalists wheeled, and met this returning assailant. In this way there was an unremitting succession of attacks for about fifty minutes. Ferguson obstinately defended himself, and repulsed every assailant; but at last he fell mortally wounded; and the second in command, seeing the contest hopeless, surrendered. Ferguson and 150 of his men lay dead on the field; as many were wounded; nearly 700 laid down their arms; and upward of 400 escaped. Among the prisoners the number of regular British soldiers did not amount to 100. The Americans lost about twenty men, who were killed on the field, and they had many wounded. They took 1,500 stand of arms. Major Ferguson's position was good; but the hill abounded with wood, and afforded the Americans, who were all riflemen, an opportunity of fighting in their own way, and of firing from behind trees.

The Americans hanged ten of their prisoners on the spot, pleading the guilt of the individuals who suffered, and the example of the British, who had executed a greater number of Americans. Those rude warriors, whose enterprise was the spontaneous impulse of their patriotism or revenge, who acknowledged no superior authority, and who were guided by no superior counsels, having achieved their victory and attained their object, dispersed and returned home Most of the prisoners were soon after released.

The ruin of Ferguson's detachment, from which so much had been expected, was a severe blow to Cornwallis: it disconcerted his plans, and prevented his progress northward. On the 14th of October, as soon after obtaining certain information of the fall of Major Ferguson as the army could be put in motion, he

FIG. 149.—Death of Ferguson.

left Charlotte, where Ferguson was to have met him, and began his retreat toward South Carolina. In that retrograde movement the army suffered severely; for several days it rained incessantly; the roads were almost impassable; the soldiers had no tents, and at night encamped in the woods in an unhealthy climate. The army was ill supplied with provisions: sometimes the men had beef, but no bread; at other times bread, but no beef. Once they subsisted during five days on Indian corn collected as it stood in the fields. Five ears were the daily allowance of two men; and it seemed as if the hand of Providence was about to requite them for the murderous barbarities they had inflicted on inoffensive women and children.

In these trying circumstances, the American loyalists who had joined the royal standard were of great service; but their services were ill requited, and several of them, disgusted by the abusive language, and even blows, which they received from some of the officers, left the army for ever. At length the troops passed the Catawba, and on the 29th of October reached Wynnesborough, an intermediate station between Camden and Ninety Six.

During those movements of the British army, the Americans were not idle. Defeated, but not subdued, they were active in preparing to renew the struggle. After the defeat and dispersion of his army at Camden, General Gates fled to Charlotte, eighty miles from the field of battle. There he halted, to collect the straggling fugitives, and to endeavor, from the wreck of his discomfited army, to form a force with which he might check or impede the advancing foe. He was soon joined by Generals Smallwood and Gist, and about 150 dispirited officers and soldiers. Most of the militia who escaped returned home; and General Caswell was ordered to assemble those of the neighboring counties. Major Anderson, of the third Maryland regiment, who had collected a number of fugitives not far from the field of battle, proceeded toward Charlotte by easy marches in order to give stragglers time to join him. But as Charlotte was utterly inde fensible, and as no barrier lay between it and the enemy, General Gates retreated to Salisbury, and sent Colonel Williams, accompanied by another officer, on the road leading to Camden, to gain information of the movements of Cornwallis, and to direct such stragglers as he met to hasten to Salisbury. From Salisbury General Gates proceeded to Hillsborough, where he intended to assemble an army with which he might contend for the southern provinces.

At Hillsborough every exertion was made to collect and organize a military force; and ere long General Gates was again at the head of 1,400 men. Even before the royal army entered North Carolina, that state had called out the second division of its militia, under Generals Davidson and Sumner; and they were joined by the volunteer cavalry under Colonel Davie.

When Cornwallis entered Charlotte, General Gates ordered General Smallwood to take post at the fords of the Yadkin, in order to dispute the passage of the river; and Morgan, who had often distinguished himself by his courage and activity, and who had joined the southern army with the rank of brigadier-general, was employed with a light corps to harass the enemy.

When Cornwallis retreated, General Gates advanced to Charlotte; he stationed General Smallwood farther down the Catawba on the road to Camden, and ordered General Morgan to some distance in his front. Such was the position of the troops when General Gates was superseded in the command of the southern army.

On the 5th of October, congress passed a resolution, requiring the commander-in-chief to order a court of inquiry into the conduct of Major-General Gates, as commander of the southern army; and to appoint another officer to that command till such inquiry should be made. The order of congress to inquire into the conduct of General Gates was dissatisfactory to the best American officers: it was afterward dispensed with, and Gates restored to a command in the army.

Meanwhile, General Washington recommended Major-General Greene to congress, as a person qualified to command the southern army. Nathaniel Greene, a native of Rhode Island, was brought up among the quakers, but was cast out of their society when he joined the army. He was in camp when General Washington took the command before Boston; and, by his activity, intrepidity, and good conduct, gained the confidence of the commander-in-chief in a high degree, who recommended him as an officer in whose ability, fortitude, and integrity, he could trust. Writing on the subject to Mr. Matthews, a delegate of South Carolina, he said: "I think I am giving you a general; but what can a general do without men, without arms, without clothes, without stores, without provisions?" Greene did not discredit the recommendation of his superior, nor disappoint the hopes of his country. In his progress southward, he visited the governors and legislatures of the states through which he passed; but in some parts of the country found the people so hostile, that he was not without apprehensions of personal danger.

On the 2d of December, General Greene arrived at Charlotte, and informed General Gates of his commission. That was the first official notice which General Gates received of his removal from the command of the southern army. Next day Gates resigned the command of the army with becoming dignity and patriotism, and Greene behaved toward him with the most polite attention.

In a few hours after General Greene entered on his command, he received the report of one of Morgan's foraging parties, not far from Camden. The party advanced to the vicinity of the British posts at Clermont, which was viewed by Colonel Washington, who saw that it was too strong to be taken by small arms and cavalry, the only weapons and force present; he therefore had recourse to stratagem. Having made an imposing show of part of his men, and having placed the trunk of a pine-tree in such a situation as, at a distance, to have the appearance of a cannon, he summoned the post to surrender, and it yielded without firing a shot. The militia-Colonel Rugely and 112 men whom he had collected in the place were made prisoners. This event elated General Greene's army, and was considered by them as a good omen of success under their new leader.

General Greene's situation was embarrassing: his army was feeble, consisting, on the 8th of December, of 2,029 infantry, of whom 1,482 were in camp and 547 in detachments; 821 were continentals, and 1,208 were militia. Besides these there were 90 cavalry, 60 artillerymen, and 128 continentals on extra service, constituting in all a force of 2,307 men.

In North Carolina there were many loyalists, and hostilities were carried on between them and their republican neighbors with the most rancorous animosity. They pursued, plundered, and massacred each other with the ruthless fury of beasts of prey; and, even without the presence of contending armies, threatened, by their mutual violence, to render the province a scene of carnage and devastation. The country was thinly inhabited, and abounded in woods and swamps. The cultivated parts were laid waste by hostile factions, and no magazines for the army were provided. The troops were almost naked, and General Greene was obliged to procure subsistence for them day by day: yet, in these circumstances, he was expected instantly to drive the British from the southern provinces. He was sensible that everything depended on public opinion, and felt the difficulty of at once preserving the good will and promoting the interests of the people. He was well aware that by rushing into precipitate measures he might gain their momentary approbation, but would ruin their cause. After maturely considering all circumstances, he resolved to divide his forces and carry on a desultory warfare.

In order to repress some irregularities which had been practised in the army, he was obliged to have recourse to severity, and succeeded in establishing more exact discipline than had been formerly enforced. At a very early period of his command he received a letter from Cornwallis, complaining of the treatment of the prisoners taken at King's mountain, and stating that he had found himself obliged to make some retaliation. General Greene replied that he was too much a stranger to the transaction at King's mountain to reply fully on that point; but alleged that the excesses at that place must have been committed by volunteers independent of the army, and that what had been done there was only in imitation of the example set by Cornwallis himself. He also complained of the transportation of the inhabitants of Charleston to St. Augustine, as a violation of the articles of capitulation.

This epistolary correspondence was soon succeeded by more active operations. General Greene found that he could not long remain at Charlotte, for the country between that place and Camden, having been traversed by the contending armies, was quite exhausted. In order, therefore, to procure subsistence for his troops, as well as to distract and harass the enemy, the American general though full aware of the danger of such a measure, felt himself constrained to divide his little army.

General Morgan had been invested with the command of the light troops by General Gates; and General Greene placed him at the head of one of the divisions of his army, consisting of nearly 400 infantry under Lieutenant-Colonel Howard, 170 Virginia riflemen under Major Triplett, and 80 light dragoons under Lieutenant-Colonel Washington. With this small force Morgan was sent to the south of the Catawba to observe the British at Wynnesborough and Camden, and to shift for himself, but was directed to risk as little as possible. On the 25th of December he took a position toward the western frontier of South Carolina, not far from the confluence of the Pacolet and Broad rivers, and about fifty miles northwest from Wynnesborough. With the other division of his army General Greene left Charlotte on the 20th of the same month; and, on the 29th, arrived at Hick's corner, on the east side of the Pedee, opposite the Cheraw hills, about seventy miles northeast from Wynnesborough, where he remained some time. He marched to that place in the hope of finding more plentiful subsistence for his troops; but his difficulties in that respect were not much diminished, for the country was almost laid waste by the cruel feuds of the hostile factions.

General Morgan did not long remain inactive. On the 27th of December he detached Colonel Washington with his dragoons and 200 militia, who next day marched forty miles, surprised a body of loyalists at Ninety-Six, killed or wounded 150 of them, and took forty prisoners, without sustaining any loss. At that time Morgan was joined by Major M'Dowal with 200 North Carolina, and by Colonel Pickens with 70 South Carolina militia.

The British were assailed not only with the force under Greene and Morgan, but were also obliged to watch other adversaries not less active and enterprising. Sumpter had been defeated by Tarleton on the 18th of August, and his followers dispersed: but that daring and indefatigable partisan did not long remain quiet. He was soon again at the head of a considerable band, and had frequent skirmishes with his adversaries. Always changing his position about Enoree, Broad, and Tiger rivers, he infested the British posts in that quarter. On the 12th of November he was attacked at Broad river by Major Wemyss; but repulsed the party, and made the major prisoner. On the 20th of the same month he was attacked by Colonel Tarleton at Black Stocks near Tiger river: the encounter was sharp and obstinate; Tarleton was repulsed with loss; but Sumpter was wounded in the battle, and, being unfitted for active service, his followers dispersed. Sumpter showed much humanity to his prisoners. Although Major Wemyss had deliberately hanged Mr. Cusack in Cheraw district, and although he had in his pocket a list of several houses burnt by his orders, yet he met with every indulgence. At Black Stocks the wounded were kindly treated by the Americans, who, although irritated by the sanguinary excesses committed on non-combatants by their cruel opponents, were yet too noble and magnanimous to retaliate.

Other partisan chiefs arose, and among them General Marion held a distinguished place. That gentleman had commanded a regiment in Charleston at the time of the siege; but having received a wound which fractured his leg, and being incapable of discharging the active duties of his office, he withdrew from the town. He was created a brigadier-general by Governor Rutledge. On the advance of General Gates, having procured a band of followers, he penetrated to the Santee, harassed the British detachments, and discouraged the loyalists. After the defeat of the Americans at Camden, he rescued a party of continental prisoners who were under a British guard. So ill was he provided with arms, that he was obliged to forge the saws of the sawmills into rude swords for his horsemen; and so scanty was his ammunition, that at times he engaged when he had not three cartridges to each of his party. He secured himself from pursuit in the recesses of the forest, and in deep swamps.

In order to discourage his followers, Major Wemyss burned many houses on the Pedee, Lynch's creek, and Black river, on pretence that their proprietors were followers of Marion: but that severe policy only strengthened the hands of the daring leader; for despair and revenge made these ruined citizens cleave to his standard. He became so troublesome that Tarleton was sent against him, but was unable to bring him to action.

Cornwallis impatiently waited the arrival of reinforcements. After the victory at Camden, when he was flushed with the sanguine hope, not only of over-running North Carolina, but of invading Virginia, General Leslie was detached from New York to the southward with a considerable body of troops, and, according to orders, landed in Virginia, expecting to meet the southern army in that state. On finding himself unable to accomplish his lofty schemes, and obliged to fall back into South Carolina, Cornwallis ordered General Leslie to reimbark and sail for Charleston. He arrived there on the 13th of December, and on the 19th began his march with 1,500 men to join Cornwallis, who resolved to begin offensive operations immediately on the arrival of his reinforcements; but, in the meantime, alarmed by the movements of Morgan for the safety of the British post at Ninety-Six, he detached Lieutenant-Colonel Tarleton with the light and legion infantry, the fusileers or 7th regiment, the first battalion of the 71st regiment, 350 cavalry, two field-pieces, and an adequate number of the royal artillery, in all about 1,100 men, with orders to strike a blow at Morgan, and drive him out of the province. As Tarleton's force was known to be superior to that under Morgan, no doubt whatever was entertained of the precipitate flight or total discomfiture of the Americans.

Meanwhile Cornwallis left Wynnesborough, and proceeded toward the northwest, between the Broad and Catawba rivers. General Leslie, who had halted at Camden, in order to conceal from the Americans as long as possible the road which the British army was to take, was now ordered to advance up the Catawba and join the main body on its march. By this route Cornwallis hoped to intercept Morgan if he should escape Tarleton, or perhaps to get between General Greene and Virginia, and compel him to fight before the arrival of his expected reinforcements. The British generals, encumbered with baggage and military stores, marching through bad roads, and a country intersected by rivulets which were often swollen by the rains, advanced but slowly. Colonel Tarleton, however, with his light troops, proceeded with great celerity, and overtook Morgan, probably sooner than was expected.

On the 14th of January, 1781, General Morgan was informed of the movements of the British army, and got notice of the march of Tarleton and of the force under his command. Sensible of his danger, he began to retreat, and crossed the Pacolet, the passage of which he was inclined to dispute; but, on being told that Tarleton had forded the river six miles above him, he made a precipitate retreat; and at ten at night, on the 16th of January, the British took possession of the ground which the Americans had left a few hours before.

Although his troops were much fatigued by several days' hard marching through a difficult country, yet, determined that the enemy should not escape, Tarleton resumed the pursuit at three next morning, leaving his baggage behind under a guard, with orders not to move till break of day. Morgan, though retreating, was not inclined to flee. By great exertions he might have crossed Broad river, or reached a hilly tract of country before he could have been overtaken. He was inferior to Tarleton in the number of his troops, but more so in their quality; as a considerable part of his force consisted of militia, and the British cavalry were three times more numerous than the American. But Morgan, who had great confidence both in himself and in his men, was apprehensive of being overtaken before he could pass Broad river, and he chose rather to fight voluntarily than to be forced to a battle. Therefore, having been joined by some militia under Colonel Pickens, he halted at a place called the Cow-Pens, about three miles from the line of separation between North and South Carolina. Before daylight, on the morning of the 17th of January, he was informed of the near approach of Colonel Tarleton, and instantly prepared to receive him.

The ground on which General Morgan halted had no great advantages; but his dispositions were judicious. On rising ground, in an open wood, he drew up his continental troops and Triplett's corps, amounting together to nearly 500 men, under Lieutenant-Colonel Howard. Colonel Washington, with his cavalry was posted in their rear, behind the eminence, ready to act as occasion might require. At a small distance, in front of his continentals, was a line of militia under Colonel Pickens and Major M'Dowell: and 150 yards in front of Pickens was stationed a battalion of North Carolina and Georgia volunteers under Major Cunningham, with orders to give one discharge on the approaching enemy, and then to retreat and join the militia. Pickens was directed, when he could no longer keep his ground, to fall back, with a retreating fire, and form on the right of the continentals.

Scarcely were those dispositions made when the British van appeared. Colonel Tarleton, who had been informed by two prisoners of Morgan's position and strength, instantly formed his troops. The light and legion infantry, and the 7th regiment, and a captain with fifty dragoons on each flank, constituted his first line: the first battalion of the 71st regiment and the rest of the cavalry composed the reserve. Formerly Tarleton had succeeded by sudden and impetuous assaults; and, entertaining no doubt of speedy and complete victory on the present occasion, he led on his men to the attack with characteristic ardor, even before his troops were well formed. The British rushed forward impetuously, shouting and firing as they advanced. The American volunteers, after a single discharge, retreated to the militia under Pickens. The British advanced rapidly, and furiously attacked the militia, who soon gave way, and sought shelter in the rear of the continentals. Tarleton eagerly pressed on: but the continentals, undismayed by the retreat of the militia, received him firmly, and an obstinate conflict ensued. Tarleton ordered up his reserve; and the continental line was shaken by the violence of the onset. Morgan ordered his men to retreat to the summit of the eminence, and was instantly obeyed. The British, whose ranks were somewhat thinned, exhausted by the previous march and by the struggle in which they had been engaged, and believing the victory won, pursued in some disorder; but, on reaching the top of the hill, Howard ordered his men to wheel and face the enemy: they instantly obeyed, and met the pursuing foe with a well-directed and deadly fire. This unexpected and destructive volley threw the British into some confusion, which Howard observing, ordered his men to charge them with the bayonet. Their obedience was as prompt as before; and the British line was soon broken. About the same moment, Washington routed the cavalry on the British right, who had pursued the fleeing militia, and were cutting them down on the left and even in the rear of the continentals. Ordering his men not to fire a pistol, Washington charged the British cavalry sword in hand. The conflict was sharp, but not of long duration. The British were driven from the ground with considerable loss, and closely pursued. Howard and Washington pressed the advantage which they had gained: many of the militia rallied, and joined in the battle. In a few minutes after the British had been pursuing the enemy, without a doubt of victory, the fortune of the day entirely changed: their artillery-men were killed, their cannon taken, and the greater part of the infantry compelled to lay down their arms. Tarleton with about forty horse, made a furious charge on Washington's cavalry; but the battle was irrecoverably lost, and he was reluctantly obliged to retreat. Upward of 200 of his cavalry, who had not been engaged, fled through the woods with the utmost precipitation, bearing away with them such of the officers as endeavored to oppose their flight. The only part of the infantry which escaped, was the detachment left to guard the baggage, which they destroyed when informed of the defeat, and, mounting the wagon and spare horses, hastily retreated to the army. The cavalry arrived in camp in two divisions: one in the evening, with the tidings of their disastrous discomfiture, and the other, under Tarleton himself, appeared next morning.

In this battle the British had ten commissioned officers and upward of 100 privates killed. More than 500 were made prisoners, nearly 200 of whom, including 29 commissioned officers, were wounded. Two pieces of artillery, two standards, 800 muskets, 35 baggage-wagons, and about 100 horses, fell into the hands of the Americans, whose loss amounted only to twelve men killed, and sixty wounded. The British force under Tarleton has been commonly estimated at 1,100 men, and the American army, as stated by General Morgan, in his official report to General Greene, written two days after the battle, at only 800.

Formerly Tarleton had been successful by the celerity of his movements, and by the impetuosity of his sudden and unexpected attacks, chiefly on raw troops. But at the Cow-Pens he was opposed to an officer as daring as himself, and who was prepared to receive him at the head of a band of veterans. Seldom has a battle in which the number of combatants was so small produced such important consequences; for the loss of the light infantry not only considerably diminished the force, but also crippled the movements of Cornwallis during the campaign.

Cornwallis was at Turkey creek, twenty-five miles from the Cow-Pens, confident of the success of his detachment, or at least without the slightest apprehension of its defeat. He was between Green and Morgan; and it was a matter of much importance to prevent their junction, and to overthrow the one of them while he could receive no support from the other. For that purpose he had marched up Broad river, and instructed General Leslie to proceed on the banks of the Catawba, in order to keep the Americans in a state of uncertainty concerning the route which he intended to pursue; but the unexpected defeat of his detachment was an occurrence equally mortifying and perplexing, and nothing remained but to endeavor to compensate the disaster by the rapidity of his movements and the decision of his conduct.

He was as near the fords of the Catawba as Morgan; and flattered himself that, elated with victory and encumbered with prisoners and baggage, that officer might yet be overtaken before he could pass those fords. Accordingly, on the 18th of January he formed a junction with General Leslie, and on the 19th began his remarkable pursuit of Morgan. In order the more certainly to accomplish his end, at Ramsour's Mills he destroyed the whole of his superfluous baggage. He set the example by considerably diminishing the quantity of his own, and was readily imitated by his officers, although some of them suffered much less by the measure. He retained no wagons, except those loaded with hospital stores and ammunition, and four empty ones for the accommodation of the sick and wounded. But notwithstanding all his privations and exertions, he ultimately missed his aim; for General Morgan displayed as much prudence and activity after his victory as bravery in gaining it. Fully aware of his danger, he left behind him, under a flag of truce, such of the wounded as could not be moved, with surgeons to attend them; and, scarcely giving his men time to breathe, he sent off his prisoners, under an escort of militia, and followed with his regular troops and cavalry, bringing up the rear in person. He crossed Broad river at the upper fords, hastened to the Catawba, which he reached on the evening of the 28th, and safely passed it with his prisoners and troops next day; his rear having gained the northern bank only about two hours before the van of the British army appeared on the opposite side.

Much rain had fallen on the mountains a short time before, and it rained incessantly during the night. The river rose, and in the morning was impassable. It was two days before the inundation subsided; and, in that interval, Morgan sent off his prisoners toward Charlotteville in Virginia, under an escort of militia; and they were soon beyond the reach of pursuit. The Americans regarded the swelling of the river with pious gratitude, as an interposition of Heaven in their behalf, and looked forward with increased confidence to the day of ultimate success.

General Morgan called for the assistance of the neighboring militia, and prepared to dispute the passage of the river; but, on the 31st of January, while he lay at Sherwood's ford, General Greene unexpectedly appeared in camp, and took on himself the command. Toward the end of December, General Greene, as already mentioned, took a position at Hick's creek, on the east side of the Pedee; and had in camp 1,100 continental and state troops fit for service. On the 12th of January he was joined by Colonel Lee's partisan legion, which arrived from the north, and consisted of 100 well-mounted horsemen, and 120 infantry. This reinforcement was next day despatched on a secret expedition; and, in order to divert the attention of the enemy from the movements of the legion, Major Anderson, with a small detachment, was sent down the Pedee. On the night of the 24th, Lee surprised Georgetown, and killed some of the garrison; but the greater part fled into the fort, which Lee was not in a condition to besiege.

On hearing of Morgan's victory and danger, General Greene's great aim was to effect the junction of his two divisions. Accordingly he called in his detachments; and, leaving the division at Hick's creek, under the command of General Huger and Colonel Otho Holland Williams, and accompanied only by one aid-de-camp and two or three mounted militia-men, he set out to meet Morgan, in the persuasion that on the spot he could better direct the movements of the troops than by any written instructions. On his journey he was informed that Cornwallis was in rapid pursuit of Morgan; he therefore despatched instructions to Huger and Williams to march as fast as possible in order to join Morgan's division at Charlotte or Salisbury, as circumstances might permit. After a ride of 150 miles, Greene arrived in Morgan's camp on the 31st.

On the evening of the 31st of January, the river had subsided, but the fords were all guarded. Cornwallis, however, resolved to attempt the passage; and, in order to perplex the Americans, made a show of intending to cross at different points. Colonel Webster with one division of the army, was sent to Beattie's ford to cannonade the enemy on the opposite bank, and make a feint of attempting to force the passage; but the real attempt was to be made at a private ford near M'Cowan's. For that purpose the division of the army under the immediate orders of Cornwallis, left their ground at one in the morning of the 1st of February, and arrived at the ford toward dawn of day. The fires on the opposite bank showed the British commander that the ford, though a private one, was not neglected. General Davidson, with 300 militia, had been sent on the preceding evening to guard it; and was directed by General Greene to post his men close by the side of the river; he, however, stationed only a small party on the bank, while the rest were encamped at some distance.

Although Cornwallis perceived that he would meet with opposition, yet he determined to force the passage. The river was about 500 yards wide, three feet deep, and the stream rapid. The light infantry of the guards, under Colonel Hall, accompanied by a guide, first entered the ford: they were followed by the grenadiers, who were succeeded by the battalions; the men moving in platoons, in order to support each other against the rapidity of the current. When near the middle of the river, they were challenged by an American sentinel, who, receiving no answer, after challenging thrice, gave the alarm by firing his musket. The party on the bank instantly turned out, and began to fire in the line of the ford. On the first discharge the guide fled, and Colonel Hall, ignorant of the direction of the ford, led his men straight across the river. This carried the column considerably above the termination of the ford, and consequently took them out of the line of the American fire, which, in the darkness of the morning, was kept up in the direction of the ford, and fell diagonally on the rear of the grenadiers. As soon as Davidson perceived the direction of the British column, he led his men to the point where it was about to land. But, before he arrived, the light infantry had overcome all difficulties, and were ascending the bank and forming. While passing the river, in obedience to orders, they reserved their fire, and, on gaining the bank, soon put the militia to flight. Davidson was the last to retreat, and, on mounting his horse to retire, he received a mortal wound.

The defeat of Davidson opened the passage of the river. All the American parties retreated, and on the same day the rest of the British army crossed at Beattie's ford. Tarleton, with the cavalry and the 23d regiment, was sent in pursuit of the militia; and being informed on his march that the neighboring militia were assembling at Tarrant's tavern, about ten miles distant, he hastened with the cavalry to that place. About 500 militia were assembled, and seemed not unprepared to receive him. He attacked them, and soon defeated and dispersed them with considerable slaughter, and the British army received no further trouble from the militia till it passed the Yadkin.

General Greene now retreated and marched so rapidly that he passed the Yadkin at the trading ford on the night between the 2d and 3d of February, partly by fording and partly by means of boats and flats. So closely was he pursued that the British van was often in sight of the American rear; and a sharp conflict happened not far from the ford, between a body of American riflemen and the advanced guard of the British army, when the latter obtained possession of a few wagons. General Greene secured all the boats on the south side: and here it again happened as at the Catawba; the river suddenly rose, by reason of the preceding rains, and the British were unable to pass. This second escape by the swelling of the waters was interpreted by the Americans as a visible interposition of Heaven in their behalf, and inspired them with a lofty enthusiasm in that cause which seemed to be the peculiar care of Omnipotence.

The river being unfordable, and still continuing to rise, all the boats being removed, and the weather appearing unsettled, Cornwallis resolved to march up the south bank of the Yadkin about twenty-five miles up to the shallow fords near its source, which are commonly passable. General Greene, released from the immediate pressure of his pursuers, continued his march northward, and on the 7th of February joined his division under Huger and Williams near Guilford courthouse. Thus Cornwallis missed his first aim, which was, to recover the prisoners, to retaliate the blow which Morgan had given at the Cow-Pens, to prevent the junction of the two divisions of the American army, and to overwhelm one or both of them.

General Greene's army was inferior to the force under Cornwallis; and therefore the British general deemed it important to get between Virginia and General Greene, and to compel him to fight before he was strengthened by his expected reinforcements. Accordingly, although his army was without tents, and, like the Americans, obliged to subsist on what it could hastily procure in a rapid march, he resolved not to abandon the pursuit of the enemy.

General Greene's infantry amounted to 2,000 men, and he had between 200 and 300 cavalry; but his equipments were greatly inferior to those of the British. He believed Cornwallis to have upward of 2,500 men, and he therefore determined to avoid a battle if possible. His aim was to retire into Virginia; that of Cornwallis was to prevent the execution of that movement, and to fight the Americans without delay.

The river Dan, the largest and most southern branch of the Roanoke, separates North Carolina from Virginia: and the British general was informed that the lower fords of that river were impassable in winter; that the ferries were distant from each other; and that no sufficient number of boats or flats could be collected at any one ferry to transport the American army in a convenient time. He reasonably concluded that if he could prevent General Greene from passing the upper fords, he might overtake and overwhelm him before he could cross at the lower ferries.

Dix's ferry, about fifty miles from Guildford courthouse, was in the direct road to Virginia; but the British were as near it as the Americans, and it was impossible to bring up boats from the lower ferries against the rapid current of the river to transport the Americans before the arrival of the British. That route, therefore, was abandoned as impracticable. But there are two other ferries, Boyd's and Irwin's, only four miles distant from each other, considerably farther down the river, and about seventy miles from Guildford courthouse. The Americans were nearest those ferries by about twenty-five miles, the whole distance between the two armies; and consequently, in that direction, they had by so much the start of their pursuing enemies. Besides, all the boats at Dix's and the intermediate ferries could easily be conducted down the stream to Boyd's and Irwin's. An officer, therefore, with a few men, was instantly despatched to perform that service.

In order to cover his retreat, and to check the pursuing enemy, General Greene formed a light corps out of Lee's legion, Howard's infantry, Washington's cavalry, and some Virginia riflemen under Major Campbell, amounting to 700 men, the flower of the southern army. As General Morgan was severely indisposed, the command of these light troops was given to Colonel Otho Holland Williams.

Having refreshed his troops, and made the necessary arrangements, on the morning of the 10th of February, General Greene left Guildford courthouse on his march toward the Dan; and was pursued by Cornwallis, who had been detained by the long circuit which he was obliged to make in order to pass the Yadkin. The retreat and pursuit were equally rapid; but the boldness and activity of the American light troops compelled the British to march compactly and with caution; for on one occasion Colonel Lee charged the advanced cavalry of the British army suddenly and furiously, killed a number, and made some prisoners. General Greene's precautions and preparations for passing the Dan were successful; and on the 14th of February, he crossed that river at Boyd's and Irwin's ferries, with his army, baggage, and stores. Although his light troops had marched forty miles that day, yet the last of them had scarcely reached the northern bank, when the advanced guard of the British army appeared on the other side of the river.

The escape of General Greene into Virginia, without a battle, and without any loss, except a few wagons at the Yadkin, was a severe disappointment to Cornwallis. The pursuit was at an end, and the Americans safe; for the river was deep, all the boats were removed from the south side, and the American army was posted on the opposite bank; General Greene's prudence and activity having accomplished what was deemed impracticable.

In this retreat and pursuit of more than 200 miles, both armies endured excessive fatigue and hardships. Want of tents, bad roads, heavy rains, swollen rivulets, and scarcity of provisions, were privations and sufferings common to each.

The men were often thoroughly wetted, without any means of drying themselves till the moisture was evaporated by the heat of their bodies. The inclement season of the year aggravated their sufferings. But under these trials the British soldiers had great advantages, for they were provided with shoes, and comfortably clothed. But the Americans were in rags, and many of them barefooted: the blood flowing from the gashes in their naked feet marked their line of march. Yet both armies bore all with patient fortitude and without a murmur. The Americans did not lose a single sentinel by desertion.

Cornwallis entirely failed in his attempts against General Greene; but he was consoled by the reflection that he had completely driven the enemy out of North Carolina, and that now there was nothing to hinder the loyal inhabitants from openly espousing his cause and reinforcing his army. By easy marches he fell back to Hillsborough, where, on the 20th of the month, he erected the royal standard, and called on the people to join his army, and assist him in restoring order and constitutional government in the country.

Originally, in North Carolina, the loyalists were more numerous than in any of the other colonies; but unsuccessful insurrections had considerably cooled their zeal and diminished their numbers. Some had left the province, and joined the royal army in South Carolina; and many, rendered cautious by experience, resolved to watch the course of events, and not rashly to expose their lives and fortunes in a doubtful and hazardous cause. Considerable numbers, however, determined to encounter every risk, and made preparations for repairing to the royal standard. But those proceedings were soon checked; for General Greene, aware of the inclinations of many of the people, on the 18th sent Lee's legion across the Dan, into North Carolina, to watch the royal army, counteract the proclamation, and intimidate the loyalists; and, being reinforced by 600 Virginia militia, under General Stevens, on the 21st and 22d of February he repassed the river with his whole army, and advanced toward the British encampment. In order to perplex and harass Cornwallis, and to discourage the loyalists, he sent forward his light troops to hover round the British quarters; while, with his main body, he proceeded slowly, by the route most favorable for forming a junction with some North Carolina and Virginia militia who were returning from a war with the Cherokees. With the force then under his command, he had no intention of hazarding a general action; but he knew that his presence in the province would overawe the loyalists, and encouraged the friends of congress.

Cornwallis was indefatigable in exciting to arms the adherents of royal government. In one day he imbodied seven independent companies; and considerable numbers were assembling in order to join his army. Colonel Tarleton, with part of the legion, was detached over the Haw river, to protect and conduct to camp a body of loyalists who had agreed to meet at O'Neil's plantation. General Pickens and Colonel Lee got notice of Tarleton's movements and design, and concerted measures for attacking him and frustrating his intentions. Lee, with his cavalry, was to fall upon Tarleton; while Pickens, with his militia, was to disperse the loyalists. On the evening of the 25th the loyalists were paraded in a lane leading to O'Neil's house, when Lee entered it with his cavalry. At first he mistook them for Pickens's militia, who, he imagined, had reached the place before him. They were equally in error with respect to him. They mistook his cavalry for Tarleton's. Lee, however, on observing the red rag on their hat, the badge of loyalty, soon became sensible of their real character; but he resolved to pass on toward Tarleton, leaving the tories to Pickens. That officer with his militia soon came up: a firing between him and the loyalists immediately began; and Lee, perceiving that Tarleton, who was within a mile, would be alarmed, and could not now be surprised, instantly wheeled and fell upon the astonished loyalists, who, as he was cutting them down, exclaimed that they were the king's best friends.

On hearing the firing, Tarleton, who was refreshing his men about a mile from the bloody scene, instantly mounted, recrossed the Haw, and hastened to Hillsborough. He met some loyalists on their way to camp, and, mistaking them for provincial militia, put them to the sabre. Thus these unfortunate persons were massacred equally by those whom they came to assist and those whom they meant to oppose. General Greene recrossing the Dan, and the massacre of Colonel Pyle's corps, disconcerted the measures of Cornwallis, and so completely intimidated the loyal inhabitants that few of them afterward repaired to the royal standard.

The country about Hillsborough, having been traversed by both armies, was nearly exhausted; and it was obvious that the royal army could not long remain at that place. Although Cornwallis, in his proclamation, had allowed forty days to the loyal inhabitants to come in, yet, on the 27th of February, only six days after issuing the proclamation, he found it expedient to decamp from Hillsborough. He passed the Haw, a branch of Cape Fear river, and took a position on Allamanee creek, in order to procure provisions for his troops, and to protect the numerous loyal inhabitants residing between the Haw and Deep river.

As Cornwallis retreated, General Greene advanced, passed the northern branch of the Haw, and encamped between Troublesome creek and Ready Fork. He assumed a confident air, although he did not yet feel himself strong enough to hazard a battle; and, in order to avoid a surprise, he changed his ground every night, without disclosing to any person beforehand the new position which he intended to take. In his difficult and critical movement to check an enemy whom he durst not encounter, and to maintain positions favorable to a junction with his expected reinforcements, General Greene was greatly assisted by an active light infanty and a daring body of cavalry, who penetrated the country in every direction, and so overawed the loyalists that Cornwallis found it difficult to procure information on which he could rely.

After several movements the American light troops and some militia took post on the branches of Reedy Fork, while General Greene, with his main body, lay at some distance toward Guilford courthouse. Early in the morning of the 6th of March, Cornwallis, under cover of a thick fog, passed the Allamanee, and marched toward Reedy Fork to beat up the quarters of the light troops, and to bring General Greene to a battle if a favorable opportunity presented itself. A sharp encounter ensued, and some loss was sustained on each side. The Americans retreated, but no important advantage was gained over them. General Greene fell back to the iron-works on Troublesome creek, and Cornwallis returned to his station near the quaker's meetinghouse at the forks of Deep river.

At length General Greene received all the reinforcements which he expected; therefore he again advanced, and took a position near Guilford courthouse, within about ten miles of the British encampment. On the 13th of March his army amounted to 4,261 men, including 180 cavalry, under Colonels Washington and Lee. The continental infantry amounted to 1,490. The rest of the army consisted of the Virginia militia, commanded by General Stevens; and of the North Carolina militia, under Generals Butler and Eaton. Hitherto General Greene had studiously avoided a battle; but having received all his reinforce ments, he now resolved to risk a general engagement. His movements indica ted his intention; and Cornwallis readily embraced the proffered opportunity of a battle. Accordingly, on the evening of the 14th of March, he sent off his baggage under a proper escort to Bell's mills, on Deep river, and early next morning put his army in motion toward Guilford courthouse.

General Greene, who was meditating an attack on the British, had his men prepared for action, when the firing of his advanced parties gave him notice of the approach of the English army. About three miles in front of the American encampment, the van of the royal troops, consisting of the cavalry, the light infantry of the guards, and the yagers, under Colonel Tarleton, fell in with the American advanced guard, consisting of Lee's legion, with some riflemen under Campbell and Lynch. A severe conflict ensued, and was obstinately maintained on both sides till the appearance of the 23d regiment to support Tarleton made Lee hastily retreat. During this skirmish General Greene put his army in order of battle, about a mile from Guildford courthouse. The whole country presented the appearance of a vast wilderness covered with tall trees and a thick underwood, interspersed with a few cleared fields. General Greene drew up his army in three lines on a large hill, surrounded by other woody eminences: his first line, composed entirely of the militia of North Carolina, and amounting to 1,060 men, exclusive of officers, under Generals Butler and Eaton, was advantageously posted on the edge of the wood, behind a strong rail fence, with an extensive open field in front of their centre, through which ran the great road to Salisbury; on it, in the centre of the line, were place two field-pieces. The second line, consisting of the two brigades of Virginia militia, amounting to 1,123 men under Generals Stevens and Lawson, was drawn up in the wood, about 300 yards behind the first, and on both sides of the great road to Salisbury. The third line, posted about 300 yards behind the second, consisted of the Virginia regular troops under General Huger, on the right, and the Maryland brigade under Colonel Williams on the left: this line was drawn up obliquely, with its left diverging from the second line, and partly in open ground. Washington, with his cavalry and some riflemen, formed a corps of observation on the right flank; and Lee's legion, with a body of riflemen under Campbell and Preston, covered the left. The baggage was sent off to the iron-works on Troublesome creek, where the army was ordered to rendezvous in case of defeat.

After the rencounter between Lee and Tarleton, Cornwallis continued his march toward the American army; and as soon as the head of the column appeared in sight, it was met by a cannonade from the two six-pounders stationed on the road. The British returned the fire. Cornwallis instantly made his dispositions for the attack. The 71st regiment, and the regiment of Bosc, led by General Leslie, supported by the first battalion of the guards under Colonel Norton, formed his right wing. The 23d and 33d regiments, commanded by Lieutenant-Colonel Webster, supported by the grenadiers and second battalion of the guards under General O'Hara, formed the left. The light infantry of the guards, and the yagers, with the cavalry, formed a corps of observation; the artillery was in the centre. The British army amounted to upward of 2,000 men.

The dispositions having been made, the line was ordered to advance, and it moved forward. When the British were at the distance of 140 yards, the American first line began to fire; but, although most advantageously posted, many of them, without even firing their loaded muskets or being fired upon, threw down their arms, ran into the woods, and made the best of their way to their respective homes. Few, even of those who remained, gave more than a second discharge; but, on receiving the fire of the British, they fled precipitately, in spite of the efforts of their officers to rally them, and sought refuge behind the second line. The British steadily advanced, but experienced more resistance from the Virginia militia than they had done from those of North Carolina. The Virginians maintained the conflict till Stevens, perceiving their inability any longer to withstand the shock, ordered a retreat. That officer, though wounded, did not leave the field. The British suffered considerably in their conflict with the American second line; but, nevertheless, they advanced steadily against the continentals under Huger and Williams. The British line was unavoidably a good deal broken by the different degrees of resistance it had experienced at different points, by impediments arising from the thickness of the woods and the inequalities of the ground, and by being extended to the right and left in order to present a front equal to that of the enemy: the whole, however, moved on, and the second battalion of the guards, under Colonel Stuart, first reached the open ground on which the greater part of the continentals were drawn up; and, impatient to signalize themselves, impetuously rushed on the second Maryland regiment, which, instead of firmly meeting the charge, fled in confusion. The guards eagerly pursued them, and took two six-pounders which had been abandoned; but they were arrested in their progress by a destructive fire from the first Maryland regiment, which threw them into some confusion: at that critical moment Washington's cavalry made a furious charge upon them, and were followed by the first Maryland regiment with fixed bayonets. The guards were completely broken, with much slaughter, and the two field-pieces were retaken; but, the British advancing both on the right and left, the Americans in their turn were compelled to retreat, and the two six-pounders were again retaken. These two field-pieces had been lost by the British at Saratoga; they were recovered by Cornwallis at the battle of Camden, were retaken by Morgan at the Cow-Pens, and after changing masters several times on the field of Guildford courthouse, ultimately on that day remained in possession of the British. After a hard-fought battle of nearly two hours, the royal army prevailed; and General Greene was obliged with reluctance to direct a retreat, which was performed with regularity and good order.

After the engagement had ceased on the left and centre of the British line, a firing was still heard on the right, where General Leslie commanded; it was occasioned by some riflemen, who, availing themselves of the woody nature of the ground, kept up a distant and irregular discharge. Tarleton was sent to disperse them, which he accomplished, after receiving a slight wound. The 23d and 71st regiments were sent in pursuit; but, when the British general was fully informed of the circumstances of the day, and of the severe loss which he had sustained, he recalled them. General Greene continued his retreat to Reedy Fork, three miles from the field of battle. After passing the stream he drew up his men, and halted for some time to collect the stragglers, and then retired to Speedwell's iron-works on Troublesome creek, ten miles from Guildford courthouse, which was the appointed place of assembling the army in case of discomfiture.

This was one of the severest battles in the course of the war. In every engagement where General Greene commanded, many of the Americans fought obstinately, and in this action, the Virginia militia fought bravely; and Stevens's brigade did not retreat till that officer, who had received a ball in his thigh, seeing his men about to be charged with the bayonet, and sensible that they could not stand such a mode of attack, both from their state of discipline and their want of that weapon, ordered a retreat. A considerable number of the continentals were new levies; and although much inferior to veteran troops, yet in general they displayed a good deal of firmness, and part of the American army manifested much bravery. General Greene lost four field-pieces, which were the whole of his artillery, and two wagons. About 300 of the continentals, and 100 of the Virginia militia, were killed or wounded. Among the former was Major Anderson of the Maryland line, much lamented by his countrymen; among the latter was General Huger, besides General Stevens. Of the North Carolina militia six were killed and three wounded, and 552 were missing. Of the Virginia militia 294 were missing. Few of the missing were made prisoners; they returned home, and never rejoined the army; so that General Greene sustained a great diminution of numbers.

The British lost several valuable officers, and more than a third of the troops engaged in the battle fell. According to the official returns, the loss of the British amounted to 532, of whom 93 were killed on the field, 413 were wounded, and 26 were missing.

After the battle, the field presented an afflicting spectacle: it was strewed, to a considerable extent, with the dead and wounded. The victors collected the wounded as soon as, in all the circumstances of the case, they were able ; but could afford them no adequate assistance, for they were without tents, and there were no houses near to shelter the sufferers. Besides, the troops had marched several miles in the morning, had no provisions for themselves on that day, and consequently could give nothing to their bleeding companions. The succeeding night was extremely dark and wet, and the piercing shrieks of the dying falling on the ear amid the deep gloom, and under torrents of rain, penetrated every feeling heart with anguish ; but, though melting with compassion, they were unable to afford even the shadow of relief. Ere morning death rescued many of the miserable sufferers from their pangs.

Cornwallis, however, had gained no permanent advantage. His army, which was weak before, was much diminished. He made every possible exertion, and employed all the means at his disposal to the best advantage. After an obstinate conflict, he had dislodged the enemy from an advantageous position, and driven him from the field ; but his embarrassments were not relieved. So far from being able to follow up his victory and pursue General Greene, he was obliged to fall back, although the motives which led to the battle of Guildford courthouse were little weakened. The British army was so much diminished, and the difficulty of finding subsistence in that part of the country was so great, that on the third day after the battle he began a retreat, leaving a number of the wounded, who could not properly be removed, at the quaker's meetinghouse, under the protection of a flag of truce. The battle of Guildford courthouse may be considered as the first step in a series of movements which terminated in the overthrow of the British power in America.

CHAPTER XII.

Instead of returning to South Carolina, Cornwallis retired to Cross creek, on a branch of Cape Fear river, where there was a friendly settlement of Scottish highlanders, and afterward to Wilmington, about 100 miles lower on the same river. Before his departure from Wynnesborough in pursuit of Morgan and Greene, Cornwallis had directed Colonel Balfour, the commandant of Charleston, to send a sufficient force by sea, to take possession of Wilmington in North Carolina, situated near the mouth of Cape Fear river. Balfour intrusted the execution of this enterprise to Major Craig, who, about the end of January, entered the place after a slight resistance. He carefully fortified himself, and made his post respectable.

For the convenience of his sick and wounded, and for procuring subsistence to his army, Cornwallis by easy marches proceeded toward Cross creek, in the hope that there the troops would be plentifully supplied, and the sick and wounded receive that comfortable accommodation and those refreshments of which they stood greatly in need. He arrived at Cross creek about the beginning of April, where he had to encounter new disappointments. Forage for four days could not be procured within twenty miles ; and the communication by water with Wilmington was found impracticable ; for the river is narrow, the banks in many places are high, and the inhabitants of a considerable part of the intervening country were extremely hostile. In all these circumstances, Cornwallis was obliged to proceed toward Wilmington, the vicinity of which place he reached on the 7th of April. There, for a while, we shall leave him, and attend to the operations of General Greene.

When General Greene took his position at the iron-works on Troublesome creek, after the battle of Guildford courthouse, he expected that Cornwallis would follow up his advantage, and attack him without delay. He therefore prepared again to fight. His army, indeed, was much diminished; but he had lost more in numbers than in effective strength. The militia, many of whom had returned home, had shown themselves very inefficient in the field. As soon as he received certain information that, instead of pursuing, Cornwallis was retreating, he resolved to follow him, and advanced accordingly. On arriving at the quakers' meetinghouse, he found the wounded British and American officers and soldiers who had been left behind; but he had no means of making any adequate provision for them. In that distressing case, General Greene addressed a letter to the quakers in the vicinity, in which he told them that he had been brought up in their persuasion, and that now they had an opportunity of exercising their humanity, without distinction of parties, both to the wounded British and Americans, who without their friendly aid must perish. His appeal was not disregarded; for the quakers immediately furnished the requisite supplies for the hospital.

General Greene, who was now in his turn the pursuer, followed Cornwallis so closely, that skirmishes occasionally happened between his advanced parties and the rear-guard of the British army: but no conflict of importance ensued. On the morning of the 28th of March he arrived at Ramsay's mills, on Deep river, a strong post, which the British had evacuated a few hours before, crossing the river by a bridge erected for the purpose. There General Greene paused, and meditated on his future movements. His army had for some time past suffered much from heavy rains, deep roads, and scarcity of provisions. On reaching Ramsay's mills, his men were starving with hunger. The troops were much exhausted, and stood in need of repose and refreshment. Besides, in that critical state of the campaign, he found himself reduced to a handful of continentals. Most of the North Carolina militia had left the army. The Virginia militia had been called out for six weeks only; that period was nearly expired and the place of those who were about to return home was not yet filled up by those who were to succeed them. Small as his army was, he found great difficulty in procuring subsistence for it.

Cornwallis had fairly the start of the Americans, and was advancing to a place where he would find more plentiful supplies, and easily communicate with the sea; so that General Greene was sensible that with the force then under his command he could make no impression on him. He resolved, therefore, instead of following his opponent, to proceed to South Carolina. That step, he thought, would oblige Cornwallis either to follow him or to abandon his posts in the upper parts of the southern states. If he followed him, North Carolina would be relieved, and enabled to raise its quota of men for the continental service; but if he remained in that state, or proceeded to the northward, it was likely that the greater part of the British posts in South Carolina and Georgia would be reduced, and that those states would be restored to the Union. But he entertained little apprehension of Cornwallis being able, with the force then under his command, to make any permanent impression on the powerful state of Virginia.

On the departure of the militia, General Greene's army was reduced to the regular troops of Virginia, Maryland, and Delaware, amounting to about 1,700 men, including cavalry and artillery; and the British army, under the immediate command of Cornwallis, was still less numerous, not exceeding 1,500 men. So small was the force with which Great Britain and the United States were eagerly contending for an extensive and valuable tract of country.

Having refreshed his troops, and collected provisions for a few days, General Greene moved from Ramsay's mills, on Deep river, on the 5th of April, toward Camden; and on the morning of the 20th of the same month encamped at Log town, in sight of the British works at that place.

Cornwallis had not been without apprehensions of General Greene's proceeding to South Carolina, and had despatched several messengers to Lord Rawdon, who commanded at Camden, to prepare him for such an event; but not one of these messengers reached the place of his destination. Soon after his arrival at Wilmington, Cornwallis received certain information that General Greene had actually made the apprehended movement; and it threw him into much perplexity. He was alarmed for the safety of Rawdon; but, though desirous of assisting him, he was convinced that the Americans were already so far advanced that it was impossible for him to arrive at Camden in time to succor Rawdon, if he should need succor. His lordship's fate and that of his garrison would probably be decided long before he could reach them; and if General Greene should be successful at Camden, he, by attempting to relieve it, might be hemmed in between the great rivers, and exposed to the most imminent hazard. On the other hand, if Rawdon should defeat General Greene, there would be no need of his assistance. A movement so perilous in the execution, and promising so little in the result, was abandoned, and Rawdon left to his own resources. An uncommonly active campaign was now about to open in South Carolina and Georgia. The importance of the prize, the talents of the generals, the courage and sufferings of the soldiers, and the accumulated miseries of the inhabitants, all contributed to give the struggle for those states a degree of interest seldom felt in military transactions in which such small armies are engaged.

Fig. 150.—Lord Rawdon.

When Cornwallis entered North Carolina, the command of South Carolina and Georgia was committed to Lord Rawdon; and, for the security of the British power in those provinces, a line of posts was continued from Charleston, by the way of Camden and Ninety-Six, to Augusta in Georgia. Camden was the most important point in the line, and there Rawdon had taken post with a garrison of about 900 men. On the day before he left Ramsay's mills, General Greene sent Colonel Lee with his legion to join General Marion, and surprise an intermediate post, which, like other stations of the kind, was but slightly fortified, and garrisoned by a few regulars, and such of the militia of the country as attached themselves to the British interest.

General Marion on the northeast, and General Sumpter on the southwes parts of South Carolina, each at the head of a small party of mounted followers, had maintained a bold but ineffectual warfare; and from their feeble and desultory efforts no serious apprehensions were entertained: but after the arrival of General Greene in South Carolina, they proved useful auxiliaries and troublesome enemies.

Lee joined Marion; and, on the 15th of April, they unexpectedly presented themselves before Fort Watson, a British post on the Santee. It was an Indian mound, rising 30 or 40 feet above the level of the plain. Neither the garrison nor the assailants had artillery; but in a few days the Americans constructed a work on an unusual plan, which overlooked the fort, and from the top of which the riflemen fired with such unerring aim that not a man of the garrison could show himself without certain destruction. On the 23d, the garrison, consisting of 114 men, capitulated.

General Greene hoped to arrive at Camden before Rawdon got notice of his march; but the inhabitants of the territories through which he passed were disaffected to the revolutionary cause; and he was obliged to forage with the same precautions as if he had been in an enemy's country; consequently his progress was slower than he had expected; Rawdon had received early information of his advance, and was ready to receive him when he appeared before Camden on the 20th of April.

Camden was a village situated on a plain, covered on the south by the Wateree, a river which higher up is called the Catawba; and below, after its confluence with the Congaree from the south, assumes the name of the Santee. On the east of it flowed a rivulet called Pinetree creek; on the north and west sides it was defended by a strong chain of redoubts, six in number, extending from the river to the creek. General Greene, whose force at that time amounted only to about 1,200 men, felt himself unable either to storm or completely to invest the place. He encamped before it to wait for the arrival of the militia whom he expected, and to be in readiness to improve any favorable opportunity that might occur; but he had not been long in that position when he was informed that Colonel Watson was marching up the Santee to join Rawdon. General Greene was sensible that, if that reinforcement arrived safely in Camden, he would be unable to maintain his ground before the place. He resolved to intercept Watson; which could be accomplished only by movements too rapid for the presence of baggage and artillery. In order to rid himself of these incumbrances, he sent them under the care of Colonel Carrington and some North Carolina militia to Lynch's creek, nearly 20 miles north from Camden, and moved his camp to the east of that place on the road to Charleston. But Watson, having been interrupted by Marion and Lee, did not arrive so soon as was expected; and Greene found it difficult to procure provisions for his men in his new position. On the 24th he sent an order to Carrington to join him with the baggage and artillery at Hobkerk's hill, an eminence rather more than a mile north from Camden on the road to the Waxhaws. On the same day he marched his army to that place; where the left of his encampment was covered by a swamp, and the hill, as well as the ground between it and Camden, abounded with trees and underwood.

At that time a drummer deserted from General Greene, and informed Rawdon of the absence of his militia, artillery, and baggage. That officer immediately resolved to seize the favorable opportunity, and to attack the American general while destitute of artillery, and unsupported by the militia, or by Marion and Lee. Accordingly, on the morning of the 25th, at the head of about 900 men, he marched from Camden to attack General Greene's camp; and, by making a circuit, and keeping close to the edge of the swamp, under cover of the woods he gained the left flank of the Americans, where the hill was most accessible, undiscovered. While the Americans were cooking their provisions, and General Greene at breakfast, the alarm was given by the outposts firing on the British van. At that critical moment the militia and the cannon arrived, and General Greene soon had his army in order of battle. The Virginia brigade, under General Huger, was on the right; the Maryland brigade, under Colonel Williams, was on the left; and the artillery in the centre. The North Carolina militia, under Colonel Reade, formed a second line; Captain Kirkwood, with the light infantry, was placed in front, to support the advanced parties, and to retard the progress of the British troops. So confident was General Greene of victory that he ordered Lieutenant-Colonel Washington, with his cavalry, to turn the right flank of the British, and to charge them in the rear.

Meanwhile the American advanced parties and Kirkwood's infantry, after a brisk fire, were driven in; and Rawdon advanced steadily to attack the main body of the American army. The 63d regiment, supported by the volunteers of Ireland, formed his right; the king's American regiment, supported by Captain Robertson's corps, composed his left; the New York volunteers were in the centre. The North Carolina volunteers and cavalry were in the rear, and formed a reserve.

After viewing the British army, and observing the narrow front which it presented, General Greene, sanguine in his hopes of success, ordered the second Maryland regiment to attack its right flank, a part of the Virginia troops to assail its left, and the rest of the Virginia and Maryland continentals to march down the hill and oppose it in front. Thus the British army was to be assailed in front, on both flanks, and in the rear.

Rawdon, perceiving General Greene's intention, quickly extended his front, by bringing the Irish volunteers forward into the line. The firing became very close, and though the American column which descended the hill was supported by a destructive discharge of grape-shot from the artillery, yet that part of the continentals was soon broken by the British troops, and fell back in confusion. Their officers were unable to rally them. The British gained the summit of the hill; and General Greene, surprised and mortified at the sudden and unexpected reverse, and apprehensive of the utter discomfiture and ruin of his army, ordered such of his continentals as were still unbroken, and his militia, who had not been engaged, to retreat. Washington, who had gained the rear of the British army, and made a number of prisoners, seeing the infantry driven from the field, paroled some wounded officers and retired, carrying with him about fifty prisoners, among whom were the royal surgeons.

In the confusion the American cannon were run down the hill, and concealed from the British among some bushes; but, in his retreat, Washington observed and drew them off. The pursuit was continued nearly three miles, but was ultimately checked by a furious charge made by Washington, with a body of cavalry. The retreat from the field was conducted in good order; and the Americans carried off all their baggage, artillery, and some prisoners. They halted for the night at Saunder's creek, four miles from Hobkerk's hill; and next day proceeded to Rugely's mills, twelve miles from Camden. After the engagement the British returned to Camden.

Hobkerk's hill was a hard-fought battle; and, considering the numbers engaged, each party suffered considerable loss. The Americans had nearly 300 men killed, wounded, or missing; and among them were some valuable officers. In killed, wounded, and missing, the loss of the British amounted to 258, out of about 900 who were on the field.

The battle of Hobkerk's hill, like that of Guildford courthouse, was of no permanent advantage to the British. For Rawdon was in no condition to follow up the advantage which he had gained: General Greene retreated no farther than Rugely's mills; and the presence of his army, together with the activity and courage of his followers, fomented the spirit of disaffection to the British authority which had manifested itself in many parts of the southern provinces, and kept Rawdon in a very uneasy and critical situation. Knowing that the British troops could not long remain in Camden without receiving fresh supplies from Charleston or the country, General Greene sent a reinforcement to Marion on the road to Nelson's ferry; and on the 3d of May he passed the Wateree with the remainder of his army, and from time to time took such positions as would most effectually prevent the garrison of Camden from receiving any supplies.

Colonel Watson, as has been already mentioned, was marching with upward of 400 men to reinforce Rawdon. Marion and Lee having obtained information of his route, resolved to obstruct his progress, and took post so judiciously at the fords, that Watson was obliged to alter his course. He marched down the north side of the Santee, crossed it near its mouth, with incredible labor advanced up its southern bank, recrossed it above the encampment of Marion and Lee, but a little below the confluence of its two great branches the Congaree and Wateree, and arrived safely at Camden with his detachment on the 7th of May.

This reinforcement gave Rawdon a decided superiority, and he resolved instantly to avail himself of it. Accordingly, next night he marched against General Greene, with the intention of attacking him in his camp; but that officer, apprized of the reinforcement, and aware that it would immediately be employed against him, left the ground which he had lately occupied, passed the Wateree retired to a greater distance from Camden, and took a strong position behind Saunder's creek. Rawdon followed him, and drove in his outposts; but, after attentively viewing his camp at all points, he was convinced that it could not be forced without a loss which he was in no condition to sustain; therefore he returned to Camden.

Rawdon's situation had now become extremely critical. Marion and Lee were exerting themselves with much activity and success against the chain of British posts, and the communications were every day becoming more difficult. It was necessary to diminish the number of posts, and to confine them within a narrower range. Accordingly, on the 10th of May, the British general burned the jail, mills, some private houses, part of his own stores, evacuated Camden, and retired, by Nelson's ferry, to the south of Santee, leaving behind him about thirty of his own sick and wounded, and as many Americans who had fallen into his hands in the battle of Hobkerk's hill.

After the evacuation of Camden, several of the British posts fell in rapid succession. On the 11th the garrison of Orangeburgh, consisting of seventy militia and twelve regulars, yielded to Sumpter. Marion and Lee, after taking Fort Watson, crossed the Santee and marched against Fort Motte, situated on the south side of the Congaree, a little above its confluence with the Wateree; they invested it on the 8th of May, and carried on their approaches so vigorously, that, after a brave defence, the garrison, consisting of sixty-five men, capitulated on the 12th. Georgetown, a post on the Black river, was reduced by a detachment of Marion's corps; and, on the 15th, Fort Grandby, a post at Friday's ferry, on the south side of the Congaree, thirty miles above Fort Motte, garrisoned by 350 men, chiefly militia, surrendered to Lee.

The presence of General Greene's army, the activity and success of his adherents, and the retreat of Rawdon, made the smothered disaffection of the inhabitants burst into a flame; and the greater part of the province openly revolted from the British authority. In that critical emergency, Rawdon retreated to Monk's corner, a position which enabled him to cover those districts from which

Charleston drew its more immediate supplies. General Greene, having succeeded in reducing so many of the British posts, and in forcing Rawdon to retire to Monk's corner, instead of following his lordship, turned his attention toward the western parts of the province, and to the upper posts in Georgia. He ordered Colonel Pickens to assemble the militia of Ninety-Six; and, on the day after the surrender of Fort Grandby, sent Lee to join him.

On the reduction of Georgia and South Carolina by the British in 1780, many of the most determined friends of congress in the upper parts of those states retreated across the mountains or fled into North Carolina; but the greater number, despairing of the popular cause, submitted to the conquerors, flattering themselves with the hope of being allowed to live in peace and in the secure enjoyment of their property. But when these men, accustomed to live on their lands in a state of rude independence, found themselves treated with overbearing insolence, plundered with unsparing rapacity, and compelled to take up arms against their countrymen, all their former predilections returned, and a spirit of bitter hostility to the royal authority was engendered.

When the British army, leaving only feeble garrisons behind, marched to the northward in the career of victory and conquest, this spirit soon manifested itself. Colonel Clarke with some adherents marched against the British garrison at Augusta. But Lieutenant-Colonel Cruger, who commanded at Ninety-Six, proceeded to the relief of Colonel Brown, the commandant of Augusta. Clarke was obliged to flee, and that premature insurrection was suppressed. Such of Clarke's adherents as fell into the hands of Colonel Brown were treated with the utmost rigor. But the spirit of opposition to the royal authority, though damped, was not extinguished: armed parties, commonly acting without any concert, daily multiplied, and disturbed the peace of the British garrisons. Captain M'Koy, with a few daring adventurers, infested the banks of the Savannah, and took some boats going up the river with supplies to Augusta: he defeated a party sent against him by Colonel Brown; but, though joined by Colonel Harden and his band, he was afterward defeated by Brown, and his followers for a while dispersed.

These desultory encounters were now succeeded by more regular and steady operations. Colonel Clarke, with indefatigable zeal, had again returned to his native province; and a number of militia, under General Pickens, assembled in the vicinity of Augusta. On the fall of Fort Granby, Colonel Lee without delay marched toward Pickens's camp, and in four days effected a junction with him. Their first attempt was against Fort Golphin or Dreadnought, at Silver bluff, on the Carolina side of the river Savannah, which was garrisoned by seventy men: on the 1st of May it surrendered to a detachment of Lee's legion under Captain Rudolph.

Pickens and Lee now turned their united arms against Fort Cornwallis at Augusta: they carried on their approaches against the place with skill and activity; but Colonel Brown made a most obstinate defence. In the course of the siege several batteries were raised which overlooked the fort, and two of them were within thirty yards of the parapet; from these the American riflemen fired with such deadly aim, that every man who showed himself was instantly shot. The garrison almost buried themselves under ground; but their valor was unavailing, and on the 5th of June they, to the number of 300 men, surrendered by capitulation. The Americans had about forty men killed or wounded in the course of the siege.

The British officers at Augusta, by their severities, had rendered themselves singularly obnoxious to the inhabitants of the surrounding country; and after the surrender, Lieutenant-Colonel Grierson was shot dead by an unknown marksman, who escaped detection, although 100 guineas of reward were offered for the discovery of the murderer. It was with difficulty that Colonel Brown was saved from a similar fate: he had lately hanged thirteen American prisoners, and delivered up some to the Indians, who put them to death with all those tortures which Indian ingenuity has devised, and which savage ferocity only can inflict. To save him from the vengeance of the enraged colonists, his conquerors escorted him safely to Savannah. At Silver Bluff, Mrs. M'Koy obtained permission to speak with him, and addressed him in the following manner:—"Colonel Brown, in the late day of your prosperity I visited your camp, and on my knees begged the life of my son; but you were deaf to my supplications. You hanged him, though only a beardless youth, before my face. These eyes have seen him scalped by the savages under your immediate command, and for no better reason than because his name was M'Koy. As you are now a prisoner to the leaders of my country, for the present I lay aside all thoughts of revenge; but when you resume your sword, I will go 500 miles to demand satisfaction at the point of it for the murder of my son." If Brown was a man of any sensibility, he must have felt acutely at this singular insult.

While those operations were going on in Georgia, General Greene with his main army marched against the British post at Ninety-Six, in South Carolina. Ninety-Six (so named because it is ninety-six miles from the town of Kecowee in the territory of the Cherokees), at the time when it came into the possession of the British troops in 1780, like other villages on the frontiers of the colonies, was surrounded by a palisade to defend it against any sudden irruption of the Indians. But the British garrison had added some new works, the most important of which was on the right of the village, and, from its form, was called The Star. It consisted of sixteen salient and re-entering angles, with a dry ditch and abatis. On the left of the place was a valley through which flowed a rivulet that supplied the village with water; on the one side the valley was commanded by the prison, which was converted into a blockhouse, and on the other by a stockade fort in which a blockhouse had been erected. The garrison consisted of 550 men, 350 of whom were regulars, commanded by Lieutenant-Colonel Cruger. There were only three pieces of artillery in the place.

When Lord Rawdon found himself under the necessity of evacuating Camden and of retiring to Monk's Corner, he was fully sensible of the danger to which the post of Ninety-Six was exposed. He sent several messengers with instructions to Colonel Cruger to abandon the post, retire to Augusta, unite his force to that of Colonel Brown, and afterward act according to his own discretion. Lest his messengers should be intercepted, he desired Colonel Balfour, commandant of Charleston, to transmit similar instructions. But the disaffection of the province to the British interest had now become so strong, and the roads leading to Ninety-Six were so effectually guarded, that not one of those messengers reached that place: hence Colonel Cruger remained without instructions, and in complete ignorance of the state of the British army in the province. His being left in ignorance he felt as an ominous circumstance: he was well aware of the hostility of the people, and not without apprehensions of a visit from the American army. In these circumstances he made every preparation for defending his post with vigor: officers and men diligently labored on the works, and by their united exertions a bank of earth, parapet high, was thrown up round the town, and strengthened by an abatis; blockhouses were erected, traverses made covered, communications constructed, and the garrison prepared for a vigorous defence.

On the 22d of May, after the works were finished, the American army under General Greene, consisting of nearly 1,000 men, appeared, and encamped in a wood within cannon-shot of the place. In the course of the ensuing night, General Greene erected two works within seventy paces of the fortifications; bu about eleven next forenoon a party, supported by a brisk cannonade from the three pieces of artillery which had been mounted on the Star, and by a close discharge of musketry from the parapet, sallied out, killed such of the Americans as fell in their way, demolished their works, and carried off their intrenching tools. General Greene put his army in motion to support his men in the trenches; but so expeditiously was the enterprise performed, that the sallying party returned within the works with little loss.

On the night of the 23d, General Greene again broke ground, but at the more cautious distance of 400 yards. Though interrupted by frequent sallies, yet the Americans labored so indefatigably that their second parallel was finished by the 3d of June. On that day they summoned the garrison; but, on being answered that Lieutenant-Colonel Cruger would defend his post to the last extremity, they carried on their approaches with unabated vigor. The batteries of the second parallel were opened, and a heavy cross-fire enfiladed several of the works. They pushed on a sap against the Star, and advanced their batteries, one of which, constructed of gabions, was erected within thirty-five yards of the abatis, and raised forty feet high, so as to overlook the works of the garrison. Riflemen, posted on the top of it, did considerable execution; and their fire proved so destructive to the men who worked the artillery on the Star, that the guns were abandoned during the day, and used only in the night.

Augusta, as already mentioned, capitulated on the 5th of June; and while Colonel Brown was sent off under an escort to Savannah, Colonel Lee, with the rest of his prisoners, about 300 in number, proceeded to join General Greene at Ninety-Six. He arrived there on the 8th of June; and, in the hope of making some impression on the garrison by the appearance of the prisoners, marched them in full view of the British works in all the parade of military triumph. Strengthened by this reinforcement, General Greene, who hitherto had carried on his approaches against the Star solely, commenced operations, under the direction of Colonel Lee, against the works on the left of the town also, which commanded the water. The approaches were made with vigor, and the defence conducted with skill and persevering valor. But the siege was carried on in such a manner, that every effort of the besieged must soon have been overpowered, and the garrison compelled to surrender. From this mortification they were saved by the approach of Rawdon. The smallness of the force under his command, and the disaffection of the province, had compelled him for some time to remain near Charleston for the security of that important post; but on the 3d of June he received a seasonable reinforcement from Britain, consisting of the 3d, 19th, and 30th regiments, a detachment from the guards, and a considerable number of recruits, the whole under the command of Lieutenant-Colonel Gould. This accession to his strength enabled him once more to overrun the province.

On the 7th of June, Rawdon left Charleston with part of the reinforcements, and, being joined by the troops at Monk's Corner, marched to the relief of Ninety-Six at the head of about 2,000 men. In their rapid progress over the whole extent of South Carolina, through a wild country, and under the beams of a scorching sun, the sufferings of his troops were severe; but they advanced with celerity to the assistance of their brave companions in arms. On the 11th of June, General Greene received notice of Rawdon's march, and immediately sent orders to Sumpter to assemble his militia, keep in front of the British army. and make every effort to retard its progress. To enable him the more effectually to accomplish this purpose, all the cavalry were detached to his assistance. But Rawdon passed Sumpter a little below the junction of the Saluda and Broad rivers, and that officer was never able to regain his front.

Meanwhile the siege was vigorously pressed, in order to force a capitulation before the arrival of Rawdon: but the courage and obstinacy of the garrison were equal to the activity of the assailants. Sallies were occasionally made, and every attack was met with intrepidity. The garrison was hard pressed, and toward the close of the siege afflicted by want of water; for every person who, during the day, ventured to approach the rivulet, was instantly shot; and the only resource in order to procure a scanty supply was to send naked negroes to the stream during the night, when their bodies could not be distinguished from the trees around them.

On the side of the Star, the besiegers had formed their third parallel, and carried a mine and two trenches within a few feet of the ditch. Having no heavy cannon, they mounted their field-pieces on batteries which overlooked the fort at the distance of only 140 yards; and riflemen were stationed on an elevated place for the protection of the workmen, so that not a man could show himself on the works with impunity. The garrison was nearly reduced to extremities, and in a few days must have been under the necessity of surrendering. But General Greene knew that Rawdon was fast approaching with a superior force, and that, unless he succeeded against the place, he must soon retreat. Unwilling to abandon a prize almost within his grasp, he, on the 18th of June, made a furious assault on the place, and was supported by a heavy cannonade from the batteries, and a close discharge of musketry from the lines. On the left of the village the assailants were successful, and made a lodgement in the works; but on the right, after a desperate conflict of nearly an hour, General Greene found it necessary to call off his men, who retreated before a fierce sally of the besieged. He now sent off his heavy baggage, and next day retreated. On the 20th he crossed the Saluda, and encamped on Little river. During the siege he lost 155 men: the garrison had eighty-five killed or wounded.

On the morning of the 21st, Rawdon arrived at Ninety-Six, and in the evening of the same day set out in pursuit of General Greene; but his indefatigable adversary, having sent off his sick and wounded, retreated before him on the road to Charlotte, in Virginia, dismantling the corn-mills by the way, in order to render the subsistence of his pursuers more difficult. Rawdon advanced to the Enoree, when, despairing of overtaking the Americans, he returned to Ninety-Six. General Greene's retreat ceased with the pursuit. Rawdon found it necessary to evacuate Ninety-Six, and contract his posts; and, after remaining only two days at Ninety-Six, began his march to the Congaree, with 800 infantry and 600 cavalry, expecting to be there joined by a strong reinforcement, which had been ordered from Charleston. That reinforcement had not set out so early as was intended, and the letter informing Rawdon of the delay had been intercepted.

The British commander probably believed that General Greene was driven out of South Carolina; but that officer had only retreated behind Broad river; and no sooner did he hear of the divisions of the British forces, than he returned toward the Congaree. Soon after Rawdon's arrival on the last-named river, one of his foraging parties was surprised by Lee's legion within a mile of the British camp, and about forty cavalry made prisoners. The appearance of the American light troops in that part of the country convinced his lordship that General Greene was not far off. He retreated toward Orangeburgh, where he arrived in safety after some interruption from the American light troops, and where he was joined by the expected reinforcements from Charleston, under Lieutenant-Colonel Stuart. That reinforcement Marion endeavored to interrupt, but failed in his main purpose, and gained only a few wagons.

On the Congaree General Greene was joined by Marion and Sumpter with 1,000 men; and on the 11th of July marched toward Orangeburgh, with the intention of attacking the British army in its camp: but on arriving there next day, found it so strongly posted that he did not venture to make any attempt upon it. While there, General Greene was informed that Ninety-Six was evacuated, and that Lieutenant-Colonel Cruger was on his march to Orangeburgh; but the river, which for thirty miles was passable at no point except that commanded by Rawdon's position, presented an insuperable barrier to any attempt on Cruger. General Greene, therefore retreated over the Congaree, and marched to the high hills of Santee. In order, however, to alarm Rawdon for his lower posts, he, on the 13th, when leaving the vicinity of Orangeburgh, detached Sumpter, Marion, and Lee, toward Monk's Corner and Dorchester. Those officers proceeded by different routes, took a number of wagons with provisions and baggage, and some prisoners; but, after hard fighting, the main body of the British effected their retreat.

The weather now became extremely warm; and in that climate the intense heat of summer as effectually stops military operations as the rigor of winter in higher latitudes. In that interval of inaction, Rawdon availed himself of leave of absence, obtained some time before on account of ill health, and embarked for Europe. On his departure, the command of the troops at Orangeburgh devolved on Lieutenant-Colonel Stuart.

General Greene reached the high hills of Santee on the 16th of July, and remained there till the 22d of August. For six months his army had been incessantly employed in marching and fighting; and though he had gained no victory, and had been repulsed with slaughter from one siege, yet he had not only kept the field, but had compelled the British to abandon all their posts in the interior parts of the country. The activity, prudence, courage, and perseverance, of General Greene had been of incalculable value to the cause in which he was engaged.

After the retreat of General Greene, Colonel Stuart proceeded with the British army to the Congaree, and encamped near its confluence with the Wateree. General Greene, while reposing on the high hills of Santee, was reinforced by a brigade of continental troops from North Carolina, so that his army amounted to 2,500 men. He was still eagerly intent on his purpose of wresting the southern provinces from the hands of the British; and accordingly, on the 22d of August, as soon as the intense heat began to abate, he left the hills of Santee, and proceeded toward Colonel Stuart's encampment. In a straight line, the two armies were only fifteen miles from each other; but two large rivers intervened, which could not be easily passed without a circuit of seventy miles. Colonel Stuart felt himself in security, and his parties spread widely over the country in order to collect provisions. Marion and Washington were detached to check them, and several smart skirmishes ensued.

On leaving the high hills of Santee, General Greene marched up the Wateree to the vicinity of Camden, where he crossed the river, and proceeded to Friday's ferry on the Congaree, where he was joined by General Pickens and his militia, and the state troops of South Carolina, commanded by Colonel Henderson. On, the approach of the American army, Colonel Stuart retired about forty miles, and took a position at Eutaw springs, sixty miles north from Charleston, where he was reinforced by a detachment which had escorted a convoy of provisions to that place. General Greene followed him, by easy marches, in order to give Marion time to join him. On the 7th of September, about seven miles from Eutaw springs, that officer, with his detachment, arrived in camp; and it was resolved to attack the British army next day.

At four in the morning of the 8th of September, the American army advanced toward the British encampment in the following order: the South and North Carolina militia, commanded by Generals Pickens and Marion, formed the first line; the second was composed of continental troops; the North Carolina brigade, under General Sumner, was on the right; that of Virginia, commanded by Lieutenant-Colonel Campbell, was in the centre; and that of Maryland, under Colonel Williams, was on the left. The legion of Lee covered the right flank, and the state troops of South Carolina, under Colonel Henderson, covered the left; Washington's cavalry and Kirkwood's infantry formed the reserve. Two three-pounders were attached to the first line, and two six-pounders to the second. The legion and state troops marched in front, with orders to fall back on the flanks when the British line was formed.

At six in the morning, two deserters from the American army entered the British camp, and informed Colonel Stuart of General Greene's approach; but little credit was given to their report. At that time a British party was out in quest of vegetables, on the road by which the Americans were advancing. About four miles from the camp at Eutaw, that party was attacked by the American van, and driven in with loss. Their return convinced Colonel Stuart of the approach of the Americans, and the British army was soon drawn up obliquely across the road on the height near the Eutaw springs. Major Marjoribanks, with the flank battalion, was on the right of the road, his right being covered by a rivulet, while his left was covered by a high, thick hedge. Two pieces of artillery, supported by a party of infantry, occupied the road; the rest of the British line extended in an oblique direction on the left of the road.

The firing began between two and three miles from the British camp. The British light parties were driven in on their main body; and the first line of the Americans attacked with great impetuosity. The militia displayed an unusual degree of firmness, but were obliged slowly to give way. The North Carolina troops advanced to support them with much intrepidity. Colonels Williams and Campbell were ordered to charge with the bayonet; and part of the British troops, unable to withstand the shock, gave way and fled; but the veterans, who had been inured to hard service, met the advancing bayonet with the same weapon. For a short time the conflicting ranks were intermingled, and the officers fought hand to hand. At that critical moment, Lee, who had turned the left flank of the British, charged them in the rear. They were broken and driven off the field, and their artillery fell into the hands of the Americans, who eagerly pressed on their retreating adversaries.

At that juncture, the British commander ordered Major Sheridan, with a detachment, to take post in a large three-story brick house, which was in the rear of the army on the right, while another occupied an adjoining palisaded garden, and some close shrubbery ground. The Americans made the most desperate efforts to dislodge them from their posts; but every attack was unsuccessful. Four pieces of artillery were brought to bear on the house, but made no impression on its solid walls. A close and destructive fire was kept up from the doors and windows of the house, as well as from the strong adjoining ground. Almost all the artillerymen were killed or wounded; and the cannon had been pushed so near the house that they could not be brought off, but were left behind. Colonel Washington attempted to turn the right flank of the British, and charge them in the rear; but his horse was shot under him, and he was wounded and made prisoner. After every attempt to dislodge the British from their strong position had failed, General Greene drew off his men; and, collecting his wounded, retired with his prisoners to the ground which he had left in the morning, there being no water nearer to refresh his fainting troops.

This obstinate and sanguinary conflict lasted almost four hours. We may estimate each of the armies at between 2,000 and 3,000 men; and, in proportion to the number of combatants, the loss on both sides was great. The Americans lost 555 in killed, wounded, and missing, of whom 137 were left dead on the field; 60 commissioned officers were among the sufferers, of whom 17 were killed on the spot, and four mortally wounded. Among the slain was Lieutenant-Colonel Campbell, of Virginia, whose death was particularly regretted. The British lost 693 men; of whom 85 were killed, 351 wounded, and 257 missing; 3 commissioned officers were killed, 16 wounded, and 10 missing.

Each party claimed the victory: the Americans, because they had driven the British from their first position; and the British, because the Americans had been obliged to retire from the field. In the early part of the battle, General Greene had decidedly the advantage; but the British commander ultimately kept his ground.

The British remained on the field on the night after the battle; but next afternoon destroyed part of their stores, and began to retreat toward Monk's Corner, leaving about seventy of their wounded at Eutaw, who afterward fell into the hands of the Americans. About fourteen miles from the field of battle, Colonel Stuart was met by a reinforcement under Major M'Arthur marching from Charleston to his assistance. Thus strengthened, he proceeded to Monk's Corner.

General Greene marched to his former encampment on the high hills of Santee. Both parties had suffered so much at the battle of Eutaw springs, that neither was in a condition to undertake offensive operations; indeed, the battle of Eutaw was the last engagement of importance in the southern provinces. A number of rencounters happened: but none of them were of much consequence. The British soon retreated to the quarterhouse on Charleston Neck, and confined their operations to the defence of the posts in that vicinity. The interior of the country which had lately been under their dominion, was abandoned, and their chief aim was the security of Charleston, the capital of South Carolina. In the southern provinces the campaign of 1781 was uncommonly active. The exertions and sufferings of the army were great; but the troops were not the only sufferers; the inhabitants were exposed to many calamities. The success of Colonel Campbell at Savannah laid Georgia and the Carolinas open to all the horrors which attend the movements of conflicting armies, and the rage of civil dissensions, for two years.

In those provinces the inhabitants were nearly divided between the British and American interests, and, under the names of *tories* and *whigs*, exercised a savage hostility against each other, threatening the entire depopulation of the country. Besides, each of the contending armies, claiming the provinces as its own, showed no mercy to those who, in the fluctuations of war, abandoned its cause or opposed its pretensions. In the vicinity of Camden, General Greene in one day hanged eight deserters from the American army; and the British officers commanding in South Carolina were by no means slow in similar acts of sanguinary vengeance. Numbers were put to death as deserters and traitors at the different British posts. One of those executions, that of Colonel Haynes, happened at Charleston, on the 4th of August, while Lord Rawdon was in that town preparing to sail for Europe, and threatened to produce the most sanguinary consequences.

Colonel Haynes had served in the American militia during the siege of Charleston; but after the capitulation of that place, and the expulsion of the American army from the province, he was, by several concurring circumstances, constrained, with much reluctance, to subscribe a declaration of allegiance to the British government, being assured that his services against his country would not be required. He was allowed to return to his family; but, in violation of the special condition on which he had signed the declaration, he was soon called on to take up arms against his countrymen, and was at length threatened with close confinement in case of further refusal. Colonel Haynes considered this breach of contract on the part of the British, and their inability to afford him the protection promised in reward of his allegiance, as absolving him from the obligations into which he had entered; and accordingly he returned to the American standard. In the month of July he was taken prisoner, confined in a loathsome dungeon, and, by the arbitrary mandate of Lord Rawdon and Colonel Balfour, without trial, hanged at Charleston. He behaved with much firmness and dignity, and his fate awakened a strong sensation.

General Greene, with his army, was then at the high hills of Santee; and, as a considerable part of the province was wrested from the hands of the British, he was extremely indignant on the occasion, and demanded of the royal commanders their reasons for this execution. He received a letter from Colonel Balfour, acknowledging that it was the result of a joint order from Lord Rawdon and himself, but in obedience to the most express directions of Cornwallis, to put to death those who should be found in arms after having been, at their own request, received as subjects since the capitulation of Charleston and the clear conquest of the province in 1780. The irritation in General Greene's army on the occasion was great; and the officers petitioned him to retaliate the execution of Colonel Haynes. Accordingly, General Greene soon afterward issued a proclamation, threatening to make British officers the objects of retaliatory vengeance.

By the execution of Colonel Haynes the British gained no advantage whatever. It excited a lively sympathy for the sufferer, and indignation against his enemies. If meant as a retaliation for the execution of Major André, it was without dignity. Its justice was questionable; and it received no countenance from sound policy. It seems to have proceeded rather from the petty irritation of disappointed ambition, than from the cool dictates of enlightened justice or political wisdom.

In the end of November, General Greene with a detachment of his army suddenly appeared before the British post at Dorchester; and, after some skirmishing, the British garrison retired to the vicinity of Charleston. General Greene posted his troops on both sides of the river Ashley; completely covered the country from the Cooper to the Edisto; and confined the British to Charleston Neck and the neighboring islands. In Georgia, the British force was concentrated at Savannah. Thus, in the course of the campaign, all the interior parts of those provinces were wrested from the British government, and restored to the American Union. In that service General Greene was greatly assisted by a small, but active, indefatigable, and daring body of cavalry.

During this campaign, an expedition was conducted by General Pickens against the Cherokees, who had been instigated by the British, by promises of rewards for scalps, &c., to take up the hatchet against the Americans. The savages were vanquished, and compelled to sue for peace.

CHAPTER XIII.

Having brought the active campaign of 1781 in the southern states to a close, we shall now return to the northward, glance at the general condition of American affairs in the early part of the year, and then attend to the military operations on the Hudson and in Virginia.

Congress had called for an army of 37,000 men, to be in camp on the 1st of January. The resolution, as usual, was too late; but, even although it had been promulgated in due time, it is not likely that so large a force could have been brought into the field. The deficiencies and delays on the part of the several states exceeded all reasonable anticipation. At no time during this active and interesting campaign did the regular force, drawn from Pennsylvania to Georgia inclusive, amount to 3,000 men. So late as the month of April, the states from New Jersey to New Hampshire inclusive had furnished only 5,000 infantry ; but this force was slowly and gradually increased : till, in the month of May, including cavalry and artillery, which never exceeded 1,000 men, it presented a total of about 7,000, of whom upward of 4,000 might have been relied on in active service. A considerable part of this small force arrived in camp too late to acquire, during the campaign, that discipline which is essential to military success. Inadequate as this army was for asserting the independence of the country, the prospect of being unable to support it was still more alarming. The men were in rags : clothing had long been expected from Europe, but had not yet arrived, and the disappointment was severely felt.

The magazines were ill supplied ; the troops were often almost starving ; and the army ready to be dissolved for want of food. The arsenals were nearly empty. Instead of having the requisites of a well-appointed army, everything was deficient ; and there was little prospect of being better provided, for money was as scarce as food and military stores. Congress had resolved to issue no more bills on the credit of the Union ; and the care of supplying the army was devolved upon the several states, according to a rule established by that body. Even when the states had collected the specified provisions, the quartermaster-general had no funds to pay for the transportation of them to the army, to accomplish which, military impressment was resorted to, in a most offensive degree. Congress was surrounded with difficulties : the several states were callous and dilatory ; and American affairs wore an aspect of debility and decay.

To deepen the general gloom, there were portentous rumors of preparations for savage warfare along the whole extent of the western frontier : and of an invasion on the side of Canada. In the midst of financial difficulties, and apprehensions of attack both from foreign and domestic enemies, a new and alarming danger appeared, in a quarter where it was little expected, and which threatened to consummate the ruin of American independence. The privations and sufferings of the troops had been uncommonly great. To the usual hardships of a military life were added nakedness and hunger, under that rigor of climate which whets the appetite, and renders clothing absolutely necessary. By the depreciation of the paper currency their pay was little more than nominal, and it was many months in arrear.

Besides those evils, which were common to the whole army, the troops of Pennsylvania imagined that they labored under peculiar grievances. Their officers had engaged them for three years, or during the war. On the expiration of three years, the soldiers thought themselves entitled to a discharge : the officers alleged, that they were engaged for the war. The large bounties given to those who were not bound by previous enlistment heightened the discontent of the soldiers, and made them more zealous in asserting what they thought their right. In the first transports of their patriotism they had readily enlisted ; but men will not long willingly submit to immediate and unprofitable hardships, in the prospect of distant and contingent rewards.

The discontents engendered by the causes now mentioned had for some time been increasing ; and, on the 1st of January, 1781, broke out into open and almost universal mutiny of the troops of Pennsylvania. On a signal given, the greater part of the non-commissioned officers and privates paraded under arms, declaring their intention of marching to the seat of congress, to obtain a redress of grievances, or to abandon the service. The officers made every exertion to bring them back to their duty, but in vain : in the attempt a captain was killed, and several other persons wounded. General Wayne interposed ; but, on cock ing his pistols at some of the most audacious of the mutineers, several bayonets were at his breast, the men exclaiming : "We respect you, we love you ; but you are a dead man if you fire ! Do not mistake us : we are not going to the enemy ; on the contrary, were they to come out, you should see us fight under you with as much resolution and alacrity as ever ; but we wish a redress of grievances, and will no longer be amused." Such of the Pennsylvania troops as had at first taken no part in the disturbance were prevailed on to join the mutineers ; and the whole, amounting to 1,300 men, with six field-pieces, marched from Morristown, under temporary officers of their own election. General Washington's headquarters were then at New Windsor, on the North river.

Next day General Wayne and Colonels Butter and Stewart, officers who in a high degree enjoyed the confidence and affection of the troops, followed the mutineers ; but, though civilly received, they could not succeed in adjusting the differences, or in restoring subordination. On the third day the mutineers resumed their march, and in the morning arrived at Princeton. Congress and the Pennsylvania government, as well as General Washington, were much alarmed by this mutiny ; fearing the example might be contagious, and lead to the dissolution of the feeble American army. Therefore a committee of congress, with the governor and some members of the executive council of Pennsylvania, set out from Philadelphia for the purpose of allaying this dangerous commotion.

Sir Henry Clinton, who heard of the mutiny on the morning of the 3d, was equally active in endeavoring to turn it to the advantage of his government. He ordered a large corps to be in readiness to march on a moment's notice ; and sent two American spies by way of Amboy, and two by way of Elizabethtown, as agents from himself to treat with the mutineers. But two of the persons employed were actually spies on himself, and soon disclosed his proposals to the American authorities. The two real spies, on reaching Princeton, were seized by the mutineers, and afterward delivered up to General Wayne, by whom they were tried and executed on the 10th.

At first the mutineers declined leaving Princeton ; but, finding their demands would be substantially complied with, they marched to Trenton on the 9th, and before the 15th the matter was so far settled that the committee of congress left Trenton and returned to Philadelphia. All who had enlisted for three years, or during the war, were to be discharged ; and in cases where the terms of enlistment could not be produced, the oath of the soldier was to be received as evidence on the point. They were to receive immediate certificates for the depreciation on their pay, and their arrears were to be settled as soon as circumstances would admit. On those terms about one half of the Pennsylvania troops obtained their discharge.

The success of the Pennsylvania troops, in exacting from their country by violence what had been denied to the claims of equity, produced a similar spirit of insubordination in another division of the army. On the night of the 20th of January, about 160 of the Jersey brigade, which was quartered at Pompton, complaining of grievances similar to those of the Pennsylvania line, and hoping for equal success, rose in arms, and marched to Chatham, with the view of prevailing on some of their comrades stationed there to join them. Their number was not formidable ; and General Washington, knowing that he might depend on the fidelity of the greater part of his troops, detached General Robert Howe against the mutineers, with orders to force them to unconditional submission, and to execute some of the most turbulent of them on the spot. These orders were promptly obeyed, and two of the ringleaders were put to death.

Sir Henry Clinton, as in the case of the Pennsylvanians, endeavored to take advantage of the mutiny of the Jersey brigade. He sent emissaries to negotiate with them, and detached General Robertson with 3,000 men to Staten Island, to be in readiness to support them, if they should accede to his proposals; but the mutiny was so speedily crushed that his emissaries had no time to act.

These commotions among the soldiers awakened congress to a sense of its danger, and rendered it more attentive in soothing the army than it had hitherto been. It raised about three months' pay in specie; and even that small sum was gratefully received by the troops, who considered it a token that the civil authorities were not entirely regardless of their sufferings or indifferent to their comfort. But, in attempting to escape one danger, congress felt itself exposed to another scarcely less alarming. The means used to sooth the army irritated the people. The troops were scantily supplied; and yet the inhabitants murmured at the contributions levied upon them.

Hitherto the United States had been held together by a very slender bond. The powers of congress were limited; and it was not to be expected that thirteen independent states, each jealous of its liberty, power, and property, would promptly, harmoniously, and vigorously, combine their strength during a protracted, expensive, and bloody struggle. But though every man of discernment was sensible of the propriety of increasing the powers of congress, and consequently of leaving less in the hands of the state legislatures, yet the several states, having once been in possession of power, felt no inclination to relinquish any part of their authority, how incompetent soever they might be to the advantageous exercise of it: thus the concentration of a due degree of power in the hands of congress was a measure which could not be easily accomplished.

The war had continued much longer than the Americans had originally anticipated; and the natural resources of the country were so much exhausted, that it became apparent the war could not be carried on without a foreign loan; and France was the only country to which congress could look for pecuniary aid. Accordingly, Lieutenant-Colonel Laurens was employed on this mission; and, besides endeavoring to negotiate a loan, was instructed to press on the French monarch the advantage of maintaining a naval superiority in the American seas. While the energies of America were thus paralysed by the financial difficulties of congress, the mutinous spirit of part of the army, and the apathy of several of the states, the British interest in the provinces seemed in a prosperous condition. General Greene maintained a doubtful and hazardous struggle against Cornwallis on the northern frontier of North Carolina. A British detachment from New York made a deep impression on Virginia, where the resistance was neither so prompt nor so vigorous as had been expected from the strength of that state and the unanimity of its citizens.

The untoward condition of American affairs could not be concealed from the British ministry, who flattered themselves that they would soon compel General Washington and his feeble army to take refuge in the states of New England, and that they would reduce all the provinces south of the Hudson to submission to the British crown. But exertions on the one side, and reverses on the other, which neither had anticipated, were soon to change the relative state of the contending parties.

The business of the executive had hitherto been conducted by committees of congress. This system was at length superseded by a minister of foreign affairs, a superintendent of finance, a secretary of war, and a secretary of the navy. Such was the tardy progress of congress, that the year was far spent before this improvement could be completed.

From the relative position and strength of the hostile armies on the Hudson, neither could hope to gain any decisive advantage. The force under the American commander-in-chief was entirely inadequate to attack New York; and Sir Henry Clinton had no prospect of being able to force the strong posts of General Washington in the highlands. Neither party could do more than carry on a petty and desultory warfare. Hitherto the Americans had received no direct aid from the French army. Ever since its arrival, the fleet of that nation had been blockaded at Newport; and the land forces remained in a position to co-operate with the fleet for mutual defence.

About the middle of January, the British fleet was overtaken by a storm off the east end of Long Island, and sustained so much loss and damage as to give the French fleet a temporary superiority on the coast. Destouches, the French admiral, was prevailed on to seize that opportunity of sending a small force to the Chesapeake bay to act against Arnold, who was then pillaging Virginia; but that force returned to Newport, without accomplishing anything except taking the Romulus, a fifty-gun ship, on her way from Charleston to Chesapeake bay. General Washington, unwilling to relinquish the attempt against Arnold, repaired to Newport; and, on the 6th of March, had a conference with the French commanders, at which it was agreed that the whole fleet should immediately sail to the Chesapeake, with a detachment of troops on board; but, owing to unforeseen circumstances, it was the evening of the 8th before the fleet left the harbor.

Meanwhile due notice of the expedition was sent to the American officers commanding in Virginia, and instructions to co-operate with their allies. From this enterprise General Washington entertained sanguine expectations of being able to apprehend Arnold; and directed the Marquis de la Fayette to grant him no terms which would save him from the consequences of his crimes. However, the delay in the sailing of the fleet frustrated the design of the American commander-in-chief.

Admiral Arbuthnot, having repaired his damages, pursued, and on the 16th overtook the French fleet, off the capes of Virginia. An indecisive engagement ensued, in which each party claimed the victory; but the object of the French expedition was defeated, and the fleet returned to Newport.

The British began their hostile operations against America in the provinces of New England; but there they met with such a stubborn resistance as soon induced them to abandon that part of the country, and to direct their attacks against more vulnerable points. New York had been less hostile to the parent state; and there they effected a lodgement, with the view of separating the middle from the northern colonies. From that station the war had been carried on with doubtful success. In 1776, an attempt against Charleston was gallantly repulsed; and for some years the southern states enjoyed the reward of the brave defence of Fort Moultrie. In 1780, however, the British arms were more successful in that quarter, and when, toward the close of the campaign, and in the early part of 1781, it was believed that Cornwallis had subdued Georgia and the Carolinas, measures were concerted for invading Virginia also, which had hitherto escaped the scourge of war.

By means of Chesapeake bay and the great rivers which fall into it, that state is particularly open to incursory depredations by a power which has an undisputed naval superiority. Chesapeake bay is a remarkable gulf or inland sea. Its entrance, between Capes Henry and Charles, is twelve miles wide. At first it runs straight into the land, but afterward turns northward, and extends in that direction upward of 150 miles. It is generally about nine fathoms deep, and varies in breadth from five to upward of twenty miles. Its shores are indented with bays and projecting points; and the James, York, Rappahannock, Potomac, and Susquehannah, large and navigable rivers, besides a number of smaller streams, pour their waters into it. The same causes which so much exposed the state to invasion by means of a superior naval force, prevent the speedy concentration of a large body of militia at any one point.

Toward the end of October, 1780, General Leslie entered Chesapeake bay, landed at Portsmouth, and began to fortify himself there with about 3,000 men. But, on experiencing unexpected and increasing difficulties in the Carolinas, Cornwallis directed that officer with his detachment to proceed to Charleston. The invasion of Virginia, however, though interrupted, was not relinquished. Sir Henry Clinton resolved to prosecute the war with vigor in that quarter; and in the end of the year sent the notorious General Arnold, with 1,600 men, to Chesapeake bay. That officer sailed up James' river, and on the 4th of January, 1781, landed at Westover, 140 miles from the capes, and twenty-five below Richmond, the capital of the state, which stands on the north side of the river at the falls or rapids.

Major-General Baron Steuben, who commanded in that part of Virginia,

Fig. 151.—Baron Steuben.

thought the expedition was intended against Petersburgh, situated on the Appomattox, which falls into James river a little above Westover. At that place a considerable quantity of stores had been collected for the use of the southern army; and those stores the baron caused his feeble body of raw troops, scarcely amounting to 300 men, to remove to a place of greater security.

At Westover, Arnold landed with the greater part of his troops, and marched directly toward Richmond. A few regulars who were in that vicinity, and some militia, were ordered to impede his progress; but their weak efforts were ineffectual. Meanwhile, Steuben made every exertion to remove the stores from Richmond, carrying them partly across the river, and partly to West Ham at the head of the rapids.

On the day after landing at Westover, Arnold entered Richmond, with little opposition. There he halted with 500 men, and sent Lieutenant-Colonel Simcoe forward with other 500 to West Ham, where he burned and destroyed a valuable foundry, a boring mill, a powder magazine, and a considerable quantity of military stores. Colonel Simcoe returned to Richmond, where the public property, as well as a large quantity of rum and salt belonging to individuals, were destroyed. After completing the work of destruction at Richmond, Arnold returned to Westover on the 7th; and, after some skirmishing, reimbarked on the 10th, sailed down he river, destroying on his way the stores at Smithfield and Mackay's mills, and on the 20th arrived at Portsmouth, where he manifested an intention of establishing a permanent post. In this expedition Arnold, while he destroyed a large quantity of military stores and other valuable property of different kinds, stated his loss at only seven men killed and twenty-three wounded.

Baron Steuben being in no condition to attack Arnold at Portsmouth, was careful to station his troops at the most convenient passes leading from that place into the country, in order to afford the inhabitants all the protection in his power. It was while Arnold lay at Portsmouth, that General Washington formed the plan of apprehending him, which failed through the backwardness of the French to engage in it.

As Arnold's force was not sufficient to make any deep and permanent impression on the powerful state of Virginia, the British commander-in-chief resolved to increase it; and for that purpose, about the middle of March, sent General Philips with 2,000 chosen men from New York to Chesapeake bay. General Philips arrived at Portsmouth on the 26th; and, being the superior officer, took the command of the army in Virginia.

After employing some time in completing the fortifications of Portsmouth, General Philips began offensive operations, with a force much superior to what congress could oppose to him in that part of the country. On the 18th of April he embarked 2,500 men on board his smaller vessels, and sailed up James river in order to destroy everything that had escaped the ravages of Arnold. He landed at Burrel's ferry, and marched to Williamsburgh, the former seat of government in Virginia. A small body of militia assembled there retreated on his approach, and he entered the place without opposition. He sent parties through all the lower district of that narrow tract of land, which lies between James and York rivers, who destroyed all public stores and property which fell in their way. He then reimbarked, sailed up the river to City point, where he landed on the afternoon of the 24th, and next day marched to Petersburgh, where he destroyed an immense quantity of tobacco and other property, together with the vessels lying in the river.

Baron Steuben was unable to make any effectual resistance to this ruthless work of devastation. The regular troops of the state had been sent to reinforce General Greene, and the militia then in the field did not much exceed 2,000. Even although the whole of that number could have been collected at any one point, yet with that kind of force no enterprise of importance could be undertaken. To have hazarded a battle with the militia against regular troops would only have been to ensure defeat, the loss of arms, and the consequent discouragement of the country. Steuben had the mortification to see the state laid waste, without being able to relieve it; and after some slight skirmishing he retreated toward Richmond.

Arnold was detached to Osborne's, a small village on the south side of James river, fifteen miles below Richmond; while General Philips marched to Chesterfield courthouse, which had been appointed the place of rendezvous for the new levies of Virginia, where he destroyed the barracks and some public stores which had not been removed. About half way between Osborne's and Richmond, a few small armed vessels which had been collected to co-operate with the French against Portsmouth, after a slight resistance, were scuttled and set on fire by their crews, who joined the militia and fled.

On the 30th of April, Generals Philips and Arnold reunited their forces near Osborne's and marched against Manchester, a small town on the south bank of James river, opposite Richmond, where, as usual, they set fire to the warehouses and consumed the tobacco and other property.

At that critical and disastrous period in the history of Virginia, the Marquis de la Fayette arrived from the northward to take the command of the military force in that state. This young nobleman had early espoused the cause of America with all the enthusiasm of an ardent and generous mind, and had manifested such a lively zeal for the interests of the Union as secured to him the entire confidence both of the American commander-in-chief and of congress. When the attempt was meditated against Arnold at Portsmouth, he was appointed to command the troops to be employed in the enterprise; but on the abandonment of the expedition by the naval force of France he returned from Annapolis in Maryland, where he had arrived, and proceeded to the head of Elk river, at which place he received orders to take the command of the troops in Virginia.

When the Marquis de la Fayette marched to the southward on the meditated enterprise against Arnold, the troops which he carried along with him were drawn chiefly from the northern states; and, as it was believed the expedition would be of short duration, they were ill provided for a southern campaign, and had imbibed strong prejudices against the climate. When they understood that the duty would be more permanent than had been at first expected, numbers of them deserted. But, appealing to their honor, the marquis at length succeeded in inspiring his troops with the resolution of braving every danger and enduring every privation in the cause of their country. In order to encourage them, that young nobleman, as careless of fortune as he was ambitious of fame, borrowed money on his own personal credit from the merchants of Baltimore to purchase shoes, linen, and other necessaries, for his detachment; and the ladies of that city, with patriotic zeal, took charge of immediately making the summer clothes of the troops.

The marquis arrived at Richmond with his detachment on the evening before General Philips entered Manchester; and, instead of attempting to pass the river in the face of that officer, the British general marched back to Bermuda Hundreds, a point of land formed by the junction of James river and the Appomattox, destroying much valuable property on his way. Embarking his army, he sailed down the river as far as Hog's island, where the van of his fleet arrived on the 5th day of May.

On the return of the British down the river, the marquis sent small parties to follow them and watch their motions, while he established his headquarters behind the river Chicahominy, at some distance from Richmond. On the 7th of May, General Philips received a letter from Cornwallis, informing him of his lordship's march into Virginia, and mentioning Petersburgh as the place at which he expected to meet the British troops in that province. General Philips immediately returned up the river, landed one division at Brandon, while another proceeded to City point; and on the 9th, those two divisions met at Petersburgh, where their arrival was so unexpected that they took prisoners some of La Fayette's officers, who had been sent to that place for the purpose of collecting boats to convey his troops across the river. Meanwhile General Philips was seized with fever, and was so ill on reaching Petersburgh as to be unable to give orders. The progress of his disease was rapid, and he died four days afterward, when the command of the troops devolved on Arnold.

We formerly left Cornwallis at Wilmington, in North Carolina, on the 7th of April. There he remained eighteen days, in order to refresh his exhausted troops; and having resolved, after much deliberation, to proceed northward, on the 25th of the month he set out on his march into Virginia, a distance of 300 miles. In his progress, he met with little opposition. Colonel Tarleton, with 180 cavalry and 60 mounted infantry, preceded the army, and easily dispersed any bodies of militia that were assembling to interrupt it. On the 20th of May Cornwallis reached Petersburgh, and took the command of the British troops in Virginia. He felt his force decidedly superior to that opposed to him, and exulted in the prospect of success. Undervaluing the talents and resources of the Marquis de la Fayette, his young opponent, he incautiously wrote to Europe, in a letter which was intercepted, "*The boy can not escape me.*"

On being informed that General Philips, in returning up the river, had landed at Brandon on the southern bank, and that Cornwallis was marching northward, the marquis perceived that a junction of their forces was intended; and suspecting that Petersburgh was the appointed place of meeting, he endeavored to anticipate them in the occupation of that town. But the march of General Philips was so rapid that he entered it before him, and frustrated his design. The marquis, with his little army, consisting of 1,000 continentals, 2,000 militia, and 60 dragoons, took a position at Richmond and exerted himself in removing the military stores to places of greater security.

On the 24th of May, Cornwallis left Petersburgh, crossed James river at Westover, thirty miles below La Fayette's encampment, and, being joined by a reinforcement from New York, marched at the head of upward of 4,000 veterans toward Richmond. But the marquis evacuated that town on the 27th, and retired toward the back country; inclining his march toward the north, so that he might easily form a junction with General Wayne, who was hastening to reinforce him with 800 men of the Pennsylvania line. Cornwallis eagerly pursued his retreating foe as far as the upper part of Hanover county; but, finding it impossible to overtake the marquis, or to prevent his junction with General Wayne, he at length altered the course of his march, and turned his attention to more attainable objects.

In his progress he destroyed much public property. That of individuals also was plundered or consumed, under pretext of cutting the sinews of war; so that Virginia, which had long escaped hostile ravages, now experienced its full share of the public calamity. Cornwallis took the horses from the stables of private gentlemen, formed an efficient cavalry, and mounted many of his infantry; so that he could move considerable detachments with uncommon rapidity.

Being thus provided with the means of rapid marches, he planned an expedition against Charlotteville, where the general assembly of Virginia was then sitting, deliberating on the means necessary for the prosecution of the war. The assembly had been sitting at Richmond, but, on the approach of the British army, had retired to Charlotteville, which stands on the bank of the Rivanna, high up the river. At that place there were some military stores; but the British prisoners were removed from it and conducted toward Pennsylvania.

The force under Tarleton, in the expedition against Charlotteville, consisted of 180 cavalry and seventy mounted infantry of the 23d regiment. At first the second battalion of the 71st regiment was ordered to accompany him, but the officers of that regiment presented a memorial to Cornwallis, representing their unwillingness to serve under that officer, who had commanded at the Cow-Pens, where the first battalion of their regiment were made prisoners. They were therefore attached to Simcoe's corps, and the 23d regiment appointed to accompany Tarleton, who on that occasion displayed his usual activity, and advanced so rapidly toward the place of destination, that it was by mere accident that the inhabitants of Charlotteville heard of his approach before he entered the town, and that all the members of the assembly of Virginia were not made prisoners. But Mr. Janiette, a private gentleman, observing Tarleton's march, suspecting his design, mounted a fleet horse, and, by following a short and unfrequented road, reached the town two hours before the British cavalry entered it. The greater part of the legislative assembly escaped and re-assembled at Staunton, beyond the Blue Ridge; only seven of them were made prisoners. Tarleton destroyed all the public stores at Charlotteville; and sent Captain M'Leod, with a troop of horse, to Mr. Jefferson's mansion three miles farther, in order to apprehend that gentleman and some other individuals who were understood to be there, but with instructions to commit no depredations. Mr. Jefferson and his friends made their escape; but M'Leod punctually obeyed his orders; and, after remaining eighteen hours in the house, left it and all it contained uninjured; conduct which was very rare, especially in Virginia.

Colonel Tarleton having executed his commission at Charlotteville, hastened down the Rivanna to co-operate with Colonel Simcoe, who had been sent with a detachment of 500 men, chiefly infantry, in order to surprise Baron Steuben, who was then at Point of Fork, formed by the confluence of the Rivanna and Fluvanna, the two great branches which constitute James river. He had upward of 500 raw troops and a considerable quantity of stores under his protection; and waited for the militia to the south of James river, who had been directed to assemble at Point of Fork.

Colonel Simcoe's progress had not been so rapid as that of Tarleton; but so skilfully had he conducted his march, that though Steuben had heard of Tarleton's expedition against Charlotteville, yet he had received no notice of Simcoe's approach to his own encampment; but, as a measure of precaution, he left Point of Fork and took a position on the south side of the Fluvanna, securing all the boats on the southern bank. Colonel Simcoe's detachment unexpectedly appeared; and the baron, mistaking it for the van of the British army, retreated precipitately during the night, leaving behind him part of the stores, which were next day destroyed by Colonel Simcoe. The baron did not halt till he was thirty miles from Point of Fork.

In Virginia the British had committed fearful devastations, and had destroyed much valuable property; but Cornwallis, though at the head of a superior army, had gained no important advantage over his opponent. He had pushed the Marquis de la Fayette across the Rappahannock, but was unable to prevent his junction with General Wayne, which was accomplished at Rackoon ford on the 7th of June. The marquis immediately repassed the Rappahannock, and advanced toward the British army.

In the course of those movements Cornwallis had got completely between the marquis and the stores of the state, which were deposited at different places, but principally at Albemarle old courthouse high up the Fluvanna, on the south side of the river. Those stores were an object of importance to both armies; and, early in June, the British commander, after having dispensed with the services of Arnold, and allowed him to return to New York, directed his march to Albemarle courthouse. The marquis was anxious to preserve his magazines; and, while the British army was more than a day's march from Albemarle courthouse, by a rapid and unexpected movement he suddenly appeared in its vicinity. The British general easily penetrated his design; and, being between him and his magazines, took a position near the road, so that he could attack him with advantage if he attempted to advance. During the night, however, the marquis discovered and cleared a nearer but long disused road, and passed the British army unobserved; and, in the morning, Cornwallis, with surprise and mortification, saw his adversary strongly posted between him and the stores.

Perceiving that the Americans could not be attacked unless under great disadvantages, and believing their force greater than it really was, Cornwallis abandoned his enterprise and began a retrograde movement, and, in two night marches, fell back upward of fifty miles. On the 17th of June he entered Richmond, but left it on the 20th, and continued his route to Williamsburgh, where the main body of his army arrived on the 25th.

The American army followed him at a cautious distance. On the 19th the marquis was joined by Steuben with his detachment, which increased the American army to 4,000 men; of whom 2,000 were regulars. but only 1,500 were disciplined troops. That of Cornwallis appears to have been somewhat more numerous, and consisted entirely of veterans: it was also provided with a well-mounted body of cavalry, which had spread terror and devastation over the country, and greatly intimidated the militia.

Though the marquis kept about twenty miles behind the main body of the British army, yet his light parties hung on its rear, and skirmishes occasionally ensued. A sharp encounter happened near Williamsburgh between the advanced guard of the Americans, under Colonel Butler, and the rear guard of the British under Colonel Simcoe, in which both suffered considerable loss. Part of the British army marched to Colonel Simcoe's assistance, and the Americans were obliged to retreat. Although the marquis encouraged skirmishes and partial conflicts, yet, distrusting his new levies and militia, he cautiously avoided a general battle. While the British army remained at Williamsburgh, the Americans occupied a strong encampment twenty miles from that place.

During the various movements of the troops in Virginia, property to a great amount, both public and private, was destroyed. Among other articles 2,000 hogsheads of tobacco were burned; individuals suffered severely, and the resources of the state were considerably impaired. While the army traversed the country, carrying devastation in its train, ships-of-war sailed up the rivers, pillaged the farms, received fugitive negroes, and, in some instances, laid the houses in ashes. Early in the spring a British frigate went up the Potomac to General Washington's mansion at Mount Vernon, and demanded from the steward a quantity of provisions, which was granted in order to save the property. This compliance, however, was not satisfactory to the American commander-in-chief, who declared that it would have been more agreeable to him to have left the enemy to take what they pleased by force, even at the risk of burning his house and property.

Though the militia showed no alacrity in taking the field, and though less resistance was made to the royal arms in Virginia than had been expected from such a powerful state, yet very little inclination manifested itself among the people to support the British cause. Some loyalists in a remote part of the province were easily reduced to unconditional submission by General Morgan, whom ill health had obliged to quit the army; but who, on this occasion, put himself at the head of a few mounted riflemen to subdue the insurgents.

We will here introduce the adventure of Charles Morgan, commonly called *Charlie* by his comrades. Charlie was a shrewd private of the Jersey brigade, a good soldier, and had attracted the notice of the Marquis de la Fayette. In the course of the movements on James river, the marquis was anxious to procure exact information of the force under Cornwallis, and, if possible, to penetrate his lordship's designs; he considered Charlie as a proper agent for the accomplishment of his purposes, and proposed to him to enter the British camp in the character of a deserter, but in reality as a spy. Charlie undertook the perilous enterprise, merely stipulating that, if he were detected, the marquis should cause it to be inserted in the Jersey newspapers, that he was acting under the orders of his commanding officer.

The pretended deserter entered the British lines and was conducted into the presence of Cornwallis. On being questioned by that nobleman concerning his motives for desertion, he replied, "that he had been with the American army from the beginning of the war, and that while under General Washington he was satisfied; but that now they had put them under a Frenchman, he did not like it, and therefore had deserted." Charlie was received without suspicion, was punctual in discharging his duty as a soldier, and carefully observed everything that passed. One day while on duty with his comrades, Cornwallis, who was in close conversation with some of his officers, called him and asked, "How long will it take the marquis to cross James river?" "Three hours, my lord," was the answer. "Three hours!" exclaimed his lordship, "will it not take three days?" "No, my lord," said Charlie; "the marquis has so many boats, each boat will carry so many men; and if your lordship will take the trouble of calculating, you will find he can cross in three hours." Turning to his officers, the earl said, in the hearing of the American, "The scheme will not do."

Charlie was now resolved to abandon his new friends: and for that purpose plied his comrades with grog till they were all in high spirits with the liquor. He then began to complain of the wants in the British camp, extolled the plentiful provision enjoyed by the Americans, and concluded by proposing to them to desert: they agreed to accompany him, and left it to him to manage the sentinels. To the first he offered, in a very friendly manner, a draught of rum from his canteen; but, while the soldier was drinking, Charlie seized his arms, and then proposed to him to desert with them, which he did through necessity. The second sentinel was served in the same way; and Charlie hastened to the American camp at the head of seven British deserters. On presenting himself before his employer, the marquis exclaimed, "Ah, Charlie! have you got back?" "Yes, sir," was the answer, "and have brought seven more with me." The marquis offered him money, but he declined accepting it, and only desired to have his gun again: the marquis then proposed to raise him to the rank of a corporal or serjeant, but Charlie's reply was, "I will not have any promotion; I have abilities for a common soldier, and have a good character: should I be promoted, my abilities may not answer, and I may lose my character." He, however, generously requested for his fellow-soldiers, who were not so well supplied with stockings, shoes, and clothing as himself, the marquis's interference to procure a supply of their wants.

For some time after entering Virginia, Cornwallis entertained the most flattering hopes of success. He was at the head of an army, which no force in that province was able to resist; and he felt no doubt of succeeding against the Marquis de la Fayette. But that young officer eluded his most active exertions, frustrated some of his schemes, and now hung upon him with an army, which, though still inferior, was nevertheless formidable, and daily increasing in strength. But new disappointments and more mortifying events awaited this active nobleman. While at Williamsburgh he received a requisition from Sir Henry Clinton for part of the troops under his command: the commander-in-chief having discovered that an attack was meditated on New York, thought his garrison insufficient for the defence of that place, and wished part of the troops in Virginia to be sent to his assistance. Cornwallis prepared to comply with Sir Henry Clinton's requisition; and, believing that with the remaining troops he would be unable to maintain himself at Williamsburgh, he resolved to pass James river and retire to Portsmouth. On the 30th of June he apprized the commander-in-chief of his resolution.

On the 4th of July the army marched from Williamsburgh, and encamped on the bank of James river, so as to cover a ford leading into the island of Jamestown. On the 5th and 6th, the baggage and some of the troops passed the ford; but the main body of the army kept its ground.

On the morning of the 5th of July, the Marquis de la Fayette left his encampment, crossed the Chickahominy, pushed his light troops near the British position and advanced with the continentals to make an attempt on the British rear, after their main body had passed the river. On the afternoon of the 6th, the marquis was told that the main body of the British army had crossed the ford, and that a rear guard only remained behind; an opinion which the British general artfully encouraged by the judicious manner in which he posted his troops. General Wayne, imagining that he had to fight a rear guard only, advanced boldly against the enemy ; but in a short time he unexpectedly found himself in presence of the British army drawn up to receive him. Instant retreat he considered impracticable, and thought the boldest course the most safe. With 800 men he made a brisk attack ; and for some minutes the conflict was sharp and bloody. But La Fayette, discovering the mistake, ordered a retreat, which was made with precipitation, leaving two pieces of cannon in the hands of the British. The Americans retired behind a morass ; and, it being nearly dark, Cornwallis, suspecting an ambuscade, ordered no pursuit. In this encounter, the Americans had 118 men, including ten officers, killed, wounded, or taken prisoners. The loss of the British was not so great, amounting to five officers, and about seventy privates. In the course of the night the British passed into the island ; whence soon afterward they proceeded to Portsmouth.

The troops required by the commander-in-chief were embarked ; but, before they sailed, despatches arrived from New York countermanding the order. At the same time, the commander-in-chief deprecated the thought of abandoning the Chesapeake, stating, that as soon as the season for military operations in that quarter returned, he would probably send thither all the disposable troops under his command, and recommending the establishment of a defensive post for the reception of ships-of-the-line, either at York, on the river of that name, or at Point Comfort in Hampton Road. Cornwallis accordingly ordered Point Comfort and York to be surveyed by engineers and officers of the navy, from whose report it appeared that works constructed on old Point Comfort could neither defend the entrance into Hampton Road, nor afford protection to ships lying there ; and as it was admitted that Portsmouth was not a station of the description required, Cornwallis thought his instructions left him no alternative but to fortify York and Gloucester, as the only points capable of affording the requisite protection to ships-of-the-line. Measures were accordingly taken for seizing and fortifying those places, and for evacuating Portsmouth. Part of the army proceeded, in boats and transports, up the Chesapeake and York river, and, on the 1st of August, took possession of Yorktown and Gloucester Point, the former on the south, the latter on the north side of the river. The evacuation of Portsmouth was completed ; and on the 22d the British force in Virginia concentrated at York and Gloucester. Here we shall leave Cornwallis and his army diligently fortifying themselves, and for a while turn our attention to the northward.

In the early part of the year the affairs of congress wore a gloomy and alarming aspect : the finances were exhausted, the troops mutinous, the army much diminished in numbers, and the soldiers who remained with the standards of their country, were in a state of entire destitution. The necessity of a foreign loan and of European auxiliaries was obvious ; and an early application for both had been made to France. But, how well disposed soever that power was to grant the desired assistance, compliance was no easy matter : for the treasury had enough to do in answering the national demands necessarily made on it, and was little able to supply foreign wants. As a signal proof of friendship, however, the French monarch gave his allies a donation of six millions of livres, and promised to support them with a strong naval and military armament.

Early in May, the Count de Barras, who had been appointed to the command of the French fleet on the American coast, arrived at Boston, accompanied by the Viscount de Rochambeau, commander of the land forces. An interview between General Washington and the French commanders was immediately appointed to be held at Wethersfield, on the 21st ; but some movements of the British fleet made De Barras repair to Newport, while the two generals met at the appointed place, and agreed on a plan of the campaign. It was resolved to unite the French and American armies on the Hudson, and to commence vigorous operations against New York. The regular army at that station was estimated at only 4,500 men; and though Sir Henry Clinton might be able to reinforce it with 5,000 or 6,000 militia, yet it was believed he could not maintain the post, without recalling a considerable part of his troops from the southward, and enfeebling the operations of the British in that quarter; in which case it was resolved to make a vigorous attack on the point which presented the best prospect of success.

General Washington immediately required the states of New England to have 5,000 militia in readiness to march, wherever they might be called for; and sent an account of the conference at Wethersfield to congress. His despatch was intercepted in the Jerseys, and carried to Sir Henry Clinton; who, alarmed by the plan which it disclosed, made the requisition, already mentioned, of part of the troops under Cornwallis, and took diligent precautions for maintaining his post against the meditated attack.

Meanwhile the several states of the Union were extremely dilatory in furnishing their contingents of troops, and it was found difficult to procure subsistence for the small number of men already in the field.

In consequence of this dilatory spirit, when the troops left their winter quarters in the month of June, and encamped at Peekskill, the army under Washington did not amount to 5,000 men. This force was so much inferior to what had been contemplated when the plan of operations was agreed on at Wethersfield, that it became doubtful whether it would be expedient to adhere to that plan. But the deficiency of the American force was in some measure compensated by the arrival at Boston of a reinforcement of 1,500 men to the army under Rochambeau.

The hope of terminating the war in the course of the campaign, encouraged the states to make some exertions. Small as was their military force, it was difficult to find subsistence for the troops; and, even after the army had taken the field, there was reason to apprehend that it would be obliged to abandon the objects of the campaign for want of provisions. In that critical juncture of American affairs, when the government was without money and without credit, the finances of the Union were intrusted to Mr. Robert Morris, a member of congress for Pennsylvania, a man of capital, and of much sagacity and mercantile enterprise. He extensively pledged his personal credit for articles of the first necessity to the army; and, by an honorable fulfilment of his engagements, did much to restore public credit and confidence. It was owing mainly to his exertions that the active and decisive operations of the campaign were not greatly impeded or entirely defeated, by want of subsistence to the army, and of the means of transporting military stores.

In this way, and by a liberal and judicious application of his own resources an individual afforded the supplies which government was unable to furnish.

The French troops marched from Newport and Boston toward the Hudson. Both in quarters and on the route their behavior was exemplary, and gained the respect and good-will of the inhabitants. Toward the end of June, General Washington put his army in motion; and, learning that a royal detachment had passed into the Jerseys, he formed a plan to surprise the British posts on the north end of York island; but it did not succeed; and General Lincoln, who commanded the Americans, being attacked by a strong British party, a sharp conflict ensued. General Washington marched with his main body to support his detachment, but on his advance the British retired into their works at Kingsbridge.

Having failed in his design of surprising the British posts, General Washington withdrew to Valentine's hill, and afterward to Dobb's ferry. While encamped there, on the 6th of July, the van of the long-expected French reinforcements was seen winding down the neighboring heights. The arrival of those friendly strangers elevated the minds of the Americans, who received them with sincere congratulations. General Washington labored, by personal attentions, to conciliate the good-will of his allies, and used all the means in his power to prevent those mutual jealousies and irritations which frequently prevail between troops of different nations serving in the same army. An attack on New York was still meditated, and every exertion made to prepare for its execution; but with the determination, if it should prove impracticable, vigorously to prosecute some more attainable object.

On the evening of the 21st of July, the greater part of the American and part of the French troops left their encampment; and, marching rapidly during the night, appeared in order of battle before the British works at Kingsbridge, at four next morning. Generals Washington and Rochambeau, with the general officers and engineers, viewed the British lines, in their whole extent, from right to left, and the same was again done next morning. But, on the afternoon of the 23d, they returned to their former encampment, without having made any attempt on the British works.

At that time the new levies arrived slowly in the American camp; and many of those who were sent were unfit for active service. The several states discovered much backwardness in complying with the requisitions of congress, so that there was reason to apprehend that the number of troops necessary for besieging New York could not be procured. This made General Washington turn his thoughts more seriously to the southward than he had hitherto done; but all his movements confirmed Sir Henry Clinton in the belief that an attack on New York was in contemplation. As the British commander-in-chief, however, at that time received about 3,000 troops from Europe, he thought himself able to defend his post, without withdrawing any part of the force from Virginia. Therefore he countermanded the requisition which he had before sent to Cornwallis for part of the troops under his command. The troops were embarked before the arrival of the counter order; and of their embarcation the Marquis de la Fayette sent notice to General Washington. On the reception of new instructions, however, as formerly mentioned, they were relanded, and remained in Virginia.

No great operation could be undertaken against the British armies, so long as their navy had the undisputed command of the coast, and of the great navigable rivers. The Americans had accordingly made an earnest application to the court of France for such a fleet as might be capable of keeping in check the British navy in those seas, and of affording effectual assistance to the land forces. That application was not unsuccessful; and, toward the middle of August, the agreeable information was received of the approach of a powerful French fleet to the American coast.

Early in March, the Count de Grasse sailed from Brest with twenty-five ships-of-the-line, five of which were destined for the East, and twenty for the West Indies. After an indecisive encounter, in the straits of St. Lucie, with Sir Samuel Hood, whom Sir George Rodney, the British admiral in the West Indies, had detached to intercept him, Count de Grasse formed a junction with the ships of his sovereign on that station, and had a fleet superior to that of the British in the West Indies. De Grasse gave the Americans notice that he would visit their coast in the month of August, and take his station in Chesapeake bay; but that his continuance there could only be of short duration. This despatch at once determined General Washington's resolution with respect to the main point of attack; and, as it was necessary that the projected operation should be accomplished within a very limited time, prompt decision and indefatigable exertion were indispensable. Though it was now finally resolved that Virginia should be the grand scene of action, yet it was prudent to conceal to the last moment this determination from Sir Henry Clinton, and still to maintain the appearance of threatening New York.

The defence of the strong posts on the Hudson or North river was intrusted to General Heath, who was instructed to protect the adjacent country as far as he was able; and for that purpose a respectable force was put under his command. Every preparation of which circumstances admitted was made to facilitate the march to the southward. General Washington was to take the command of the expedition, and to employ in it all the French troops, and a strong detachment of the American army.

On the 19th of August, a considerable corps was ordered to cross the Hudson at Dobb's ferry, and to take a position between Springfield and Chatham, where they were directed to cover some bakehouses, which it was rumored were to be immediately constructed in the vicinity of those places, in order to encourage the belief that there the troops intended to establish a permanent post. On the 20th and 21st the main body of the Americans passed the river at King's ferry; but the French made a longer circuit, and did not complete the passage till the 25th. Desirous of concealing his object as long as possible, General Washington continued his march some time in such a direction as still to keep up the appearance of threatening New York. When concealment was no longer practicable, he marched southward with the utmost celerity. His movements had been of such a doubtful nature, that Sir Henry Clinton, it is said, was not convinced of his real destination till he crossed the Delaware.

Great exertions had been made to procure funds for putting the army in motion; but, after exhausting every other resource, General Washington was obliged to have recourse to Count Rochambeau for a supply of cash, which he received.

On the 30th of August, at three in the afternoon, the combined American and French armies entered Philadelphia, where they were received with ringing of bells, firing of guns, bonfires, illuminations at night, and every demonstration of joy. Meanwhile, Count de Grasse, with 3,000 troops on board, sailed from Cape François with a valuable fleet of merchantmen, which he conducted out of danger, and then steered for Chesapeake bay with twenty-eight sail-of-the-line and several frigates. Toward the end of August he cast anchor just within the capes extending across from Cape Henry to the middle ground. There an officer from the Marquis de la Fayette waited on the count, and gave him full information concerning the posture of affairs in Virginia, and the intended plan of operations against the British army in that state.

Cornwallis was diligently fortifying himself at York and Gloucester; the Marquis de la Fayette was in a position on James river to prevent his escape into North Carolina, and the combined army was hastening southward to attack him. In order to co-operate against Cornwallis, De Grasse detached four ships-of-the-line and some frigates to block up the entrance of York river, and to carry the land forces which he had brought with him, under the Marquis de St. Simon, to La Fayette's camp. The rest of his fleet remained at the entrance of the bay.

Sir George Rodney, who commanded the British fleet in the West Indies, was not ignorant that the count intended to sail for America; but, knowing that the merchant vessels which he convoyed from Cape François were loaded with valuable cargoes, the British admiral believed that he would send the greater part of his fleet along with them to Europe, and would visit the American coast with a small squadron only. Accordingly, Sir George Rodney detached Sir Samuel Hood with fourteen sail-of-the-line to America, as a sufficient force to counteract the operations of the French in that quarter. Admiral Hood reached the capes of Virginia on the 25th of August, a few days before De Grasse entered the bay; and, finding no enemy there, sailed for Sandy Hook, where he arrived on the 28th of August.

Admiral Graves, who had succeeded Admiral Arbuthnot in the command of the British fleet on the American station, was then lying at New York with seven sail-of-the-line; but two of his ships had been damaged in a cruise near Boston, and were under repair. At the same time that Admiral Hood gave information of the expected arrival of De Grasse on the American coast, notice was received of the sailing of De Barras with his fleet from Newport. Admiral Graves, therefore, without waiting for his two ships which were under repair, put to sea on the 31st of August, with nineteen sail-of-the-line, and steered to the southward.

On reaching the capes of the Chesapeake early on the morning of the 5th of September, he discovered the French fleet, consisting of twenty-four ships-of-the-line, lying at anchor in the entrance of the bay. Neither admiral had any previous knowledge of the vicinity of the other till the fleets were actually seen. The British stretched into the bay: and soon as Count de Grasse ascertained their hostile character, he ordered his ships to slip their cables, form the line as they could come up, without regard to their specified stations, and put to sea. The British fleet entering the bay, and the French leaving it, they were necessarily sailing in different directions; but Admiral Graves put his ships on the same tack with the French; and, about four in the afternoon, a battle began between the van and centre of the fleets, which continued till night. Both sustained considerable damage. The fleets continued in sight of each other for five days; but De Grasse's object was not to fight unless to cover Chesapeake bay; and Admiral Graves, owing to the inferiority of his force and the crippled state of several of his ships, was unable to compel him to renew the engagement.

On the 10th, Count de Grasse bore away for the Chesapeake, and anchored within the capes next day, when he had the satisfaction to find that Admiral de Barras, with his fleet from Newport, and fourteen transports laden with heavy artillery and other military stores for carrying on a siege, had safely arrived during his absence. That officer sailed from Newport on the 25th of August, and, making a long circuit to avoid the British, entered the bay while the contending fleets were at sea. Admiral Graves followed the French fleet to the Chesapeake; but, on arriving there, he found the entrance guarded by a force with which he was unable to contend. He then sailed for New York, and left Count de Grasse in the undisputed possession of the bay.

While these naval operations were going on, the land forces were not less actively employed in the prosecution of their respective purposes. The immediate aim of the one party was to overwhelm Cornwallis and his army at Yorktown, that of the other to rescue him from their grasp. As soon as Sir Henry Clinton was convinced of General Washington's intention of proceeding to the southward, with a view to bring him back, he employed Arnold, with a sufficient naval and military force, on an expedition against New London. Arnold passed from Long Island, and on the forenoon of the 6th of September landed his troops on both sides of the harbor; those on the New London side being under his own immediate orders, and those on the Groton side commanded by Lieutenant-Colonel Eyre. As the works at New London were very imperfect, no vigorous resistance was there made, and the place was taken possession of with little loss. But Fort Griswolde, on the Groton side, was in a more finished state, and the small garrison made a desperate defence. The British entered the fort at the point of the bayonet; when, though opposition ceased, a murderous carnage ensued. Few Americans had fallen when the British entered the works, but eighty-five were killed, sixty wounded, most of them mortally, and the remainder, seventy in number, were made prisoners. The loss of the British was considerable. A great quantity of valuable property was destroyed, and the town much injured.

The loss sustained by the Americans at New London was great; but that predatory incursion had no effect in diverting General Washington from his purpose, or in retarding his march southward. From Philadelphia the allied armies pursued their route, partly to the head of Elk river, which falls into the northern extremity of Chesapeake bay, and partly to Baltimore, at which places they embarked on board of transports furnished by the French fleet, and the last division of them landed at Williamsburgh on the 25th of September. Generals Washington and Rochambeau, and their attendants, proceeded to the same place by land, and reached it ten days before the troops. Virginia had suffered extremely in the course of the campaign: the inhabitants were clamorous for the appearance of the commander-in-chief in his native state, and hailed his arrival with acclamations of joy.

Generals Washington and Rochambeau immediately repaired on board De Grasse's ship, in order to concert a joint plan of operations against Cornwallis. De Grasse, convinced that every exertion would be made to relieve his lordship, and being told that Admiral Digby had arrived at New York with a reinforcement of six ships-of-the-line, expected to be attacked by a force little inferior to his own; and deeming the station which he then occupied unfavorable to a naval engagement, he was strongly inclined to leave the bay, and to meet the enemy in the open sea. General Washington, fully aware of all the casualties which might occur to prevent his return, and to defeat the previous arrangements, used every argument to dissuade the French admiral from his purpose, and prevailed with him to remain in the bay.

As Count de Grasse could continue only a short time on that station, every exertion was made to proceed against Cornwallis at Yorktown, a small village on the southern bank of the river York, in which ships-of-the-line can ride in perfect safety. A long peninsular tract of land, only eight miles broad, lies between James and York rivers. Opposite Yorktown is Gloucester point, which projects considerably into the river, the breadth of which at that place does not exceed a mile. Cornwallis had taken possession of both these places, and diligently fortified them. The communication between them was commanded by his batteries, and by some ships-of-war which lay in the river under cover of his guns. The main body of his army was encamped near Yorktown, beyond some outer redoubts and fieldworks calculated to retard the approach of an enemy. Colonel Tarleton, with 600 or 700 men, occupied Gloucester point.

The combined army, amounting to upward of 11,000 men, exclusive of the Virginia militia, was assembled in the vicinity of Williamsburgh; and on the morning of the 28th of September marched by different routes toward Yorktown. About midday the heads of the columns reached the ground assigned them; and, after driving in the outposts and some cavalry, encamped for the night. The next day was employed in viewing the British works, and in arranging the plan of attack. At the same time that the combined army encamped before Yorktown, the French fleet anchored at the mouth of the river, and completely prevented the British from escaping by water, as well as from receiving supplies or reinforcements in that way. The legion of Lauzun and a brigade of militia, amounting to upward of 4,000 men, commanded by the French General de Choisé, were sent across the river to watch Gloucester point, and to enclose the British on that side.

On the 30th Yorktown was invested. The French troops formed the left wing of the combined army, extending from the river above the town to a morass in front of it: the Americans composed the right wing, and occupied the ground

FIG. 152 Yorktown, Virginia.

between the morass and the river below the town. Till the 6th of October the besieging army was assiduously employed in disembarking its heavy artillery and military stores, and in conveying them to camp from the landing place in James river, a distance of six miles.

On the night of the 6th the first parallel was begun, 600 yards from the British works. The night was dark, rainy, and well adapted for such a service; and in the course of it the besiegers did not lose a man. Their operations seem not to have been suspected by the besieged till daylight disclosed them in the morning, when the trenches were so far advanced as in a good measure to cover the workmen from the fire of the garrison. By the afternoon of the 9th, the batteries were completed, notwithstanding the most strenuous opposition from the besieged, and immediately opened on the town. From that time an incessant cannonade was kept up; and the continual discharge of shot and shells from twenty-four and eighteen-pounders, and ten-inch mortars, damaged the unfinished works on the left of the town, silenced the guns mounted on them, and occasioned a considerable loss of men. Some of the shot and shells from the batteries passed over the town, reached the shipping in the harbor, and set on fire the Charon of forty-four guns, and three large transports, which were entirely consumed. In this action Alexander Hamilton distinguished himself.

Fig. 153.—Monument of Hamilton.

On the night of the 11th, the besiegers, laboring with indefatigable perseverance, began their second parallel, 300 yards nearer the British works than the first; and the three succeeding days were assiduously employed in completing

FIGS. 154, 155.—Marquis de La Fayette and his French soldiers

it. During that interval the fire of the garrison was more destructive than at any other period of the siege. The men in the trenches were particularly annoyed by two redoubts toward the left of the British works, and about 200 yards in front of them. Of these it was necessary to gain possession; and on the 14th preparations were made to carry them both by storm. In order to avail himself of the spirit of emulation which existed between the troops of the two nations, and to avoid any cause of jealousy to either, the attack of the one redoubt was committed to the French, and that of the other to the Americans. The latter were commanded by the Marquis de la Fayette, and the former by the Baron de Viominel.

On the evening of the 14th, as soon as it was dark, the parties marched to the assault with unloaded arms. The redoubt which the Americans attacked was defended by a major, some inferior officers, and forty-five privates. The assailants advanced with such rapidity, without returning a shot to the heavy fire with which they were received, that in a few minutes they were in possession of the work, having had eight men killed, and twenty-eight wounded, in the attack. Eight British privates were killed; the major, a captain, an ensign, and seventeen privates, were made prisoners. The rest escaped. Although the Americans were highly exasperated by the recent massacre of their countrymen in Fort Griswolde by Arnold's detachment, yet not a man of the British was injured after resistance ceased. Retaliation had been talked of, but was not exercised.

The French party advanced with equal courage and rapidity, and were successful; but as the fortification which they attacked was occupied by a greater force, the defence was more vigorous, and the loss of the assailants more severe. There were 120 men in the redoubt; of whom eighteen were killed, and forty-two taken prisoners: the rest made their escape. The French lost nearly 100 men killed or wounded. During the night these two redoubts were included in the second parallel; and, in the course of next day, some howitzers were placed on them, which in the afternoon opened on the besieged.

Cornwallis and his garrison had done all that brave men could do to defend their post. But the industry of the besiegers was persevering, and their approaches rapid. The condition of the British was becoming desperate. In every quarter their works were torn to pieces by the fire of the assailants. The batteries already playing upon them had nearly silenced all their guns; and the second parallel was about to open on them, which in a few hours would render the place untenable.

Owing to the weakness of his garrison, occasioned by sickness and the fire of the besiegers, Cornwallis could not spare large sallying parties; but in the present distressing crisis, he resolved to make every effort to impede the progress of the enemy, and to preserve his post to the last extremity. For this purpose, a little before daybreak on the morning of the 16th of October, about 350 men, under the command of Lieutenant-Colonel Abercrombie, sallied out against two batteries, which seemed in the greatest state of forwardness. They attacked with great impetuosity, killed or wounded a considerable number of the French troops who had charge of the works, spiked eleven guns, and returned with little loss. This exploit was of no permanent advantage to the garrison; for the guns, having been hastily spiked, were soon again rendered fit for service.

About four in the afternoon several batteries of the second parallel opened on the garrison, and it was obvious that, in the course of next day, all the batteries of that parallel, mounting a most formidable artillery, would be ready to play on the town. The shattered works of the garrison were in no condition to sustain such a tremendous fire. In the whole front which was attacked the British could no

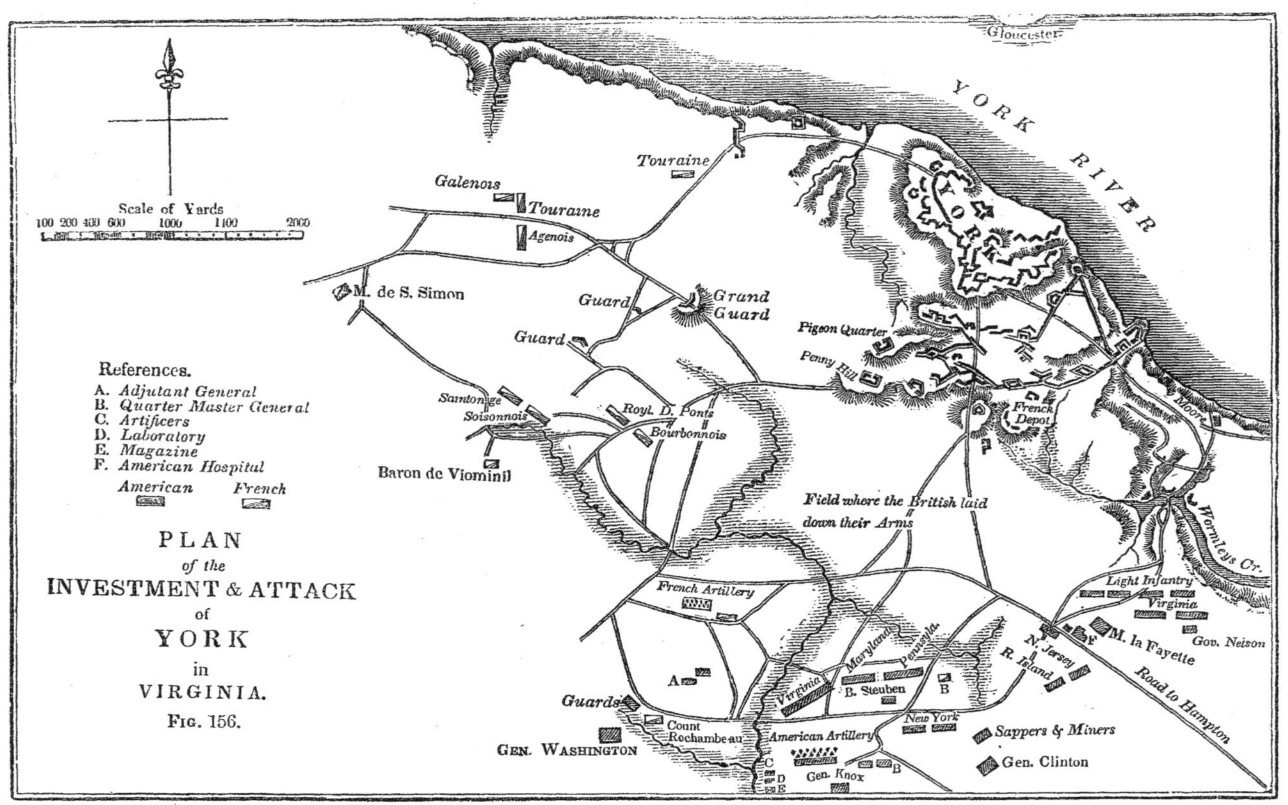

PLAN of the INVESTMENT & ATTACK of YORK in VIRGINIA.
FIG. 156.

show a single gun, and their shells were nearly exhausted. In this extremity, Cornwallis formed the desperate resolution of crossing the river during the night, with his effective force, and attempting to escape to the northward. His plan was, to leave behind his sick, baggage, and all incumbrances; to attack De Choisé, who commanded on the Gloucester side, with his whole force; to mount his own infantry, partly with the hostile cavalry, which he had no doubt of seizing, and partly with such horses as he might find by the way; to hasten toward the fords of the great rivers in the upper country, and then, turning northward, to pass through Maryland, Pennsylvania, and the Jerseys, and join the army at New York. The plan was hazardous, and presented little prospect of success; but in the forlorn circumstances of the garrison, anything that offered a glimpse of hope was reckoned preferable to the humiliation of an immediate surrender.

In prosecution of this perilous enterprise, the light infantry, most of the guards, and a part of the 23d regiment, embarked in boats, passed the river, and landed at Gloucester point before midnight. A storm then arose, which rendered the return of the boats and the transportation of the rest of the troops equally impracticable. In that divided state of the British forces, the morning of the 17th of October dawned, when the batteries of the combined armies opened on the garrison at Yorktown. As the attempt to escape was entirely defeated by the storm, the troops that had been carried to Gloucester point were brought back in the course of the forenoon, without much loss, though the passage was exposed to the artillery of the besiegers. The British works were in ruins; the garrison was weakened by disease and death, and exhausted by incessant fatigue. Every ray of hope was extinguished. It would have been madness any longer to attempt to defend the post, and to expose the brave garrison to the danger of an assault, which would soon have been made on the place.

At ten in the forenoon of the 17th, Cornwallis sent out a flag of truce, with a letter to General Washington, proposing a cessation of hostilities for twenty-four hours, in order to give time to adjust terms for the surrender of the forts at Yorktown and Gloucester point. To this letter the American general immediately returned an answer, expressing his ardent desire to spare the further effusion of blood, and his readiness to listen to such terms as were admissible; but that he could not consent to lose time in fruitless negotiations, and desired that, previous to the meeting of commissioners, his lordship's proposals should be transmitted in writing, for which purpose a suspension of hostilities for two hours should be granted. The terms offered by Cornwallis, although not all deemed admissible, were such as induced the opinion that no great difficulty would occur in adjusting the conditions of capitulation; and the suspension of hostilities was continued through the night. Meanwhile, in order to avoid the delay of useless discussion, General Washington drew up and transmitted to Cornwallis such articles as he was willing to grant, informing his lordship that, if he approved of them, commissioners might be immediately appointed to reduce them to form. Accordingly, Viscount Noailles and Lieutenant-Colonel Laurens, whose father was then a prisoner in the tower of London, on the 18th met Colonel Dundas and Major Ross of the British army at Moore's house, in the rear of the first parallel. They prepared a rough draught, but were unable definitely to arrange the terms of capitulation. The draught was to be submitted to Cornwallis: but General Washington, resolved to admit of no delay, directed the articles to be transcribed; and, on the morning of the 19th, sent them to his lordship, with a letter expressing his expectation that they would be signed by eleven, and that the garrison would march out at two in the afternoon. Finding that no better terms could be obtained, Cornwallis, on the 19th of October, surrendered the posts of Yorktown and Gloucester point to the combined armies of America and France, on condition that his troops should receive the same honors of war

Fig. 157.—Moore's House at Yorktown.

which had been granted to the garrison of Charleston, when it surrendered to Sir Henry Clinton. The army, artillery, arms, accoutrements, military chest, and public stores of every description, were surrendered to General Washington; the ships in the harbor, and the seamen, to Count de Grasse.

Cornwallis wished to obtain permission for his European troops to return home, on condition of not serving against America, France, or their allies, during the war, but this was refused; and it was agreed that they should remain prisoners of war in Virginia, Maryland, and Pennsylvania, accompanied by a due proportion of officers for their protection and government. The British general was also desirous of securing from punishment such Americans as had joined the royal standard, but this was refused, on the plea that it was a point which belonged to the civil authority, and on which the military power was not competent to decide. But the end was gained in an indirect way; for Cornwallis was permitted to send the Bonetta sloop-of-war unsearched to New York, with despatches to the commander-in-chief, and to put on board as many soldiers as he thought proper, to be accounted for in any subsequent exchange.

The officers and soldiers were allowed to retain their private property. Such officers as were not required to remain with the troops were permitted to return to Europe, or to reside in any part of America not in possession of the British troops. The garrison marched out of the town with colors cased, and with the drums beating a British or German march. General Lincoln was appointed to receive the surrender in precisely the same way in which his own had been received at Charleston. Exclusive of seamen, nearly 7,000 persons surrendered, about 4,000 of whom were fit for duty. During the siege, the garrison lost, in killed, wounded, and prisoners, 552 men.

By the surrender of the posts of Yorktown and Gloucester point, the Americans gained possession of a large train of artillery, consisting of seventy-five brass and sixty-nine iron cannon, howitzers, and mortars, with a considerable quantity of arms, ammunition, military stores, and provisions. One frigate, two ships of twenty guns each, a number of transports and other vessels, and about 1,500 seamen, surrendered to Count de Grasse, his most Christian majesty's admiral. The combined army at Yorktown may be estimated at 16,000 men; consisting of 7,000 French, 5,500 continentals, and 3,500 militia. Their loss during the siege amounted to about 300 killed and wounded.

General Washington felt all the importance of the conquest which he had achieved. His troops had displayed indefatigable industry joined with much bravery; and, in general orders of the 20th, he acknowledged their merits, thanking all the officers and men for their services. The engineers and artillerymen had particularly distinguished themselves, and were mentioned in terms of high commendation. The general offered his best acknowledgments to Count de Rochambeau and his officers and men: the important co-operation of Count de Grasse was also duly appreciated. The capture of Cornwallis and his army raised the shout of triumph and joy throughout America, particularly in Virginia: it was like the exultation of a pastoral people over the death of the lion which had cruelly ravaged their flocks, and spread terror through their dwellings.

The unfortunate are commonly blamed, and their want of success imputed to misconduct. From such censure Cornwallis has not escaped, although it is difficult to perceive any distinct ground for blaming his military career. It is easy to find fault on the retrospect of a series of events after they are past, when the whole can be contemplated in all their bearings and relations; but it is not so easy to discern the wisest course while the events are in progress and the issue uncertain. Concerning the movement of Cornwallis from Ramsay's mills to Cross creek and Wilmington, different opinions may be entertained; but his lordship was strongly drawn toward Virginia by the force acting there under

Generals Arnold and Philips; and, after he entered the province, he did all that activity could perform to attain his end. If he had been to leave Virginia at all, and proceed to the southward, the time for beginning that movement was when he found it expedient to retire from the vicinity of Albemarle courthouse; but then such a step would, in all probability, have been generally condemned, and would certainly have been disagreeable to the commander-in-chief, who purposed to carry on vigorous operations in that quarter.

After Cornwallis took possession of Yorktown, in obedience, as he thought, to his orders, retreat became nearly impracticable; for the Marquis de la Fayette took post on James river, and was prepared to dispute his passage southward; and, although he had escaped that nobleman, yet he would have been pursued and also obliged to encounter General Greene at the passage of the great rivers which lay between him and Charleston. Besides, he was encouraged to remain in Virginia by the promise of assistance, which Sir Henry Clinton was unable to afford in time to save him.

The attack on Cornwallis was conceived in the true spirit of military enterprise; but a concurrence of many favorable circumstances was necessary in order to its successful execution. It was a combined effort by sea and land, carried on by different leaders, and liable to the uncertainty of winds and waves. Superiority by sea was indispensably requisite; and the whole scheme was endangered by the appearance of Admiral Hood at Chesapeake bay. The arrival of De Barras, the return of De Grasse after his encounter with Admiral Hood, all combined against the British, who, after behaving like brave men, were compelled to surrender themselves prisoners-of-war.

Sir Henry Clinton was not ignorant of the perilous situation of Cornwallis, and was anxious to relieve him: but the fleet had sustained considerable damage in the battle with De Grasse, and some time was necessarily spent in repairing it. During that interval, four ships-of-the-line arrived from Europe and two from the West Indies. At length the commander-in-chief embarked with 7,000 of his best troops, but was unable to sail from Sandy Hook till the 19th, the day on which Cornwallis surrendered. The fleet, consisting of twenty-five ships-of-the-line, two vessels of fifty guns each, and eight frigates, arrived off the Chesapeake on the 24th, when the commander-in-chief had the mortification to be informed of the event of the 19th.

CHAPTER XIV.

General Washington used all his influence to detain Count de Grasse some time longer on the coast, to assist in the reduction of Charleston; but the orders of his court, ulterior projects, and his engagements with the Spaniards, put it out of the power of the French admiral to continue so long in America as was required. He, however, remained some days in the bay, in order to cover the embarcation of the troops and of the ordnance to be conveyed by water to the head of the Elk. Some brigades proceeded by land to join their companions at that place. Some cavalry marched to join General Greene; but the French troops, under Count Rochambeau, remained in Virginia, to be in readiness to march to the south or north, as the circumstances of the next campaign might require. On the 27th the troops of St. Simon began to embark, in order to return to the West Indies; and early in November Count de Grasse sailed for that quarter. General Washington proceeded to Philadelphia, where he arrived on the 27th of November, and the Marquis de la Fayette returned to Europe.

The capture of Cornwallis was the most decisive event of this glorious war. The military operations in America were afterward languid and desultory; few in number, and unimportant in their nature; injurious or fatal, indeed, to individuals, but of little public advantage or loss to either of the contending parties.

While General Washington was marching against Cornwallis, the loyalists of North Carolina, under M'Neil and M'Dougall, made themselves masters of Hillsborough, and took a number of prisoners. M'Neil and some of his followers were killed in a rencounter with the friends of congress. M'Dougall was pursued; but effected his escape with a number of prisoners to Wilmington.

Late in October Major Ross made an incursion into the country on the Mohawk at the head of 500 men, regulars, rangers, and Indians. Colonel Willet, with about an equal force, found him at Johnstown. An engagement ensued, when part of the Americans fled without any apparent cause; but as the rest maintained their ground, the British retreated. Willet, with a select party, pursued them; and, on the morning of the 30th, overtook their rear at a ford on Canada creek. He immediately attacked them, killed a number, and put the rest to flight. Among the slain was Walter Butler, who perpetrated the massacre at Cherry Valley. He asked quarter; but was reminded of Cherry Valley, and instantly despatched.

The convention of Saratoga was a severe blow to the British arms; but the surrender of Cornwallis at Yorktown was still more decisive. It produced a great change in America, and gave a new and more cheering aspect to the affairs of the Union. In the early part of the year, the cause of the states was in a drooping condition, and American freedom seemed verging to ruin. Congress was surrounded with embarrassments, and victory had fled from their standards. The success of Morgan at the Cow-Pens and the exertions of Greene dissipated the gloom in the south; but, in the middle and northern provinces nothing had occurred to awaken hope and stimulate exertion. The capture, however, of Cornwallis and his army, which was achieved by a remarkable concurrence of good conduct and fortunate circumstances, altered the face of things. Congress, the state governments, and all the classes of the people, exulted with joy. A brighter sun shone on their heads, elevated their hopes, and invigorated their exertions. The clamors of the discontented were silenced, the hearts of the desponding reanimated, and the wavering confirmed in their attachment to the Union. A new impulse was given to the public mind; but, above all, the ray of peace, which seemed now to burst through the gloom of war, was grateful to their souls.

If the effects of the surrender of Yorktown were great in America, they were not less in Europe. The government and people of Britain entertained the most sanguine hopes from the operations of the army in Virginia. The expense of the war was heavy, and every year increasing. The people murmured under the load; but were encouraged to bear with patience, in the hope of being soon relieved, and ultimately reimbursed by the exclusive trade of the subjugated provinces. Many flattered themselves that the campaign in Virginia would annihilate the power of congress, and put an end to the contest.

In the midst of these fond anticipations, the news of the surrender at Yorktown arrived, and struck both the ministry and people with amazement and dismay. The blow was equally severe and unexpected. It laid their towering hopes in the dust, and filled them with painful apprehensions. They now discovered, what former experience had been unable to teach them, that a country may be overrun, but can not easily be subdued, while the minds of the people continue hostile. They who before disapproved of the war now spoke of it in terms of the strongest reprobation, and many who formerly had given it their zealous support began to express a desire of peace. The public mind underwent a great change, and sentiments which not long before met only with scorn and detestation became popular and fashionable; such a fluctuating thing is public opinion.

Parliament met on the 27th of November, and in the king's speech the disasters in America were not dissembled, but were urged as a motive for the vigorous prosecution of the war. Addresses, in the usual form, were moved; which brought on animated debates, in which some of the ministry expressed their intention of altering the plan of the war, and of merely retaining possession of those posts which they held in America, and of directing their main efforts against France, Spain, and Holland. In both houses of parliament the addresses were carried by large majorities. About that time Mr. Laurens, who had been detained a close prisoner in the Tower, of which Cornwallis was governor, was released.

Though ministry carried the address by triumphant majorities, yet the popular feeling became strong against the continuance of the war. The lord mayor and aldermen of the city of London, a great influential body, whose sentiments serve as a sort of political barometer, the indications of which it is imprudent to disregard, voted an address favorable to peace, which, owing to a difference on a point of ceremony, was not presented, but it was published. All classes became weary of the protracted struggle; the house of commons began to waver, and, on the 27th of February, the opposition carried an address against the prolongation of the war in America.

We now return to America, where the first thing that meets us is one of those painful incidents which result from the infuriated passions engendered by civil commotions. On the 24th of March, Captain Haddy, who commanded the troops in a blockhouse on the river Tom in New Jersey, was attacked, overpowered, and made prisoner by a party of loyalists from New York. In a few days afterward, they led him out and hanged him, with a label on his breast declaring that he was put to death in retaliation for some of their brethren who had suffered a similar fate. General Washington took up the matter seriously; submitted it to his officers, laid it before congress, and wrote to the British general, demanding that the perpetrators of the horrid deed should be given up, and threatening retaliation in case of refusal. The British general ordered a court-martial to inquire into the offence. It acquitted the person accused. General Washington ordered a British prisoner of equal rank with Haddy to be chosen by lot, and sent to Philadelphia, that he might suffer as a retaliatory victim. The lot fell on Captain Asgill, an English youth of only nineteen years of age, and respectably connected. Great interest was made to save the life of this young gentleman: he was ultimately set free; but was long kept in a state of painful suspense.

During winter, the states labored to prepare for another campaign; but, owing to the exhaustion of the country, the preparations went on slowly. Every one wished to devolve the burden on his neighbor, and every state seemed afraid of bearing more than its share of the war. Notwithstanding the late success in the southern states, and brilliant issue of the campaign in Virginia, there was much disinclination to vigorous exertions. The troops were few in number, and almost destitute of every necessary. Many of them were almost naked, and nearly all were ill fed. Every department was without money and without credit. Discontent was general among the officers and soldiers, and severe measures were necessary to check a mutinous spirit in the army. Fortunately for America, while the resources of congress were exhausted, and everything was hastening to ruin, the people of Britain also had become weary of the war, and it was found expedient to change the ministry. The new servants of the crown did not inherit the military propensities of their predecessors, but were inclined to conciliation and peace.

One of the last acts of the late administration was to appoint Sir Guy Carleton afterward Lord Dorchester, commander-in-chief in America, in the room of Sir Henry Clinton; and the new ministry continued him in that high office. He took the command at New York early in May; and being also, in conjunction with Admiral Digby, appointed a commissioner to negotiate a peace, he soon communicated to General Washington copies of the votes of parliament respecting peace; and also a bill which had been introduced by the ministry to authorize his majesty to conclude a peace with the colonies of North America. Those papers, he said, manifested the dispositions of the government and people of Britain toward America; and if they were met with a corresponding temper, both inclination and duty would lead him to act in the spirit of conciliation. He had addressed to congress, he said, a letter containing the same communications; and he requested of General Washington a passport for the person who was to deliver it.

The American commander immediately forwarded the communications to congress; but as the bill to enable the king to conclude peace with America had not then passed into a law; as there was no assurance that the present commissioners were empowered to offer any other terms than those which had been already rejected; as congress was suspicious that the offers were merely intended to amuse and put them off their guard, that they might be successfully attacked when reposing in security; and as they were resolved to enter into no separate treaty, the passport was refused. Both armies, however, lay inactive. There was no peace, and there was no war. Sir Guy Carleton undertook no offensive operation; and the army of General Washington was too feeble to attack New York. On the Hudson, the summer passed away in inactivity.

Early in August, General Washington received a letter from Sir Guy Carleton and Admiral Digby, informing him that negotiations for a general peace were begun at Paris; that the independence of the thirteen United States would be acknowledged; that Mr. Laurens was set at liberty; and that passports were preparing for such Americans as had been hitherto detained prisoners in Britain. This letter was soon followed by another from Sir Guy Carlton, in which he declared that he no longer saw any object of contest, and therefore disapproved of the continuance of hostilities either by sea or land, as tending to increase the miseries of individuals, without any public advantage to either party. He added, that, in consequence of this opinion, he had restrained the practice of detaching Indian parties against the frontiers of the United States, and had recalled those which were in the field. Those communications seem to have awakened the jealousy of the French minister in America; and, in order to allay his suspicions, congress renewed its resolution not to enter into any discussion for a pacification but in concert with his most Christian majesty.

Although the inactivity which prevailed in the north was, in a certain measure, communicated to the southern army, yet some desultory hostilities happened in that quarter. General St. Clair, who conducted the reinforcements from Yorktown toward the south, reached General Greene's headquarters early in January. He had been ordered to take the post of Wilmington on his way; but the British garrison evacuated that place before his arrival, and he met with no detention there.

St. Clair experienced no hostile interruption; the number of his troops, however was so much diminished by the casualties of a long march, that his reinforcement did little more than supply the place in Greene's army of those soldiers who had been entitled to their discharge on the last day of December

But feeble as the southern army was, yet, on St. Clair's arrival, General Greene detached General Wayne across the Santee, to protect the state of Georgia. On his approach, General Clarke, who commanded the British troops in that province, amounting to about 1,000 regular soldiers, besides militia, concentrated his force in the town of Savannah. Wayne insulted his outposts, and some sharp but useless skirmishes ensued. On the 11th of July, the garrison evacuated the town of Savannah, and retired from the province.

General Leslie commanded in Charleston, and held the place till the 14th of December, though the intention of evacuating it was announced in the general orders of the 7th of August. In that interval, General Leslie humanely proposed to General Greene a suspension of hostilities; to which the stern and inflexible American did not consider himself empowered to accede. In the same spirit of conciliation, General Leslie offered full payment for rice and other provisions sent into the town, but threatened to take them without compensation if withheld. General Greene, suspecting that it was intended to collect a large quantity of rice in Charleston to supply the army while it acted against the French islands in the West Indies, declined the arrangement. The consequence was, that the British made some foraging incursions into the country, and skirmishes ensued. In themselves these skirmishes were unimportant; but they derived a lively interest from the death of Lieutenant-Colonel Laurens, who fell in one of them, to the deep regret of his countrymen, among whom he was universally esteemed and beloved.

While the Americans slumbered on their arms, the war which their quarrel had engendered was actively carried on in other quarters of the world. In the West Indies the French fleet had long been successful; but, on the 12th of April, Count de Grasse was entirely defeated and taken prisoner by Admiral Rodney, which restored the balance to a kind of equilibrium, and threatened a prolongation of the struggle. In the month of July, the French army in Virginia marched northward, and reached the states of New England in October. It was given out that they were to winter there; but the real intention was to transport them to the West Indies, for which purpose the Marquis de Vaudreuil, with a fleet of fifteen sail-of-the-line, arrived at Boston on the 10th of August. By the long continuance of the contest, and by mutual reverses, all parties were now become tired of war and desirous of peace. Negotiations for a general pacification were going on at Paris, but were protracted by the mutual jealousies and interfering claims of the several parties interested. Great Britain admitted the independence of the thirteen United States, and so removed a great cause of the war; but the boundaries of the states, and their share in the fisheries on the banks of Newfoundland, were not so easily adjusted, and on both of these points France and Spain seemed unfriendly to the wishes of America.

After a tedious and intricate negotiation, in which the firmness, judgment, and penetration of the American commissioners, were exercised, preliminary articles of peace were signed on the 30th of November; and news of the conclusion of a general peace reached the United States early next April.

A line running through the middle of the great lakes and their connecting waters, and from a certain point on the St. Lawrence to the bottom of the bay of Fundy, was agreed to as the northern boundary of the states; and their western frontier was to rest on the Mississippi. It was stipulated that British creditors should be allowed to recover their debts in the United States; that congress should recommend to the several states the restoration of the estates of real British subjects which had been confiscated during the war; and that no further confiscations should be made.

On the 19th of April, 1783, the day which completed the eighth year of the

Fig. 158.—Acknowledgment of American Independence by France.

war, the cessation of hostilities with Great Britain was, by order of General Washington, proclaimed in the American camp. A number of negroes, who had once belonged to American citizens, were sent off by the British. This produced an interview between Generals Carleton and Washington, at Tappan, on the 6th of May, which ended without any decisive result.

On the 25th of November the British troops evacuated New York, and an American detachment, under General Knox, took possession of the town. General Washington and Governor Clinton, accompanied by a number of civil and military officers and respectable citizens, soon afterward entered the city; and the Americans, after a struggle which had lasted eight years, gained full and undisputed possession of the provinces.

The independence of the United States was acknowledged, and peace with Great Britain concluded: but the dangers of America were not at an end. She had succeeded in repelling foreign aggression; but was threatened with ruin by internal dissension. In the interval between the cessation of hostilities and the disbanding of the troops, congress found itself in a trying and perilous situation. Their army was in a state of high dissatisfaction and irritation. In October, 1780, a season of danger and alarm, congress promised half-pay to the officers on the conclusion of peace. That promise they now seemed neither very able nor willing to perform. The danger had passed away, and the spirit of liberality, engendered by fear, had evaporated. The state legislatures affected much jealousy of what they called their liberty, but discovered little inclination to fulfil their obligations to those who had been instrumental in establishing it. The chicanery, evasions, and subterfuges even of congress deprived it of the respect and sympathy due to unsullied honor in distress. Spotless integrity is the brightest ornament and best shield of nations, as well as of individuals. The shuffling policy of congress roused the indignation of the officers of the army, many of whom manifested an inclination to procure redress of their own wrongs with the same weapons which had asserted the independence of their country.

In the month of December, 1782, soon after going into winter quarters, the officers presented a memorial and petition to congress, and deputed a committee of their number to call its attention to the subject. They had shed their blood, spent their time, and wasted their substance, in the service of their country. Large arrears were due to them, and they had received liberal promises; but there was no certain prospect that the arrears would ever be paid, and there was much reason to suspect that there was no serious intention to perform the promises. After all their sufferings and sacrifices, they had nothing before them but the melancholy prospect of being discharged without even money to carry them to their respective homes, and of being cast naked on the world, and spending old age in penury and neglect, after having lost the prime of life in vindicating the claims and establishing the independence of an ungrateful people.

To men who had long and zealously served their country in the midst of the greatest hardships and wants, these were irritating considerations. Accordingly, early in March, on receiving a letter from their committee in Philadelphia, purporting that their solicitations had not been successful, meetings of the officers were held to consider what measures should be adopted for obtaining redress of their grievances. An ably written address was circulated through the army, inviting a general meeting of the officers at a given time and place.

"*To the Officers of the Army.*

"GENTLEMEN: A fellow-soldier, whose interests and affections bind him strongly to you, whose past sufferings have been as great, and whose future fortunes may be as desperate as yours, would beg leave to address you. Age has its claims, and rank is not without its pretensions to advise; but, though unsupported by both,

FIG. 159.—Statue of Hamilton.

he flatters himself that the plain language of sincerity and experience will neither be unheard nor unregarded.

"Like many of you, he loved private life, and left it with regret. He left it, determined to retire from the field with the necessity that called him to it, and not till then—not till the enemies of his country, the slaves of power and the hirelings of injustice, were compelled to abandon their schemes, and acknowledge America as terrible in arms as she had been humble in remonstrance. With this object in view, he has long shared in your toils and mingled in your dangers. He has felt the cold hand of poverty wlthout a murmur, and has seen the insolence of wealth without a sigh. But, too much under the direction of his wishes, and sometimes weak enough to mistake desire for opinion, he has till lately, very lately, believed in the justice of his country. He hoped that, as the clouds of adversity scattered, and as the sunshine of peace and better fortune broke in upon us, the coldness and severity of government would relax, and that more than justice, that gratitude, would blaze forth upon those hands which had upheld her, in the darkest stages of her passage, from impending servitude to acknowledged independence. But faith has its limits as well as temper, and there are points beyond which neither can be stretched without sinking into cowardice or plunging into credulity. This, my friends, I conceive to be your situation. Hurried to the very verge of both, another step would ruin you for ever. To be tame and unprovoked when injuries press hard upon you, is more than weakness; but to look up for kinder usage, without one manly effort of your own, would fix your character, and show the world how richly you deserve those chains you broke. To guard against this evil, let us take a review of the ground upon which we now stand, and thence carry our thoughts forward for a moment into the unexplored field of expedient. After a pursuit of seven long years, the object for which we set out is at length brought within our reach. Yes, my friends, that suffering courage of yours was active once—it has conducted the United States of America through a doubtful and a bloody war; it has placed her in the chair of independence, and peace returns again—to bless whom? A country willing to redress your wrongs, cherish your worth, and reward your services? A country courting your return to private life with tears of gratitude and smiles of admiration—longing to divide with you the independency which your gallantry has given, and those riches which your wounds have preserved? Is this the case? or is it rather a country that tramples upon your rights, disdains your cries, and insults your distresses? Have you not more than once suggested your wishes, and made known your wants, to congress—wants and wishes which gratitude and policy should have anticipated rather than evaded? And have you not lately, in the meek language of entreating memorials, begged from their justice what you could no longer expect from their favor? How have you been answered? Let the letter which you are called to consider to-morrow reply.

"If this then be your treatment while the swords you wear are necessary for the defence of America, what have you to expect from peace, when your voice shall sink, and your strength dissipate, by division—when those very swords, the instruments and companions of your glory, shall be taken from your sides, and no remaining mark of military distinction left but your wants, infirmities, and scars? Can you then consent to be the only sufferers by this revolution; and, retiring from the field, grow old in poverty, wretchedness, and contempt? Can you consent to wade through the vile mire of dependancy, and owe the miserable remnant of that life to charity, which has hitherto been spent in honor? If you can, go, and carry with you the jest of tories and the scorn of whigs; the ridicule, and, what is worse, the pity, of the world! Go, starve and be forgotten! But, if your spirit should revolt at this—if you have sense enough to discover and spirit enough to oppose tyranny, under whatever garb it may assume, whether it be the plain coat of republicanism or the splendid robe of royalty—if you have yet learned to discriminate between a people and a cause, between men and principles—awake, attend to your situation, and redress yourselves! If the present moment be lost, every future effort is in vain, and your threats then will be as empty as your entreaties now.

"I would advise you, therefore, to come to some final opinion upon what you can bear, and what you will suffer. If your determination be in any proportion to your wrongs, carry your appeal from the justice, to the fears, of government. Change the milk-and-water style of your last memorial; assume a bolder tone, decent, but lively, spirited, and determined; and suspect the man who would advise to more moderation and longer forbearance. Let two or three men, who can feel as well as write, be appointed to draw up your last *remonstrance;* for I would no longer give it the suing, soft, unsuccessful epithet of *memorial.* Let it be represented, in language that will neither dishonor you by its rudeness nor betray you by its fears, what has been promised by congress, and what has been performed; how long and how patiently you have suffered; how little you have asked, and how much of that little has been denied. Tell them, that though you were the first, and would wish to be the last, to encounter danger, though despair itself can never drive you into dishonor, it may drive you from the field; that the wound, often irritated, and never healed, may at length become incurable; and that the slightest mark of malignity from congress, now, must operate like the grave, and part you for ever. That, in any political event, the army has its alternative: if peace, that nothing shall separate you from your arms but death; if war, that, courting the auspices and inviting the directions of your illustrious leader, you will retire to some unsettled country, smile in your turn, and 'mock when their fear cometh on.' But let it represent also, that should they comply with the request of your late memorial, it would make you more happy, and them more respectable. That while war should continue, you would follow their standard into the field; and when it came to an end, you would withdraw into the shade of private life, and give the world another subject of wonder and applause—an army victorious over its enemies, victorious over itself."

General Washington's Speech at the Meeting of Officers.

"GENTLEMEN: By an anonymous summons an attempt has been made to convene you together; how inconsistent with the rules of propriety, how unmilitary, and how subversive of all order and discipline, let the good sense of the army decide. In the moment of this summons, another anonymous production was sent into circulation, addressed more to the feelings and passions than to the judgment of the army. The author of the piece is entitled to much credit for the goodness of his pen; and I could wish he had as much credit for the rectitude of his heart: for, as men see through different optics, and are induced by the reflecting faculties of the mind to use different means to attain the same end, the author of the address should have had more charity than to mark for suspicion the man who should recommend moderation and longer forbearance; or, in other words, who should not think as he thinks, and act as he advises.

"But he had another plan in view, in which candor and liberality of sentiment, regard to justice, and love of country, have no part; and he was right to insinuate the darkest suspicion to effect the blackest design. That the address was drawn with great art, and is designed to answer the most insidious purposes; that it is calculated to impress the mind with an idea of premeditated injustice in the sovereign power of the United States, and rouse all the resentments which must unavoidably flow from such a belief; that the secret mover of this scheme, whoever he may be, intended to take advantage of the passions while they were warmed by the recollection of past distresses, without giving time for cool, deliberative thinking, and that composure of mind which is so necessary to give dignity and stability to measures, is rendered too obvious, by the mode of conducting the business, to need other proofs than a reference to the proceedings.

"Thus much, gentlemen, I have thought it incumbent on me to observe to you, to show upon what principles I opposed the irregular and hasty meeting which was proposed to have been held on Tuesday last, and not because I wanted a disposition to give you every opportunity, consistent with your own honor and the dignity of the army, to make known your grievances. If my conduct, therefore, has not evinced to you that I have been a faithful friend to the army, my declaration of it at this time would be equally unavailing and improper. But, as I was among the first who embarked in the cause of our common country; as I have never left your side one moment, but when called from you on public duty; as I have been the constant companion and witness of your distresses, and not among the last to feel and acknowledge your merits; as I have ever considered my own military reputation as inseparably connected with that of the army; as my heart has ever expanded with joy when I have heard its praises, and my indignation has arisen when the mouth of detraction has been opened against it; it can scarcely be supposed, at this stage of the war, that I am indifferent to its interests. But how are they to be promoted? The way is plain, says the anonymous addresser. If war continues, remove into the unsettled country; there establish yourselves, and leave an ungrateful country to defend itself. But who are they to defend? Our wives, our children, our farms, and other property which we leave behind us? or, in this state of hostile preparation, are we to take the first two (the latter can not be removed), to perish in the wilderness with hunger, cold, and nakedness?

"If peace takes place, never sheath your swords, says he, until you have obtained full and ample justice. This dreadful alternative of either deserting our country in the extremest hour of her distress, or turning our arms against it, which is the apparent object, unless congress can be compelled into instant compliance, has something so shocking in it, that humanity revolts at the idea. My God! what can this writer have in view by recommending such measures? Can he be a friend to the army? Can he be a friend to this country? Rather, is he not an insidious foe; some emissary, perhaps, from New York, plotting the ruin of both, by sowing the seeds of discord and separation between the civil and military powers of the continent? And what a compliment does he pay to our understandings, when he recommends measures, in either alternative, impracticable in their nature?

"But here, gentlemen, I will drop the curtain, because it would be as imprudent in me to assign my reasons for this opinion, as it would be insulting to your conception to suppose you stood in need of them. A moment's reflection will convince every dispassionate mind of the physical impossibility of carrying either proposal into execution. There might, gentlemen, be an impropriety in my taking notice, in this address to you, of an anonymous production; but the manner in which that performance has been introduced to the army, the effect it was intended to have, together with some other circumstances, will amply justify my observation on the tendency of that writing.

"With respect to the advice given by the author, to suspect the man who should recommend moderate measures, I spurn it, as every man, who regards that liberty and reveres that justice for which we contend, undoubtedly must; for, if men are to be precluded from offering their sentiments on a matter which may involve the most serious and alarming consequences that can invite the consideration of mankind, reason is of no use to us. The freedom of speech may

be taken away, and dumb and silent we may be led like sheep to the slaughter. I can not in justice to my own belief, and what I have great reason to conceive is the intention of congress, conclude this address, without giving it as my decided opinion, that that honorable body entertain exalted sentiments of the services of the army, and, from a full conviction of its merits and sufferings, will do it complete justice. That their endeavors to discover and establish funds for this purpose have been unwearied, and will not cease till they have succeeded, I have not a doubt; but, like all other large bodies, where there is a variety of different interests to reconcile, their determinations are slow. Why, then, should we distrust them; and, in consequence of that distrust, adopt measures which may cast a shade over that glory which has been so justly acquired, and tarnish the reputation of an army which is celebrated through all Europe for its fortitude and patriotism? And for what is this done? To bring the object we seek nearer? No; most certainly, in my opinion, it will cast it at a greater distance. For myself (and I take no merit for giving the assurance, being induced to it from principles of gratitude, veracity, and justice, and a grateful sense of the confidence you have ever placed in me), a recollection of the cheerful assistance and prompt obedience I have experienced from you under every vicissitude of fortune, and the sincere affection I feel for an army I have so long had the honor to command, will oblige me to declare, in this public and solemn manner, that in the attainment of complete justice for all your toils and dangers, and in the gratification of every wish, so far as may be done consistently with the great duty I owe to my country, and those powers we are bound to respect, you may freely command my services to the utmost extent of my abilities.

"While I give you these assurances, and pledge myself in the most unequivocal manner to exert whatever abilities I am possessed of in your favor, let me entreat you, gentlemen, on your part, not to take any measures which, viewed in the calm light of reason, will lessen the dignity, and sully the glory, you have hitherto maintained. Let me request you to rely on the plighted faith of your country, and place a full confidence in the purity of the intentions of congress, that, previous to your dissolution as an army, they will cause all your accounts to be fairly liquidated, as directed in the resolutions which were published to you two days ago; and that they will adopt the most effectual measures in their power to render ample justice to you for your faithful and meritorious services. And let me conjure you, in the name of our common country, as you value your own sacred honor, as you respect the rights of humanity, and as you regard the military and national character of America, to express your utmost horror and detestation of the man who wishes, under any specious pretences, to overturn the liberties of our country; and who wickedly attempts to open the flood-gates of civil discord, and deluge our rising empire in blood.

"By thus determining, and thus acting, you will pursue the plain and direct road to the attainment of your wishes; you will defeat the insidious designs of our enemies, who are compelled to resort from open force to secret artifice; you will give one more distinguished proof of unexampled patriotism and patient virtue rising superior to the pressure of the most complicated sufferings; and you will, by the dignity of your conduct, afford occasion for posterity to say, when speaking of the glorious example you have exhibited to mankind: 'Had this day been wanting, the world had never seen the last stage of perfection to which human nature is capable of attaining.'"

That eloquent and impassioned production greatly increased the sensation which before existed: the crisis was alarming. Even in the army of a firmly established government, such a general spirit of dissatisfaction would have been unpleasant; but in a new, feeble, and tottering government, and in an army ill trained to strict subordination, the occurrence was far more formidable. The

Fig. 161.—Residence of Washington.—Mount Vernon

sagacious General Washington clearly saw the danger, and prohibited the proposed meeting; but, deeming it safer to direct and weaken the current than immediately to oppose it, he appointed a similar meeting on a subsequent day. General Gates, as the senior officer of rank, presided. General Washington, who had been diligent in preparing the minds of the officers for the occasion, addressed the assembly, strongly combated the address, and, by his sound reasoning and high influential character, succeeded in dissipating the storm.

These proceedings of the officers induced congress to pay some regard to its promises, and to commute the half-pay for a sum equal to five years' full pay. It was insulted by a body of lately-raised troops of Pennsylvania, and much agitation prevailed in the army. But as the dread of foreign enemies subsided, the state governments became careless of the claims and comfort of their defenders. To disband an army in a state of irritation, and to which large arrears were due, many of whom had not money to supply their most pressing wants, or to defray their expenses on the way home, was a dangerous experiment; but it was ultimately executed without any convulsion.

General Washington's military career was now about to close; and, on the 4th of December, he met the principal officers of the army at Frances' tavern. The officers assembled at noon, and their revered and beloved commander soon entered the room. His emotions were too strong to be concealed: filling a glass, and addressing the officers, he said: "With a heart full of love and gratitude, I now take leave of you, and devoutly wish that your latter days may be as prosperous and happy as your former ones have been honorable." Having drank, he added, "I can not come to take each of you by the hand, but shall be obliged to you if each of you will come and take me by the hand." In the midst of profound silence, and with the liveliest sensibility and tenderness, each of the officers took him by the hand; and, at the close of the affecting ceremony, they all accompanied him to Whitehall, where a barge was in readiness to carry him across the river. Having embarked, General Washington turned round to his late companions-in-arms, took off his hat, respectfully bowed to them, and bade them a silent farewell. They returned the compliment, and went back in mute procession to the place where they had assembled.

Congress was then sitting at Annapolis in Maryland; and thither General Washington proceeded, for the purpose of resigning that power which he had so successfully exercised. He remained a few days in Philadelphia, in order to settle his accounts with the treasury; and, on the 19th of December, arrived at Annapolis. At noon, on the 23d, in presence of a numerous company of spectators, he resigned his commission into the hands of congress; and afterward retired to his patrimonial mansion at Mount Vernon.

In the course of the revolution, a number of men of no mean abilities arose, both in the military and civil departments; but General Washington appears with pre-eminent lustre among them all; not only by the brilliancy of his genius, but by the soundness of his understanding, and the moral dignity of his character. His courage was unquestionable, and it was governed by discretion. His glory, however, lies in the moral excellence of his character, his spotless integrity, disinterested patriotism, general humanity, invincible fortitude, and inflexible perseverance. In trying times, he occupied the most difficult situation in which a man can be placed. At the head of an unorganized militia, unaccustomed to military subordination, he was exposed to clamor and calumny, and sometimes fettered by the presumption of rulers, who were forward to decide on what they did not understand, to enjoin measures the consequences of which they did not foresee, and to dictate on subjects of which they had but a very imperfect knowledge. He was unmoved by the clamors of the former; and he bore, with invincible patience, the aberrations of the latter; he remonstrated and reasoned with them, and often succeeded in setting them right. With a steady hand he steered the vessel amid the terrors of the storm, and through fearful breakers brought it safe into port. America owes him much, and seems not insensible of the obligation; but the best mode for the Americans to show their gratitude would be to imitate his virtues, and the character of every American to reflect the moral image of General Washington.

APPENDIX.

CONSTITUTION OF THE UNITED STATES.

We, the people of the United States, in order to form a more perfect union establish justice, insure domestic tranquillity, provide for the common defence promote the general welfare, and secure the blessings of liberty to ourselves and our posterity, do ordain and establish this constitution for the United States of America.

ARTICLE I.

Section 1.—1. All legislative powers herein granted, shall be vested in a congress of the United States, which shall consist of a senate and house of representatives.

Section 2.—1. The house of representatives shall be composed of members chosen every second year, by the people of the several states; and the electors in each state shall have the qualifications requisite for electors of the most numerous branch of the state legislature. 2. No person shall be a representative who shall not have attained to the age of twenty-five years, and been seven years a citizen of the United States, and who shall not, when elected, be an inhabitant of that state in which he shall be chosen. 3. Representatives and direct taxes shall be apportioned among the several states which may be included within this union, according to their respective numbers, which shall be determined by adding to the whole number of free persons, including those bound to service for a term of years, and excluding Indians not taxed, three fifths of all other persons. The actual enumeration shall be made within three years after the first meeting of the congress of the United States, and within every subsequent term of ten years, in such manner as they shall by law direct. The number of representatives shall not exceed one for every thirty thousand, but each state shall have at least one representative; and until such enumeration shall be made, the state of New Hampshire shall be entitled to choose three; Massachusetts, eight; Rhode Island and Providence Plantations, one; Connecticut, five; New York, six; New Jersey, four; Pennsylvania, eight; Delaware, one; Maryland, six; Virginia, ten; North Carolina, five; South Carolina, five; and Georgia, three. 4. When vacancies happen in the representation from any state, the executive authority thereof shall issue writs of election to fill up such vacancies. 5. The house of representatives shall choose their speaker and other officers, and shall have the sole power of impeachment.

Section 3.—1. The senate of the United States shall be composed of two senators from each state, chosen by the legislature thereof, for six years; and each senator shall have one vote. 2. Immediately after they shall be assembled, in consequence of the first election, they shall be divided, as equally as may be, into three classes. The seats of the senators of the first class shall be vacated at the expiration of the second year, of the second class at the expiration of the fourth year, and of the third class at the expiration of the sixth year, so that one third may be chosen every second year ; and if vacancies happen, by resignation or otherwise, during the recess of the legislature of any state, the executive thereof may make temporary appointments until the next meeting of the legislature, which shall then fill such vacancies. 3. No person shall be a senator who shall not have attained to the age of thirty years, and been nine years a citizen of the United States, and who shall not, when elected, be an inhabitant of that state for which he shall be chosen. 4. The vice-president of the United States shall be president of the senate, but shall have no vote, unless they be equally divided. 5. The senate shall choose their other officers, and also a president pro tempore, in the absence of the vice president, or when he shall exercise the office of president of the United States. 6. The senate shall have the sole power to try all impeachments. When sitting for that purpose, they shall be on oath or affirmation. When the president of the United States is tried, the chief justice shall preside; and no person shall be convicted without the concurrence of two thirds of the members present. 7. Judgment, in cases of impeachment, shall not extend further than to removal from office, and disqualification to hold and enjoy any office of honor, trust, or profit, under the United States ; but the party convicted shall nevertheless be liable and subject to indictment, trial, judgment, and punishment, according to law.

Section 4.—1. The times, places, and manner of holding elections for senators and representatives, shall be prescribed in each state by the legislature thereof; but the congress may, at any time, by law, make or alter such regulations, except as to the places of choosing senators. 2. The congress shall assemble at least once in every year, and such meeting shall be on the first Monday in December, unless they shall by law appoint a different day.

Section 5.—1. Each house shall be the judge of the elections, returns, and qualifications of its own members; and a majority of each shall constitute a quorum to do business; but a smaller number may adjourn from day to day, and may be authorized to compel the attendance of absent members, in such manner and under such penalties as each house may provide. 2. Each house may determine the rules of its proceedings, punish its members for disorderly behavior, and, with the concurrence of two thirds, expel a member. 3. Each house shall keep a journal of its proceedings, and from time to time publish the same, excepting such parts as may in their judgment require secresy ; and the yeas and nays of the members of either house, on any question, shall, at the desire of one fifth of those present, be entered on the journal. 4. Neither house, during the session of congress, shall, without the consent of the other, adjourn for more than three days, nor to any other place than that in which the two houses shall be sitting.

Section 6.—1. The senators and representatives shall receive a compensation for their services, to be ascertained by law, and paid out of the treasury of the United States. They shall, in all cases, except treason, felony, and breach of the peace, be privileged from arrest during their attendance at the session of their respective houses, and in going to or returning from the same ; and for any speech or debate in either house, they shall not be questioned in any other place. 2. No senator or representative shall, during the time for which he was elected, be appointed to any civil office under the authority of the United States, which shall have been created, or the emoluments whereof shall have been increased, during such time ; and no person holding any office under the United States shall be a member of either house during his continuance in office.

Section 7.—1. All bills for raising revenue shall originate in the house of representatives ; but the senate may propose or concur with amendments, as on other bills. 2 Every bill which shall have passed the house of representatives and the senate, shall, before it become a law, be presented to the president of the United States; if he approve, he shall sign it; but if not, he shall return it, with his objections, to that house in which it shall have originated, who shall enter the objection at large on their journal, and proceed to reconsider it. If, after such reconsideration, two thirds of that house shall agree to pass the bill, it shall be sent, together with the objections, to the other house, by which it shall be likewise reconsidered, and if approved by two thirds of that house, it shall become a law. But in all such cases, the votes of both houses shall be determined by yeas and nays, and the names of the persons voting for and against the bill shall be entered on the journal of each house respectively. If any bill shall not be returned by the president within ten days (Sundays excepted) after it shall have been presented to him, the same shall be a law in like manner as if he had signed it, unless the congress by their adjournment prevent its return; in which case it shall not be a law. 3. Every order, resolution, or vote, to which the concurrence of the senate and house of representatives may be necessary (except on a question of adjournment), shall be presented to the president of the United States; and before the same shall take effect, shall be approved by him, or being disapproved by him, shall be repassed by two thirds of the senate and house of representatives, according to the rules and limitations prescribed in the case of a bill.

Section 8.—The congress shall have power—1. To lay and collect taxes, duties, imposts, and excises; to pay the debts and provide for the common defence and general welfare of the United States; but all duties, imposts, and excises, shall be uniform throughout the United States: 2. To borrow money on the credit of the United States: 3. To regulate commerce with foreign nations, and among the several states, and with the Indian tribes: 4. To establish a uniform rule of naturalization, and uniform laws on the subject of bankruptcies throughout the United States: 5. To coin money, regulate the value thereof, and of foreign coins, and fix the standard of weights and measures: 6. To provide for the punishment of counterfeiting the securities and current coin of the United States: 7. To establish postoffices and postroads: 8. To promote the progress of science and useful arts, by securing for limited times, to authors and inventors, the exclusive right to their respective writings and discoveries: 9. To constitute tribunals inferior to the supreme court: To define and punish piracies and felonies committed on the high seas, and offences against the law of na tions: 10. To declare war, grant letters of marque and reprisal, and make rules concerning captures on land and water: 11. To raise and support armies; but no appropriation of money to that use shall be for a longer term than two years: 12. To provide and maintain a navy: 13. To makes rules for the government and regulation of the land and naval forces: 14. To provide for calling forth the militia to execute the laws of the union, suppress insurrections, and repel invasions: 15. To provide for organizing, arming, and disciplining the militia, and for governing such part of them as may be employed in the service of the United States, reserving to the states respectively the appointment of the officers, and the authority of training the militia according to the discipline prescribed by congress: 16. To exercise exclusive legislation in all cases whatsoever over such district (not exceeding ten miles square), as may, by cession of particular states, and the acceptance of congress, become the seat of government of the United States, and to exercise like authority over all places purchased, by the consent of the legislature of the state in which the same shall be, for the erection of forts, magazines, arsenals, dock-yards, and other needful buildings:—and, 17. To make all laws which shall be necessary and proper for carrying into execution the foregoing powers, and all other powers vested by this constitution in the government of the United States, or in any department or officer thereof

Section 9.—1. The migration or importation of such persons as any of the states now existing shall think proper to admit, shall not be prohibited by the congress prior to the year one thousand eight hundred and eight, but a tax or duty may be imposed on such importation, not exceeding ten dollars for each person. 2. The privilege of the writ of habeas corpus shall not be suspended, unless when, in cases of rebellion or invasion, the public safety may require it. 3. No bill of attainder, or ex-post-facto law, shall be passed. 4. No capitation or other direct tax shall be laid, unless in proportion to the census or enumeration herein before directed to be taken. 5. No tax or duty shall be laid on articles exported from any state. No preference shall be given by any regulation of commerce or revenue, to the ports of any one state over those of another: nor shall vessels bound to or from one state, be obliged to enter, clear, or pay duties in another. 6. No money shall be drawn from the treasury but in consequence of appropriations made by law: and a regular statement and account of the receipts and expenditures of all public money shall be published from time to time. 7. No title of nobility shall be granted by the United States, and no person holding any office of profit or trust under them, shall, without the consent of the congress, accept of any present, emolument, office, or title of anykind whatever, from any king, prince, or foreign state.

Section 10.—1. No state shall enter into any treaty, alliance, or confederation; grant letters of marque and reprisal; coin money; emit bills of credit; make anything but gold and silver coin a tender in payment of debts; pass any bill of attainder, ex-post-facto law, or law impairing the obligation of contracts; or grant any title of nobility. 2. No state shall, without the consent of the congress, lay any imposts or duties on imports or exports, except what may be absolutely necessary for executing its inspection laws; and the neat produce of all duties and imposts, laid by any state on imports or exports, shall be for the use of the treasury of the United States, and all such laws shall be subject to the revision and control of the congress. No state shall, without the consent of the congress, lay any duty of tunnage, keep troops or ships-of-war in time of peace, enter into any agreement or compact with another state, or with a foreign power, or engage in war unless actually invaded, or in such imminent danger as will not admit of delay.

ARTICLE II.

Section 1.—1. The executive power shall be vested in a president of the United States of America. He shall hold his office during the term of four years, and, together with the vice-president, chosen for the same term, be elected as follows: 2. Each state shall appoint, in such manner as the legislature thereof may direct, a number of electors, equal to the whole number of senators and representatives to which the state may be entitled in the congress; but no senator or representative, or person holding an office of trust or profit under the United States, shall be appointed an elector. [3. The electors shall meet in their respective states, and vote by ballot for two persons, of whom one at least shall not be an inhabitant of the same state with themselves. And they shall make a list of all the persons voted for, and of the number of votes for each; which list they shall sign and certify, and transmit sealed to the seat of the government of the United States, directed to the president of the senate. The president of the senate shall, in the presence of the senate and house of representatives, open all the certificates, and the votes shall then be counted. The person having the greatest number of votes shall be the president, if such number be a majority of the whole number of electors appointed; and if there be more than one who have such majority, and have an equal number of votes, then the house of representatives shall immediately choose by ballot one of them for president; and if no person have a majority, then, from the five highest on the list, the said house shall, in like manner, choose the president. But in choosing the president, the vote shall be taken by states, the representation from each state having one vote; a quorum for this purpose shall consist of a member or members from two thirds of the states, and a majority of all the states shall be necessary to a choice. In every case, after the choice of the president, the person having the greatest number of votes of the electors, shall be the vice-president. But if there should remain two or more who have equal votes, the senate shall choose from them, by ballot, the vice-president.]* 4. The congress may determine the time of choosing the electors, and the day on which they shall give their votes; which day shall be the same throughout the United States. 5. No person, except a natural-born citizen, or a citizen of the United States at the time of the adoption of this constitution, shall be eligible to the office of president: neither shall any person be eligible to that office, who shall not have attained to the age of thirty-five years, and been fourteen years a resident within the United States. 6. In case of the removal of the president from office, or of his death, resignation, or inability to discharge the powers and duties of the said office, the same shall devolve on the vice-president, and the congress may, by law, provide for the case of removal, death, resignation, or inability, both of the president and vice-president, declaring what officer shall then act as president, and such officer shall act accordingly, until the disability be removed, or a president shall be elected. 7. The president shall, at stated times, receive for his services a compensation, which shall neither be increased nor diminished during the period for which he shall have been elected, and he shall not receive within that period any other emolument from the United States, or any of them. 8. Before he enter on the execution of his office, he shall take the following oath or affirmation: 9. "I do solemnly swear (or affirm) that I will faithfully execute the office of president of the United States, and will, to the best of my ability, preserve, protect, and defend the constitution of the United States."

Section 2.—1. The president shall be commander-in-chief of the army and navy of the United States, and of the militia of the several states, when called into the actual service of the United States; he may require the opinion, in writing, of the principal officer in each of the executive departments, upon any subject relating to the duties of their respective offices; and he shall have power to grant reprieves and pardons for offences against the United States, except in cases of impeachment. 2. He shall have power, by and with the advice and consent of the senate, to make treaties, provided two thirds of the senators present concur: and he shall nominate, and, by and with the advice and consent of the senate, shall appoint ambassadors, other public ministers and consuls, judges of the supreme court, and all other officers of the United States, whose appointments are not herein otherwise provided for, and which shall be established by law. But the congress may, by law, vest the appointment of such inferior officers as they think proper, in the president alone, in the courts of law, or in the heads of departments. 3. The president shall have power to fill up all vacancies that may happen during the recess of the senate, by granting commissions which shall expire at the end of their next session.

Section 3.—1. He shall, from time to time, give to congress information of the state of the Union, and recommend to their consideration such measures as he shall judge necessary and expedient: he may, on extraordinary occasions, convene both houses or either of them, and, in case of disagreement between them, with respect to the time of adjournment, he may adjourn them to such time as he shall think proper; he shall receive ambassadors and other public ministers; he shall take care that the laws be faithfully executed; and shall commission all the officers of the United States.

* This clause was annulled by the 12th article under amendments.

Section 4.—1. The president, vice-president, and all civil officers of the United States, shall be removed from office on impeachment for, and conviction of, treason, bribery, or other high crimes and misdemeanors.

ARTICLE III.

Section 1.—1. The judicial power of the United States shall be vested in one supreme court, and in such inferior courts as the congress may, from time to time, ordain and establish. The judges, both of the supreme and inferior courts shall hold their offices during good behavior; and shall, at stated times, receive for their services a compensation, which shall not be diminished during their continuance in office.

Section 2.—1. The judicial power shall extend to all cases in law and equity, arising under this constitution, the laws of the United States, and treaties made, or which shall be made, under their authority: to all cases affecting ambassadors, other public ministers, and consuls; to all cases of admiralty and maritime jurisdiction; to controversies to which the United States shall be a party; to controversies between two or more states; between a state and citizens of another state; between citizens of different states; between citizens of the same state claiming lands under grants of different states; and between a state, or the citizens thereof, and foreign states, citizens, or subjects. 2. In all cases affecting ambassadors, other public ministers, and consuls, and those in which a state shall be a party, the supreme court shall have original jurisdiction. In all the other cases before mentioned, the supreme court shall have appellate jurisdiction, both as to law and fact, with such exceptions, and under such regulations, as the congress shall make. 3. The trial of all crimes, except in cases of impeachment, shall be by jury, and such trial shall be held in the state where the said crime shall have been committed; but when not committed within any state, the trial shall be at such place or places as the congress may by law have directed.

Section 3.—1. Treason against the United States shall consist only in levying war against them, or in adhering to their enemies, giving them aid and comfort. No person shall be convicted of treason unless on the testimony of two witnesses to the same overt act, or on confession in open court. 2. The congress shall have power to declare the punishment of treason; but no attainder of treason shall work corruption of blood, or forfeiture, except during the life of the person attainted.

ARTICLE IV.

Section 1.—1. Full faith and credit shall be given in each state to the public acts, records, and judicial proceedings of every other state. And the congress may, by general laws, prescribe the manner in which such acts, records, and proceedings, shall be proved, and the effect thereof.

Section 2.—1. The citizens in each state shall be entitled to all privileges and immunities of citizens in the several states. 2. A person charged in any state with treason, felony, or other crime, who shall flee from justice, and be found in another state, shall, on demand of the executive authority of the state from which he fled, be delivered up, to be removed to the state having jurisdiction of the crime. 3. No person held to service or labor in one state, under the laws thereof, escaping into another, shall, in consequence of any law or regulation therein, be discharged from such service or labor; but shall be delivered up on claim of the party to whom such service or labor may be due.

Section 3.—1. New states may be admitted by the congress into this union; but no new state shall be formed or erected within the jurisdiction of any other state, nor any state be formed by the junction of two or more states, or parts of states, without the consent of the legislatures of the states concerned as well as of the congress. 2. The congress shall have power to dispose of, and make all needful rules and regulations respecting the territory or other property belonging to the United States; and nothing in this constitution shall be so construed as to prejudice any claims of the United States, or of any particular state.

Section 4.—1. The United States shall guaranty to every state in this union, a republican form of government, and shall protect each of them against invasion; and, on application of the legislature, or of the executive (when the legislature can not be convened), against domestic violence.

ARTICLE V.

1. The congress, whenever two thirds of both houses shall deem it necessary, shall propose amendments to this constitution; or, on the application of the legislatures of two thirds of the several states, shall call a convention for proposing amendments, which, in either case, shall be valid to all intents and purposes, as part of this constitution, when ratified by the legislatures of three fourths of the several states, or by conventions in three fourths thereof, as the one or the other mode of ratification may be proposed by the congress; provided, that no amendment which may be made prior to the year one thousand eight hundred and eight, shall in any manner affect the first and fourth clauses in the ninth section of the first article; and that no state, without its consent, shall be deprived of its equal suffrage in the senate.

ARTICLE VI.

1. All debts contracted, and engagements entered into, before the adoption of this constitution, shall be as valid against the United States under this constitution, as under the confederation. 2. This constitution, and the laws of the United States which shall be made in pursuance thereof, and all treaties made, or which shall be made, under the authority of the United States, shall be the supreme law of the land; and the judges in every state shall be bound thereby; anything in the constitution or laws of any state to the contrary notwithstanding. 3. The senators and representatives before mentioned, and the members of the several state legislatures, and all executive and judicial officers, both of the United States and of the several states, shall be bound by oath or affirmation to support this constitution; but no religious test shall ever be required as a qualification to any office or public trust under the United States.

ARTICLE VII.

1. The ratification of the conventions of nine states shall be sufficient for the establishment of this constitution between the states so ratifying the same.

Done in convention, by the unanimous consent of the states present, the seventeenth day of September, in the year of our Lord one thousand seven hundred and eighty-seven, and of the independence of the United States of America, the twelfth. In witness whereof, we have hereunto subscribed our names

GEORGE WASHINGTON,
President, and Deputy from Virginia

New Hampshire.
JOHN LANGDON,
NICHOLAS GILMAN.

Massachusetts.
NATHANIEL GORHAM,
RUFUS KING.

Connecticut.
WM. SAMUEL JOHNSON,
ROGER SHERMAN.

New York.
ALEXANDER HAMILTON

New Jersey.
WILLIAM LIVINGSTON,
DAVID BEARLY,
WILLIAM PATERSON,
JONATHAN DAYTON

Pennsylvania.
BENJAMIN FRANKLIN,
THOMAS MIFFLIN,
ROBERT MORRIS,
GEORGE CLYMER,
THOMAS FITZSIMONS,
JARED INGERSOLL,
JAMES WILSON,
GOVERNEUR MORRIS.

Delaware.
GEORGE READ,
GUNNING BEDFORD, JR.,
JOHN DICKINSON,
RICHARD BASSETT,
JACOB BROOM.

Maryland.
JAMES M'HENRY,
DANL. OF ST. TH. JENIFER,
DANIEL CARROLL.

Virginia.
JOHN BLAIR,
JAMES MADISON, JR.

North Carolina.
WILLIAM BLOUNT,
RICHARD DOBBS SPAIGHT,
HUGH WILLIAMSON.

South Carolina.
JOHN RUTLEDGE,
CHARLES C. PINCKNEY,
CHARLES PINCKNEY,
PIERCE BUTLER.

Georgia.
WILLIAM FEW,
ABRAHAM BALDWIN,

ATTEST, WILLIAM JACKSON, SEC.

[Congress, at their first session under the constitution, held in the city of New York, in 1789, proposed to the legislatures of the several states, twelve amendments, ten of which only were adopted. They are the first ten of the following amendments; and they were ratified by three fourths, the constitutional number of the states, on the 15th of December, 1791. The 11th amendment was proposed at the first session of the third congress, and was declared in a message from the president of the United States to both houses of congress, dated the 8th of January, 1798, to have been adopted by the constitutional number of states. The 12th amendment, which was proposed at the first session of the eighth congress, was adopted by the constitutional number of states in the year 1804, according to a public notice by the secretary of state, dated the 25th of September, 1804.]

AMENDMENTS

To the constitution of the United States, ratified according to the provisions of the fifth article of the foregoing constitution.

ART. 1. Congress shall make no law respecting an establishment of religion, or prohibiting the free exercise thereof; or abridging the freedom of speech, or of the press; or the right of the people peaceably to assemble, and to petition the government for a redress of grievances.

ART. 2. A well-regulated militia being necessary to the security of a free state, the right of the people to keep and bear arms shall not be infringed.

ART. 3. No soldier shall, in time of peace, be quartered in any house without the consent of the owner; nor in time of war, but in a manner to be prescribed by law.

ART. 4. The right of the people to be secured in their persons, houses, papers, and effects, against unreasonable searches and seizures, shall not be violated; and no warrants shall issue but upon probable cause, supported by oath or affirmation, and particularly describing the place to be searched, and the persons or things to be seized.

ART. 5. No person shall be held to answer for a capital or otherwise infamous crime, unless on a presentment or indictment of a grand jury, except in cases arising in the land or naval forces, or in the militia, when in actual service, in time of war or public danger; nor shall any person be subject for the same offence to be twice put in jeopardy of life or limb; nor shall be compelled, in any criminal case, to be a witness against himself, nor be deprived of life, liberty, or property, without due process of law; nor shall private property be taken for public use, without just compensation.

ART. 6. In all criminal prosecutions, the accused shall enjoy the right to a speedy and public trial, by an impartial jury of the state and district wherein the crime shall have been committed, which district shall have been previously ascertained by law, and to be informed of the nature and cause of the accusation; to be confronted with the witnesses against him; to have compulsory process for obtaining witnesses in his favor; and to have the assistance of counsel for his defence.

ART. 7. In suits at common law, where the value in controversy shall exceed twenty dollars, the right of trial by jury shall be preserved; and no fact tried by a jury shall be otherwise re-examined in any court of the United States, than according to the rules of the common law.

ART. 8. Excessive bail shall not be required, nor excessive fines imposed, nor cruel and unusual punishments inflicted.

ART. 9. The enumerations in the constitution of certain rights, shall not be construed to deny or disparage others retained by the people.

ART. 10. The powers not delegated to the United States by the constitution, nor prohibited by it to the states, are reserved to the states respectively, or to the people.

ART. 11. The judicial power of the United States shall not be construed to extend to any suit in law or equity, commenced or prosecuted against one of the United States by citizens of another state, or by citizens or subjects of any foreign state.

ART. 12.—1. The electors shall meet in their respective states, and vote by ballot for president and vice-president, one of whom, at least, shall not be an inhabitant of the same state with themselves; they shall name in their ballots the person voted for as president, and in distinct ballots the person voted for as vice-president; and they shall make distinct lists of all persons voted for as president, and of all persons voted for as vice president, and of the number of votes for each, which lists they shall sign and certify, and transmit sealed to the seat of the government of the United States, directed to the president of the senate; the president of the senate shall, in the presence of the senate and house of representatives, open all the certificates, and the votes shall then be counted; the person having the greatest number of votes for president, shall be the president, if such number be a majority of the whole number of electors appointed: and if no person have such majority, then from the persons having the highest numbers, not exceeding three, on the list of those voted for as president, the house of representatives shall choose immediately, by ballot, the president. But, in choosing the president, the votes shall be taken by states, the representation from each state having one vote; a quorum for this purpose shall consist of a member or members from two thirds of the states, and a majority of all the states shall be necessary to a choice. And if the house of representatives shall not choose a president whenever the choice shall devolve upon them, before the fourth day of March next following, then the vice-president shall act as president, as in case of the death or other constitutional disability of the president.

2. The person having the greatest number of votes as vice-president, shall be the vice-president, if such number be a majority of the whole number of electors appointed; and if no person have a majority, then from the two highest numbers on the list, the senate shall choose the vice-president; a quorum for the purpose shall consist of two thirds of the whole number of senators, and a majority of the whole number shall be necessary to a choice.

3. But no person constitutionally ineligible to the office of president, shall be eligible to that of vice-president of the United States.

THE END.

TO ALL PERSONS INTERESTED IN the diffusion of Useful Knowledge. Valuable Books for Public, Private, and District School Libraries. SEARS' PICTORIAL FAMILY LIBRARY. TWELVE VOLUMES, *large octavo, substantially bound in leather.* Embellished with more than TWO THOUSAND ENGRAVINGS, *designed and executed by the most Eminent Artists of England and America.*

The entire series of Mr. Sears' Pictorial Works has been examined, and strongly recommended to Superintendents, Trustees, and Teachers of Schools, by the following distinguished gentlemen: His Excellency HAMILTON FISH, Governor of the State of New York; Hon. CHRISTOPHER MORGAN, Secretary of State, and Superintendent of Common Schools, N. Y.; T. ROMEYN BECK, M. D., Secretary of the Regents of the University, N. Y.; the LEGISLATIVE COMMITTEE on Colleges, Academies, and Common Schools; Rev. EDWARD HITCHCOCK, LL. D., President of Amherst College, and Professor of Geology, Massachusetts.

From his Excellency HAMILTON FISH, *Governor of the State of New York.*

ALBANY, *April* 10, 1849.

Mr. ROBERT SEARS:—

Dear Sir: I have not had time, amid other engagements, for a very thorough examination of the series of Pictorial Works which you have been so kind as to send me. I have, however, examined them sufficiently to justify me in saying, that they are compiled with care, and are highly interesting and useful Family Books, pure in their moral tendency, and replete with valuable information. They are *good* books, and worthy of a place in our *District School Libraries.*

HAMILTON FISH.

From the Hon. CHRISTOPHER MORGAN, *Secretary of State, and Superintendent of Common Schools.*

STATE OF NEW YORK, *Secretary's Office,*
Department of Common Schools, ALBANY, *April* 10, 1849.

Mr. ROBERT SEARS,—Sir: I have examined your series of *Pictorial Works;* I find them to contain a large amount of valuable information, and take pleasure in cheerfully recommending them as *suitable Books* to be introduced into the *Common* and *District School Libraries* of this State.

CHRISTOPHER MORGAN.

Recommendation of Hon. ROBERT H. PRUYN, GABRIEL P. DISOSWAY, JAMES D. BUTTON, JAMES W. BEEKMAN, *and* ALONZO JOHNSON, *Committee on Colleges, Academies, and Common Schools.*

NEW YORK LEGISLATURE, *April,* 5, 1849.

We have examined the PICTORIAL WORKS* edited and published by Mr. ROBERT SEARS, 128 Nassau street, New York, prepared for DISTRICT SCHOOL LIBRARIES, and are of the opinion that they deserve a place in these institutions—designed as they are for the diffusion of Useful Knowledge.

* The Works alluded to, as having been examined and recommended for the libraries, are as follows: "A New and Popular Description of the United States."—"Pictorial History of the American Revolution."—"Scenes and Sketches of Continental Europe."—"Description of Great Britain and Ireland."—"Pictorial Family Annual."—"Treasury of Knowledge."—"Information for the People."—"The Family Instructor."—"Pictorial Sunday-Book."—"Bible Biography."—"Bible History."—Second Series of the "Wonders of the World."

ROBERT H. PRUYN, *Chairman,*
GABRIEL P. DISOSWAY,
JAMES D. BUTTON,
JAMES W. BEEKMAN,
ALONZO JOHNSON.

From T. ROMEYN BECK, M. D., *Secretary of the Regents of the University, New York.*

Office of the Secretary of the Regents of the University,
ALBANY, *March* 12, 1849.

Mr. ROBERT SEARS,—Sir: I have given as much time as possible to an examination of your *Pictorial Works.* They are all interesting: compiled evidently with much care, and profusely illustrated with Engravings. I can not imagine more useful books to be introduced to *Families,* and *particularly to our District School Libraries* and *Academies.* You appear to have followed in the track of the "Library of Useful Knowledge," and the publications of William and Robert Chambers, and will, I doubt not, be rewarded with a portion of the popularity that has followed them in Great Britain. It is not, by any means, the least of the recommendations of your Books, that their morality is pure, and that they contain few lines which, on mature reflection, you would need to blot.

T. ROMEYN BECK.

From Rev. EDWARD HITCHCOCK, LL. D., *President of Amherst College, and Professor of Geology, Massachusetts.*

AMHERST COLLEGE, *Dec.* 25, 1848.

Mr. ROBERT SEARS,—Dear Sir: I have looked over the entire series of your valuable Publications with much interest and profit; and am quite surprised at the amount of literary labor you have performed, and the research it must have cost you to obtain so many fine illustrations, while you have an active superintendence of an extensive business. I am also gratified at the decidedly moral and religious influence which your books will exert, and can not but hope that they will do much to counteract the effects of that light and immoral literature which deluges the land, and like the frogs of Egypt comes up even into the kneading-troughs of our kitchens. May you live long to follow out and perfect your plans.

EDWARD HITCHCOCK.

AMERICAN BOOKS IN ENGLAND.

THE following letter is from the REV. THOMAS TIMPSON, an able and pious minister in London, the author of many valuable theological and other works; and a person who has distinguished himself as the originator of various benevolent movements in that great city. It breathes a spirit of peace and good-will toward America, creditable alike to the head and the heart of the writer. To such sentiments we heartily respond, and hope the peace and intercourse now existing between England and America, may long be preserved inviolable.—*Ed. American Saturday Courier.*

"LONDON (ENG.) *March* 22, 1847.

"MR. ROBERT SEARS:

"*My Dear Sir:* I am constrained by a sense of obligation, to testify to you on the part of myself, my sons, and my daughters, the inexpressible gratification that we feel in the possession of the sixteen volumes of your beautiful works which now adorn my library with their elegant bindings. I look at them with astonishment, as I reflect on their having been the production of one individual; comprehending, as they do, so large a variety of the most important subjects, and compiled, as their valuable contents show, from a vast number of the best publications, and by a gentleman otherwise engaged in an extensive business! Having been honored with the commission to offer a set of them to Victoria, queen of Great Britain—and which she has graciously accepted—I examined these volumes more particularly; and I feel admiration of their excellent and useful information, their pure and Christian morality, and their truly scriptural theology. I may most justly apply to you, what a reverend doctor of America once said to me, after examination of my rather numerous publications—'I have not observed a line of all your writings, which you may wish to blot out when you come to die.' I considered that a very high compliment from such a judge.

"By your publications, you have made all classes through the whole community in the United States very greatly your debtors. This they are in some good measure acknowledging, as I perceive, by the large and increasing demand for your valuable works; but the man who has placed in their hands *illustrated pictorial* volumes, relating to such a variety of that which is wonderful in 'nature, art, and mind;' so much that is instructive in biography and history; and what is most divinely consoling in religion and the oracles of God—in forms well adapted to promote the edification of all classes, especially those in the peculiar condition of the millions so widely scattered, as the people of your vastly-extended Union, can not easily be remunerated for the requisite expenditure of mental and physical labor, with the large amount of property employed in producing these works.

"'The Pictorial Family Instructor,' the 'Wonders of the World,' the 'History of the American Revolution,' and 'Information for the People,' must be invaluable treasures to the rising members of thousands of families throughout America; especially because of the necessarily limited sphere of observation on men and manners existing in the 'Old World;' while the 'Description of Great Britain and Ireland,' will afford them the most ennobling ideas concerning the people, the riches, and glory of their 'fatherland' and the 'mother-country.' For this good service we are indebted to you as Britons.

"Your 'Bible Biography,' 'Pictorial Sunday Book,' and 'History of the Bible,' can not fail to be highly prized by those of a more religious or established Christian character; on account of the precious stores of pure divinity which they contain, and the concentration of the rays of heavenly light which they throw upon the Scriptures. You can not wonder that I rejoice to see my name and labors so prominently placed in one of your volumes, with my 'Thirty Dissertations' on the Scriptures, from my 'Key to the Bible,' in your 'Bible Biography.'

"It is natural for you to wish my judgment—as that of an Englishman, more particularly—upon your 'Description of Great Britain and Ireland.' Regarding this work especially, as I am acquainted with most parts of this country, I beg to assure you that it does very great credit to your talents, research, and industry; the information, I perceive, is derived from the best sources, and the pictorial representations are good—many of them equal to those of the same kind published in England. You have done wisely by giving so extended an account of London, our wonderful metropolis: for, though Edinburgh and Dublin are truly splendid cities, as the ancient capitals of the kingdoms of Scotland and Ireland; and, while Birmingham, Bristol, Leeds, Sheffield, Manchester, Liverpool, and Glasgow, are really magnificent as provincial boroughs, great manufacturing centres, and emporiums of trade—London, with its sister-city of Westminster, is the seat and source of intelligence, commerce, wealth, legislation, and government of the vast British empire. The palaces of the sovereign and the mansions of the nobility are grand. No language or pictorial description can, however, adequately represent our mighty metropolis to a stranger; yourself, on a personal survey, will be like the queen of Sheba in her visit to King Solomon and Jerusalem.

"One word as to the spirit of your writings. I admire exceedingly the benevolence, liberality, and enlarged philanthropy, which they all breathe; indicating the author to be in the best sense, 'A CITIZEN OF THE WORLD.' I cordially delight in the unsectarian Christian spirit which pervades those that are religious; this is worthy your profession as a follower of the world's Redeemer, and as to your work on 'Great Britain and Ireland,' I tender you my warmest thanks for the noble sentiments it expresses. I can not look upon the Americans but as our own brethren. As an Englishman, I feel the full force of the significant expression uttered by some of our profound worldly politicians—'ENGLAND AND AMERICA *against* ALL THE WORLD!' but as a minister of the blessed 'PRINCE OF PEACE,' the Redeemer of all nations, I would rather say, what in my judgment your work is happily designed and adapted to promote, and the whole body of British Christians would joyfully echo my words—'ENGLAND AND AMERICA *for* ALL THE WORLD!' May we continue increasingly to co-operate, by the Bible, Missions, and Commerce, in promoting the intelligence, liberty, and happiness of every people!

"I am convinced that the two countries are deeply interested in the prosperity of each other. Our people are one in blood, one in language, one in science and art, and one in religion. Ourselves mutually united in the bonds of peace and friendly intercourse, both must prosper, and essentially serve each other; and, increasing in population, by our moral influence, our intelligence, religion, liberty, and commerce—all improved and perfected—we may be the means of removing the ten thousand evils of despotism, superstition, and false religion, which afflict the great nations of Europe, Asia, Africa, and many parts of America, and of regenerating the world, under the gracious providence of God.

"Wishing you success in your various noble, benevolent, and Christian enterprises, and that your life and health may long be preserved, to enjoy the fruits of your labors on earth, I remain, yours, in Christian esteem,

"THOMAS TIMPSON."

PRESENTATION OF MR. SEARS' PICTORIAL WORKS TO HER MAJESTY QUEEN VICTORIA.

PRESENTATION OF MR. SEARS' PICTORIAL WORKS,

TO HER MAJESTY QUEEN VICTORIA.

(*See Engraving.*)

BUCKINGHAM PALACE, *May* 17, 1847.

MR. ROBERT SEARS —

Sir: Some short time since, several important and interesting works, compiled and published by you, were presented, in your name, for the Queen's acceptance, through the Rev. Mr. Timpson. An official acknowledgment of the receipt and acceptance of these volumes was conveyed to Mr. Timpson from Sir George Grey, the Secretary for the Home Department: but I have, since that period, been honored with the Queen's commands to convey to you the expression of Her Majesty's thanks for your attention in forwarding these works for her acceptance, and her satisfaction at the kind sentiments expressed, by your desire, in Mr. Timpson's letter which accompanied them.

I am, Sir, your very ob't serv't,

J. H. GLOVER,

Librarian to Her Majesty.

From the New York Sun, Dec. 29, 1846.

AMERICAN PUBLICATIONS FOR QUEEN VICTORIA. Evidences of American progress in literature, science, and art, are constantly presenting themselves. Our latest efforts are startling to the "mother-country," who now begins to find a sturdy competitor, if not an equal, in her promising daughter. These legitimate branches of competition are eminently calculated to strengthen the bonds of friendship, and perpetuate the blessings of those amicable relations at present existing between the two nations. These reflections were suggested by a pleasing incident which came to our knowledge yesterday. Our readers are probably all acquainted with the series of excellent family books issued by Mr. Robert Sears, of this city, and we presume there are few who are not acquainted with the principal incidents in Mr. Sears' own life—his beginning in this city as a poor journeyman, and the subsequent achievements which he accomplished by perseverance, morality, honest labor, and a liberal patronage of the popular advertising newspapers. The reputation of his books having extended to England, and being considered there equal to many of their own best publications, he received an intimation from an eminent divine, the Rev. Thomas Timpson, of London, and others, that a complete set of them would be an appropriate present to her Majesty. Accordingly, Mr. Sears sends out, by the steamer of the 1st January, the "Pictorial Illustrations of the Bible," the "Bible Biography," the "Pictorial Wonders of the World," the "Pictorial Family Library," the "Pictorial History of the American Revolution," the "Pictorial History of the Bible," the "Guide to Knowledge," the "Pictorial Sunday Book," the "Pictorial Description of Great Britain and Ireland," and "Information for the People," being thirteen magnificent volumes in all. They are superbly bound in morocco, and ornamented with beautiful designs in gilt. The following presentation is written inside of each:—

Presented to her Most Gracious Majesty,

VICTORIA,

Queen of Great Britain and Ireland,

With the utmost respect, by the Compiler and Publisher,

ROBERT SEARS,

New York (U. S. A.), January 1, 1847.

MR. SEARS' PRESENT TO THE QUEEN.—Our readers, says the New York Sun, will recollect that a few months since we alluded to the gratifying fact that Mr. Robert Sears, of this city, had forwarded a complete set of all his interesting pictorial publications to the Queen of England. The following article respecting their safe arrival and presentation may prove interesting to our readers. It is copied from the *London Patriot*, of Feb. 22, 1847:—

"AMERICAN PRESENT TO THE QUEEN.—Many in this country will be interested in learning, that a present of books from America, has recently been made to our Gracious Queen, by an eminent publisher in New York. These works are, 'The History of the Bible,' 'Description of Great Britain and Ireland,' 'Information for the People,' &c. They are profusely illustrated with fine engravings on wood, printed in imperial octavo, sumptuously bound in Turkey morocco, and very elegantly gilded, exhibiting admirable specimens of the progress that is being made in typographical and artistical skill in the United States. The present was sent from America to the care of the Rev. Thomas Timpson, by whom it was forwarded to the Right Hon. Sir George Grey, Bart., the Home Secretary, for presentation to the Queen. Sir George, in a polite letter, has assured Mr. Timpson that he has complied with his request, and that her Majesty had graciously accepted the volumes. Reflecting on this gratifying fact, and remembering that the vast republic of the New World possesses our language, laws, literature, and religion, and our blood flowing in their veins, every true patriot and Christian must feel delighted, and pray that a perfect cordiality and everlasting peace may be enjoyed between the two great nations, that this enterprise may be mutually beneficial, and the means of universal good to all the nations upon earth, especially in diffusing the Gospel."

IF half the pains now taken by interested politicians on both sides of the ocean, to rend asunder, derange, and disunite, were used to calm, pacify, soothe and unite mankind, in a short period our world would become a paradise, a garden of love, riches, honor, and wealth; in fact everything noble, good, or great. *Peace and Good Will* would not only form a part of the religion of the Christian world, but would constitute true religion itself. All that is wanting in order to accomplish this great end is, for each one to feel that *we are all one family:* and to allow no separate or sectional party, thought, or word, to go forth, either printed, written, or spoken.

CIRCULAR FOR FAMILIES.

TO ALL PERSONS INTERESTED IN THE DIFFUSION OF USEFUL KNOWLEDGE.

A Book for the Wives and Children of the Farmer, Mechanic, Laborer, Physician, Lawyer, and Divine—for Persons in every sphere and station of Life, and for Followers of every Pursuit—

For Public, Private, and District School Libraries.

Extract from the First Message to Congress of the Father of his Country, January 8, 1790.

"There is nothing that can better deserve our patronage than the promotion of science and literature. Knowledge is in every country the surest basis of public happiness; and in one in which the measures of government receive their impression so immediately from the sense of the community as in ours, it is proportionably essential. To the security of a free constitution it contributes in various ways. By convincing those who are intrusted with the public administration, that every valuable end of government is best answered by the enlightened confidence of the people, and by teaching the people themselves to know and to value their own rights; to discern and provide against invasions of them; to distinguish between oppression and the exercise of lawful authority — between burdens arising from a disregard to their convenience and those resulting from the inevitable exigences of society; to discriminate the spirit of liberty from that of licentiousness—cherishing the first, avoiding the last, and uniting a speedy but temperate vigilance against encroachment with an inviolable respect to the laws." WASHINGTON.

The following Work has been prepared with great care, and at an enormous expense, combining the useful with the agreeable, the solid with the ornamental; and designed, by replacing the cheap trash which overruns the country, to disseminate, broadcast, the seeds of virtue and religion—to supply literary food of a moral, attractive, and useful character—to extend far and wide the roots of a true and lofty patriotism—and, by making good citizens of the rising generation, to throw a firm bulwark around our free and noble institutions. The title is as follows:—

SEARS' NEW AND POPULAR PICTORIAL

DESCRIPTION OF THE UNITED STATES:

CONTAINING AN ACCOUNT OF THE TOPOGRAPHY, SETTLEMENT, HISTORY, REVOLUTIONARY AND OTHER INTERESTING EVENTS, STATISTICS, PROGRESS IN AGRICULTURE, MANUFACTURES, AND POPULATION, &C., &C., OF EACH STATE IN THE UNION. ILLUSTRATED WITH

TWO HUNDRED ENGRAVINGS

of the principal Cities, Places, Buildings, Scenery, Curiosities, Seals of the States, &c., &c.

COMPLETE IN ONE OCTAVO VOLUME OF 600 PAGES, ELEGANTLY BOUND IN GILT PICTORIAL MUSLIN.

Retail Price $2.50.

☞ We have prepared this volume at great expense: the type large, clear, and handsome; paper smooth and white; binding strong and substantial; engravings neat and appropriate. This work is decidedly the cheapest and most popular ever issued from the American press; and, from the orders already received for it, we are satisfied it is destined to have an immense sale throughout our vast extended country. From peculiar circumstances we are able to offer this book extremely low to book-pedlars, postmasters, and others, who may feel disposed to act as agents.

☞ The principles of morality and of a *well-regulated* FREEDOM are introduced with sufficient frequency throughout its pages; the editor exercising a careful discrimination, while honestly desirous of enlarging its circumference, not to admit within the circle the elements of licentiousness, to which we are liable in the present state of society. Let every parent remember it is to an EDUCATION wisely and liberally provided for our people, America owes her proud superiority over other nations. This will preserve a love of freedom, and detestation of oppression, pure and unadulterated, in the young and rising generation. ☞ For further particulars, please address (post-paid),

S. M. FENNER, WOODSTOCK, CONN.

General Agent for Rhode Island, and Connecticut east of Connecticut River.

V.

New and Interesting Pictorial Work.

JUST PUBLISHED,

SCENES AND SKETCHES
IN
CONTINENTAL EUROPE;

EMBRACING DESCRIPTIONS OF

France, Portugal, Spain, Italy, Sicily, Switzerland, Belgium, and Holland,

Together with Views and Notices of the principal objects of interest in Paris, Rouen, Lisbon, Madrid, Barcelona, Pisa, Leghorn, Rome, Naples, Herculaneum, Pompeii, Pæstum, Palermo, Malta, Venice, Milan, Geneva, Furnes, Brussels, Tyrol, Antwerp, Rotterdam, Amsterdam, Waterloo, &c., &c.

Carefully Compiled from the best and latest Sources,

BY ROBERT SEARS.

EMBELLISHED WITH NUMEROUS ENGRAVINGS.

Complete in one imperial volume 8vo., of 550 pages, elegantly bound in gilt pictorial muslin.

Price Two Dollars and a half.

This work is intended as a companion to the "Pictorial Description of Great Britain," and will be found a valuable aid to every one seeking information respecting the countries described.

VI.

SEARS' INFORMATION FOR THE PEOPLE.

A splendidly Illustrated Work, comprising the finest series of Embellishments ever presented to the American public—in one handsome, large octavo volume, of 550 pages, elegantly bound.

Price only $2 50.

This splendid volume comprises within itself

A COMPLETE LIBRARY OF USEFUL AND ENTERTAINING KNOWLEDGE,

condensed in form, familiar in style, and copious in information, embracing an extensive range of subjects in Literature, Science, and Art.

VII.

*** JUST PUBLISHED—A valuable, illustrated Work, for Families, Schools, and Libraries, complete in one large and splendid 8vo. volume of 550 pages, elegantly bound in muslin, gilt, printed with large type, and embellished with beautiful **Engravings.**

☞ PRICE $2 50. ☜

The title of the Work is as follows:—

SEARS' PICTORIAL FAMILY LIBRARY,

OR

DIGEST OF GENERAL KNOWLEDGE:

Comprising a complete circle of useful and entertaining information, designed for FAMILY READING: compiled from the latest and best authorities, and embracing the various divisions of

HISTORY, BIOGRAPHY, LITERATURE, GEOGRAPHY, NATURAL HISTORY,

AND THE OTHER SCIENCES.

Illustrated with Numerous Engravings.

VIII.

A BOOK FOR EVERY FAMILY!

To the People of America.

A beautifully-illustrated Volume—purely American in its character and design—forming a large and handsome octavo, of between Four and Five Hundred pages: with several hundred Engravings! Retail price $2—bound in muslin, gilt. The title of the Works is as follows:—

PICTORIAL HISTORY
OF THE
AMERICAN REVOLUTION.

With an Account of the Early History of the Country, the Constitution of the United States, and a Chronological Index.

Illustrated with several hundred engravings.

IX.

THE WONDERS OF THE WORLD!

SECOND SERIES, IN TWO PARTS:

PART I.—WONDERS OF NATURE—containing a Description of the Races of Men, Manners and Customs of various Nations, Beasts, Birds, Trees, Plants, Mountains, Volcanoes, Rivers, &c., &c.

PART II.—WONDERS OF ART—or Descriptions of Mechanical Inventions, Automatons, Cities, Buildings, Curiosities, Ruins, Antiquities, &c., &c.

EDITED BY ROBERT SEARS.

With 400 Illustrative Embellishments.

The whole complete in one volume of 550 pages, in emblematic gilt binding; making an interesting and instructive work for all classes of readers. Price **$2.50.**

X.

THE

Pictorial Family Bible:

BEING

THE OLD AND NEW TESTAMENTS,

According to the authorized Version. With full Marginal References; Tables of the Weights and Measures of the Scriptures; a full Chronology, from the Latin of Calovius; a steel engraved Family Record, for Births, Marriages, and Deaths; a superb and authentic Map of Palestine and the Holy Land: Illustrated by

ONE THOUSAND ENGRAVINGS,

Representing Places, Costumes, Antiquities, Birds, Beasts, Reptiles, Plants, Minerals, Insects, Coins, Medals, Trees, and Historical Events, from the most authentic sources. Each Chapter commences with an illuminated letter. The whole printed upon superfine paper, and substantially and elegantly bound in one quarto volume of fifteen hundred pages.

☞ The Text, together with the Marginal References, is printed from the standard edition of the American Bible Society.

Price only Six Dollars.

www.ingramcontent.com/pod-product-compliance
Lightning Source LLC
LaVergne TN
LVHW021135110826
845150LV00005B/1039

* 9 7 8 1 4 2 5 5 4 9 2 9 9 *